Student-Involved
Classroom Assessment

Student-Involved
Classroom Assessment

3rd Edition

RICHARD J. STIGGINS

Assessment Training Institute

Merrill
Prentice Hall

Upper Saddle River, New Jersey
Columbus, Ohio

Library of Congress Cataloging-in-Publication Data
Stiggins, Richard J.
    Student-involved classroom assessment / Richard J. Stiggins.—3rd ed.
       p.   cm.
    Rev. ed. of: Student-centered classroom assessment, 2nd ed. ©1997.
    Includes bibliographical references and index.
    ISBN 0-13-022537-1
    1. Educational tests and measurements—United States. 2. Examinations—
United States.   I. Stiggins, Richard J. Student-centered assessment. II. Title.

  LB3051.S8536   2001
  371.26—dc21   00-055395

Vice President and Publisher: Jeffery W. Johnston
Executive Editor: Kevin M. Davis
Development Editor: Hope Madden
Editorial Assistant: Christina Kalisch
Production Editor: Mary M. Irvin and Julie Peters
Design Coordinator: Diane C. Lorenzo
Text Design: Ceri Fitzgerald/STELLARViSIONs
Cover Design: Jeff Vanik
Cover Photo: © Bob Daemmrich Photography
Production Manager: Laura Messerly
Electronic Text Management: Marilyn Wilson Phelps, Karen L. Bretz,
   Melanie N. Ortega
Director of Marketing: Kevin Flanagan
Marketing Manager: Amy June
Marketing Services Manager: Krista Groshong

This book was set in ITC Century by Prentice Hall and was printed and bound by
R. R. Donnelley & Sons Company. The cover was printed by Phoenix Color Corp.

10 9 8 7 6 5 4 3 2
ISBN: 0-13-022537-1

For Kris,
our new science teacher
and a continuing source of pride
for her mom and me

Acknowledgments

In this third edition of *Student-Involved Classroom Assessment*, we at the Assessment Training Institute present a very exciting new vision of the relationship between assessment and effective schools. This innovative vision finds its power not in the assessment methods we use, but in how we can use assessment to help our students want to learn. We advocate the use of student-involved classroom assessment to help our students gain confidence in themselves as learners. Those students who believe that they can learn try harder than those who have given up on themselves.

This vision presented herein is not mine alone. Rather, it represents the collective wisdom of many. I claim only to be an able learner who is blessed with a team of outstanding teachers from whom to learn. The starting lineup on this team included Judy Arter, ATI National Training Director, and ATI Associates Kathy Busick, Jan Chappuis, and Kris Bridgeford. They studied early drafts and helped me overcome my own lack of understanding and clarity. As a team, we all learned much from each other.

Judy contributed far more than mere reactions to my draft manuscripts. When I found myself tangled in my ideas (a frequent occurrence), she helped me sort them out. When I needed an example to illustrate a key point, she always came up with the perfect choice. When I needed encouragement, she always offered supportive thoughts. Thank you, Judy.

In addition, Judy and Kathy co-authored the very practical workbook *Practice with Student-Involved Classroom Assessment*, designed to help educators use the assessment strategies described herein to build student confidence. This workbook, combined with the series of interactive videos developed by ATI, support this introductory assessment text with an unprecedented array of learning aids.

The task of compiling and coordinating the production of the various draft manuscripts at ATI in Portland fell to Jennifer Letter. Jen was more patient than I deserve and more organized than I could ever be. Thanks also to ATI teammates who contributed to the effort: Sharon Lippert, Joelle Irvine, and Barbara Carnegie.

Special thanks also to Kevin Davis, Executive Editor at Merrill, who saw the potential of our ideas when we proposed the first edition and has remained the champion of our work ever since. For this third edition, Kevin was ably assisted by Julie Peters and Mary Irvin, Senior Production Editors, and Development Editor Hope Madden.

All three editions of this book have been copy edited by Robert Marcum. Though he is neither an educator nor an assessment specialist, Robert has consistently understood and believed in our mission of building student confidence. This commitment has permitted him to add focus, clarity, and economy to our presentation.

Others have assisted us by reviewing draft chapters. Primary among these is Susan Brookhart of Duquesne University, whose insightful commentary through the development of all three editions has consistently stood out as extremely helpful. Others have included John Creswell of Edinboro University, Bruce Frey of Kansas University, Daniel Kmitta of the University of Idaho, Ronald Marso of Bowling Green State University, Katherine Ryan of the University of Illinois, and Mike Trevisan of Washington State University. This text has been improved markedly by their insightful criticism.

Finally, another warm thank you to my wife and partner, Nancy Bridgeford, to whom the second edition of this book was dedicated. Nancy patiently listens to my ideas at all hours and always seems to know when to offer encouragement.

Thank you, everyone. As educators, we know far more collectively than any of us does alone. When we pool our insights as a community of learners, and when we combine this with a dedication to the academic and personal well-being of our students, we prepare ourselves to succeed as teachers.

Rick Stiggins

Discover the Companion Website Accompanying This Book

The Prentice Hall Companion Website: A Virtual Learning Environment

Technology is a constantly growing and changing aspect of our field that is creating a need for content and resources. To address this emerging need, we have developed an online learning environment for students and professors alike—Companion Websites—to support our textbooks.

In creating a Companion Website, our goal is to build on and enhance what the textbook already offers. For this reason, the content for each user-friendly website is organized by chapter and provides the professor and student with a variety of meaningful resources. Common features of a Companion Website include:

For the Professor

Every Companion Website integrates **Syllabus Manager**™, an online syllabus creation and management utility.

- **Syllabus Manager**™ provides you, the instructor, with an easy, step-by-step process to create and revise syllabi, with direct links into Companion Website and other online content without having to learn HTML.

- Students may logon to your syllabus during any study session. All they need to know is the web address for the Companion Website, and the password you've assigned to your syllabus.

- After you have created a syllabus using **Syllabus Manager**™, students may enter the syllabus for their course section from any point in the Companion Website.

- Class dates are highlighted in white and assignment due dates appear in blue. Clicking on a date, the student is shown the list of activities for the assignment. The activities for each assignment are linked directly to actual content, saving time for students.

- Adding assignments consists of clicking on the desired due date, then filling in the details of the assignment—name of the assignment, instructions, and whether or not it is a one-time or repeating assignment.

- In addition, links to other activities can be created easily. If the activity is online, a URL can be entered in the space provided, and it will be linked automatically in the final syllabus.

- Your completed syllabus is hosted on our servers, allowing convenient updates from any computer on the Internet. Changes you make to your syllabus are immediately available to your students at their next login.

For the Student

- **Chapter Objectives**—outline key concepts from the text
- **Interactive Self-quizzes**—complete with hints and automatic grading that provide immediate feedback for students

  After students submit their answers for the interactive self-quizzes, the Companion Website Results Reporter computes a percentage grade, provides a graphic representation of how many questions were answered correctly and incorrectly, and gives a question-by-question analysis of the quiz. Students are given the option to send their quiz to up to four email addresses (professor, teaching assistant, study partner, etc.).

- **Message Board**—serves as a virtual bulletin board to post–or respond to–questions or comments to a national audience

- **Chat** — real-time chat with anyone who is using the text anywhere in the country—ideal for discussion and study groups, class projects, etc.

- **Web Destinations**—links to www sites that relate to chapter content

- **Additional Resources**—access to chapter-specific or general content that enhances material found in the text

To take advantage of these resources, please visit the *Student-Involved Classroom Assessment* Companion Website at

www.prenhall.com/stiggins

Brief Contents

Contents

Chapter 10   Performance Assessment of Skills and Products 295

Chapter 11   Assessing Dispositions   337

PART IV   Effective Communication about Student Achievement   367

Chapter 12   Classroom Perspectives on Standardized Testing   375

Chapter 13   Report Cards   409

Chapter 14   Portfolios: Capturing the Details   467

Chapter 15   Communicating with Conferences   491

Student-Involved
Classroom Assessment

Understanding the Classroom Assessment Challenge

This is where we begin a journey together through the realm of classroom assessment. Welcome. I'll be your guide. Call me Rick.

To introduce the topic, let me briefly frame your classroom assessment tasks and challenges in commonsense terms. Then we'll explore together a variety of concrete, productive ways for you to fulfill your assessment responsibilities.

I have two goals for you. By the end of our time together, you will

- Understand the meaning of excellence in classroom assessment.
- Make a personal professional commitment to meeting standards of assessment excellence.

Do a good job of assessing day to day in the classroom and your students will prosper and learn much there. Fail to meet standards of sound practice and someone is likely to get hurt.

Let me illustrate what it looks like when someone gets hurt. Our daughter, Kristen, arrived home one afternoon full of gloom when she was in third grade. She said she knew we

were going to be angry with her. She presented us with a sheet of paper—the third-grade size with the wide lines. On it, she had written a story. Her assignment was to write about someone or something she cares deeply about. She wrote of Kelly, a small kitten that had come to be part of our family, but who had to return to the farm after two weeks because of allergies. Kelly's departure had been like the loss of a family member. We all had cried.

On the sheet of paper was an emergent writer's version of this story—not sophisticated, but poignant. Krissy's recounting of events was accurate and her story captured her very strong sadness and disappointment at losing her new little friend. She did a pretty darn good job of writing, for a beginner.

At the bottom of the page, below the story, was a big red circled "F"! We asked her why, and she told us that the teacher said she had better improve or she would fail. Questioning further, we found that her teacher had said that students were to fill the page with writing. Krissy had used only three-quarters of the page, so she hadn't followed directions and so deserved an F.

When she had finished telling us this story, Kristen Ann put the sheet of paper down on the kitchen table and, with a very discouraged look, said in an intimidated voice, "I'll never be a good writer anyway," and left the room. My recollection of that moment remains vivid after 20 years.

In fact, she had *succeeded* at hitting the achievement target. She produced some pretty good writing. But her confidence in herself as a writer was deeply shaken because her teacher failed to disentangle her expectation that students comply with directions with her expectation that they demonstrate the ability to write well. As a result, both the assessment and the feedback had a destructive impact on this student. Without question, it's quite easy to see if the page is full. But is that the point? It's somewhat more challenging to assess accurately and to formulate and deliver understandable and timely feedback that permits a student to remain confident about her ability to continue to grow as a writer.

The classroom assessment challenge boils down to a relatively brief series of questions:

- Do you know and understand what it means to succeed academically in your classroom—what it looks like when your students are making progress toward success?

- Can you transform your vision of success into assessment exercises and scoring schemes that provide dependable information about student success?

- Do you know and understand how to use both the assessment process and its results to help students both to believe in themselves as learners and to strive for academic success?

To be more specific, as teachers, our job is to maximize our students' learning. To reach this goal, we must constantly develop and deliver accurate information about student achievement; in other words, we must know and understand the following:

- *Why we are conducting any assessment.* This means that we must identify the information needs of those who will use the assessment results.

- *What achievement we wish to assess.* We must identify the achievement targets (goals, objectives, expectations, standards) that we expect our students to hit.

- *What assessment method to use in any particular situation.* This requires that we (1) identify a method that accurately reflects our expectations and (2) create assessment exercises and scoring procedures that tell us how well students have met those expectations.

- *How much evidence of achievement to gather.* We must assemble those exercises into an array (a sample) that spans the full range of our expectations.

- *What can go wrong with any assessment and how to prevent problems.* We need to be vigilant that bias does not creep into our assessment, distorting results.

Classroom assessments can be developed well or poorly. Part I of this book (Chapters 1–4) is about this difference. If you assess well, students can prosper. If you assess poorly, students are placed directly in harm's way. Our collective professional, ethical, and moral responsibility as teachers is to see to it that all assessments are done well. My intent is to help you develop the professional knowhow, or *assessment literacy*, to fulfill this critical responsibility.

In addition, we may use assessments well or poorly. Again, as teachers our challenge is to understand how to use them to benefit students. But beyond this understanding is the need for every one of us to make a personal professional commitment to supporting students' well-being through the effective use of classroom assessment.

We need to avoid assessment environments steeped in mystery and illusion, intimidation and vulnerability, stress and anxiety. They are unhealthy because they are built on a motivational model fueled by uncertainty and fear of failure. Maximum anxiety does not lead to maximum learning. Rather, confidence in one's self as a learner leads to student success and school effectiveness. In Part I, I will tell you why this is true.

Today, many teachers are creating more constructive classroom assessment environments than previously existed. They see assessment playing a different role, and have access to the tools and materials they need to make this happen, including the following:

- A clear and complete collection of standards *defining the achievement targets* that their students are to hit

- A carefully developed sense of the *different information needs of different assessment users*

- The ability to create *accurate assessments* of those targets

- Strategies for *sampling* student performance efficiently

- An understanding of possible *sources of bias* and how to control them

- The capacity to *communicate results* effectively

- The wisdom to use both classroom assessment processes and their results to *build student confidence as learners*

These teachers understand that the most important instructional decisions—that is, the decisions that bear most directly on student success in school—are made by students themselves. To make those decisions well, students need continuous access to understandable information about their own improvement as

readers, writers, math problem solvers, and the like. When they are partners in the assessment process, these teachers tell me, it's almost shocking how fast they can grow. It's surprising what students can and will do if we just don't prevent it! The purpose of this book is to give you the tools to enable you to join the ranks of these enlightened teachers.

This is not to say that decisions made by teachers, parents, principals, superintendents, or school board members are unimportant. Indeed, they are crucial. But these are not the people who are in charge of learning. Learners are in charge of learning. If they don't *want* to learn, or don't feel *able* to learn, they *won't* learn. So, as teachers, our driving questions must be, How can we help our students *want* to learn? How can we help them believe they are capable of learning?

I believe that these are essentially classroom assessment questions. This book is about how to use the day-to-day classroom assessment process to turn learners on to the possibility of success. It's about helping them feel in complete control of their own success. It's about putting in place in your classroom the conditions necessary to avoid assessments that destroy student confidence. It's about assessment without victims.

A Roadmap of Our Journey

In the chapters that follow, we lay the foundation of professional competence you need to meet standards of excellence in classroom assessment. The four chapters of Part I add detail to the vision of quality classroom assessment alluded to here. Chapter 1 offers a reexamination of the relationship between assessment and student motivation. The other three chapters frame commonsense standards of classroom assessment quality: Chapter 2 profiles assessment users, Chapter 3 defines achievement targets, and Chapter 4 explains how to select proper assessment methods, given users and targets.

The four chapters of Part II analyze the impressive array of assessment methods available to teachers wishing to build and maintain a productive, student-involved assessment environment. This phase of our journey takes you inside four assessment methods: selected response (e.g., multiple choice, true/false) assessments, essay assessments, performance assessments, and assessments based on direct personal communication with students.

In Part III, we will explore the backroads of how to apply these methods to a variety of different kinds of achievement, including mastery of content knowledge, reasoning proficiencies, performance skills, and product development capabilities.

In Part IV, we detail the options for delivering assessment results into the hands of many users, such as students, parents, other teachers, administrators, and so on, in timely and understandable terms.

This book will help you form the framework of your assessment literacy. From this, you must build your own classroom assessment environments. I will teach you about the options at your disposal through careful use of examples from a variety of academic disciplines. But remember, you can only understand sound assessment practices when you see them play out in your own real-world context. You must experiment with the assessment and communication options described herein to see how they fit into your particular assessment world.

From time to time, I will ask you to reflect on your own assessment experiences or on your reactions to the ideas I am sharing. Other times, I will invite you to practice applying the strategies being offered. Please take time to do these things. They represent a critically important part of your learning. Never forget that, during this journey, the responsibility for your learning resides with *you*. I am just your guide. In this sense, we model the relationship that must exist between you and your students.

Important Learning Aids

In designing this presentation, I have woven in several learning aids intended to help you connect the ideas and strategies presented to your personal experiences and classroom realities.

Travel Guides

As we travel together, we will be joined on occasion by some residents of the realm of classroom assessment. They have a wealth of experience with student-involved classroom assessment, record keeping, and communication to share in very practical terms. Our companions will include Emily, a high school student, Ms. Weatherby, her English teacher, Ms. Smith, another high school teacher, and Mr. Lopez, a third-grade teacher. Fictitious characters, they represent composite portraits of real people with whom I have worked over the years. Their assignment is to share their personal thoughts, emotions, and experiences in dealing with the challenges of classroom assessment and in finding solutions.

Connecting to Your Experiences

Periodically you will encounter "Times for Reflection" asking you to relate an idea to your personal perceptions or to think about something before moving on. The success of our joint efforts on behalf of sound classroom assessment will hinge on your ability to construct your own personal meaning of the material presented. You must fit these new ideas into your existing structure of knowledge and understanding of assessment. "Times for

Reflection" will help you do just that, so please take them seriously.

Vocabulary Is Important

In this book, I intend to deal with assessment matters in commonsense terms using everyday language. However, I occasionally will adopt a term or phrase for particular practices or concepts that we touch on repeatedly. I define these terms where I introduce them.

Technical Notes

Although my primary goal is for you to learn to apply practical assessment strategies, another is for you to become familiar with the technical side of assessment. For example, I want you to understand what experts are talking about when they refer to the "validity" and "reliability" of an assessment. When we touch on a matter of technical importance I will append a brief but informative "Technical Note" to the margin of the text. Watch for the ☉ Technical Note icon.

Time and Energy Savers

It is most important that you understand why high-quality classroom assessment effectively used to benefit student learning is an immense time saver for teachers. It can make everyone's job far easier—students, teachers, and parents. So, periodically I will offer suggestions that promise time and energy savings, noting them in the margin. Watch for the ⏱ Time Saver icon.

Lots of Opportunities to Practice

To help you integrate the ideas presented herein into your teaching practices, we have developed a variety of opportunities for you to practice applying student-involved classroom assessment strategies and methods.

Practice Exercises

We conclude each chapter with a set of "Exercises for Self-Assessment." Please take these seriously. Do not treat this book as a piece of literature that you merely read. Rather, regard it as a book you "do." It will serve you productively only if you experiment with the assessment options offered. These exercises are designed to expand your understanding in preparation for that experimentation.

Workbook

To provide you with further practice, we have developed an accompanying workbook, *Practice with Student-Involved Classroom Assessment*. Coauthored by Judy Arter and Kathy Busick, this learning aid offers an array of provocative opportunities for risk-free experimentation and learning, including the following:

- Case studies that ask you to confront real-world classroom assessment dilemmas and use what you are learning to find solutions

- Examples of unsound assessments that you can practice fixing

- Examples of high-quality assessments for you to study and learn from

- Projects that you can complete to meld these ideas directly into your classroom

The most interesting of these actually model here in your adult learning context the very student-involved assessment, record-keeping, and communication strategies that we recommend for your classroom. For instance, one such activity asks you to develop your own "Classroom Assessment Portfolio," a collection of examples of your classroom assessments that you assemble over time, along with self-reflections that capture your improvement as a classroom assessor during the course of your study of this text. We summarize the workbook exercises for each chapter at the end of the chapter. Watch for the 📖 Workbook icon.

This workbook is available from Merrill Education for use in college and university course settings. Contact Merrill at 1-800-922-0579, or visit their Website (http://www.prenhall.com). You also may order the workbook directly from the Assessment Training Institute (ATI) for use in inservice professional training contexts. Please contact ATI at 1-800-480-3060, or visit our Website (http://www.assessmentinst.com).

Companion Website

Merrill and ATI have teamed up to create a Companion Website (http://www.prenhall.com/stiggins) for those using this text in university courses. Among other features, this learning aid helps students work through the Exercises for Self-Assessment that appear at the end of each chapter, and suggests resources for further study for those seeking deeper understanding of key topics.

Video Support

ATI has developed a set of interactive video training packages to assist those using this text. Each presentation reviews key points made in its associated chapter(s) and provides structured practice in their application. These videos are useful both in university courses and with local learning teams for inservice professional development. Each available video, listed here, is described in detail at the end of its associated chapter.

Video Package

Imagine! Assessments That Energize Students (Ch. 1, 2)

Creating Sound Classroom Assessments (Ch. 2-4)

Common Sense Paper and Pencil Testing (Ch. 5, 6)

Assessing Reasoning in the Classroom (Ch. 9)

Report Card Grading: Strategies and Solutions (Ch. 13)

Student-Involved Conferences (Ch. 15)

Contact ATI at 1-800-480-3060 or visit our Website (http://www.assessmentinst.com) for details on how to obtain these interactive video packages.

Let Your Reflection and Practice Start Here

If you are using the workbook, *Practice with Student-Involved Classroom Assessment*, you can turn to it now and find the following activities awaiting your attention:

- *Where Am I Now?* We highly recommend this activity. It is important to set a baseline of your current confidence and understanding of student-involved classroom assessment prior to beginning your studies. That way, you will be able to track your own growth over time. The workbook contains specific instruments and procedures to help you do just that. Turn to Part I Introduction, Activity 1.

- *Establishing Group Norms.* If you are planning to study this book as a member of a learning team, we strongly recommend that you and your teammates establish your expectations of each other from the outset. Only then can you create a comfortable climate conducive to risk-free experimentation and learning. Part I Introduction, Activity 2 provides specific procedures for building a cooperative team environment.

- *Team Assets.* Once again, if you have formed a learning team, you will find it advantageous to identify the strengths each member brings to the learning situation. The team then can lean on each other as they grow together. To complete this team analysis, turn to Part I Introduction, Activity 3.

A Story of Classroom Assessment Success

CHAPTER FOCUS

This chapter answers the following guiding question:

> What does it look like and how is learning enhanced when classroom assessment is working to its full productive potential to motive student learning?

To find answers, we need to understand the following critical points:

1. The most powerful forms and applications of assessment take place day to day in the classroom.
2. Those applications reach their full potential only if the teacher adheres to certain principles of sound assessment practice.

A Vision of Success

Visualize yourself at a particularly important meeting of the school board in the district where you teach. This is the once-a-year meeting at which the district presents the annual report of standardized test scores to the board and the media. Every year it's the same: Will scores be up or down? How will you compare to national norms? How will your district compare to others in the area?

What most present don't realize as the meeting begins is that, this year, they are in for a big surprise with respect to both the achievement information to be presented and the manner of the presentation.

The audience includes a young woman named Emily, a junior at the high school, sitting in the back of the room with her parents. She knows she will be a big part of the surprise. She's only a little nervous. She understands how important her role is. It has been quite a year for her, unlike any she has ever experienced in school before. She also knows her parents and teacher are as proud of her as she is of herself.

The assistant superintendent begins by reminding the board and the rest of the audience that the district uses standardized tests that sample broad domains of achievement with just a few multiple-choice test items. Much that we value, she points out, must be assessed using other methods. She promises to provide an example later in the presentation. Emily's dad nudges her and they both smile.

Having set the stage, the assistant superintendent turns to carefully prepared charts depicting average student performance in each important achievement category tested. Results are summarized by grade and building, concluding with a clear description of how district results had changed from the year before and from previous years. As she proceeds, board members ask questions and receive clarification. Some scores are down slightly; some are up. Participants discuss possible reasons. This is a routine annual presentation that proceeds as expected.

Next comes the break from routine. Having completed the first part of the presentation, the assistant superintendent explains how the district has gathered some new information about one important aspect of student achievement. As the board knows, she points out, the district has implemented a new writing program in the high school to address the issue of poor writing skills among graduates. As part of their preparation for this program, the English faculty attended a summer institute on assessing writing proficiency and integrating such assessments into the teaching and learning process. The English department was confident that this kind of professional development and program revision would produce much higher levels of writing proficiency.

For the second half of the evening's assessment presentation, the high school English department faculty shares the results of their evaluation of the new writing program.

As the very first step in this presentation, the English chair, Ms. Weatherby, who also happens to be Emily's English teacher, distributes a sample of student writing to the board members (with the student's name removed), asking them to read and evaluate this writing. They do so, expressing their dismay aloud as they go. They are indignant in their commentary on these samples of student work. One board member reports in exasperation that, if these represent the results of that new writing program, the community has been had. The board member is right. These are, in fact, pretty weak pieces of work. Emily's mom puts her arm around her daughter's shoulder and hugs her.

But Ms. Weatherby urges patience and asks the board members to be very specific in stating what they don't like about this work. As the board registers its complaints, the faculty records the criticisms on chart paper for all to see. The list is long, including everything from repetitiveness to disorganization to short, choppy sentences and disconnected ideas.

Next, the teacher distributes another sample of student writing, asking the board to read and evaluate it. Ah, this, they report, is more like it! This work is much better! But be specific, the chair demands. What do you like about this work? They list positive aspects: good choice of words, sound sentence structure, clever ideas, and so on. Emily is ready to burst! She squeezes her mom's hand.

The reason she's so full of pride at this moment is that this has been a special year for her and her classmates. For the first time ever, they became partners with their English teachers in managing their own improvement as writers. Early in the year, Ms. Weatherby (Ms. W, they all call her) made it crystal clear to Emily that she was, in fact, not a very good writer and that just trying hard to get better was not going to be enough. She expected Emily to *be* better—nothing else would suffice.

Ms. W started the year by working with students to set high writing standards, including understanding quality performance in word choice, sentence structure, organization, and voice, and sharing some new "analytical scoring guides" written just for students. Each explained the differences between good and poor-quality writing in understandable ways. When Emily and her teacher evaluated her first two pieces of writing using these standards, she received very low ratings. Not very good. . . .

But she also began to study samples of writing her teacher supplied that Emily could see were very good. Slowly, she began to understand *why* they were good. The differences between these and her work started to become clear. Ms. W began to share examples and strategies that would help her writing improve one step at a time. As she practiced with these and time passed, Emily and her classmates kept samples of their old writing to compare to their new writing, and they began to build portfolios. Thus, she literally began to watch her own writing skills improve before her very eyes. At midyear, her parents were invited in for a conference at which Emily, not Ms. Weatherby, shared the contents of her portfolio and discussed her emerging writing skills. Emily remembers sharing thoughts about some aspects of her writing that had become very strong and some examples of things she still needed to work on. Now, the year was at an end and here she sat waiting for her turn to speak to the school board about all of this. What a year!

Now, having set the board up by having them analyze, evaluate, and compare these two samples of student work, Ms. W springs the surprise: The two pieces of writing they had just evaluated, one of less sophistication and one of outstanding quality, were produced by the same writer at the beginning and at the end of the school year! This, she reports, is evidence of the kind of impact the new writing program is having on student writing proficiency.

Needless to say, all are impressed. However, one board member wonders aloud, "Have all your students improved in this way?" Having anticipated the question, the rest of the English faculty joins the presentation and produces carefully prepared charts depicting dramatic changes in typical student performance over time on rating scales for each of six clearly articulated dimensions of good writing. They accompany their description of student performance on each scale with actual samples of student work illustrating various levels of proficiency.

Further, Ms. W informs the board that the student whose improvement has been so dramatically illustrated with the work they have just analyzed is present at this school board meeting, along with her parents. This student is ready to talk with the board about the nature of her learning experience. Emily, you're on!

Interest among the board members runs high. Emily talks about how she has come to understand the truly important differences between good and bad writing. She refers to differences she had not understood before, how she has learned to assess her own writing and to fix it when it doesn't "work well," and how she and her classmates have learned to talk with her teacher and each other about what it means to write well. Ms. W talks about the improved focus of writing instruction, increase in student motivation, and important positive changes in the very nature of the student–teacher relationship.

A board member asks Emily if she likes to write. She reports, "I do now!" This board member turns to Emily's parents and asks their impression of all of this. They report with pride that they had never seen so much evidence before of Emily's achievement and most of it came from Emily herself. Emily had never been called on to lead the parent-teacher conference before. They had no idea she was so articulate. They loved it. Their daughter's pride in and accountability for achievement had skyrocketed in the past year.

As the meeting ends, it is clear to all in attendance that evening that this two-part assessment presentation—one part from standardized test scores and one from students, teachers, and the classroom—reveals that assessment is in balance in this district. The test scores cover part of the picture and classroom assessment evidence completes the achievement picture. There are good feelings all around. The accountability needs of the community are being satisfied and the new writing program is working to improve student achievement. Obviously, this story has a happy ending.

Can you visualize yourself walking out of the boardroom at the end of the evening, hearing parents wish they had had such an experience in high school? I sure can. Can't you just anticipate the wording of the memo of congratulations the superintendent will soon write to the English department? How about the story that will appear in the newspaper tomorrow, right next to the report of test scores? *Everyone involved here, from Emily to her classmates to parents to teachers to assessment director to (at the end) school board members, understood how to use assessment to promote student success and effective schools.*

The Keys to Success

What were the active ingredients in this success? To begin with, the faculty understood who is in charge of learning—not them, not the principal, not parents, not school board members, but the students themselves. Therefore, assessment was never a teacher-centered activity, carried out by the teacher to meet the teacher's needs. Rather, it was a student-centered activity, in which Emily and her classmates consistently assessed their own achievement repeatedly over time, so they and their parents could watch the improvement. To be sure, Ms. W controlled writing content and evaluation criteria, and made important decisions based on assessment results. But she also shared the wisdom and power that come from being able to assess the quality of writing. She showed her students the secrets to their own success.

In this way, Ms. W used assessment and its results to build, not destroy, her students' confidence in themselves as writers. The faculty understood that those who believe the target is within reach for them will keep striving. Those who see the target as being beyond reach will give up in hopelessness.

Second, they understood that students can remain self-confident only if they know and understand where they are now in relation to an ultimate vision of success. Ms. W began her program of writing instruction with a highly refined vision of what good writing looks like and shared that vision of excellence with her students from the beginning. Students could continually see the distance closing between their present position and their goal. This turned out to be incredibly empowering for them.

Third, Ms. W and her colleagues knew that their assessments of student achievement had to be very accurate. Writing exercises had to elicit the right kinds of writing. Scoring procedures needed to focus on the important facets of good writing. As faculty members, they needed to train themselves to apply those scoring standards dependably—to avoid making biased judgments about student work.

But, just as important, Ms. W understood that she also had to train her students to make dependable judgments about the quality of their own work. This represents the heart of competence. Any student who cannot evaluate the quality of her own writing and fix it when it isn't working cannot become an independent, lifelong writer.

The final key to success was the great care taken to communicate effectively about student achievement. Whether Ms. W was discussing with Emily improvements needed or achieved in her work or sharing with the school board summary information about average student performance, she took pains to speak simply, to the point, and with examples to ensure that her meaning was clear.

Success from the Student's Point of View

The day after the board meeting, I interviewed Emily about the evening's events. As you read, think about how our conversation centers on what really works for Emily.

Rick	You did a nice job at the school board meeting last night, Emily.
Emily	Thanks. What pleases me most is that, last year, I could never have done it.
Rick	What's changed from last year?
Emily	I guess I'm more confident. I knew what had happened for me in English class and I wanted to tell them my story.
Rick	You became a confident writer.
Emily	Yeah, but that's not what I mean. Last night at the board meeting I was more than a good writer. I felt good talking

	about my writing and how I'd improved. It's like, I understand what I've learned and I have a way to describe it.
RICK	Let's talk about Emily the confident writer. What were you thinking last night when the board members were reacting to your initial writing sample—the one that wasn't very good? Still confident?
EMILY	Mom helped. She squeezed my hand and I remember she whispered in my ear, "You'll show 'em!" That helped me handle it. It's funny, I was listening to their comments to see if they knew anything about good writing. I wondered if they understood as much about it as I do—like, maybe they needed to take Ms. Weatherby's class.
RICK	How did they do?
EMILY	Pretty well, actually. They found the problems in my early work and described them pretty well. When I first started last fall, I wouldn't have been able to do that. I was a terrible writer.
RICK	How do you know that?
EMILY	I understand where I was, how little I could do. No organization. I didn't even know my own voice. No one had ever taken the time to show me the secrets. I'd never learned to analyze my writing. I wouldn't have known what to look for or how to describe it. That's part of what Ms. Weatherby taught us.
RICK	Say more about what she taught you.
EMILY	To begin with, she taught us to do what the board members did last night: analyze other people's writing. We looked at newspaper editorials, passages from books we were reading, letters friends had sent us. She wanted us to see what made those pieces work or not work.
RICK	Why do you suppose she started you there?
EMILY	Well, she would read a piece to us and then we'd brainstorm what made it good or bad. Pretty soon, we began to see patterns—things that worked or didn't work. She wanted us to begin to see and hear stuff as she read out loud.
RICK	Like what?
EMILY	Well, look, here's my early piece from the meeting last night. See, just read it!

Time for Reflection

Please take time to read Emily's beginning of the year writing sample in Figure 1.1 before you read on.

BEGINNING OF THE YEAR Writing Sample

Computers are a thing of the future. They help us in thousands of ways. Computers are a help to our lives. They make things easier. They help us to keep track of information.

Computers are simple to use. Anyone can learn how. You do not have to be a computer expert to operate a computer. You just need to know a few basic things.

Computers can be robots that will change our lives. Robots are really computers! Robots do a lot of the work that humans used to do. This makes our lives much easier. Robots build cars and do many other tasks that humans used to do. When robots learn to do more, they will take over most of our work. This will free humans to do other kinds of things. You can also communicate on computers. It is much faster than mail! You can look up information, too. You can find information on anything at all on a computer.

Computers are changing the work and changing the way we work and communicate. In many ways, computers are changing our lives and making our lives better and easier.

END OF THE YEAR Writing Sample

So there I was, my face aglow with the reflection on my computer screen, trying to come up with the next line for my essay. Writing it was akin to Chinese water torture, as I could never seem to end it. It dragged on and on, a never-ending babble of stuff.

Suddenly, unexpectedly—I felt an ending coming on. I could wrap this thing up in four or five sentences, and this dreadful assignment would be over. I'd be free.

I had not saved yet, and decided I would do so now. I clasped the slick, white mouse in my hand, slid it over the mouse pad, and watched as the black arrow progressed toward the "File" menu. By accident, I clicked the mouse button just to the left of paragraph 66. I saw a flash and the next thing I knew, I was back to square one. I stared at the blank screen for a moment in disbelief. Where was my essay? My ten-billion-page masterpiece? Gone?! No—that couldn't be! Not after all the work I had done! Would a computer be that unforgiving? That unfeeling? Didn't it care about me at all?

I decided not to give up hope just yet. The secret was to remain calm. After all, my file had to be somewhere—right? That's what all the manuals say—"It's in there *somewhere.*" I went back to the "File" menu, much more carefully this time. First, I tried a friendly sounding category called "Find File." No luck there; I hadn't given the file a name.

Ah, then I had a brainstorm. I could simply go up to "Undo." Yes, that would be my savior! A simple click of a button and my problem would be solved! I went to Undo, but it looked a bit fuzzy. Not a good sign. That means there is nothing to undo. Don't panic ... don't panic ...

I decided to try to exit the program, not really knowing what I would accomplish by this but feeling more than a little desperate. Next, I clicked on the icon that would allow me back in to word processing. A small sign appeared, telling me that my program was being used by another user. Another user? What's it talking about? *I'm* the only user, you idiot! Or at least I'm trying to be a user! Give me my paper back! Right now!

I clicked on the icon again and again—to no avail. Click ... click ... clickclickclickCLICKCLICKCLICK!!!! Without warning, a thin cloud of smoke began to rise from the back of the computer. I didn't know whether to laugh or cry. Sighing, I opened my desk drawer, and pulled out a tablet and pen. It was going to be a long day.

Figure 1.1
Emily's writing samples
Source: Personal writing by Nikki Spandel. Reprinted by permission.

EMILY

It's correct—no mistakes. But these short, choppy sentences don't work. And it doesn't say anything or go anywhere. It's just disconnected thoughts. It doesn't grab you and hold your attention. Then it just stops. See, we needed to learn how to fix these things in our own writing.

Now look at my other piece. Let me read it to you, so you can hear the rhythm of these sentences (She reads aloud). Ms. W taught us to read our writing out loud to hear how to fix it.

Time for Reflection

Now please read Emily's end of the year writing sample in Figure 1.1 before you read on.

EMILY

In this one, I tried to tell about the feelings of frustration that happen when humans use machines. See, I think the voice in this piece comes from the feeling that "We've all been there." Everyone who works with computers has had this experience—or something close to it. A tiny writer's problem (not being able to find a good ending) turns into a major problem (losing the whole document). This idea makes the piece clear and organized. I think the reader can picture this poor, frustrated writer at her computer, wanting, trying to communicate in a human way—but finding that the computer is just as frustrated with her!

RICK

You sound just like you did last night.

EMILY

I'm always like this about my writing now. I know what works. Sentences are important. So is voice. So are organization and word choice—all that stuff. If you do it right, it works and you know it.

RICK

What else did your teacher do to help you?

EMILY

When we were first getting started, Ms. Weatherby gave us a big stack of student papers she'd collected over the years—some good, some bad, and everything in between. Our assignment was to sort them into four stacks based on quality, from real good to real bad. When we were done, we compared who put what papers in which piles and then we talked about why—we argued, really. Soon, we began to describe what the differences were among the piles. From here, Ms. W helped us develop the six five-point rating scales that we used for the rest of the year to analyze, evaluate, and improve our writing.

RICK

When did you begin to write and then evaluate your own work?

EMILY

As soon as we finished the rating scales.

RICK

Your own and each other's work?

EMILY	Only our own to begin with. Ms. W said she didn't want anyone being embarrassed. We all had a lot to learn. It was supposed to be private until we began to trust our own judgments. She kept saying, "Trust me. You'll get better at this and then you can share."
RICK	Did you ever move on to evaluating each other's work?
EMILY	You bet. When we began to trust ourselves and each other, we were free to ask classmates for opinions. But Ms. Weatherby was very clear about saying that we could only give opinions in the form of ratings, with specific descriptions of what we saw in the work we evaluated. No blanket judgments, like this is good or bad. And we were always supposed to be honest. If we couldn't see how to help someone improve a piece, we were supposed to say so.
RICK	Then what?
EMILY	Lots of practice—all year. I've still got my writing portfolio full of practice, see? It starts out pretty bad back in the fall and slowly gets pretty good toward spring. This is where the two pieces came from that the board read last night. I picked them. I talk about the changes in my writing in the self-reflections in here. My portfolio tells the whole story. Want to look through it?
RICK	I sure do. What do you think Ms. Weatherby did right?
EMILY	Nobody had ever been so clear with me before about what it took to be really good at school stuff. It's like, there's no mystery—no need to psych her out. She said, "I won't ever surprise you, trust me. I'll show you what I want and I don't want any excuses. But you've got to deliver good writing in this class. You don't deliver, you don't succeed."
RICK	What else did she do right?
EMILY	A bunch of us were talking about this the other day. She trusted us. Every so often, she would give us something she had written, so we could evaluate her work. She listened to our comments and said it really helped her. We were her teachers! That was so cool!
RICK	Anything else?
EMILY	You know, she was the first teacher ever to tell me that it was okay to fail. But just at first, like, when you're trying to do something new. But we couldn't keep failing. We had to get a little better each time. If we didn't, it was our own fault. She didn't want us to give up on ourselves. If we kept improving, over time, we could learn to write well. I wish every teacher would do that. She would say, "There's no shortage of success around here. You learn to write well, you get an 'A.' My goal is to have everyone learn to write well and deserve an 'A.'"

| Rick | Thanks for filling in the details, Em. |
| Emily | Thank you for asking! |

Some Students Aren't So Lucky

Sadly, for every such positive story, in which sound assessment feeds into productive instruction and important learning, there may be another with a far less constructive, perhaps even painful, ending. Remember the story of our daughter Krissy and Kelly the kitten? Some unfortunate students may be mired in classrooms in which they are forced to try to guess the meaning of academic success. Their teachers may lack a vision of success or may focus on an incorrect one. Or they might choose to keep the secrets of success a mystery in order to retain power and control in the classroom. When their students guess at the valued target and guess wrong, they fail the assessment. But they fail not from lack of motivation, but from lack of insight as to what they are supposed to achieve. This can be very discouraging. It destroys confidence. These students may well have succeeded had they been given the opportunity to strive for a clear objective.

Then there are those students who prepare well, master the required material, and fail anyway because the teacher prepares a poor-quality test, thus mismeasuring achievement. Student achievement may also be mismeasured because a teacher places blind faith in the quality of the tests that accompanied the textbook, when in fact that confidence is misplaced. In addition, some students fail not because of low achievement, but because their teacher's subjective performance assessment judgments are riddled with the effects of unconscious bias.

> **TECHNICAL NOTE**
>
> Tests made up of poor-quality exercises or that are scored using inappropriate procedures yield scores that misrepresent student achievement. The results of such assessments are said to be **BIASED**. They are distorted, and inaccurate.

Still further, school boards might make poor policy decisions because members fail to understand what their district's standardized tests do and don't measure, thus misinterpreting the meaning of the scores these tests produce. The list of problems could go on and on.

When these and other such problems arise, an environment of assessment illiteracy dominates, assessments will be of poor quality, and students are placed directly in harm's way.

Our Common Mission

Our joint challenge in this book is to begin or to carry on with the professional development needed to ensure your assessment literacy. *Assessment literates* are those who understand the basic principles of sound assessment. But just understanding the meaning of sound assessment will not suffice. We must demand adherence to high standards by acting purposefully to meet those standards in all assessment contexts and by pointing out to others when their assessments fail to measure up. As we implement assessments in the classroom or the boardroom, we must know how sound assessment relates to quality instruction and must strive to maintain a balanced use of assessment alternatives.

As you will see, assessments serve many masters, take many different forms, can reflect many different kinds of achievement, and can fall prey to any of a variety of different problems that may lead to inaccurate evaluation. When our journey is complete you will have developed your own framework for understanding all of the options, what can go wrong, and how to prevent assessment problems. In short, you will be prepared to assemble the parts of the classroom assessment puzzle as artfully as Ms. Weatherby does.

But underpinning all that we cover, all that we illustrate with examples, all that you practice applying, must be one guiding aspiration: Like Ms. W, *your job as a teacher is to teach yourself out of a job.* It is to take your students to a place where they no longer need you to tell them whether they have done well—to a place where they know in their minds and hearts how they have performed because *they know the meaning of success.* We seek classrooms where there are no surprises and no excuses.

> Assessment takes time and energy to carry out. The more of that work you can share with your students, the more time you have to teach; but more importantly, the more they learn!

A Set of Guiding Principles

In the chapters that follow, I will share a vast array of assessment tools, strategies, admonitions, and examples all aimed at making assessment work well for you. As we proceed, you will find certain themes recurring. These are graphically portrayed in Figure 1.2, and are addressed in greater detail in the remainder of this chapter. They represent both important assessment realities teachers face in classrooms and important values that I personally have come to hold about classroom assessment. I share them with you here at the outset as interrelated themes that map the path to quality. The order in which they are presented is unimportant. All are profoundly important. Together, they represent the foundation of your preparation to assess well in the classroom.

As you read, reflect on Emily, the high school writing student in the chapter's opening vignette, and you will see why I started our journey together in this way.

Guiding Principle 1: Students Are the Key Assessment Users

Students are the most important users of assessment results. In our opening vignette, Emily and her classmates learned to improve because they learned to compare their own performance to a clearly stated set of standards of quality performance. They learned to understand these standards through direct interaction with their teachers, based on practice in the presence of regular ongoing feedback on their progress via classroom assessments.

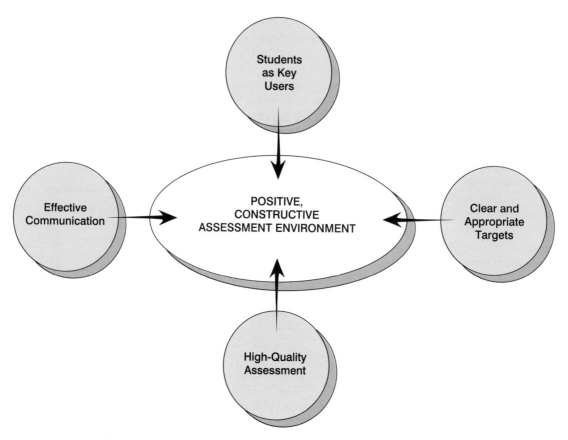

Figure 1.2
A critical blend of guiding principles

Consider the role of student as consumer of assessment results: *Right from the time students arrive at school, they look to their teachers for evidence of their success. If that early evidence suggests that they are succeeding, what begins to grow in them is a sense of hopefulness and an expectation of more success in the future. This in turn fuels the motivation to try, which fuels even more success.* The basis of this upward spiral is the evidence of their own achievement, which students receive from their teachers based on ongoing classroom assessments. Thus, classroom assessment information is the essential fuel that powers the learning system for students.

However, when the evidence suggests to students that they are not succeeding in this place called school, what can then begin to grow in them is a sense of hopelessness and an expectation of more failure in the future. This can rob them of the motivation to try, which in turn can lead to more failure. In this downward spiral, here again we see consequences of classroom assessment evidence, but this time as the fuel that drives the motivation *not* to try.

I do not mean to imply that all assessment results should be positive simply to keep students involved and motivated. On the contrary, if students are not meeting your high standards, your assessments must accurately reflect that fact. But if those results reflect a lack of academic success, you must act to change your instructional approach to prevent the pattern of failure from becoming chronic. You must find a different formula that brings to students hope of future success. Ongoing classroom assessments are your best tool for revealing that success to them.

There are many important assessment users at all levels of the educational process. We will study them in depth in Chapter 2. However, only students use the assessment results to set expectations of themselves. Students decide how high to aim based on their sense of the probability that they will succeed. They estimate the probability of future success based on their record of past success as reflected in their prior classroom assessment experience. *No single decision or combination of decisions made by any other party exerts greater influence on student success.*

Guiding Principle 2: Clear and Appropriate Targets Are Essential

The quality of any assessment depends first and foremost on how clearly and appropriately we define the achievement target we are assessing. In the opening vignette, a breakthrough in student writing achievement occurred because the English faculty returned from that summer institute with a shared vision of writing proficiency. They built their program, and thus the competence of their students, around that vision.

You cannot accurately assess academic achievement targets that you have not defined precisely. There are many different kinds of valued achievement expectations within our educational system, from mastering content knowledge to complex problem solving, from performing a flute recital to speaking Spanish to writing a strong term paper. All are important. But to assess them well, you must ask yourself: Do I know what it means to do it well? Precisely what does it mean to succeed academically? You are ready to assess only when you can answer these questions with clarity and confidence.

If your job is to teach students to become better writers, you had better start with a highly refined vision of what good writing looks like and a sense of how to help your students meet that standard. If your mission is to promote math problem-solving proficiency, you had better be a confident, competent master of that performance domain yourself. Without a sense of final destination reflected in your standards, and signposts along the way against which to check students' progress, you will have difficulty being an effective teacher.

Guiding Principle 3: Accurate Assessment Is a Must

High-quality assessment is essential in all assessment contexts. Sound assessments satisfy five specific quality standards: (1) clear targets; (2) focused purpose;

(3) proper method; (4) sound sampling; and (5) accurate and free from bias and distortion. All assessments must meet all standards. No exceptions can be tolerated, because to violate any of them is to risk inaccuracy, placing student academic well-being in jeopardy. Figure 1.3 illustrates these five standards. This is the first of many discussions and illustrations of these quality standards that permeate this book. On this first pass, I intend only to give you a general sense of the meaning of *quality*.

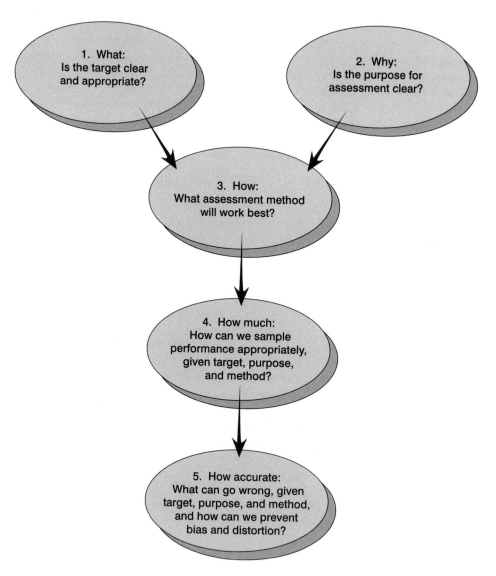

Figure 1.3
Keys to sound assessment

Clear Targets

First, sound assessments arise from and reflect clear achievement targets (as in Guiding Principle 2). You can ask this question about any assessment: Can the developer and user provide a clear and appropriate description of the specific achievement expectation(s) it is designed to reflect? If the answer is yes, proceed to the next quality criterion. If the answer is no, realize that there is a very real danger of inaccurate assessment. As educators, we must all be confident, competent masters of the achievement targets we expect our students to master.

In the chapters that follow, I will reveal why most teachers need to assess four interrelated forms of achievement expectation day to day in their classrooms. We almost always expect our students to master (meaning know and understand) *content* knowledge sufficiently to be able to use it productively to *reason* and solve problems. In addition, many teachers expect their students to develop specified *performance skills* and be able to use them productively to *create products* that meet certain standards of quality. I hold these same kinds of expectations for you as you use this book to learn about assessment. Quality standard number one asks that those who develop or select classroom assessments begin that process with a refined sense of the specific knowledge, reasoning, skill, and product expectations they hold for their students. In other words, *you must understand what you are assessing*.

> Assessment experts say that an assessment that accurately reflects its intended target is **VALID**; it possesses the attribute of **CONTENT VALIDITY**.

Focused Purpose

This standard asks that you begin any assessment design with a clear sense of *why* you are conducting the assessment. It is impossible to develop a quality assessment unless and until you know how you will use the results it produces. So again, about any assessment you can ask: Does the developer understand the intended uses and has the developer taken users' needs into account in developing and implementing the assessment?

In Chapter 2, we discuss the information needs of several different assessment users at three levels of concern. First, there are those who use assessment results at the classroom level: students, teachers, and parents. Each user brings certain information needs to the classroom assessment table, and schools must meet all needs to be effective. Then there are users at the instructional support level (principals, support teachers, curriculum personnel, etc.), and finally those at the policy level (superintendents, school board members, state department personnel, etc.). Each brings unique information needs and has a right to have those needs met by our assessment systems. There is no single assessment capable of meeting all of these different needs. Thus, the developer of any assessment must start with a clear sense of whose needs the assessment will meet.

> Assessment experts say that an assessment that serves its intended purpose is **VALID**; it provides the information needed to do the job.

Proper Method

A sound assessment examines student achievement through the use of a method that is, in fact, capable of reflecting the valued target. To test mastery of scientific knowledge, you might use a multiple-choice test. But when your challenge is to assess the ability to speak Spanish fluently, you must turn to another method altogether. As stated, you have several different kinds of achievement to assess. As you will see in later chapters, you have several different assessment methods to use to reflect them. These include *selected response* methods (multiple choice, true/false, matching, and fill in), *essay* assessments, *performance assessments* (based on observation and judgment), and direct *personal communication* with students (talking with them). Your classroom assessment challenge is to know how to match the method with the intended target. About any assessment, you can ask: Is the method used here capable of accurately reflecting the kinds of outcomes the user wishes to assess? If the answer is yes, proceed to the next criterion. If it is no, be aware that student achievement is about to be a victim of inaccurate assessment.

Sound Sampling

Almost all assessments rely on a sample of all the exercises you could have included if time were unlimited and the test could be infinitely long. A sound assessment offers a representative sample that is large enough to yield confident conclusions about how the respondent would have done given all possible exercises. The realities of classroom life require that you generalize from your sample to the total performance arena being assessed. Each different classroom assessment context places its own special constraints on sampling procedures. Your responsibility is to know how to adjust your sampling strategies as context varies to produce results of maximum accuracy at minimum cost in time and effort. About any assessment, you can ask: Have I gathered enough information of the right kind, so I can draw confident conclusions about student achievement? If the answer is yes, proceed. If it is no, consumers of assessment information may be misinformed.

Assessments that fail to sample the achievement target in a complete representative manner are **INVALID**.

Accurate Assessment Free from Bias and Distortion

This final criterion demands that you design, develop, and use assessments in ways that permit you to control for all sources of bias and distortion that can cause your results to misrepresent real student achievement. Again, each assessment context presents its own unique sources of interference with accurate assessment. Each assessment method permits errors to creep in when you let your guard down. With multiple-choice tests, for example, poorly written or culturally biased test items can harm the quality of resulting scores. With performance assessments, evaluator prejudice can bias judgments. So it is with all methods. Your challenge is to know all sources of bias and distortion that can rob assessment results of clear and appropriate meaning and to know how to head off those problems before they get a foothold. About any assessment, you can ask: Have the important sources of bias been accounted for during development and use? If the answer is no, you must take action to address sources of error that are not accounted for.

Violate any of these five criteria and you place students at risk. Problems arise when assessments are developed and used by those who fail to understand the valued target, fail to identify user needs, rely on an improper assessment method, sample achievement inadequately, or introduce bias. Unsound assessments can lead to misdiagnosed needs, failure to provide needed instructional support, use of inappropriate instructional approaches, counterproductive grouping of students, and misinformation provided to student and parent decision makers.

> Assessment experts tell us to eliminate errors of measurement due to bias to maximize the **RELIABILITY** of our assessments.
>
> TECHNICAL NOTE

Guiding Principle 4: Sound Assessments Must Be Accompanied by Effective Communication

Mention assessment and the first thoughts that come to mind are of scores, numbers, and grades attached to very briefly labeled forms of achievement such as reading, writing, science, math, and the like. The underlying meaning of these single-word labels is rarely explicated. In contrast, in our opening vignette the English faculty started with a clear vision of the meaning of academic success in their classrooms and communicated that meaning effectively to their students, parents, and school board members through the thoughtful use of performance rating schemes combined with examples of student performance, both of which reflected their vision. Sound assessment requires clear thinking and effective communication, not merely the quantification of ill-defined achievement targets.

While many assessments do translate levels of achievement into scores, we are coming to understand two important realities more and more clearly. First, numbers are not the only way to communicate about achievement. We can use words, pictures, illustrations, examples, and many other means to convey this information. Second, the symbols we use as the basis of our communication about student achievement are only as meaningful and useful as the definitions of achievement that underpin them and the quality of the assessments used to produce them.

Assessment-literate educators are critical consumers of assessment information. They are constantly asking, "Precisely what is being assessed here and how do I know what the results mean?" They do not rest until they achieve clear thinking and effective communication, both in their own assessments and those of others.

A Final Thought

Teachers direct both the assessments that determine what students learn and how those students feel about that learning. In our opening account, the assessments that contributed to a stronger writing program were not the districtwide tests reported at the beginning of the board presentation. Rather, the critical assessments were those the English teachers conducted in their classrooms from the beginning through the end of the school year.

Yet, in most educational contexts, standardized test results (district, state, national, or even international) command all of the resources, news coverage, and political power, as though they were the only assessments that count. *They are not.* While these highly visible assessments do contribute to the quality of schools, they are not in the same league as teachers' classroom assessments in terms of their direct impact on student well-being.

Almost all of the assessment events that take place in students' lives happen at the behest of their teachers. Teachers spend as much as one-third of their professional time on assessment-related activities (Stiggins & Conklin, 1992). They make new decisions every few minutes about how to interact with their students. Most decisions are informed by some kind of classroom assessment of student achievement—asking questions and interpreting answers, watching students perform, examining homework assignments, and using tests and quizzes, among other means. Assessment is almost continuous in classrooms.

Clearly, classroom assessments are the ones most available to teachers. They also are most closely aligned with day-to-day instruction and are most influential in terms of their contribution to student success. *Without question, as a teacher, you control the assessment systems that determine your school's effectiveness.*

The guiding theme of this book is that the greatest potential value of classroom assessment is realized when we open the process up and welcome students in as full partners. Please understand that I do not simply mean having students trade test papers or homework assignments so they can grade each other's work. That's strictly clerical stuff. This concept of full partnership, as Emily and her classmates learned, goes far deeper.

Scriven (personal communication, 1995) provides a sense of the different levels of student involvement in assessment. Starting with very superficial involvement, each level brings students further into the actual assessment equation. Students can do the following:

- Take the test and receive the grade
- Be invited to offer the teacher comments on how to improve the test
- Suggest possible assessment exercises
- Actually develop assessment exercises
- Assist the teacher in devising scoring criteria
- Create the scoring criteria on their own
- Apply scoring criteria to the evaluation of their own performance
- Come to understand how assessment and evaluation affect their own academic success
- Come to see how their own self-assessment relates to the teacher's assessment and to their own academic success

Students who participate in the thoughtful analysis of quality work, so as to identify its critical elements or to internalize valued achievement targets, become better performers. When students learn to apply those standards so thoroughly that they can confidently and competently evaluate their own and each other's work, they are well down the road to becoming better performers in their own right. Consider Emily's case in the opening vignette. Her teacher helped her to internalize key elements of good writing so she could understand the shortcomings of her own writing, take responsibility for improving them, and watch herself improve. Her confidence and competence in being a partner in her classroom assessment came through loud and clear, both in the parent-teacher conference she led at midyear and in her commentary to the school board at the end of the year. I offer many specific suggestions for melding assessment and instruction in this way throughout this text on "student-involved" classroom assessment.

Time for Reflection

In your past, did you ever work with a teacher who succeeded in turning an assessment event into a positive, constructive learning experience for you? Specifically, how did that teacher do so? What do you think might be some keys to turning assessment experiences into learning experiences for students?

Summary: The Importance of Accurate Assessment

The guiding principles discussed in this chapter (and illustrated with Emily's experience) form the foundation of the assessment wisdom all educators must master in order to manage classroom assessment environments effectively.

Teachers who are prepared to meet the challenges of classroom assessment understand that they need to do their assessment homework and be ready to think clearly and to communicate effectively at assessment time. They understand why it is critical to be able to share their expectations with students and their families and why it is essential that they conduct high-quality assessments that accurately reflect achievement expectations.

Well-prepared teachers realize that they themselves lie at the heart of the assessment process in schools and they take that responsi-

bility very seriously. Unfortunately, as you shall see in the next chapter, as a society and as a community of professional educators, we have done little to support teachers over the decades in fulfilling this responsibility. Fortunately, this is changing, as professional development in assessment is becoming a high educational priority.

Competent teachers understand the complexities of aligning a range of valued achievement targets with appropriate assessment methods so as to produce information on student achievement that both they and their students can count on to be accurate. They understand the meaning of sound assessment and they know how to use all of the assessment tools at their disposal to produce accurate information.

Effective classroom assessors/teachers understand the interpersonal dynamics of classroom assessment and know how to set students up for success, in part through using the appropriate assessment as a teaching tool. They know how to make students full partners in defining the valued targets of instruction and in transforming those definitions into quality assessments.

As teachers bring students into the assessment process, thus demystifying the meaning of success in the classroom, they acknowledge that students use assessment results to make the decisions that ultimately will determine if school does or does not work for them. Our collective classroom assessment responsibility is to be sure students have the information they need, in a form they understand, and in time to use it effectively.

Exercises for Self-Assessment

1. Scan the chapter focusing on Emily's experience and list as many benefits as you can of student involvement in assessment, record keeping, and communication. What conclusion do you draw about the power of this teaching and assessment strategy?

2. What do you believe are the major dangers or limitations of student involvement? Why do you believe this?

3. Restate each of the four guiding principles in your own words, including the standards of assessment quality discussed in Principle 3.

4. The most prominent admonition articulated in this chapter is that your job as a teacher is to strive to "teach yourself out of a job." What does this mean? Why is it important?

 You may go to the Companion Website at www.prenhall.com/stiggins and answer these questions in the Self-Assessment module.

Final Chapter Reflection

Each chapter in this text will conclude with a brief and consistent set of questions for you to reflect on to solidify your understanding and ease your transition to subsequent chapters. Please take time to record your answers. They will help you make key connections as we continue our journey through the realm of classroom assessment.

1. *What are the three most important new insights to come to you as a result of your study of this chapter?*
2. *What questions come to mind now about classroom assessment that you hope to have answered in subsequent chapters?*

Workbook Activities

Those of you using the workbook, *Practice with Student-Involved Classroom Assessment*, as part of your study of this material will find the following activities and others included for Chapter 1:

- *Discussion.*   The research paper, "Inside the Black Box," presents compelling evidence that high-quality, student-involved classroom assessment leads to greater student achievement. It describes the changes in classroom assessment practice that need to occur in order to tap that positive impact, reinforcing the power of student involvement in classroom assessment. Turn to the workbook to learn how to access this paper for review and discussion.

- *Pop Quiz.*   A cartoon depicts the role of assessment in determining the direction and intensity of student motivation to learn. This activity asks you to identify which students are most likely to be motivated by the classroom assessment situation depicted and to state why.

- *Our Own Experiences with Assessment and Implications for Practice.*   This personal reflection activity connects your own personal experiences with assessment to motivation and sound practice.

2

The Role of Assessment in Helping Students Succeed

CHAPTER FOCUS

This chapter addresses the following guiding question:

> What contributions can and should assessment make in helping students strive for and achieve success in school?

The following key understandings help us derive our answer:

1. Assessments serve many purposes in school; that is, they inform a variety of users. All users are important and deserve accurate, timely, and understandable information about student achievement.

2. In the order of priorities, students are the most important assessment users, followed by their teachers, their parents, and then other school and district personnel.

3. To understand these priorities, one must carefully examine and come to understand the relationship between assessment and student motivation.

We are going to explore specific strategies for meeting each of the standards of assessment quality referred to under Principle 3 in Chapter 1. As we go, we will use Figure 2.1 as our road map. In this chapter, we will deal with the shaded bubble of Figure 2.1, the need to begin the development of any assessment with a clear sense of purpose.

Assessment, Decision Making, and School Effectiveness

We assess to gather information about student achievement to help us make important decisions. For instance, teachers assess to find out what students know and

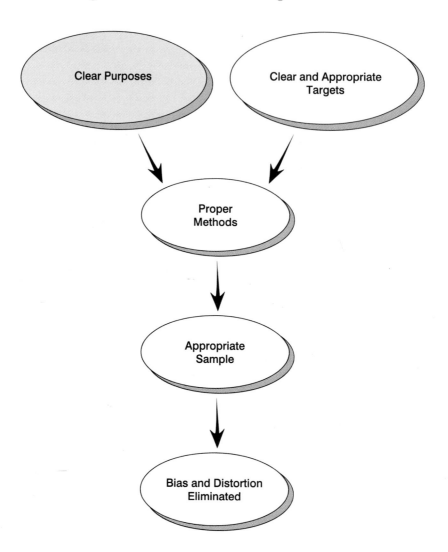

Figure 2.1
Standard of sound assessment 1: Clear purpose

can do in order to diagnose their needs, pace instruction, or to assign grades, among other purposes. School districts assess to help the school board or the community decide if school programs are working and how best to spend district resources. The kind of information that teachers need to guide instruction day to day in the classroom is different from the information that a school board needs for its overall K–12 program decision making. Thus, assessments must be designed or selected to fit into specific decision-making contexts. The decision maker's needs dictate the kind(s) of information that a given assessment must produce.

Assessments serve many masters in schools. Different assessment contexts bring different information needs, requiring different assessment procedures. Thus, no single assessment is capable of serving all users' information needs.

To understand the range of roles assessment plays in schooling, we must see the big assessment picture. That big picture shows us that assessment serves the following users:

- Classroom-level users (teachers, students, and parents)
- Those who provide teachers with instructional support (principals, curriculum specialists, counselors, etc.)
- Policy makers (legislators, school board members, superintendents, etc.)

At the classroom level, assessment can serve two key purposes: (1) it can serve as a powerful teaching tool, particularly when students are involved in the process; and (2) results can inform a variety of instructional decisions. In Chapter 1 we established student involvement as a learning strategy. In this chapter, we examine classroom assessment's role as a decision-making tool.

Let's analyze the full array of decisions that quality achievement information can help the various users make.

Focus on Users and Uses

The many and varied ways that assessment results can inform decision makers are spelled out in Tables 2.1, 2.2, and 2.3. These tables describe how each assessment user's roles and responsibilities contribute to student success by depicting three levels at which assessment results can come into play.

The first level of use is in the classroom. Students, teachers, and parents gather and use the results of student assessments to inform a variety of decisions that influence both student motivation and their level of success. Some of these call for the formative use of assessment: How can we help students improve? Others use assessment in a summative manner: Did the student learn enough?

The second level is that of instructional support. Decision makers at this level provide teachers with whatever backup they may need in the form of curricular, professional development, and/or resource support. Backup may come from the department, building, or district level, or beyond. In this case, formative applications examine assessment results to see what teachers may need to be more effective. Summative uses center on such questions as, Did the new reading program we purchased work effectively?

> The **VALIDITY** of an assessment is evaluated, in part, in terms of its ability to serve the information needs of its intended users.

The final level of assessment user is policy makers, including the superintendent, the school board, public officials (appointed and elected), and citizens of the community. They establish achievement standards to guide instruction in classrooms and then demand evidence of achievement to verify that students are meeting the standards. Based on the evidence they receive, they allocate district resources to overcome weaknesses, set personnel policies to regulate who gets to teach, and set procedural policies that guide teaching practices. Once again, we find both formative and summative applications.

Taken together, all three sets of assessment users make the decisions that determine whether schools work for any individual child, or for all children considered collectively. While I am of the opinion that decisions made at the classroom level (Table 2.1) contribute the most to student success, please understand that all parties listed in Tables 2.2 and 2.3 make important decisions, too; their information needs also deserve careful attention.

Table 2.1
Sample questions that we use assessment to answer at the classroom level

Assessment User	Sample Questions
Student	Am I succeeding?
	Am I improving over time?
	Do I know what it means to succeed here?
	What should I do next to succeed?
	What help do I need to succeed?
	Do I feel in control of my own success?
	Does my teacher think I'm capable of success?
	Do I think I'm capable of success?
	Is the learning worth the effort?
	How am I doing in relation to my classmates?
	Where do I want all of this to take me?
Teacher	Are my students improving?
	Is it because of me?
	What does this student need?
	Is this student capable of learning this?
	What do these students need?
	What are their strengths that we can build on?
	How should I group my students?
	Am I going too fast, too slow, too far, not far enough?
	Am I improving as a teacher?
	How can I improve?
	Did that teaching strategy work?
	What do I say at parent/teacher conferences?
	What grade do I put on the report card?
Parent	Is my child learning new things—growing?
	Is my child succeeding?
	Is my child keeping up?
	Are we doing enough at home to support the teacher?
	What does my child need to succeed?
	Does the teacher know what my child needs?
	Is this teacher doing a good job?
	Is this a good school? District?

Column one of each table lists decision makers whose decisions are (or can be) informed by assessment results. Column two presents questions these decision makers ask whose answers are based at least in part on assessment results of some kind. These tables are not intended to be exhaustive.

Table 2.2
Sample questions that we use assessment to answer at the instructional support level

Assessment User	Sample Questions
Principal	How do we define success in terms of student learning?
	Is this teacher producing results in the form of student learning?
	How can I help this teacher improve?
	Is instruction in our building producing results?
	Is instruction at each grade level producing results?
	Are our students qualifying for college?
	Are our students prepared for the workplace?
	Do we need professional development as a faculty to improve?
	How shall we allocate building resources to achieve success?
Mentor Teacher	Is this new teacher producing results?
	What does this new teacher need to improve?
Curriculum Director	How do we define success in terms of student achievement?
	Is our program of instruction working?
	What adjustments do we need to make in our curriculum?
Special Services	Who needs (qualifies for) special educational services?
	Is our program of services helping students?
	What assistance does this student need to succeed?

Table 2.3
Sample questions that we use assessment to answer at the policy-making level

Assessment User	Sample Questions
Superintendent	Are our programs of instruction producing results in terms of student learning?
	Is each building principal producing results?
	Which schools deserve or need more or fewer resources?
School Board	Are our students learning and succeeding?
	Is the superintendent producing results?
State Department of Education	Are programs across the state producing results?
	Are individual school districts producing results?
Citizen/Legislature	Are our students achieving in ways that prepare them to become productive citizens?

Time for Reflection

Before continuing, please study Tables 2.1, 2.2, and 2.3 carefully. Based on the information provided in each, jot down what conclusions or generalizations you can draw about assessment's role in promoting student success. When you have done this for all three tables, read on.

Classroom Users

After reflecting on the classroom-level questions listed in Table 2.1, can you imagine the dire consequences for student success if students, teachers, and parents were to try to answer them based on misinformation about student achievement due to inaccurate classroom assessment? What if students were not hitting the target, but the assessments said they were succeeding? What if they were succeeding, but the assessments said they were not?

Clearly, inaccurate assessments would lead to misdiagnosis of student needs on the part of the teacher, failure to understand which instructional strategies work and which do not, and communication of misinformation to parents, among other problems.

The point is that accurate information derived from quality classroom assessments is essential for instruction to work effectively and for students to learn. In addition, the following critically important generalizations are warranted on the basis of analyzing the questions in Table 2.1:

- Although we most often think of students as the examinees and not as examiners, they clearly are assessors of their own academic progress, and they use those results in compelling ways.

- Given the manner in which assessment results fit into day-to-day classroom decision making, assessment must be a regularly occurring process in all cases. These are continually recurring decisions. This is precisely why classroom assessment events are so much more frequent in a student's life than are annual, formal standardized tests.

- At this level, assessment virtually always focuses on individual students' mastery of specified material. You, the teacher, must set standards of acceptable achievement if your assessments are to show whether students have succeeded.

Instructional Support Users

We can see the following patterns emerge from the information presented in Table 2.2:

- In every case, the decisions to be made focus on the instructional program or the teacher.

- Typically, the focus is not on the individual student but is rather on group performance.

- Decisions are made infrequently and thus assessment need only be periodic (typically once a year), not continuous.

- At this level, heavy reliance is placed on the use of assessment results in which assessment instruments or procedures must be held constant across classrooms. In other words, some standardization is required if sound information and good decisions are to result.

For all these reasons, this is the domain of the standardized test.

Policy-Level Users

We can make the following generalizations on the basis of the information in Table 2.3:

- The focus is on broad domains of achievement, not specific objectives of instruction.

- As with the instructional support level, results summarized across students (group results) fill the need.

- As with the instructional support level, periodic assessment will suffice.

- At this level too, assessment procedures must be standardized across contexts and over time. The decisions to be made require it.

Again, this is the domain of the standardized test.

Generalizations about Users and Uses

Having reflected on these three tables, do any general conclusions come to your mind regarding the role of assessment in determining and enhancing the effectiveness of schools? Try the following and see if you agree:

- Obviously, assessment is intricately woven into the effectiveness of school functioning. Often the depth and complexity of the contributions of the various assessment levels are surprising to many educators. As teachers and instructional leaders, we must all face this complexity and come to terms with it.

- Students count on many people at all levels and in all decision-making contexts to use sound assessment results in productive ways. Every question listed in the tables is critical to student well-being. This is why we must continually strive for the highest-quality assessment. It is a moral, ethical, and professional imperative of the highest order.

- Considering the tables together, it is clear that both information gathered continuously on individual student mastery of specified material and information gathered periodically for the purpose of comparing students serve important roles. Different users need different information at different times in different forms to do their jobs.

Given this summary of all of the decision-oriented users and uses of assessment, it becomes clear that we need to maintain a balanced perspective about assessment's valuable role at all levels. High-quality classroom assessment serving its important users must be balanced with high-quality standardized assessment serving its important users.

At the risk of appearing redundant, let me reiterate the importance of *accurate* assessment at all levels, especially at the classroom level. If teachers are devising and using poor-quality assessments day to day in their classrooms, all other levels of assessment become irrelevant. If day-to-day decisions are being made on the basis of inaccurate classroom assessment results, sound assessments and decisions at instructional support or policy levels cannot overcome the damage that will result.

The Assessment/Student Success Equation

Of the above links between assessment and decision making, the link most central to student success and school effectiveness is that between assessment and student decision making. This is because hidden inside that linking mechanism is the critically important bond between assessment and student motivation. Perhaps you read past it very fast and didn't notice, but Table 2.1 listed one question that students ask routinely that comes to the heart of this matter: *Is the learning worth the effort?* Depending on their answer, students will or will not expend effort and will or will not learn.

It is in this sense that classroom assessment fuels the engine that drives instruction and student learning. That engine is *student motivation*. Please understand that the only students who learn are those who want to learn. Let's remain clear about who is in charge of the learning. It is not teachers, parents, principals, superintendents, school boards, or state legislatures. The responsible party is each individual learner.

This leads to the age-old question: How do you help your students want to learn? I contend that this represents a classroom assessment question first and foremost. You can enhance or destroy students' desire to succeed in school more quickly and permanently through your use of assessment than with any other tools you have at your disposal. Therefore, I have concluded that the teacher's most important challenge is to effectively manage the relationship between assessment and student motivation. Let me defend this proposition.

Our Evolving Sense of What Motivates

How can you help your students want to learn? We have evolved answers to this question over the years and each iteration has led us to more powerful insights. Let me share a bit of that historical perspective.

Reward and Punishment as Motivators
The theory of learning that has exerted greatest influence on school efforts to motivate is known as *behaviorism*. Proponents of this theory explain how or why we

learn as a function of schedules of rewards and punishments (Skinner, 1974). We tend to repeat behavior that is regularly reinforced within our environment. Behavior that is repeatedly punished is likely to be extinguished and to disappear. Therefore, by manipulating rewards teachers can encourage learners to repeat academically productive behavior and by administering punishment to eliminate behavior unlikely to result in learning. This theory of motivation has spread so deeply into our classrooms and into society at large that it has now become an unquestioned "truth."

In the classroom, assessment has served as the primary mechanism triggering those rewards and punishments. High test scores and grades are thought to reinforce the behavior that resulted in substantial learning, while failing test scores and grades are supposed to punish and thus extinguish the behavior that resulted in insufficient learning. Sounds like a pretty straightforward way to promote the pursuit of academic excellence, doesn't it?

However, another social psychologist, Kohn (1993), cautions that this seductive simplicity masks an underlying truth: Students don't all respond in the same ways to reward and punishment. For many, using grades as rewards and punishments does not motivate learning in productive ways. Indeed, he contends, it has just the opposite effect. From a comprehensive review of decades of research, Kohn concludes that the use of extrinsic sources of motivation, such as stars, stickers, trophies, and grades, can bring students to believe that learning activities are not worth doing in their own right, thus undermining students' natural curiosity to find out how and why things work as they do.

Among others, he cites the research findings of Condry (1977), who concluded that people do the following when offered rewards:

> . . . choose easier tasks, are less efficient in using the information available to solve novel problems, and tend to be answer oriented and more illogical in their problem-solving strategies. They seem to work harder and produce more activity, but the activity is of a lower quality, contains more errors, and is more stereotyped and less creative than the work of comparable nonrewarded subjects working on the same problems. (quoted in Kohn, 1993, pp. 471-72)

Time for Reflection

Think about your own schooling experiences. Can you think of an instance in which your pursuit of a reward or avoidance of a punishment in school carried with it negative consequences for your actual level of achievement?

Assuming that these researchers correctly describe what is at least a very complicated relationship of behaviorism and student motivation, and they provide a compelling body of research to defend their position, we are forced to ask the question, If test scores and grades don't necessarily result in greater learning for all students, what other motivational strategies do we have at our disposal to encourage them to strive to attain academic excellence?

Causal Attribution as a Path to High Achievement

Part of the answer may lie in the work of Weiner (1974), who developed a theory of motivation that expands on the idea of reward and punishment in a very interesting manner. He contends that we are driven by an internal reality or filter that helps us interpret who is in control of or responsible for our personal successes and failures. This is called *attribution theory*.

Basically, students who attribute their academic successes to their own ability and hard work are said to hold an *internal locus of control* over those successes. They see themselves as able. Thus, when faced with a learning challenge, they are likely to feel in control of the situation, to anticipate success, and to invest whatever it takes to attain it.

However, there also are those who attribute their successes to others. Their interpretation holds that success in school probably resulted from good luck or the hard work of a good teacher. In their minds, they are not in control of the reward and punishment contingencies, someone else is. These students have an *external locus of control*.

To encourage students to put forth the effort required to be productive learners, we must strive to help them develop a sense of pride at having tried hard. If we can show them that hard work can pay off with academic success, they will be in control of the reasons for their success. This will prepare them to face new challenges with confidence and the motivation to succeed. In this sense, our goal is to help students feel that if they try, they have the resources to learn.

In a very real sense, this represents the school version of the American dream. Hard work is its own reward. Pull yourself up by your bootstraps with hard work. We value this because we feel, logically, that those who try to learn succeed more than those who don't try. In reality, however, just as with behaviorism, life is more complicated than this set of values would imply.

The connection of effort to achievement is relatively easy to make for academically successful students. But what about students who fail to achieve and who attribute that failure to their own lack of ability? What do we do with students who try hard and fail anyway? How do we keep them from giving up in the face of insurmountable odds? How do we keep these students from feeling unable to control their own well-being in school? The bottom line is, how do we keep them from giving up on themselves and on their teachers?

Further, how do we deal with students who attribute the reasons for academic failure to a system that is "out to get them," to drive them from school? Or students who lack the courage to risk trying out of fear that they might fail, because of uncertainty about who really is in control? Where does the motivation come from for these students to invest whatever it takes to find some level of academic success?

Maintaining Self-Worth as a Path to High Achievement

The answers to these questions may lie in the work of Covington (1992), centering on the concept of student self-worth. He points out that school presents students with a special "ability game" that can be difficult to win. "In this game, the amount of effort students expend provides clear information about their ability status. For instance, if students succeed without much effort, especially if the task is difficult, then estimates of their ability increase; but should they try hard and fail anyway, especially if the task is easy, attributions to low ability are likely to follow" (pp. 16–17).

Covington's perspective is that students' prime objective in schools is to maintain a sense of ability, a sense that they can do it, if they try. But in a cruel twist of this perspective, many students consciously choose to not study and not achieve because if they try and fail they damage that internally held and publicly perceived sense of capability, the basis of their self-worth. They feel it is better to maintain at least some degree of uncertainty, and therefore some degree of self-esteem, by not investing in the system.

Of course, not all students see themselves or school in this self-doubting way. Some are distinctly more positive in asserting an internal locus of control. Covington (citing Skinner, Welborn, & Connell, 1990) differentiates between success- and failure-oriented students. This orientation influences how they see themselves in the competitive arena of the classroom:

> When children believe that they can exert control over success in school, they perform better on cognitive tasks. And, when children succeed in school they are more likely to view school performance as a controllable outcome. . . . Children who are not doing well in school will perceive themselves as having no control over academic success and failures and these beliefs will subsequently generate performances that serve to confirm their beliefs. (Skinner et al., 1990, as cited in Covington, 1992, p. 38)

So far, this sounds just like Weiner (1974) on attribution theory. However, Covington (1992) then departs from his predecessors in offering us a trichotomy of student perceptions of self-worth: (1) success-oriented students, those who are academically competent; (2) failure avoiders, who are uncertain about the probability of success; and (3) failure acceptors, who see themselves as doomed from the outset. He describes the first two orientations through the following examples of Losa and John.

Losa believes in herself as capable of success in the classroom. Her frequent success reaffirms this self-concept. When failure does occur in school (a rare occurrence), she quickly infers that she didn't try hard enough or didn't understand the task well enough to perform well on it. In this sense, failure is not a threat. It does not lead to a sense of incompetence but rather one of ignorance: "There must be something I missed, something correctable if I just work harder and smarter." In the face of failure, she relies on her sense of her own ability to infer a problem that leaves her feeling guilty but optimistic. As a result, she continues to try and does better the next time. The steps in her reasoning are depicted in Figure 2.2. Under all circumstances, she's safe because she has desensitized herself to the potentially negative effects of evaluation. She has the inner resources to comfortably risk something new.

John, on the other hand, is a self-doubting, apathetic high school senior whose reasoning is depicted in Figure 2.3. When faced with an academic challenge, his first thought is that he just isn't able to succeed. This yields shame and pessimism,

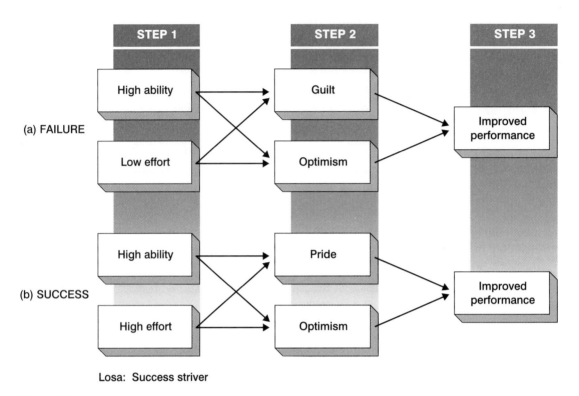

Figure 2.2
The steps in the reasoning of Losa, a success-oriented student
Source: From *Making the Grade: A Self-worth Perspective on Motivation and School Reform* (p. 56) by
M. V. Covington, 1992, New York: Cambridge University Press. Reprinted by permission of Cambridge
University Press.

which contribute to a lack of effort. When he fails, it reinforces his feelings of inadequacy. This leads to greater feelings of shame and pessimism which, in turn, yield more poor performance. This cycle can become debilitating. To illustrate, John can even extend this counterproductive self-concept to those occasions when he succeeds. His internal sense of low ability can leave him worrying that he really didn't deserve the high grade. Further, he might be concerned that someone might discover that he's really only a high-achieving impostor. He lacks any sense of pride in accomplishment that would reassure him about his future prospects of high grades, thinking instead that he was just lucky to do well this time. In effect, John can snatch defeat from the jaws of imminent victory, resulting once again in a kind of pessimism that promises more poor performance in the future. Under no circumstances is he safe, making it very difficult to risk trying something new or that might require a stretch on his part.

This is where John's apathy comes from. Covington (1992) points out that John is not "unmotivated" at all. Rather, he is highly motivated; but, he's highly

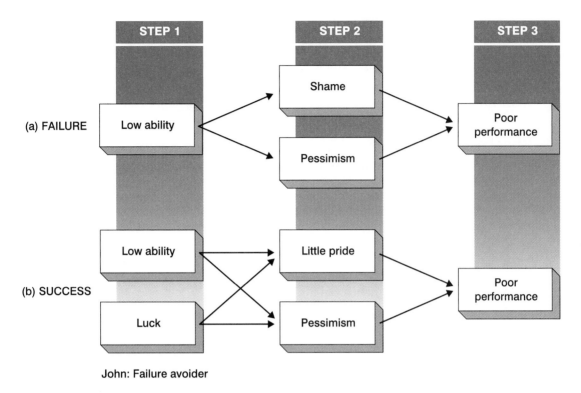

Figure 2.3

The steps in the reasoning of John, a failure avoider

Source: From *Making the Grade: A Self-worth Perspective on Motivation and School Reform* (p. 58) by M. V. Covington, 1992, New York: Cambridge University Press. Reprinted by permission of Cambridge University Press.

motivated to behave in counterproductive ways from an academic achievement point of view.

To complete the picture, in a similar situation we also can find failure-accepting students. They are even more trapped than John. These students have experienced so much failure over such a long period of time that they have given up completely on themselves and school. There is no desire to "try" left in them and thus they are assured of virtually never succeeding academically. As a result, they are constantly bombarded with compelling evidence of their own "stupidity." Soon they become numbed to the onslaught and become mental dropouts. Covington (1992) refers to this as "learned helplessness." Even if they happen to succeed at something, these students are sure to credit blind luck, disregard any message of possible competence, and remain enmeshed in a tangle of doom. Such students feel absolutely no control over what happens to them in school and therefore are always vulnerable. Taking the risks needed to learn is not only beyond their reach, it's also beyond their frame of reference.

Time for Reflection

As you reflect on your own school experiences, which category do you fall into now? Can you remember classmates that fell into the other two categories? If you are teaching now, who among your students fit into these categories?

Keeping Perspective

Clearly, any teacher's goal must be to help students maintain the internal sense that (1) they can do the work, and (2) the work is worth doing. But be very careful here, on two fronts.

First, do not interpret this to mean that the academic work to be done must be made easy. The subtle but critical difference is this: You must be sure yourself and then convince your students that the work to be done is challenging, that there is always a risk of failure, but that risk is not a reason to stop trying. You must help them understand that they cannot succeed unless they face the fact that they are going to fail sometimes. We all do. But if they learn to manage that risk, they will come to see that persistence is the key to success. You must convince them that the risk is worth taking.

Second, remain aware of the fact that many forces impinge on a student's academic self-concept. Primary among these is the student's family—primarily early childrearing practices. Obviously, teachers have no control over these. Further, even during the school years, many things are happening in students' lives that affect their perceptions of self-worth. Most of these happen outside the classroom, again beyond your control.

For these reasons, it is imperative that you maintain perspective on the extent to which you alone can help a student overcome a sense of a lack of academic ability. But if you team up with parents in a common mission of trying to help, the combined forces can be quite powerful. Assessment, record-keeping, and communication strategies that include both students and parents in the process can tap that power.

Exploring the Real-World Implications

When I was in school, my teachers employed a specific set of reward and punishment-driven motivators to keep students on task. They delivered a very clear message about consequences. I'll bet you received this same message from your teachers: "You should work hard and learn a great deal. Because if you do, good things will happen to you. For example, if you study hard, you will get high scores on the classroom tests and quizzes. You will perform well on assignments and projects. In short, the gradebook will bear a record of your strong academic performance.

"That strong record will pay off, too, because it will permit me to put high grades on your report card. Accumulate enough of those As and Bs and that will entitle you to be promoted to the next grade or to receive credit for course completion or to graduate or to get into college or to get scholarships or to get a good job. Good things come to those who work hard and learn a lot."

As I reflect on this, the word *bribery* comes to mind—the systematic manipulation of incentives, reinforcers, rewards.

This message came in a negative form, too: "You should work hard and learn a lot. Because if you do not, bad things will happen to you. If you don't study and learn, you will accumulate a very weak academic record, low scores, poor performance. This is a bad thing because it will result in failing grades. Accumulate enough of those Fs and you will be retained at the same grade level or you will not receive credit or you will not graduate or get into college or get scholarships or get a good job. Only bad things will result if you don't work hard and learn a lot."

In this case, the word *intimidation* comes to mind—the manipulation of either punishments or the promise of dire consequences. Threaten this, my teachers thought, and students will work hard and learning will result.

Time for Reflection

Before we delve more deeply into the assessment–motivation relationship, please take a few minutes to complete this exercise: Create a 2 x 2 table to cover an 8½ x 11 piece of paper. Label the two columns "System Works" and "Does Not Work." Label the rows "Who Are They?" And "Why?" In the upper left of the four cells of this table, describe those students for whom the reward and punishment–driven behavior management system of motivation works in that it results in a great deal of student learning. How would you characterize them? What proportion of the student population falls into this category? In the cell below it see if you can explain why it works for them. What does it do for them that keeps them going? Next, in the upper right, describe those students for whom the system does not work and below that, why. When you have filled in the cells and thought through your results, please read on.

Understanding the Complexity

Isn't this a system in which the rich get richer? But be careful. That is not a bad thing, in the sense that those who learn a great deal get to learn a great deal more. Someone is benefiting from this motivational system. The antecedents are strong support and high expectations at home, including early childrearing practices that teach kids how to succeed. Those who experience early success gain the confidence needed to risk trying for even more. They expect to succeed and behave accordingly.

But isn't it also a case where the poor get poorer? Students who experience early failure, lose confidence in themselves, stop trying, and find themselves failing even more frequently. At some point, it becomes just too risky, from their point of view, to expose themselves to further punishment. They lose confidence and give up in hopelessness. This is a bad thing in contexts in which they need to meet academic standards.

As it turns out, *confidence is the key to student success in all learning situations*. In the behavior management system, where tests and grades underpin rewards and punishments, some students gain confidence and learn to continue to take the risks of trying to learn more. But others lose confidence and stop trying. In other words, if we assume that our traditional motivation system is working well or can work well for all students, we are being naïve. If our assessment practices continue to reflect this naïvete, we will continue to lose those students who give up in hopelessness. In my opinion, this is an unacceptable loss.

Why Is This Important?

To see why this is important in the context of your study of classroom assessment practices, think about the profoundly important changes that are happening in the mission of schools. Most of us grew up in schools whose mission was to sort us from the highest achiever to the lowest. The index of school effectiveness was a dependable rank order at the end of high school. We were not expected to meet any absolute achievement standards.

But in the 1980s and 1990s, the business community began to say, "We hired those who were very high in your rank order and they couldn't read or write well enough to do the job. Just sorting them is not enough anymore. We demand competence. We want every student to be a capable reader, writer, math problem solver."

So states and districts and schools began to establish achievement standards—competencies that all students must master to be promoted or to graduate. Thus, society's mission for its schools changed. Schools that merely sort are no longer deemed effective if all graduates do not meet prescribed academic achievement standards.

Hidden inside this shift in schooling's mission is an immense and important paradox. In schools where the mission is to rank students from the highest to the lowest achiever, if some students work hard and learn a great deal, that's good, because they are available to occupy places high in the rank order. And if some students give up in hopelessness and stop trying along the way, that turns out to be a good thing too, because we need to have them occupy places low in the rank order. The result is maximum variance in achievement and a dependable sorting of all students.

Now change the mission to one of ensuring competence. In this case, if some students work hard and learn a great deal, again, that is a good thing. They will strive for and meet prescribed standards. But now if some students give up in hopelessness, that becomes a distinctly bad thing, because they will not even try to meet standards.

The problem is that, as we enter the twenty-first century, schools will be held accountable for increasing the proportion of their students who meet state standards. That means schools that used to accept students giving up must now keep them from losing confidence. They must find those students who already have developed a sense of futility in their schooling and reverse their academic self-concepts. In other words, our success as educators in standards-driven schools turns, not on our ability to motivate bright high achievers, but on our ability to rekindle the desire to learn among those students who have given up on themselves and on us.

Here is the practical significance of this issue: Let's say you live in a state in which policy makers have just "raised the bar" by setting very high achievement standards for all students. And further, let's say they develop a new state assessment system reflecting those standards and administer it statewide. And finally, say the percentage of students meeting and not meeting state standards looks like the following:

Meet Standards	30%
Do Not Meet Standards	70%

Which group probably includes a relatively large percentage of students for whom the reward and punishment–driven behavior management system of motivation works? The 30 percent who met standards. And which group probably includes a relatively large percentage for whom the traditional system of motivation does not work? The 70 percent group.

Now think about the shift in your educational mission. You are to take students who are in the "do not meet standards" category and move them to the "meet standards" level. How do you do that when the motivational system around which we have built the American educational system is not working for them? Under these circumstances, why not change the manner in which you motivate? But change to what? Are there options to reward and punishment that might work for these students? Indeed there are.

Tapping the Wellspring of Motivation Within

As teachers, our challenge comes in two parts: (1) keep students from losing confidence in themselves as learners to begin with, and (2) rekindle confidence among those students who have lost faith in themselves as capable learners.

It's tempting to conceive of the latter case as a self-concept problem; that is, as a personal/emotional issue. If we can just raise these students' self-concept, they will become capable learners. I believe that this is counterproductive, because it confronts the problem from the wrong direction. Rather, we conceptualize the problem far more productively if we see this first as a classroom assessment problem.

If these students are to come to believe in themselves, then they must first experience some believable (credible) form of academic success as reflected in a real and rigorous classroom assessment. A small success can rekindle a small spark of confidence, which, in turn, encourages more trying. If that new trying brings more success, their academic self-concept will begin to shift in a positive direction. Our goal then is to perpetuate that cycle. To see clear examples of this principle at work, view (or watch again) the movie *Stand and Deliver*. Mr. Escalante uses assessment to put students in touch with their own emerging competence. This begins to build their confidence, which ultimately pays off in their ability to risk failure to find immense success.

The direction of the effect is critical. First comes academic success, then comes confidence. With increased confidence comes the belief that learning just may be possible. Success must be framed in terms of academic attainments that students think represent a significant stretch for them. Focused effort with an expectation of success is essential. Students must come honestly to believe that what counts here—indeed the only thing that counts here—is the learning that results. They must believe that any level of effort that does not produce learning has no value in your classroom and that they are capable of learning.

The evidence that students attend to in order to renew their faith in themselves as learners cannot come once a year from summative district, state, national, or international standardized tests. The crucial evidence will come to them moment to moment through continuous formative classroom assessment. This places you, the classroom teacher as assessor, directly at the heart of the relations among assessment, student motivation, and school effectiveness.

Thus, the essential school improvement question from an assessment point of view is this: Are teachers skilled enough to use assessment to either (1) keep all learners from losing confidence in themselves to begin with, or (2) rebuild that confidence once it has been destroyed?

For those students who are motivated to work hard and learn by the prospect of rewards, teachers can rely on them to encourage effort. But what do we do when that system has lost its motivational power in the eyes of some (perhaps many!) students?

The Case for Student Involvement

We have alternatives to our tradition of manipulating rewards and punishments. We can turn to a constellation of three tools that, taken together, can tap an unlimited wellspring of motivation that resides within each learner:

- Student-involved classroom assessment
- Student-involved record keeping
- Student-involved communication

Together, they redefine how to use assessment to turn students on to the power and joy of learning. Here's why:

Each teacher's instructional task is to take students to the very edges of their academic capabilities. This is where new learning begins. But to learn, students must be willing to take the risk of stepping off that edge—to take the risk of trying something new, something they might not be very good at at first. If students perceive that failure is a bad thing, then stepping off that edge can be very scary business. It's natural for students to ask, What if I try and fail? I'll embarrass myself in front of my classmates! My parents will ground me!

If you hear no other part of my message in this book about the role of assessment in schools, HEAR ME ON THIS: *Your challenge as a teacher—indeed, the art and heart of your profession—is to take your students to their personal edges with enough confidence in themselves and enough trust in you, their teacher, to go ahead and step off when you ask them to. They must dare to risk failure.* Your students must know that it's true of all people that when we try to learn to do something new, we may not be very good at first and that's okay! Your instructional challenge is to help them believe that their early failures hold the seeds of their later success.

In other words, as teachers, we must help students accept that no one is an expert the first time they try something. There is a learning curve that starts low and progresses upward. Emily was not a good writer at the beginning of the year. You may not be good at developing assessments when you first start. But she improved and so will you. Wise teachers use *student-involved classroom assessment, record keeping, and communication* as instructional interventions to teach that improvement is always possible. They define *success* as continuous improvement and rely on classroom assessment to help everyone track that improvement.

Student-involved classroom assessment opens up assessment development and brings students in as full partners. We begin early on, starting with a clear and appropriate vision of what we want students to master. We invite students to learn about the criteria by which their work will be judged. We teach these lessons by having students actually devise sample assessment exercises and scoring criteria. These examples permit students to see where they are now in relation to where we want them to be. Thus the path to success becomes clear to them; there will be no surprises and no excuses.

Student-involved record keeping brings them into the process of monitoring improvements in their achievement through repeated self-assessment over time. They learn to apply appropriate criteria to the evaluation of their own practice work. One way to accomplish this is by having students build portfolios of evidence of their success over time, including periodic self-reflections about the changes they see. In effect, we use repeated student-involved classroom assessments to hold a mirror up, permitting students to watch themselves grow—to help them chart and thus feel in control of their own success. This can be a powerful confidence builder.

Student-involved communication brings them into the process of sharing information with others about their success. One way to do this is through the use of student-led parent-teacher conferences. In my opinion, this is the biggest breakthrough to happen in communicating about student achievement in the last century. When students are prepared well over an extended period to tell the story of their own success (or lack thereof), they seem to experience a fundamental shift in their internal sense of responsibility for that success. The pride in accomplishment that students feel when they have a positive story to tell and then tell it convincingly using concrete evidence can be immensely motivational. Mark my words, your students will feel an immense sense of personal accountability when they know that they will have to tell their parents about the specifics of their achievement. Most will work very hard to avoid the prospect of having to justify their failure to achieve.

In these three ways, you can use student involvement to help them see, understand, and appreciate their own continuing and productive journey of achievement.

This is exactly what Ms. Weatherby did to help Emily and her classmates understand her achievement expectations, find and follow the path of success, and feel in charge of, rather than victimized by, the assessment process. In these ways, student involvement in assessment, record keeping, and communication helped them to build the self-confidence needed to keep stepping off the edge of their current capabilities into new learning adventures.

You will know you are succeeding in helping your students to achieve internal control as they less and less frequently ask, "How am I doing?"

Understanding How to Motivate

From their very earliest school experiences, students draw life-shaping conclusions about themselves as learners on the basis of the information provided them as a result of classroom assessments. They decide if they are capable of succeeding. They decide whether it is worth trying. They decide if they can have confidence in themselves as learners and in their teachers. They decide whether to risk investing in the schooling experience.

In this sense, the relationship between assessment and student motivation is complex indeed. Do not be so naïve as to believe that you can force students to care merely by manipulating schedules of reinforcement and punishment. The downside risk is that such a simplistic system of motivation will become a game for students, breeding cynicism, not learning.

The alternative is to find ways to help students learn to respond to more than external motivational forces. We need to help them go on internal control—to learn to take responsibility for their own academic success. Let me now detail the conditions that must exist to achieve this kind of positively motivating and constructively energizing assessment environment.

There is much that we teachers must do if we are to help students find the take-charge learner that resides within each of them. Remember the Guiding Principles of Chapter 1: We must be crystal clear about the achievement targets we want our students to hit, so we can reveal those expectations to them. We must know how to develop high-quality classroom assessments of various kinds, so we can accurately determine if they are succeeding. We must master the craft knowledge of student involvement in assessment, record keeping, and communication, if we are to help them see that they can take control. We must understand the principles of effective communication about student achievement and also know how to involve students productively in those processes.

One Success Along the Road to Excellence

One of the keys to Emily's development as a confident writer is found during her transformation from a poor writer who lacked confidence to a proficient writer who knew she was good. Ms. Weatherby helped by providing a learning environment in which young writers received continuous, understandable, and credible feedback on how to improve their writing. Each student gained a clear understanding of the attributes of good writing, together with the vocabulary needed to communicate with Ms. W and the class about their work. The following story about one learning experience in Emily's transformation reveals how Ms. W helped them succeed and feel in control of that success.

One assignment during the year called for each student to read four novels by the same author, develop a thesis statement, and write a term paper in defense of that thesis.

Ms. W began by giving her students a copy of a term paper from the past that was of outstanding quality. Their homework assignment? Read the paper overnight and make a list of the elements that made it outstanding. The next day they pooled their ideas by brainstorming a list of student opinions about those qualities. They saved this list.

Then she gave them a term paper that was of dismal quality. Once again, they were to read it and be prepared to tell her what made it inferior. The next day, they brainstormed a list of these elements.

On the third day, working as an entire class, they carried out a very thoughtful comparative analysis of the differences between the two lists—attributes of good and bad term papers. Their goal was to boil their lists down to the essential ingredients that really captured the differences between these two papers. They finally agreed on six elements of difference, including the quality of ideas, the organization of those ideas, the mustering of support materials from the books read, and so on.

Next, Ms. W divided the class into teams of four or five and assigned one of the six term paper elements to each team, along with a two-part assignment:

1. Write a definition of your element.
2. Develop the basis of a three-point rating scale defining what a term paper would look like when, with respect to your element, if it was (1) outstanding, (2) of very poor quality, and (3) in between.

Each team had to reflect on different levels of quality, collect their ideas, develop a presentation, and share their definitions and initial rating scales with the class. This presentation was not graded. It was a way to stimulate discussion, even debate, among students about the meaning of each of the key attributes of a term paper. As a result of these presentations, Emily and her classmates developed a clearer sense of how a term paper can vary in quality. During the process, Ms. W actually helped the class expand its three-point rating scale to five points so they would be able to track their own improvement more precisely as they revised their papers.

Ms. Weatherby was now a week into this unit and no term paper had been written yet. She had taken her students with her into the process of devising the product-based performance criteria that would be used to evaluate their work. She had revealed to them the keys to their ultimate success—showing them what was required *before* they wrote.

Then they drafted their papers and, working in different teams, read and provided feedback to each other in terms of their specific vision of excellence. When students first drafted their papers, many received ratings of "1" on most attributes of their initial papers. But this "failure" was not cause for hopelessness, as they worked in a workshop-style classroom in which they were assured of continuous, dependable feedback that permitted them to keep improving their paper. They could revise, based on feedback from the team, as many times as needed. The paper was done when the student said it was done.

Let's be clear about something here. This is not about students setting the standards or defining academic success, although they contributed. Ms. W knew where she wanted them to end up when they started developing the rating scales. She could have just run off copies of her version of excellence and given each student a copy. But she did not. Rather, she chose to lead her students to a vision of term paper excellence through a series of inferences that resulted in students' clear understanding of that vision and some ownership of it, too.

Remember the edge metaphor used previously? Surely you can see that Ms. Weatherby brought her students to the edge of their writing capabilities when she assigned the term paper. When they took the risk and stepped off, they were guaranteed that they would not disappear down into the chasm and crash, because the rating scales they had developed represented the rocks they could stand on as they walked across.

When they first drafted their papers, their work might have been rated with all 1s and 2s. But upon revision based on feedback from teammates, the next draft got 2s and 3s, and then 3s and 4s. Ultimately, if they stuck with it, their papers would receive 5s on all six rating scales. Success!

 Assessment experts tell us that the **VALIDITY** of an assessment is determined in part by its impact on learning. The greater its impact, the more valid it is.

Her students collected a portfolio of early drafts and thus were able to look back and reflect on what they did to improve their work. The result was a strong feeling of internal control over their own academic well-being. Each student who invested the time and energy, like Emily, became a more confident writer.

Summary: Sound Assessment and Student Involvement Are Essential

Imagine yourself as a student in a classroom in which all of the decisions that influence the quality of your learning experience are being made on the basis of highly accurate information about your achievement. Imagine that your teacher is developing and being informed by the highest-quality classroom assessments. Your teacher is helping you see and believe in your own improvement. In addition, everyone who supports your teacher with resources and ideas is being informed by the highest-quality

assessments. The result would be a foundation of information about you and your academic growth that would allow everyone to do all in their power to help you succeed in the classroom. In Chapter 1, Emily learned in that kind of environment, at least with respect to her writing. The positive results were obvious.

Now imagine yourself trapped in a classroom in which the various decisions listed in Tables 2.1, 2.2, and 2.3 are being made on the basis of inaccurate information about your achievement due to inept assessment. Your teacher would be misdiagnosing your needs, selecting counterproductive instructional strategies, assigning incorrect grades, and so on. In addition, those who provided support at all levels would be drawing incorrect conclusions about the kinds and amounts of support needed, for individual special-needs students, for classrooms as a whole, and for entire buildings. In short, the consequences would be dire for learners. Now imagine that those students are second graders who are just beginning to get a sense of themselves as learners. Surely you can see that the negative consequences of the mismeasurement of their achievement could be long lasting.

In other words, what if a student reads the assessment results, sees the signs of failure and gives up in hopelessness when, in fact, those assessment results were inaccurate and the student had really succeeded and hit the target? The impact could be serious. This is precisely why *all assessments used at all levels absolutely must meet standards of quality and produce accurate results*.

Conceive of the linkage between assessment and effective schools as a team effort. Each decision maker, from the classroom (including students!) to the living room to the board room and beyond, is a team member with a key role to play. If any member is misinformed about student achievement due to inappropriate or ineffective assessment—from either the classroom or standardized tests—then poor decisions will result, reducing the effectiveness of the overall team effort. The consequences for student confidence and academic achievement are obvious.

Exercises for Self-Assessment

1. Table 2.1 lists examples of questions for each user that we use assessments to help us answer. For each user, try to extend each list. What additional questions need answers? When you have run out of new ideas, identify what you believe to be the five most important questions for each user and place them in order of importance. What kind of information (assessment results) will the user need to answer each?

2. Build a chart that includes four rows, one for each of the motivational systems discussed in this chapter: behavior management (Skinner), causal attribution (Weiner), self-worth (Covington) and student-involved assessment. Add four columns to your chart, each headed as follows, and fill in the cells of the table with your best ideas:

- Primary motivator
- Strengths
- Weaknesses

3. During our discussion of the use of rewards and punishments to motivate, I implied that, if some students will work hard and learn a lot in the pursuit of rewards, you should use that motivator to their advantage. But I also implied that the use of punishment to cause students to want to learn is very dangerous business. Given the material covered in this chapter, why do you suppose that both statements might be true?

4. Using Figures 2.2 and 2.3 about Losa's and John's reasoning, make a similar diagram that represents the reasoning of a failure acceptor, in the face of (1) failure and (2) success.

You may go to the Companion Website at www.prenhall.com/stiggins and answer these questions in the Self-Assessment module.

Final Chapter Reflection

1. *What are the three most important new insights to come to you as a result of your study of this chapter?*
2. *Which of your previous questions about assessment can you now answer based on your study of this chapter?*
3. *What new questions have come to mind as a result of your study of this chapter that you hope to have answered as your study continues?*
4. *For practicing teachers only:* *What do you plan to do differently in assessment in your classroom as a result of your study of this book so far?*

   For those in preservice study only: *As you think about the classroom assessment environment that you hope to create for your students, how has your thinking changed as a result of your study of this book so far?*

Workbook Activities

Those of you using the workbook, *Practice with Student-Involved Classroom Assessment*, as part of your study of this material will find the following activities and others included for Chapter 2:

- *Balance in Assessment.* Whose needs would not be met if large-scale assessment were not done? Whose needs would not be met if classroom assessment information were not available? This reflection and discussion activity emphasizes the need for balanced assessment.

- *Interview Others on Their Uses of Assessment.* This activity guides you through interviewing a colleague (inservice) or a professor (preservice) on the way they use assessments in the

classroom. You will more clearly understand current practice based on these interviews.

- *Student Assessment Questionnaire.* What do students think of the assessments they are encountering? How do they come to understand and use the results? This activity gives you the opportunity to ask them.

- *What Went Wrong?* You pick one of two real case studies that illustrate undesireable impacts of assessment on students. Discussion questions revolve around causes and countermeasures to prevent serious problems.

- *Imagine! Video.* See "Video Support" following.

- *Analyze Sample Assessments for Clear Users and Uses.*   What does it look like in an actual classroom assessment when the users and uses are made clear? You apply standards of good practice to analyze sample assessments.

Video Support

The ATI interactive video training package, *Imagine! Assessments that Energize Students*, carefully analyzes the relationship between assessment and student motivation. It combines a historical perspective with a look to the future to argue for a redefinition of that relationship. Brief video segments alternate with hands-on activities to bring the power of student-involved assessment to the fore, and to help you learn to apply it.

3

Defining Classroom Achievement Targets

CHAPTER FOCUS

This chapter answers the following guiding question:

What kinds of achievement must teachers assess in the classroom?

From your study of this chapter, you will understand the following enduring principles:

1. If our goals are accurate assessment and academic success for students, teachers must clearly and completely define the achievement targets that students are to hit.

2. Achievement targets must center on the truly important proficiencies students are to master.

3. Further, we can categorize these achievement expectations in ways that help us understand how to assess them accurately.

Continuing to Define Quality Assessment

In Chapters 1 and 2, we began to uncover the secrets of excellence in classroom assessment. The first secret is to begin development of any assessment with a clear sense of our purpose. We must know why we are conducting the assessment—exactly who will be the assessment user(s) and how they will use it. Different users need different information in different forms at different times to do their jobs. No single assessment can meet everyone's needs. Sometimes the users are students themselves trying to decide if the learning is worth the risk of attaining it. Sometimes the users are teachers trying to diagnose student needs. Other times they are principals, parents, school board members, and so on. Each brings different information needs to the assessment context.

In this chapter, we move on to the second secret to excellence in classroom assessment: clear targets (Figure 3.1). We must clearly define what we are assessing. What do we expect our students to achieve? Teachers who cannot define the student characteristic(s) that they wish to assess will have great difficulty developing assessment exercises and evaluation criteria that reflect their expectations.

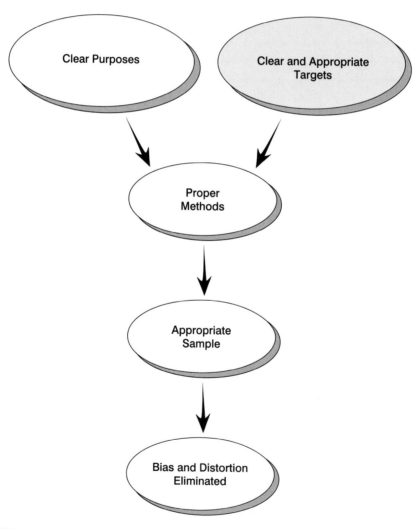

Figure 3.1
Standard of sound assessment 2: Clear targets

Further, they will find it impossible both to share a clear vision of success with their students in terms that their students understand and to select instructional strategies that promise and deliver student success.

Teachers faced with the responsibility of evaluating students' reading proficiency, for example, but who lack a clear vision of what proficient readers are able to do, will be ineffective. Not only must they recognize a proficient reader when they see or hear one, but they also must be able to diagnose the needs of nonreaders and know how to help them. Regardless of the subject or level of education, only those with sharp visions of valued achievement expectations can effectively and efficiently assess student attainment of those expectations.

For this reason, we devote this entire chapter to defining achievement targets for purposes of assessment. Just as you form a foundation of quality assessment by clarifying your purpose, so too do you shape that foundation by beginning assessment with a refined vision of the meaning of academic success. As you strive to define your achievement targets, both as guideposts for instruction and as bases for your classroom assessments, you can benefit from recent advances made by specialists in virtually all subject matter arenas. Our understanding of achievement success, of what students need to learn to succeed during and after school, is clearer today than at any time previously. The work of reading specialists, for example, permits teachers schooled in that work to produce more and better readers today than ever before. And so it is with writing, and with reasoning and problem solving in math, science, and other disciplines. We will explore those developments and their assessment implications in depth in later chapters.

What Is a "Target"?

A *target* defines academic success, what we want students to know and be able to do. Think of a target with its bull's-eye in the middle. That center circle defines the highest level of performance students can achieve; a very high-quality piece of writing, the most fluent oral reading, the highest possible score on a math problem-solving test. Each outside ring on the target defines a level of performance further from the highest level. As students improve, they need to understand that they are progressing toward the bull's-eye.

Our collective goal is that the largest possible percentage of our students get there. To reach that goal, we must define for ourselves and for them where "there" is. What are the attributes of a good piece of writing, such as Emily's end of year sample from Chapter 1? How does this level of performance differ from the outer rings of the target? Ms. Weatherby knew and gave Emily the insights she needed to understand as well.

We have used a variety of labels over the years to identify achievement expectations. We have called them *goals* and *objectives*. Other times we have referred to *scope* and *sequence*. *Proficiencies* or *academic attainments*, we also sometimes called them. Recent popular terms are *standards* and *benchmarks*. These terms all refer to the same basic concept, the definition of *academic success*.

Our achievement expectations form a solid foundation for classroom assessment when they meet certain standards of quality. We describe these standards in the following subsections.

Targets Are Clearly Stated

Our achievement expectations must be written in clear language and offered in public for all to see. The language should be clear enough that all concerned with their attainment can understand what they mean. When achievement targets are clearly stated, different teachers who read and paraphrase them interpret them to mean essentially the same thing. Indeed, I believe that the clarity of our academic standards hinges on our ability to translate them into "kid-friendly" language, so those we expect to hit the target can understand precisely what we expect of them.

From a slightly different perspective, one criterion by which we should judge the appropriateness of our achievement expectations is our ability to provide samples of student work that demonstrate different levels of proficiency.

Targets Are Specific

We can define achievement expectations at different levels of specificity. They can begin at a very general level:

> The student understands and applies the concepts and procedures of mathematics.

From here we can progress to higher levels of specificity, by subdividing the general statement into its component parts:

> The student understands and can apply concepts and procedures from number sense.

> The student understands and can apply concepts and procedures of measurement.

> From geometry, and so on.

It is common to define state and local achievement "standards" at these levels of specificity. And even these can be further subdivided. For instance, number sense includes number and numeration, computation, and estimation.

Individually, our challenge is to be clear with our students about the focus and level of specificity of the achievement expectations we will hold them accountable for in our classrooms. Then, as teachers, we are responsible for devising properly focused opportunities to learn and classroom assessment exercises with scoring procedures that reflect the agreed level of specificity.

Targets Center on What Is Truly Important

But beyond this, our achievement expectations cannot merely be a matter of local opinion. Rather, they must be steeped in the best thinking of leading experts in the field. We don't get to vote on what it means to be a good writer. Those traits have been clearly defined in our professional literature. Whether students are doing good science or solving math problems effectively are not matters of opinion. As teachers it is our personal and collective responsibility to continue to study that professional literature to stay in touch with current thinking in the fields we teach.

Targets Fit into a Big Picture

In a similar sense, the achievement expectations held as important in any particular classroom cannot be merely a matter of the judgment of that particular teacher. Rather, they must fit into a continuously progressing curriculum that guides instruction across grade levels in that school and district. The overall curriculum should define ascending levels of competence that spiral through grade levels, mapping a journey to academic excellence. Each teacher's goals and objectives, therefore, must arise directly from what has come before and lead to what will follow.

Targets Fit Comfortably into the Teacher's Repertoire

So, as a classroom teacher, it will fall to you to deliver instruction and to conduct classroom assessments that focus on an assigned set of achievement expectations. To fulfill this responsibility, you must become a confident, competent master of the achievement targets that you expect your students to hit. This doesn't mean, for example, that elementary teachers need to be masters of high school physics. But it does mean they must thoroughly and completely understand those big ideas and concepts in physics that their students must master at this particular point on their journey to high school physics and beyond. I will say much more about this later in the chapter.

An Example

Figure 3.2 presents sample learning requirements for the state of Washington. These represent just a subset of the essential learning objectives that Washington educators feel are important for their students, and are stated at a general statewide level of specificity. But they are *clearly stated* and *specific*. Washington educators have developed benchmarks that define continuous progress in attainment through grades 4, 7, and 10. A sample of these is seen in Figure 3.3. It remains a local responsibility to be sure that each teacher is able to deliver them.

WRITING

1. The student writes clearly and effectively.

   To meet this standard, the student will:

   1.1 develop concept and design

   develop a topic or theme; organize written thoughts with a clear beginning, middle, and end; use transitional sentences and phrases to connect related ideas; write coherently and effectively

   1.2 use style appropriate to the audience and purpose

   use voice, word choice, and sentence fluency for intended style and audience

   1.3 apply writing conventions

   know and apply correct spelling, grammar, sentence structure, punctuation, and capitalization

SCIENCE

1. The student understands and uses scientific concepts and principles

   To meet this standard, the student will:

   1.1 use properties to identify, describe, and categorize substances, materials, and objects, and use characteristics to categorize living things

   1.2 recognize the components, structure, and organization of systems and the interconnections within and among them

   1.3 understand how interactions within and among systems cause changes in matter and energy

---

Figure 3.2
Sample state of Washington learning requirements
Source: Washington State Office of Superintendent of Public Instruction. Reprinted by permission.

The Benefits of Clear and Appropriate Targets

Any energy you invest in becoming clear about your targets will pay big dividends at assessment time. First of all, it will provide a sharp focus for your assessment exercises and scoring procedures. The result will be high-quality assessments—the remainder of this book details how. But in addition, three other very valuable benefits will result if you can articulate your expectations in appropriate terms.

Limits on Teacher Accountability

One major benefit of defining specific achievement targets is that you set the limits of your own professional responsibility. These limits provide you with a standard by which to gauge your own success as a teacher. In short, defining targets helps you control your own professional destiny.

The student understands and uses different skills and strategies to read.

To meet this standard, the student will: (1)

Components	Benchmark 1–Grade 4	Benchmark 2–Grade 7 (3)	Benchmark 3 – Grade 10
1.1 use word recognition and word meaning skills (2)	apply phonetic principles to read, including sounding out, using initial letters, and using common letter patterns to make sense of whole words use language structure to understand reading materials, including sentence structure, prefixes, suffixes, contractions, (7) and simple abbreviations	➡ apply phonetic principles to read, including sounding out initial letters and using common letter patterns to make sense of whole words (4) ➡ use language structure to understand reading materials, including sentence structure, prefixes, suffixes, contractions, (7) and simple abbreviations	➡ apply phonetic principles to read, including sounding out, using initial letters, and using common letter patterns to make sense of whole words (4) ➡ use language structure to understand reading materials, including sentence structure, prefixes, suffixes, contractions, (7) and simple abbreviations
1.5 use features of non-fiction text and computer software (2)	locate and use text organizers (title headings, (6) table of contents, index, captions, alphabetizing, numbering, glossaries, etc.) recognize organizational features of electronic (5) information such as *pull-down menus, key word searches, icons,* etc.	use organizational features of printed text (titles, headings, table of contents, indexes, glossaries, prefaces, appendices, captions, etc.) use organization features of electronic information microfiche headings and numberings, CD-ROMS, Internet, etc.	use complex organizational features of printed text (titles, headings, table of contents, indexes, glossaries, prefaces, appendices, captions, citations, endnotes, etc.) use features of electronic information (electronic bulletin boards and databases, e-mail, etc.)

(1) Essential Academic Learning Requirement: A statement of what students should know and be able to do at the completion of their K–12 education. These statements are purposefully broad and are intended to serve as guideposts to school districts and give teachers flexibility in designing curriculum, teaching strategies, and planning instruction.

(2) Components: The key components to each Essential Academic Learning Requirement. The components are intended to describe broad categories of student behaviors or actions.

(3) Benchmark: A point in time that may be used to measure student progress. Designed to help educators organize and make sense of a complex process of interaction between the student, the teacher, and the learning process. TBD means "to be determined" in science, social studies, arts, and health and fitness.

(4) ➡   The text repeats for each benchmark. The arrow means that the skills or materials used become increasingly complex.

(5) Content *for example* or *such as* (italics):   Provides examples of skills contained in the benchmarks so that parents and students can more clearly see the particular skills students are being asked to acquire.

(6) Parentheses (   ) indicate material or types of material that are included in the test specifications for reading, writing, and communication.

(7) Each set of indicators demonstrates the developmental, cumulative nature of learning. For example, young readers should be able to progress independently through the steps of the reading process but will read simpler materials than maturing learners.

Figure 3.3
Sample Washington learning requirement broken down into grade-level benchmarks
Source: Washington State Office of Superintendent of Public Instruction. Reprinted by permission.

With clearly stated student expectations in hand, expectations that have been verified as appropriate by your supervisors, if all goes well, you will be able to say, "I am a successful teacher. My students have attained the achievement targets that were assigned to me as my instructional responsibility." Hopefully, you will gain both the internal and external rewards of your own clearly defined and documented success.

From a slightly different point of view, in effect, this prevents you from being trapped with unlimited accountability where, by default, you are held responsible for producing in your students virtually any human characteristic that anyone has ever defined as desirable! No one can hope to succeed under the weight of such expectations. There will always be someone out there pointing to some valued outcome, complaining that schools failed them. This is a trap to which many educators fall prey. Clear targets set limits and set teachers and schools up for success by defining and delimiting responsibilities.

But Mind the Risks.   We would be naïve if we failed to acknowledge that the clear and public definition of achievement expectations carries with it potential risks for teachers. Accountability is a double-edged sword. To the extent that we are clear and public about our expectations and rigorous in our assessments, we open ourselves up to the possibility that some students may not be able to hit the target after instruction. Your own assessments might provide concrete, irrefutable assessment evidence of this. There will be no hiding. In effect, your supervisor may be able to use your own focused, high-quality classroom assessment to muster evidence that you did not succeed in doing what you were hired to do: produce achievement results.

As a community of professionals, I think each of us must face this possibility. If I succeed as a teacher and my students hit the target, I want an acknowledgement of that success. If my students fail to hit the target I want to know it, and I want to know why they failed.

I can think of at least five possible reasons why my students might not have learned:

1. They lacked the prerequisites needed to achieve what I expected of them.
2. I didn't understand the target to begin with, and so could not convey it appropriately.
3. My instructional methods, strategies, and materials were inappropriate.
4. My students lacked the confidence to risk trying—the motivation to strive for success.
5. Some force(s) outside of school and beyond my control (home environment, for example) interfered with and inhibited learning.

If I am a professional educator whose students failed to hit the target, I must know which problem(s) held sway in my case if I expect to remedy the situation. Only when I know what went wrong can I make the kinds of decisions and take the kinds of action that will promote success for me and my students next time.

For example, if my students lacked prerequisites (reason 1), I need to work with my colleagues at lower grades to be sure our respective curricula mesh. If I lack mastery of the valued targets myself or fail to implement solid instruction (reasons 2 or 3), I have to take responsibility for some pretty serious professional development. Similarly, if my students lack confidence or motivation (reason 4), I may need to investigate with them the reasons for their lack of motivation and plan a course of action that will teach me new and better motivational tactics. And finally, if reason 5 applies, and the home–school partnership is contributing to academic failure, then I need to contact the community beyond school to seek solutions.

As a teacher employed in a school setting committed to helping all students meet state or local academic standards, my success hinges on my understanding the reasons for any lack of success.

Time for Reflection

What other reasons can you think of to explain why students might fail?
What action might you take to counter each if it came up?

Note that I can choose the proper corrective action if and only if I take the risks of (1) gathering dependable information about student success or failure using my own high-quality classroom assessments, and (2) becoming enough of a classroom researcher to uncover the causes of student failure. If I as a teacher simply bury my head in the sand and blame my students for not caring or not trying, I may doom them to long-term failure for reasons beyond their control. Thus, when they fail, I must risk finding out why. If it is my fault or if I can contribute to fixing the problem in any way, I must act accordingly.

I believe that the risk is greatly reduced when I start out with clear and specific targets. If I can share the vision with my students, they can hit it! If I have no target, how can they hit it? When I start with a sharp vision of success, we both profit. This brings us to the next benefit.

Benefits in Student Motivation

I must know which achievement targets I expect my students to hit if I am to share that meaning of success with them. If I can help them understand these expectations, I set them up to take responsibility for their own success. The motivational implications of this for students can be immense.

Personalize this! Say you are a student facing a test. A great deal of material has been covered. You have no idea what will be emphasized on the test. You study your heart out but, alas, you concentrate on the wrong material. Nice try, but you fail. How do you feel when this happens? How are you likely to behave the next time a test comes up under these same circumstances?

Now, say you are facing another test. A great deal of material has been covered. But your teacher, who has a complete understanding of the field, points out the parts that are critical for you to know. The rest will always be there in the text for you to look up when you need it. Further, the teacher provides lots of practice in applying the knowledge in solving real-world problems and emphasizes that this is a second key target of the course. You study in a very focused manner, concentrating on the important material and its application. Your result is a high score on the test. Good effort—you succeed. Again, how do you feel? How are you likely to behave the next time a test comes up under these circumstances?

Given clear requirements for success, students are better able to gauge the appropriateness of their own preparation and thus gain control over their own academic well-being. Students who feel in control of their own chances for success are more likely to care and to strive for excellence.

The fact is that virtually all students start school with the desire to please by becoming competent. They really want to learn the things school offers—to read, write, explore the mysteries of science. Part of the challenge of keeping them on track is for us to remain clear among ourselves and with them about what success means and how to get there.

A Manageable Teacher Workload

Time Saver: In our research on the task demands of classroom assessment, my colleagues and I determined that typical teachers can spend as much as one-third of their available professional time involved in assessment-related activities. That's a lot of time! In fact, in many classrooms it may be too much time. Greater efficiency in assessment is possible.

Clear achievement targets can contribute to that greater efficiency. Here's why: Any assessment is a sample of all the questions we could have asked if the test were infinitely long. But because time is always limited, we can never probe all important dimensions of achievement. So we sample, asking as many questions as we can within the allotted time. A sound assessment asks a representative set of questions, allowing us to infer a student's performance on the entire domain of material from that student's performance on the shorter sample.

As you will see later, sound sampling is another key standard of sound assessment. The **VALIDITY** of an assessment is, in part, a function of the extent to which it covers the important material.

If we have set clear limits on our valued target, then we have set a clear sampling frame. This allows us to sample with maximum efficiency and confidence (i.e., to gather just enough information on student achievement without wasting time overtesting). Let me illustrate.

If I want my students to master specific content knowledge, say in history or science, I can devise the most powerful (accurate and efficient) test of that knowledge most easily when I have done the following:

1. Set clearly defined limits on what they are to learn.

2. Established which elements of that knowledge are most important.

3. Sampled those elements with just enough assessment exercises to lead me to a confident conclusion about student learning without wasting time gathering too much evidence.

Similarly, if I select an achievement target in the arena of reasoning and problem solving, I will be confident of student mastery of those proficiencies most quickly (i.e., based on the fewest possible exercises) if I am crystal clear about my definitions of reasoning and problem solving. If my vision of success is vague, I will need more evidence gathered over a longer period of time before I feel certain that my students have hit the target.

For a clear example of the power of focused targets, see Figure 3.4. I can begin my reading instruction with a cloudy sense of what it means to be a proficient

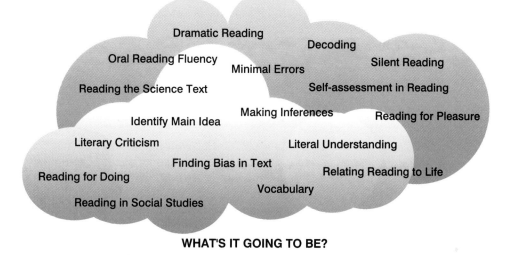

The Unclear Vision

Dramatic Reading

Decoding

Oral Reading Fluency

Silent Reading

Minimal Errors

Reading the Science Text

Self-assessment in Reading

Making Inferences

Reading for Pleasure

Identify Main Idea

Literary Criticism

Literal Understanding

Finding Bias in Text

Reading for Doing

Relating Reading to Life

Vocabulary

Reading in Social Studies

WHAT'S IT GOING TO BE?

A More Focused Vision

Washington State's Second-Grade Reading Proficiencies:
- Decoding Proficiency
- Oral Reading Fluency and Rate
- Simple Recall of What Is Read

NOW WE'RE ZEROING IN ON WHAT TO ASSESS!

Figure 3.4
Achievement targets defined: What it means to be a good reader

reader, or I can zero in on a clear and specific meaning. Which do you think is most likely to lead to focused classroom assessment?

When I have a clear sense of the desired ends, I can use the assessment methods that are most efficient for the situation. In the next chapter, we will discuss four alternative assessment methods. (In Part II of this book I discuss each of these methods in detail.) I will argue that different methods fit different kinds of targets. It will become clear that some methods produce certain kinds of achievement information more efficiently than do others. Skillful classroom assessors match methods to targets so as to produce maximum information with minimum invested assessment time. This is part of the art of classroom assessment. Your skill as an artist increases with the clarity of your vision of important learning.

There you have several compelling reasons to invest energy up front to become clear about the meaning of success in your classroom. To make it easier for you to define success for yourself and your students, let's set some limits for the range of possible targets.

Types of Achievement Targets

All right, so clearly defined targets are useful. But, you might now ask, how do I make my targets clear? What is it that I must describe about them? The first step in answering these questions is to understand that we ask our students to learn a number of different kinds of things. Our challenge as teachers is to understand which of these is relevant for our particular students at any particular point in their academic development.

As my colleagues and I analyzed the task demands of classroom assessment, we tried to discern categories of targets that seemed to make sense to teachers (Stiggins & Conklin, 1992). We collected, studied, categorized, and tried to understand the various kinds of valued expectations reflected in teachers' classroom activities and assessments. The following categories or types of achievement targets emerged as important:

- *Knowledge*—mastery of substantive subject matter content, where mastery includes both knowing and understanding it
- *Reasoning*—the ability to use that knowledge and understanding to figure things out and to solve problems
- *Performance Skills*—the development of proficiency in doing something where it is the process that is important, such as playing a musical instrument, reading aloud, speaking in a second language, or using psychomotor skills
- *Products*—the ability to create tangible products, such as term papers, science fair models, and art products, that meet certain standards of quality and that present concrete evidence of academic proficiency
- *Dispositions*—the development of certain kinds of feelings, such as attitudes, interests, and motivational intentions

As you will see, these categories are quite useful to our thinking about classroom assessment because they subsume all possible targets, are easy to understand, relate to one another in significant ways, and (now here's the important part!) have clear links to different kinds of assessment. But before we discuss assessment, let's more thoroughly understand these categories of achievement targets.

A Note of Caution

For clarity, I discuss these targets in the order listed. Because the targets build on one another, I can use this order to reveal important aspects of their interrelationships. But there also is danger in my doing this, because imposing order can mislead you with respect to the totality of their relationships. Let me explain.

Because I refer first to knowledge and understanding (sometimes even calling them a "foundation") you may infer that your students must learn content before approaching any other targets. This is incorrect.

Students are natural thinkers, and sometimes they may use this natural thinking process to help them figure things out and come to new understandings. As they become more proficient reasoners and problem solvers under your leadership, they become more capable of independently generating new knowledge and understanding; the two can interact, growing together.

Further, students can experiment with applying new reasoning and performance skills as they learn to create new products. As they refine their reasoning and performance capabilities, their products improve in quality; again, they all grow together. In the process, they figure out how to reason through a problem more effectively, building on their existing knowledge and understanding of how to create quality products.

These relationships among forms of achievement are important. They are dynamically interrelated targets that spiral toward academic excellence together. As a teacher, if I know how I'd like the parts to fit into a dynamic whole, when the need arises I can help my students pull out certain parts (say, gaps in their understanding), examine them closely, and identify where difficulties may reside. For this reason, as a classroom assessor I must be prepared to assess any of the components of academic excellence: knowledge and understanding, reasoning, performance skills, or product development capabilities.

Knowledge and Understanding Targets

When we were growing up, we were asked to learn important content. What happened in 1066? Who signed the Declaration of Independence? Name the Presidents of the United States in order. What does the symbol "Au" refer to on the periodic table of elements? Learn this vocabulary for a quiz on Friday . . . Here is your spelling list for this week . . . Learn the multiplication tables.

We had to memorize these things by test time or fail. And, in fact, at least some of what we learned in this way was important. For example, we would never have developed the ability to communicate our ideas if we had not mastered sufficient vocabulary. We would not have attained proficiency in speaking a second language if we had not learned the vocabulary and syntax of that language. We would have remained incapable of reading and understanding our science text if we had not learned to understand at least some science content.

If such knowledge is prerequisite to mastery of more sophisticated achievements, then part of our jobs as teachers is to be sure our students gain control of that content. This is precisely why I have structured this book in part to help you know and understand some of the foundations of sound assessment. You cannot do the classroom assessment part of the teaching job well unless you know certain things. In that sense this knowledge represents a foundation of your teaching competence.

But this is not merely about making students memorize content and then regurgitate it for a test. Such work, we now understand, will not lead to academic success. There are several reasons for this.

First, knowing something is not the same as understanding it. To understand content, students need to see how it fits into the larger schema of the academic discipline they are studying. Without such connection, knowledge is useless.

Second, in this information age, the world does not operate merely on facts stored in our brains. I am every bit as much a master of content if I know where to find it as if I know it outright. This way of knowing is becoming increasingly important as technology continues to permeate our society.

And finally, there are ways to come to "know" that do not rely on memorization. I can come to know because I figured it out and the resulting insight left an indelible impression. I can come to know because frequent use of certain knowledge leaves a residue.

In short, mastering (meaning *gaining control over*) content knowledge is a complex enterprise. Let me fill in some details.

To Know and to Understand Are Not the Same.   The world around me is full of wonderful things that I know but that I just don't understand. For instance, the Golden Gate Bridge arches beautifully over San Francisco Bay. But I don't understand the structures that keep it from falling into the bay. I know that my computer will save the text that I am composing. But I don't understand how it does this. The French say, "C'est la même chose." I can say this. But I don't understand what it means. Thus, for me these represent useless information.

On the other hand, the world is also full of things that I know and understand. Airplanes whisk me across the country and don't fall out of the sky. I understand that this is because of the vacuum formed under the wing when air accelerates over the top of that wing. I can say and spell the science word *watershed* and I understand what it means. I even understand why it is an important environmental science concept. I can read and understand guidebooks on fly fishing because I know and understand the physics of a fly line in motion.

I submit that merely knowing but not understanding leaves learners unable to make use of what they have learned. Memorizing the multiplication tables without understanding the underlying mathematical concept does not make that knowledge useful. Learning to mimic French phrases cannot lead to effective communication. But knowing and understanding those phrases will.

Therefore, as a classroom teacher/assessor, I must know and understand what I expect my students to master. Further, I must be prepared to assess my students' understanding of what they claim to know.

Two Ways of "Knowing".   When I was a student, consequences were dire if anyone was caught with a crib sheet in a test. We were expected to know it outright. We were expected to have burned the content into the neural connections of our brains by whatever means. Remember all the tricks? Flash cards. Repetition—over and over. Cramming. All nighters. Playing recordings while sleeping. If we didn't memorize it, we failed. There can be no question, some of that stuff stuck and that's a good thing. Regardless of how one gets there, knowing something outright can be a powerful way of knowing. But this is not the only way of coming to know.

The reason, as stated previously, is that I am every bit as much a master of content if I know where to find it as if I know it outright. In other words, the world does not operate solely on information retrieved only from memory. To see what I mean, just try to fill out your income tax return, operate a new computer, or use an unfamiliar transit system without referring to the appropriate (hopefully well written!) user's guide. When we confront such challenges in real adult life, we rely on what we know to help us find what we don't know.

In short, this "knowledge" category of achievement targets includes both those targets (core facts, concepts, relationships, and principles) that students must learn outright to function within an academic discipline and those targets they tap as needed through their use of reference resources. Each presents its own unique classroom assessment challenges. And remember, each way of "knowing" must be accompanied by "understanding."

The Structure of Understanding.   There is a danger lurking just below the surface of any conversation about student mastery of content in school. We have a habit of thinking of content knowledge as knowledge of facts. What happened in 1066? Who was the tenth president? When was the Louisiana Purchase made? What words did Abraham Lincoln speak at Gettysburg? The danger is that such details will be valued and learned as disconnected facts only. Television game shows often perpetuate this sense of "learnedness."

An alternative vision of academic excellence is advanced by those who contend that these facts form into categories that lead us to deeper understanding and that this deeper understanding is what our students should master. Erickson (1998) contends that

> Every content-based discipline has a core of conceptual, essential understandings. In this age of knowledge overload, students need a mental schema to pattern or sort information. As they progress through the grades, students build conceptual structures in the brain as they relate new examples to past learnings. This means that teachers, in writing curricula, need to identify conceptual ideas, often stated as essential understandings, that are developmentally appropriate for the age level of their students. Conceptual understandings become more sophisticated from elementary through secondary and post secondary schools. I would not expect to see, in a concept-based (idea-centered curriculum), the same essential understandings at the high school level that I see in the elementary curriculum. (pp. 51–52)

Many who have written of these structures of knowledge and understanding define them in terms of ascending levels of generality. Again, Erickson helps us see the big picture with the graphic depiction in Figure 3.5 and with this example:

Theory:	Migration is a psychologically driven response to meet an internal need.
General Principle:	People migrate to meet a variety of needs. Migration may lead to new opportunities or greater freedom.
Concepts:	Migration
	Needs
	Opportunity
	Freedom
Topic:	Westward migration
Facts:	Lewis and Clark explored the Pacific Northwest.
	Early American settlers migrated west.
	Early American settlers looked for new opportunities. (Erickson, 1998, p. 52)

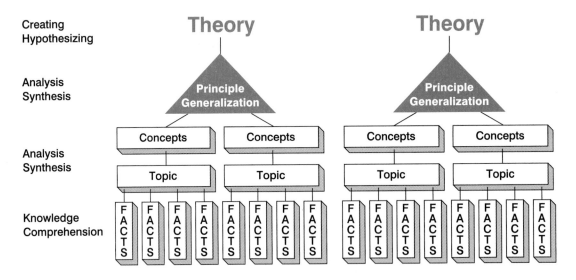

Figure 3.5
Erickson's structure of knowledge
Source: Reprinted from *Concept-Based Curriculum and Instruction: Teaching beyond the Facts* (p. 5) by H. L. Erickson, 1998, Thousand Oaks, CA: Corwin. Reprinted by permission.

Unless our students have this kind of big picture into which to plug the examples they learn, they will have difficulty understanding them. Our teaching and our classroom assessments must venture beyond merely helping students know the facts.

Here's another example that starts at the fact end and works toward enduring (timeless), universal (transferable) and encompassing concepts:

Fact:	Fossils and rocks that are identical appear in vastly different places on the earth's surface.
Topic:	The study of rocks and fossils
Constellation of concepts that transfer:	Continents
	Layers of the earth's surface
	The nature of biological and geological evidence
General Principle:	Pieces of the earth's surface have moved.
Theory:	Continental drift

To be clear, facts may well be worth knowing outright, or they may be worthy of the effort needed to retrieve through the use of reference. But that value resides in the understanding that accompanies knowing. Wiggins and McTighe (1999) refer to "enduring understandings" as big ideas that

- Have enduring value beyond the classroom
- Reside at the heart of the academic discipline
- Raise questions and require interrogation, analysis, exemplification to grasp completely
- Offer potential for engaging students—like to be provocative, stimulating (pp. 29–30)

Big ideas yield essential questions that guide exploration of a discipline. They cite Bruner to illustrate:

> One of the organizing concepts in biology is the question, What function does it serve?—a question premised on the assumption that everything one finds in an organism serves some function or it probably would not have survived. Other general ideas are related to this question. The student who makes progress in biology learns to ask the question more and more subtlely, to relate more and more things to it. (Bruner [1960], cited in Wiggins & McTighe, 1999, p. 28)

Wiggins and McTighe (1999) pose additional essential questions from other contexts: "Must a story have a moral? How does an organism's structure enable it to survive in its environment? What is light? Is U.S. history a history of progress?" (p. 31).

To help our students know and understand content, we ourselves must be masters of the disciplines we expect them to master. Thus, we must be prepared to share the topics, concepts, generalizations, and theories that hold facts together.

Further, as a classroom teacher, part of your job is to devise assessment exercises that require students to demonstrate their understanding of those connections.

Relationship to Other Proficiencies.   The foundation of academic competence rests on knowledge and understanding. I know that this is not the trendy position to be taking in the field of education today. We are supposed to be attending to "higher-order thinking" and process skills. I agree that these, too, are important. But there is a danger lurking here.

In our haste to embrace "higher-order thinking," we deemphasize what we have a tradition of calling "lower-order thinking." But what have we traditionally defined as "lower order?" The mastery of content knowledge. So by deemphasizing content mastery, we in effect deny our students access to the very content they need to solve the problems that we want them to solve. Does that make sense to you? Let me illustrate my point.

We cannot, for example, solve math problems (clearly a reasoning competence) without a foundational knowledge of math facts, number systems, and/or problem-solving procedures. Nor can we speak a foreign language skillfully without mastery of its vocabulary, syntax, and structure. It is impossible to write a quality essay in English without a practical knowledge of letters, words, sentences, paragraphs, and grammar, as well as an understanding of how to write in an organized and coherent manner. We cannot read with comprehension if we lack sufficient background about the material presented in the text. We cannot respond to an essay question on the Civil War in history class unless we know something about the Civil War! In every performance domain, there is a basis of knowledge underpinning competence.

Understand, however, that this foundation of knowledge is never sufficient for finding solutions to complex problems. It is merely one essential ingredient. To succeed, we must combine the necessary knowledge with appropriate patterns of reasoning. The essential point is that there is no such thing as content-free thinking. I will amplify this point in the next section.

At any point in instruction, a teacher concerned about student attainment of the building blocks of competence might legitimately hold as the valued target that students master some important basic knowledge. At such a time, assessing student mastery of that knowledge might very well make sense.

Time for Reflection

Identify the academic discipline you regard as your greatest strength. How strong is your underlying knowledge of facts, concepts, and generalizations in that area? Think about your weakest area of academic performance. How strong is your knowledge and understanding base there? How critical is a strong, basic understanding of facts, concepts, and generalizations to academic success?

Reasoning Targets

Having students master content merely for the sake of knowing it and for no other reason is a complete waste of their time and ours. It is virtually always the case that we want students to be able to use their knowledge and understanding to reason, to figure things out, to solve certain kinds of problems. For example, we want them to

- Analyze and solve story problems in math because those problems mimic life after school
- Compare current or past political events or leaders because they need to be active citizens
- Reason inductively and deductively in science to find solutions to everyday problems
- Evaluate opposing positions on social and scientific issues because life constantly requires critical thinking

We want them to use what they know within the problem context to achieve a desired solution.

If we hold such targets as valuable for students, it is incumbent on us to define precisely what we mean by *reasoning and problem-solving proficiency*. Exactly what does it mean to reason "analytically"? It means that we take things apart and see what's inside them. But what does it mean to do it well? That's the key question. What does it mean to reason "comparatively"? We do this when we think about similarities and differences. But when and how is that relevant? Another key question. What does it mean to categorize, synthesize, to reason inductively or deductively? What *is* critical thinking, anyway? Not only must we be clear about the underlying structure of these patterns of reasoning, but we must help students understand and take possession of them, too. And, of course, we must be ready to translate each pattern into classroom assessment exercises and scoring procedures.

We'll explore these patterns in detail in later chapters. Obviously, they represent important forms of achievement. The key to our success in helping students master them is to understand that any form of reasoning can be done either well or poorly. Our assessment challenge lies in knowing the difference. Our success in helping students learn to monitor the quality of their own reasoning—a critical part of lifelong learning—is to *help them learn the difference*.

In the case of reasoning, as with all achievement targets, we who presume to help students master effective reasoning must first ourselves become confident, competent masters of these patterns. In other words, we must strive to meet standards of intellectual rigor in our own thinking if we are to make this vision come alive in our students' minds. If we do not, then we remain unprepared to devise assessments that reflect sound reasoning.

Relationship to Other Targets.   We can use our reasoning powers to generate new knowledge and understanding. When I combine two things that I knew before into an insight that I hadn't realized before, that insight can remain with me for future use. Further, my reasoning powers can serve as antecedents to skillful performance or product development—the next two kinds of targets. You'll see how as you read on.

Performance Skill Targets

In most classrooms, there are things teachers want their students to be able to do, instances for which the measure of attainment is students' ability to demonstrate that they can perform or behave in a certain way. For example, at the primary-grade level, a teacher might expect to see certain fundamental social interaction behaviors or the earliest oral reading fluency skills. At the elementary level, a teacher might observe student performance in cooperative group activities. In middle school or junior high, manipulation of a science lab apparatus might be important. And at the high school level, public speaking or the ability to converse in a second language might be a valued outcome.

In all of these cases, success lies in "doing it well." The assessment challenge lies in being able to define in clear terms, using words, examples, or both, what it *means* to do it well—to read fluently, work productively as a team member, or carry out the steps in a lab experiment. To assess well, we must provide opportunities for students to show their skills, so we can observe and evaluate while they are performing.

Relationship to Other Targets.   Note that two necessary conditions for performing skillfully are first, that students master prerequisite procedural knowledge, and second, that they have the reasoning power to use that knowledge appropriately in performance. For example, I cannot produce a quality written product unless I have handwriting or computer keyboarding skills *and* the language mastery necessary to write fluently and coherently. I cannot produce a quality art or craft product unless I am proficient at using the tools of that medium *and* understand how to mold the raw material into my desired final form. Thus, knowledge and reasoning outcomes form the foundations of skill outcomes. However, it is critical that we understand that, in this category, the student's performance objective is to put all the foundational and reasoning proficiencies together and to be skillful. This is precisely why achievement-related skills often represent complex targets requiring quite sophisticated assessments. Success in creating products—the next kind of target—virtually always hinges on the ability to perform some kinds of skills. Performance skills underpin product development.

Product Development Targets

Yet another way for students to succeed academically is through creating quality products, tangible entities that exist independently of the performer, but that present evidence in their quality that the student has mastered foundational knowledge, requisite reasoning and problem-solving proficiencies, and specific production skills.

For example, a high school social studies teacher might have students prepare a term paper. A technology teacher might ask students to repair a computer. An elementary school teacher might challenge students to create a model or diorama. A primary-grade teacher might collect samples of student artwork. A classic example of this kind of target that crosses grade levels is the ability to create high-quality written products or writing samples, tangible products that contain within them evidence of the writer's proficiency.

In all cases, success lies in creating products that possess certain key attributes. The assessment challenge is to be able to define clearly and understandably, in writing and/or through example, what those attributes are. We must be able to specify exactly how high- and low-quality products differ.

Relationship to Other Targets. Note once again that successful performance arises out of student mastery of prerequisite knowledge and through the application of appropriate reasoning strategies. In addition, students will probably need to perform certain predefined steps to create the desired product. Prerequisite achievement thus underpins the creation of quality products, but evidence of ultimate success resides in the product itself. Does it meet standards of quality or does it not?

Dispositional Targets

This final category of aspirations for our students is quite broad and complex. It includes those characteristics that go beyond academic achievement into the realms of affective and personal feeling states, such as attitudes, sense of academic self-confidence, or interest in something that motivationally predisposes a person to act or not act.

Many teachers set as goals, for example, that students will develop positive academic self-concepts or positive attitudes toward school subjects predisposing them to strive for excellence. Without question, we want our students to develop strong interests, as well as a strong sense of internal control over their own academic well-being. We may define each disposition in terms of three essential elements:

- It is directed at some specific object.
- It has a positive or negative direction.
- It can vary in level of intensity, from strong to weak.

In other words, attitudes, values, and interests don't exist in a vacuum. Rather, they are focused on certain aspects of our lives. We have attitudes about self, school, subjects, classmates, and teachers. We hold values about politics, work, and learning. We are interested in doing, reading, and discussing certain things. Thus, dispositions are directed toward certain objects, ideas, people, and so on.

Further, our feelings about things are positive, neutral, or negative. Our academic self-concepts are positive or negative. We hold positive or negative attitudes. Our values are for or against things. We are passionate or disinterested. Thus, direction is important. In school, we seek to impart positive dispositions toward learning new things.

Dispositions vary in their intensity. Sometimes we feel very strongly positive or negative about things. Sometimes we feel less strongly. Sometimes the intensity is too weak to ascertain its direction. Intensity varies. Positive learning experiences can result when teachers are in touch with students' dispositions (either as individuals or as a group) and when teachers can put students in touch with their own feelings about important issues. Obviously, however, we cannot know students feelings about things unless we ask. That requires assessment.

Because these affective and social dimensions are quite complex, thoughtful assessment is essential. We define success in assessing them exactly as we do success in assessing achievement: Sound assessment requires a crystal-clear vision or understanding of the characteristic(s) to be assessed. Only then can we select a proper assessment method, devise a sampling procedure, and control sources of bias and distortion so as to accurately assess direction and intensity of feelings about specified objects.

Summary of Targets

We have discussed four different but interrelated visions of achievement plus the affective component of student learning. Knowledge and understanding are important. Reasoning and problem solving require application of that knowledge. Knowledge and reasoning are required for successful skill performance and/or product development. And dispositions very often result from success or a lack of success in academic performance. But once again, remember that these can all grow and change in dynamic, interrelated ways within students. Table 3.1 presents sample achievement targets from various academic disciplines. Read down each column.

Time for Reflection

Let's say we wanted to extend Table 3.1 to include three more columns. Identify examples of knowledge, reasoning, skill, product, and dispositional targets that would be relevant for Foreign Language (spoken and written, separately) and for Social Studies.

I have seen a problem emerging across the country arising from our collective tendency as educators to be trendy. Back in the 1950s, 1960s, 1970s, and even early 1980s, schools were almost obsessed with student mastery of content and reasoning. Performance skills and product development capabilities were less important.

From the mid 1980s until now, however, our deeper understanding of the complexity of achievement targets has led us to embrace the importance of performance skill and product targets almost to the exclusion of knowledge and reasoning targets. Let me show you when this can be a problem.

A young middle schooler in our neighborhood was being taught by a science teacher who was into "project-based learning." The project-based assignment she gave to her students was to create a complex machine that involved the use of five

Table 3.1
Sample achievement targets across school subjects

Achievement Target	Reading	Writing	Music	Science	Math
Know and Understand	Sight vocabulary Background knowledge required by text	Vocabulary needed to communicate Mechanics of usage Knowledge of topic	Instrument mechanics Musical notation	Science facts and concepts	Number meaning Math facts Numeration systems
Reason	Process the text and comprehend the meaning	Choose words and syntactic elements to convey message Evaluate text quality	Evaluate tonal quality	Hypotheses testing Classifying species	Identify and apply algorithms to solve problems
Performance Skills	Oral reading fluency	Letter formation Keyboarding skills	Instrument fingering Breath control	Manipulate lab apparatus correctly	Use manipulatives while solving problem
Products	Diagram revealing comprehension	Samples of original text	Original composition written in musical notation	Written lab report Science fair model	Diagram depicting problem solution
Dispositions	"I like to read."	"I can write well."	"Music is important to me."	"Science is worth understanding."	"Math is useful in real life."

simple machines. They were to use building skills to create a product to meet certain standards of quality. But nowhere during her instruction did she give students the opportunity to learn what a "simple machine" was. In short, the knowledge and understanding foundations of success were completely overlooked. To be successful, students need all of the pieces in the puzzle.

Step one in planning instruction or designing assessments is to specify the type(s) of target(s) students are to hit. As you will see later, once a target is defined, the process of designing assessments is quite easy. The toughest part by far is coming up with the clear and complete vision!

Sources of Information about Achievement Targets

Teachers can search out, identify, and set limits on the achievement targets that are to represent their particular teaching responsibilities in two ways: through thorough professional preparation and thoughtful planning (teamwork!) with colleagues. Let's explore each.

Professional Preparation

Solid professional preparation to teach provides the foundation for clear and appropriate achievement targets. Put simply, if you intend to teach something, you had better understand it inside and out! Maximum teaching effectiveness arises from having a complete sense of the meaning of quality performance, including a complete understanding of the foundational knowledge and kinds of reasoning and problem-solving skills students need to master to achieve success.

In my years of work in the arena of writing assessment, I have worked with teachers who have been given the responsibility of teaching students to write, but who have only the vaguest notion of what it means to write well. They feel uncertain, and their students struggle. On the other hand, I also have met many teachers who possess a refined vision of success in this performance domain and have seen their students blossom as young writers. These two groups of teachers prepared very differently to meet this professional challenge, and that difference showed in student achievement.

Those who would teach science concepts must first understand those concepts. Those who aspire to being math teachers must first develop a highly refined mental picture of those concepts, and so on. If you would assess in these or any other performance domains you must first become master of the required material yourself. Five ways for you to reach this goal are to (1) be a lifelong learner, (2) participate in available training, (3) understand your state and local academic achievement standards, (4) network with fellow professionals, and (5) remain current with the literature of your field.

Lifelong Learning. Be the same kind of lifelong learner you want your students to become. Take personal responsibility to become good at what you expect your students to be good at. If you seek to help them become good writers, for example, become one yourself. Study, practice, strive to publish your work. Become a proficient performer yourself and commit to your own ongoing improvement, regardless of the target(s) you hold as valuable for your students.

Teacher Training. If you are currently involved in an undergraduate or graduate-level teacher training program, be sure your discipline-based curriculum and instructional methods courses (e.g., in reading, writing, math, science, etc.) reflect the best current thinking about definitions of academic success. Early on in each course, ask specific questions of your professors and evaluate their answers critically.

For example, ask them what vision of student success they believe should govern teaching in this arena. What definition of high achievement do they hold as being most appropriate for students and why? They should be able to provide a written description of the vision they value, and they should be able to cite references from professional literature to support the reasons they hold those particular values. Ask if there is universal agreement among members of the profession that this is the best definition. If not, what alternative visions of excellence in student performance are valued? Why do your professors reject them?

Also inquire about how your professors plan to assess your mastery of those visions of successful student achievement. They should be able to provide specific examples of the assessment exercises and scoring criteria they plan to use.

Evaluate the meaning of student success your professors convey to you. Does it make sense to you? Can you master this vision with sufficient depth to convey it to your students comfortably? I understand that I am asking you to do something that will require a stretch on your part to evaluate their responses to your queries. After all, you're there to learn about achievement targets. However, as a teacher, you must be able to evaluate ideas as you learn them.

I also realize that I am asking you to do something that will require diplomacy on your part, because you do not hold the power in this communication with your professors. But in one sense you do: Their job is to help you become a successful teacher. They have dedicated their professional lives to that effort. If your professors are committed to student well-being, they will welcome your "critical consumer" inquiries. (In fact, among the professors I know personally, you will gain great respect just for asking!)

State and Local Achievement Standards. While the ultimate responsibility for your preparation as a teacher falls to you and you alone, excellent support is available. As noted earlier, our emergence into the era of standards-driven education has spurred a great deal of high-powered reexamination of important achievement expectations. This is a boon to teachers because in virtually every field, we have at our disposal definitions of achievement targets that hold the promise of allowing us to produce better achievers faster than ever before. This applies to reading, writing, science, math, reasoning and problem solving, foreign languages, and many other subjects. Virtually every state and lots of local districts have standards of academic excellence, typically developed by teams of experienced teachers from within the state. Contact your state department of education for information about them. Many school districts engage their faculty in the collaborative effort of devising achievement standards for students in their community.

Be advised, however, that standards developed in these contexts typically are articulated in the form of goals or objectives. Two examples appear in Figure 3.6, one in history and the other in writing. As a classroom teacher, it is your responsibility to transform such objectives into the achievement targets that your students must hit to become proficient. *What do students need to know to meet this standard? What patterns of reasoning must they be able to apply? What performance skills, if any, are called for? What products must they be prepared to create?* Figure 3.6 illustrates this conversion process for the two achievement standards listed. I will offer more examples in later chapters.

Professional Networks and Literature

Another way to prepare as a teacher is to contact the appropriate local and national professional associations of teachers. Most have assembled commissions of their members to translate current research into practical guidelines for teachers, and many regularly publish journals to disseminate this research. Work with the resource personnel in your professional library if you have one. Often they can route special articles and information to you when they arrive. College and university libraries represent additional repositories of valuable information and support personnel. In addition, you can always search the Internet for information on valued achievement targets.

You can also find help in understanding important targets by studying textbooks adopted for use in your district, text support materials, and district curriculum guides and frameworks. These might represent state, district, school, or even departmental statements of valued targets.

Tap all of these sources to build your own sense of understanding and confidence in the field of study in which you teach. I cannot overstate how much this will help when it comes to generating high-quality classroom assessment. *In fact, it has been my experience in over 20 years of research that the single most common barrier to sound classroom assessment is teachers' lack of vision of appropriate achievement targets within the subjects they are supposed to teach.* Focused visions lead to sound assessments.

Building a Team Effort

One key part of the process of establishing achievement standards for students is to analyze each goal to determine the enabling objectives, the attainment of which are prerequisite to accomplishing the ultimate goal. If we want students to be competent communicators, for example, what competencies must they attain in what

---

Sample State Standard

History: Students will evaluate different interpretations of historical events.

The teacher must translate this into relevant classroom targets:

Knowledge and Understanding: Students must know and understand each historical event, and must understand each of the alternative interpretations to be evaluated. The teacher must determine if students are to know those things outright or if they can use reference materials to retrieve the required knowledge.

Reasoning: Evaluative reasoning requires judgment about the quality of each interpretation. Thus students must demonstrate both an understanding of the criteria by which one judges the quality of an interpretation and the ability to apply these criteria.

Performance Skills: None required

Products: None required

Sample State Standard

Writing: Students will use styles appropriate for their audience and purpose, including proper use of voice, word choice, and sentence fluency.

The teacher must translate this into relevant classroom targets:

Knowledge and Understanding: Writers must possess appropriate understanding of the concept of style as evidenced in voice, word choice, and sentence structure. In addition, students must possess knowledge of the topic they are to write about.

Reasoning: Writers must be able to figure out how to make sound voice, word choice, and sentence construction decisions while composing original text. The assessment must provide evidence of this ability.

Performance Skills: One of two kinds of performance will be required. Either respondents will write longhand or will compose text on a keyboard. Each requires its own kind of skill competence.

Products: The final evidence of competence will be written products that present evidence of the ability to write effectively to different audiences.

Figure 3.6
Converting state standards to classroom achievement targets

order to learn to read, write, speak, and listen? We can learn the components of each of these from the professional literature and thus establish those critical building blocks of competence.

   Once we identify those building blocks, then the various members of our professional team of educators must collaborate with one another both within and across grade levels to decide how to (1) fit the blocks into the curriculum at various grade levels of instruction and (2) define how they will support the ultimate goal: developing competent communicators. What teachers will have responsibility for supporting student attainment of which blocks? How shall teachers communicate with each other and with parents and students about progress? How shall all involved devise and conduct the assessments that inform instructional decision making? These are the classroom-level issues that teachers and instructional support personnel must address together to lay the foundation for student success.

A Final Reminder: The Targets in Your Classroom Are Your Responsibility

As a teacher, you may or may not practice your profession in a community that engages in the kind of integrated planning outlined here. You may or may not practice in a school in which staff collaborate in articulating achievement targets across grade levels or subjects. In short, you may or may not receive the kind of school and community support needed to do a thorough job of generating a continuous progress portrait of success for students.

Nevertheless, each of us has a responsibility to our particular students to be clear, specific, and correct about our achievement expectations. The point is, while all of the aforementioned school and community planning work is being carried out (if conducted at all), tomorrow in your classroom, or as soon as you enter a classroom for the first time, there will be a group of students wanting and needing to master content knowledge, learn to solve problems, master important performance skills, create important products, and/or develop certain dispositions. They count on you to know what these things mean and to know how to teach and assess them. *When it comes to being clear about what it means to be successful in your classroom, the responsibility stops with you, regardless of what else is going on around you! Embrace that responsibility.*

Summary: Clear Targets Are Key

In this part of our journey into the realm of classroom assessment, I have argued that the quality of any assessment rests on the clarity of the assessor's understanding of the achievement target(s) to be assessed. We have identified five kinds of interrelated expectations as useful in thinking about and planning for assessment and for integrating it into your instruction:

- Mastering content knowledge (including understanding)
- Using that knowledge to reason and solve problems

- Demonstrating certain kinds of performance skills
- Creating certain kinds of products
- Developing certain dispositions

Each teacher faces the challenge of specifying desired targets in the classroom, relying on a commitment to lifelong learning, strong professional preparation, community input, and collegial teamwork within the school to support this effort.

When we are clear, benefits accrue for all involved. Limits of teacher accountability are established, setting teachers up for time savings and greater success. Limits of student accountability are established, setting students up for success. And, the huge assessment workload faced by teachers becomes more manageable.

I urge that you specify clear expectations in your classroom. Do so in writing and publish them for all to see. Eliminate the mystery surrounding the meaning of success in your classroom by letting your students see your vision. If they can see it, they can hit it. But if they cannot see it, their challenge turns into pin the tail on the donkey—blindfolded, of course.

Exercises for Self-Assessment

1. Reread the important benefits of specifying clear and appropriate targets and rewrite them in your own words.

2. Identify the major risks to teachers of being explicit about targets and be sure these make sense to you.

3. List and define the five kinds of achievement targets presented in this chapter. Make them part of that portion of your structure of knowledge that you learn outright—that you don't have to look up to recall.

4. Identify, in your own words, available sources of information and guidance in selecting and defining valued targets.

5. Translate each of the five kinds of targets into a real example of a significant target that you hit during your own school experience.

6. Explain in your own words the relationships that exist between and among the five kinds of achievement targets.

 You may go to the Companion Website at www.prenhall.com/stiggins and answer these questions in the Self-Assessment module.

Final Chapter Reflection

1. *What are the three most important new insights to come to you as a result of your study of this chapter?*
2. *Which of your previous questions about assessment can you now answer based on your study of this chapter?*
3. *What new questions have come to mind as a result of your study of this chapter that you hope to have answered as your study continues?*
4. For practicing teachers only: *What do you plan to do differently in assessment in your classroom as a result of your study of this book so far?*

   For those in preservice study only: *As you think about the classroom assessment environment that you hope to create for your students, how has your thinking changed as a result of your study of this book so far?*

Workbook Activities

Those of you using the workbook, *Practice with Student-Involved Classroom Assessment*, as part of your study of this material will find the following activities and others included for Chapter 3:

- *What's Worth Assessing?*   This real-world case study asks whether the targets assessed are worth the time devoted to assessing them.

- *Inviting Students into the Target.*   This exercise provides practice in transforming achievement targets into "student-friendly" language and in investigating whether your descriptions are, in fact, clear to students.

- *What's in a Standard?*   In this exercise, you go inside broad achievement standards to determine the implied classroom achievement targets. This practice helps you see how to connect state standards, for example, to classroom assessment and instruction.

- *Write a Letter.*   If you are a practicing teacher, write a letter to a parent describing what achievement targets you expect your students to master. Or, if you are a student yourself, write a letter to your course instructor outlining your understanding of the achievement targets for a course you are taking.

- *You Build Assessment into One of Your Instructional Units—Assignment 1.* This activity kicks off a project that continues throughout the workbook, in which you plan and develop all of the assessments needed to determine student mastery of the valued achievement targets in one of your own units of instruction. You begin here by identifying the knowledge, reasoning, performance skill, product, and/or disposition targets for your unit of instruction.

Understanding Our Assessment Alternatives

CHAPTER FOCUS

This chapter answers the following guiding question:

> What is the best assessment method?

Through your study of this chapter you will understand the following important principles:

1. We have a variety of assessment methods from which to choose for any particular classroom assessment situation.
2. The method of choice in any particular classroom assessment context is a function of the desired achievement target and the purpose for the assessment; that is, the context dictates the best assessment method.
3. Once we select a method, we must understand how to use it correctly.

Selecting an Assessment Method

Having introduced the range of purposes for and targets of classroom assessment, we now turn to the issue of selecting proper assessment methods. The assessment method of choice in any classroom context is a direct function of the purpose and the target. There are many possible reasons to assess. Different uses require different results. Different results require different modes of assessment.

There are many possible achievement targets. Different targets require different methods of assessment, too. Thus, without knowledge of purpose and target, it is impossible to devise a sound assessment. Now let's understand how the various assessment methods that we have at our disposal fit into the puzzle (Figure 4.1).

We're going to study four basic assessment methods, all of which are familiar to you: selected response assessments, essay assessments, performance assessments, and assessments that rely on direct personal communication with students. Each provides its own special form of evidence of student proficiency. I introduce them in this chapter, and will devote an entire chapter to each method in Part II, studying each in depth in terms of design, development, advantages, disadvantages, and keys to effective use in the classroom.

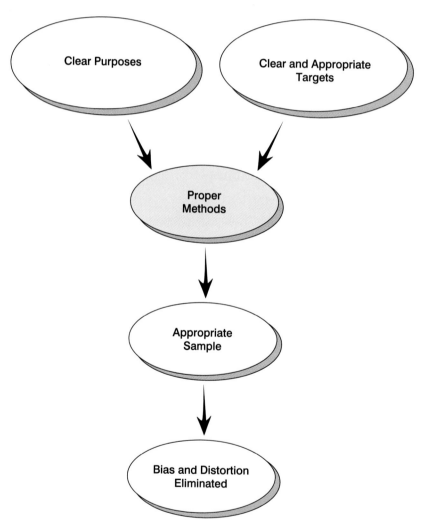

Figure 4.1
How assessment methods fit in

We will analyze how each of these four assessment methods aligns with the four kinds of achievement targets plus dispositions discussed in Chapter 3. In essence, we will see which methods make sense with each target and which do not. We will do this by filling in the cells of Figure 4.2 with commentary on viable matches.

The Assessment Options

The artistry of classroom assessment requires that teachers orchestrate a careful alignment among purposes, targets, and methods. For example, an assessment of instrumental music proficiency is likely to look very different from an assessment of scientific understanding. The former relies on the assessor to listen to and subjectively judge proficiency. The latter can be accomplished with a set of exercises scored correct or incorrect, yielding a score reflecting proficiency. Different targets, different assessment methods.

Note also that an assessment of instrumental music proficiency for the purpose of planning a student's next lesson demands a different kind of assessment from one designed to determine who receives a scholarship to the conservatory. The former requires a narrowly focused, brief assessment; the latter a much larger, more diverse sampling of proficiency. As purpose varies, so does the definition of a sound assessment.

	SELECTED RESPONSE	ESSAY	PERFORMANCE ASSESSMENT	PERSONAL COMMUNICATION
Know				
Reason				
Skills				
Products				
Dispositions				

Figure 4.2
A plan for matching assessment methods with achievement targets

Once the purpose and target have been specified, then and only then can a proper assessment method be selected, developed, and administered, so as to yield sound results for the user. The process is much like assembling a jigsaw puzzle; only those pieces that belong together will fit properly.

We're going to study the range of alternative assessment methods available to meet your combined purpose and target needs in the classroom. In addition, we will examine how to connect methods with targets and how to pick a method that really will reflect the target you wish to assess.

Selected Response Assessment

This category includes all of the objectively scored paper and pencil test formats. Respondents are asked a series of questions, each of which is accompanied by a range of alternative responses. Their task is to select either the correct or the best answer from among the options. The index of achievement in this instance is the number or proportion of questions answered correctly.

Format options within this category include the following:

- multiple-choice items
- true/false items
- matching exercises
- short answer fill-in items

I realize that fill-in-the-blank items do require a response originating from within a respondent's mind, but I include it in this category because it calls for a very brief answer that typically is counted right or wrong.

Standardized achievement test batteries often rely on selected response assessment methodology. So do the chapter tests that accompany many textbooks.

Essay Assessment

In this case, respondents are provided with an exercise (or set of exercises) that calls for them to prepare an original written answer. Respondents might answer questions about content knowledge or provide an explanation of the solution to a complex problem. They might be asked to compare historical events, interpret scientific information, or solve open-ended math problems, where they must show and explain all their work. The examiner reads this original written response and evaluates it by applying specified scoring criteria.

Evidence of achievement is seen in the conceptual substance of the response (i.e., ideas expressed and the manner in which they are tied together). What the score typically tells teachers and students is the number of points attained out of a total number of points possible.

Performance Assessment

In this case, respondents actually carry out a specified activity under the watchful eye of an evaluator, who observes their performance and makes judgments as to the quality of achievement demonstrated. Performance assessments can be based either on observations of the process while respondents are demonstrating skills, or on the evaluation of products created. In this sense, like essay assessments, performance assessments have two parts: a performance task or assignment and a set of scoring guides.

> Assessment experts sometimes refer to essay and performance assessments as "constructed response" assessments, to differentiate them from the "selected response" types.
>
> **TECHNICAL NOTE**

Respondents may evidence achievement by carrying out a proper sequence of activities or by doing something in the appropriate manner. Examples include musical performance, reading aloud, communicating conversationally in a second language, or carrying out some motor activity, as in the case of physical education or dance. In this case, it is the doing that counts. The index of achievement typically is a performance rating or profile of ratings reflecting levels of quality in the performance.

Or, respondents may demonstrate proficiency by creating complex achievement-related products intended to meet certain standards of quality. The product resulting from performance must exist as an entity separate from the performer, as in the case of term papers, science fair exhibits, and art or craft creations. The assessor examines the tangible product to see if those attributes of quality are indeed present. In this instance, it is not so much the process of creating that counts (although that may be evaluated, too) but rather the characteristics of the creation itself. Again in this case, the index of achievement is the rating(s) of product quality.

Personal Communication as Assessment

One of the most common ways teachers gather information about day-to-day student achievement in the classroom is to talk with them! We don't often think of this as assessment in the same sense as a multiple-choice test or a performance assessment. But on reflection, it will become clear to you that certain forms of personal communication definitely do assess student achievement.

These forms of personal communication include questions posed and answered during instruction, interviews, conferences, conversations, listening during class discussions, and oral examinations. The examiner listens to responses and either (1) judges them right or wrong if correctness is the criterion, or (2) makes subjective judgments according to some continuum of quality. Personal communication is a very flexible means of assessment that we can bring into play literally at a moment's notice. While it certainly is not as efficient as some other options when we must assess many students, it can probe achievement far more deeply than can the other alternatives.

Time for Reflection

Think about the assessments you have experienced in the classroom, either as a student or as a teacher, and identify two specific examples from your personal experience of each of the four assessment methods described in this section.

Keep the Options in Balance

As you assess in your classroom, strive to maintain a balanced perspective regarding the viability of these assessment options. For decades, one method dominated: the objectively scored multiple-choice (selected response) test. We were not balanced in our use of assessment methods. As a result, some very important achievement targets that cannot be translated into this method were not assessed. This was especially true in the context of standardized testing, where selected response methods have been used extensively.

As we moved through the 1980s, however, we began to experience a backlash against those decades of domination of one method. As pointed out earlier, we began to embrace a more complex array of valued achievement expectations, and this required that we make more extensive use of such alternatives as essay and performance assessment.

As a result of this swing in values, however, if we aren't careful we may go out of balance in the other direction. By this, I mean we risk trading our prior obsession with multiple-choice tests for a new obsession with performance assessments. Neither method is inherently superior to another. I'll explain why later in this chapter. We can prevent this problem only by knowing what method to use and when and how to use each of them well.

Some Notes about Methods

If you're tuned into the current assessment scene, you may be asking, "What about the very popular alternative called 'portfolio assessment?' Doesn't that represent a fifth method?"

I regard portfolios as a wonderful idea, and devote an entire chapter to their use in assessment and instruction in Part IV. However, I do not regard portfolios as a separate assessment method. Rather, they represent an excellent means of collecting diverse evidence of student achievement (gathered using a variety of the methods described in this chapter) and assembling it into a coherent whole. In short, portfolios are a means of *communicating* about student effort, growth, or achievement status at a point in time.

Note also that three of the four assessment methods described call for students to develop complex original responses. They require them to prepare extended written responses, demonstrate complex performance skills, create multidimensional products, or participate in one-on-one communication, all of which take more time to administer and certainly more time to score than, say, true/false test items. Thus, if the amount of assessment time is held constant, selected response assessments can provide a much larger sample of performance per unit of assessment time.

Given this reality, you might ask, why not just use the most efficient option, selected response, every time? The reason is that selected response assessment formats cannot accurately depict all of the kinds of achievement we expect of our students. Different kinds of assessment methods align with different kinds of achievement targets. We shall explore these relationships next.

Matching Methods with Targets

The art of classroom assessment revolves around the teacher's ability to blend different kinds of achievement targets, with all the forms and nuances of each, with four kinds of assessment methods, with all the variations in format that come with each method. Your object, given a choice of methods, is to identify and choose the most efficient for your specific context. Sounds like a pretty big job, doesn't it! But, as it turns out, the recipes for creating these blends are not complicated. Besides, make proper matches and you save immense amounts of time and make your teaching job (plus your students' learning job) a great deal easier.

As you saw in Figure 4.2, we visualize this blending by crossing the five kinds of outcomes with the four methods to create a table depicting the various matches of targets to methods. We may then explore the nature and practicality of the match within each cell of this table. The result, though not a simple picture, is both understandable and practical. Table 4.1 presents brief descriptions of the various matches.

Important Things to Remember

As you read Table 4.1, please keep the following key points in mind:

Remember the Targets.   First, remember that the various kinds of achievement targets we are discussing are interrelated, each building on and contributing to the others. Problem solving involves application of knowledge. You can't solve math or science problems without applying math or science knowledge and understanding. Once attained, problem solutions can become part of our structure of knowledge. For example, the first time I tried to replace a headlight in my car I was working without instructions. I had to reason it through—figure it out. The second time, my prior problem-solving experience told me exactly what to do. I didn't have to figure it out again. I knew it.

Performance skills represent procedural knowledge and problem-solving proficiencies in action. Given what I know about how to play basketball, I anticipate (a reasoning proficiency) a teammate's cut to the basket and make a perfect pass for an easy basket.

Quality products result from combining knowledge, reasoning, and performance skills in the right ways. To write a quality term paper, the author must combine knowledge of the English language with knowledge of the topic, figure out the message to be communicated, and skillfully render ideas to paper via keyboard or cursive writing. Teachers who are concerned with building student competence must be sure students have the opportunity to develop the prerequisite knowledge, understanding, reasoning proficiency, and writing or keyboarding skills. As students develop those building blocks of term paper success, from time to time the teacher might need to separate out the component parts (knowledge, reasoning, or skills) to be sure they are developing as desired. If they are, down the road, a quality term paper is likely to result.

Remember What We're Seeing.   Second, remember that assessments provide us with external indicators of the internal mental states we call *achievement*. These indicators are visible manifestations that we can see and evaluate. In other words, we can't just lift the tops off students' heads and look inside to see if math problem-solving proficiency is in there. So, we administer an assessment in the form of several math problems to gather evidence of proficiency from which we infer mastery of the desired target. One important key to selecting an acceptable method for any particular form of achievement is to choose the method that permits us to draw the most accurate inference. Thus, a refined vision of the achievement target we are assessing is the foundation for our selection of a method.

Remember Our Goal.   Finally, as stated before, any assessment represents a sample of all the exercises we could have posed if the assessment were infinitely long. A sound assessment relies on a sample that is systematically representative of all the possibilities. We use performance on the sample to infer how much of the target students have mastered.

Our goal in assessment design is to use the most powerful assessment option we can. Power derives from the accuracy and efficiency with which a method can represent our valued standard. We always want the highest-resolution picture of that valued target we can get using the smallest possible sample of student performance; maximum information for minimum cost.

As you read Table 4.1, I hope you can see more clearly why it is crucial to understand the achievement target in order to select a proper assessment method. This cannot be overstated: *Different targets require different methods.*

Time for Reflection

Please study Table 4.1 now and then read on.

A startling realization came to me as I worked through the cells of this table, thinking about which methods matched what outcomes: almost every cell offered a viable match at some level. But some matches are clearly far stronger than others; that is, some get to the heart of the valued target better than others. For example,

Table 4.1
Links between achievement targets and assessment methods

TARGET TO BE ASSESSED	ASSESSMENT METHOD			
	SELECTED RESPONSE	ESSAY	PERFORMANCE ASSESSMENT	PERSONAL COMMUNICATION
KNOWLEDGE & UNDERSTANDING	Multiple choice, true/false, matching, and fill-in can sample mastery of elements of knowledge	Essay exercises can tap understanding of relationships among elements of knowledge	Not a good choice for this target—three other options preferred	Can ask questions, evaluate answers, and infer mastery, but a time-consuming option
REASONING PROFICIENCY	Can assess application of some patterns of reasoning	Written descriptions of complex problem solutions can provide a window into reasoning proficiency	Can watch students solve some problems or examine some products and infer about reasoning proficiency	Can ask student to "think aloud" or can ask followup questions to probe reasoning
PERFORMANCE SKILLS	Can assess mastery of the prerequisites of knowledge and understandings prerequisite to skillful performance, but cannot rely on these to tap the skill itself		Can observe and evaluate skills as they are being performed	Strong match when skill is oral communication proficiency; also can assess mastery of knowledge prerequisite to skillful performance
ABILITY TO CREATE PRODUCTS	Can only assess mastery of the understandings prerequisite to the ability to create quality products	Can assess mastery of knowledge prerequisite to product development; brief essays can provide evidence of writing proficiency	Can assess (1) proficiency in carrying out steps in product development, and (2) attributes of the product itself	Can probe procedural knowledge and knowledge of attributes of quality products, but not product quality
DISPOSITIONS	Selected response questionnaire items can tap student feelings	Open-ended questionnaire items can probe dispositions	Can infer dispositions from behavior and products	Can talk with students about their feelings

without question, the best way to assess writing proficiency is to rely on performance assessment and have students create written products. But we also can use selected response or personal communication to help students determine if they have mastered the knowledge base that underpins effective writing. This can help those who struggle to write well. Such assessments aren't intended to accurately depict writing. Rather, for the teacher striving to create writers, they provide accurate representations of key prerequisites to effective writing. Thus, for instructional purposes, they represent useful assessment alternatives.

The realization that all methods have the potential of contributing at least some useful information about most kinds of classroom outcomes is very good news, because it tells us that we have a variety of tools at our disposal to help us help students learn.

How, then, do we decide which one to use? In the best of all possible worlds where both our time to assess and our assessment resources are unlimited, we choose the cell that affords us the most accurate depiction of our desired target. But, in the real world, we must select the assessment methods that come closest to representing our valued targets and that at the same time fit into the resource realities of our classrooms. Though compromise is inevitable, we can work some pretty good tradeoffs between fidelity and cost of assessment if we know what we're doing.

To illustrate, let's move across Table 4.1 from left to right, one row at a time. Strive to see the big picture. We are looking at the forest now. We'll concentrate on examining the trees in rich detail later.

Remember, This Is Just the First Pass.   The plan for aligning achievement targets and assessment methods that I am about to share is going to sound somewhat complex to you at first. Just remember that this is only our first time through! The remainder of the book is about how to make these matches work to the benefit of your students. All I expect here is that the possibilities make sense to you. I do not expect you to complete your study of this chapter with a feeling of comfort that you know it all.

Remember to Be Practical.   Sometimes I find myself debating with teachers about which kind of assessment (what column of Table 4.1) a particular example represents. For instance, is a term paper an example of a product-based performance assessment or is it an extended essay? Is an assessment of foreign language proficiency a teacher carries out by conversing with a student a skill-based performance assessment or personal communication?

These are intellectual debates more than practical matters. The fact is that methods overlap. Table 4.1's purpose is not to make fine distinctions. Rather, it is to let you know and understand the full array of options at your disposal. The key to your success is to pick a method that fits your context and learn to use it well. That turns on knowing how to devise and use each method, not on how to classify it.

Assessing Knowledge and Understanding

Selected Response.   We all know that we can use selected response, objective paper and pencil tests to measure student mastery of facts, concepts, and even generalizations. Typically, these assessments tend to test mastery of disconnected elements of knowledge, such as knowledge of United States history, spelling, vocabulary, earth science, and the like.

These tests are efficient in that we can administer large numbers of multiple-choice or true/false test items per unit of testing time. Thus, they permit us to sample widely and draw relatively confident generalizations from the content sampled. For this reason, when the target is knowledge mastery, selected response formats fit nicely into the resource realities of most classrooms.

But remember, even with this most traditional of all assessment methods, things can go wrong. For instance, what if respondents can't read well? A non-reader (or student whose first language is not English) might actually know the material but score low because of poor reading proficiency. If we conclude that his low score means a lack of knowledge, we would be wrong. We'll explore these and other potential sources of mismeasurement in later chapters.

Essay.   When the domain of knowledge is defined not as elements in isolation but rather as larger concepts and important generalizations (à la Erickson) where knowledge is structured in complex ways, we can test student mastery using the essay format. Examples of larger information chunks we might ask students to know are the causes of westward migration in U.S. history or differences among igneous, metamorphic, and sedimentary rocks.

In this case, we sample with fewer exercises, because each exercise requires longer response times, and each provides us with relatively more information than any single selected response item would. Further, essay assessments present us with a more complex scoring challenge, and not just in terms of the time it takes. Because we must subjectively judge response quality, not just count it right or wrong, bias can creep in if we are not cautious. And remember, in this case, students also must bring writing proficiency into the assessment context. We must remain aware of the danger that students might know and understand the material but be unable to communicate it in this manner.

Performance Assessment.   When it comes to the match between performance assessment and mastery of content knowledge, things quickly become complicated. The match is not always a strong one. To see what I mean, consider a brief example.

Let's say we ask a student to complete a rather complex performance involving a process leading to a final product, as in the case of carrying out a science lab experiment to identify an unknown substance. If the student successfully identifies the substance, then we know that she possesses the prerequisite knowledge of science and lab procedures to solve the problem. In this case, the match between performance assessment and assessment of mastery of knowledge is a strong one.

However, to understand the complexity of this match, consider the instance in which the student fails to accurately identify the substance. Is her failure due to lack of knowledge? Or does the student possess the required knowledge and fail to use it to reason productively? Or does the student possess the knowledge and reason productively, but fail to use the lab apparatus skillfully? At the time the student fails to perform successfully, we just don't know.

Now here's the key point: We cannot know the real reason for failure unless and until we follow up the performance assessment with one of the other assessment methods (selected response, essay, or personal communication—probably the natural choice in this case). We must ask a few questions to find out if the prerequisite knowledge was there to start with. But if our initial goal was to assess mastery of content knowledge, why go through all this hassle? Why not just turn to one of the other three options from the outset?

If my reason for assessing is to certify lab technicians, I don't care why the student failed. But if I am a teacher whose job is to help students learn to perform well in science, I must know why this student failed or I have no way to help her perform adequately in the future.

As an important aside, I submit that a primary reason why large-scale standardized assessments, whether objective tests or performance assessments, have historically had so little impact on teachers in classrooms is that they leave teachers not knowing the reasons for student failures. They reveal only high- or low-level performance, which from a public accountability point of view may be good enough. But, from the teacher's point of view, they simply don't reveal which explanation for failure is correct. They fail to suggest actions the teacher can follow. *Only sound classroom assessments can do this.*

Personal Communication.   The final option for assessing mastery of knowledge is direct personal communication with students, for example, by asking questions and evaluating answers. This is a good match across all grade levels, especially with limited amounts of knowledge to be mastered, few students to be assessed, and in contexts where we need not store records of performance for long periods of time.

The reason I impose these conditions is that this obviously is a time- and labor-intensive assessment method. So if our domain of knowledge to assess is large, we are faced with the need to ask a large number of questions to cover it well. That just doesn't fit the resource realities in most classrooms. Further, if the number of students to be assessed is large, this option may not allow enough time to sample each student's achievement representatively. And, if we must store records of performance over an extended period of time, written records will be needed for each student over a broad sample of questions. This, too, eats up a lot of time and energy.

Assessment via personal communication works best in those situations when teachers are checking student mastery of critical content during instruction in order to make quick, ongoing adjustments as needed. Further, sometimes with some students in some contexts, it is the only method that will yield accurate information. For various reasons, some students just cannot or will not participate in the other forms of assessment, such as those who experience debilitating evaluation anxiety, have difficulty reading English, have severe learning or communication disabilities, or simply refuse to "test."

Time for Reflection

Now to review, go back to Table 4.1 and read across the Knowledge and Understanding row.

Assessing Reasoning Proficiency

In most classrooms, at all grade levels, we want students to be able to use the knowledge they master in productive ways to reason and solve problems. There are many ways to define what it means to be a proficient problem solver. We discuss many of these alternative definitions and their assessment throughout this book. For now, let me cite a few sample patterns of reasoning as a point of departure for discussing assessment in this important arena.

One kind of reasoning we value is *evaluative* or *critical thinking*, the ability to make judgments and defend them through rigorous application of standards or criteria. Just as movie or restaurant critics evaluate according to criteria, so students can evaluate the quality of a piece of literature or the strength of a scientific argument. This is critical thinking in action.

Another commonly valued pattern of reasoning is *analytical*, the ability to break things down into component parts, and to see how the parts work together. Yet another pattern involves using foundational knowledge to *compare and contrast* things, to infer similarities and differences.

How does one assess these kinds of reasoning targets? Our four methodological choices all provide excellent options when we possess both a clear vision of what we wish to assess and sufficient craft knowledge of the assessment methods.

Selected Response.   For example, we can use selected response exercises to determine if students can reason well. We can use them, for example, to see if students who have read a story can analyze things, compare them, or draw inferences or conclusions. Consider the following examples of questions from a reading test:

- *Analytical reasoning:* Which of the following sequences of plot elements properly depicts the order of events in the story we read today? (Offer response options, only one of which is correct.)

- *Comparative reasoning:* What is one essential difference between the story we read today and the one we read yesterday? (Offer response options, only one of which is correct.)

- *Drawing generalizations:* If you had to choose a theme from among those listed below for the story we read today, which would be best? (Offer response options, one of which is best.)

Assuming that these are novel questions posed immediately after reading the story, so students had no opportunity to memorize the answers, they ask students to dip into their knowledge base (about the story) and use it to reason. Students who see themselves becoming increasingly proficient at responding to questions like these become increasingly confident readers. This can be powerful.

I continue to be surprised by how many educators believe that selected response exercises can test only recall of content. While they can do this very well, this assessment mode is more flexible than many people think, as the previous examples illustrate. There are limits, however.

Evaluative reasoning—expressing and defending a point of view—cannot be tested using multiple-choice or true/false items because this kind of reasoning requires at least a written expression of the defense. Further, problems that are multifaceted and complex, involving several steps, the application of several different patterns of reasoning, and/or several problem solvers working together, as real-world problems often do, demand more complex assessment methods. But for some kinds of reasoning, selected response can work.

Essay.   This represents an excellent way to assess student reasoning and problem solving. Student writing provides an ideal window into student thinking. In fact, very often, students can be encouraged to look through this window and assess their own reasoning and problem solving. Teachers can devise highly challenging exercises that ask students to analyze, compare, draw complex inferences, evaluate, or use some combination of these proficiencies, depicting their reasoning in written form.

Of course, the key to evaluating the quality of student responses to such exercises is for the assessor to understand the pattern of reasoning required and be able to detect its presence in student writing. This calls for exercises that really do ask students to reason through an issue or figure something out, not just regurgitate something that they learned earlier. And these exercises must be accompanied by clear and appropriate scoring criteria that reflect sound reasoning, not just content mastery.

Performance Assessment.   Once again, here we have another excellent option that is applicable across all grade levels. We can watch students in the act of problem solving in a science lab, for example, and draw inferences about their proficiency. To the extent that they carry out proper procedures or find solutions when stymied, they reveal their ability to carry out a pattern of reasoning. When we watch students work with math manipulatives to demonstrate a problem solution or figure out how to manipulate computer software to accomplish something that they haven't done before, we can literally see their reasoning unfolding in their actions.

However, again, drawing conclusions about reasoning proficiency on the basis of the quality of student products can be risky. If performance is weak, did the student fail to perform because of a lack of foundational knowledge, failure to reason productively, or lack of motivation? As previously stated, without follow-up assessment by other means, we just don't know.

If we don't follow-up with supplemental assessment, and thereby infer the wrong cause of failure, at the very least our remedy is likely to be inefficient. We may waste valuable time reteaching material already mastered or teaching reasoning skills already developed.

Personal Communication.   One of the strongest matches between target and assessment method in Table 4.1 is the use of personal communication to evaluate student reasoning. Teachers can do any or all of the following:

- Ask questions that probe the clarity, accuracy, relevance, depth, and breadth of reasoning.
- Have students ask each other questions and listen for evidence of sound reasoning.
- Have students reason out loud, describing their thinking as they confront a problem.
- Have students recount their reasoning processes.
- Ask students to evaluate each other's reasoning.
- Simply listen attentively during class discussions for evidence of sound, appropriate reasoning.

Just talking informally with students can reveal so much, when we know what we're looking for! However, with this method, it will always take time to carry out the assessment and to keep accurate records of results.

Time for Reflection

Now for a review, go back to Table 4.1 and read across the Reasoning Proficiency row.

Assessing Mastery of Performance Skills

When our assessment goal is to find out if students can demonstrate performance skills, such as play a role in a dramatic performance, fluently speak in a second language, effectively give a formal speech, or interact with classmates in socially acceptable ways, then there is just one way to assess. We must observe them while they are exhibiting the desired behaviors and make judgments as to their quality. This calls for performance assessment. There is no other choice. Each of the other options falls short for this kind of target.

But sometimes limited resources make it impossible to assess the actual skill. At those times, we may need to go for second best and come as close to the real target as we can. We have several options when we need to trade high fidelity for greater efficiency in skills assessment. We can use selected response test items to determine whether students can recognize the right behaviors. For example, given a number of performance demonstrations (on video, perhaps), can respondents identify the best? Or, we may use a multiple-choice format to see if students know the proper sequence of activities to carry out when that is relevant to the outcome.

Given several descriptions of a procedure, can respondents identify the correct one? We can also use this method to ask if students have mastered the vocabulary needed to communicate about desired skills.

Realize, however, that such tests assess only prerequisites to effective performance, the building blocks to competence. They cannot assess examinees' actual levels of skill in performing.

With this same limitation, we could have students write essays about the criteria they might use to evaluate performance in a vocal music competition, knowledge that might well represent an important foundation for performing well in such a competition. But, of course, this will fall short of a real test of performance. Only performance assessment will suffice.

Finally, personal communication represents an excellent means of skills assessment when the skills in question have to do with oral communication proficiency, such as speaking a foreign language. For such an outcome, this is the highest-fidelity assessment option. For other kinds of performance skills, however, personal communication falls short of providing direct data on students' abilities.

Time for Reflection

Now to review, go back to Table 4.1 and read across the Performance Skills row.

Assessing Proficiency in Creating Products

The same limitations discussed for skills assessment apply here. If our assessment goal is to determine whether students can create a certain kind of achievement-related product, there is no other way to assess than to have them actually create one. In fact, performance assessment represents the only means of direct assessment. The best test of the ability to throw a ceramic pot is the quality of the finished product itself. The best test of the ability to set up a scientific apparatus is the completed arrangement. The best test of the ability to write a term paper is the finished paper.

Again, we could use a selected response assessment format to see if students can pick out a quality product from among several choices. Or, we could test knowledge of a quality product's key attributes. But these are limited substitutes for assessment that actually asks students to create the product.

It is also possible to have students answer questions, write brief essays, or just discuss informally the key attributes of a carefully crafted object, such as a cabinet in shop class (personal communication). In this way, we can be sure they start with the key understandings they need—a necessary, but not sufficient, condition for success. Then students won't waste valuable time working on projects they are not prepared to succeed on.

But ultimately the real issue is whether students can create a carefully crafted cabinet. When that is the question, product-based performance assessment is the method of choice.

When we wish to assess writing proficiency by judging the quality of students' written products, we have two methodological choices. One is to have them write brief essays. The other is to have them produce much longer performance assessment products, such as term or research papers. Both are acceptable when accompanied by high-quality scoring criteria reflecting attributes of good writing.

Time for Reflection

Now to review, go back to Table 4.1 and read across the Ability to Create Products row.

Assessing Dispositions

The range of assessment methods available to tap the various dimensions of dispositions is wide indeed.

Let's take a minute to review some of the student characteristics that fall under this heading. Affective dimensions of individuals that might be the object of classroom assessment include attitudes, values, interests, self-concept, and motivation. Remember, as stated earlier, the focus of assessment in this case is to determine the direction and intensity of student feelings about different school-related issues. When it comes to dispositions, we typically seek strong positive affect: positive attitudes about school, subjects, classmates, and so on; strong values about hard work; a strong positive academic self-concept; and strong positive motivation or seriousness of purpose. But negative attitudes about drugs, for example, are important, too.

The key to success in assessing these things, as usual, is a clear and appropriate definition of the characteristic to be assessed. Given a clear understanding, could we translate such targets into selected response questions? You bet! But our collection of such items won't be a test per se, it would more properly be considered a *questionnaire*.

Selected Response Questionnaire.   Many selected response item formats are very useful for such highly structured questionnaires. For instance, we could offer students statements and ask if they agree, disagree, or are undecided. Or, we could ask them to select from among a list of adjectives those that most accurately apply to themselves or to some other object. This assessment realm is rich with useful options.

Written Response Questionnaire.   Essay questions are another viable option for tapping dispositions. We can write open-ended questionnaire items that ask students to describe both the direction and intensity of their feelings about any particular object. After more than 20 years of in-school and in-classroom research on classroom assessment practices, one of the most startling insights for me has been how rarely teachers use questionnaires to gather affective information from their students, information that could make everyone's job much easier. In fact, the act of seeking student opinion can yield its own very positive impact on student dispositions. They may be honored to know that you care what they feel about aspects of the classroom.

Performance Observations.   The match between affective targets and performance assessment is a bit more complex, however, because of the nature of the inferences we must draw. In this case, I urge caution. It certainly is possible to look at samples of student performance or at student-created products and draw conclusions about attitudes, values, and motivational dispositions with respect to that particular project. If students demonstrate high levels of achievement, their attitude was probably strongly positive, they probably valued the project and their work, and they probably were disposed to work hard to perform well. Just remember, such inferences on your part can be wrong. There is also some chance that such students are just coping well with a frustrating academic challenge, are angry about the project, in fact, and just don't want you to know it.

Care must be exercised at the low end of the performance continuum, too. When performance is poor, there are many possible explanations, only one of which is a poor attitude and lack of motivation. Only additional followup assessment will reveal the real reason for failure to perform.

Personal Communication.   One excellent way in which to conduct such a followup is direct personal communication with students. In the right atmosphere, students will talk openly and honestly about the strength and direction of their dispositions. The keys to success, of course, are to be able to establish that open, trusting environment and to know what kinds of questions to ask to tap important affect.

Time for Reflection

Now for a review, go back to Table 4.1 and read across the Dispositions row.

Remember Our Standards of Assessment Quality

If our goal in classroom assessment is to gather dependable evidence of student achievement, then, our challenges are clearly framed. First, we must make sure we know why we are assessing. Who will use the results and how?

Second, we must clearly define the achievement targets we wish to assess. We cannot develop assessment exercises or scoring criteria for achievement expectations that we have not clearly, completely and appropriately defined.

Next, as you can now see, we must be sure we select an assessment method capable of reflecting the valued achievement. Different assessment contexts (purposes and targets) afford us opportunities to use different assessment methods.

In addition, once we select an assessment method, we need to use that method in a manner calculated to present us with an accurate portrait of achievement. This means two things. First, we must assemble enough of the right kinds of exercises (test items, if you will) to sample student performance in a representative manner. We need enough evidence to lead us to a confident conclusion about each student's achievement without wasting time gathering too much.

An Assessment can be valid **ONLY** if it relies on a method capable of accurately reflecting the intended target.

Further, we must understand that each method carries with it a list of things that can go wrong—that can yield misleading information about student achievement. As it turns out, distortions in assessment results can creep in from many sources, including the assessment itself, the evaluator, the students, and the test administration environment. Part of assessment literacy is understanding those potential sources of bias and knowing what to do by way of assessment development and implementation to prevent such problems. In Parts II and III of this book I discuss how to sample achievement appropriately and how to avoid bias.

The final standard of excellence in assessment requires that we use the assessment productively to benefit our students. Certainly, that means we must communicate assessment results accurately. Just as we have choices among different achievement targets and assessment methods, so too do we have choices among different ways of sharing results. We can rely on test scores, grades, performance ratings, portfolios of student work, and student-led conferences, to mention a few options. Part IV of this book offers instruction on how to use these options well.

Consider Student Involvement!

However, as you know by now, the effective use of classroom assessment includes much more than effective communication. The basic premise of this book is that we can involve students actively in classroom assessment and from this derive great motivational and learning benefits. In subsequent chapters, I will entice you with very interesting ways to involve students. But as an advance organizer, consider the following:

- What if you involve your students in actually writing practice multiple-choice test items that tap important patterns of reasoning?

- What if they practice devising essay exercises, as well as scoring procedures for evaluating the quality of answers?

- How about providing them with sample pieces of writing to practice scoring?

- Could your students themselves create performance assessment exercises that tap your chosen performance skill and product targets?

- Could they develop scoring guides for evaluating their own performance?

Sprinkled throughout the chapters of Parts II and III are intriguing answers to these questions—ways to use student involvement to unlock the secrets of their own academic success right before their very eyes.

Roadblocks to Quality Assessment

Just defining standards of quality assessment gets us nowhere, however, if those standards remain unattainable in the classroom. And the fact is, these standards have remained very difficult for teachers to meet in U.S. classrooms for decades. There are several reasons for this and I want you to understand them. As a teacher/classroom assessor, you will confront and will need to come to terms with three roadblocks to quality assessment.

The first barrier arises from within us. It is our own emotions about the prospect of having our performance assessed and evaluated. This scares many of us, even as adults. These strong negative feelings about assessment and evaluation stand in the way of quality assessment in your classroom if they prevent you from being willing to both take the risk and invest the mental energy needed to rigorously assess your students' achievement and hold yourself accountable for that achievement.

The second barrier is time. When teachers lack time to learn about quality assessment and time to carry out sound assessment practices, quality suffers. The vast majority of teachers don't feel that they have time to participate in such professional development or time to assess well in the classroom.

The final barrier to quality classroom assessment is a lack of understanding of how to assess well. This gap in professional understanding keeps many teachers from carrying out sound practices.

Let's understand each barrier and then talk about how to remove all three.

Barrier 1: Our Emotions

As adults, many of us harbor some very strong emotions about the prospect of being evaluated. Most of us grew up in classrooms in which assessment was a distinctly dangerous enterprise. It left us feeling at risk. If we didn't study for an exam, we knew we risked being judged failures. But even if we did prepare carefully, there was always the chance that something could go wrong. I'm reminded of the bumper sticker I saw recently that read, "As long as there are tests in schools, there will be prayer in schools." These feelings of vulnerability form part of our foundation of adult feelings about assessment and evaluation.

These emotions run deep. I'm struck by how many teachers tell me that they have the recurring dream that they are back in school, they haven't been going to class, and are far behind in their work, and the final exam is tomorrow. In this case, the residual emotion is one of guilt. Even if we prepare carefully, what if it isn't enough? Another bumper sticker I saw read, "My teacher was a travel agent for guilt trips." Guilt—the gift that keeps on giving!

Please understand I do not contend that these were always counterproductive emotions. They caused many of us to behave in academically responsible and productive ways. However, as I work with teachers and administrators (all of whom are former kids, by the way) I find few who want to return to their "golden school days," mostly because of the testing environment.

The accumulation of these emotions leads some to infer that assessment is a topic to avoid. When educators draw this conclusion, the unfortunate consequence is that they become closed to the possibility of creating an assessment environment that is more positive and productive than the one we all grew up in. We have no prior experiences that leave us able to conceive of assessment and evaluation as processes that might be friendly.

Such fear of assessment can prevent us from learning what we need to know about assessment in order to practice our profession, and that lack of knowhow keeps us from being able to build quality assessments into our classroom teaching and learning. It is a barrier to sound assessment.

Time for Reflection

Based on Emily's experience at the beginning of Chapter 1 (read it again, along with the interview with her that follows it), what do you think are likely to be her emotional associations with the prospect of being evaluated?

There's another dimension of vulnerability that becomes important in this context. The ideas offered in this book are not without their downside risks for teachers. Consider this teacher's point of view in terms of barriers to quality assessment:

> "You're telling me to be clear about my achievement expectations, right? (Yes.) And you want me to be public about those achievement targets, so all can see them, including my students, right? (Yes.) And you want me to conduct rigorous assessments that accurately reflect my students' achievement, right? (Yes.) And then you want me to make those results public for all to see and use in their decision making? (Yes.)
>
> "But wait a minute. What if those results reveal, beyond a shadow of a doubt, that my students didn't learn? You want me to be public with rigorous evidence of that?! To use my own evidence to bring down the wrath of whoever on me?! I'm not sure that's smart. (Why?) Well it's simple. What if their failure isn't my fault? What if it's due to factors that are beyond my control, like severe learning disabilities, a poor home environment or peer group pressures? What if I'm doing the best job I can—working very hard—but they're not contributing their part? Nevertheless, who's going to get blamed for the failure? I am! See, here I go again being victimized by assessment. It's not fair.
>
> "I think it's smarter on my part to remain vague and very private about my achievement expectations. Further, I think I should couch my assessments in such gradebook exotica that no one could ever look in there and see what's really happened. It's just a lot safer for me that way. I won't be unjustly accused."

This teacher frames the ultimate accountability challenge. As a teacher, if I am not sure I can deliver learning, for whatever reason, I may feel the need to protect myself. Any teacher who seeks that kind of safety may not be willing to meet standards of quality assessment. That's a barrier.

Barrier 2: Lack of Time to Assess Well

Perhaps the most prominent barrier to quality assessment from the teacher's point of view is the lack of time to assess well. Listen as our two experienced teachers discuss the issues:

MS. SMITH	I just can't handle any more of this school improvement stuff! First it's cooperative learning, then it's thematic instruction and integrated learning. Now they want us to muck around with the schedules. You know, now, we're "restructuring." Wow, so many changes. Oh, and by the way, when am I supposed to teach?
MR. LOPEZ	I hear ya. And on top of that, there's all the new assessment practices we're supposed to be using. Like performance assessment—observe 'em and judge 'em. Why can't I just give 'em a test like I used to? I don't have time to do all that work.
MS. SMITH	Have you tried it?
MR. LOPEZ	I have some. And I can see how performance assessment fits sometimes. But where do I get the time?
MS. SMITH	We just added a whole new emphasis on technology on top of the traditional curriculum. Now I've gotta learn all that stuff myself.
MR. LOPEZ	You gonna do it?
MS. SMITH	Not as a volunteer, no way. But I may get drafted.
MR. LOPEZ	I know what you mean.
MS. SMITH	(With a smirk.) I need a staff: a whole team of "assistant teachers" to delegate stuff to!
MR. LOPEZ	Forget it! You're the only worker in your teaching world. Always have been, always will be!
MS. SMITH	Which means I better get to work on these grades. Have you ever seen a gradebook like this? (Holds it up.) I've got 185 students this year!

This dialogue, an interchange any experienced teacher will recognize, touches on several specific issues that trouble teachers deeply. These issues are pertinent here because, if they're valid, each represents a strong barrier to assessment quality.

For example, the broadening scope of the curriculum means teachers must assess an ever-expanding array of forms of student achievement. Teachers don't have time to assess more. Without question, the curriculum is evolving to include more achievement targets (such as with the addition of important technology and health-related topics), more complexity within the various targets (such as our enhanced understanding of what it means to be a proficient reader or writer), and more complex ways of integrating the curriculum across disciplines. Add to this mix a rapid expansion in recommended instructional imperatives, like cooperative learning and inclusion of diverse ability levels in the same classroom, along with the opportunity to be involved in school-based decision making and, whew! one could be overwhelmed. How can we assess even more when we have too little time to cover it all, let alone assess it all, now?

Further, currently popular assessment methods, such as performance assessment, are labor intensive. Teachers don't have time to do labor-intensive assessment. Teachers say, "The more I assess and the more labor intensive my assessment methods, the more work I, the teacher, am forced to do. I have to make up the exercises. I must devise the scoring scheme. I must administer the exercises. I must do all of the scoring (tons of fun with essay tests or performance assessments!). I must record the results and try to summarize them all for the parent-teacher conference, which I must plan and conduct. There is no one here to help me do this work."

Next, we must confront labor-intensive record-keeping methods: the grade-book with one line per student including handwritten records of performance on assignments, projects, quizzes, tests, presentations, and so on. And top this off with the need to summarize it all, assign report card grades, and get it all in to the office accurately and on time and you have a nightmare of hectic activity.

As the chapters of this book unfold, I will offer specific ways to get past these time barriers (Figure 4.3). We must find ways to assess less, not more. We must rely on assessment methods that are as efficient as they can be. We must spread the work of assessment across as many shoulders as possible, including students and their families, being sure to do so according to the principles of sound teaching and learning. And we must rely on modern information-processing technologies whenever possible to reduce our record-keeping and communication workloads. We will touch on all of these factors in subsequent chapters.

Barrier 3: Lack of Assessment Expertise

This is the easiest of the three roadblocks to understand. We cannot meet standards of quality if we don't know what those standards are or how to achieve them in any particular classroom assessment context. We remove this barrier by developing the expertise we need to meet the various challenges that emerge. The benefits of developing that expertise are immense.

After reflecting on the first two barriers to quality—our emotions about evaluation and lack of time—it becomes clear that this final barrier represents the key to their removal and thus a clear path to quality. Only by attaining a sufficiently high level of assessment literacy—that is, an understanding of the principles of sound assessment—can we gain access to the equipment needed to remove the other barriers. We remain fearful about assessment mysteries that we don't understand. We can't use our assessment wisdom to make our assessment job faster, easier, and better if we don't understand the assessment economies we have at our disposal. *Assessment literacy is the key*.

Figure 4.3
Help is on the way!

Summary: A Vision of Excellence in Classroom Assessment

Sound classroom assessments arise from a clear sense of purpose, clear and appropriate targets, and the sampling of student performance using a proper assessment method. A proper method is one that provides the most direct view of student performance, permitting the strongest inferences from the assessment results to the actual status of the achievement target.

In this chapter, we have described four assessment methods and discussed how we might use them selectively to tap student achievement on a range of school outcomes. Given the range of our valued school outcomes, we will need to apply all of the assessment tools we have at our disposal: selected response tests, essay exercises, performance assessments, and direct personal communication with students. No single method can serve all of our assessment needs at all grade levels. We must learn to use all available methods. If we do, the results will be better information about student success gathered in less time.

But to gain access to these tools and learn to apply them productively, we must confront and overcome the fear of assessment that seemed to hold us hostage in our youth. We must school our communities on the differences between sound and unsound assessments. And we must find teachers the time to assess well, while at the same time providing them with the right tools to do the job.

In the chapters that follow, we provide the instruction and practice needed to become assessment literate. In Parts II and III we will explore achievement targets, assessment methods, and their alignment in greater depth. As we go, we will address the sampling and quality-control guidelines needed to use each assessment method well. We also will explore using student-involved assessment as a motivational and teaching tool. Finally, we will conclude our journey in Part IV with several chapters on strategies for effective communication about student achievement, strategies designed to meet the diverse information needs of all assessment users.

Exercises for Self-Assessment

1. List and define each of the four basic assessment methods. Identify format options within each method.

2. Scan the chapter again and recreate Table 4.1 in your own words.

3. List the three roadblocks to quality discussed in this chapter and in your own words describe how each could keep a teacher from meeting standards of assessment quality.

4. How can assessment literacy help us progress toward effective schools by helping us remove other barriers to quality?

5. If you were forced to select only one method for assessing each of the four kinds of achievement targets discussed in this chapter (not including dispositions), which method would you choose for each and why?

6. If your supervisor's objective was to evaluate your teaching proficiency, what assessment method(s) should she or he use and why? (Be careful here! Pause to reflect on the active ingredients of good teaching before answering.)

You may go to the Companion Website at www.prenhall.com/stiggins and answer these questions in the Self-Assessment module.

Final Chapter Reflection

1. What are the three most important new insights to come to you as a result of your study of this chapter?
2. Which of your previous questions about assessment can you now answer based on your study of this chapter?
3. What new questions have come to mind as a result of your study of this chapter that you hope to have answered as your study continues?
4. For practicing teachers only: *What do you plan to do differently in assessment in your classroom as a result of your study of this book so far?*

   For those in preservice study only: *As you think about the classroom assessment environment that you hope to create for your students, how has your thinking changed as a result of your study of this book so far?*

Workbook Activities

Those of you using the workbook, *Practice with Student-Involved Classroom Assessment*, as part of your study of this material will find the following activities and others included for Chapter 4:

- *How Purpose Affects Method.* Much attention is given in this chapter to the target/method match. But this exercise helps you see how different users also might rely on different methods to serve different purposes.

- *What's the Learning Here?* You are given several samples of student work and asked to determine why some students did not succeed. If you cannot tell from the evidence provided, what other assessments might you conduct to find out?

- *What Questions Do You Have about Matching Targets to Methods?* This activity permits you to practice matching targets to methods and deepens your understanding of how to find the powerful matches.

- *Analyze Sample Assessments for Target/Method Match.* You practice using a set of clear criteria for judging the appropriateness of matches in specific real-world classroom assessment contexts.

- *Unit Building Activity, Assignment 2: Making Your Matches.* This is the second part of the ongoing series of activities in which you apply key concepts discussed in the textbook to an actual unit of instruction you are building. (Note: These assignments are offered at the end of every chapter throughout the workbook.)

Video Support

Creating Sound Classroom Assessments. This ATI interactive video training package reviews the various kinds of targets, describes the available assessment methods, explores target/method match and discusses barriers and ways around them.

Workbook Activities for Part I (Chapters 1–4)

The workbook also offers activities at the end of each of the four parts of the text to tie the chapters of that part together in practical ways. The following activities and others are offered for the end of Part I.

- *What Does It Mean to "Set High Standards?"*   This real-world case study asks you to address issues of unclear targets, unclear purposes, and the motivational implications of each.

- *Show What You Know.*   This activity provides several different options for personal reflection that allow you to collect your understandings from Part I: concept mapping, drawing, writing a letter, or outlining major learnings.

- *Build Your Own Portfolio.*   The workbook offers a plan for you to build a portfolio of evidence of your own increasing classroom assessment competence and confidence. This activity suggests specific portfolio entries to be made at the end of Part I of the text. (Note: These portfolio entry assignments appear at the end of each part of the book.)

II

Understanding Assessment Methods

The fabric of your classroom assessment environment must be woven from four basic assessment methods: selected response, essay, performance assessment, and personal communication. Each is the focus of a chapter in Part II. Your challenge is to use these methods to create a continuously evolving portrait of each student's achievement, keeping your students in touch with and feeling in control of their own growth. In this way, they can continue to believe in themselves as learners.

Chapter 5 describes selected response methods of assessment: multiple choice, true/false, matching, and short answer fill-in. Their power lies in their great efficiency.

Chapter 6 offers guidance in developing and using essay assessments. In this case, students construct brief written responses to essay questions, which you then read and score.

Chapter 7 explores the basics of currently popular performance assessment methods, assessments based on teacher observation and professional judgment. This option offers a variety of ways to evaluate students' performance skills and the products they create.

Chapter 8 details a set of assessment options not normally thought of as part of classroom assessment: direct personal interaction or personal communication with students. Teachers can and often do learn a great deal about achievement by talking to their students. We will explore how to do this well.

None of these assessment methods is inherently superior to the others. Each is capable of providing vivid insights into student learning in certain contexts, when in the hands of a competent user. At the same time, however, each also can be done poorly. An assessment-literate classroom teacher knows the difference and is committed to carrying out sound assessment practices.

We continue to remain in close contact with the five bubbles that capture our standards of assessment quality, as depicted in the following figure. In Part I, we addressed matters of purpose and target. In Part II, we will explore when to use each method well by thinking more about target–method match, rules of evidence for sampling, and how to avoid common forms of bias. And, of course, within each chapter of Part II we also will explore specific ways to involve students in developing and implementing assessments.

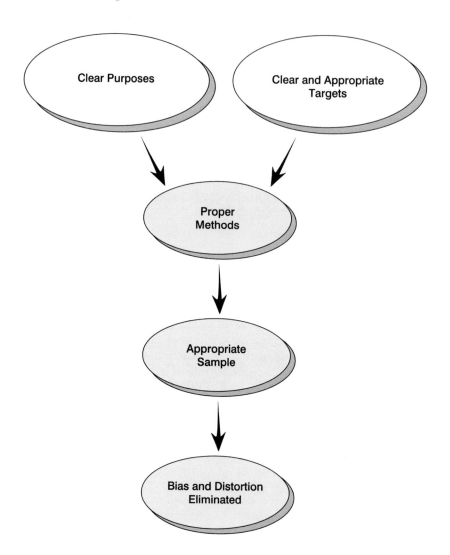

There are three specific reasons why it is critical that you understand how to design and use the assessment methods described in Part II.

First and most obviously, you will need to design and develop assessments to use in your classroom. Your curriculum will include important achievement targets that will require you to use a variety of formats. As those assessment opportunities arise, you will need to know how to pick a proper method and develop exercises and scoring guides that reflect your desired targets.

The second reason to understand the differences between sound and unsound assessments is that at times you may want to use instruments and procedures that others have developed. In these cases, you must know how to review and evaluate the quality of these assessments before using them.

For instance, you may want to use tests that come with a particular textbook. Text publishers often ask their authors to develop tests to accompany their textbooks as an aid to teachers and, frankly, as a marketing device to save teachers from the time-consuming work of developing their own tests. If those who develop these textbook-embedded tests are familiar with the achievement targets established for the book and knowledgeable about the development of sound tests, then everyone wins. The publisher sells books, teachers save time and effort, and students benefit from sound assessment during instruction.

Problems arise, however, if the test designers did not understand the intended targets and/or were not trained in developing sound tests. When this occurs, unsound tests result and student achievement will be inaccurately assessed.

What is the likelihood that this will occur? As a teacher, you will never know the skill level of those who designed the assessments that come with your textbooks. This leaves you with two choices: Trust the text author and publisher to have done a good job and assume that the tests are sound, or conduct your own quality control check on these tests. This should be a no brainer; anyone who places blind faith in text authors or publishers to be assessment literate may be placing their students directly in harm's way. *Don't do this.* But to conduct your own quality control verification, you must be prepared to be a critical consumer and to thoroughly investigate quality.

An experienced high school teacher friend of mine tells an interesting story that carries with it important advice about the assessment materials that come with textbooks:

> "I served on a committee several years ago charged with adopting a new history textbook. As we reviewed the available options, publishers all made a big deal about the support they offered along with their texts. One such support was tests. I'll never forget one publisher's representative telling us, 'Buy our product and you won't have to worry about test develop-

ment ever again. We have them all developed for you. Just copy and distribute them to your students.'
>
> "Luckily, we checked on these unit tests and they were a huge surprise. The text listed objectives and even included discussion questions that asked students to use their history knowledge in solving problems. This was one of the things we liked best about that particular book—a real reasoning and problem-solving approach to history. But all we found in the file of assessments were multiple-choice tests measuring recall of trivial facts. It was as if the text and test authors never talked to each other. They were on completely different wavelengths, a total mismatch."

Over the years, colleagues have shared variations on this same story. We have to be very careful. Just because a test comes with a really good textbook and happens to be typeset or even computerized is no guarantee of quality. Teachers have to be ready to verify that quality.

Never forget that you, the teacher, are the last line of defense against mismeasuring student achievement using previously developed assessments. Whether you play the role of test developer or gatekeeper, in the final analysis *you* are responsible for the quality of the tests you use in your classroom.

The final reason you need to understand the meaning of quality assessments may surprise you. But it too is very important. You may need to act in your own best interest when *your own* achievement is being assessed. Now, I'm not referring to you the teacher. I'm talking about you the undergraduate or graduate student facing the prospect of taking tests your professors develop and use. It is in your best interest to know if these assessments, which can influence your life in profoundly important ways, are sound or unsound.

If an assessment happens to be unsound in ways that are clear to you, then it is important that you identify the flaws in its design that are likely to render the score inaccurate as an estimate of your real achievement or that of your classmates. I know this presents a challenge in diplomacy. It can be risky to point out these kinds of problems to those in power positions. But if we let obvious sources of mismeasurement go unchecked, not only do we allow ourselves to be mistreated, but we also miss golden opportunities to strike a blow on behalf of higher levels of assessment literacy throughout the educational system. When the opportunity presents itself, you can and should take advantage of such "teachable moments" to diplomatically help your professors understand and adhere to accepted standards of quality assessment.

Selected Response Assessment: Flexible and Efficient

CHAPTER FOCUS

This chapter answers the following guiding question:

> When and how do I use the selected response method of assessment most effectively?

You will come to understand the following principles from your study of this chapter:

1. Selected response assessments align well with knowledge and understanding targets, as well as with some patterns of reasoning.
2. We can efficiently develop these assessments in three steps: blueprinting, focusing, and item writing.
3. This method can fall prey to avoidable sources of bias that can distort results if users are not careful.
4. By involving our students in developing and using selected response assessments, we can set them up for confident, energetic, and successful learning.

As we start this part of our journey, keep our big picture in mind. Figure 5.1 crosses our five achievement targets with the four methods of assessment. In this chapter, we will be dealing in depth with the shaded areas.

The Most Traditional Assessment Methods

Consider multiple-choice, true/false, matching and fill-in tests. These represent what many people think of as the "real" tests—the kind we've all come to know

	SELECTED RESPONSE	ESSAY	PERFORMANCE ASSESSMENT	PERSONAL COMMUNICATION
Know				
Reason				
Skills				
Products				
Dispositions				

Figure 5.1
Aligning achievement targets and assessment methods

and love or fear, depending on our personal experience. Have you ever noticed how many people contend that they were never "good test takers" in school? This usually is the kind of test to which they refer.

In Chapter 4, we established the balanced perspective that we can rely on selected response assessment formats to provide high-quality information about certain kinds of important student achievement. But to take advantage of selected response assessments, we must be clear about the achievement targets for which they are appropriate. In addition, we must understand how to sample student achievement efficiently by means of test items and how to control for those bedeviling sources of bias that can creep into any assessment. Over the years, it has been difficult for many educators to delve into these matters, because the lore and mysterious complexity of these tests has rendered them unapproachable.

For most of us, our testing experience began with those once-a-year standardized achievement and/or intelligence tests. (Personally, I never seemed to finish those before my teacher called, "Time's up!" No one ever explained why they wouldn't let me finish. But rules were rules.) Soon, the scores came back and went into our "permanent record," even though no one ever seemed to know what those scores meant. It was all rather mysterious.

As we grew older, we began to care more deeply about grades and grade point averages. At the same time, our teachers tended to rely more and more on tests consisting of "right or wrong" items. Remember exchanging papers so we could score our neighbor's test as the teacher read the right answer? I remember that my teachers' reliance on these kinds of assessments increased through middle school and high school.

Next came college admissions tests and even greater mysteries. No one seemed to know what was coming as test time approached, least of all our teachers. Nevertheless, we knew we had better be "on" that day. A whole Saturday morning, literally hours, of nothing but multiple-choice test items. And when we finished, we had no idea how well we had done. Remember? Then the scores came back and once again no one knew what they really meant—but, they had to be high!

This is the lore of selected response tests. We've all experienced them, we have plenty of emotions tied to them and, to this day, we have lots of questions about them. My goal in this chapter is to eliminate the mystery surrounding this assessment method. We'll cover the basics of the various selected response formats. Then, in subsequent chapters we'll explore a variety of classroom assessment and standardized test applications.

The Foundations of Quality

To begin with, we need to think about two quality control factors that form the foundation for the appropriate use of selected response assessment. First, certain realities of life in classrooms can and should contribute to your decision about when to use this option. You must know that the context is right.

Second, almost from the time of their first appearance on the educational scene in the 1920s, selected response assessments have carried an air of objectivity or scientific precision—an apparent freedom from the fallibility of human judgment—that belies the underlying reality. The fact is, the development and use of this "objective" form of assessment is riddled with teachers' subjective professional judgments. As a result, judgmental errors may occur and students can be placed directly in harm's way. You need to understand how to prevent such occurrences.

Context Factors

It is appropriate to consider using selected response formats only when you are absolutely certain students have a sufficiently high level of reading proficiency to be able to understand the exercises. Students' mastery of the material being assessed is always confounded with their ability to read the exercises. Therefore, if you are administering a selected response test of knowledge mastery or problem solving to poor readers, nonreaders, or students whose first language is not English, you must in some way help them overcome their reading difficulty. It is only through such adjustments that you can disentangle subject mastery from reading proficiency and obtain an accurate estimate of achievement.

Further, it is a good idea to turn to this method of assessment when you can take advantage of already-developed, available, high-quality assessments. Why waste time on new development when others already have done the work for you? But again, you must verify quality; you cannot and should not assume it.

It is particularly appropriate to use selected response assessments when you need to take advantage of the efficiency of the method. Once developed, you can administer selected response tests to large numbers of students at the same time and score them very quickly. These tests can be very efficient.

Consider this method when the scope of your knowledge and reasoning achievement target is broad. When students have much material to master, you will need relatively large samples of test items to cover all the important material. These tests can cover a broad array of information in limited testing time.

In the classroom, use selected response assessment only when time permits students to respond to all test items. In the past, sometimes our teachers would rank students on the basis of speed and accuracy. Very often, tests carried tight time limits by design. Not all students finished the test. However, as we are now concerned more about competence, assessment must focus on mastery of the required material, with less emphasis on speed. Test items not attempted fail to contribute useful information about students' levels of learning. For this reason, it is best to opt for "power" tests, which permit every student to at least attempt each test item.

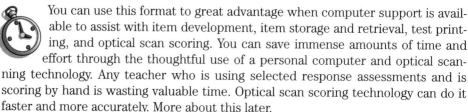 You can use this format to great advantage when computer support is available to assist with item development, item storage and retrieval, test printing, and optical scan scoring. You can save immense amounts of time and effort through the thoughtful use of a personal computer and optical scanning technology. Any teacher who is using selected response assessments and is scoring by hand is wasting valuable time. Optical scan scoring technology can do it faster and more accurately. More about this later.

The Role of Teacher Judgment in "Objective" Assessment

I have chosen the label *selected response assessment* rather than the more traditional label *objective test* because the latter connotes an absence of subjectivity in development or use. In truth, subjectivity—that is, matters of teacher/assessor judgment—permeate all facets of selected response assessment. In fact, whenever we use selected response assessments, if we are not careful, there is the danger that subjectivity can give rise to inaccurate assessments. Be advised that we know how to avoid those problems. But that takes attention to detail. All assessments are made up of the following:

1. Exercises designed to elicit some response from students
2. An evaluation scheme that allows the user to interpret the quality of that response

Let's be very clear about the fact that the renowned "objectivity" in selected response assessment applies *only* to the scoring system. It has nothing to do with the exercise side of the equation.

Well-written multiple-choice test items, for example, allow for just one best answer or a limited set of acceptable answers. This leads to the "objective" scoring of responses as being right or wrong. No judgment required. Students' answers are either right or wrong.

However, developing exercises that form the basis of this kind of test involves a major helping of the test author's subjective professional judgment. The developer decides what learnings to transform into exercises, how many questions to pose on a test, how to word each question, what the best or correct answers will be, and which incorrect answers to offer as choices, if needed.

All assessments, regardless of method, arise from the assessor's professional judgment. So we will address this matter again in each of the following three chapters. All assessments reflect the assessor's biases or perspectives. The key to your effective use of sound classroom assessment as a part of instruction is to make sure that your perspectives or instructional priorities are clear and public for your students from the outset. This way, they have a chance to see and understand what it means to be successful.

> Assessment experts tell us that "objective" (right/wrong) scoring tends to keep evaluator (subjective) bias from influencing scores, thus resulting in a more **RELIABLE** assessment.
>
> TECHNICAL NOTE

Matching Selected Response Assessments to Achievement Targets

In Chapter 4, we touched on strategies for aligning the various assessment methods with the different kinds of achievement targets. Let's continue that discussion now by examining the kinds of targets that we can effectively translate into selected response formats. Select the best answer for the following question:

> Which of the following test item formats can be used to assess both students' mastery of content knowledge and their abilities to use that knowledge to reason and solve problems?
> 1. Multiple choice
> 2. True/false
> 3. Matching
> 4. Short answer fill-in
> 5. All of the above

The best answer is 5, all of the above. All four formats can tap both knowledge mastery and reasoning, two of the four basic kinds of achievement targets discussed in earlier chapters.

Assessing Knowledge Mastery

We can use selected response test items to assess student mastery of subject matter knowledge. To fully understand this match, we must understand three essential concepts.

1. Mastery Requires Both Knowing and Understanding   Students can know things but not understand them. Shepard (1997) provides us with a classic illustration of the difference.* When students were presented with the following problem, 86 percent of them answered it correctly:

$$\begin{array}{r} 4 \\ \times 3 \\ \hline \end{array}$$
    A. 9
    B. 12
    C. 15
    D. 18

But when confronted with the same problem in a manner that requires conceptual understanding the results were quite different. Here's an example:

Which choice goes with:

   X   X   X   X

   X   X   X   X

   X   X   X   X

A. $3 \times 4 =$
B. $3 + 4 =$
C. $3 \times 12 =$

This time, only 55 percent of those same students were able to answer correctly. For many, rote learning of the answer (first problem) did not result in conceptual understanding of the mathematics involved (second problem).

If we expect students to know and understand, we must teach for and assess knowing and understanding. Selected response assessment formats can help us with that.

2. We Have Two Ways to Retrieve Knowledge   We can retrieve knowledge directly from memory if we have learned it outright. Or, we can retrieve knowledge from reference resources if we know where and how to find it. Both are relevant in this "online" information age, with the explosion in the amount of available knowledge and the easy access to information worldwide. In the real adult world, we

---

*From *Measuring Achievement: What Does It Mean to Test for Robust Understanding?* (n.p.) by L. A. Shepard, 1997, Princeton, NJ: Educational Testing Service. Copyright 1997 by ETS Policy Information Center. Reprinted by permission of Educational Testing Service.

meet the challenges of everyday life by combining what we know already with what we look up or learn from others as we need it.

So it must be in our expectations for our students. We must be clear about what we expect them to learn outright. We must differentiate that from the content we expect them to be able to retrieve from reference if and when they need it. In addition, we must be prepared to assess both forms of content mastery. Selected response assessment can often help us do so.

Again, remember that both forms of "knowing" are useless if not accompanied by understanding. Our selected response exercises must tap understanding as well.

3. Useable Knowledge Takes Several Interrelated Forms   We spoke of this in Chapter 3, in our discussion of the different kinds of achievement. Knowledge can take the form of facts, concepts, general principles, and so on. Skillful selected response item writers can use multiple-choice, true/false, matching, and fill-in test items to tap student mastery of knowledge in any or all of these forms, whether we expect students to know the material outright or retrieve it from references.

Admittedly, we have used selected response over the decades far more often to test material supposedly learned outright than in any other form. But let's not lose sight of the fact that we can use interpretive exercises (offering a text passage, a map, or a data table with associated questions), open-book examinations, and take-home exams to see if students can find and interpret information that we do not expect them to learn outright. As stated earlier, this has become an important life skill.

Remember, though, that we have established that merely knowing, and even understanding, something is of little value if one is not proficient at using that knowledge productively to reason and solve problems. We address this next.

Assessing Reasoning

When we ask students to dip into their knowledge and understanding and to use what they know in novel ways to figure something out, we ask them to *reason*. To assess this well, at testing time we must present them with new test items that they have not seen before to see if they can reason their way through the problems we present. For example, we might ask students to demonstrate proficiency in figuring out one or more of the following:

- How things are alike or different
- How something can be subdivided into its component parts or how the parts work together
- The main idea or theme of a story just read
- The proper conclusion to be drawn from a science experiment
- The insights that can be derived from a provided data chart

It is a common misconception that selected response assessments can tap only student mastery of specific facts. Nothing could be further from the truth, as you will see. They can do much more.

In this case our teaching challenges are to (1) make sure students have access to the knowledge they need to solve such problems, and (2) provide them with lots of guided practice in applying specified patterns of reasoning. But at assessment time, we must leave them alone to see if they can combine the two successfully.

Skillful selected response test item writers can use multiple-choice, true/false, matching, and fill-in test items to tap the various other forms of student reasoning included in their curriculum. But again, to do so, these items must present students with novel problems. They cannot simply ask students to regurgitate solutions to problems solved previously and then memorized. We will study examples of such test items in later chapters.

Assessing Performance Skills

We cannot use selected response test formats to assess student mastery of performance skills such as speaking, drama, physical education, interacting socially, tuning an engine, and the like. But we can use them to assess mastery of at least some of the procedural knowledge and understanding prerequisite to being able to demonstrate such skills. For instance, if we use a performance assessment to determine that students are unable to communicate effectively in a second language, we might follow up with another assessment method to see if they know the vocabulary. Or, if students are unable to adequately solve a math problem, we might follow up by assessing their knowledge of the procedures for solving such problems. If students fail to carry out a science lab procedure correctly, we can use selected response formats to ask whether they understand the science to which the experiment relates or if they know and understand the steps in the lab process.

Assessing Products

Selected response exercises cannot help us determine if students can create quality products. They cannot tap proficiency in building a structurally sound model bridge, creating an authentic model of a native village, or producing an artistic creation that meets specified standards of quality. But they can test students' prerequisite knowledge of the attributes of a quality product. Students who don't know the attributes of a sound bridge are unlikely to be able to make the right kind of model. Students who cannot distinguish a quality product from an inferior one are unlikely to be able to produce quality. Selected response assessments can test these prerequisites.

Please understand that foundational knowledge is only a prerequisite to success. It is never sufficient merely to know and understand, but it is *always* essential.

Assessing Dispositions

In a different vein, we can develop questionnaire items to tap student attitudes, values, motivational dispositions, and other affective states, items that ask students to select from among a limited number of response options. Questions inquiring about preferred extracurricular activities, for example, might offer a series of choices. Attitude scales might offer a statement about a particular feeling, such as, "School is a place where my academic needs are met"; the responses might ask students if they agree, disagree, or are undecided. These formats can be excellent ways to tap both the direction and intensity of student feelings about important aspects of school or classroom life.

The remainder of this chapter deals only with the design of selected response assessments of student achievement. In Chapter 11, we will discuss in depth the assessment of dispositions.

Summary of Target Matches

While we certainly can't reach all of the achievement targets we value with selected response exercises, we can tap parts of many of them. We can test student mastery of content knowledge, including what they learn outright and what they learn to retrieve through effective use of reference materials. In addition, we can tap a variety of kinds of reasoning and problem solving, including analytical, comparative, and other kinds of inferential reasoning proficiencies. And we can get at some of the underpinnings of successful performance in more complex arenas, assessing knowledge of appropriate procedures, and/or understanding of the key attributes of quality products. Table 5.1 summarizes the Selected Response column of our comprehensive targets-by-methods chart.

The Steps in Assessment Development

Described in its simplest form, the selected response assessment is developed in three steps, each of which requires the application of special professional competence:

Table 5.1
Selected response: Assessment of achievement targets

Target to be Assessed	Selected Response
Knowledge & Understanding	Multiple choice, true/false, matching, and fill-in can sample mastery of elements of knowledge
Reasoning Proficiency	Can assess application of some patterns of reasoning
Performance Skills	Can assess mastery of the knowledge prerequisite to skillful performance, but cannot rely on these to tap the skill itself
Ability to Create Products	Can assess mastery of the knowledge prerequisite to the ability to create quality products, but cannot assess the quality of products themselves
Dispositions	Selected response questionnaire items can tap student feelings

1. Develop an assessment plan or blueprint that identifies an appropriate sample of achievement.

2. Identify the specific elements of knowledge, understanding, and reasoning to be assessed.

3. Transform those elements into assessment exercises or test items.

The steps of test planning and identifying elements to be assessed are the same for all four test item formats, so we will deal with those together. Then we will discuss how to write quality test items using each individual format.

Time for Reflection

As you proceed through the following pages on assessment development, make a list of how you think you might involve your students in this process in ways that will maximize their confidence and learning.

Step 1: Preparing a Blueprint

Building a test without a plan is like building a house without a blueprint. Two things are going to happen, and both are bad. First, the construction process is going to take much longer than you hope; second, the final product is not going to be what you expect. In developing selected response assessments, a carefully developed blueprint is everything. Plan well and the test will almost automatically develop itself. Fail to plan and you will struggle. In fact, the practice of test blueprinting will save you more time than any other single idea offered in this text.

Besides making test development easier and more efficient, test blueprinting offers an opportunity for teachers and students to clarify achievement expectations, to sharpen their vision of what it means to be successful. As you will see, planning absolutely requires that the test developer delve deeply into the material under study, to understand both the underlying structure of the knowledge students are to master and the nuances of solving problems using that knowledge. Without this clarity and depth of vision, it will be impossible to develop sound assessments.

In the classroom, teachers have two types of test blueprints from which to choose. One is called a *table of test specifications*, the other a list of *instructional objectives*. Choose whichever you like, both work. They are essentially equally effective as test planning devices, as you shall see.

Table of Specifications as a Blueprint.   To explain how the table of test specifications works, we must first consider the individual assessment exercise or test question. Any question requires respondents to do two things: (1) gain access to a specific piece of information (either from memory or reference materials), and (2) use that knowledge to carry out a cognitive operation (i.e., to solve some kind of problem).

For example, you might construct a test item based on knowledge of a piece of literature and ask respondents simply to demonstrate the ability to retrieve it from memory:

Who were the main characters in the story?

Or, you might ask respondents to recall two elements of content knowledge from literature and relate one to the other, as in this comparison item:

What is one similarity between two prominent characters in this story?

In this case, respondents must dip into their reservoir of knowledge about the two characters (prerequisite knowledge), understand the various facets of each, and find elements that are similar (comparative reasoning). So it is in the case of all such test questions: Elements of knowledge are carried into some reasoning process.

The table of test specifications takes advantage of this combination of knowledge retrieval and its application to permit you to develop a plan that promises to sample both in a predetermined manner. Table 5.2 is a simple example of such a table. For our example, pretend that you are teaching a class in Government. In this table, we find your plan for a unit test. The test is to include 40 questions worth one point each. You choose this number because you feel you need this many questions to adequately sample the knowledge and reasoning students need to master and your students can attempt all 40 in the available time.

On the left, you subdivide the content into three basic categories: Alternative Forms of Government, Structure of U.S. Government, and Rights and Responsibilities of Citizens. Each category obviously contains many elements of knowledge within it, some of which you will transform into test items later. But for now, note in the last column that you have decided to include 15 questions covering knowledge of Forms, 10 on U.S. Government, and 15 on Responsibilities. These numbers reflect your sense of the relative importance of these three categories of material.

Table 5.2
Sample table of test specifications

Content	Know & Understand	Comparative Reasoning	Classification Reasoning	Total
Alternative Forms of Government	9 questions	5	1	15
Structure of U.S. Government	4	5	1	10
Rights and Responsibilities of Citizens	7	5	3	15
Total	20	15	5	40

Time for Reflection

Before reading on, think about how a teacher might establish sampling priorities. Why might some categories in a blueprint receive more questions than others? How have you set these priorities in the past, if you are now a classroom teacher? What important factors must a teacher consider in making these decisions?

The difference in the number of items assigned to each category might reflect any or all of the following:

- Amount of instructional time spent on each
- Amount of material in each category
- Relative importance of material in each category for later learning
- Important relationships among various ideas

This is an important part of the art of classroom assessment: As a teacher, your special insights about the nature and capabilities of your students and the nature and amount of material you want them to master must guide you in setting these priorities. Given this particular body of material, as a teacher/test developer, you must ask, What should be my areas of greatest emphasis now if I am to prepare students for important concepts and general principles they will confront later in their education?

Now let's continue with your table of specifications. Notice the columns in Table 5.2. Three patterns of reasoning appear, representing three different kinds of cognitive actions required of respondents: demonstrate understanding of the content, reason comparatively using elements of content, and use knowledge and reason to classify elements of content. Your target priorities are reflected at the bottom of each column: 20 understanding items, 15 comparison items, and 5 items requiring classification.

Remember, if the test and your instruction are to align well—that is, if the test is to reflect the results of instruction accurately and fairly—then students need to have been provided with opportunities to (1) master the essential content and (2) practice with the valued patterns of reasoning. It's only fair.

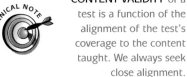

Assessment experts tell us that the **CONTENT VALIDITY** of a test is a function of the alignment of the test's coverage to the content taught. We always seek close alignment.

Once you have defined categories and specified row and column totals (which does not take long when *you* understand the material), you need only spread the numbers of questions into the cells of the table so that they add up to the row and column totals. This will generate a plan to guide you in writing a set of test questions that will systematically sample both content and reasoning priorities as established.

How do you decide how many and what rows and columns to include in a table of test specifications? There are no rigid rules. You can include as many rows and columns as make sense for your particular unit and test. This aspect of test development is as much art as science. You should consider the following factors with respect to blueprint categories for content:

1. Look for natural subdivisions in the material presented in a text, such as chapters or major sections within chapters. These are likely to reflect natural subdivisions of material generally accepted by experts in the field. Each chapter or section might become a row in your table of specifications.

2. Be sure categories have clearly marked limits and are large enough to contain a number of important elements of knowledge within each. As you will see, you will sample these elements during item writing and you need a clear sampling plan.

3. Use subdivisions of content that are likely to make sense to students as a result of their studies. Ultimately, you want them to see the vision, too.

4. Analyze state and local academic achievement standards, benchmarks, and learning requirements for important content categories.

The patterns of reasoning (columns) in your test blueprint should have the following characteristics:

1. Patterns should have clear labels and underlying meanings. Many options have been carefully researched and defined. I will say more about these, and provide examples, in Chapter 9.

2. Categories should be so familiar and comfortable to you that you can almost automatically pose exercises that demand student thinking in those terms.

3. Each category should represent kinds of reasoning and problem solving that occur in the real world.

4. All categories should represent kinds of reasoning students can come to understand and converse about as a result of experience and practice during instruction.

Be careful as you plan for this! The textbook you use may simply supply the content. You may have to establish the patterns of reasoning yourself. The bottom line is this: The categories of content, kinds of reasoning tested, and proportion of items assigned to each should reflect the target priorities communicated to students during instruction. *Students can hit any target they can see and that holds still for them!*

Instructional Objectives as Assessment Blueprints.   You also may build your assessment from a list of instructional objectives. To accomplish this, understand that objectives, like each cell in your table of specifications, specify the knowledge students must bring to bear and the action they must take (recall it, analyze it, compare it, and so on). Following are examples of such objectives:

Students will be able to compare and contrast different forms of government.

Students will understand a citizen's voting rights and responsibilities.

Note that you need not write each objective so as to define targets at a high level of specific detail. Rather, like cells in a table of specifications, they can set frames around categories that contain many possible test items within them. Sound objectives answer the question, What knowledge must respondents use to perform what cognitive activity? Later, you can prepare test items that ask students to retrieve required knowledge and use it to figure out the right answer. More about that later in this chapter.

Blueprints Really Help.   The frames you place around content and reasoning by devising tables of specifications and lists of instructional objectives are very important for three reasons. First and foremost, they define success for students, giving them more control over their own fate. So be sure to share your expectations with them. Turn the spotlight on your expectations so all can see them.

Second, clearly written expectations in the form of tables of test specifications and lists of objectives set limits on your accountability for your students' learning. With thoughtful plans in place, you are no longer responsible for seeing to it that every student knows every single fact about the subject. Rather, students need to know and understand specific parts and know how to reason using that information. When your students can hit such a complex target, you are a supreme success as a teacher, and there can be no question about it.

Third, once your overall plan is assembled, it becomes possible for you to develop more than one form of the same test. This can be very useful when you need to protect test security, such as when you need another form for students who were absent or who must retake the test for some reason. You can develop two tests (or more, if you like) made up of different items that you know sample the same content and reasoning patterns. This means that you provide all students with the same chance of success regardless of when they take the test.

Time for Reflection

Let's say you have developed a table of test specifications and two forms of your test. You need to keep one secure for administration as your final exam. This leaves you a "spare test" to use as you see fit to maximize student learning. How might you involve your students during instruction in productive ways with that "spare" assessment?

Summary of Step 1.   The first step in selected response assessment development is to formulate a plan or blueprint. Sound plans can be developed only when you yourself have attained complete mastery of the material (knowledge and reasoning) that you expect your students to master. Given that foundation, you can either (1) design a table of test specifications, or (2) prepare a list of instructional objectives. Any cell of the table or any objective will represent the union of two essential elements: some content knowledge students must retrieve via memory or reference and some cognitive act they must carry out using that material.

Using tables of specifications or lists of objectives allows you to connect the test directly to instructional priorities. In this way, these plans also set limits on the meaning of student (and therefore teacher) success, thus maximizing the chances that you and your students will each achieve the levels of excellence that you seek.

Besides, your test development goes much faster when sharply focused in this way. Still further, the sharper your focus the easier it is to involve students in assessment development. Are you keeping your list of ways to involve them?

Step 2: Selecting Material to Assess

After developing your table of specifications or list of objectives, you must select the specific and individual elements of knowledge and reasoning around which you will create test items. In Table 5.2, the cell crossing Alternative Forms of Government with Know & Understand requires the construction of nine test questions. Your next key test development question is, Can these nine questions test any facts or concepts that I wish? How do I decide which of the huge number of facts, concepts, and general principles about alternative forms of government to include in the assessment?

There are two factors to consider in answering such a question: (1) coverage of the full range of material in the unit, and (2) the relative importance of the elements within. Let me explain how these come into play.

Coverage of Material.   As previously stated, any set of assessment exercises really only represents a sample of all of the questions you could ask if the assessment were infinitely long. Clearly, if you were to test student mastery of every aspect of government, we'd be talking about an impossibly long test! The most efficient way to prevent this problem (and to create tests that fit into reasonable time limits) is to include questions that cover as much of the important material as possible. Then assume that each student's score reflects relative mastery of the entire domain of knowledge and understanding sampled. A student who answers 80 percent of the questions on the assessment correctly probably has mastered about 80 percent of the material in the entire domain sampled.

To understand this, think about commonly used polling techniques. Pollsters cannot afford to ask every citizen's opinion. So they select a sample of voters, ask them to express their opinions, and then estimate from this carefully selected sample how the general population probably feels on key issues.

In test development, we do exactly the same thing with assessment questions. If we thoughtfully sample larger bodies of content and reasoning, then the percentage of questions students answer correctly on the test will let us estimate the proportion of the larger body of knowledge that they have mastered.

But precisely what portion of the larger domain do we sample on our test? Can we pick just any set of facts, test them, and then generalize? The answer is no. Here is another place where classroom assessment becomes an art. We must select a sample (a subset) of all possible *important elements* of knowledge and understanding.

Assessment specialists call the sampled categories **CONTENT DOMAINS**. A valid assessment systematically covers, and is therefore representative of, its domain.

Who decides what is important, and how do they do it? If you are to develop the assessment, you do! If the textbook publisher developed the test and you are considering using it, you must establish your classroom achievement standards and must evaluate the text-embedded test to see if it accurately represents them. If the book covers more than students can master during your time with them, you must select from among the array of possibilities what to emphasize. This is yet another reason why you must have immersed yourself in your subject(s), so you know what is important.

But there are other places to turn to for advice in determining which material is important. For example, the textbook's author will highlight and emphasize the most important material in lists of objectives and chapter summaries, as will any accompanying teacher's guides. In addition, state, district, building, and/or department curriculum guidelines typically spell out priorities at some level. Sometimes, just taking time to talk with colleagues about instructional priorities can help.

Other valuable sources of guidance in articulating valued knowledge and reasoning targets are the various national and state professional associations of teachers, such as science, mathematics, English, and so on. Nearly every such association has assembled a commission within the past five years to identify and publish standards of excellence for student achievement in their domain. You should be familiar with any national standards of student performance held as valuable by teachers in your field.

But even with all of this help, in the end, you must decide what is important to test within each cell of your table of specifications or within each instructional objective you specify in your classroom. And so it is that, even though you might use an "objective test" format, the material tested is very much a matter of your professional judgment.

Please understand that this subjectivity is not a problem as long as you (1) are in touch with priorities in your school subject(s), (2) specify your valued achievement targets carefully, and (3) communicate them to your students. No one can do this work for you. You must possess the vision, and it must be a sound and appropriate one, given the students you teach and the latest thinking about the disciplines you teach and assess.

Identifying Important Elements.   In this section, I offer a practical and efficient means of transforming your vision, whether expressed in a table of specifications or a list of objectives, into quality test questions. Here is another strategy that promises to save you immense amounts of test development time while improving the quality of your tests.

Capture the elements you wish to test in the form of clearly stated sentences that reflect important elements of content and stipulate the kind of cognitive operation respondents must carry out. In the test development field, such statements are called *propositions*. As you shall see, propositions save you time in assessment development.

But before I illustrate them, I need to ask you to accept something on faith now, which I will verify for you later through example: When you have identified and listed all of the propositions that form the basis of your test, that test is 95 percent developed! While the work remaining is not trivial, I promise you that it will go so fast it will make your head spin. If you invest your time up front in identifying those things students should know and be able to do, the rest of your test development will be almost automatic.

To collect these propositions, or basic units of test items, begin by reviewing the material you will sample on the test, keeping your table of specifications or instructional objectives close at hand.

Refer to Table 5.2 once again. You need a total of 20 Knowledge & Understanding test items (bottom of column 1). Nine of these must arise from content related to Alternative Forms of Government. So as you review this material, you seek out and write down, say, 15 to 20 statements that capture important facts, concepts, or enduring understandings about Alternative Forms of Government that you think every student should know and understand. I recommend collecting about twice as many propositions as you will need to fill your final quota of test items. That way, if you need to replace some later or if you want to develop two parallel forms of the same test, you have your active ingredients (that is, additional propositions) ready to go. Remember, those collected must reflect the most important material. As you collect propositions, use clearly stated sentences like these:

> *Three common forms of government are monarchies, dictatorships, and democracies.*

> *In democracies, the power to govern is secured by vote of the people.*

And by the way, item writing is easier when you state propositions in your own words. That process forces you to understand what it is you are going for in the questions. Don't lift them verbatim from the text.

Time for Reflection

Are you thinking about how to use that parallel form of your test during instruction to maximize student learning? Hint: Think student-involved assessment.

Likewise, your table of specifications calls for four questions in the Know and Understand/Structure of U.S. Government cell. Here are two sample propositions:

> *The three branches of U.S. government are legislative, judicial, and executive.*

> *Under the system of checks and balances, the executive branch balances the legislative branch through its ability to veto legislation.*

Once you have written your propositions for the cell of the first column of Table 5.2, move on to the next column, this time crossing the content categories with Comparative Reasoning. Note from the blueprint that you need 5 of these in each cell, for a total of 15. Given this expectation, try to identify and state 10 important propositions for each cell. Here's an example from the row on Structure of U.S. Government:

A difference between the U.S. Senate and House of Representatives is the term of office.

And so you proceed through all nine cells of the table, seeking out and writing down more propositions than you will need. In effect, you are creating a list of elements of the material that it is important for students to learn. Note that you have not yet attempted to write any test questions.

Remember our general sampling goal: For any given body of material, we must collect enough test propositions to confidently generalize that students' performance on the sample (score on the test) reflects their proportional mastery of the whole. We know we can't ask everything. But we need to be sure to ask enough. It's a matter of judgment and, as the test creator, you are the judge.

A Note on Propositions Focused on Student Reasoning.   When you wish to assess your students' ability to use their knowledge to figure things out—that is, to *reason*, your challenge is to state propositions reflecting important learning that you may not have explicitly covered in class. That is, they may represent the kinds of comparative inferences you want them to be able to draw using their own knowledge of government and their understanding of the comparison process—they apply the concepts of similarity and difference. To test their ability to reason on their feet, then, you must present cognitive challenges at assessment time that demand more than mastery of foundational knowledge.

To reach this goal, a very special relationship must exist between the questions that appear on the test and your preceding instruction: The item must present a problem for which students (1) have had the opportunity to master appropriate prerequisite knowledge but (2) have not had the opportunity to use it to solve this particular problem. The assessment exercise challenges them to reason it out right there on the spot.

Certainly, students must dip into their reservoir of available knowledge. That is, they must retrieve the requisite information if they are to reason productively. But the aim of these propositions can be to convey more than retrieval from memory, when the goal of instruction is more than just knowing. If you want students to make the leap, for example, from just knowing something to analyzing or comparing (that is, to reasoning), you must write propositions representing inferences you expect them to make. It is not acceptable for them to have solved the problem before and memorized the answer for later regurgitation. You want them to be able to use their knowledge to figure things out at assessment time. Otherwise, you have not assessed their reasoning powers.

Completing Step 2.   Once you have completed your collection of propositions tapping critically important learnings to be assessed—remember, you have been writing twice as many as you need—you must make the final cut. At this time, it is wise to step back from this list of propositions, review them one more time, and ask yourself, Do these really provide a composite picture of what I think are the important knowledge and reasoning targets of this unit? If you really know and understand the material and know how it relates to what students will confront in the future, weak propositions will jump out at you. If you find weak entries, remove them. When the list meets your highest standards of coverage, you are ready to select the specific number needed to actually fill the cells of the table.

Just remember to keep those that do not make the final cut. They will come in very handy during instruction, as you will see later. Are you keeping your list of student involvement ideas?

Additional Thoughts on Steps 1 and 2

Without question, these are not simple test development steps. And, reasonably, you may be asking, How does he expect me to find time to do all of this and teach, too? Stick with me through the third and final test development step and it will become apparent why all of this planning saves you a great deal of time and effort.

Also, this kind of test development quickly becomes second nature to those who practice and master it. I promise you, if you are not confident that you have mastered all of the content or reasoning targets that you value when you start test development, by the time you finish designing some tests in this way, you will have a much stronger handle on them. In this sense, the very process of test development is an excellent professional growth experience.

Step 3: Building Test Items from Propositions

Previously, I noted that developing a high-quality test plan and specifying propositions represent 95 percent of the work in selected response test development. Complete the list of propositions and the test will almost develop itself from that point on. The reason lies in the fact that each proposition captures a complete and coherent thought. Professional test developers understand that the key to fast and effective item writing is to be sure to start with a complete and coherent thought about each fact, concept, general principle, or matter of inference that you intend to test.

Once you have a proposition in hand, you can spin any kind of selected response item out of it that you wish. Let me illustrate with the following proposition from the cell in Table 5.2 that crosses Alternative Forms of Government with Know & Understand:

In a monarchy, the right to govern is secured through birth.

To generate a true/false item out of this proposition that is true, you can simply include the proposition on the test as stated! The proposition is a true true/false test item as written. This is always the case in well-stated propositions.

If you want a false true/false item, simply make one part of the proposition false:

In a monarchy, the right to govern is secured through the approval of those governed.

To convert this proposition to a fill-in item, simply leave out the phrase dealing with the effect and ask a question:

How is the right to govern secured in a monarchy?

If you desire a multiple-choice item, add a number of response options, only one of which is correct.

How is the right to govern secured in a monarchy?
   a.   *With military power*
   b.   *Through birth*
   c.   *By popular vote*
   d.   *Through purchase*

Mark my words: Every well-conceived and clearly stated proposition, whether requiring retrieval of knowledge or its application in a problem-solving context, is an automatic source of test questions.

Here's another example, this time requiring Comparative Reasoning using an understanding of Structure of U.S. Government. In its initial statement, it is a true true/false question:

The executive and legislative branches of U.S. government differ in that the latter is elected directly by the people.

As a false true/false question:

Members of executive and legislative branches are both elected directly by the people.

As a fill-in item:

Election of members of the executive and legislative branches differs in what way?

As a multiple-choice item:

Election of members of the executive and legislative branches differs in what way?
   a.   *Legislators are restricted by term limits; presidents are not*
   b.   *Legislators are elected directly; presidents are not*
   c.   *One must register to vote for legislators; not for president*

Invest your time and effort up front learning the underlying structure of the material you teach, and finding the important propositions. These are the keys to the rapid development of sound selected response assessments.

Once you have identified the format(s) you plan to use, a few simple keys will aid you in developing sound test items. Some of these guidelines apply to all formats; others are unique to each particular format. They all have the effect of helping respondents understand exactly what you, the item writer, are going for in posing the exercise.

General Item Writing Guidelines.   These tend to focus on the form of the item. The simplicity of their advice belies their power to improve your tests, believe me.

1. Write clearly in a sharply focused manner.   Good selected response assessment development is first and foremost an exercise in clear communication. Follow the rules of grammar—tests are as much a public reflection of your professional standards as any other product you create. Include only material essential to framing the question. Be brief and clear. Your goal is to test mastery of the material, not students' ability to figure out what you're asking!

Not this:

When scientists rely on magnets in the development of electric motors they need to know about the poles, which are?

But this:*

What are the poles of a magnet called?
    a.   Anode and cathode
    b.   North and south
    c.   Strong and weak
    d.   Attract and repel

2. Ask a question.   When using multiple-choice and fill-in formats, minimize the use of incomplete statements as exercises. When you force yourself to ask a question, you force yourself to express a complete thought in the stem or trigger part of the question, which usually promotes respondents' clear understanding.

Not this:

Between 1950 and 1965
    a.   Interest rates increased.
    b.   Interest rates decreased.
    c.   Interest rates fluctuated greatly.
    d.   Interest rates did not change.

But this:

What was the trend in interest rates between 1950 and 1965?
    a.   Increased only
    b.   Decreased only
    c.   Increased, then decreased
    d.   Remained unchanged

3. Aim for the lowest possible reading level.   This is an attempt to control for the inevitable confounding of reading proficiency and mastery of the material in students' scores. You do not want to let students' reading proficiency prevent them from demonstrating that they really know the material. Minimize sentence length

---

*Item adapted from *Handbook on formative and summative evaluation of student learning* (p. 592, item A.4-n-2.211) by B. S. Bloom, J. T. Hastings, and G. F. Madaus, 1971, New York: McGraw-Hill. Copyright 1971 by McGraw-Hill, Inc. Adapted by permission of the publisher.

and syntactic complexity and eliminate unnecessarily difficult or unfamiliar vocabulary. For an example, see the previous magnet questions.

4. Eliminate clues to the correct answer either within the question or across questions within a test. When grammatical clues within items or material presented in other items give away the correct answer, students get items right for the wrong reasons. The result is misinformation about their true achievement.

Not this:

All of these are examples of a bird that flies, *except* an
   a.   Ostrich
   b.   Falcon
   c.   Cormorant
   d.   Robin

(The article *an* at the end of the stem requires a response beginning with a vowel. As only one is offered, it must be correct.)

Not this either:

Which of the following are examples of birds that do not fly?
   a.   Falcon
   b.   Ostrich and penguin
   c.   Cormorant
   d.   Robin

(The question calls for a plural response. As only one is offered, it must be correct.)

TECHNICAL NOTE

When students answer test items right for the wrong reasons, assessment experts call these **ERRORS OF MEASUREMENT**. They make a test unreliable.

5. If you write the test questions, have a qualified colleague read them through at least once to ensure accuracy. This is especially true of your really high-stakes tests, such as big unit tests and final exams. No one is perfect. We all overlook simple mistakes. Having a willing colleague review your work takes just a few minutes and can save a great deal of time and eliminate problems in the long run. Don't get your ego so tied up in your assessment that you can't take needed constructive criticism.

6. And please, double check the scoring key for accuracy before scoring. Enough said!

Guidelines for Multiple-Choice Exercises   When developing multiple-choice test items, keep these few simple, yet powerful, guidelines in mind:

1. Repeated for emphasis: Ask a complete question to get the item started, if you can. This has the effect of placing the item's focus in the stem, not in the response options. (See the previous interest rate example.)

2. If you find yourself repeating the same words at the beginning of each response option, reword the stem to move the repetitive material up there.

This will clarify the problem and make it more efficient for respondents to read. (Again, see the interest rate example.)

3. Be sure there is only one correct or best answer.   This is where that colleague's independent review can help. Remember, it is acceptable to ask respondents to select a best answer from among a set of answers, all of which are correct. Just be sure to word the question so as to make their task clear.

4. Word response options as briefly as possible and be sure they are grammatically parallel.   This has two desirable effects. First, it makes items easier to read. Second, it helps eliminate grammatical clues to the correct answer. (See the second bird example.)

Not this:

Why did colonists come to the United States?
- a.   To escape heavy taxation by their native governments
- b.   Religion
- c.   They sought the adventure of living among Native Americans in the new land
- d.   There was the promise of great wealth in the new world
- e.   More than one of the above answers

But this:

Why did colonists migrate to the United States?
- a.   To escape taxation
- b.   For religious freedom
- c.   For adventure
- d.   More than one of the above

5. Vary the number of response options presented as appropriate to pose the problem you want your students to solve.   While it is best to design multiple-choice questions around three, four, or five response options, it is permissible to vary the number of response options offered across items within the same test. Please try not to use "all of the above" or "none of the above" to fill up spaces just because you can't think of other incorrect answers. In fact, sound practice suggests limiting their use to those few times when they fit comfortably into the context of the question. Some teachers find it effective to include more than one correct answer and ask the student to find them all, when appropriate. *This means those questions should be worth more than one point.* They need to count for as many points as there are correct answers. For example:

Which of the labels provided represents a classification category for types of rocks? (Identify all correct answers[*])
1.   Geologic
2.   Metamorphic*
3.   Sandstone
4.   Igneous*

By the way, here's a simple, yet crafty, multiple-choice test item writing tip: If you compose a multiple-choice item and find that you cannot think of enough plausible incorrect responses, include the item on a test the first time as a fill-in question. As your students respond, those who get it wrong will provide you with the full range of viable incorrect responses you need the next time you use it.

Guidelines for True/False Exercises   You have only one simple guideline to follow here: Make the item *entirely* true or false *as stated*. Complex "idea salads" including some truth and some falsehood just confuse the issue. Precisely what is the proposition you are testing? State it and move on to the next one.

Not this:

From the Continental Divide, located in the Appalachian Mountains, water flows into either the Pacific Ocean or the Mississippi River.

But this:

The Continental Divide is located in the Appalachian Mountains.

Guidelines for Matching Items   When developing matching exercises, which are really complex multiple-choice items with a number of stems offered along with a number of response options, follow all of the multiple-choice guidelines offered previously. In addition, observe the following guidelines:

1. State the matching challenge up front with a clear and concise set of directions specifying what is to be matched.

2. Keep the list of things to be matched short.   The maximum number of options is 10. Shorter is better. This minimizes the information processing and idea juggling respondents must do to be successful.

3. Keep the list of things to be matched homogeneous.   Don't mix events with dates or with names. Again, idea salads confuse the issue. Focus the exercise. Figure 5.2 offers a list of alignments that work well.

Figure 5.2
Relationships that can provide a basis for strong matching exercises
Source: From *Measurement and Assessment in Teaching*, 7th ed. (p. 167) by R. L. Linn and N. E. Gronlund, 1995, Upper Saddle River, NJ: Merrill/Prentice Hall. Reprinted by permission.

Persons	Achievements
Dates	Events
Terms	Definitions
Rules	Examples
Symbols	Concepts
Authors	Book titles
Foreign words	English equivalents
Machines	Uses
Plants/animals	Classifications
Principles	Illustrations
Objects	Names of objects
Parts	Functions

4. Keep the list of response options brief in their wording and parallel in construction.   Pose the matching challenge in clear, straightforward language.

5. Include more response options than stems and permit students to use response options more than once.   This has the effect of making it impossible for students to arrive at the correct response purely through a process of elimination. If students answer correctly using elimination and you infer that they have mastered the material, you will be wrong.

Not this:

_____ 1.	Texas	A. $7,200,000
_____ 2.	Hawaii	B. Chicago
_____ 3.	New York	C. Liberty Bell
_____ 4.	Illinois	D. Augusta
_____ 5.	Louisiana	E. Cornhusker
_____ 6.	Florida	F. Mardi Gras
_____ 7.	Massachusetts	G. 50th State
_____ 8.	Alaska	H. Austin
_____ 9.	Maine	I. Everglades
_____10.	California	J. 1066
_____11.	Nebraska	K. Dover
_____12.	Pennsylvania	L. San Andreas Fault
		M. Salem
		N. 1620
		O. Statue of Liberty

But this:

Directions: The New England states are listed in the left-hand column and capital cities in the right-hand column. Place the letter corresponding to the capital city in the space next to the state in which that city is located. Responses may be used only once.

States   **Capital Cities**

_____ 1.	Connecticut	A. Augusta
_____ 2.	Maine	B. Boston
_____ 3.	Massachusetts	C. Brunswick
_____ 4.	New Hampshire	D. Concord
_____ 5.	Rhode Island	E. Hartford
_____ 6.	Vermont	F. Montpelier
		G. New Haven
		H. Providence

Guidelines for Fill-in Items.   Here are three simple guidelines to follow:

1. Ask respondents a question and provide space for an answer.   This forces you to express a complete thought. The use of incomplete statements as item stems is acceptable. But if you use them, be sure to capture the essence of the problem in that stem.

2. Try to stick to one blank per item.   Come to the point. Ask one question, get one answer, and move on to the next question. Simple language, complete communication, clear conclusions. Does the student know the answer or not?

Not this:

In the percussion section of the orchestra are located _____, _____, _____, and _____.

But this:

In what section of the orchestra is the kettle drum found?

_____

3. Don't let the length of the line to be filled in be a clue as to the length or nature of the correct response.   This may seem elementary, but it happens. Again, this can misinform you about students' real levels of achievement.

Mixing Formats Together.   The creative assessment developer also can generate some interesting and useful assessment exercises by mixing the various formats. For example, mix true/false and multiple-choice formats to create exercises in which respondents must label a statement true or false and select the response option that gives the proper reason it is so. For example:

As employment increases, the danger of inflation increases.
    a.   True, because consumers are willing to pay higher prices
    b.   True, because the money supply increases
    c.   False, because wages and inflation are statistically unrelated to one another
    d.   False, because the government controls inflation

Or, mix multiple-choice or true/false questions with the fill-in format by asking students to select the correct response and fill in the reason it is correct. As a variation, ask why incorrect responses are incorrect, too.

Time for Reflection

Can you recall any variations of these formats used by your own teachers that you found to be challenging, creative, or especially effective? Can you think of combinations of these formats that might be useful?

Guidelines for Interpretive Exercises.   Here's another simple but effective assessment development idea: Let's say you wish to use selected response formats to assess student reasoning and problem-solving proficiency. But let's also say you are not sure all of your students have the same solid background in the content, or you want to see them apply content you don't expect them to know outright. In these contexts, you can turn to what is called an *interpretive exercise*. With this format, you provide information to respondents in the form of a brief passage, chart, table, or figure and then ask a series of questions calling for them to interpret or apply that material. For example:*

Here is a graph of Bill's weekly allowance distribution.

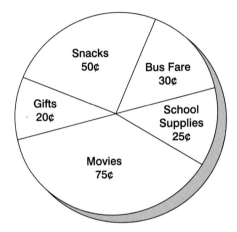

1.   What is the ratio of the amount Bill spends for school supplies to the amount he spends for movies?
     a.   7:2
     b.   1:3
     c.   2:7
     d.   3:1

2.   What would be the best title for this graph?
     a.   Bill's weekly allowance
     b.   Bill's money graph
     c.   Bill's weekly expenditures
     D.   Bill's money planning

More General Guidelines.   Finally, here are a few simple guidelines for setting up your test as a whole that will maximize the accuracy of the results:

1. Make sure your students know the point value for each assessment exercise. This helps them use their time wisely.

2. Start each test with relatively easy items. This will give students a chance to get test anxiety under control.

3. Present all questions of like format together (all multiple choice together, all fill-in, etc.)

4. Be sure all parts of a question appear on the same page of the test.

5. Make sure all copies are clear and readable.

Summary of Step 3.   In this step, you transformed propositions into assessment questions. This can be a very quick and easy process. Regardless of the item format, however, clarity and focused simplicity must be hallmarks of your exercises. Always try to ask questions. Strive to eliminate inappropriate clues to the correct answer, seek one clearly correct answer whenever possible and appropriate, ask a colleague to review important tests, and follow just a few simple format-specific guidelines for item construction. Figure 5.3 presents a summary of these guidelines collected for convenient use.

Further, remember to help students perform up to their potential by providing clear and complete instructions, letting students know how each exercise contributes to the total test score, starting with easy items, and making sure the test is readable.

General guidelines for all formats

____ Items clearly written and focused

____ Question posed

____ Lowest possible reading level

____ Irrelevant clues eliminated

____ Items reviewed by colleague

____ Scoring key double checked

Guidelines for multiple-choice items

____ Item stem poses a direct question

____ Repetition eliminated from response options

____ One best or correct answer

____ Response options are brief and parallel

____ Number of response options offered fits item context

Guideline for true/false items

____ Statement is entirely true or false as presented

Guidelines for matching exercises

____ Clear directions given

____ List of items to be matched is brief

____ List consists of homogeneous entries

____ Response options are brief and parallel

____ Extra response options offered

Guidelines for fill-in items

____ A direct question is posed

____ One blank is needed to respond

____ Length of blank is not a clue

Figure 5.3
Test item quality checklist

Fine Tuning Assessment Applications

As we plan our development and use of selected response assessments, we must think critically about such issues as when to use each of the four formats, how to evaluate tests developed by others, and how technology might help us in our endeavor.

Selecting from Among the Four Formats

How do we decide which selected response format (multiple-choice, true/false, matching, or fill-in) to use in any particular assessment context?

In general, the first three—multiple choice, true/false, and matching—are preferable when scoring efficiency is an issue, especially if an optical scan machine scoring service is available. When these formats fit the achievement targets, students are old enough to respond by bubbling in answer sheets (generally from grade 4), and scoring can be automated, multiple-choice, true/false, and matching formats can be big time savers. Unfortunately, until computer technology allows us to scan and evaluate student writing, short answer fill-in items are going to take longer to score. (Incidentally, the technology exists today to scan actual student work into the computer. But its evaluation still requires the human eye and mind.)

On the other hand, fill-in exercises are preferable when we wish to control for guessing. And make no mistake about it, guessing can be an issue. If a student guesses an item right and we infer that the right answer means the student has mastered the material, we are wrong. We have mismeasured that student's real achievement.

Guessing a correct answer represents another kind of "error of measurement" that leads to unreliable assessment.

Given a true/false test, respondents who rely on blind guessing alone will answer about half of the items correctly. With multiple-choice, the approximate percent they will guess right depends on the number of response options: tests made up of four-choice items yield a guessing score of about 25 percent correct; five-choice, roughly 20 percent. Notice that respondents who can confidently eliminate two options in a four-choice multiple choice item before guessing raise their odds of guessing correctly from 1 in 4 to 1 in 2! Our heart must go out to students who score below the chance or guessing score on a selected response test. Not only are such students misinformed, but they're unlucky! Fill-in items, on the other hand, greatly reduce the chances of success through guessing alone.

Multiple-choice items are preferable when we can identify one correct or best answer and at the same time identify a number of viable incorrect responses (also known as *distractors*). On its surface, this might sound obvious. But think about it. If we formulate our distractors carefully, we can use multiple-choice items to uncover common misunderstandings and to diagnose students' needs. Let me illustrate.

If we were to start with a math problem and solve it correctly, we have identified the correct response (response option 1). Next, we can solve that same problem making a common mistake on purpose. Say we carry that mistake all the way to an answer. This yields response option 2, and it will be incorrect. But if anyone chooses that incorrect response option when they take the test, we will know what mistake they made. Next, we solve the same problem making another kind of common mistake, and another viable incorrect response results (response option 3). We continue until we have as many incorrect response options as needed. Thus, each incorrect response can provide useful information about the students who choose it, if we develop the item thoughtfully.

If we administer such a test and analyze how many students selected each response option for each item (which we may do very easily with currently available optical scan test scoring technology and item analysis software packages), we gain clear insights into common misconceptions among our students. Multiple-choice exercises developed in this way can serve to identify student needs with a minimum investment of testing time.

True/false exercises are most useful when we have a great deal of material to cover and want to ask a large number of questions per unit of testing time, or when we have much to cover and limited testing time, because they require very short response times. They also are usable when we either cannot think of or don't want to take the time to generate lists of viable distractors for multiple-choice items.

The greatest strength of matching items lies in their efficiency. When carefully developed to include homogeneous elements, they are in effect several multiple-choice items presented at once. Each premise statement to be matched triggers a new multiple-choice test item and all items in a matching exercise offer the same set of multiple response options. They can be used to assess mastery of knowledge and/or reasoning and problem solving, although most tend to center on recall of associations.

Working Backwards to Verify Test Quality

We have come a long way in this chapter depicting a three-step test development process, from blueprints to propositions to test items. Before we leave this topic, let's discuss a natural extension of this process. This idea may already have occurred to you.

You can reverse this entire process in order to evaluate previously developed tests, such as those that come with a textbook or those you have developed in previous years. To do this, begin at the test item level: Do the items themselves adhere to the few critical guidelines presented previously? If they do not, there is obvious reason for concern about test quality. If they do, proceed to the next level of analysis.

At this level, you can transform the items into the propositions that they reflect. You accomplish this by doing the following:

- Combine the multiple-choice item stem with the correct response.
- True true/false items already are propositions.
- Make false true/false items true to derive the proposition.

- Match up elements in matching exercises.
- Fill in the blanks of short answer items.

Then, analyze the resulting list of propositions, asking, Do these reflect the priorities in my instruction? Next, collect the propositions into like groups to determine the instructional objectives they represent or to create a table of specifications depicting the overall picture of the test, including the proportional representation of content and thinking. Again, ask, Do these reflect priorities as I see them?

This backward analysis can both reveal the flaws in previously developed tests and help you understand the nature of the revisions needed to bring the test up to your standards of quality.

Getting Help from Technology

Today's technology can greatly ease the workload associated with selected response assessment. One time- and labor-saving device of immense potential is the personal computer. Many textbook publishers, test publishers, and other service providers have developed computerized test item banks. The packages often include disks full of developed test exercises grouped and coded by content, type of reasoning involved, grade level, and subject. Software packages are also available to ease the word processing load of test construction, should you choose to create your own. On the Internet, access the Wested Website (http://www.wested.org/acwt) to review a compilation of such software or call them at 415-565-3000 and request the "Assessment Software Database."

To illustrate the level of sophistication of this technology, IPS Publishing of Vancouver, Washington, has developed thousands of computer algorithms, or software routines, capable of automatically generating literally millions of high-quality mathematics test exercises on command. Exercises generated reflect specific learning objectives cross-referenced to nearly all of the texts used across the United States and Canada in elementary arithmetic through advanced college-level mathematics.

Another application that can save teachers immense amounts of time and provide students with dependable feedback that they are improving is offered by the Accelerated Reader and Accelerated Math programs of Advantage Learning Systems of Wisconsin Rapids, Wisconsin. These systems provide teachers with easy-to-use classroom assessments of reading comprehension and math problem-solving proficiency that motivate students by keeping them in touch with their own increasing competence as readers and math problem solvers.

Yet another application of technology that demands mention earlier is optical scanners, or test scoring machines that produce results very quickly. Not only can these machines generate test scores, but currently available versions can analyze test items to tell you how your students did collectively on each item. If that is not diagnostic of the impact of your instruction and students' learning, diagnosis will never be possible!

Further, software described in the aforementioned WestEd database can help you link objectives, assessments, and student records into new and very efficient ways of building electronic portfolios. The good news is that these technologies are now quite affordable.

I will continue to refer to applications of technology in classroom assessment as our journey progresses, particularly in Part III of this text. But for now, let's stick with the test development process itself.

Barriers to Sound Selected Response Assessment

Recall that, in earlier chapters, we listed five key attributes of a sound assessment:

- clear targets
- clear purposes
- proper method
- appropriate sampling
- control of bias

These also reflect the things that can go wrong—that can keep a student's test score from being an accurate reflection of that student's real level of achievement. Listed in Figure 5.4, by way of summary, are many of the sources of mismeasurement touched in this chapter, together with actions you can take to prevent these problems. These remedies can help you develop sound selected response assessments.

Student Involvement in Selected Response Assessment

Time for Reflection

Have you been collecting possible ideas for student involvement as you have been reading this chapter? If so, review your list before you proceed. If not, before you read further, take a minute to think more about this. In what specific ways can you bring your students into selected response assessment development and use in ways that maximize their confidence and learning?

I have said from the outset that classroom assessment can serve two important purposes. One is to provide information for teacher, student, and parent to use in informing the various decisions they must make. The other is as a highly motivational teaching tool. Figure 5.5 presents specific ways to weave selected response assessment development and use into the very fabric of your teaching and learning

Potential Sources of Problems	Suggested Remedies
Lack of vision of the priority target	Carefully analyze the material to be tested to find the knowledge and reasoning targets.
	Find truly important learning propositions.
Wrong method for the target	Use selected response methods to assess mastery of knowledge and appropriate kinds of reasoning only.
	Selected response can test prerequisites of effective skill and product performance, but not performance itself.
Inappropriate sampling:	
• Not representative of important propositions	Know the material and plan the test to thoroughly cover the target.
• Sample too small	Include enough items to cover key concepts.
• Sample too large for time available	Shorten cautiously so as to maintain enough to support confident student learning conclusions.
Sources of bias:	
• Student-centered problems	
• Cannot read well enough to respond	Lower reading level of test or offer reading support.
• Insufficient time to respond	Shorten test or allow more time.
• Poor-quality test items	Learn and follow both general and format-specific guidelines for writing quality items.
	Seek review by a colleague.
• Scoring errors	Double check answer key; use it carefully.

Figure 5.4
Avoiding problems with selected response tests and quizzes

environment. Many of these suggestions reflect an idea planted earlier in the chapter. Remember when I asked you who else might become involved in the process of assessment development and use in order to lighten your classroom assessment workload? The coworkers to whom I referred are your students.

Figure 5.5 represents only the beginning of a practically endless list of ways to do this. You can and should generate ideas to add to it. These uses of selected response assessment all contribute to one huge key to student success: Students can hit any target that they can see and that holds still for them. These strategies serve to remove the mystery surrounding the meaning of academic success. They bring students into the process of defining that meaning (under your watchful leadership) and give them control over their own well-being.

- Develop a table of test specifications for a final unit test *before* ever teaching the unit. A clear vision of the valued outcomes will result and you can tailor instruction to promote student success.
- Share a copy of that plan with every student. Review it carefully at the beginning of the unit and explain your expectations at that time. Now students and teacher share the same vision.
- Involve students in the process of devising the test plan, or involve them from time to time in checking back to the blueprint (1) to see together—as partners—if you might need to make adjustments in the test plan and/or (2) to chart your progress together.
- Once you have the test plan completed, develop a few test items each day as the unit unfolds. Such items certainly would reflect timely instructional priorities. Further, at the end of the unit, the final exam would be all done and ready to go! This eliminates the last-minute anxiety of test development and improves test quality.
- Involve students in writing practice test items. Think of the benefits: students will have to evaluate the importance of the various elements of content, and they will have to become proficient in using the kinds of reasoning and problem solving valued in your classroom. Developing sample test items provides high-fidelity practice in doing these things.
- As a variation on that theme, provide unlabeled exercises and have students practice (1) placing them in the proper cell of the test blueprint, and (2) answering them.
- As another variation, have students evaluate the quality of the tests that came with the textbook—do they match your plan developed for instruction?
- Have students use the test blueprint to predict how they are going to do on each part of the test before they take it. Then have them analyze how they did, part by part, after taking it. If the first test is for practice, such an analysis will provide valuable information to help them plan their preparation for the real thing.
- Have students work in teams, with each team given responsibility for finding ways to help everyone in class score high in one cell, row, or column of a table of specifications or one objective.
- Use lists of unit objectives and tables of test specifications to communicate among teachers about instructional priorities, so as to arrive at a clearer understanding of how those priorities fit together across instructional levels or school buildings.
- Store test items by content and reasoning category for reuse. If your item record also includes information on how students did on each item (say, the percentage that got it right), you could revise instruction next time for items students had trouble with. Incidentally, this represents an excellent place to use your personal computer to advantage as a test item storage and retrieval system.

Figure 5.5
Ideas for student-involved assessment

Summary: Productive Selected Response Assessment

During this phase of our journey through the realm of educational assessment we have considered multiple-choice, true/false, matching, and fill-in test item formats. We established at the beginning of the chapter that these options often are labeled "objective" tests because of the manner in which they are scored. When test items are carefully developed, answers are right or wrong. No judgment is involved. However, the teacher's professional judgment does play a major role in all other facets of this kind of assessment, from test planning, to selecting material to test, to writing the test items. For this reason, it is essential that all selected response test developers closely follow procedures for creating sound tests. Those procedures were the topic of this chapter.

We discussed the match between selected response assessment methods and the four basic kinds of achievement targets plus dispositions that are serving as signposts for our journey. These selected response formats can serve to assess students' mastery of content knowledge and understanding, ability to reason in important ways, and mastery of some of the procedural knowledge that underpins both the development of performance skills and the creation of complex products.

As we examined the test development process itself, we explored several context factors that extend beyond just the consideration of match to target that must be taken into account in choosing selected response assessment. These included factors related to students' reading abilities and to the kinds of support services available to the user.

Also under the heading of test development, we explored a three-step developmental sequence: test planning, identifying propositions to test, and test item writing. We reviewed a limited number of specific item and test development tactics within each step that promise to decrease test development time and increase test quality. These tactics hold the promise of saving teachers immense amounts of time in test development. Not only do they result in quick and easy test item development, but teachers can store both test blueprints and items on their personal computer for convenient reuse later.

We closed with a list of specific ways to bring students into the assessment as full partners. Note that we are not referring merely to exchanging papers at test scoring time. Rather, we are talking about far deeper involvement so students can come to understand valued targets, assist in designing assessment exercises, and understand how to interpret and use assessment results. These ideas also hold the promise of making the teacher's assessment job much easier.

Exercises for Self-Assessment

1. In your own words, describe the specific kinds of achievement targets that can be transformed into selected response formats and those that cannot.

2. Make a checklist of factors to take into account when considering the selected response option.

3. What are the key considerations in devising a sound sample of selected response items?

4. Make a chart listing the four selected response formats as rows and the following as columns: principal advantages, limitations, and when to use. Review this chapter and fill in the cells of the table.

5. Make a one-page chart listing your own abbreviations of the general and format-specific guidelines for item writing presented in Figure 5.3. Keep it handy for reference if and when you consider selected response assessment.

 You may go to the Companion Website at www.prenhall.com/stiggins and answer these questions in the Self-Assessment module.

Final Chapter Reflection

1. *What are the three most important new insights to come to you as a result of your study of this chapter?*
2. *Which of your previous questions about assessment can you now answer based on your study of this chapter?*
3. *What new questions have come to mind as a result of your study of this chapter that you hope to have answered as your study continues?*
4. *For practicing teachers only: What do you plan to do differently in assessment in your classroom as a result of your study of this book so far?*

   For those in preservice study only: As you think about the classroom assessment environment that you hope to create for your students, how has your thinking changed as a result of your study of this book so far?

 ## Workbook Activities

Those of you using the workbook, *Practice with Student-Involved Classroom Assessment*, as part of your study of this material will find the following activities and others included for Chapter 5:

- *Write Propositions and Test Questions.* The trickiest part of Chapter 5 is identifying important learnings and transforming them into propositions. This activity provides practice.

- *Test of Franzipanics.*   Even though every multiple-choice question on this test is complete nonsense, you can answer them all correctly. Find out why and learn key lessons about good item writing.

- *Setting Up a Tropical Fish Tank.*   Using a real unit of instruction (complete with a test at the end) you can be the sleuth to determine the strengths and weaknesses of the test specifications, the link between the test specifications and the test questions, and the quality of the test questions themselves.

- *Try This With Students.*   Figure 5.5 in the textbook presents 11 suggestions for involving students with selected response test assessment to boost achievement. You get to try some.

Video Support

The ATI interactive video training package, entitled *Common Sense Paper and Pencil Assessments*, reinforces much of what is covered in the text about selected response assessment, with several opportunities for specific practice.

6

Essay Assessment: Subjective and Powerful

CHAPTER FOCUS

This chapter answers the following guiding question:

When and how do I use the essay mode of assessment most effectively?

Your study of this chapter will help you understand the following important principles:

1. Essay assessment aligns well with knowledge and understanding targets, as well as various patterns of reasoning.
2. Essays can be efficiently developed in three steps: assessment planning, exercise development, and preparation to score student responses.
3. This method can fall prey to avoidable sources of bias that can distort results if users are not careful.
4. By involving your students in essay assessment development and use, you can set them up for energetic and successful learning.

As we start this part of our journey, keep the big picture in mind. Figure 6.1 is a duplicate of Figure 4.2, which matched the five targets with four methods of assessment. In this chapter, we will be dealing in depth with the shaded areas.

Introducing Assessment Based on Teacher Judgment

The essay form of assessment may have the greatest untapped potential of any of the four assessment methods discussed in this book. The time has come for us to begin to take greater advantage of this rich assessment option.

	SELECTED RESPONSE	ESSAY	PERFORMANCE ASSESSMENT	PERSONAL COMMUNICATION
Know				
Reason				
Skills				
Products				
Dispositions				

Figure 6.1
Aligning achievement targets and assessment methods

Our changing social and economic circumstances, along with our increasingly technical world, demand that schools assist students in mastering increasingly complex forms of achievement. As a result, during the 1980s and 1990s, these more sophisticated achievement targets spawned interest in assessment methods able to tap the greater depth of our achievement expectations. We began to sense the insufficiency of selected response assessment. So, we began to explore richer assessment methods.

One result has been renewed interest in essay assessment—the method, by the way, that dominated student evaluation until the appearance of the multiple-choice format in the 1920s. In essay assessment, students create brief original written responses to essay exercises posed by their teacher, who then reads their responses and judges quality.

This chapter explores the potential of the essay assessment alternative and reviews this assessment methodology's three major strengths:

- Essays can delve into students' attainment of some complex and sophisticated achievement targets, such as their understanding of connections among elements of knowledge or their reasoning proficiency.

- Essays can assess these outcomes at a relatively low cost in terms of teacher time and energy.

- Essay assessment can be integrated productively into teaching and learning, especially through student involvement.

As with all modes of assessment, if we are not careful, problems can crop up. For instance, we are likely to inaccurately assess student achievement if we

- Lack a sufficiently clear vision of the kinds of outcomes to be learned and therefore assessed
- Do not connect the essay format to the proper kinds of achievement targets
- Use this method with students who lack sufficient writing skills to convey their achievement of content or reasoning skills
- Do not representatively sample the achievement target
- Disregard the many sources of bias that can invade subjective assessments

This chapter is about how to avoid those problems. Further, we will continue to explore ways to turn assessment into a learning experience through student involvement. Let's start with an example.

Essay Assessment at Work in the Classroom

A professor acquaintance of mine uses essay exercises exclusively for his final examinations in the classroom assessment course that he teaches for teachers and school administrators. His students are like you—they're becoming assessment literate. He reports that he likes the essay method in this context because it allows him to do the following:

1. Present exercises that depict relatively complex real-world classroom assessment dilemmas.
2. Ask his students to use their assessment methodology knowledge, understanding, and reasoning abilities to describe how they would resolve each dilemma if confronted with it in their classroom.

Obviously, he could obtain a more "authentic" assessment of their proficiency if he could place his students in a real classroom and observe them solving real classroom assessment problems. But because that kind of authenticity is beyond reach, he turns to an essay test and effectively gains insight into their achievement.

The Assessment.   The professor samples the achievement of his students using 10 essay exercises on each final exam. He chooses them from a pool of exercises that he and his students have devised over the years to represent an array of classroom assessment challenges teachers face in real classrooms. He feels 10 exercises sample well enough to permit him to generalize to the examinees' overall competence.

For practice, this professor regularly involves his students in developing exercises and scoring criteria similar but not identical to those that will appear on the exam. During instruction, sometimes students respond to each other's practice exercises and apply scoring guides to evaluating each other's work. Remember, this must be for practice only—to help them improve and track their own growth. The results play no role in determining their grades. The exercises that appear on the "official" final exam ask students to use their knowledge to solve novel problems presented at that time.

For each exercise on the actual final exam, he establishes performance expectations in advance by specifying either one best solution or a set of acceptable solutions to the classroom assessment problem presented. The professor carefully translates these expectations into predetermined scoring guidelines for each exercise. He tells students up front how many points are associated with each exercise, and they strive to attain as many of those points as they can.

Following is a sample of one of his exercises, along with its scoring criteria. It reveals the kind of real-world complexity that the professor can attain with the essay mode of assessment.

Sample Essay Exercise:

Assume you are a French teacher with many years of teaching experience. You place great value on the development of speaking proficiency as an outcome of your instruction. Therefore, you rely heavily on assessments where you listen to and evaluate performance. But a problem has arisen. Parents of students who attained very high scores on your written tests are complaining that their children are receiving lower grades on their report cards. The principal wants to be sure your judgments of student proficiency are sound and so has asked you to explain and defend your procedures. Describe at least three specific quality standards that your oral proficiency exams would need to meet for you to be confident that your exams truly reflect what students can do; provide the rationale for each. (2 points for each procedure and rationale, total = 6 points.)

Score Responses as Follows:

2 points if the student's response lists any of these six procedures and defends each as a key to conducting sound performance assessments:

- Specify clear performance criteria
- Sample performance over several exercises
- Apply systematic rating procedures
- Maintain complete and accurate records
- Use published performance assessments to verify results of classroom assessments
- Use multiple observers to corroborate

Also award 2 points if the response lists any of the following and defends them as attributes of sound assessments:

- Specifies a clear instructional objective
- Relies on a proper assessment method
- Samples performance well
- Controls for sources of rater bias

All other responses receive no points.

The professor claims that, over the years, these final exams have become very much a part of his classroom teaching and learning process. Let's explore why this might be the case.

The Process.   The professor conducts this as a take-home exam, so as to maximize the amount of time students can spend reflecting and responding, and learning as they do so. His students report that they do, in fact, spend a considerable amount of time preparing their responses. Further, students receive the exercises a few at a time throughout the term, as the professor presents the material needed to address the various problems. This has the effect of making the achievement targets perfectly clear to the students, thus helping them focus their learning and reduce test anxiety. It also focuses study and spreads the extra learning time and effort over the entire term.

As take-home exams, these obviously are open-book exams. The professor covers a great deal of material about assessment in this course and reports that he does not expect students to memorize it all, any more than he expects his physician to memorize all of the treatment options she has at her disposal.

Rather, each student receives a text and a parallel set of resource materials. Over the course, students learn how to use these reference materials. Hopefully, after the course is over, they will keep their "library" of assessment ideas handy for classroom use. The open-book exam format encourages them to learn the overall organizational structure of these materials for both present and later use.

The Scoring.   At the end of the term, when students hand in their final exam for scoring (all 10 exercises come in together), the professor applies the predetermined scoring guides in evaluating each response to each exercise. Because enrollment can exceed 50 students per class, he has had to find ways to maximize reading and scoring efficiency. The single biggest time saver, he reports, is to have the scoring criteria clearly in mind before beginning. Next is to score all responses to one exercise at one time and then move on to the next exercise.

The Feedback.   Students receive feedback on their performance in the following forms:

- Points assigned to each part of each response
- Brief written rationale for the score, suggesting factors they might have overlooked
- The total number of points summed over all exercises
- A grade based on comparing the total score to a predetermined set of cutoff scores for each grade

Students who attain grades that are lower than their expectations for themselves can rework any exercise(s) any time and resubmit their exam for reevaluation. If reevaluation of their written work and a personal discussion with the professor reveals that they have completed more productive study and have attained a higher level of proficiency, the professor submits a change of grade at once. This procedure has the effect of extending the learning time beyond the limits of a single term when necessary. However, the professor accepts resubmissions for one subsequent term only.

Time for Reflection

If you took a course from a professor who practiced these assessment procedures (and perhaps you have), what would you expect to be the effect on your learning? Do you think it might help you learn more? If so, how? What general lessons about the use of essay assessment can we learn from these examples?

The Impact.   The professor reports that scoring all responses to a single exercise together helps him to integrate assessment into instruction in another important way. After reading 50 attempts to solve a relatively complex classroom assessment problem, he assures me that he knows which facets of his instruction were effective and which were not. When his students successfully resolve the classroom assessment dilemma presented in an exercise, he reports, he uses this as evidence of his instruction's effectiveness. But when the professor has failed to set his students up for success in solving some kind of classroom assessment problem, it becomes painfully obvious in paper after paper. He knows without question which phase of instruction did not work. Next term, he revises instruction in the hope that his students will perform better on similar exercises.

The impact on students is clear, too. A high percentage of them do very well on these exams. They report that they spend more time on these exercises than on other exams, and that they truly must study, analyze, and reflect deeply on the material covered in class and required readings to find solutions to the problems presented. In addition, they welcome the opportunity to rework the material when necessary to score higher.

Without question, this particular professor's assessment and grading procedures will not work in all contexts. In a very real sense, he works in what most teachers would regard as an ideal world: a manageable number of students and few preparations.

However, my point in telling you this story is not to convince you to adopt his procedures. Rather, it is to make the point that *essay assessment can contribute to the effectiveness of a learning community in which teacher and students enter into a partnership with a mutual goal of maximum achievement.*

We will explore how you might do this in your classroom, given your realities.

The Foundations of Assessment Quality

To begin with, we need to think about two quality control factors that form the foundation of the appropriate use of this mode of assessment. First, certain realities of life in classrooms can and should contribute to your decision about when to use this option. You must know that the context is right.

Second, essay assessments represent the first of three assessment methods we will discuss over the next few chapters that are subjective by their very nature. You may recall that selected response assessments, we said, rely on matters of professional judgment in the setting of the target and design of the assessment exercises, but scoring typically is not a matter of judgment. By design, answers to well-constructed selected response items are right or wrong. The number of right answers produces a score that is not a matter of judgment, either. With essay assessments, professional judgment plays a big role in scoring, too.

Context Factors

Essay assessment is not for every teacher and every classroom. For instance, it cannot work in primary grades where students are not yet writers. So obviously, certain conditions need to be satisfied for it to fit into the assessment context. You will need to consider the classroom context factors delineated in Figure 6.2 before deciding whether the essay format is appropriate for the particular achievement target you are assessing. Attention to these factors will help you use this format most effectively.

> **TECHNICAL NOTE**
>
> When students are confronted with an assessment that relies on a means of communication that they cannot use, the results will misrepresent their achievement; they will be biased.

- *The respondents' level of writing proficiency*. This is absolutely critical. If students lack writing skill, it is impossible to use this mode of communication to gather useful information about their achievement. Writing proficiency is always confounded with achievement in this format. If students cannot write, we must select another method of assessment. It is the only fair way.

- *The availability of already developed high-quality essay exercises with associated scoring criteria*. If the work has already been done by you, your colleagues, or by the textbook author, and essays are ready to go, then go with them. Just be sure to verify quality.

- *The number of students to be evaluated*. The smaller the group, the shorter the overall time needed to do the scoring. The larger the group, the more time you need. Plan accordingly.

- *The number of exercises needed to sample the material and the length of responses to be read and scored*. The smaller the number of exercises needed to provide an adequate sample of material and the shorter the response, the less time will be needed for scoring. Most assessment experts recommend the use of more shorter exercises rather than fewer exercises requiring longer responses. The more exercises you use, the easier it is to sample the domain representatively.

- *The amount of person time available to read and evaluate responses*. This need not be only teacher time, although your time should be a major consideration. Sometimes, essay scoring support can come from students, teacher aides, or even from qualified parents. Be advised, however, of the two keys to being able to take advantage of such scoring assistance:

  1. Develop clear and appropriate scoring criteria and procedures.
  2. Train all scorers to apply those standards fairly and consistently.

Figure 6.2
Context factors in the use of essay assessment.

The Role of Teacher Judgment in Essay Assessment

In the case of essay tests, professional judgment plays a role in both development and scoring. This means there are more ways for unwanted bias to creep into the assessment results, placing the attainment of meaningful scores in jeopardy. That, in turn, means that users of this methodology must be doubly vigilant against potential problems. However, there are ways to create "subjective" (or judgmental) assessment tools in a systematic way that can ultimately make them one of the most versatile tools at our disposal.

Perhaps the most critical message of Part II of this book is this: *Assessments that rely on professional judgment to evaluate student work can produce dependable results leading to effective instruction only if they are carefully developed using proper assessment development procedures.*

In the case of essay assessments, teacher judgment is involved in the following aspects:

- Establishing the underlying achievement target
- Selecting the component parts of that target to include in the assessment
- Preparing essay exercises themselves
- Devising scoring criteria
- Conducting the scoring process itself

In the case of essay assessment, as with any form of assessment, the responsibility for avoiding problems and for ensuring quality rests squarely with you, the teacher! Those who thoroughly comprehend the content and patterns of reasoning to be mastered are in an excellent position to plan exercises and scoring schemes that fit the valued outcomes of instruction. It is only through developing and using strong exercises and appropriate scoring criteria that you may avoid errors in measuring student achievement attributable to evaluator or rater bias. These are the foundations of quality.

Matching Method to Target

Essay assessments have a potential contribution to make in assessing key dimensions of student learning in all five categories of valued targets, knowledge, reasoning, skills, products, and dispositions (affect).

Assessing Knowledge and Understanding

Most experts advise against using essays to assess student mastery of subject matter knowledge, when the targets are conceived of as specific facts or concepts students are to learn. The primary reason is that we have better options at our disposal for tapping this kind of outcome. Selected response assessment formats provide a more efficient means of assessment that, at the same time, allow for a more precise and controlled sampling of the achievement domain.

Selected response test formats are more efficient than essays in this case for two reasons. First, you can ask more multiple-choice questions than essay questions per unit of testing time because multiple-choice response time is so much shorter. So, you can provide a broader sample of performance per unit of time with selected response items than with essay exercises. Second, scoring selected response items is much faster than scoring essays.

Nevertheless, I argue in favor of using the essay format for assessing student mastery of content knowledge. Let me explain.

In discussing the design and development of selected response items, I described a planning process that began with a broad domain of content, divided into categories for the table of specifications. Then I suggested further subdividing these into collections of important propositions, any one of which might be transformed into a specifically focused test item. In such test development, elements of knowledge become quite narrow and disconnected from one another.

However, this is not the only way to conceive of the knowledge we want our students to master. We may also conceive of larger units of knowledge, each containing numerous important smaller elements within it that all relate to one another in some important way. For example, we might want students to know all of the parts of a particular ecosystem in science and to understand how they are related to one another. You might recall our Chapter 3 discussion of knowledge in terms of enduring principles, the understanding of which requires mastery of certain concepts that tie together certain facts. It is the *relationships among ideas* that are key. An essay assessment can help us evaluate student attainment of this depth of mastery.

Following is an example of such an exercise that a science teacher might use on a final exam in a biology course to find out if students know and understand the water cycle.

Describe how evaporation and condensation operate in the context of the water cycle. Be sure to include all key elements in the cycle and how they relate to one another. (20 points)

We can use such exercises in an open-book exam, too, if we wish to assess mastery of such complex understanding through the use of reference materials. With essay assessments, we are seeking a readout of the more complex cognitive map of the learner. One of the most common complaints against the selected response form of assessment is that it compartmentalizes learning too much—students demonstrate mastery of discrete bits of knowledge but need not integrate it into a larger whole. Students familiar with and expecting essay assessments know that such integration is important.

Assessing Reasoning

A real strength of essay assessment is in assessing reasoning proficiency. At assessment time, we can present complex problems that ask learners to bring their subject matter knowledge, understanding, and reasoning skills together to find a solution. In instances where we cannot directly observe knowledge application or can't see the mental process of reasoning unfold, we can ask students to describe the results of their reasoning in their essays. From this, we infer the state of their understanding and their ability to use it in problem-solving contexts.

We can ask them to analyze, compare, draw inferences, and/or think critically in virtually any subject matter area. Furthermore, we can pose problems that require integrating material from two or more subjects and/or applying more than one pattern of reasoning. The key question here would be, Do students know how and when to use the knowledge they have at their disposal to reason and solve problems? Here is an example from a "science, technology, and society" course taught by a middle school teacher:

> *Using what you know about the causes of air pollution in cities, propose two potentially useful solutions. Analyze each in terms of its strengths and weaknesses. (20 points)*

Remember, however, the keys to success in assessing student reasoning with essays are the same as the keys to success with selected response:

1. Assessors must possess a highly refined vision of what they mean by the terms "reasoning and problem solving." (We discuss this in detail in Chapter 9.)

2. Assessors must know how to translate that vision into clear, focused essay exercises and scoring criteria.

3. The exercises must present problems to students that are new at the time of the assessment (i.e., problems for which students must figure out a response on the spot).

Assessing Performance Skills

If our valued achievement target holds that students become proficient in demonstrating specific performance skills, then there is only one acceptable way to assess proficiency: we must observe actual performance and judge its quality. For instance, say we want to find out if students can perform certain complex behaviors, such as participating collaboratively in a group, communicating orally in a second language, debating a controversial issue in social studies, or carrying out the steps in a science experiment. In these cases, standards of sound assessment require that we give students the opportunity to demonstrate group participation skills, speak the language, debate, or conduct an actual lab experiment.

There is no way to use an essay to assess these kinds of performances. An essay exercise would not be and could not be "authentic." It would not, could not, accurately depict real performance.

However, there are some important related outcomes that we can tap with the essay format. For instance, we can use the essay to assess mastery of some of the complex knowledge, understanding, and even problem-solving proficiencies prerequisite to performing the skill in question.

For example, if students do not know and understand the functions of different pieces of science lab equipment, there is no way that they will successfully complete the lab work. We could devise an essay question to see if they have mastered that prerequisite knowledge and understanding. Thus, we could use the essay format to assess student attainment of some of the building blocks of performance skill competence.

Assessing Products

Again in this case, if our valued target holds that students be able to create a specified kind of product that reflects certain attributes (such as a model, a craft product, or an artistic creation), the only high-fidelity way to assess the outcome is to have them actually create the product—a performance assessment. Only then can we evaluate it according to established standards of quality.

However, essays can provide insight into whether students know and understand the attributes of or steps in the process of creating a quality product. The results of such an essay assessment might be useful in a classroom context where we are working on building the foundations of competence. We can use essay assessments in these contexts, however, only if we remain constantly aware of the fact that being able to write about a good product and being able to create that product are different things.

Assessing Writing as a Product   One kind of product we often ask students to create is samples of their writing. Without question, student responses to essay exercises do represent original written constructions, and we therefore can evaluate them in terms of the demonstrated writing proficiency. However, in this context we *must* be sure not to confound our content and/or reasoning criteria with our criteria for good writing. They are not the same. We must make sure our students know which criteria are important in *all* contexts.

Most often, we evaluate writing proficiency by using more formal and systematic writing assessments, research report assignments, term papers, and so on. It is tempting to think of a term paper as just a long essay assessment tapping mastery of larger knowledge structures and/or complex thinking.

However, these bigger written products are different from responses to essay exercises, largely because of subtle but important differences in the nature of the criteria we use to evaluate each.

When students write in response to an essay exercise, we evaluate in terms of criteria that focus on their mastery of the kind(s) of content and/or reasoning needed to answer the question adequately. In this case, writing is the tool we use to gather evidence of mastery—it is not the focus of the assessment. It is the substantial ideas found in the writing, the ideas expressed, that go under the microscope.

But when writing is the medium used to produce a term paper or research report, the criteria used to evaluate performance typically include issues of form as well as those of content. When students use written language as a medium of communication, we also may evaluate their writing in terms of organization, sentence fluency, word choice, voice (i.e., the extent to which the writer's personality comes through to the reader), and other important factors.

Further, we can evaluate research reports and term papers in terms of presentation format, use of graphs and tables, and use and citation of references. When matters of form come into play, I think of writing as an achievement-related product and my list of key aspects of good performance begins to grow. We will discuss this more in Chapter 7.

Assessing Dispositions

Students' writing can also provide a window into their motivations or attitudes. When we ask them specific questions about the direction and intensity of their feelings about focused aspects of their schooling, in an environment where honesty is accepted, students can and will inform us about their attitudes, interests, and levels of motivation. Questionnaires containing open-ended questions can produce student responses that are full of profoundly important insights into the affective and social climate of a school or classroom.

Chapter 11 deals in detail with issues and procedures related to assessing dispositions using this and other methods.

Summary of Target Matches

On the whole, essay assessment is a very flexible option. It can provide useful information on a variety of targets. We can use it to evaluate student mastery of larger structures of knowledge, whether learned outright or mastered through the use of reference materials. We certainly can tap student reasoning and problem-solving skills. We can assess mastery of the complex procedural knowledge that is prerequisite to skilled performance and/or the creation of quality products. And finally, we also can explore student motivations and attitudes in rich and useful ways through student writing. Table 6.1 provides a quick summary.

Developing Essay Assessments

We are about to begin the section of this chapter dealing with designing and developing sound essay exercises and scoring criteria. Before we do, please do the following two things:

Time for Reflection

Important activities to complete before reading on:
  1. Draft an essay exercise that could appear on a final exam on this
     chapter of this book that asks respondents to describe the relationships

*among essay assessment and the various achievement targets:
knowledge, problem solving, and so on. Also, draft a scoring guide for
your exercise. Be sure both your exercise and scoring guide are as
complete as you can make them.*

*Keep these drafts handy, and refer to them as we discuss procedures for
developing and scoring essay assessments. The purpose for this exercise
is to provide you with an opportunity to try this before learning some of
the intricacies of essay development. This will create a context within
which you may understand the design suggestions offered. So don't read
on until you do this work!*

*2. As you read, collect a list of ideas for how you might involve your
students in essay assessment development and use in ways that will
maximize their learning and make this labor-intensive assessment
method easier for you to apply in your classroom.*

Designing and developing essay assessments involves three steps:

1. Assessment planning
2. Exercise development
3. Scoring preparation

Test planning for this form of assessment is very much like planning selected response assessments. While exercise development is a bit easier, scoring preparation is much more challenging.

Assessment Planning

The challenge, as always, is to begin with clearly articulated achievement targets. In this case, the target will reflect both the components of knowledge and the patterns of reasoning respondents must master. Consequently, once again we have the option of starting with either a table of test specifications or a list of instructional objectives.

Table 6.1
Essay: Assessment of achievement targets

Target to Be Assessed	Essay
Knowledge & Understanding	Essay exercises can tap understanding of relationships among elements of knowledge
Reasoning Proficiency	Written descriptions of complex problem solutions can provide a window into reasoning proficiency
Performance Skills	Can assess mastery of the knowledge prerequisites to skillful performance, but cannot rely on these to tap the skill itself
Ability to Create Products	Can assess writing proficiency and mastery of the knowledge necessary to create other products
Dispositions	Open-ended questionnaire items can probe dispositions

Tables of specifications for essay tests are like those used for selected response assessments in some ways, and different in others. The similarities lie in the basic framework. Table 6.2 is an example of such a table for an essay test covering material on a series of short stories read in class. As the developer of such a table, I must specify the categories of knowledge respondents will use on one axis and the patterns of reasoning I expect on the other. Row and column totals, and therefore entries in the cells of the table, once again represent the relative emphasis assigned to each.

However, with the essay table of specifications, cells each contain the number of points on the test that I have assigned to that content-reasoning combination, not the number of individual test items, as was the case in Chapter 5. When I actually construct the test, I might spread those points over one or more exercises associated with each cell.

Given 100 points for the entire exam, this plan obviously emphasizes the understanding of characters relative to the other two categories, requiring that respondents rely on that understanding to compare and evaluate. If I were to use exercises valued at 10 points each, I would need 10 exercises distributed so as to reflect these priorities.

I could translate these same values into instructional objectives, if I wish, as shown in the following list. I list these sample objectives simply to illustrate a second way of capturing and communicating the meaning of academic success reflected in the cells of the table. I need not do both the table and the objectives, but may select one or the other as a means of reflecting my valued outcomes.

- Students will be able to describe the settings, characters, and plots of the stories.
- Students will be able to infer similarities and differences in settings, plots, and characters.
- Students will be able to carry out a systematic evaluation of the quality of the stories.

Exercise Development

Essay exercises should pose problems for students to solve. But what are the attributes of a sound exercise?

One of my graduate students once described an exercise he received on a final exam at the end of his undergraduate studies. He had majored for four years in

Table 6.2
Sample table of test specifications

Content	Number of Points			
	Know	Compare	Evaluate	Total
Setting	5	15	10	30
Plot	10	10	10	30
Characters	0	20	20	40
Total	15	45	40	100

Spanish language, literature, and culture. His last final was an in-class essay exam with a 3-hour time limit. The entire exam consisted of one exercise, which posed the challenge in only two words: "Discuss Spain."

Obviously, he would have preferred a bit more detail. But haven't we all had experiences like this? One of the advantages often listed for essay tests relative to other test formats is that exercises are much easier and take less time to develop. I submit that many users turn that advantage into a liability by assuming that "easier to develop" means they don't have to put much thought into it, as evidenced in the previous example.

Another common mistake teachers make is trying to turn an essay exercise into a demonstration of their creativity. A scientist friend offered an example from his experience as a college student: "Take a walk through a late Mesozoic forest and tell me what you see." This is better than "Discuss Spain." However, even more specification is needed to set respondents up for success.

To succeed with this assessment format, we must invest thoughtful preparation time in writing exercises that challenge respondents by describing a single complete and novel task. Sound exercises do three things:

1. *Specify the knowledge students are supposed to command in preparing a response.*   For example:

During the term, we have discussed both the evolution of Spanish literature and the changing political climate in Spain during the twentieth century.

2. *Specify the kind(s) of reasoning or problem solving respondents are to carry out.*   Be clear about what respondents are to write about. For example:

During the term, we have discussed both the evolution of Spanish literature and the changing political climate in Spain during the twentieth century. Analyze these two dimensions of life in Spain, citing three instances where literature and politics may have influenced each other. Describe the mutual influences in specific terms.

3. *Point the direction to an appropriate response without giving away the answer.*   Good exercises literally list the key elements of a good response without cueing the unprepared examinee on how to succeed:

During the term, we have discussed both the evolution of Spanish literature and the changing political climate in Spain during the twentieth century. Analyze these two dimensions of life in Spain, citing three instances where you think literature and politics may have influenced each other. Describe the mutual influences in specific terms. In planning your response, think about what we learned about prominent novelists, political satirists, and prominent political figures of Spain. (5 points per instance, total = 15 points.)

Let's analyze the content of the example given at the beginning of the chapter, reproduced here.

> Assume you are a French teacher with many years of teaching experience. You place great value on the development of speaking proficiency as an outcome of your instruction. Therefore, you rely heavily on assessments where you listen to and evaluate performance. But a problem has arisen. Parents of students who attained very high scores on your written tests are complaining that their children are receiving lower grades on their report cards. The principal wants to be sure your judgments of student proficiency are sound and so has asked you to explain and defend your procedures. Describe at least three specific quality standards that your oral proficiency exams would need to meet for you to be confident that your exams truly reflect what students can do; provide the rationale for each. (2 points for each procedure and rationale, total = 6 points.)

Here's the challenge to respondents in a nutshell:

Demonstrate understanding of:	Performance assessment methodology
By using it to figure out:	Proper applications of the method in a specific context
Adhering to these standards:	Include three appropriate procedures and defend them

Time for Reflection

Please return to the essay exercise you developed at the beginning of this section of the chapter. Did you specify the knowledge respondents must use, kinds(s) of reasoning they must employ, and standards they must apply? Adjust your exercise as needed to meet these standards.

Another good way to check the quality of your essay exercises is to try to write or outline a quality response yourself. If you can, you probably have a properly focused exercise. If you cannot, it needs work.

Incidentally, when I use essays, I like to make it clear to my students that *I care far more about the content of their answer than its form*. I urge them to communicate their understanding and problem solutions to me as efficiently as they can, so I can read and score their responses as fast as possible. I urge them to use outlines and lists of ideas, examples, illustrations, charts, whatever it takes to come to the point quickly and clearly. I do not require the use of connected discourse unless it is needed to communicate their solution to the problem. I explain that I do not want them beating around the bush in the hope that somewhere, somehow, they say something worth a point or two. Believe me, this suggestion makes scoring so much easier!

Figure 6.3
Factors to consider when devising essay exercises

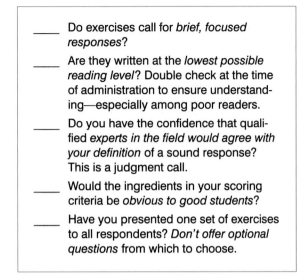

_____ Do exercises call for *brief, focused responses*?

_____ Are they written at the *lowest possible reading level*? Double check at the time of administration to ensure understanding—especially among poor readers.

_____ Do you have the confidence that qualified *experts in the field would agree with your definition* of a sound response? This is a judgment call.

_____ Would the ingredients in your scoring criteria be *obvious to good students*?

_____ Have you presented one set of exercises to all respondents? *Don't offer optional questions* from which to choose.

Figure 6.3 presents a checklist of factors to think about as you devise essay exercises. Answering these questions should assist you in constructing effective, high-quality essay exercises—those that avoid bias and distortion.

In regard to the inclusion of the last point in Figure 6.3, don't offer choices: The assessment question should always be, "Can you hit the agreed-on target?" It should never be, "Which part of the agreed-on target are you most confident that you can hit?" This latter question will always leave you uncertain about whether students have in fact mastered the material covered in exercises not selected, some of which may be crucial to later learning. When students select their own sample of performance, it can be a biased one.

Here is a final idea for exercise development: If you wish to use the essay format to assess reasoning skills, but you are not sure all students have a sufficient or equal grasp of the underlying body of knowledge, provide the knowledge needed to solve the problem and see if they can use it appropriately. This is another instance where you can use the interpretive exercise format discussed in Chapter 5. Simply provide a chart, graph, table, or paragraph of connected discourse and spin an essay or essays out of the material presented, as shown in the following example.*

> As master of the achievement domain you, not your students, should determine the sampling frame. Offering a choice of exercises is generous, but it also can lead to an invalid assessment.
>
> TECHNICAL NOTE

*Item reprinted from *Explaining American History* (p. 303) by M. Swartz and J. R. O'Connor, 1986, Englewood Cliffs, NJ: Globe. Copyright 1986 by Globe. Reprinted by permission.

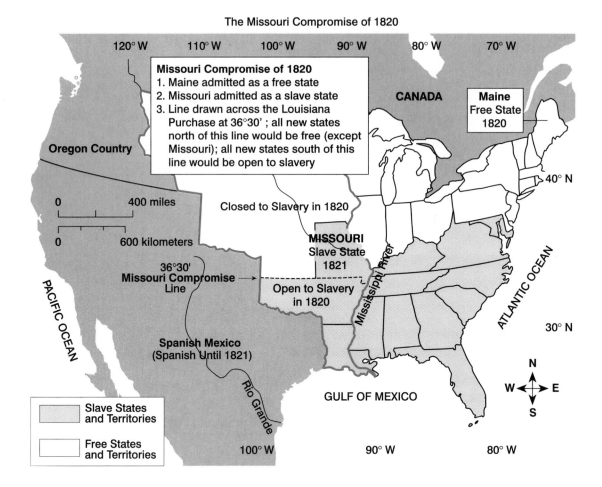

The Missouri Compromise of 1820

Missouri Compromise of 1820
1. Maine admitted as a free state
2. Missouri admitted as a slave state
3. Line drawn across the Louisiana Purchase at 36°30' ; all new states north of this line would be free (except Missouri); all new states south of this line would be open to slavery

Map Skills: The Compromise of 1820

Study the map. Then decide whether these statements are true or false. Explain your choice in a brief essay.

1. Most of the Louisiana Purchase was open to slavery.
2. Missouri was south of the line marked at 36 degrees, 30 minutes.
3. Missouri was admitted to the United States as a slave state.
4. The Mississippi River divided the free and slave territories.
5. The southwest boundary of the United States in 1820 was the Rio Grande.

Note here that "brief" essays are requested. These require only the most efficient explanation of the respondent's defense. If it's true, state why in the simplest possible terms. If it's false, again, defend your position. In some contexts extended responses are not needed to present convincing evidence of competence.

But whether we seek extended or short answers to essay exercises, we must conduct the scoring process with clearly articulated evaluative criteria in mind.

Developing Essay Scoring Procedures

Many teachers score essays by applying what I call "floating standards," in which you wait to see what responses you get to decide what you wanted. The perceived benefits of this method, I fear, are that students always appear to have achieved and will be motivated to continue learning. But this does not represent good teaching, good assessment, or sound motivation.

In that regard, I hope you will adhere to the instructional and assessment philosophy that has guided everything we have discussed up to this point: *Students can succeed if they know what it means to succeed*. State the meaning of success up front, design instruction to help students succeed, and devise and use assessments that reflect those stated standards. That includes formulating essay scoring criteria in advance and holding yourself and your students accountable for attaining those standards.

Essay scoring is a classic example of one of the most important reasoning patterns: evaluative or critical reasoning. In evaluative reasoning, one expresses one's opinion about something and defends it through the logical application of specified criteria. Theater critics evaluate plays according to certain (rarely agreed on!) criteria and publish their reviews in the newspaper. Movie critics give thumbs up or down (an evaluative judgment) and use their criteria to explain why.

These are exactly the kinds of evaluative judgments teachers must make about responses to essay exercises, as presented in this chapter, and to observed performance skill and achievement-related products, as discussed in Chapter 7. In all cases, the key to success is the clear articulation of appropriate performance criteria.

Scoring Options.   Typically, we convey evaluative judgments about essay quality in terms of the number of points attained on the exercises. Here are two acceptable ways to do this, the checklist and the rating scale.

The Checklist.   We award points when specific ingredients appear in students' answers. The French teacher example that appeared earlier in the chapter provides an example of this kind of scoring. The scoring guide calls for respondents to cover certain material. They receive points for each key point they cover. Here is the scoring guide again:

Score Responses as Follows:

2 points if the student's response lists any of these six procedures and defends each as a key to conducting sound performance assessments:

- Specify clear performance criteria
- Sample performance over several exercises
- Apply systematic rating procedures

- Maintain complete and accurate records
- Use published performance assessments to verify results of classroom assessments
- Use multiple observers to corroborate

Also award 2 points if the response lists any of the following and defends them as attributes of sound assessments:

- Specifies a clear instructional objective
- Relies on a proper assessment method
- Samples performance well
- Controls for sources of rater bias

All other responses receive no points.

Realize that, in the case of checklist scoring, each scoring guide will detail exercise-specific scoring criteria. That is, each exercise will be accompanied by its own unique scoring guide identifying the specific content ingredients required to respond well to that particular exercise. This is as opposed to a generic scoring guide that can be applied to a range of essays. Rating scales, on the other hand, can be generic.

The Rating Scale.   In this case, we define achievement in terms of one or more performance continua; for example, a five-point rating scale defines five levels of performance and we would use carefully thought-out criteria to place each student's response along that scale. Here's an example. Be advised that it is acceptable to leave points 2 and 4 to interpolate if the response falls between two score points.

5	The response is clear, focused, and accurate. Relevant points are made (in terms of the kinds of reasoning sought by the exercise) with good support (derived from the content to be used, again as spelled out in the exercise). Good connections are drawn and important insights are evident.
3	The answer is clear and somewhat focused, but not compelling. Support of points made is limited. Connections are fuzzy, leading to few important insights.
1	The response either misses the point, contains inaccurate information, or otherwise demonstrates lack of mastery of the material. Points are unclear, support is missing, and/or no insights are included.

Some teachers devise such rating scales to apply in a "holistic" manner, like this example. In this case, one overall judgment captures the teacher's evaluation of the essay. Other times teachers devise multiple "analytical" scales for the same essay, permitting them to evaluate the content coverage of the response separately from other important features. The idea is to develop as many such scales as needed to evaluate the particular material you are rating. Criteria for ratings, for example, might include these factors:

- demonstrated mastery of content
- organization of ideas
- soundness of the reasoning demonstrated

Whether using holistic or analytical scales, however, the more specific and focused the criteria, the more dependable will be the results.

Clearly, the rating scale option is more subjective than the checklist option for awarding points. However, if you have done the following three things, your generic rating scales can serve as excellent tools for evaluating essay responses:

1. Define the meaning of student success in terms of such scales in advance of assessment.
2. Provide examples to your students illustrating the differences between sound and unsound performance.
3. Provide students with guided practice in performing successfully according to your generic criteria.

Obviously, these tactics can't work with exercise-specific checklist scoring criteria. In those cases, I recommend that you involve your students with some practice exercises and scoring guides similar to those that will appear on the exam. This orients them to your expectations.

In addition to these essay scoring guidelines, experts urge that you adhere to the additional principles outlined in Figure 6.4 as you develop and apply scoring procedures.

Time for Reflection

Please return to the scoring plan you developed for your exercise at the beginning of this discussion. Did you devise a clear and appropriate set of standards? Adjust them as needed.

Barriers to Sound Essay Assessment

To summarize, you can do many things to cause a student's score on an essay test to represent that student's real level of achievement with a high degree of accuracy. Potential sources of mismeasurement appear in Figure 6.5, along with action you can take to ensure sound assessment.

- Set *realistic expectations and performance standards* that are consistent with instruction and that promise students some measure of success if they are prepared.
- Check scoring guides against a few real responses to see if any *last-minute adjustments* are needed.
- *Refer back to scoring guidelines* regularly during scoring to maintain consistency.
- *Score all responses to one exercise* before moving on to the next exercise. This does two things: It promotes consistency in your application of standards, and speeds up the scoring process.
- Score all responses to one exercise *in one sitting without interruption* to keep a clear focus on standards.
- Evaluate responses *separately for matters of content (knowledge mastery and reasoning) and matters of form (i.e., writing proficiency)*. They require the application of different criteria.
- Provide feedback in the form of *points and written commentary* if possible.
- If possible, keep the *identity of the respondent anonymous* when scoring. This keeps your knowledge of their prior performance from influencing current judgments.
- Although it is often difficult to arrange, try to have *two independent qualified readers score* the papers. In a sense, this represents the litmus test of the quality of your scoring scheme. If two readers generally agree on the level of proficiency demonstrated by the respondent, then you have evidence of relatively objective or dependable subjective scoring. But if you and a colleague disagree on the level of performance demonstrated, you have uncovered evidence of problems in the appropriateness of the criteria or the process used to train raters, and some additional work is in order. When very important decisions rest on a student's score on an essay assessment, such as promotion or graduation, double scoring is absolutely essential.

Figure 6.4
Guidelines for essay scoring

Student Involvement in Essay Assessment

Time for Reflection

Have you been collecting your list of possible ideas for student involvement? If so, review your list before you proceed. If not, before you read further, take a minute to think more about this. What specific ways can you devise to bring your students into your essay assessment development and use?

With all assessment methods, the first and most obvious way to integrate assessment into teaching and learning is to match assessment to instruction by being sure that what you assess is what you teach, and what your students (hopefully) learn. In the context of standards-based education, students deserve practice hitting the very targets for which they will be held accountable. Similarly, as a teacher,

Potential Sources of Problems	Counteraction
Lack of target clarity:	
• Underlying knowledge unclear	Carefully study the material to be mastered and outline the knowledge structures to assess.
• Patterns of reasoning unspecified	Define forms of reasoning to be assessed in clear terms (see Chapter 9 for examples).
Wrong target for essay	Limit use to assessing mastery of larger knowledge structures (where several parts must fit together) and complex reasoning.
Lack of writing proficiency on part of respondents	Select another assessment method or help them become proficient writers.
Inadequate sample of exercises	Select a representative sample of sufficient length to give you confidence, given your table of specifications.
Poor-quality exercises	Follow guidelines specified above.
Poor-quality scoring:	
• Inappropriate criteria	Redefine criteria to fit the content and reasoning expected.
• Unclear criteria	Prepare explicit expectations—in writing.
• Untrained rater	All who are to apply the scoring criteria must be prepared to do so.
• Insufficient time to read and rate	Find more raters (see Figure 6.6 for ideas), or use another method.

Figure 6.5
Avoiding problems

you deserve to be held accountable for your students' success in attaining those specified, agreed-on outcomes.

Beyond this essential perspective, Figure 6.6 presents additional ways to integrate assessment with instruction by involving students as full partners in assessing their own and each other's achievement.

This figure is intended to present enough ideas to prime the pump, but it is only a start. The list of ways to bring students into the assessment equation is as endless as your imagination. Please reflect and experiment, and find more ways. These uses of essay assessment development all contribute to that huge key to student success: making the target crystal clear for them to see and hit. These strategies serve to remove the mystery surrounding the meaning of good performance on an essay and in the classroom. They put students in control of their own academic well-being.

- As with selected response assessment, develop a blueprint for an essay test before ever teaching a unit, share that plan with students, and keep track of how well instruction is preparing them to succeed on the exam.

- Present students with unlabeled essay exercises and have them practice fitting them into the content and reasoning cells of the table of specifications.

- Have students join in on the process of writing sample exercises. To do so, they will need to begin to sharpen their focus on the intended knowledge and reasoning targets—as they do this, good teaching is happening! Be careful, though, these might best be used as examples for practice. Remember, to assess student reasoning, the exercises that actually appear on a test must present novel problems.

- Give students some sample exercises and have them evaluate their quality as test exercises, given the test blueprint.

- Have students play a role in developing the scoring criteria for some sample exercises. Give them, for example, an excellent response and a poor-quality response to a past essay exercise and have them figure out the differences.

- Bring students into the actual scoring process, thus spreading the work over more shoulders! Form scoring teams, one for each exercise on a test. Have them develop scoring criteria under your watchful eye. Offer them advice as needed to generate appropriate criteria. Then have them actually score some essays, which you double check. Discuss differences in scores assigned. Students find this kind of workshop format very engaging.

- Have students predict their performance in each cell in the table of specifications or objectives and then compare their prediction with the actual score. Were they in touch with their own achievement?

- Save essays and scoring criteria for reuse. A personal computer can help with this. If you keep information on student performance on each record (say, average score), you can adjust instruction next time to try to improve learning.

- Exchange, trade, or compare tables of specifications and/or exercises and scoring criteria with other teachers to ease the workload associated with assessment development.

Figure 6.6
Ideas for student-involved assessment

Summary: Tapping the Potential of Essays

We all have heard those stories about the same essays being given to several college professors, who assigned vastly different grades to the same pieces of work. These stories often are cited as indictments of the essay form of assessment. This is unfair.

The reasons the professors disagreed on the level of proficiency demonstrated were that they had no opportunity to discuss and arrive at common expectations. There was no development of a common view of what it meant to perform well, no communication, no preparation to devise sound exercises and to score dependably. As a result, there was no common basis for assigning grades.

If two assessors independently evaluate the same student work and agree on the level of proficiency demonstrated by each student, then that assessment is said to possess a high level of **INTER-RATER RELIABILITY**

These stories reflect supremely poor applications of a potentially sound, rich, and powerful assessment method. When placed in the hands of teachers and students who know what they are doing, essay assessments, like selected response assessments and the other methods yet to be discussed, can unlock and promote effective teaching and learning.

In this chapter, we have explored ways to tap this power by preventing many of the quality control problems that can arise in the context of naive use. We began by exploring the prominent roles in essay assessment of informed subjectivity and professional judgment. This prominence means that this method carries with it dangers of bias. We studied specific ways to prevent these dangers from becoming realities. One is to connect essay assessment to appropriate kinds of achievement targets. These include mastery of complex structures of knowledge, complex reasoning processes, some of the knowledge foundations of skill and product proficiencies, and affective outcomes.

However, the heart of the matter with respect to quality assessment is adherence to specific assessment development procedures. We studied these in three parts: assessment planning, exercise development, and preparation to score. In each case, we reviewed specific procedural guidelines.

As in Chapter 5, we closed with an array of strategies to engage students as full partners in assessment, from design and development of exercises, to scoring, to interpreting and using essay assessment results. These strategies connect assessment to teaching and learning in ways that can maximize both students' motivation to learn and their actual achievement.

Exercises for Self-Assessment

1. Refer back to the text and list three reasons for using essay assessments.

2. Summarize from memory three basic steps in essay assessment development.

3. What kinds of achievement targets can be transformed into the essay assessment format? What kinds cannot? Review the text if necessary to find the answers, then learn them outright.

4. What factors should you take into account when considering using essay assessment? Again, learn this outright. These considerations are very important.

5. Make a one-page chart with three columns listing your own tailor-made abbreviations of the information presented in Table 6.1 and in Figures 6.3, 6.4, and 6.5. Keep this handy for easy reference when you use essay assessment.

6. Write three essay exercises that tap dimensions of this chapter. When you have done so, review the list and ask yourself whether these really represent the most important learnings from this chapter.

7. Devise scoring schemes for each of your exercises.

You may go to the Companion Website at www.prenhall.com/stiggins and answer these questions in the Self-Assessment module.

Final Chapter Reflection

1. *What are the three most important new insights to come to you as a result of your study of this chapter?*

2. *Which of your previous questions about assessment can you now answer based on your study of this chapter?*

3. *What new questions have come to mind as a result of your study of this chapter that you hope to have answered as your study continues?*

4. *For practicing teachers only: What do you plan to do differently in assessment in your classroom as a result of your study of this book so far?*

   For those in preservice study only: As you think about the classroom assessment environment that you hope to create for your students, how has your thinking changed as a result of your study of this book so far?

Workbook Activities

Those of you using the workbook, *Practice with Student-Involved Classroom Assessment*, as part of your study of this material will find the following activities and others included for Chapter 6:

- *Accounting For More.* This case study is good for activating your prior knowledge of essay exams. The case brings up a situation familiar to all teachers—problems with scoring essays.

- *When to Use Essay.* This activity gives you practice in deciding when an essay format would be a match to targets and contextual factors.

- *Practice Analyzing Essay Questions.* This activity provides practice in analyzing existing essay questions for quality. Are the needed components there? Is essay the best match? What are the reasoning and knowledge targets to be assessed? You can use the supplied essay questions and/or find your own examples.

- *Assessing Conceptual Understanding.* Essay questions require performance criteria for judging the quality of responses. Sometimes what is assessed is conceptual understanding. This activity gives you practice in scoring student essays in math for conceptual understanding.

Video Support

The ATI interactive video training package, *Common Sense Paper and Pencil Assessments*, reinforces much of what is covered in the text about essay assessment, with several opportunities for specific practice.

Performance Assessment: Rich with Possibilities

This chapter answers the following guiding question:

> When and how do I use performance assessment most effectively?

You will come to understand the following principles from your study of this chapter:

1. Performance assessments permit you to rely on professional judgment to gather evidence of student reasoning proficiency, performance skills, and product development capabilities.

2. You can effectively develop performance assessments in two steps: (1) defining performance criteria; and (2) developing performance tasks or exercises.

3. This method can fall prey to avoidable sources of bias that can distort results if users are not careful.

4. By involving your students in developing and using performance assessments, you can set them up for energetic and successful learning.

As we start this part of our journey, keep our big picture in mind. Figure 7.1 crosses our achievement targets with the four modes of assessment. In this chapter, we will be dealing in depth with the shaded areas.

	SELECTED RESPONSE	ESSAY	PERFORMANCE ASSESSMENT	PERSONAL COMMUNICATION
Know				
Reason				
Skills				
Products				
Dispositions				

Figure 7.1

Aligning achievement targets and assessment methods

Assessment Based on Observation and Professional Judgment

Over the past decade, the education community has discovered the great potential of performance assessment. These assessments involve students in activities that require them to demonstrate mastery of certain performance skills or their ability to create products that meet certain standards of quality. In this case, we rely on evaluator judgment to help us tap complex achievement targets that cannot be translated into selected response or essay tests.

With performance assessments, we observe students while they are performing or we examine the products they create and evaluate the level of proficiency demonstrated. As with essay assessments, we make our subjective judgments of level of achievement by comparing student performance to predetermined standards of excellence. Our goal is to make these subjective judgments as objective (free of bias and distortion) as they can be. We accomplish this by relying on a sufficient number of quality performance tasks to sample achievement and by devising and learning to apply clear and appropriate performance criteria.

To illustrate, visualize a middle school science teacher asking students to build mousetrap cars to determine the extent to which they understand and can apply principles of energy utilization. (*Mousetrap cars* are vehicles powered by one snap of a spring-loaded mousetrap.) The goals are to (1) see who can design a car that can travel the farthest by converting "one snap of energy" into forward motion, and

(2) to help students understand the scientific principles involved. When the criteria are clear and the teacher understands how to apply them consistently, she can help students understand, not just which car won, but why—that is, how it used energy most productively.

Table 7.1 lists other examples of achievement targets that lend themselves to performance assessment. Notice that every academic discipline includes both skills and products for which we can establish performance criteria we can observe and judge. But to assess them accurately, we must be careful to zero in on the right standards of excellent performance. This chapter is about how to do that.

Although performance assessment methodology has arrived on the scene over the past few years with a flash of brilliance unprecedented since the advent of selected response test formats six decades ago, please understand that there is nothing new about performance assessment. This is not some kind of radical invention recently fabricated by opponents of traditional tests to challenge the testing industry. Rather, it is a proven method of evaluating human characteristics that has *Pit around for centuries* been in use for decades (See Linquist, 1951, and Berk, 1986, for example), for centuries, perhaps for millennia. For how long have we observed and evaluated political oratory, athletic performance, and the quality of art products, for example?

My goals for this chapter are to describe and illustrate a basic performance assessment design structure and to reveal the power of student involvement in the process. In later chapters, we will explore many more classroom applications. Chapter 9, for example, addresses performance assessment of reasoning proficiency, while Chapter 10 illustrates using performance assessment to evaluate a variety of skills and products.

Table 7.1
Achievement targets for performance assessment

Focus of Assessment	Process or Skill Target	Product Target
Reading	Oral reading fluency	Picture depicting the story
Writing	Cursive writing skill	Samples of writing
Mathematics	Manipulate objects to form sets	Model depicting math principle
Science	Lab safety procedures	Lab research report
Social Studies	Debate	Term paper
Foreign Language	Oral fluency	Model depicting cultural awareness
Art	Use of materials	Artistic creation
Physical Education	Athletic performance	Picture or diagram of quality performance
Technical Education	Computer operation	Software system designed
Vocational Education	Following prescribed procedures	Effectively repaired machine
Teamwork	Each member's contribution	Final team product
Early childhood	Social interaction skill	Artistic creation

The Promise and Perils of Performance Assessment

Proponents of performance assessment contend that, just as high-fidelity musical reproductions provide rich and accurate representations of the original music, so too can performance assessments provide high-resolution representations of those forms of achievement that stretch into life beyond school (Wiggins, 1993).

At the same time, there can be no question that performance assessment brings with it great technical challenges. This is a difficult methodology to develop and use well (Dunbar, Koretz, & Hoover, 1991). Virtually every bit of research and development done in education and business over the past decades leads to the same conclusion: Performance assessment is complex. It requires users to prepare and conduct their assessments in a thoughtful and rigorous manner. Those unwilling to invest the necessary time and energy will place their students directly in harm's way.

In this sense, performance assessment methodology is best kept in perspective. It is neither the best of all assessment methods nor is it so challenging to use that it is beyond your reach as a teacher. It is but one tool among many capable of providing effective and efficient means of assessing some of our most highly valued achievement targets. In that sense, it is a valuable tool indeed—in the hands of a competent user.

To be sure, there is nothing in this chapter that you cannot master quite easily. But don't take this methodology lightly. Just because it is subjective does not mean that we're talking about "assessment by guess and by gosh" here. There is no place in performance assessment for "intuitions" or ethereal "feelings" about student achievement. It is not acceptable for a teacher to claim to just "know" a student can do it. Credible evidence is required. It takes thorough preparation and attention to detail to attain appropriate levels of performance assessment rigor.

> *When we venture into the ethereal world of assessments that take the form of our* TECHNICAL NOTE *intuitions or feelings about student achievement, we face the greatest danger of making biased judgments that result in unreliable assessments.*

Adhere to the standards of assessment quality spelled out in earlier chapters when developing performance assessment and you can add immensely to the quality and utility of your classroom assessments. Remember, you must begin assessment development with a clear purpose and a focused vision of the achievement you are assessing. Then you must select a proper target, devise a proper sample of performance tasks, and control for all relevant sources of bias. Violate those rules (which is very easy to do in this case!) and you place your students' academic success in jeopardy.

Time for Reflection

Performance assessments are based on observation and judgment. In this case, evaluators see performance and apply standards or criteria of excellence to evaluate the level of proficiency the performer demonstrates. Can you think of instances in everyday life (outside of the school setting) where

*this mode of assessment comes into play as a matter of routine? For exam-
ple, supervisors observe and evaluate workers' performance on the job. We
observe and even operate various automobiles as we prepare to purchase
one. Can you think of other examples? Keep a few in mind as we discuss
effectively developing performance assessments for use in the classroom.*

[handwritten: Restaurants, movies / TV]

The Foundations of Quality

Once again in this case, as with selected response and essay assessment, we begin
by discussing two quality control factors that form the foundation of the appropriate use of this mode of assessment. First, certain realities of life in classrooms can
and should contribute to your decision about when to use this option. You must
know that the context is right.

Second, we must address the role of informed subjectivity and professional
judgment in creating and using performance assessments.

Context Factors

Obviously, you will want to turn to performance assessment for certain kinds of
achievement targets, like complex reasoning and problem solving, performance
skills, and product development targets. But there are other practical considerations as well.

Performance assessment is appropriate only when you can control the display
of proficiency in ways that protect students' academic self-concept. There is the
danger that the need to perform before others or display products for others to see
can raise students' anxiety to a level that distorts their performance. This requires
that you create a place for such assessments that students regard as safe, or that
you protect each student's privacy by restricting access to their work.

[handwritten: environ.]

In addition, you must be sure that each student has the opportunity to succeed. That is, all must have equal access to the resources and equipment needed to
succeed. This may mean that each student has access to materials provided at
school or to resources that you expect them to obtain at home. If circumstances
beyond their control keep them from succeeding, that's not fair.

[handwritten: success]

Consider performance assessment only when there is time to conduct it. It is a
labor-intensive method. The more students you need to evaluate, the less attractive
this option is. The more performance tasks you need to administer, the
longer the per student time cost will be and the less feasible this method
will be. Remember, one solution to a time crunch is to involve more
observers and evaluators; such as, for example, (dare I say) your students. . . .

[handwritten: Students as evaluators]

Give careful consideration to using this method when you have access to previously developed, high-quality performance tasks and scoring guides. Many are available these days. Just be sure to verify quality.

Turn to performance assessment when you have the opportunity to use it, not merely as a source of test scores—of data—but also as an instructional strategy. Perhaps the most powerful application of this method is in contexts where you can take your students inside the assessment development itself and then help them apply the result repeatedly over time to track their own success. Show them how to succeed, get out of the way, and watch with pride as they take off.

But if you do this, make sure that the learning environment that you create is one in which students understand that it's all right to perform at low levels at first, when trying something for the first time. In other words, any time we put a reticent student on display demonstrating a lack of proficiency, we risk severe damage to that student's confidence and subsequent willingness to try to learn. Take care to protect them.

Subjectivity in Performance Assessment

Professional judgment guides every aspect of design, development, and use of every performance assessment.

For instance, as the developer or user of this method, you establish the achievement target you will assess using input about educational priorities expressed in state and local curricula, your text materials, and the opinions of experts in the field. You interpret these factors and decide what you will emphasize in your classroom, all matters of your professional judgment.

Once you have identified your target(s), you select the assessment method to reflect that target. Based on your vision of the valued target and your sense of the assessment options available to you, you make the choices. You devise performance criteria, formulate performance tasks, and observe and evaluate student proficiency. Every step along the way is a matter of your professional and subjective judgment.

Over the past decade, we have come to understand that carefully trained performance assessment users, who invest the clear thinking and developmental resources needed to do a good job, can use this methodology effectively. Indeed, many of the increasingly complex achievement targets that we ask students to hit today demand that we use performance assessments and use them well. In short, in certain contexts we have no choice but to rely on subjective performance assessment. So we had better do our homework and be prepared to do a good job!

Here I must insert as strong a warning as any I present in this book: In your classroom, *you* will set the standards of achievement that your students must meet. *It is your vision that you will translate into performance criteria, performance tasks, and records of student achievement. For this reason, it is not acceptable for you to hold a vision that is wholly a matter of your personal opinion about what it means to be academically successful. Rather, your vision must have the strongest possible basis in the collective academic wisdom both of experts in the discipline within which you assess and of colleagues and associates in your school, district, and community.*

In other words, systematic assessment of student attainment of an inappropriate target is as much a waste of time as a haphazard assessment of the proper target. The only way to prevent this is for you to become a serious student of the correct definition of academic excellence in the disciplines you teach. Strive to know the patterns of reasoning, the performance skills, and the products that constitute maximum proficiency in the subjects you teach and assess.

Matching Method to Target

As your definition of the meaning of academic excellence becomes clear, it will also become clear whether performance assessment is, in fact, the method of choice in a particular context. The range of possible applications of this methodology is broad, but not infinitely so. Performance assessment can provide dependable information about student achievement of some, but not all, kinds of valued targets. In fact, one strength of performance assessment is that one application can provide evidence of student attainment of several valued achievement targets at once.

Let's examine the matches and mismatches with our targets: knowledge, reasoning, skills, products, and dispositions.

Assessing Knowledge

If the objective of your instruction is to have students master a body of knowledge, observing and judging performance or products may not be the best way to find out if they have done it. It's not that you can't assess knowledge and understanding with this method. Sometimes, under certain conditions, you can. But other times you cannot. For several reasons, most often other methods can do it far more effectively.

First, there are potential sampling problems. Assume, for example, that you ask students to participate in a group discussion conducted in Spanish as a means of assessing their mastery of vocabulary and rules of grammar. Although this is an apparently authentic performance assessment, it might lead you to incorrect conclusions about students' language mastery. They will naturally choose to use vocabulary and syntax with which they are most comfortable and confident, avoiding vocabulary and constructions unfamiliar to them. Thus, in effect, they will provide biased samples.

Besides, the topic of such a discussion might narrow the vocabulary used, again limiting the scope of your sample and restricting the breadth of the generalizations you can draw about their mastery of Spanish. One solution would be to conduct several discussions on different topics over time, a labor-intensive and time-consuming plan. For assessing such mastery of foreign language vocabulary and usage (a knowledge target), you have far more efficient choices at your disposal.

> **TECHNICAL NOTE**
> In this case the bias arises from students keeping us from finding out what they don't know. The result is an invalid assessment.

Still further, you must consider the potential problems that arise if you need to assess the language mastery of a large number of students, not least of which is the challenge of spending a great deal of time assessing. Sometimes this is just not practical.

But even more troubling is the reality that, if you try to use performance assessment to tap knowledge mastery, you will have difficulty deciding how to help students who fail to perform well. It will not be clear what went wrong to give rise to the failure. Is their inability to converse in Spanish due to a lack of knowledge of vocabulary and grammar, an inability to pronounce words, or anxiety about the public nature of the demonstration? All three are hopelessly confounded with one another in performance assessment, and it will be impossible for you to identify the problem(s) and plan a proper course of action to help these students. Thus, once again, given this knowledge target in this context, performance assessment may not be your best choice.

When assessing student mastery of content knowledge, whether learned outright or retrieved through the use of references, selected response or essay formats are usually the best choices. When larger structures of knowledge are the target (see Chapter 6), the essay mode typically is preferable. When the context permits direct, person-to-person questioning of students, asking questions and listening to answers may be the method of choice (discussed in the next chapter). All three of these options offer greater control over the material sampled in the assessment than does performance assessment.

Assessing Reasoning

Performance assessment can provide an excellent means of assessing student reasoning and problem-solving proficiencies. Given complex problems to solve, students must reason in a series of steps. While we cannot directly view their thoughts, we can use various assessment procedures that do reveal their patterns of reasoning.

For example, you might give chemistry students unidentified substances to identify and watch how they go about setting up the apparatus and carrying out the study. The performance criteria would have to reflect the proper order of activities for conducting such experiments. Those who reason well will follow the proper sequence and succeed. In this case, the process is as important as getting the right answer—the process is what you're trying to assess.

Performance assessments structured around the products students create also can provide insight into their reasoning proficiency. Consider an example in which students are to carry out a science experiment and write a research report. You may evaluate these reports in terms of the standards of a good report, if those criteria have been clearly and completely articulated. But in addition, the resulting products could provide evidence of students' reasoning while conducting the experiment and writing the report itself. You would need two sets of criteria, one reflecting the proper structure of a lab report and the other reflecting the reasoning requirements of the experiment.

Or consider the example of a product-based performance assessment in which you challenge students to build a tower out of toothpicks to hold a heavy load. The obvious criterion of quality will be the amount of weight the tower can hold. But a more precise evaluative lens might center on how builders figure out how to apply principles of effective stress distribution.

Assessing Performance Skills

The great strength of this assessment methodology lies in its ability to ask students to perform in certain ways and to provide a dependable means of evaluating that performance. Most communication skills fall in this category, as do all forms of performing, visual, and industrial arts. In fact, most real-world applications of the knowledge, understanding, and reasoning proficiencies learned in school translate into demonstrated skills. Observing students in action can be a rich and useful source of information about their attainment of very important forms of skill achievement.

Assessing Products

Herein lies the other great strength of performance assessment. There are occasions when we ask students to create complex achievement-related products. The quality of those products indicates the creator's level of achievement. If we develop sound performance criteria that reflect the key attributes of these products and learn to apply those criteria well, performance assessment can serve us as both an efficient and effective tool. We may evaluate in this way everything from written products, such as term papers and research reports, to the many forms of art and craft products. Again, many examples will follow.

Assessing Dispositions

To the extent that we can draw inferences about positive attitudes, strong interests, motivational dispositions, and/or academic self-concept based either on students' actions or on what we see in the products they create, then performance assessment can assist us here as well.

However, I urge caution. Remember, sound performance assessment (like all other assessment methods!) requires strict adherence to an established set of rules of evidence. Each assessment must:

Reflect a clear target	We must thoroughly understand and develop sound definitions of the affective targets we are assessing.
Serve a clearly articulated purpose	We must know precisely why we are assessing and what we intend to do with the results, especially tricky in the case of affective targets.

Rely on a proper method	The performance must present dependable information to us about disposition.
Sample the target appropriately	We must collect enough evidence to give us confidence in our conclusions without wasting time gathering too much.
Control for key sources of bias	We must understand the potential sources of bias in our judgments about student attitudes, values, interests, and so on and neutralize them in the context of our assessments.

When applying these standards of quality to assessing achievement targets that we're trained to teach, it is relatively easy to see the keys to assessment success. That is, our academic expertise helps us know when selected response tests, essay exercises, performance assessment, or product evaluation are likely to capture the meaning of academic success.

When it comes to student dispositions, however, most of us have had much less experience with and therefore are much less comfortable with their meaning, depth, and scope. That means successfully assessing them demands careful and thoughtful preparation.

We can watch students in action and/or examine the things they create and make inferences about their dispositions. But we can do this only if we have a clear and practiced sense of what we are looking for and why we are assessing it. I will address these issues in depth in Chapter 12.

Summary of Target–Performance Assessment Matches

Table 7.2 provides a simple summary of the alignments among performance assessment and the various kinds of achievement that we expect of our students.

Developing Performance Assessments

The **VALIDITY** of a performance assessment is a function of (a) how well the tasks sample desired performance and (b) the extent to which performance criteria tap the important keys to good performance.

We initiate the creation of performance assessments just as we initiated the development of paper and pencil tests in the previous two chapters: with a plan or blueprint. The performance assessment plan includes just two specific parts. In this case, each part asks that we make several specific design decisions within it.

After we define the purpose (users and uses) of the assessment, first, we must define the performance(s) we

Table 7.2
Performance: Assessment of achievement targets

Target to be Assessed	Selected Response
Knowledge & Understanding	Not a good choice for this target—three other options preferred
Reasoning Proficiency	Can watch students solve some problems or examine some products and infer about reasoning proficiency
Performance Skills	Can observe and evaluate skills as they are being performed
Ability to Create Products	Can assess: (1) proficiency in carrying out steps in product development, and (2) attributes of the product itself
Dispositions	Can infer dispositions from behavior and products

are evaluating. We then must prepare tasks or assignments that elicit student performance so we may evaluate it. Figure 7.2 presents an overview of the design decisions we must make as performance assessment developers. The immense potential of this form of assessment becomes apparent when we consider all of the design options available within this structure.

As we explore that structure, we will examine how one group of teachers selected from among the array of possibilities to find the design they needed to

Design Ingredient	Options
Remember to articulate your purpose: Specify user(s) and use(s). Then:	
Design Step 1: Define Performance	
A. Type of performance	Skill target, product, or both Individual, group achievement, or both
B. Develop performance criteria	Articulate the keys to successful performance Score holistically, analytically or a combination
Design Step 2: Develop Performance Tasks	
A. Nature of the event	Structured assignments Naturally occurring events
B. Task specification	Define target, conditions, criteria
C. Selecting a sample	Decide how many tasks are needed to cover the terrain

Figure 7.2
Performance assessment design framework

serve their purposes. Remember Emily, the high school English student in the school board meeting that opened Chapter 1? We will explore the assessment challenges that her English teachers faced as they endeavored to put her and her classmates in touch with their emerging proficiency as writers.

Remember Your Purpose   *why*

Remember, regardless of the assessment method, you must begin any developmental sequence with a clear sense of why you are conducting the assessments. Different assessment users need different information in different forms at different times to make informed decisions. In earlier chapters we established that classroom users need continuous access to high-resolution portraits of the achievement of each individual student. Policy makers at the local or state level, on the other hand, require fundamentally different kinds of information. They need periodic access to information about student performance on global achievement targets. Because their decisions impact broad school programs, group data will suffice. Different contexts, different information needs.

To illustrate, the kind of writing assessment that Ms. Weatherby conducted at the beginning of the school year to determine the writing strengths and weaknesses of Emily and her classmates was fundamentally different from the statewide writing assessment conducted in Emily's home state. The former centered on individual student specifics, while the latter provided the broadest of portraits of group proficiency.

Stated in general terms, *no single assessment can meet everyone's needs*. Therefore, if you or I as assessment developers do not know whose needs we expect to meet with our performance assessments, how do we build them effectively? Step 1 of the design process requires that we clarify precisely who will use the assessment results and how.

As we discuss how Ms. Weatherby and Emily's other teachers used performance assessments of writing proficiency, bear in mind that they assessed for two reasons, or to serve two purposes:

1. To help their students become better writers (students and teacher are users; they seek to understand strengths and weaknesses)
2. To gather information on improvement in student writing as part of the faculty's evaluation of the impact of their new instructional program

Design Step 1: Defining Performance

The first challenge we face as performance assessment developers is that of defining our vision of academic success. Ms. W and the English faculty at Emily's high school, for example, needed to stipulate what it meant to be a "good writer" within their program. With performance assessment, we have the freedom to select from a range of achievement target possibilities, as you shall see. In specifying the target, we must make two design decisions: What type of performance are we assessing?

And, specifically, what does good performance look like? Let's consider these in a bit more detail.

Design Decision 1A: The Type of Performance.   This design decision asks us to answer the basic question, How will successful achievement manifest itself? Where will we most easily find evidence of proficiency? That evidence might take the form of a particular set of skills or behaviors that students must demonstrate. Will we watch students "in process" while they are actually doing something? In this instance, success manifests itself in their actions. Examples of this kind of performance include oral reading fluency, public speaking proficiency, compliance with safety rules in the science lab, and productive contributions to a team effort.

Or, will we observe and judge the results of students having created something to determine proficiency? In this case, we ask students to create a particular kind of product, which we then examine to find evidence of achievement. Consider, for example, artistic creations, term papers, models, or effectively repaired machines.

Note also, that some performance assessments might focus both on skills of doing and on the product that results, such as when we assess the computer programming process and then the quality of the resulting program.

The high school faculty in Emily's school wanted to evaluate their students' writing proficiency, so they needed to see and make judgments about the quality of actual samples of student writing. They couldn't get inside their students' heads to watch the brains at work. They instead read the written products that resulted and made judgments about writing proficiency.

Actual Examples of Student Work Can Help You Focus.   To help you identify the type of performance that you will evaluate and connect that decision to the performance criteria you will use to score the assessment, you need to study examples of actual student work.

Think deeply about the nature of the achievement targets you want your students to hit. What complex patterns of reasoning? What performance skills? What products? Describe them in writing. The more precisely you can describe them, the easier it will be to design your performance assessments.

Then, find, produce, or at least precisely visualize an example of the performance. You need an example of a skill demonstration in which sound reasoning is depicted, a performance in which a high level of skill is demonstrated, or a sample product that reveals evidence of a high level of proficiency. If you cannot find, create, or visualize examples, then I question whether you will be able to assess proficiency at all. In that case, it may be time to think more deeply about your achievement expectations.

Center on Individual or Group Performance.   Understand also that, with performance assessments, you can focus your attention on the performance of individual students or on that of students working in groups. Without doubt, most classroom assessments attend to the performance of students working alone. But in these times of cooperative learning, evaluating teamwork also can require performance assessment. For instance, you might observe and judge group interaction behaviors, tracking the manner in which the group works as a whole.

In the case of Emily and her English class, the focus of attention is on the writing proficiency of each individual student. Each student must learn to write. If the individual improves, the program is working for that student. But when it comes to evaluating the impact of their instructional program, the faculty must look first at each individual and then summarize individual performance over all students within and across classes.

Design Decision 1B: Defining Performance Criteria   Performance criteria spell out in descriptive detail the nature of the expected performance. This is the part of the performance assessment where we decide and describe what counts. The challenge is to not only describe what "outstanding" performance looks like, but also to map each of the different levels of performance leading up to the highest levels.

More specifically, in designing performance criteria, we strive to find a vocabulary to use in communicating with each other and with our students about the meaning of successful performance. The key assessment question comes down to this: Do I, the teacher, know what I am looking for in performance? But the more important instructional question is this: Do I know the difference between successful and unsuccessful performance and can I convey that difference in meaningful terms to my students? Remember, students can hit any target that they can see and that holds still for them. In performance assessment contexts, we define that target in terms of the performance criteria.

Shaping Your Vision of Success.   Without question, the only way for you to be able to articulate the key attributes of good performance is for you to be a master of the skills and products that reflect the valued academic achievement targets in your classroom. Those who teach drama, music, physical education, second languages, computer operations, or other skill-based disciplines are prepared to assess well only when they possess a refined vision of the nature of expert performance and the stages learners must go through to get there. Those who instruct students in creating visual art or craft products, for example, face the challenge of classroom assessment with greatest competence and confidence when they can describe the high-quality end point in terms that neophytes understand.

Connoisseurs can recognize outstanding performance when they see it. They know a good restaurant when they find it. They can select a fine wine. They know which movies deserve a thumbs-up and which Broadway plays are worth their ticket price. Connoisseurs also can describe why they believe something is outstanding or not. However, because the evaluation criteria may vary somewhat from reviewer to reviewer, their judgments may not always agree. For restaurants, wines, movies, and plays, the standards of quality may be a matter of opinion. But, that's what makes interesting reading in newspapers and magazines.

Teachers are very much like these connoisseurs in that they too must be able to recognize and describe outstanding performance. But this is where the similarity ends. Not only can well-prepared teachers visualize and explain the meaning of success, but they also can impart that meaning to others so as to help them become outstanding performers. *In short, they don't just criticize—they inspire improvement.*

In most disciplines, the standards of excellence that characterize high-quality performance are always those held by experts in the field of study in question. Outstanding teacher/classroom assessors are those who have immersed themselves in understanding those discipline-based meanings of proficiency. Even when differences of opinion exist about the meaning of outstanding performance in a particular discipline, well-prepared teachers understand those differences and are capable of revealing them to their students.

It is this depth of understanding that we must capture in our performance expectations so we can convey it to students through instruction, example, and practice. Our performance criteria cannot exist only in the intellect of the assessor. We must translate them into words and examples for all, especially our students, to see.

In this regard, because we have behind us over a decade of significant new discipline-based performance assessment research and development, many fields of study already have developed outstanding examples of sound criteria for critical performance. Examples include writing proficiency, foreign language, mathematics, and physical education. The most accessible source of information about these developments is the national association of teachers in each discipline. Nearly every such organization has advanced written standards of student achievement in their field of study within the past few years.

But these are not the only sources to tap. Consider the following:

- District or school curriculum guides
- State and local achievement standards
- Textbooks and other published instructional materials that include the expectation that students will develop reasoning, skill, or product capabilities; these also may include assessments
- Test publishers, many of whom are developing and selling quality performance assessments
- University research centers and regional educational service centers and laboratories

But be careful! Just because it's in print does not mean it's good. Be sure to verify the quality of these assessments before using them. Let the consumer beware. . . .

As it turns out, the vision of good writing, that is, the scoring criteria, adopted by the English faculty at Emily's high school came from the summer professional development session they attended and included a set of rating scales reflecting six dimensions of effective writing. The faculty's first challenge was to understand these standards of writing excellence themselves. Then they had to transform the performance criteria into student-friendly language. They elected to bring their students into that process as partners. I'll explain later how they did that. But in the meantime, the transformation they developed appears in Figure 7.3. Please read it.

Ideas

5. My paper is clear, focused, and filled with details not everybody knows.
   - You can tell I know a lot about this topic.
   - My writing is full of interesting tidbits, but it doesn't overwhelm you.
   - I can sum up my main point in one clear sentence: _____
   - You can picture what I'm talking about. I *show* things happening *(Fred squinted)*; I don't just *tell* about them *(Fred couldn't read the small print)*.

3. Even though my writing grabs your attention here and there, it could use some spicy details.
   - I know *just* enough about this topic—but more information would make it more interesting.
   - Some "details" are things most people probably already know.
   - My topic is too big. I'm trying to tell too much. Or else it's too skimpy.
   - It might be hard to picture what I'm talking about. Not enough *showing*.
   - I'm afraid my reader will get bored and go raid the refrigerator.

1. I'm just figuring out what I want to say.
   - I need a LOT more information before I'm really ready to write.
   - I'm still thinking on paper. What's my main idea?
   - I'm not sure *anyone* reading this could picture *anything*.
   - I wouldn't want to share this aloud. It's not ready.
   - Could I sum it up in one clear sentence? No way! It's a list of stuff.

Organization

5. My paper is as clear as a good road map. It takes readers by the hand and guides them along every step.
   - My beginning hints at what's coming, and makes you want to read on.
   - Every detail falls in just the right place.
   - Nothing seems out of order.
   - You never feel lost or confused; however, there could be a surprise or two.
   - Everything connects to my main point or main story.
   - My paper ends at just the right spot, and ties everything together.

3. You can begin to see where I'm headed. If you pay attention, you can follow along pretty well.
   - I have a beginning. Will my reader be completely hooked, though?
   - Most things fit where I have put them. I might move *some* things around.
   - Usually, you can see how one idea links to another.
   - I guess everything should lead up to the most important part. Let's see, *where* would that *be*?
   - My paper has an ending. But does it tie up loose ends?

Figure 7.3
Analytical writing assessment rating scales
Source: Reprinted from *Creating Writers*, 3d ed. by V. Spandel, in press. New York: Addison-Wesley Longman. Reprinted by permission.

1. Where are we headed? I'm lost myself.
   - A beginning? Well, I might have just repeated the assignment . . .
   - I didn't know where to go next, so I wrote the first thing that came to me.
   - I'm not really sure which things to include—or what order to put them in.
   - It's a collection of stuff—kind of like a messy closet!
   - An ending? I just stopped when I ran out of things to say.

Voice

5. I have put my personal, recognizable stamp on this paper.
   - You can hear my voice *booming* through. It's *me.*
   - I care about this topic—and it shows.
   - I speak right to my audience, always thinking of questions they may have.
   - I wrote to please myself, too.
   - My writing rings with confidence.

3. What I truly think and feel shows up sometimes.
   - You might not laugh or cry when you read this, but you'll hang in there and finish reading.
   - I'm right on the edge of finding my own voice—so *close!*
   - My personality pokes out here and there. You *might* guess this was my writing.
   - It's pleasant and friendly enough, but I didn't think about my audience *all* the time. Sometimes I just wanted to get *it over with!*

1. I did not put too much energy or personality into this writing.
   - It could be hard to tell who wrote this. It could be anybody's.
   - I kept my feelings in check.
   - If I liked this topic better or knew more, I could put more life into it.
   - Audience? *What* audience? I wrote to get it done.

Word Choice

5. I picked *just* the right words to express my ideas and feelings.
   - The words and phrases I've used seem *exactly* right.
   - My phrases are colorful and lively, yet nothing's overdone.
   - I've used some everyday words in new ways. Expect a few surprises.
   - Do you have a favorite phrase or two in here? I do.
   - Every word is accurate. You won't find yourself wondering what I mean.
   - Verbs carry the meaning. I don't bury my reader in adjectives.

3. It might not tweak your imagination, but hey, it gets the basic meaning across.
   - It's functional and it gets the job done, but I can't honestly say I stretched.
   - O.K., so there are some cliches hiding in the corners.
   - I've also got a favorite phrase lurking around here *someplace.*
   - Verbs? What's wrong with a good old *is, are, was, were...?*
   - I might have over utilized the functionality of my thesaurus.
   - You can understand it, though, right? Like, nothing's really wrong.

continued

1. My reader might go, "Huh?"
   - See, I'm like this victim of vague wording and fuzzy phrasing.
   - It's, you know, kind of hard to get what I'm talking about. *I* don't even remember what I meant and *I wrote this stuff*.
   - Maybe I misutilized a word or two.
   - Some redundant phrases might be redundant.
   - I need verby power.

Sentence Fluency

5. My sentences are clear and varied —a treat to read aloud.
   - Go ahead—read it aloud. You won't need to practice.
   - Sentence variety is my middle name.
   - Hear the rhythm? Smooth, huh?
   - Deadwood has been cut. Every word counts.

3. My sentences are clear and readable.
   - My writing is *pretty* smooth and natural—you can get through it all right.
   - Some sentences should be joined together. Others might be cut in two.
   - There's a little deadwood, sure, but it doesn't bury the good ideas too badly under extra verbiage, even though I must say it won't hurt to cut some unneeded words here and there and shorten things up just a bit.
   - I guess I did get into a rut with sentence beginnings. I guess I could use more variety. I guess I'll fix that.

1. I admit it's a challenge to read aloud (even for me).
   - You might have to stop or reread now and then it just feels like one sentence picked up right in the middle of another a new sentence begins and, oh boy, I'm lost...Help! Untangle me!
   - My sentences all begin the same way. My sentences are all alike. My sentences need variety. My sentences need work.
   - Some sentences are too short. They're too short. They're really short. Way short. Short.
   - Reading this is like trying to skate on cardboard. Tough going!

Figure 7.3
continued

Conventions

5. An editor would fall asleep looking for mistakes in this paper.
   - Capitals are all in the right places.
   - Paragraphs begin at the right spots.
   - Great punctuation—grammar, too.
   - My spelling (even of difficult words) would knock your socks off.
   - I made so few errors, it would be a snap getting this ready to publish.

3. Some bothersome mistakes show up when I read carefully.
   - Spelling is correct on simple words.
   - Capitals are O.k. maybe I should look again, Though.
   - The grammar might be a little informal, but it's OK for everyday writing.
   - A few pronouns do not match what IT refers to.
   - You might stumble over my innovative! Punctuation.
   - It reads like a first draft, all right.
   - I'd definitely need to do some editing to get this ready to publish.

1. Better read it once to decode, then once again for meaning.
   - Lotsuv errers Mak? The going ruf.
   - I've forgotten some CAPS—otherS aren't Needed.
   - Look out four speling mysteaks.
   - To tell the truth, I didn't spend much time editing.
   - I'll really have to roll up my sleeves to get this ready for publishing.

---

continued

Developing Your Own Performance Criteria.   To develop performance criteria yourself, you will need to carry out a thoughtful skill or product analysis. That means you must look inside the skills or products of interest to find the active ingredients. In most cases, this is not complicated. Do it on your own, work with colleagues, or partner up with your students—it's all the same.

To illustrate, Emily and I analyze here how she and her classmates worked with Ms. W to learn the attributes of good writing through developing performance criteria. As you follow the steps described, consider other contexts where this process might come into play in your classroom. How might you use these steps to help your students understand performance criteria for some form of their achievement you are evaluating? I once watched a class of third graders go through this same process to clarify criteria for assessing upcoming dramatic presentations of historical characters they were planning for their parents. A middle school social studies teacher I know used these steps to help his students see how to improve the research reports they were about to write. As you read on, see if you can see applications of this five-step process that might be relevant in your classroom.

Discovery.   The goal in this initial step is to help students begin to discover the keys to their own success. This requires that they become partners in the task or product analysis that will identify the active ingredients contributing to different levels of proficiency. As their teacher, you engage students in answering the question, How does a good task or product differ from a poor-quality one? To do this, students must have the opportunity to see examples. Regard Emily's experience:

RICK	Em, how did Ms. W first get you started in understanding how to write well?
EMILY	She gave us a writing assignment to complete in class that day. She said we were to write an essay about someone or something that we care deeply about. I wrote about my Mom. When we were done, she gave us each a folder and told us to put it in there and put the folder away.
RICK	What next?
EMILY	A big surprise. She said she didn't want us writing anything else—not for a while anyway. She said she just wanted us to read things.
RICK	Like what?
EMILY	She gave us all copies of an essay that she had just written for a magazine. Our homework assignment was to read it and try to decide if it was any good. The tough part was that she said she didn't want us to try to please her. She wanted our honest reaction. If it's good, what makes it good? Be specific, she said. If it's not very good, tell me why.
RICK	Could you do that?
EMILY	Not very well. Oh, some kids noticed some bad things. But mostly we just thought it was real good. I mean, she's a professional writer. What do we know? Besides who wants to tick off the "grade giver?" But then she did something very interesting. She gave us a copy of an essay that she had saved from her high school years, when she was first learning to write. She told us to read that one as our next homework assignment. Same deal: Come to class the next day ready to evaluate it.
RICK	So what did you find?
EMILY	We all hoped that she meant it when she said that it's okay to be honest. It was terrible—it reminded me of me!
RICK	How did she respond to your criticism?
EMILY	She was cool. She made us be real specific. We brainstormed a list on the board of all the problems we saw in that essay. She

made us write 'em down too. Then she returned us to her first essay—the real good one—and made us do the same thing. We brainstormed another list on the board, this time of all the things that we thought made it real good. We had to write those down, too, to take with us. This time our homework assignment was to study both essays and try to figure out the ten most important differences between them. What are the things that one essay does well that are missing or done badly in the other?

RICK	What did you find?
EMILY	You should've asked me back then. Now that I really know and understand keys to good writing, those are the things that I naturally think of. But, you know, we listed differences like sentence length, the depth of ideas, good start and finish, simple words versus bigger words, that kind of stuff. Then she told us to put our lists of differences in our folders along with the essay we had written. We'd return to them later.
RICK	What came next?
EMILY	The next day, she gave us each a stack of essays—like, ten or so. She said some are very good and some are not so good. Our job was to find out which was which. She had us work in teams to sort them into four piles: Very Good, Good, So-so, and Pretty Bad. In my group, we each read each paper and then voted on which pile. Our homework that night was to get together to finish up the sorting if we didn't get done during class.
RICK	Did you agree with each other or argue about the papers?
EMILY	Sometimes we disagreed. But not much—just about two or three.
RICK	Then what?
EMILY	The next day in class, she had us compare the Pretty Bad and So-so papers to figure out what made them different. Then we compared the So-so and Good papers, and then the Good and Very Good. Once again, we brainstormed lists of important differences.
RICK	What did you make of all of this?
EMILY	As I look back now, I see that she had us discovering how the quality of writing differs. When we finished figuring out the essential differences among those four stacks of papers, Ms. W referred us back to our comparison of what was good and bad about her essays—you know, the list in our folders. The two lists were alike!

We'll return to our conversation with Emily in just a moment. But first, it has been my experience over the years that asking students to contrast examples of vastly different performances virtually always helps them zero in on how to describe performance, good and poor, in clear, understandable language.

Consolidation.   Then we begin to refine student understanding and to help them begin to build a vocabulary that both you and they can use to converse with each other about performance. This is why it is important to engage students in devising criteria, even though you know the criteria you want used. *When you share the stage with your students and involve them in defining success by having them analyze examples and choose the language to describe achievement, in effect you begin to connect them to their target.* (Please reread that sentence. It is one of the most important in the entire book. It argues for sharing with your students your vision and thus your power to evaluate. The motivational and achievement consequences can be immense.)

RICK	OK, so now you are beginning to understand different levels of writing quality. How did Ms. W use that understanding to help you?
EMILY	Well, first, she had us take our initial essays out of our folders and evaluate them. Which pile is our essay most like: Very Good, Good, So-so, or Pretty Bad? You know where mine was—thumbs down!!
RICK	Pretty discouraging.
EMILY	You bet. But she said, "Just be patient. Improvement will come pretty quickly." Since there wasn't a pile below the one I was in, I had to believe her.
RICK	Where did you go from there?
EMILY	Ms. W said that we had to start getting specific. We had long lists of attributes of different levels of performance. We had to start boiling them down. We had to get to the important stuff.
RICK	How did she do that?
EMILY	Through lots of class discussion—or, I should say, argument. She said that we were going to have to translate all of our ideas about the differences between good and bad writing into as short a list of keys to success as we could. We started by brainstorming again. This time she said if we were going to try to categorize the differences we had been analyzing into major headings, what might the headings be?
RICK	What were they?
EMILY	Our first list wasn't very short! We included, like, 15 or 20 ingredients. But then she asked things like, can any of these

be combined? Are some a lot more important than others? We actually read Ms. W's good essay again, this time out loud in class to see if it helped us zero in on keys to success. I don't remember all of our steps along the way. But this was when we had our first experience with the BIG SIX!

RICK   Which are?

EMILY   Look! I put them on the cover of my writing portfolio:

Ideas and Content—you got anything to say?

Organization—you gotta have a plan

Sentence Fluency—rhythm, rhythm, rhythm

Word Choice—accurate and precise, that's me

Voice—speak to your reader

Conventions—don't let errors distract your reader

Defining.   In this step, it is crucial to remember that the job is not merely to define successful, or high-level, performance. Rather, you seek to describe the full range of performance, so each performer can come to understand where they are now in relation to where you want them to be down the road. Only with that road map in hand can they watch themselves travel their own personal journey to excellence, feeling in complete control all along the way.

EMILY   Ms. Weatherby divided us up into collaborative teams—six teams. Then she placed the labels for our six categories in a hat and each team had to draw one out. Each team was to take the lead in helping the rest of the class learn to master their element of good writing.

RICK   How were you to do that?

EMILY   As our assignment, each team was to write a definition of their element. But we couldn't just make it up. We had to go to the library and check in the dictionary and other reference materials. And further, we needed to review the various essays we had been analyzing to find an example of strong and weak performance of our element. Then we had to prepare a presentation for the rest of the class to show them what we had learned—using the overhead projector and all!

RICK   What was that like?

EMILY   Actually, the presentations were pretty good. But Ms. W encouraged us to question and argue with each other to be

	sure we all agreed on the final definitions. We really had good discussions. The illustrations really helped.
RICK	Then did you go to the next level of detail?
EMILY	As our next assignment, Ms. W had us divide a piece of paper into three columns, labeled "high," "middle," and "low." Under the high column, we were to develop a list of words or phrases that we believed describe a piece of writing when it is of outstanding quality with respect to our particular element. Then under low, we were to describe a paper that is of poor quality on our assigned attribute. And finally, we were to describe the midrange, too. And once again, we had to make transparencies and teach the rest of the class about out rating scale. And once again, we had to bring examples to illustrate different levels of writing.
RICK	Sounds like you guys were the teachers.
EMILY	We were! Each team presented and we listened and questioned. Ms. W asked the best questions—really challenged us to see if we knew what we were talking about. She also showed us how to stretch our rating scales from three to five points. Everyone had to revise our stuff based on suggested improvements. But no one got mad. It was cool. When we were all done, Ms. W told us how proud she was of us and how much we had learned. She collected the results of each team's work and overnight put all of the rating scales on her computer and printed copies for all of us to use with our next assignments.
RICK	So you weren't done yet?
EMILY	No way! We were just getting started. Now we knew about different levels of quality but the question was, Could we learn to write well?

Please refer to Figure 7.3 to see the results of the work of Emily and her classmates: clearly stated attributes in student-friendly language.

Now remember, this is not about students setting academic standards. The vision of academic excellence is Ms. Weatherby's. She knew where her students were headed at all times. She could have simply printed these scoring criteria off, given them to her students and instructed them to "write papers that deserve 5s on all of these scales." But she didn't select that course of action. Rather, she led her students to her vision of excellence through thoughtful analysis and evaluation of their own and other's writing. The results for her students were a highly refined sense of excellence in writing, ownership in that vision, and a growing sense of how they might be able to achieve higher levels of performance.

Learning to Apply the Criteria.   The next step is to help your students learn to apply their performance criteria through practice. You accomplish this most effectively by providing them with lots of examples of performance that vary greatly in quality so they can analyze and judge quality. As this process proceeds, you can start your students down the road of discovering their own current level of performance using agreed-on rating scales. (When your students become trained raters, the work load spreads over many shoulders.) In this way, you show them where they are now in relation to where you want them to be, so they can begin to take charge of their journey to excellence. Here's how Ms. W did that, as Emily recounts it:

> "First, she returned us to the stack of papers that we had sorted into piles. You know, Very Good , So-so, and so on. Then she had us pick one paper from each pile and rate it using our six five-point performance criteria. We all rated the same four papers. Then using a show of hands, she asked us how many of us rated each paper on each criterion at each level. We didn't all agree with each other exactly. But we were pretty close. And boy, those profiles sure revealed why we had put each paper in each pile originally. They were really different.
>
> "Next, Ms. W had us go to our files and pull out the essay that we had written at the very beginning and rate it using our scales. Mine was terrible. But she said that was okay. Low ratings are not a bad thing when you're first getting started. Low ratings don't mean you've failed. They only mean you're just starting to learn about something. But, you have to start improving.
>
> "Then she gave us another writing assignment, promising that even now we probably would see improvement in the quality of our writing. As I wrote that night, I found myself thinking, Ideas and Content—Have I got anything to say?; Organization—I gotta have a plan; Sentence Fluency—rhythm, rhythm, rhythm; Word Choice—am I telling my story accurately and precisely?; Voice—am I speaking to my reader?; and Conventions—don't let errors interfere.
>
> "The next day in class, we worked in teams to read and evaluate each other's essays and we all found that this second effort was much better! Ms. W was right.
>
> "From then on we did more and more of the same. She shared samples of writing that she had found that did or didn't do something well. We dug up some, too, and shared them. We wrote a lot. Sometimes we just evaluated one or two of the six criteria. Ms. W said, when we're working on Organization, that's what we evaluate. But, she said, eventually all of the pieces have to come together."

Refining.   Revising and refining performance criteria never stops. By evaluating lots of student work over time, you tune into the keys to success with increasing focus and precision. As new insights arise, revise your criteria to reflect your best current thinking. And remember, it is not uncommon for students who are involved in the process to "outthink" their teachers and come up with criteria of excellence that you have not seen. When they do, honor their good thinking! Never regard performance criteria as "finished." Rather, always see them as works in progress.

Devising Your Own Criteria: Step-by-step.   When it comes down to devising your own performance criteria, do what Ms. Weatherby did. Her steps are listed in Table 7.3.

And remember, when students are partners in carrying out these steps, you and they join together to become a learning community. Together, you open windows to the meaning of academic success, providing your students with the words and examples they need to see that vision.

Summary: The Attributes of Truly Good Performance Criteria.   Truly good performance criteria focus on the right ingredients, are clearly and sharply focused, and are practical to use. For now, I just want you to understand what each of these means. In later chapters I will provide greater detail about each, along with examples.

Strong criteria are "on target." That means they are *clear*:

To the extent that your criteria meet these standards and you learn to apply them consistently, you erect a shield against biased judgments and unreliable assessments.

- Each element to be scored is vividly and understandably described; all language is specific and accurate.
- The guide is well organized both within and across rating scales.

They are on target when they are *compelling* or convincing in terms of their importance:

- The criteria to be evaluated center on the target of interest.
- They have a "ring of truth" about them—it is clear why each ingredient is included.
- The rating criteria are couched in the best current thinking of the academic field.

Table 7.3
Steps in devising performance criteria

Step	Activity
Discovery	Analyze examples of performance to uncover keys to success
Consolidation	Pool the resulting ideas into a coherent but concise and original set of key attributes
Definition	Develop simple definitions of the key to success and devise performance continuums for each
Application	Practice applying performance evaluation procedures until you can do so with consistency
Refinement	Always remain open to the possibility that criteria might need to be revised

In addition, they're on target when they're *complete:*

- All key facts of performance are reflected in the criteria; nothing is left out.
- Examples of student work can be found to illustrate each level of quality.

From a different perspective, the performance criteria must also be "practical." Their practicality turns in part on the sharpness of their focus. They are *precise* in focus when the following is true:

- The level of detail in ratings (holistic/analytical) fits the context.
- Scoring guides can be applied to student responses to a variety of performance tasks; that is, they are generalizeable.
- There is evidence that two teachers or two students evaluating the same piece of work independently rate it the same.
- The criteria lead to fair evaluations for all students, regardless of ethnicity, socioeconomic status, or facts other than achievement.

Criteria are practical when they are *teacher friendly*:

- Any teacher who wishes to use the scoring guide can be trained to apply the scoring criteria in a dependable manner.
- Teachers contend that having judgments about student achievement on the scales used represents useful information—information that helps them help their students.

And finally, criteria are practical when *students can use them* too, when the following are true:

- Criteria address aspects of performance that students can understand.
- They have been translated into language that students understand and can apply.
- All levels of performance can be illustrated with examples students themselves have found.

Users must ask, "Can my scoring guides serve as a pathway to improving student achievement?"

In later chapters, we will turn these lists into actual rating scales for evaluating performance assessments. We will study examples of scoring criteria of varying quality to understand more deeply what good ones look like. But first, let's finish our design framework.

What Level of Precision?   In any performance assessment context, we have two choices in the level of scoring we carry out: holistic and analytical. Both require explicit performance criteria. That is, we are never absolved from responsibility for having articulated the meaning of academic success in clear and appropriate terms.

However, these two scoring methods use the criteria in different ways and therefore fit into different contexts. When we score *analytically*, we make our judgments by considering each key dimension of performance or criterion separately, thus analyzing performance in terms of each of its elements. When we judge *holistically*, we consider all of the criteria simultaneously, making one overall evaluation of performance. The former provides a high-resolution picture of performance but takes more time and effort to accomplish. The latter provides a more general sense of performance but is much quicker.

Your choice of scoring procedure will turn on how you plan to use the results (whether you need precise detail or a general picture) and the resources you have available to conduct the assessment (whether you have time to evaluate analytically).

Some assessment contexts demand analytical evaluation of student performance. No matter how hard you try, you will not be able to diagnose student strengths or weaknesses based on holistic performance information. As a teacher, like Ms. Weatherby, you cannot help students understand and learn to replicate the fine details of sound performance by scoring their work in holistic terms.

But on the other hand, it is conceivable that you may find yourself involved in an assessment where you must evaluate the performance of hundreds of students with few resources on hand, too few resources to score analytically. Holistic scoring may be your only option.

In most classroom applications, when you need a holistic score, I recommend that you generate it by summing or averaging analytical scores. If your vision of the meaning of academic success suggests that some analytical scales are more important than others, then assign higher weights to some (by multiplying by a weighting factor) before summing. However, you must spell out in advance a rational basis for determining those weights.

It may also be acceptable to supplement a set of analytical scores with an "overall impression" rating, if you can define and describe to your students how the whole is, in fact, equal to more than the sum of the individual parts of performance.

Design Step 2: Devising Performance Tasks

Performance assessment tasks, like selected response test items and essay exercises, frame the challenge for students and set the conditions within which they are to meet that challenge. Thus, performance assessment tasks clearly and explicitly reflect the achievement target(s). Like essay exercises, sound performance assessment tasks outline a complete problem for respondents: achievement to demonstrate, conditions of the demonstration, and the standards of quality to be applied.

As specified earlier in this chapter, we face three basic design considerations when dealing with tasks in the context of performance assessment. We must determine the following:

1. The nature of the event(s), whether preplanned or naturally occurring
2. The specific ingredients of the task, defining what performers are to do
3. The number of tasks needed to sample performance

Let's delve into each in some detail.

Design Decision 2A: The Nature of the Event.   The decision about whether to rely on structured and assigned tasks, naturally occurring events, or some combination of the two should be influenced by several factors related to the assessment target(s) and the environment within which we conduct the assessment.

When we want to maintain tight control over the range of performance we see and evaluate, to ensure evaluation of specific important skills, we need structured exercises. If, for example, I want to see and hear a student communicate in a second language in a variety of social situations, I must strategically sample those instances. I cannot simply leave to chance which situations the student performs in.

Further, structured exercises and naturally occurring events can help us get at slightly different targets. When we announce a pending performance assessment and instruct students how to prepare, we intend to maximize their motivation to perform well. In fact, we often try to encourage the best possible performance by attaching a grade or telling students that observers from outside the classroom (often parents) will watch them perform. When we take these steps and build the assessment around structured exercises, we set our conditions up to assess students' best possible performance, under conditions of maximum motivation to do well.

However, sometimes our objective is not to see students' "best possible" performance. Rather, what we wish is "typical" performance, performance under conditions of regular, everyday motivation. For example, we want students to adhere to safety rules in the woodworking shop or the science lab at all times (under conditions of typical motivation), not just when they think we are evaluating them (maximum motivation to perform well). Observation during naturally occurring classroom events can allow us to get at the latter.

Here's another example: In Emily's English class, Ms. W collected samples of student writing in two ways. She gave them regular writing assignments—structured activities that they were to complete to produce evidence of proficiency. In addition, Ms. W had them write in journals about topics of interest, self reflections, and so on. When she collected and read the journals for evidence of proficiency, she conducted a spontaneous performance assessment relying on routine classroom events.

Time for Reflection

Identify a few achievement targets you think might be most effectively assessed through the unobtrusive observation of naturally occurring events. In your experience as a teacher or student, have you ever been assessed in this way? When?

In addition to motivational factors, there also are practical considerations to bear in mind in deciding whether to use structured or naturally occurring events. One is time. If normal events of the classroom afford you opportunities to gather sound evidence of proficiency without setting aside special time to present structured exercises and make associated observations, then take advantage of these naturally occurring instructional events.

Another practical matter to consider in your choice is the fact that classrooms are places just packed full of evidence of student proficiency. Think about it. Teachers and students spend more time together than do the typical parent and child or husband and wife! Students and teachers live in a world of constant interaction in which both are watching, doing, talking, and learning. A teacher's greatest assessment asset is the opportunity to observe student achievement continuously over time. This permits the accumulation of bits of evidence over extended periods of time, and makes for big samples of performance. It offers opportunities to detect patterns, to double check, and to verify.

Everything I have said about performance assessment up to this point has depicted it as rational, structured, and preplanned. But teachers know that assessment also is sometimes spontaneous. The unexpected classroom event or the briefest of unanticipated student responses can provide the ready observer with a new glimpse into student competence. Effective teachers see things. They file those things away. They accumulate evidence of proficiency. They know their students. No other assessor of student achievement has the opportunity to see students like this over time.

But beware! These kinds of spontaneous performance assessments based on on-the-spot, sometimes unobtrusive observations of naturally occurring events are fraught with as many dangers of inaccurate assessment as any other kind of performance assessment. Even in these cases, we are never absolved from adhering to the basic principles of sound assessment: clear target, clear purpose, proper method, sound sample, and control of potential bias.

You must constantly ask yourself: What did I really see? Am I drawing the right conclusion based on what I saw? How can I capture the results of this spontaneous assessment for later use (if necessary or desirable)? Anecdotal notes alone may suffice. The threats to sound assessment never disappear. So by all means, take advantage of the insights provided by classroom time spent together with your students. But as a practical classroom assessment matter, do so cautiously. Create a written record of your assessment whenever possible.

Time for Reflection

What creative, realistic ways can you think of to establish dependable records of the results of spontaneous performance assessments that happen during an instructional day? What kinds of recording devices or strategies might you use? How might you prompt students to record evidence of their own achievement or growth? journaling

Design Decision 2B: Task Specification.   Like well-developed essay exercises, sound structured performance assessment tasks specify and explain the challenge to respondents, while setting them up to succeed if they can, by doing the following:

- Identifying the specific kind(s) of performance to demonstrate
- Detailing the context and conditions within which proficiency will be demonstrated
- Reminding students of the criteria applied in evaluating performance

Following is a simple example of an exercise that does all three:

Achievement	You are to use your knowledge and understanding of how to convert energy into motion, along with your understanding of the principles of mechanics, to reason through the design for a mousetrap car. A mousetrap car converts one snap of the trap into forward motion. Then you are to build and demonstrate your car.
Conditions	Using materials provided in class and within the time limits of four class periods, please design and diagram your plan, construct the car itself, and prepare to explain why you included your key design features.
Criteria	Your performance will be evaluated in terms of the specific standards we set in class, including the clarity of your diagrammed plan, the performance and quality of your car, and your presentation explaining its design features. Scoring guides are attached.

In this way, sound performance tasks frame clear and specific problems to solve.

Design Decision 2C: Selecting a Sample.   How do we know how many exercises we need within any particular assessment to give us confidence that we are drawing dependable conclusions about student proficiency? In other words, how many samples of Emily's writing must Ms. W see to draw a dependable conclusion about her proficiency?

This can be somewhat tricky with performance assessments, because it can take quite a bit of time to develop, administer, observe, and score any single exercise. In a half-hour of testing time we can administer lots of multiple-choice test items, and thus cover much territory with our sample, because each item demands so little response time. But what if the performance assessment exercise, which typically requires a more complex demonstration, takes 15 minutes? Clearly we cannot administer as many per unit of testing time. As a result, sometimes it can be very difficult to sample performance adequately using a number of different exercises, given our classroom workload and time constraints.

Now consider the specific sampling challenges of writing assessment, for example. Because writing takes so many forms and takes place in so many different contexts, assessing overall writing proficiency can be very complex. A quality writing sample permits generalizing about student proficiency across the entire performance domain. As a result, the sample of writing exercises must include assignments calling for various kinds of writing, such as narrative, expository, and persuasive. This takes time. This is the performance assessment sampling challenge.

Some Practical Guidance.   Sampling student performance with assessment tasks always involves tradeoffs between quality of resulting information and the cost of collecting it. Few have the resources needed to gather the perfect sample of student achievement. We all compromise. The good news for you as a teacher is that you must compromise less than the large-scale assessor, primarily because you get to have more time with your students. This is precisely why I feel that the great strength and future of performance assessment lies in the classroom more than in large-scale standardized testing.

Let's define *sampling* as the purposeful assembly of tasks to collect information about student achievement in order to support conclusions about that achievement. In the classroom, often we have the luxury of being able to gather that information strategically in bits and pieces over time. If we plan and administer assessment tasks carefully, these bits can form into a representative sample of performance that is broad enough in its coverage to lead us to confident conclusions about student achievement.

Unfortunately, there are no hard and fast rules to follow in determining how many exercises it takes to yield dependable conclusions. That means we must once again speak of the art of classroom assessment. Mr. Lopez, the elementary teacher who has been providing guidance occasionally along our journey, offers practical guidance on this matter:

> I use a simple decision rule to tell me if my sample of assessment exercises has covered enough ground to justify a final conclusion about how the student is doing. Now remember, this is really a matter of my professional judgment based on prior experience with the targets and with kids. I feel that I have presented enough exercises and gathered enough instances of student performance when I am quite certain that I can accurately predict how well they would do if I gave them one additional exercise. I try to sample student achievement more than once and under a number of different circumstances. So I know I'm not guessing. After a while a teacher compiles enough information to know who's getting it and who isn't.

An Illustration.   Let's explore a real-world assessment situation to see sampling in action. Let's say we are a licensing board charged with responsibility for certifying the competence of commercial airline pilots. One specific skill we want them to demonstrate, among others, is the ability to land the plane safely. So we take candidates up on a bright, sunny, calm day and ask them to land the plane, clearly an authentic performance assessment. And let's say the first pilot does an excellent job of landing. Are you ready to certify?

If your answer is yes, I don't want you screening the pilots hired by the airlines on which I fly. Our assessment reflected only one narrow set of circumstances within which we expect our pilots to be competent. What if it's night, not bright, clear daylight? A strange airport? Windy? Raining? An emergency? These represent realities within which pilots must operate routinely. So the proper course of action in certifying competence is to see each pilot land under various conditions, so we can ensure safe landings on all occasions. To achieve this, we hang out at the airport waiting for the weather to change, permitting us to quickly take off in the plane so we can watch our candidates land under those conditions. And over the next year we exhaust the landing condition possibilities, right?

Of course not. Obviously, I'm being silly here. We have neither the time nor the patience to go through all of that with every candidate. So what do we do? We compromise. We operate within our existing resources and sample pilot performance. We have each candidate land the plane under several different conditions. And at some point, the array of instances of landing proficiency (gathered under strategically selected conditions) combine to lead us to a conclusion that each pilot has or has not mastered the skill of landing safely.

This example frames the performance assessment sampling challenge in a real-world situation that applies just as well in your classroom. How many "landings" must you see under what kinds of conditions to feel confident your students can perform according to your criteria? The science of such sampling is to have thought through the important conditions within which you will sample performance. The art is to use your resources creatively to gather enough different instances under varying conditions to bring you and your students to a confident conclusion about proficiency.

I hope you understand why you must consider the decision to be made in planning the size of your sample. Some decisions are important, like promotion to the next grade, high school graduation, or becoming licensed to practice a profession. These demand assessments that sample both more deeply and more broadly to give us confidence in the decision that results. An incorrect decision based on poor-quality assessment would have dire consequences.

But on the other hand, other decisions are not so momentous. They allow you to reconsider the decision later, if necessary, at no cost to the student. For example, if I mismeasure a student's ability to craft a complete sentence during a unit of instruction on sentence construction, I am likely to discover my error in later assessments and take proper action. When the target is narrow and the time frame brief, we can sample more narrowly and not do great harm.

Figure 7.4 identifies six factors to take into account when making sampling decisions in any particular performance assessment context. Even within these guidelines, however, remember Mr. Lopez's sampling decision rule: "I feel that I have presented enough exercises and gathered enough instances of student performance when I am quite certain that I can accurately predict how well students would do if I gave them one additional exercise." In your classroom, if you sense that you have enough evidence, draw your conclusion and act on it.

Your professional challenge is to follow the rules of sound assessment and gather enough information to minimize the chance that your conclusions are wrong. The conservative position to take in this case is to err in the direction of oversampling to increase your level of confidence in the inferences you draw about student competence. If you feel at all uncertain about the conclusion you might draw regarding the achievement of a particular student, you have no choice but to gather more information. To do otherwise is to place that student's well-being in jeopardy.

- *The Reason for the Assessment*—The more important the decision, the more sure you must be about the student's proficiency. The more sure you must be, the bigger should be your sample. Greater coverage leads to more confident conclusions about achievement.

- *The Scope of the Target*—The more narrowly focused the valued achievement target, the easier it is to cover it with a small sample. Targets broad in their scope require more exercises to cover enough material to yield confident conclusions.

- *The Coverage of Any One Exercise*—If the student's response is likely to provide a great deal of evidence of proficiency, you need not administer many such exercises. How many term papers must a student prepare to demonstrate that he or she can do it?

- *Time Available to Assess*—If you must draw conclusions about proficiency tomorrow, you have too little time to sample broadly. But as the time available to assess increases, so can the scope of your sample.

- *Consistency of Performance*—If a student demonstrates consistently very high or very low proficiency in the first few exercises, it may be safe to draw a conclusion even before you have administered all the exercises you had intended.

- *Proximity to the Standard*—If a student's performance is right on the borderline between being judged as competent or incompetent, you might need to extend the sample to be sure you know which conclusion to draw.

Figure 7.4
Practical considerations in performance assessment sampling

Time for Reflection
_____

Based on your experience, can you identify one performance skill target that you think would take several exercises to sample appropriately and another that you think could be sampled with only one, or very few, exercises? What are the most obvious differences between these two targets?

Summary: The Attributes of Truly Effective Tasks.   The bottom line for performance tasks is that they have to elicit from students the kind of response that will permit you to dependably assess proficiency. That means that each task must be on target. A task is "on target" when it is clear, compelling, and complete. Here's what I mean by each:

Clear

- The assignment clearly describes what students are to do or create.
- The conditions under which students are to perform (time limits, available resources) are spelled out.
- The task description includes a reminder to students of the criteria you will apply in evaluating the work.

Compelling

- The task relates directly to the important achievement target it is supposed to reflect; it reflects something that you want students to be able to do.
- The task seems worth doing to both you and your students.
- There is a specific time during instruction when students have the opportunity to learn to do it well.

Complete

- The instructions (assignment) given to students provide sufficient depth to assure that each student understands them.
- Key terms are either familiar to students or are defined.
- You have verified that each student understands the task.

A task is "practical" when it's developmentally appropriate, feasible for classroom use, fair for all students and one of several such tasks. Thus,

- The task is appropriate for the age and mental faculties of the students being evaluated.
- Students can perform the work with the available resources.
- The task accommodates differences (gender, ethnicity, etc.) among the students being evaluated.
- The task is one of a class of such tasks you can use over time still applying the same criteria, so students can witness their own growth.

In addition, the set of exercises that comprise an assessment, taken together, sample an appropriate range of relevant applications of the proficiency being evaluated.

Fine Tuning Your Performance Assessments

Clearly, your prime consideration in selecting an assessment method is the match of performance assessment methodology to your target. In addition, however, it is prudent to consider other practical questions when deciding if or how to use performance assessment in your classroom.

Checking for Errors in Judgment

Subjective scoring, a prospect that raises the anxiety of any assessment specialist, is the hallmark of performance assessment. We already have discussed many ways to ensure that your subjective assessment is as objective as it can be:

- Be mindful of the purpose for assessing.
- Be crystal clear about the target.
- Articulate the key elements of good performance in explicit performance criteria.
- Share those criteria with students in terms they understand.
- Learn to apply those criteria in a consistent manner.
- Double check to be sure bias does not creep into the assessment.

Under all circumstances, you want to avoid instances where students can either do well on a performance assessment without having mastered the achievement target or fail the assessment when they have, in fact, mastered the target.

Assessment experts call the process of investigating inter-rater agreement the determination of **INTER-RATER RELIABILITY**

There is a simple way to check for bias in your performance evaluations. Remember, bias occurs when factors other than the kind of achievement being assessed begin to influence rater judgment, such as examinees' gender, age, ethnic heritage, appearance, or prior academic record. You can determine the degree of objectivity of your ratings by comparing them with the judgments of another trained and qualified evaluator who independently observes and evaluates the same student performance with the intent of applying the same criteria. If, after observing and evaluating performance, two independent judges generally agree on the level of proficiency demonstrated, then you have evidence that the results reflect student proficiency. But if the judges come to significantly different conclusions, they obviously have applied different standards. You have no way of knowing which are the most appropriate. Under these circumstances the accuracy of the assessment must be called into question and the results set aside until you have thoroughly explained the reasons for those differences.

Now you may be saying, It's just not practical to determine inter-rater agreement in the classroom. It'll take too much time. Besides, where do I find a qualified second rater? And how do I determine if the other rater and I agree in our judgments?

In fact, evaluating consistency among raters need not take much time. You need not find corroboration for every performance judgment you make. Just checking a few for consistency often will suffice. Perhaps a qualified colleague could double check a select few of your performance ratings to see if they are on target.

Further, it doesn't take a high degree of technical skill to do this. Have someone who is qualified rate some student performances you already have rated, and then sit down for a few minutes and talk about any differences in your ratings. If the performance in question is a product that students created, have your colleague evaluate a few. If it's a skill, videotape a few examples. Both you and your colleague apply your criteria to one performance and check for agreement. Do you both see it about the same way? If so, go on to the next one. If not, try to resolve differences, adjusting your performance criteria as needed.

Please understand that my goal here is not to have you carry out this test of objectivity every time you conduct a performance assessment. Rather, try to understand the spirit of this test of your objectivity. An important part of the art of classroom performance assessment is the ability to sense when your performance criteria are sufficiently explicit that another judge would be able to use them effectively, if called on to do so. Further, from time to time it is a good idea to actually check whether you and another rater really do agree in applying your criteria.

The more important the performance assessment (that is, the greater its potential impact on students, such as when it is used for promotion decisions, graduation decisions, and the like), the more important it becomes that you verify inter-rater agreement.

And don't forget, you can share your criteria with your students. The process of turning them into trained raters can provide you with useful diagnostic insights. You can be assured that students who don't understand the performance rating criteria that they are trying to apply will tell you so, if you ask. This will force you to greater clarity.

Just remember, all raters must be trained to understand and apply your standards. Never assume that they are qualified to evaluate performance on the basis of prior experience if that experience does not include training in using the criteria you employ in your classroom. Have them evaluate some samples to show you they can do it. If training is needed, it very often does not take long. Figure 7.5 presents steps to follow when training raters. Remember, once they're trained, your support raters are allies forever. Just think of the benefits to you if you have a pool of trained evaluators ready to share the workload!

- Have trainees review and discuss the performance criteria. Provide clarification as needed.
- Give them a sample of work to evaluate that is of known quality to you (i.e., which you already have rated).
- Check their judgments against yours, reviewing and discussing any differences in terms of the specifics of the performance criteria.
- Give them another sample of work of known quality to evaluate.
- Compare their judgments to yours again, noting and discussing differences.
- Repeat this process until your trainee converges on your standards, as evidenced by a high degree of agreement with your judgments.
- You and the trainees evaluate a sample of work of unknown quality. Discuss any difference.
- Repeat this process until you have confidence in your new partner(s) in the evaluation process.

Figure 7.5
Steps in training raters of student performance

Barriers to Sound Performance Assessment

By way of summary, many things in the design and development of performance assessments can cause a student's real achievement to be misrepresented. Many of the potential problems and remedies are summarized in Figure 7.6.

Student Involvement in Performance Assessment

The purpose of the assessment drives the selection of observers and evaluators. When the goal is to certify that students have met performance standards for important grading, promotion, or graduation decisions, then you, the teacher, must be the assessor. The only acceptable alternative in these contexts is for you to bring into the classroom another adult rater (a qualified outside expert). Schools that ask students to do exhibitions and demonstrations, such as senior projects, science fairs, and music competitions, routinely rely on outside expert judges. In all cases, it is essential that raters be fully trained and qualified to apply the performance criteria that underpin the evaluation. High-stakes decisions hang in the balance. So we must do it right.

On the other hand, as we have established, you can use assessments as far more than simply sources of scores to inform decisions. You can use them as teaching tools. You can accomplish this in one way by using performance assessments to teach students to evaluate their own and each other's performance. The very process of learning to dependably apply performance criteria helps students become better performers, as it helps them to learn and understand key elements

Potential Sources of Problems	Recommended Remedy
Inadequate vision of the achievement target	Seek training and advice or consult the professional literature to sharpen your focus; work with colleagues in this process
Mismatch of target and method	Performance assessment aligns well with complex reasoning, performance skills and product assessments; use it only for these
Unclear performance criteria	Analyze samples of performance very carefully, working with qualified experts if necessary, to sharpen your focus
Incorrect performance criteria	Compare and contrast samples of performance of vastly different quality for real keys to success; consult the professional literature for advice; work with qualified colleagues in the process of identifying criteria
Unfocused tasks	Tap the professional literature for good tasks; seek training from qualified colleagues in task development
Biased tasks	Understand the social and linguistic backgrounds of your students; seek advice of qualified reviewers in revising and selecting tasks
Insufficient sample of tasks	Start with a clear definition of the desired achievement target; work with a team of qualified colleagues to devise new tasks and determine how many would be enough
Too little time to assess	Add trained raters . . . such as your students
Untrained raters	Train them and provide them with practice in applying criteria
Wrong scoring scheme (holistic v. analytical)	In the classroom, stick with analytical; it's just more powerful
Students don't understand the basis of your evaluations	Give them the criteria up front and teach them to apply them

Figure 7.6
Avoiding problems

of sound performance. So when the assessment is to serve instructional purposes, students can be raters, too.

And remember, some classroom situations may require relying on multiple raters to serve multiple purposes. For example, students can learn to evaluate their own work with teacher supervision, thus helping themselves and each other in the process of improving. But to do so, they too must understand the target and the criteria. Then, when the summary judgment is needed, such as to assign a final grade, you as teacher/expert can evaluate the final performance.

Imagine what it would mean if your helpers, your trained and qualified evaluators of skills or products, were your students. Not only could they be participants in the kind of rater training spelled out in Figure 7.5, but also, they might even be partners in devising the performance criteria themselves. And, once trained, what if they took charge of training some additional students, or perhaps trained their parents to be qualified raters, too? The pool of available helpers begins to grow as more participants begin to internalize the meaning of success in your classroom.

Without question, the best and most appropriate way to integrate performance assessment and instruction is to be absolutely certain that the important performance criteria serve as the goals and objectives of our instruction. As we teach students to understand and demonstrate key dimensions of performance, we prepare them to achieve the targets we value. We prepare in sound and appropriate ways to be held accountable for student learning when we are clear and public about our performance criteria, and when we do all in our power to be sure students have the opportunity to learn to hit the target.

In addition, we can make performance assessment an integral part of teaching and learning by involving students in assessment development and use in the ways listed in Figure 7.7. These activities will help increase students' control of their own academic well-being and will remove the mystery that too often surrounds the meaning of success in the classroom.

Summary: Thoughtful Development Yields Sound Assessments and Energized Students

This chapter has been about the great potential of performance assessment, with its array of design possibilities. Please refer to Table 7.1 and consider once again the variety of classroom applications. However, we have tempered the presentation with the admonition to develop and use this assessment method cautiously. Performance assessment, like other methods, brings with it specific rules of evidence. We must all strive to meet those rigorous quality control standards.

To ensure quality, we discussed the conditions that must be present for performance assessment to be used effectively. We also discussed the need to understand the role of subjectivity. We analyzed the match between performance assessment and the various kinds of achievement targets, concluding that strong matches can be developed for reasoning, skills, and products. We discussed key context factors to consider when selecting this methodology for use in the classroom, centering mostly on the importance of having in place the necessary expertise and resources.

Clearly, the heart of this chapter was our exploration of the two basic steps in developing performance assessments:

- Share the performance criteria with students at the beginning of the unit of instruction.
- Collaborate with students in keeping track of which criteria have been covered in class and which are yet to come.
- Involve students in creating prominent visual displays of important performance criteria for bulletin boards.
- Engage students in the actual development of performance exercises.
- Engage students in comparing and contrasting examples of performance, some of which reflect high-quality work and some of which do not (perhaps as part of a process of developing performance criteria).
- Involve students in the process of transforming performance criteria into checklists, rating scales, and other recording methods.
- Have students evaluate their own and each other's performance, one-on-one and/or in cooperative groups.
- Have students rate performance and then conduct studies of how much agreement (i.e., objectivity) there was among student judges; see if degree of agreement increases as students become more proficient as performers and as judges.
- Have students write about their own growth over time with respect to specified criteria.
- Have students set specific achievement goals in terms of the criteria and then keep track of their own progress.
- Store several samples of each student's performance over time, either as a portfolio or on videotape, if appropriate, and have students compare old performance to new, discussing their own growth.
- Have students predict their performance criterion-by-criterion, and then check actual evaluations to see if their predictions are accurate.

Figure 7.7
Ideas for student-involved assessment

- Clarifying performance (dealing with the nature and focus of the achievement being assessed)
- Developing performance tasks (dealing with the way we elicit performance for observation and judgment)

As we covered each step, we framed the possibilities available to you as a classroom teacher, establishing standards for sound performance criteria and performance tasks. We will return to both of those in Part III of this book, where we study examples of each.

In my opinion, the most practical part of the presentation in this chapter occurred when we devised five practical steps for formulating your own sound performance criteria, urging collaboration with students and/or colleagues in the process. This is most practical because it affords you the best opportunities for bringing students into your performance assessment development and for teaching them the most valuable lessons. We began by comparing and contrasting examples of performance to discover the active ingredients of quality. Then from there, we began to boil those ingredients down to their essence: concise statements of the meaning of academic excellence. Once you and your students learn to apply those standards to evaluating student work, you are on the road to success.

As schools continue to evolve, I predict that we will come to rely increasingly on performance assessment as part of the basis for our evaluation of student achievement. Hopefully, we will find even more and better ways of integrating performance assessment and instruction. I feel strongly that, whatever those better ways are, they will have their foundation in student involvement. Let us strive for the highest-quality, most rigorous assessments our resources will allow.

Exercises for Self-Assessment

① defining ② criteria performance task

1. Learn the two basic parts of and design decisions that guide performance assessment development so you can restate them without reference to the book. These are essential to the thoughtful application of this assessment format.

2. Referring to the text, list the aspects of performance assessment design that require professional judgment and the dangers of bias associated with each.

3. Again, referring to the text, specify in writing the kinds of achievement targets that can be transformed into the performance assessment format and those that cannot.

4. Working with a colleague or fellow student, brainstorm the key considerations in devising a sound sample of performance exercises.

5. Learn the steps in developing your own performance criteria. If you know them, you can apply them automatically as appropriate.

6. In your own words and without referring to the text, list as many ways as you can to bring students into performance assessment as partners. Then check your list against the ideas offered in this chapter.

7. Let's say two teachers fundamentally disagree on the performance criteria to apply to evaluating a particular kind of student work. How should they resolve their difference of opinion?

8. Let's say a student and teacher have a legitimate difference of opinion about the standards of excellence to apply to evaluating a particular kind of student work. What should happen then? Should the teacher simply assert ultimate authority and conduct the evaluation anyway? What are the alternatives?

9. Performance assessment is a labor-intensive method. However, sprinkled throughout this chapter are a number of ideas that can save you time and make the method more practically useable. Write down as many of them as you can recall. Then leaf back through the chapter and find and list them.

You may go to the Companion Website at www.prenhall.com/stiggins and answer these questions in the Self-Assessment module.

Final Chapter Reflection

1. *What are the three most important new insights to come to you as a result of your study of this chapter?*
2. *Which of your previous questions about assessment can you now answer based on your study of this chapter?*
3. *What new questions have come to mind as a result of your study of this chapter that you hope to have answered as your study continues?*
4. *For practicing teachers only: What do you plan to do differently in assessment in your classroom as a result of your study of this book so far?*

For those in preservice study only: As you think about the classroom assessment environment that you hope to create for your students, how has your thinking changed as a result of your study of this book so far?

Workbook Activities

Those of you using the workbook, *Practice with Student-Involved Classroom Assessment*, as part of your study of this material will find the following activities and others included for Chapter 7:

- *Achievement Targets for Performance Assessment.*   What targets are worth the time and effort for a performance assessment? This activity provides practice in deciding.

- *A Term Paper Assignment.*   This case study is good for activating prior knowledge about performance assessment. The case brings up issues about teacher workload, student motivation, and quality.

- *Help Your Students Understand Performance Criteria.*   What are the essential elements of a performance that determine quality? An analogy helps students understand what performance criteria are all about.

- *Sorting Student Work.*   A good strategy for developing performance criteria is to sort student work into piles based on quality, then analyze differences across piles. This activity provides a concrete example. Do it along with your learning team, and/or with your students.

Personal Communication: Immediate Information about Achievement

---

CHAPTER FOCUS

This chapter answers the following guiding question:

> How can I best use my interaction with my students during instruction to provide information about their achievement?

You will come to understand the following principles during this part of our journey through the realm of classroom assessment:

1. Personal communication-based assessments align well with knowledge, understanding, and reasoning targets.

2. This kind of assessment can take a variety of forms, including instructional questions and answers, class discussions, conferences and interviews, oral exams, conversations with others about students, and student journals.

3. Using personal communication in conjunction with other methods can deepen our understanding of student learning.

4. As with the other methods, this one can fall prey to avoidable sources of bias that can distort results if we are not careful.

5. By involving our students in assessments that rely on personal communication, we can set them up for energetic and successful learning.

As we start this part of our journey, keep our big picture in mind. Look at Figure 8.1. Once again, we will be dealing in depth with the shaded areas.

	SELECTED RESPONSE	ESSAY	PERFORMANCE ASSESSMENT	PERSONAL COMMUNICATION
Know				
Reason				
Skills				
Products				
Dispositions				

Figure 8.1
Aligning achievement targets and assessment methods

Classroom Interaction as Assessment

Teachers gather a great deal of valuable information about student achievement by talking with them. We seldom think of this personal communication as assessment, but it often is. At different times during teaching and learning, we might ask questions, listen to answers, and evaluate achievement, or we might conduct conferences with students that, in effect, serve as interviews that yield information about achievement. These kinds of assessments are the focus of this chapter.

You will find that the tenor of this chapter is somewhat different from that of the three previous methodology chapters. My intent is not so much to provide precise detail on procedures as it is to describe the factors to be aware of as you draw inferences about students' achievement based on what you hear from them. If you interact in a focused manner, listen attentively, and are cautious in the conclusions you draw, your personal communications with students can provide a clear window into student learning.

For example, sometimes our communications with students simply provide information that corroborates or calls into question assessment results secured through other, more structured means. Sometimes, we use question and answer exchanges during instruction to find out if the class as a whole or individual students are on track or tuned in—to monitor and adjust, if you will. In addition, we often use various forms of personal communication to encourage and evaluate student reasoning and problem solving.

As teachers, we also frequently engage in the following forms of student communication:

- Conduct conferences with students that, in effect, serve as interviews yielding information about achievement.

- Listen carefully for student contributions during class discussions to evaluate student reasoning.

- Conduct oral examinations to assess mastery of required material.

- Request that students collect their thoughts about their learning in various forms of journals, diaries, and logs.

When we use these forms of assessment with care, we can tap dimensions of achievement not easily accessed through other means. For example, an effective questioner can use properly sequenced questions to probe deeply into students' reasoning processes to help them tune in to and understand their own problem-solving approaches. Further, thoughtful questioners can effectively link assessment to instruction by using questions to uncover and immediately correct students' misconceptions or faulty reasoning.

By the same token, if we are not careful in our use of personal communication as assessment, as with other modes of assessment, we can mismeasure students' achievement. As you shall see, the list of potential pitfalls is as long as that for performance or for paper and pencil assessments. In fact, in some senses, the list of challenges to the effective use of personal communication assessment is even longer than those of other modes because we often communicate casually in an informal context, where bias can creep in without our noticing it. The good news is that we know how to overcome these potential problems.

Nowhere is classroom assessment more of an art than when using personal communication to track student growth and development. Typically, there is no table of test specifications to match against our intended target. There are no test items to check for quality, no score results. We can't check for agreement among observers to see if judgments are consistent. Personal communication is more spontaneous, more personal.

Nevertheless, you must understand and appreciate the fact that even this more artistic mode of assessment carries with it specific rules of evidence. Understand and adhere to those rules and you can derive valuable information about the attainments of your students. Disregard those rules and, just as with other forms of assessment, you can do great harm. With this form of assessment, just as with the others, you must vigilantly pursue quality.

This chapter will, once again, cover the context factors to consider when selecting this mode of assessment and the role of subjective teacher judgment. We will explore alignment to achievement targets, and the various types of personal communication available for teacher use.

The Unique Power of Personal Communication

As with other forms of assessment, you can forge a clear and complete link between your questioning strategies and the focus of instruction. Even as teaching and learning is progressing, a few strategically placed questions can help you to monitor and adjust. But beyond this, personal communication affords you some special strengths.

For example, unlike some other forms of assessment, if you are startled or puzzled by a student's response you can ask follow-up questions to dig more deeply into student thinking. In other words, you can get beyond a particular response to explore its origins. If you find misconceptions, you can take immediate action to correct them.

If we vary that theme just a bit, we come upon another power of personal communication. You can attach those follow-up questions to any other mode of assessment to gain deeper understanding of student achievement. For instance, let's say a student fails a performance assessment and you wish to discover why in order to help that student find success. You can follow up the failure with a few carefully phrased questions to see if it was due to a lack of prerequisite knowledge or to poor-quality reasoning on the student's part.

Third, also unlike some other forms of assessment, personal communication can be spontaneous, allowing you to take advantage of unexpected opportunities to assess and promote achievement. That is, when you sense a need for a bit more information on student thinking, you can strike while the iron is hot and take advantage of a teachable moment.

Fourth, personal communication is almost infinitely flexible in its applications as classroom assessment. It can focus on a range of valued outcomes. It can focus the assessment microscope on individual students or on students as a group. It can sample students and/or the material being covered. Students may volunteer to respond, or you can call on anyone. Interaction can be public or private. Questions and answers can come from either you or students. Assessment can be structured or informal. Considering the flexibility indicated here, you must agree that this is a versatile mode of assessment.

Fifth and finally, to the attentive user, students' nonverbal reactions can provide valuable insights into achievement and feelings about the material learned (or not learned). These indicators of confidence or uncertainty, excitement or boredom, and comfort or anxiety can lead you to probe more deeply into the underlying causes. This kind of perception checking can result in levels of student–teacher communication not achievable through other assessment means.

The Foundations of Ensuring Quality Assessment

As with the other three assessment methods we have studied, the quality of a personal communication-based assessment turns on its use in appropriate contexts and on your ability to manage effectively the subjectivity inherent in this method.

Context Factors

There are several contextual pitfalls to sound assessment using personal communication about which you must remain constantly aware.

A Common Language Is the Foundation.   Teacher and student must share a common language to communicate effectively. This factor has become more and more critical through the 1980s and 1990s, as ethnic and cultural diversity have increased markedly in our schools. By *common language*, I don't just mean a shared vocabulary and grammar, although these obviously are critical to communication. I also mean a common sense of the manner in which a culture shares meaning through verbal and nonverbal cues. Ethnicity and cultural heritage may differ between student and teacher. If you assess by means of personal communication, you must know how to make meaning in the language and culture of your students. When you lack that understanding, you ensure mismeasurement.

Personality Is Important as Well.   Shy, withdrawn students simply may not perform well in this kind of assessment context, regardless of their real achievement. To make these methods work, two people must connect in an open, communicative manner. For some students, this simply is too risky, often for reasons beyond your control.

> Attend carefully to these key context factors to keep bias from creeping into your assessments. This maximizes the accuracy of your assessments.

This coin has two sides: There also is the danger that students with very outgoing, aggressive personalities will try to lay down a "smoke screen" to mislead you with respect to their real achievement. But, this works only with assessors who have not prepared carefully, and who cannot stay focused. You fall prey to the dangers of bias in assessment when you allow yourself to be distracted by irrelevant factors.

You Must Allow Sufficient Time.   There must be enough time available to carry out this one-on-one form of assessment. When the target is narrow in scope and you are assessing only a few students, time may not be a factor. A question or two may suffice to provide a quick glimpse into achievement. No problem.

However, as the target broadens and the number of students increases, two time dimensions become more important. First, there must be enough time to permit you to interact with each student whose achievement you are assessing. Second, there must be sufficient time available with each student to allow you to properly sample achievement. If this time is not available, it is better to turn to another strategy that does not require such intense one-on-one contact.

Create a Safe Environment.   Personal communication works best as assessment when students feel they are in a safe learning environment. There are many ways to interpret this. One kind of safety permits them to succeed or fail in private, without an embarrassing public spotlight. For instance, in some cultures, it is unseemly to make public displays of competence—to call attention to one's self as standing above others. A safe environment accommodates a cultural imperative for these students.

Another kind of safety takes the form of a peer environment sensitive to the plight of those who perform less well and supportive of their attempts to grow. Still another kind of safety comes from having the opportunity to learn more and perform again later with the promise of a higher level of success. Nowhere is personal safety more important to sound assessment than when that assessment is conducted through public personal communication.

Students Must Understand the Need for Honesty.   Personal communication works best as assessment when students understand that sometimes as their teacher you need an honest answer, not their attempt at a best possible answer or the answer they think will please you. This mode of assessment provides its best information most efficiently when a sound interpersonal relationship exists between you and your students. Again, the key is trust. Students must know that if they give you the "socially desirable" response to a question, a response that misrepresents the truth about their achievement or feelings, then you will be less able to help them.

Accurate Records Are Key.   Because there frequently are no tangible results from assessments conducted via personal communication, such as a grade or score, records of achievement can be lost. Over a span of a few moments or hours when the communication focuses on narrow targets for a few students, this may not be a problem. But when the context includes many students, complex targets, and a requirement of extended storage, you absolutely must maintain tangible, written or taped records of some kind. If you have no means or hope of doing so when necessary, you would do better to revise your assessment plans.

Figure 8.2 summarizes these six practical keys to the effective use of assessment by means of personal communication by transforming them into seven quality control questions that you can ask about your assessments (the language key is subdivided into its two aspects).

The Role of Subjective Judgment in Personal Communication

Professional judgment, and therefore subjectivity, permeates all aspects of assessments that rely on personal communication:

- Achievement targets we set for students
- Questions we pose (and sometimes generate on the spot)
- Criteria we apply in evaluating answers (often without a great deal of time to reflect)
- Performance records we store (sometimes in memory!)
- Manner in which we retrieve those results for later use
- Interpretations we make of the results
- Various ways in which we use those results

Things to investigate:

- Do teacher and students share a common language?
- Have students attained a sufficiently high level of verbal fluency to interact effectively?
- Do students have personalities that permit them to open up enough to reveal true achievement?
- Is there sufficient time for assessment?
- Do students see the environment as safe enough to reveal their true achievement?
- Do students understand the need to reveal their true achievement?
- Can accurate records of achievement be kept?

Figure 8.2
Factors to consider when using personal communication as assessment

This subjectivity makes it imperative that, as with other assessment methods, you know and understand your achievement target and know how to translate it into clear and specific questions and other probes to generate focused information.

Let's be specific about the three reasons not to take personal communication as assessment too lightly as a source of information and as a teaching strategy. These reasons are (1) the problem of forgetting, (2) the problem of filters, and (3) the challenge of sampling.

> Here again, we find a list of potential ways that factors other than achievement can distort, or **BIAS**, assessment results.
>
> TECHNICAL NOTE

The Problem of Forgetting   The first reason for caution is that we must remain mindful of the fallibility of the human mind as a recording device. Not only can we forget and lose things in there, but also, the things we try to remember about a student's performance can change over time for various reasons, only some of which are within our control. We must act purposely to counteract this danger by conducting quality assessments and recording results before they get lost or are changed in our minds.

The Problem of Filters   We also must remain aware of and strive to understand those personal and professional filters, developed over years of experience, through which we hear and process student responses. They represent norms or standards, if you will, that allow us to interpret and act on the achievement information that comes to us through observation and personal communication.

These filters hold the potential for improving or harming assessment quality. On the good side, if we set achievement expectations based on a thorough understanding of a particular field of study and if we interpret the things students say with those clearly held and appropriate standards, we can use personal communication as a positive and productive form of assessment.

Further, if we set our expectations for individual learners on the basis of accurate information about their current levels of achievement, we maximize the chances that we will be able to assist them in achieving more. These represent appropriate uses of norms and expectations.

However, there is a dark side to these interpretive filters. They can be the source of inappropriate bias. If we set our expectations for students, not on the basis of a clear understanding of the discipline or on the basis of careful assessment of student capabilities, but on the basis of stereotypes or other convenient categories of people that are in fact unrelated to real academic achievement, we risk doing great harm indeed. If, for example, we establish professional filters by holding predetermined expectations of learners according to gender, ethnic heritage, cultural background, physical appearance, linguistic experience, our knowledge of a student's prior achievement, or any of a variety of other forms of prejudice, unrelated to actual achievement, we allow bias to creep into assessment.

The insidious aspect is that we are hardly ever aware of our own biases. We don't go around saying, "I don't like boys who are athletes," or "I have a feeling that this student can do this, even though she didn't do so on this occasion." Biases are subtle and operate even when we're trying to be as objective as possible.

We can only counter these dangers by adhering to the basic rules of sound assessment: Articulate clear targets. Transform them into sound assessment exercises and scoring guides. Sample appropriately. Control bias.

Time for Reflection

As a student, have you ever been on the losing end of a biased assessment where for some reason, your teacher's inappropriate personal or professional filters led to an incorrect assessment of your proficiency? What was that like? What effect did it have on your learning?

The Challenge of Sampling.   Just as with other forms of assessment, we can make sampling mistakes. One is to gather incorrect information by asking the wrong questions, questions that fail to reflect important forms of achievement. We sample the wrong thing, such as by asking knowledge-recall questions when we really want to get at understanding.

Another mistake is to gather too few bits of information to lead to confident conclusions about proficiency. Our sample is too small.

Still another sampling mistake is to spend too much time gathering too many bits of information. This is a problem of inefficiency. We eventually reach a point of diminishing returns, where collecting additional information is unlikely to change our conclusion about proficiency.

To avoid such sampling problems, we must seek just enough information without overdoing it. In the classroom, this is very much a matter of subjective judgment. Thus, it represents another example of a place where the art of classroom assessment, your professional judgment, comes into play.

Remember, *any assessment represents only a sample of an ideal assessment of infinite length*. The key to successful sampling in the context of personal communication is to ask a representative set of questions, one that is long enough to give you confidence in the generalizations you draw to the entire performance domain.

Example of an Easy Fit.   Mr. Lopez, the elementary teacher who has been sharing his insights during our journey, tells this story illustrative of a time when sampling challenges were relatively easy to meet:

> "I was about to start a new science reading activity on fish with my third graders. As a prereading activity, I wanted to be sure all my students had sufficient background information about fish to understand the reading. So I checked the story very carefully for vocabulary and concepts that might be stumbling blocks for my students. Then I simply asked a few strategic questions of the class, probing understanding of those words and ideas and calling on students randomly to answer. As I sampled the group's prior knowledge through questions and answers, I made mental notes about who seemed not to know some of the key material. There were only three or four. Later, I went back and questioned each of them more thoroughly to be sure. Then I helped them to learn the new material before they began reading."

In this scenario, the performance arena is quite small and focused: vocabulary and concepts from within one brief science story. Sampling by means of personal communication was simple and straightforward, and there are no real record-keeping challenges presented. Mr. Lopez simply verified understanding on the part of the students before proceeding. After that, most records of performance could go on the back burner. Mr. Lopez did make a mental note to follow up with those students who had the most difficulty, but decided that all other records could be "deleted."

Example of a More Challenging Fit.   Now here's a scenario in which the assessment challenges are more formidable: A high school health teacher wants to rely extensively on small- and large-group discussions of health-related social issues to encourage student participation in class discussions. To accomplish this, she announces at the beginning of the year that 25 percent of each student's grade will be based on the extent and quality of their participation in class. She is careful to point out that she will call on people to participate and that she expects them to be ready.

This achievement target is broader in two ways: It contains many more elements (the domain is much larger), and it spans a much longer period of time. Not only does the teacher face an immense challenge in adequately sampling each individual's performance, but also, her record-keeping challenge is much more complex and demanding. Consider the record-keeping dilemma posed by a class schedule that includes, say, four sections of eleventh-grade health, each including 30 students! Mental record keeping is not an option: When we try to store such information in our gray matter for too long, bad things happen. Besides, this qualifies as a high-stakes assessment. So the pressure is on to do it right. These are not unsolvable problems, but they take careful preparation to assess. In this sense, they represent a significant challenge to the teacher.

These two scenarios capture the essence of the quality control challenge you face when you choose to rely on personal communication as a means of assessing student achievement. You must constantly ask yourself: Is my achievement target narrow enough in its scope and short enough in its time span to allow for conscientious sampling of the performance of an individual student or students as a group? If the answer is yes, in your opinion, proceed to the next question: Is the target narrow enough in its scope and short enough in its time span to allow me to keep accurate records of performance? If the answer again is yes, proceed. *If the answer to either question is no, choose another assessment method.*

Time for Reflection

A PE teacher is about to start a new game with a class of 30 fourth graders. She thinks the rules are familiar to all, but decides to check just to be sure. So she picks a student and asks what that student should do, according to the rules, if a particular situation arises. The student answers correctly. She calls on another, seeking a second interpretation. Correct again. She infers that the class knows the rules. Soon, the game falls into disarray due to rules violations. What mistake(s) did the teacher make? What should she have done?

Avoiding Problems Due to Subjectivity.   We can avoid problems due to the fallibility of the human mind and bias only by attending to those five ever-present, important, basic attributes of sound assessment as they apply in the context of personal communication. Whether we plan or are spontaneous in our personal communication with students, we must bear these quality standards in mind. Figure 8.3 reviews these standards as they apply to personal communication as assessment.

When we meet these standards of quality, personal communication holds the promise of providing rich and useful data about student attainment of important educational outcomes. Obviously, as with other methods, one prominent key to our success is the match of our method to the various outcomes we need to assess. We discuss how to find sound matches next.

Matching Method to Target

Personal communication-based assessments can provide direct evidence of proficiency in three of our five kinds of targets and can provide insight into the student's readiness to deliver on the other two. This is a versatile assessment option.

Attribute of Quality	Defining Question
Arise from a clear and specific achievement target	Do my questions reflect the achievement target I want my students to hit?
Serve clear purposes	Why am I assessing? How will results be used?
Assure a sound representation of that target	Can the target of interest to me be accurately reflected through personal communication with the student?
Sample performance appropriately	Do I have enough evidence?
Control for unwanted interference	Am I in touch with potential sources of bias, and have I minimized the effects of personal and professional filters?

Figure 8.3
Defining issues of quality for personal communication as classroom assessment

Assessing Knowledge and Understanding

This can be done with personal communication, but you need to be cautious. Obviously, you can question students to see if they have mastered the required knowledge or can retrieve it through the effective use of reference materials. To succeed, however, you must possess a keen sense of the limits and contents of the domain of knowledge. Once again, since you cannot ask all possible questions, especially using this labor-intensive method, your questions must sample and generalize in a representative manner. And remember, knowing and understanding are not the same thing. So you will want to query both.

Assessing Reasoning

Herein lies the real strength of personal communication as a means of assessment. Skillful questioners can probe student reasoning and problem solving, both while the very thinking process is under way and retrospectively, to analyze how students reached a solution. But even more exciting is that you can use questioning to help both of you understand and enhance each other's reasoning.

For example, you can ask students to let you in on their thought processes as they analyze events or objects, describing component parts. You can probe their abilities to draw meaningful comparisons, to make simple or complex inferences, or to express and defend an opinion or point of view. There is no more powerful method for exploring student reasoning and problem solving than a conversation while students are actually trying to solve the problem. By exploring their reasoning along with them, you can provide students with the kinds of understanding and vocabulary needed to converse with you and with each other about what it means to be proficient in this performance arena.

Asking students to "think out loud" offers great promise for delving deeply into their reasoning. For example, mathematics teachers often ask students to talk about their thinking while proceeding step by step through the solution to a complex math problem. This provides a richness of insight into students' mathematical reasoning that cannot be attained in any other way. Further, as students talk through a process, you also can insert follow-up questions: Why did you take (or omit) certain steps? What would have happened if you had . . . ? Do you see any similarities between this problem and those we worked on last week? When students are unable to solve the problem, tactical questioning strategies can tell you why. Did they lack prerequisite knowledge? Analyze the problem incorrectly? Misunderstand the steps in the process? These probes permit you to find student needs and link your assessment to instruction almost immediately—there is no need to wait for the score reports to be returned!

Time for Reflection

One popular way of assessing reading comprehension these days is to have students retell a story they have just read. As the retelling unfolds, the teacher is free to ask questions as needed to probe the student's interpretation. Why do you think this kind of assessment has become so popular? What does it offer that, say, a multiple-choice test of reading comprehension does not?

Assessing Performance Skills and Products

In the previous chapter, we established that the only way to obtain direct information about student performance skills or proficiency in creating quality products is to have them actually "do" or "create" and compare their work to established standards of quality.

However, if you are a skilled teacher of "doing" or "creating" (i.e., a teacher who possesses a highly refined vision of such targets), you can ask your students to talk through a hypothetical performance, asking a few key questions along the way, and know with a certain degree of confidence whether they are likely to be proficient performers. You also can tell what aspects of their performance are likely to fall short of expectations.

This can save assessment time in the classroom. Let's say, for example, the kind of performance to be assessed is complex and the cost of time and materials required to conduct a full-blown performance assessment is quite high, as in an assessment of repairing an expensive piece of electronic equipment in a technology education class. If this teacher has some question about a particular student's proficiency and, therefore, is hesitant about investing the time and equipment needed to carry out the assessment, he could simply sit down and talk with the student. He could ask a few critical questions, and, based on the level of achievement reflected in the student's answers, infer whether it would be proper to conduct the actual assessment or offer additional instruction and more time to prepare.

In this same performance-related sense, you can ask students strategic questions to examine the following:

- Prior success in performing similar tasks
- Their sense of certainty or uncertainty about the quality of their work
- Knowledge and understanding of the criteria used to evaluate performance (i.e., key skills to be demonstrated or key attributes of quality products)
- Awareness of the steps necessary to create quality products

Based on the results of such probes, you can infer competence. But again, talking is not doing. Without question, some may be able to talk a better game than they can actually deliver. So clearly, personal communication is inferior to actual performance assessment when it comes to evaluating skill and product outcomes. But under certain circumstances, it can be an inexpensive, accessible, and instructionally relevant form of classroom assessment.

Assessing Dispositions

Herein resides another strength of personal communication as a form of assessment. Perhaps the most productive way to determine the direction and intensity of students' school-related attitudes, interests, values, or motivational dispositions is simply to ask them. An ongoing pattern of honest exchanges of points of view between you and your students can contribute much to creating powerful learning environments.

The keys to making personal communication work in the assessment of student affect are trust and open channels of communication. If students are confident that it's all right to say what they really think and feel, they will do so.

Time for Reflection

What kinds of questions might you ask a student to tap the direction and intensity of that student's true, honest feelings about the learning environment in your classroom?

Summary of Target Matches

Personal communication in its many forms can supply useful information to teachers about a variety of important educational outcomes, including mastery of subject matter knowledge, reasoning and problem solving, procedural knowledge that is prerequisite to skill and product creation proficiency, and dispositions. Table 8.1 presents a summary of matches.

To create effective matches between this method of assessment and these kinds of targets, however, you must start with a clear vision of the outcomes to be

Table 8.1
Personal communication: Assessment of achievement targets

Target to be Assessed	Personal Communication
Knowledge & Understanding	Can ask questions, evaluate answers, and infer mastery, but a time-consuming option
Reasoning Proficiency	Can ask students to "think aloud" or can ask follow-up questions to probe reasoning
Performance Skills	Strong match when skill is oral communication proficiency; also can assess mastery of knowledge prerequisite to skillful performance
Ability to Create Products	Can probe procedural knowledge and knowledge of attributes of quality products, but not product quality
Dispositions	Can talk with students about their feelings

attained. In addition, you must know how to translate that vision into clear, focused questions, share a common language, open channels of communication with students, and understand how to sample performance representatively. But none of these keys to success is powerful enough to overcome the problems that arise when your interpretive filters predispose you to be inappropriately biased in deciphering communication from students.

The Many Forms of Personal Communication as Assessment

In each case, the procedural guidelines listed here are intended to sharpen the focus (validity) of questions while minimizing the chances of inaccurate (unreliable) assessment due to bias.

Throughout the previous discussion of quality control, we have addressed personal communication as a mode of assessment. As with the other three modes, this one includes a variety of assessment formats: questioning, conferences and interviews, class discussions, oral examinations, and journals and logs. We will define each format and identify several keys to its effective use in the classroom.

Instructional Questions and Answers

This has been a foundation of education since before Socrates. As instruction proceeds, either the teacher or the students themselves pose questions for others to answer. This activity promotes thinking and learning, and also provides information about achievement. The teacher listens to answers, interprets them in terms of internally held standards, infers the respondent's level of attainment, and proceeds accordingly.

The following keys to successful use will help you take advantage of the strengths of this as an assessment format, while overcoming weaknesses:

- Plan key questions in advance of instruction, so as to ensure proper alignment with the target and with students' capabilities.

- Ask clear, brief questions that help students focus on a relatively narrow range of acceptable responses.

- Probe various kinds of reasoning, not just recall of facts and information.

- Ask the question first and then call on the person who is to respond. This will have the effect of keeping all students on focus.

- Call on both volunteer and nonvolunteer respondents. This, too, will keep all students on task.

- Keep mental records of performance only for a few students at a time and over no more than a day or two. Written records are essential for large numbers of students over longer periods.

- Acknowledge correct or high-quality responses; probe incorrect responses for underlying reasons. Also regarding incorrect or low-quality responses, remember that the public display of achievement (or the lack thereof) links closely to self-concept. Strive to leave respondents with something positive to grow on.

- After posing a question, wait for a response. Let respondents know that you always expect a response and will wait for as long as it takes.

While this last suggestion, allowing time for students to respond, turns out to be surprisingly difficult to do, research reviewed and summarized by Rowe (1978) reveals many benefits. These effects appear to be most positive when we give traditionally low-achieving students time to respond:

- The length of student responses increases.

- The number of unsolicited but appropriate responses increases.

- Failure to respond decreases.

- Student confidence increases.

- The incidence of creative, speculative responses increases.

- Student-centered interaction increases, while teacher-centered teaching decreases.

- Students defend inferences better.

- The number of questions asked by students increases.

- Slow students contribute more.

- Discipline problems decrease.

- Teachers tend to view their class as including fewer academically weak students.

- Teachers are less likely to expect only their brighter students to respond.

If we can force ourselves not to fill the silence with the sound of our own voices and can wait for responses to brief, clearly focused questions, not only do we obtain sound assessment information, but also, in effect we integrate assessment deeply into the instructional process.

And remember, some students are taught in their family cultures to avoid circumstances where they appear to be holding themselves up as being more knowledgeable than others. Thus, there is the danger of bias. They may well know the answer to your question even though they don't respond to you. To avoid problems with this kind of bias, learn about the cultures of your students.

The Nature of Questions.   If our objective is to help our students become active strategic thinkers, using their new insights to make meaning—as opposed to training them to be robots regurgitating what they have learned—the questions we pose for them are crucial to their success.

Hunkins (1995) summarizes concisely the various ways that questioning can draw students into constructing their own meaning from the material they study. Table 8.2 presents a list of questioning techniques that serve specific learning functions and that have particular instructional implications. In effect, each of these techniques turns the questioning into a partnership between teacher and student, making students responsible in part for the success of the interchange. In these ways, we encourage students to begin to evaluate the quality of their own responses.

Questions need not always flow from teacher to student. Students can ask themselves key questions and then discuss their answers with you, their teacher. For example, here are some questions that can focus student reflection on their reading experiences:

Understanding	Did I understand what I read?
Ease	Was the reading easy or difficult for me?
Meaning	Did I learn anything from this? If so, what?
Evaluation	Was it well written?
Pleasure	Did I like what I read?

These and similar questions can provide an excellent basis from which to encourage students to think aloud in conversation with you about their reading.

Conferences and Interviews

Some student-teacher conferences serve as structured or unstructured audits of student achievement, in which the objective is to talk about what students have learned and have yet to learn. Teachers and students talk directly and openly about levels of student attainment, comfort with the material the students are mastering, specific needs, interests, and desires, and/or any other achievement-related topics that contribute to an effective teaching and learning environment. In effect, teachers and students speak together in the service of understanding how to work effectively together.

Table 8.2
Questioning techniques that draw students into learning

Technique	Function	Examples	Instructional Implications
Probing	Encourages in-depth response; clarifies respondent's intent	How do you know that?	Must demand and provide time for response; encourages respondent to dig deeper in processing the question.
Clarification	Probes the precise meaning of response and prevents misinterpretation	What do you mean by that?	Sets the expectation that "vague" responses are unacceptable and encourages thoughtful, precise answers.
Elaboration	Adds depth to response; encourages respondent to bring in more information	Can you share an example?	Curriculum must offer enough depth of information on key topics to permit elaboration
Redirection	Encourages respondents to approach a problem from a different perspective	What if you approached the problem from this direction?	Instruction must encourage flexibility in thinking, so respondents know when and how to redirect.
Supporting	Furnishes respondent with cognitive and affective encouragement	That's right. But how did you come to that conclusion? Or That's not correct. But what made you think that?	Classroom assessment environment must help students feel that it is safe to take risks and that they are valued as questioners.

Note: Adapted from *Teaching Thinking Through Effective Questioning* (p. 216) by F. P. Hunkins, 1995, Norwood, MA: Christopher-Gordon Publishers, Inc. Adapted by permission.

Remember, interviews or conferences need not be conceived as every-pupil, standardized affairs, with each event a carbon copy of the others. You might meet with only one student, if it fills a communication need. Also, interviews or conferences might well vary in their focus with students who have different needs. The following are keys to your successful use of conference and interview assessment formats:

- Both participants must be open to honest communication and willing to examine the real, important aspects of teaching and learning.

- Keep your interview questions sharply focused on your content and reasoning achievement targets.

- Carefully think out and plan your questions in advance. Remember, students can share in their preparation.

- Plan for enough uninterrupted time to conduct the entire interview or conference.
- Be sure to conclude each interview with a summary of the lessons learned and their implications for how you and the student will work together in the future.

One important strength of the interview or conference as a mode of assessment lies in the impact it can have on your student–teacher relationships. When conducted in a context where you have been up front about expectations, students understand the achievement target, and all involved are invested in student success, conferences have the effect of empowering students to take responsibility for at least part of the assessment of their own progress. Conducted in a context where everyone is committed to success and where academic success is clearly and openly defined, interviews inform and motivate both you and your students.

Class Discussions

When students participate in class discussions, the things they say reveal a great deal about their achievements and their feelings. Discussions are teacher- or student-led group interactions in which the material to be mastered is explored from various perspectives. Teachers listen to the interaction, evaluate the quality of student contributions, and infer individual student or group achievement. Clearly, class discussions have the simultaneous effect of promoting both student learning and their ability to use what they know.

To take advantage of the strengths of this method of assessment, while minimizing the impact of potential weaknesses, follow these keys to successful use:

- Prepare questions or discussion issues in advance to focus sharply on the intended achievement target.
- Be sure to differentiate between achievement targets that are a matter of the content of students' contributions and targets that are a matter of the form of their communication. Be clear about the meaning of success in both cases.
- Involve students in preparing for discussions, being sure their questions and key issues are part of the mix.
- Rely on debate or other team formats to maximize the number of students who can be directly involved. Pay special attention to involving low achievers.
- Formalize the discussion format to the extent that different roles are identified, such as moderator, team leader, spokesperson, recorder, and so on, to maximize the number of students who have the opportunity to present evidence of their achievement.
- Remember, the public display of achievement represents a risk that links that achievement (or the lack thereof) to self-concept. Be aware of those times when that risk must be controlled a bit for student good.

- Provide those students who have a more reserved personal style or whose cultures disdain public displays of competence with other equally acceptable means of demonstrating achievement.

- Contexts where achievement information derived from participation in discussion is to influence high-stakes decisions, such as a grade, *require* dependable written or taped records of performance.

The great strength of class discussion as assessment is in its ability to reveal the depth and quality of students' reasoning, their abilities to analyze, compare, infer, and defend points of view. The great danger of this method is the difficulty of sampling student performance in a complete and equitable manner. You must take care to structure discussions thoughtfully if you use them as assessments.

Oral Examinations

In European educational traditions and current assessment practices, the oral examination still plays a strong role. Teachers plan and pose exercises for their students, who reflect and provide oral responses. Teachers listen to and interpret those responses, evaluating quality and inferring levels of achievement.

In a very real sense, this is like essay assessment, discussed in Chapter 7, but with the added benefit of being able to ask follow-up questions.

While the oral examination tradition lost favor in the United States with the advent of selected response assessment, it still has great potential for use today, especially given the increasing complexity of our valued educational targets and the complexity and cost of setting up higher-fidelity performance assessments.

You can take advantage of the strengths of this format by adhering to some simple keys to its successful use, in effect the quality control guidelines listed in Chapter 7 for the development of quality essay assessments:

- Develop brief exercises that focus on the desired target.

- Rely on exercises that identify the knowledge to be brought to bear, specify the kind of reasoning students are to use, and identify the standards you will apply in evaluating responses.

- Develop written scoring criteria in advance of the assessment.

- Be sure criteria separate content and reasoning targets from facility with verbal expression.

- Prepare in advance to accommodate the needs of any students who may confront language proficiency barriers.

- Have a checklist, rating scale, or other method of recording results ready to use at the time of the assessment.

- If necessary, record responses for later reevaluation.

Clearly, the major argument against this format of assessment is the amount of time it takes to administer oral exams. However, you can overcome part of this problem by bringing students into the assessment process as partners. If you adhere to the guidelines listed above and spread the work of administering and scoring over many shoulders, you may derive great benefit from oral assessment.

Journals and Logs

Sometimes personal communication-based assessment can take a written form. Students can share views, experiences, insights, and information about important learnings by writing about them. You can derive clear and useful information by assigning writing tasks that cause students to center on particularly important achievement targets. Further, you can then provide them with written feedback.

Four particular forms bear consideration: response journals, personal writing journals or diaries, dialog journals, and learning logs. These are infinitely flexible ways of permitting students to communicate about their learning, while at the same time practicing their writing and applying valued patterns of reasoning. In addition, because these written records accumulate over time, you can use them to help students reflect on their improvement as achievers.

Response journals are most useful in situations where you ask students to read and construct meaning from literature, such as in the context of reading and English instruction. As they read, students write about their reactions. Typically, you would provide structured assignments to guide them, including such tasks as the following:

- Analyze characters in terms of key attributes or contribution to the story.
- Analyze evolving story lines, plots, or story events.
- Compare one piece of literature or character to another.
- Anticipate or predict upcoming events.
- Evaluate either the piece as a whole or specific parts in terms of appropriate criteria.
- Suggest ways to change or improve character, plot, or setting, defending such suggestions.

Teachers who use response journals report that it is an excellent way to permit students to practice applying reasoning patterns, and to increase the intensity of student involvement with their reading. Further, it can provide a means for students to keep track of all the things they have read, building in them a sense of accomplishment in this facet of their reading.

Personal writing journals or *diaries* represent the least structured of the journal options. In this case, you would give students time during each instructional day to write in their journals. The focus of their writing is up to them, as is the amount they write. Sometimes you evaluate the writing, sometimes it is merely for practice. When you evaluate it, either you, or the student, or both, make judgments. Often young writers are encouraged to use their journals to experiment with new forms of writing, such as dramatic dialogue, poetry, or some other art form. Some teachers suggest to their students that they use personal journals as a place to store ideas for future writing topics. This represents an excellent way to gain insight into the quality of student writing when students are operating at typical levels of motivation to write well. Because there is no high-stakes assessment under way, they do not have to strive for excellence. They can write for the fun of it and still provide both themselves and you with evidence over time of their improvement as writers.

Dialogue journals capture conversations between students and teachers in the truest sense of that idea. As teaching and learning proceed, students write messages to you conveying thoughts and ideas about the achievement expected, self-evaluations of progress, points of confusion, important new insights, and so on, and periodically give you their journals. You then read the messages and reply, clarifying as needed, evaluating an idea, amplifying a key point, and so on, and return the journals to the students. This process links you and each of your students in a personal communication partnership.

Learning logs ask students to keep ongoing written records of the following aspects of their studies:

- Achievement targets they have mastered
- Targets they have found useful and important
- Targets they are having difficulty mastering
- Learning experiences (instructional strategies) that worked particularly well for them
- Experiences that did not work for them
- Questions that have come up along the way that they want help with
- Ideas for important study topics or learning strategies that they might like to try in the future

The goal in the case of learning logs is to have students reflect on, analyze, describe, and evaluate their learning experiences, successes, and challenges, writing about the conclusions they draw. You have the freedom to be more or less structured in using learning logs. Certain circumstances may benefit from a high degree of structure, such as when you want students to center on and practice with a particular pattern of reasoning. In these cases, you would carefully structure learning log assignments. Under other circumstances, you may give students a great deal of freedom in logging their learning experiences. In any case, you can learn a great deal about students' academic self-concepts and achievements by viewing them through this window.

Student Involvement in Personal Communication

Because instruction is conducted in large part through personal interaction between teacher and student, in a very real sense students are always partners in personal communication-based forms of assessment. Nevertheless, we can list a variety of concrete strategies for helping this partnership reach its full potential. To see what I mean, study the ideas listed in Figure 8.4.

- Minimize the number of questions posed that simply require yes or no answers. Seek more complex responses as a matter of routine, so students come to expect it.
- Have students pose questions that tap different patterns of reasoning.
- Wait for a response. Let students know that you expect an answer and will not let them off the hook by allowing them to remain silent. Once they speak, the channels of communication are open.
- Keep the whole class involved by calling on non-volunteers, asking students to add to what someone just said, and asking them to signal if they agree or disagree.
- Turn leadership for discussion over to students; they can ask questions of each other or of you (put your own reasoning power on the line in public once in a while).
- Ask students to paraphrase each other's questions and responses.
- Ask students to address key questions in small groups, so more students can be involved.
- Offer students opportunities to become oral examiners, posing questions of each other.
- Ask students to keep track of changes in the depth of their own questions over time, such as through the use of tally sheets and diaries.
- Designate one or two students to be observers and recorders during discussions, noting who responds to what kinds of questions and how well; other teachers can do this too.
- Engage students in peer and self-assessment of performance in discussions.
- Schedule regular interviews with students, one-on-one or in groups.
- Schedule times when your students can interview you to get your impressions about how well things are going for them as individuals and as a group.

Figure 8.4
Ideas for student-involved assessment

Summary: Assessment as Sharing, Person-to-Person

The key to success in using personal communication to assess student achievement is to remember that, just because assessment is sometimes casual, informal, unstructured, and/or spontaneous, this does not mean we can let our guard down with respect to standards of assessment quality. In fact, we must be even more vigilant than with other forms of assessment, because it is so easy to allow personal filters, poor sampling techniques, and/or inadequate record keeping to interfere with sound assessment.

When we attend to quality standards, we use our interactions with students to assess important achievement targets, including mastery of knowledge, reasoning, and dispositions. We also can assess student mastery of knowledge and reasoning prerequisites to performance skills and product development capabilities. But remember, to tap the skills and products themselves, performance assessment is required.

Thus, like the other three modes of assessment, this one is quite flexible. Even though we typically don't refer to personal communication as assessment, if we start with a clear and appropriate vision, translate it into thoughtful probes, sample performance appropriately, and attend to key sources of bias, we can generate quality information in this manner.

So can students. Whether in whole-class discussions, smaller collaborative groups, or working with a partner, students can be assessors, too. They can ask questions of each other, listen to responses, infer achievement, and communicate feedback to each other. Beware, however. The ability to communicate effectively in an assessment context is not "wired in" from birth. Both you and your students must practice it, to hone it as an assessment skill.

Exercises for Self-Assessment

1. Identify three specific combinations of assessment purpose (user and use) and achievement targets that define classroom contexts in which you believe that personal communication would be the best method of assessment. For each, state why.

2. Refer to the text and list the strengths, limitations, and keys to effective use of the five formats of personal communication assessment: instructional questions and answers, conferences and interviews, class discussions, oral exams, and journals and logs.

3. Referring to the text, identify and describe in your own words the key considerations in sampling student performance via personal communication.

4. Learn the list shown in Figure 8.4 of ways to engage students in assessment using personal communication.

5. Assume that, as a first-grade teacher, you are about to read a story about volcanoes. To ensure that your students will understand the story, you want to be sure they know the meanings of several key words the author uses. You decide to ask a few questions of the class before beginning. How would you handle this assessment situation? Would personal communication play a role? If so, how? How might you appropriately sample achievement?

6. Assume you are a high school chemistry teacher needing to verify student adherence to safety rules in the science lab. How would you do so? What role might assessment via personal communication play? How might you appropriately sample performance?

7. Do you feel that assessment based on personal communication could be more beneficial to students and their academic well-being when used for some purposes than others? If so, for what classroom assessment purposes might they be most helpful? Why? Be specific.

You may go to the Companion Website at www.prenhall.com/stiggins and answer these questions in the Self-Assessment module.

Final Chapter Reflection

1. *What are the three most important new insights to come to you as a result of your study of this chapter?*
2. *Which of your previous questions about assessment can you now answer based on your study of this chapter?*
3. *What new questions have come to mind as a result of your study of this chapter that you hope to have answered as your study continues?*
4. *For practicing teachers only: What do you plan to do differently in assessment in your classroom as a result of your study of this book so far?*

   For those in preservice study only: As you think about the classroom assessment environment that you hope to create for your students, how has your thinking changed as a result of your study of this book so far?

Workbook Activities

Those of you using the workbook, *Practice with Student-Involved Classroom Assessment*, as part of your study of this material will find the following activities and others included for Chapter 8:

- *What Types of Personal Communication Assessment Have You Experienced? And What are the Potential Sources of Bias and Distortion?* The title says it all—you collect your own personal insights, learning the important lessons.

- *Scored Discussion.* This activity provides practice with identifying quality performance when students are interacting during classroom discussions. We provide a simple scoring guide—you do the rest.

Workbook Activities for the End of Part II

When you have completed your studies of Chapters 5 through 8, these activities can tie those experiences together:

- *Analyze Sample Assessments for Sampling Problems and Potential Sources of Bias.*   What does it look like in an actual classroom assessment when there are technical problems? You use the rubrics for Sampling and Bias and Distortion to analyze the sample assessments. You practice using real assessments.

- *Show What You Know.*   This activity provides several different options for personal reflection that allow you to collect your understandings from Part II of the book: concept mapping, drawing, writing a letter, or outlining major learnings.

Classroom Applications

We began our journey together in Chapter 1 understanding that this book is about the assessment options that you have at your disposal. In this book I do not prescribe the best way to assess. The art of classroom assessment is that of making the right choices from among the options for each particular assessment context. It should be clear to you by now why we started with this perspective.

In Part I, we established the fact that assessments serve a variety of educational purposes. They inform policy makers, program planners, parents, and students and teachers in the classroom. One of your keys to classroom assessment success is to build each assessment with a clear understanding of your intended purpose. Who will use the results and how?

Also in Part I, we established that sound assessments arise from clearly articulated achievement expectations. You must begin assessment development with a clear sense of the knowledge, the patterns of reasoning, performance skills, and product development capabilities that you expect your students to master. A second key to your success is to identify the specific achievement standards

that will guide your instruction, as they also will guide your assessment development.

Finally in Part I, we framed your choices in aligning different assessment methods to your valued achievement targets. Another key to your success in classroom assessment is to select the right method for the particular context.

With this basic framework of challenges in mind, then, in Part II we delved more deeply into each of the four assessment methods you have at your disposal. In effect, we zeroed in on each column of our guiding Target-by-Methods matrix. We framed quality control standards, assessment development steps, and ideas for student involvement in selected response, essay, performance, and personal communication-based assessment. These methods, as they subdivide into their various format options, represent the color palette from which you must spin your classroom assessment art. In Part II, I provided details that will help you select the proper method for each situation to create a quality assessment.

Now, as we begin Part III, we reorient the rows of our Targets-by-Methods matrix. Each chapter addresses a different kind of achievement target. This will help you do the following:

1. Analyze the kinds of achievement targets that you want your students to master.

2. Understand how different kinds of achievement targets relate to (build on) one another.

3. Gain confidence in selecting proper assessment methods and in transforming your expectations into quality classroom assessment exercises and scoring criteria.

4. Gain further insight into when and how to involve students in your assessment development and use.

In Chapter 9, you learn more about assessing knowledge, understanding, and reasoning. We will discuss how reasoning proficiencies come alive in adult life. Then we'll illustrate how they manifest themselves in students' academic lives. Out of these will come conclusions about specific patterns of reasoning that must be priorities in the school curriculum. These are the patterns that you must teach and assess, because they are the patterns over which students must gain control if they are to learn to monitor the quality of their own reasoning—a critical lifelong learner proficiency. If you are to set students up for success in this regard, you must be clear about what you mean by "reasoning proficiency." One of the main goals of this chapter is to help you sort through the dozens of different ways reasoning is defined in our professional literature, to form your vision of success to convey to your students. Remember, you yourself must master the reasoning achievement targets that you expect your students to master.

Chapter 10 centers on performance skill and product targets. This takes us back once again to the topic of performance assessment methodology. This time, I will isolate each part of performance assessment development and show you more detailed keys to your success. You will learn more about the assessment of performance skills and product development capabilities by analyzing and evaluating applications that span the range of grade levels and school subjects. You will learn to apply a set of evaluative criteria in judging the quality of performance assessment scoring guides and tasks. As we go, as usual, we will explore the potential of student involvement in assessment development and use.

Finally, Chapter 11 offers the tools you need to help your students monitor (and hopefully take responsibility for!) their own dispositions. In each chapter of Part II, I promised to fill in details later about assessing our fifth expectation of students: their affective characteristics. Here it is. We'll explore some critically important ground rules for venturing into this very specialized domain of classroom assessment. Then we'll analyze some of the very creative classroom assessment options you have at your disposal.

If you are ready, then, let Part III of our journey begin.

Assessing Reasoning Proficiency

CHAPTER FOCUS

This chapter answers the following guiding question:

> How can I help my students become confident, competent masters of their own reasoning and problem-solving proficiencies?

Through reading this chapter you will come to understand the following general principles:

1. Adult problem solvers succeed in their professions because they have learned to use their knowledge and understanding in predictable ways; that is, they solve real-life problems using certain consistent patterns of reasoning.

2. The heart of academic competence includes the ability to use knowledge and understanding to figure things out in the same patterned ways as required to solve real-life problems.

3. Our classroom assessment challenges, then, are to understand those predictable patterns of reasoning ourselves, assess them accurately, and share the patterns and assessment responsibilities with our students.

As you read this chapter, continue to keep in mind our big classroom assessment picture. The shaded areas of Figure 9.1 indicate the relevant achievement targets and assessment methods.

	SELECTED RESPONSE	ESSAY	PERFORMANCE ASSESSMENT	PERSONAL COMMUNICATION
Know				
Reason				
Skills				
Products				
Dispositions				

Figure 9.1
Aligning achievement targets and assessment methods

First Understand Reasoning, Then You Can Assess It

The challenges of teaching and assessing reasoning proficiency come in two parts. First, we must define what it means to reason well, and then we must transform that vision into (1) assessment exercises that ask students to reason and (2) scoring criteria reflecting sound reasoning.

I worry about our preparedness to do this. As I travel the continent offering workshops on assessing reasoning, I start every session with three questions. First, I ask participating teachers, "How many of you expect your students to become proficient at reasoning and solving problems as a result of the time spent in your classroom?" Virtually every teacher in every audience will raise her or his hand. Then I ask the next question: "How many of you can define for me *precisely* what patterns of reasoning you expect your students to master?" Almost no hands go up.

Given this response, my third question becomes moot: "How many of you can assure me that you use quality assessments to gather dependable information about your students' reasoning proficiency?" In the absence of a sharply focused vision of this target, quality assessment (not to mention effective teaching and learning) remains beyond reach.

The fact is that we have been imprecise in defining what it means to be good at this thing called "reasoning." We have been vague in our conceptualizations and as a result our vocabulary doesn't have a precise shared meaning. Over the past few years, I have been collecting the terminology of the reasoning curriculum. Every time I hear or read a term or phrase an educator uses in this domain, I enter it in a file on my computer. Here is a sampling of my collection:

Abstracting	Hypothesizing
Analogous reasoning	Induction
Analytical thinking	Inferences
A priori reasoning	Intelligence
Classifying	Judgmental thinking
Cognition	Justifying
Cognitive abilities	Logical thinking
Comparison	Math problem solving
Comprehending	Metacognition
Constructing meaning	Metaphorical thinking
Contrasting	Multiple intelligences
Creative thinking	(lots of them!)
Critical abilities	Mustering support
Critical spirit	Patterns of reasoning
Critical thinking	Predicting
Decision making	Problem solving
Deduction	Rational thinking
Drawing conclusions	Reasoning
Drawing generalizations	Reflective judgment
Evaluative thinking	Reflective thinking
Explaining	Scientific reasoning
Fair-minded thinking	Sound thinking
Figuring things out	Summarizing
Formal operations	Synthesizing
Good thinking	Thinking
Habits of mind	Understanding
Higher-order thinking	

If we expect our students to come to terms with all of this, we must do the same. That is, we need to be circumspect in our use of terms and in our development of definitions. When we set limits on achievement targets and define them clearly, everyone's job gets easier; both instruction and assessment become more sharply focused and efficient. Remember, *students can hit any target that they can see and that holds still for them.* But just look at that list. It looks more like a thundercloud boiling over our heads than a sharply defined set of achievement targets at which our students can aim. They wouldn't want to hit it—they'd want to take cover from it!

What does it mean to use one's knowledge and understanding to reason well? How, for example, do students who perform the following acts demonstrate reasoning proficiency?

- Write a good critical review of a movie.
- Solve a complex math problem.
- Successfully debate an issue.
- Predict the results of a science experiment.
- Combine understandings from science and social studies to solve an environmental problem.

How do we determine if students have met appropriate standards of excellence in reasoning?

These points illustrate the complexity of the achievement target and classroom assessment issues we confront in this chapter. But I have good news! As we endeavor to define and assess reasoning and problem-solving proficiencies, we can stand on the shoulders of some very good educators who have worked hard to define them and to create sound assessment ideas. Because of them, we are in a better position today than ever before to help more students reason effectively.

As you shall see, all four basic forms of assessment—selected response, essay, performance assessment, and personal communication—have important contributions to make to the assessment of reasoning. We can comfortably translate a variety of important forms of reasoning into selected response formats. Others are better triggered with carefully crafted essay exercises, performance exercises, or thoughtful dialogue with students. We will examine examples of all of these.

Guiding Principles

Before we get into the details, however, let me share some guidelines that should influence your work in this arena. I have summarized these in Figure 9.2 following the discussion.

Guideline 1: All Reasoning Arises from Knowledge and Understanding

Never forget that all reasoning arises from a basis of knowledge and understanding. Without that base, no problem will be solved. This is why I believe that the common practice of differentiating between "higher-order" and "lower-order" thinking has reduced, not enhanced, school effectiveness. Here's why: When we differentiate in this manner, unfortunately, the honor of being labeled "lower-order thinking" always goes to the mastery and understanding of content knowledge. As a result, by placing curricular emphasis on higher-order thinking and deemphasizing lower-order we in effect deprive students of access to the very content understandings that they need to solve the complex problems we expect them to be able to handle.

There is no such thing as "content-free" reasoning. My auto mechanic can diagnose the reason for my car problems in large part because he knows and understands the systems that make my car run. My attorney can help me with my legal problems because she has studied and learned the law. CPAs prepare taxes correctly because they know proper procedures. My physician can help me get well because he knows the human body and understands medical remedies. Chefs create culinary delights because they know and understand how ingredients blend to look and taste good. You will develop sound assessments in your classroom in part because of the knowledge and understanding you acquire from studying the *content* of this book.

Now to be sure, just knowing and understanding doesn't ensure that you will solve any particular problem. You must use that knowledge intelligently to reason through and figure out the solution. But the foundational understanding is essential. Your classroom assessments must attend to this reality if they are to be of high quality.

Guideline 2: Acknowledge Two Ways of "Knowing"

As a teacher, you can help your students "know" in two ways, both of which only have value if accompanied by understanding. Knowledge retrieved through the effective use of reference is every bit as powerful as knowledge retrieved from memory, when the objective is to solve problems. Most of us grew up in an educational environment in which one was judged to be a master of content if one knew it outright and understood it. But, to reiterate a key point, this is not the only way of knowing and understanding.

I am also the master of knowledge when I can retrieve it when I need it, efficiently and in a useable form. Thank heaven my physician, my tax accountant, and my auto mechanic have learned this lesson! They cannot know outright all that they need to know to help me solve my problems. But it is crucial to my well-being that they know where to go to get the answers they need to questions that concern my health, my relationship with the IRS, and my car.

In other words, there are two ways for me to be a master of knowledge: burn it into the neural circuits of my mind or know where to find it when I need it. Hopefully, my memory will always hold much for me to remember and use productively. But in this information age (and at my age!), I must now acknowledge that the library and the Internet will always hold more. As we discuss the meaning and assessment of reasoning proficiency in this chapter, let's agree to allow for both ways of knowing, as both can provide an excellent basis for successful problem solving.

Guideline 3: Realize That Students Are Natural Thinkers

Virtually all students arrive at school from day one as natural thinkers. You don't have to teach them to think. Rather, you must help them learn to focus and structure their thinking into reasoning. The vast majority of students possess those cognitive abilities they need to survive and even prosper in school and beyond. Hidden within them is the capacity to interact purposefully with their world, confronting problems, reflecting on solutions, solving problems, and deriving or constructing personal meaning from experience.

But there's a problem. According to critical thinking expert Richard Paul (1995), the unschooled human mind is a mixed bag of good and bad thinking, of sharp focus and fuzzy thinking, of ignorance and sound knowledge, of accurate conceptions and misconceptions, of misunderstanding and important insight, of open-mindedness and prejudice. Our challenge as teachers is to help students learn to clean out and organize their mental houses as needed, to clear out the garbage and let sound reasoning prevail. With certain exceptions, students bring with them all the thinking tools they need to reason effectively. We must help them understand how to structure or pattern their use of these tools. We must help them understand how to evaluate the quality of their own reasoning and problem solving. We can do this by involving them in assessing their own reasoning.

Guideline 4: Formulate Clear Targets

Strive to formulate clear reasoning targets, being sure to clarify in your own mind the knowledge and understanding foundations that underpin your reasoning expectations.

Of the kinds of achievement targets discussed in this book, *none places a greater premium on our own sharp vision of the valued target than does reasoning*. Each of us must enter our classroom with a refined conceptual understanding of the reasoning process, the vocabulary needed to communicate effectively about it, and the strategies needed to share both the vision and its vocabulary with our students. Without such a clear sense of the kinds of reasoning students are to master and the standards of quality we will apply, both we and our students will remain adrift in uncertainty about their success. Here's why:

Remember how the various kinds of achievement targets that we have discussed work together to promote academic success? Only when essential prerequisite knowledge is available can we use that knowledge to reason and solve problems. Remember also that we can reason things through to generate new insights, thus building new knowledge and understanding through good problem solving. Reasoning is one way of generating understanding. So these targets intertwine.

Further, knowledge and reasoning proficiencies underpin complex performance skills that, in turn, lead to the ability to create quality achievement-related products. By successfully figuring out how to use our skills to make something new, we gain new understanding of how to be successful. So once again, we see the interrelationship among these four achievement targets. Each is indispensable. In essence, they all grow together.

So, as students progress through the grades and come to comprehend ever more complex and differentiated arrays of knowledge, they can solve more and more complex problems. This, in turn, permits them to master increasingly sophisticated performance skills and to create products of increasing complexity. And, as they grow, students gain confidence in themselves as problem solvers, predisposing them (that is, permitting them to take the risks required) to strive for further, even more sophisticated, academic excellence. Thus, it becomes clear that sound reasoning represents a critical building block in the development of academic competence.

As you study reasoning proficiencies, plan how to share your vision with your students, and as you design your assessments, be sure to do the following:

1. Develop a vision of reasoning achievement targets that you can believe in and invest time in mastering yourself, a framework you can become so comfortable with that you can effortlessly integrate its valued reasoning processes into every nook and cranny of your classroom. *I urge you, take this responsibility very seriously.*

2. Be sure your vision of reasoning makes sense in the real world, that it reflects the manner in which individuals solve important everyday problems. The standards we apply in evaluating the quality of student reasoning should be the same as those we use in adult life.

3. Work with your colleagues to achieve consistency across grade levels and academic disciplines in the reasoning patterns you expect students to master. If everyone does their own thing, students are left to guess at how to hit a constantly moving target. But if you and your colleagues are consistent in conceptualization and vocabulary, your students can learn to confidently apply their prior understandings.

4. You must be able to translate the forms of reasoning you teach and the standards of quality you apply into terms that make sense to your students. You also must be able to translate the acts of reasoning and problem solving into terms they can integrate and use in their academic and personal lives. You must share with them both a conceptual understanding of your expectations and a vocabulary they can use to converse with you about reasoning.

Guideline 5: Ask Novel Questions

Only novel questions at testing time can tap reasoning proficiency. *Sound assessment requires that respondents see assessment exercises for the first time at the time they are to respond.* Throughout this chapter I will make consistent reference to this need to present novel exercises if you wish to gain insight into student reasoning. Ms. Casey, a member of the social studies faculty in Emily's high school, explains why:

> The validity of any assessment of reasoning is, in part, a function of the novelty of the problems presented.

   "In one of my classes, we study various forms of government. My students are expected to master specific knowledge about different governmental structures. As they learn about the various structures, from time to time I ask them to brainstorm a list of similarities and differences between and among different governments, to compare them. Other times, I ask them to use what they know to draw conclusions about the functions of government. As they do, we write their ideas on the chalkboard. These both require complex reasoning, right? I regard these as challenging, but always engaging, exercises. Sometimes, my kids struggle with them.

"But let's say we do the brainstorming comparison exercise to glean important similarities and differences between two countries' governments. After we list their responses on the chalkboard, I tell my students how important that list of similarities and differences is, and inform them that they had better learn it because it will be on the final exam next week. When this same exercise, which tapped rich comparative reasoning during class, appears as an essay exercise on the final, all it measures is recall.

"Any time my instructions ask my students to respond from memory, the assessment taps mastery of content they've already learned or the solution to a problem solved before and that is all, regardless of what the exercise looks like. So how do we get beyond knowledge mastery at testing time? By posing questions that students have never seen before. These are the only kinds of exercises that engage the wheels of their reasoning."

Her in-class brainstorming task assesses more than mastery of knowledge because she asks students to do more than simply remember what they know about government. When the challenge is new, students must dip into their knowledge, retrieve the right information, and use it in practiced, productive reasoning. If they have seen the question before, there is no guarantee that they must perform these steps.

Please do not infer from this that turning an in-class reasoning exercise into recall items on a test is necessarily a bad idea. Sometimes, you might regard results of such classroom activities as well worth knowing outright. When this happens, by all means put them on the test—but as knowledge mastery exercises, nothing else. When you want more, you must present students with novel exercises that require that they figure something out.

You do not have to be the only one assessing your students' reasoning proficiencies. Given conceptual understanding of important reasoning processes, standards of good reasoning, and a vocabulary that permits them to converse about their reasoning, students can monitor their own and each other's reasoning, enjoy being part of the process, and learn a great deal along the way! Your job as a teacher is to begin with a vision of how to use knowledge and understanding to reason in productive ways. Then you must share that vision with students, to teach them to monitor their own reasoning, and to offer positive support as they come to terms and become confident with their own reasoning powers. Figure 9.2 recaps the five guidelines we have discussed here.

1. Never forget that all reasoning arises from a basis of knowledge and understanding. Without that base, no problem will be solved.

2. Acknowledge two ways of "knowing," both of which only have value if accompanied by understanding.

3. Realize that virtually all students come to you as natural thinkers. You don't have to teach them to think. Rather you must help them learn to focus and structure their thinking into reasoning.

4. Strive to formulate clear reasoning targets, being sure to clarify in your own mind the knowledge and understanding foundations that underpin your reasoning expectations.

5. Pose only novel questions at testing time to tap reasoning proficiency.

Figure 9.2
Guidelines for assessing reasoning

Reasoning in the Adult World

Our adult personal and professional lives demand that we use our knowledge and understanding to figure things out. For instance, as wise, informed consumers, whether we're buying vegetables, computers, cars, or homes, we strive to make informed decisions. We compare the options in terms of costs and benefits and then decide which to purchase. These are critical consumer decisions. They involve applying comparison shopping and critical or evaluative reasoning.

My physician must also reason effectively. Here's how he describes his version:

"When patients come to me for help, first I ask them to describe their symptoms. As they do, I check their description against what I know from previous experience. If that process leads me to a confident conclusion about the cause, I begin to evaluate treatment options to decide which one will be most effective. On follow up, if the patient gets better, then I conclude that my hypothesis was confirmed and my service to that patient is complete. If the symptoms don't disappear, I go to the next-best treatment option, and the next, and so on until I find one that works. But, if my initial interview fails to confirm a diagnosis, then I form a hypothesis about what might be wrong and call for lab tests, X-rays, or other evidence to confirm or reject my hypothesis. If the test results confirm my hunch, then we go to the treatment phase. If not, I seek even more evidence to help me make an accurate diagnosis. I might even ask for help from a knowledgeable and experienced physician specialist."

Think about the patterns of reasoning that count here. Obviously, all reasoning in this case arises from the doctor's foundation of knowledge and understanding of the human body and of treatment options. But among the keys to success are his ability to do the following:

- Synthesize symptoms into a pattern—an inference about what might be causing the problem.
- Compare this case to prior cases in terms of what might help.
- Understand when he needs more information.
- Evaluate treatment options.
- Predict which one will work best.

But understand that, at this point, his inference about the cause of the symptoms and the likely effect of treatment are only hypotheses. Ultimately, only the record of the patient's subsequent recovery will tell if the doctor reasoned effectively.

My attorney faces a different reasoning challenge. She must analyze circumstances to uncover legal issues:

> "My clients come to me for legal advice. That can mean that a conflict has arisen. My client has come to differences with someone. My job is to listen to my clients' description of their problems, trying to comprehend the circumstances and analyze their cases for legal issues. Then I must evaluate their positions in terms of the law to see if they are justified in taking those positions. In law school, I learned to identify legal issues, research the law and apply the law to the facts of any particular case. To evaluate my client's prospects in a legal action, often I go online or into the law library, look up similar cases, and compare the case to others that have been adjudicated before. I analyze them to find precedents that bolster our case. Based on my evaluation of the circumstances and my application of the law as I read and interpret it, I lay out possible courses of action for my client to compare, evaluate, and select. I always accompany this with my judgment about what I believe to be the best course."

Legal action virtually always turns on matters of judgment—applications of evaluative reasoning (a.k.a. *critical thinking*). What is the proper resolution to the dispute? That depends on the criteria or standards of fairness applied and how the facts of the dispute play out given those standards. My attorney must do the following:

- Analyze her client's perspectives on the case.
- Deduce the legal issues.
- Evaluate how they stand relative to legal precedent.
- Offer her best possible recommendations.

My auto mechanic describes his reasoning job in ways that sound a great deal like my physician:

> "It helps me in fixing ailing cars if I know about the various systems of the car I am asked to repair and what functions they serve. This is important

because it helps me analyze and isolate possible causes. If I know the kind of car, then I can compare this case to my previous experience and see if that suggests an explanation of the problem. If I am unfamiliar with the particular make of car, then I have to rely heavily on the factory-prepared maintenance manual to tell me what I need to know. I ask the owner to describe what's wrong. I'm happy when he or she simply describes symptoms and when they occur—not what they think is causing the problems. I am overjoyed when I can reproduce the symptoms while the owner is still there. I need this evidence to infer what's wrong. That's my job. Once I have the problem described, then I begin to hypothesize what might be causing it. These days, I am able to rely more and more on the on-board diagnostics to provide more detailed information about the problem. Then, once I think I have it diagnosed, I evaluate my repair options and begin to make the repairs needed to correct the problem. With each repair, I test the vehicle to see if the symptoms have disappeared. Hopefully that happens right away."

To see a different kind of reasoning problem, consider the work of the life insurance provider. Here we find a challenge in mathematical reasoning:

"First, I need to know the age, health, and lifestyle of my client. From this, I can estimate how long a client is likely to live. The client's age classification tells me approximately when I will have to pay her or his family the amount of the death benefit stipulated on the policy. Most people don't realize that I must figure this out from a financial or business point of view. You see, I have to calculate how much I must charge the client in premiums per month to collect enough money over the years to cover the death benefit of the policy, my business expenses, and a small profit for me. The thing that makes calculations so complicated is that, as I receive premium payments over time, I can invest them and use the proceeds to help me cover those costs. But I never know what my rate of return will be for sure. Besides, what if the client dies earlier than expected? We insurance providers work hard to try to figure these things out."

Some of the reasoning patterns that emerge as being of value here are as follows:

- Classification—classifying the client into a risk category
- Prediction—predicting the long-term status of each category of client
- Application—applying mathematical algorithms to estimate expected costs and return on investment

Finally, let me share a picture of reasoning processes "painted" for me by an artist friend who is also an art teacher. While I am compelled to reproduce this image in words, it is apparent that artists often reason in shapes and colors:

"I often teach my art students to think artistically by starting to see the big picture of what they wish to create—to understand the whole before beginning to think backwards and analyzing its component parts. In my art, I try to visualize the whole, completed visual image and then bring it to life. If I cannot see it to start with, I cannot create it. Then I try to teach students to work with their tools to make the piece "look good" in terms of their own image. Humans have a strong sense of balance, rhythm, and pattern, not to mention a personal and very emotional reaction to color. I want them to tap into those resources in themselves. When the piece isn't coming together, sometimes my students come to me for help. Then I have to revert to words. We have to talk about art. I suggest ways to move shapes, add elements, and tinker with things. But they must return to matters of form, color, and light, comparing the work before them to their initial image. They must continue to strive to make it feel right. To "reason" in art is to resolve design problems or to give an idea form."[1]

In this case, we see the entire artistic piece being viewed as the synergy or synthesis of its ingredients. In addition, students evaluate their artistic creations by comparing them to standards of good work.

Time for Reflection

Select another profession or hobby (race car driver, airplane pilot, chef, bridge player, chess player, etc.) of your choosing and figure out what problems the participant needs to solve. What patterns of reasoning are required?

Patterns of Reasoning

How then should we understand and help students learn what it means to reason well? The answer lies in understanding various ways to organize our thinking and how those ways must come together to solve problems. Let's start by exploring a few of the commonly referenced forms of reasoning. Then we'll explore their dynamic interrelationships.

In the real-world examples presented previously, we found instances of the need to see relationships by reasoning analytically, comparatively, or in an evaluative manner. Real-life thinkers need to be able to synthesize, classify, and reason inductively or deductively. Let's think together about what these inferring processes really mean.

As you read about these different ways of reasoning, you will see that each has its own definition. Each can be illustrated in understandable terms. Nevertheless, as the examples reveal, *reasoning patterns are rarely used independently of one another.* Rather, these patterns blend to bring us to problem solutions. For now, as you read about each pattern, take a few seconds to see if you can identify some of the ways they fit together. We'll discuss those connections later.

---

[1] Special thanks to artist and educator Annie Painter, Dr. Pete Perry, auto mechanic Rick Westcott, and attorney Lois Beran for describing the reasoning processes of their professions.

Just to be sure you see the path ahead, I intend to argue that students must know and understand these patterns if they are to be able to use them productively to reason and solve problems. Therefore, they have a place among our valued achievement targets. We need to be ready to teach and assess student mastery of each. But more important, *we must prepare our students to be lifelong assessors of the quality of their own reasoning.*

Analytical Reasoning

Remember in our earlier discussions of performance and writing assessment where we drew the distinction between holistic and analytical scoring? In *holistic* scoring we consider all of the performance criteria together and synthesize our judgments into one overall score. In *analytical* scoring, we break performance down into its component parts (word choice, organization, voice, and the like), evaluating and assigning a score to each part. It is this sense of the meaning of *analytical* that we are speaking of here.

When we reason analytically, we draw inferences about the component parts of something: its ingredients, internal functioning, and how its parts fit together. When reporters do "news analysis" they go into a story in greater depth to study its parts. When we try to figure out how a machine works (to go inside and see how the pieces fit and work together) we are reasoning analytically. When we try to infer what goes into making something good, like food, a movie, or a teacher, we are involved in analytical reasoning. Figure 9.3 analyzes and presents a graphic representation of this pattern of reasoning, analyzing key assessment topics.

In this case, our instructional challenges are to be sure that students have access to whatever knowledge and understanding they need to analyze something and that they have guided practice in exercising their analytical thought processes.

Our assessment challenge is to ask them to tap into that knowledge base and apply their reasoning skills to a novel analytical task. For example, in literature, we might provide practice in doing character analysis by having students read a new story (gathering knowledge of a new character) and asking them to generate an original analysis of this character they have just "met."

As a teacher, I want my students to know exactly what is called for whenever I ask them to "analyze" something. I might even put a chart on the wall detailing the analysis process and highlighting examples of analytical inferences. These might include character analyses from literature, story line or plot analyses, breakdown diagrams of machines, or depictions of the subparts of a scientific process such as the water cycle. I want students to recognize when analysis is needed and to understand how to apply that pattern of reasoning in novel problem situations.

Synthesizing

Let's say you have just finished helping students analyze the structure of two short stories. Then, you have them pool or synthesize these into a set of generalizations about the typical structure of a short story. Thus two different sources of knowl-

Questions that help students reason *analytically*:

1. What is it that I wish to analyze?
2. Why is analysis relevant?
3. What are the relevant parts, subdivisions, or categories?
4. How do the parts relate to each other?
5. How do the parts come together to create the whole?

Key concepts that underpin *analytical* reasoning:

- Interrelated parts of a whole
- Components
- Ingredients

Graphic representation of an example:

Reasoning Task: Analyze the ingredients of assessment quality covered in this book:

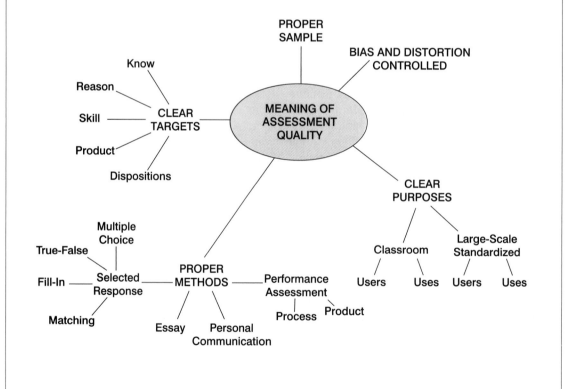

Figure 9.3
Understanding analytical reasoning

edge and understanding about short stories are integrated. This is synthesizing. You then ask them to draw the following inference: How does the story you just read align with what you know about the typical structure that you just developed? Figure 9.4 presents a description of synthesis.

When thinkers achieve synthesis they use reasoning to generate new insight and understanding. Remember in Chapter 3 when we discussed Lynn Erickson's conceptualization of understanding? Refer to Figure 3.5. Starting at the bottom, factual examples are synthesized into key concepts and these concepts lead us to general principles. It is an act of synthesis for students to derive the generalizations that can be drawn from a set of examples.

We find a great deal of interest being expressed these days in the development of "integrated" or "thematic" instruction or curriculum. This often is described as being different from discipline-based instruction, in which students study separately math, science, writing skills, and so on. Thematic instruction encourages students to bring knowledge and productive patterns of reasoning together from several disciplines, as they explore their particular theme, whether it be the study of a particular culture, scientific problem, or social issue. Such curricula place a pre-

---

Questions that help students *synthesize*:

1. What is the problem to be solved by combining ideas?
2. Why is synthesis relevant in this context?
3. What are the various understandings that can be combined to help?
4. How do those parts fit together to help us find a solution?

Key concepts underpinning *synthesis*:

- Convergence
- Generalization
- Whole is more than the sum of its parts

An example of *synthesis*:

Understanding #1: My personal experience has shown me that students who are involved in the ongoing assessment of their own achievement are much more highly motivated to learn than are those who are not involved.

Understanding #2: The professional literature in both reading and writing instruction tell us that students must learn to monitor their own comprehension and the quality of their own writing to become independently literate adults.

Understanding #3: Research from around the world provides irrefutable evidence that students who are deeply involved in high-quality classroom assessment environments learn more.

Synthesis: It would be a very good idea for me, the teacher, to involve my students in assessment, record keeping, and communication to increase motivation.

Figure 9.4
Understanding synthesis as a pattern of reasoning

mium on synthesizing insights from divergent sources and present wonderfully rich opportunities to develop and assess student mastery of this pattern of reasoning.

Comparative Reasoning

Comparative reasoning refers to the process of figuring out or inferring how things are either alike or different. Sometimes we compare in terms of similarities, other times we contrast in terms of differences, still other times we do both. To understand this kind of reasoning, we must see that those who are proficient begin with a clear understanding of the things they are to compare. Then they identify the dimensions of each that they will examine for similarities or differences. And finally, they detail the comparison, highlighting why those particular points are important. Here are simple examples: In what way are these two poems alike and different? Given this early and this late work by this particular author, how are they different in style? How are these insects alike and different? Figure 9.5 illustrates the structure.

Questions that help students *compare* and *contrast*:
1. What is to be compared?
2. Why is it relevant to draw the comparison?
3. Upon what basis will we compare them?
4. How are they alike?
5. How are they different?
6. What important lessons can we learn from this *comparison*?

Key concepts:
• Similar
• Different

Example:
Compare classroom and stardardized assessment

Criterion	Classroom Assessment	Standardized Test
Focus	Narrow Targets	Broad Targets
Developer	Teacher	Test Publisher
Frequency	Continuous	Once-a-year
Users	Teacher Student Parent	Principal Curriculum Director Superintendent School Board Legislator

Figure 9.5
Understanding comparative reasoning

Questions that can focus students' *classification*:
1. Classify what?
2. Into what categories?
3. Why is it relevant to do so?
4. What elements into what categories?
5. What is the basis of (our reasoning behind) each proper match?

Key concepts:
- Objects have characteristics
- Categories have characteristics
- Alignment in terms of characteristics

Example:
Classify each instructional objective on the left in terms of the kind of achievement target that it represents.

Objective	Target
Read aloud fluently	Understand content knowledge
Know the causes of the Great Depression	Pattern of reasoning
Speak a second language fluently	Performance skill
Predict the results of an experiment	Product development
Set up the science lab apparatus properly	
Learn a poem	
Create a model dwelling	
Compare two characteristics from literature	

Figure 9.6
Understanding the reasoning that underpins classification

Classifying

Sometimes, life presents us with reasoning challenges that ask us to categorize or classify things. When we budget, we classify expenses. When we analyze how we use our time, we organize events into different categories. In science, we classify plants and animals. In politics, we categorize issues and candidates. To reason productively in this manner, we must first know the defining parameters of each category and the attributes of those things we are classifying. Then we can compare each item with the categorical options and infer its appropriate group (Figure 9.6).

Induction and Deduction

In the case of *inductive* reasoning, we reason productively when we can infer principles, draw conclusions, or glean generalizations from accumulated evidence. Induction results from a synthesis. Reasoning travels from particular facts to a general rule or principle. Here are two examples:

Now that you have read this story, what do you think is its general theme or message?

Given the evidence provided in this article about the stock market [note that this is an example of using knowledge gained through reference], what is the relationship between interest rates and stock values?

We help students gain control over their inductive reasoning proficiency when we make sure they have the opportunity to access the proper knowledge from which important rules or principles arise and when we provide guided practice in drawing inferences, conclusions, or generalizations.

We also reason when we apply a general rule or principle to find the solution to a problem. This is *deductive* reasoning. Here, reasoning travels from the general to the specific:

Given your theory about criminal behavior, who did the killing?

Given what you know about the role of a tragic hero in classic literature, if this character is a tragic hero, what do you think will happen next in the story?

If the chemical test yields this result, what element is it?

Obviously, the key instructional challenge is to be sure students have the opportunity to learn and understand the rules, generalizations, or principles we want them to apply. Then and only then can we assess their reasoning proficiency by presenting them with novel contexts within which to apply those rules.

Evaluative Reasoning

We reason in an evaluative manner when we apply certain criteria to judge the value or appropriateness of something. The quality of the reasoning turns on our ability to logically or dependably apply proper judgmental criteria. Synonyms for this pattern of reasoning include *critical thinking* and *judgmental reasoning*.

Within the context of our journey together, the very process of evaluating the quality of student work in terms of some predetermined achievement standards, such as writing assessment, is a classic example of evaluative reasoning. When we express and defend a point of view or opinion, we reason in an evaluative manner. When we judge the quality of an assessment using our five standards of quality, we reason evaluatively.

Our instructional task is to help students understand the criteria they should be applying when they defend their point of view on an issue. Who is the best candidate for mayor? That's a matter of opinion. What are the important characteristics of a good mayor? As we discuss these criteria in class, we must address how to apply these standards logically.

Our assessment challenge is to determine if students are able to apply those criteria appropriately, given a novel evaluative challenge. Students who are able to appropriately evaluate a piece of writing they have never seen before using a learned set of analytical rating scales are demonstrating proficiency in evaluative reasoning. It is in this sense that I say this entire book is about developing critical thinkers.

Why These Patterns?

Remember earlier in the chapter when I presented the long list of terms used in our professional literature to characterize reasoning? Of all those labels, you might wonder why I chose to describe the six used here. I have three reasons.

First, I sought to describe what people normally think of as reasoning processes. I wanted as few patterns as possible that, at the same time, covered sufficient ground to provide the most commonsense meaning of reasoning. This would make the list comprehensive but manageable. It needed to be practical. These patterns are simple and understandable, and at the same time describe what happens in the real world.

Second, I finally realized that there is no final "truth" in the universe with respect to defining *reasoning*. As I studied the professional literature, I found a variety of labels for patterns. Classification systems abound. Every scholar has a different opinion about the truth. So I tried to glean from these various opinions the things they had in common. The patterns described here have a foundation in current thinking about reasoning.

Third, I wanted patterns that I could describe and illustrate in terms that students (including you!) could master. The fact that we can diagram each pattern and easily find examples makes them approachable by our students. That's a good thing.

But remember, after studying and reflecting on the reasoning targets that you want your students to master, you may find other classifications or definitions that work better for you. That's fine. Just be clear enough about your vision of excellence in reasoning to be practical, based on the best current understanding, and student-friendly.

Summary: Note the Relationships among Patterns

As I wrote about these patterns of reasoning and the classroom applications above, I tried to use descriptive vocabulary so you could see key connections. I hope that your study of and reflection on the six organizing structures permitted you to notice some important connections among them. I have listed some here to establish the dynamic nature of reasoning. Your own reasoning may be different. If you are seeing rich relationships, you are reasoning productively.

- All reasoning consists of seeing relationships—of drawing inferences.
- Synthesis requires inductive inference; that is, we do it well when we can infer or see the unity arising from divergent parts.
- Complex comparisons require a prior step of analyzing the things to be compared to infer or identify potential points of similarity and difference.
- Classification involves comparison of each item to be classified to the attributes of each category to infer which goes where.
- Inductive inference requires that we compare the pieces of evidence at hand to see what they have in common.

- Evaluation often requires analysis and comparison of different points of view before coming to judgment.

- Evaluative judgments about the quality of any reasoning can be made if we have standards for what it means to do it well.

- Knowledge may not just be a prerequisite of sound reasoning. It also can be the result of *good* reasoning. We can rely on reasoning to help us generate new understandings. An inference drawn once through careful reasoning can become a strong part of one's structure of knowledge and understanding. For example, careful analysis of the keys to success provides insight in the form of performance criteria by which to evaluate the quality of student performance in the future.

So it is that different ways of reasoning form a puzzle whose pieces can fit together in various ways to permit you and your students to figure things out. It is appropriate to help students see and understand the different organizing structures.

Students who encounter a new math problem, debate a volatile social issue, or confront an unknown substance in a science lab bring all of these ways of reasoning into play in a rapid-fire manner, analyzing the problem to infer what knowledge bases they must bring to bear. Beyond school, when students are confronted with a drug pusher, make career choices, or deal with the demands of peer pressure, they must think clearly and select a proper course of action. Those who are masters of their own reasoning and who know how to use their minds effectively have a strong chance of generating productive responses to such circumstances.

Before we address the assessment of reasoning, let's collect a few additional insights about what it means to be a proficient reasoner.

Reasoning in the Classroom

Just as we can identify patterns of reasoning as they play out in the work worlds of various professions, so too can we see these patterns come alive in the context of school subjects. Virtually every academic discipline can be defined in part in terms of the patterns of reasoning it uses to solve problems. In the sections that follow, I intend to show you that success in reading, writing, math problem solving, science, and social studies, among others involves far more than merely learning the content. Each also requires clear and appropriate reasoning. If this truly is the case, then we teachers had better be clear about the patterns of reasoning that count in our classrooms, and we had better be prepared to share those valued targets with our students in a manner that sets them up to learn to evaluate the effectiveness of their own reasoning.

Reading IS Reasoning

Reading experts tell us that reading doesn't just involve reasoning—it is, quite literally, reasoning in action. Reading comprehension is reasoning carried out in the reader's mind. In our minds, each of us holds our own mental copies of the world as we understand it. When we read, we compare what the author says to us in the text with our mental models to determine (infer) if we need to change or maintain our sense of the world. This is the active process of comprehending that we, the reader, control. In independently competent readers, this process is automatic. We don't do it at a conscious level.

Thus, reading specialists tell us, we comprehend or understand written text only when we can bring to that text (1) the appropriate structure of prior knowledge and (2) the text decoding and processing strategies needed to apprehend the author's message. If either is missing, we will not be able to construct the meaning. This is why most of us cannot understand textbooks on nuclear physics. We lack the appropriate mental models. This is why we have difficulty reading a book written in a foreign language that we have not mastered. We can't apprehend the message.

Let me illustrate with a simple simulation. *This is important: Follow the steps that I outline below in order.* Think through each step in order before moving on to the next.

STEP 1:   Please read the passage presented in Figure 9.7. Do you comprehend it? What do you think the author is writing about? Please write down your answer.

STEP 2:   If you had difficulty comprehending (and I bet that you did), why did you find this passage difficult to understand? What's the problem here? What's missing? Think about it.

STEP 3:   What did you find yourself doing as you read to try to help yourself construct your own meaning? What text-processing strategies did you switch to as you tried to figure it out?

STEP 4:   Please think about these things: As you read, you handled the text just fine. You could read the words and you understood the syntax. But as you

---

For some it is highly unsettling to come into close contact with them. It is far worse to gain control over and deliberately inflict pain on them. The revulsion caused by this punishment is so strong that many will not take part in it at all. But there is another group of people who seem to revel in the contact and punishment, as well as the rewards associated with both. Members of this group share modes of dress, talk and deportment. Then there is another group of people who shun the whole enterprise—contact, punishment and rewards alike. Members of this group are as varied as all humanity. But there also is a fourth group not previously mentioned for whose sake attention to this activity is undertaken. They too harm their victims, though they do so without intention of cruelty. They simply follow their own necessities. Theirs is the cruelest punishment of all. Sometimes, but not always, they themselves suffer as a result.

Figure 9.7
Reading passage

compared the author's message to your mental picture, you began to sense a problem. Because the pronouns in the passage have no referents, in effect, I deprived you of the essential connection to your prior structure of knowledge. Result? You were unable to construct your own meaning.

Now, here is the critically important point of this exercise: As you read, you knew you were not getting it! You were monitoring your own comprehension, and when you had difficulty, you changed strategies. Do you see the point? *Self-assessment of one's own comprehension resides at the very heart of reading proficiency.* Those who cannot monitor their own comprehension (an active reasoning process) while they are reading and who cannot change reading strategies when necessary to obtain meaning cannot become independently functioning competent readers. These, then are the reasoning processes that underpin reading proficiency.

STEP 5:   Now I am going to give you the information you need to construct that meaning. I am going to tell you what the above passage is about. Then I want you to reread it, once again, monitoring your own comprehension. This will be like an out-of-body experience! As you go, you can watch (monitor) yourself inferring meaning (comprehending). Every word and sentence will unfold in your mind like a blossom opening. Are you ready? This is a passage about using worms as bait for fishing. Enjoy!

Consider the classroom assessment implications of this exercise. First we must assess to determine if students comprehend text, that is, if they can construct proper meaning. If they cannot, then we must assess to diagnose which is missing, the prerequisite knowledge, text-processing proficiencies, or both. Only then can we help them.

To assess comprehension, we can rely on multiple-choice items that ask them to infer the main idea. We can ask them to write an essay analyzing the parts of the material read. We can ask them to retell the story in a manner that lets us know that they understood it. We have many choices. But all point in the same direction. We use these methods to tell us if our students are constructing proper meaning of the text that they read. As their text-processing sophistication increases over time and their mental copies of the world become more complex and differentiated, then they can read more complex material with comprehension. If they can play a role in the assessments that reveal that growth, they can become increasingly confident readers.

So equally important in the classroom assessment challenge is helping students learn to monitor their own comprehension—that is, the quality of their own reasoning in a reading context. We can do this in many ways. For instance, we can have them retell the story or recount the key points in something they have read and then compare that to an accurate retelling, noting similarities and differences. We can have them read aloud, stopping to think aloud about the meaning they are deriving. We can watch for instances in personal reading time when students stop reading for the purpose of doing something obviously calculated on their part to sharpen their own comprehension. For instance, they might go for a dictionary to find a word meaning or read a passage aloud to someone, asking for help in understanding. We can have them pose a question that requires comprehension and then have them answer it themselves. By doing these things consistently over time, they can watch themselves grow and feel empowered as readers.

Writing IS Reasoning

Just as the process of reading is reasoning happening as we comprehend, so too is writing reasoning. When we compose new text, we analyze what we wish to say, infer how to say it well, evaluate our results to see if we have met our standards of effective communication, and revise if necessary until it "works".

Once again, let me illustrate. Same deal, follow the steps in order. Do not go on until you have completed each step:

STEP 1:   Start with a clean sheet of paper and a pen and write a brief essay. Here is the topic: There has been much discussion recently about the advisability of developing national educational standards and a national standardized test. Do you think this is a good or bad idea? Why? Please write a very brief (one-paragraph) essay stating your position.

STEP 2:   I submit that the text you just finished writing came into existence on the page before you as a result of your focused decision making. What specific decisions did you have to make in composing your text? List as many as you can. Be sure to examine the work on that piece of paper very carefully as you do this. Be quite literal. What were your key decisions?

STEP 3:   Compare your list to mine that follows. To compose your original text, you had to decide the following:

- Your position on the issue
- How to support your position
- What audience to write to and what style the reader will listen to
- How to organize your presentation of these ideas
- What words to use to convey your meaning
- How to construct sentences that would communicate your meaning
- How to structure your paragraph to help readers understand

As an independently functioning adult writer, you know and understand that if you make good decisions about these things you get good text. If you make poor decisions you get text that is weak in its defense, disorganized, unclear, lacks idea flow, and is difficult for readers to understand. In short, you are in control of the quality of your text.

Here's how: Because you know these things, *as you were composing you were monitoring the quality of your newly created text. And when and if you found something that was not working you fixed it.* Again I ask, do you see the point?! Self-assessment of the quality of one's own writing lies at the very heart of writing proficiency.

Those who cannot (1) monitor the quality of their own writing in terms of standards of good writing and (2) know how to fix it when it isn't working cannot become independently functioning competent adult writers. This is the evaluative reasoning process that forms the foundation of writing proficiency.

How, then, do we help students gain control over the quality of their writing? We accomplish this by turning over to them the evaluative criteria (the standards of good writing) they need to monitor and adjust it. If we teach them to apply those criteria to their own work and show them how to improve in terms of specific and relevant dimensions of quality, we put students in charge of the reasoning that permits them to pursue excellence in writing in the classroom and beyond.

To see an example, please turn to Chapter 7 and review Figure 7.3, the student-friendly version of a six-trait analytical writing assessment scoring model. By helping students internalize these kinds of standards of excellence, we permit them to reason as follows:

- Compare any piece of their original work to a continuum of quality
- See where it is now on that continuum
- Infer what changes will make it better

Reasoning in Mathematics

Math problem solving is reasoning. Each problem presents a challenge to be solved in several steps. First, we must analyze the problem to understand its relevant parts. Second, we must dip into our math knowledge and understanding to determine what kind of problem it represents (classification). This allows us to deduce what math algorithm, rules, and principles to apply to find an acceptable solution. Finally, we must actually apply those procedures to generate a solution, evaluating along the way to see if it seems reasonable.

According to Greg Hall, a math specialist with whom I work, when we are proficient math problem solvers, we use our prior knowledge and understanding in different ways depending on the context. If the problem is routine and familiar, we recall the proper procedures immediately, retrieve procedures from memory, apply them, and arrive at a solution. In this case, our problem solving is straightforward.

When we confront a problem that appears to be routine but is unfamiliar, then our reasoning has another step. Once again, we must analyze the problem to understand its parts. But then we must compare the new problem to those successfully solved in the past to determine which classification it fits. This step helps us evaluate options and deduce which concepts and procedures we might either adopt or adapt to find a solution. Once we develop a strategy, we then carry it out to that solution. In this case our reasoning is more complex.

Even more challenging is the context where the problem is neither familiar nor routine. When we confront problems for which we can recall no previous experience with similar problems, we face a different kind of challenge. Problem analysis is still the first step, as we strive to understand the focus of the problem. But then we must tap into references and resources that reveal to us how to solve similar problems. In effect, we have to add new classifications of math problems to our understanding to find one that fits. Then we must apply new concepts and procedures and experiment with solutions, evaluating as we go, until we find one that seems reasonable. This is the most sophisticated form of mathematical reasoning.

Because we understand this process more deeply today than ever before, in most cases, assessments of math problem-solving proficiency go beyond merely checking to see if students arrived at the correct answer. Typically, these assessments present a problem and ask students to solve it, showing all work. But in addition, more and more teachers are asking their students to write a brief paragraph explaining how they arrived at their solution. Student responses are evaluated in terms of the quality of the reasoning demonstrated.

For example, student responses to open-ended math problems can be evaluated using criteria such as those presented in Figure 9.8. Students are instructed to show all work and write a brief essay describing the reasoning behind their solution. The process is broken down into "Conceptual Understanding" and "Strategies and Reasoning." Note also that each includes clear and complete definitions of each proficiency level.

Clearly, this way of thinking about assessing math problem-solving proficiency must be seen as a priority in classroom assessment, where teachers seek to help students understand and evaluate the quality of their own proficiencies.

Reasoning in Science

Science, obviously, also involves reasoning. Scientists pose hypotheses, make predictions, gather data, analyze, and draw conclusions regarding their starting hypotheses. These are the key steps in scientific reasoning. Remember, we use these steps most productively when we are masters of the science content knowledge needed to solve complex problems.

Scientists also rely extensively on classification systems to organize their knowledge and understanding. They classify elements, plants, animals, rocks, and so on. When doing field studies, they compare specimens to category attributes to classify them. Physicians become scientists when they investigate the viability of new drugs by conducting field trials to determine the effects of new treatments of disease.

To assess proficiency in reasoning in science contexts, we can ask students to dip into their knowledge bases and derive answers to reasoning questions, or we can provide them with tables of data or figures depicting scientific phenomenon and ask them questions that require analysis, synthesis, or comparison of the information presented. We can ask them to demonstrate their reasoning in their responses to essay exercises that seek analysis, comparisons, or defense of opinion. We can have them create more complex performance assessment products in the form of laboratory reports. Just remember, when the assessments are subjective, the performance criteria that we apply must reflect the expected pattern(s) of reasoning. When we (their teachers) understand the patterns of reasoning that students are to demonstrate, we can devise criteria that reflect the key elements of those patterns.

	Emerging	Developing	Proficient	Exemplary
Conceptual Understanding *Key Question: Does the student's interpretation of the problem using mathematical representations and procedures accurately reflect the important mathematics in the problem?*	1. Your mathematical representations of the problem were incorrect. 2. You used the wrong information in trying to solve the problem. 3. The mathematical procedures you used would not lead to a correct solution. 4. You used mathematical terminology incorrectly.	1. Your choice of forms to represent the problem was inefficient or inaccurate. 2. Your response was not completely related to the problem. 3. The mathematical procedures you used would lead to a partially correct solution. 4. You used mathematical terminology imprecisely.	1. Your choices of mathematical representations of the problem were appropriate. 2. You used all relevant information from the problem in your solution. 3. The mathematical procedures you chose would lead to a correct solution. 4. You used mathematical terminology correctly.	1. Your choice of mathematical representations helped clarify the problem's meaning. 2. You uncovered hidden or implied information not readily apparent. 3. You chose mathematical procedures that would lead to an element solution. 4. You used mathematical terminology precisely.
Strategies and Reasoning *Key Question: Is there evidence that the student proceeded from a plan, applied appropriate strategies, and followed a logical and verifiable process toward a solution?*	1. Your strategies were not appropriate for the problem. 2. You didn't seem to know where to begin. 3. Your reasoning did not support your work. 4. There was no apparent relationship between your representations and the task. 5. There was no apparent logic to your solution. 6. Your approach to the problem would not lead to a correct solution.	1. You used an oversimplified approach to the problem. 2. You offered little or no explanation of your strategies. 3. Some of your representations accurately depicted aspects of the problem. 4. You sometimes made leaps in your logic that were hard to follow. 5. Your process led to a partially complete solution.	1. You chose appropriate, efficient strategies for solving the problem. 2. You justified each step of your work. 3. Your representation(s) fit the task. 4. The logic in your solution was apparent. 5. Your process would lead to a complete, correct solution of the problem.	1. You chose innovative and insightful strategies for solving the problem. 2. You *proved* that your solution was correct and that your approach was valid. 3. You provided examples and/or counterexamples to support your solution. 4. You used a sophisticated approach to solve the problem.

Figure 9.8

Mathematics problem-solving scoring guide

Source: From Northwest Regional Educational Laboratory Mathematics and Science Education Center, 1999. Reprinted by permission.

Reasoning in Social Studies

The social studies context is rich with possibilities for developing and assessing student reasoning proficiency. For instance, we can ask students to analyze events to understand how they transpired. We can ask them to synthesize their knowledge and understanding of multiple events or historical figures to infer important generalizations. Obviously, it is relevant in social studies contexts to compare and contrast things, to classify them, and to express and defend an opinion or point of view (evaluative reasoning or critical thinking).

We can use selected response items to assess knowledge and understanding, as well as simple comparisons, some classifications, and simple inferences. However, for more complex patterns of reasoning such as evaluation and complex problems that require applying multiple patterns of reasoning we must use assessment methods that permit us to probe more deeply, such as essay and performance assessment.

For example, a performance assessment of high school historical investigations might rely on scoring guides such as those shown in Figure 9.9. First, they address the importance of knowing and understanding history. Then they call for applying that knowledge in a critical thinking context. Note once again the clear definition of performance levels.

One Final Point

One question often posed by primary-grade teachers during my workshops on assessing reasoning is, How do I know what is developmentally appropriate for my students? At what age can students be expected to think? Mr. Lopez, our elementary teacher guide, has some thoughts on this topic:

"I'll never forget when I first started my career as a first-grade teacher. I thought my job was to begin to fill their little heads with the knowledge of the world. Somewhere, I had learned that they weren't ready to figure things out yet. That was not "developmentally appropriate." Someone told me that Piaget said there were stages they go through and my kids weren't there yet. The textbooks we used and the curriculum outline I was given said, in effect, that I needed to rely pretty much on direct instruction and rehearsal to teach them what they needed to know. I was into lots of rote learning.

"But something began to trouble me right from the start. I remember Amy. One time I just happened to walk past her desk while she was working on a simple word puzzle. She was stumped, so I filled in a blank for her. Well, you'd think I had just insulted her best friend. 'No,' she complained, nudging me away, 'I wanted to figure it out myself. I can do it. Don't help me.'

"Then there was the time Bart was really frustrated with a math problem. Unlike Amy, he wanted my help. But I was busy with other students on another project and asked him to be patient. Patience was never Bart's long suit. Right then, Esteban came up and said he could help Bart figure it out. They worked together.

	Level I Minimal Achievement	Level II Rudimentary Achievement	Level III Commendable Achievement	Level IV Superior Achievement	Level V Exceptional Achievement
Knowledge and Use of History	Reiterates one or two facts without complete accuracy. Deals only briefly and vaguely with concepts or the issues. Barely indicates any previous historical knowledge. Relies heavily on the information provided.	Provides only basic facts with only some degree of accuracy. Refers to information to explain at least one issue or concept in general terms. Limited use of previous historical knowledge without complete accuracy. Major reliance on the information provided.	Relates only major facts to the basic issues with a fair degree of accuracy. Analyzes information to explain at least one issue or concept with substantive support. Uses general ideas from previous historical knowledge with fair degree of accuracy.	Offers accurate analysis of the documents. Provides facts to relate to the major issues involved. Uses previous general historical knowledge to examine issues involved.	Offers accurate analysis of the information and issue. Provides a variety of facts to explore major and minor issues and concepts involved. Extensively uses previous historical knowledge to provide an in-depth understanding of the problem and to relate it to the past and possible future situations.
Critical Thinking	Demonstrates little understanding and only limited comprehension of scope of problem or issues. Employs only the most basic parts of information provided. Mixes fact and opinion in developing a viewpoint. States conclusion after hasty or cursory look at only one or two pieces of information. Does not consider consequences.	Demonstrates only a very general understanding of scope of problem. Focuses on a single issue. Employs only the information provided. May include opinion as well as fact in developing a position. States conclusion after limited examination of evidence with little concern for consequences.	Demonstrates a general understanding of scope of problem and more than one of the issues involved. Employs the main points of information from the documents and at least the general idea from personal knowledge to develop a position. Builds conclusion on examination of information and some consideration of consequences.	Demonstrating clear understanding of scope of problem and at least two central issues. Uses the main points of information from the documents and personal knowledge that is relevant and consistent in developing a position. Builds conclusion on examination of the major evidence. Considers at least one alternative action and the possible consequences.	Demonstrates a clear accurate understanding of the scope of the problem and the ramifications of the issues involved. Employs all information from the documents and extensive personal knowledge that is factually relevant, accurate, and consistent in the development of a position. Bases conclusion on a thorough examination of the evidence, an exploration of reasonable alternatives and an evaluation of consequences.

Figure 9.9

California Assessment Program—History–Social Science grade 11 scoring guide: Group performance task. Reprinted by permission.

"Several other such incidents finally helped me get it through my thick skull that I had been wrong about these kids. When the light finally went on, I began to realize that they are thinkers. Their growing little brains are working just fine, thank you very much. They aren't just empty boxes for me to fill with knowledge. They can be problem solvers if I just give them a chance. From then on, we began to have some real fun and to do some serious learning by figuring things out together."

Mr. Lopez is right. The conventional wisdom is that the vast majority of students can reason from the day they arrive at school. From the outset, they can figure out what things are made of (analysis), how ideas can fit together (synthesis), how things are alike and different (comparison), how to categorize, and how to draw simple inductive and deductive inferences. However, in the early grades, they are severely limited in the range of knowledge and understanding they bring to their reasoning challenges, especially when it comes to school subjects. Nevertheless, they can practice reasoning using the knowledge they have. But as they do, our job is to help them move past misconceptions and prejudices in their understanding. We must help them clean out and rebuild their understanding. Our challenge is to show them how to use their abilities to figure things out as they confront increasingly complex academic challenges through their school years.

Matching Method to Target

Transforming reasoning targets into selected response test items, essay exercises, performance tasks, or discussion or interview questions is straightforward, once we understand the reasoning pattern. In all cases, we must pose novel challenges that ask students to tap what they know and to use that to find answers. In effect, they have to reason "on their feet" to answer the questions or solve the problems that we pose for them on assessments. Before we examine some examples, let me share a set of related insights that I have found useful.

When Assessing Reasoning, the Question Is Everything!

Paul (1995) suggests that the questions we pose in reasoning contexts fall into three categories:

1. Those with one right answer, for which students' reasoning leads them to correct or incorrect answers.

2. Those with relatively better or worse answers, depending on the quality of students' reasoning.

3. Those with as many different answers as there are human preferences.

Questions that fall into category one arise from disciplines within which we have an acknowledged system for determining one correct answer, such as mathematics. Questions that call for applying established bodies of knowledge and reasoning principles fit here:

Combining what this map tells you about average rainfall with your knowledge of how plants grow, where on the map would you expect to find the highest-yielding agricultural regions?

Time for Reflection

What pattern(s) of reasoning do you see reflected in this question? As you go, reflect also on the pattern(s) you see in each of the next three questions presented in the text.

These types of questions permit effective use of selected response assessment because they lead to a right answer. Personal communication may also be a suitable assessment method if the context is right.

Questions in category two require that respondents understand the issue at hand, bring accurate and appropriate knowledge and understanding to bear, and figure out a sound answer:

How did differences in the natural resources available to the Axis and Allied powers contribute to the outcome of World War II?

In this case, there is no single correct answer. Rather, the quality of the response turns on the quality of the respondent's reasoning. This type of question lends itself to essay assessment, which requires subjective evaluation criteria reflecting the relevant reasoning quality.

This second category also can include selected response questions that call for the best answer from among several correct answers. These cases require effective reasoning to make the important differentiation among response options.

Category three questions are matters of personal opinion or personal preference:

Which car do you prefer?

What kind of vacation do you wish to take?

These kinds of questions require evaluative reasoning—personal standards provide the basis for determining the preference. In the classroom, these kinds of questions can be tricky. Not only can people vary in their opinion, but they also can value different criteria in arriving at their position. Thus both the question and the answer relate only to personal well-being and not to academic appropriateness.

However, these kinds of questions do afford us engaging ways to put students in touch with the underlying structure of evaluative reasoning and standards of sound reasoning. We can help them understand that good decisions rely on access to accurate information about their choices, establishing sound evaluative criteria, and applying those criteria logically. Then we can help them generalize from matters of personal preference to academic judgments.

Selected Response

Sometimes we can effectively and efficiently assess student reasoning proficiency by posing novel questions that lead respondents to one best answer if they reason appropriately. We can translate five of the six ways discussed at the beginning of the chapter into such test exercises, if we wish. The one exception is evaluative reasoning, which requires students to formulate and present an original defense of their judgment. More about this later. Study the examples offered in Figure 9.10. To help you generate good questions tapping the various patterns of reasoning, consider using test question "triggers" such as those listed in Figure 9.11.

In all such cases, the questioner must understand the form(s) of reasoning required to answer the question correctly—that is, we must anticipate the proper inference. There may be just one or more than one defensible answer, but the array of possibilities must be clear. If there is more than one, we must advise respondents to use their reasoning skills to find the best one or all correct responses. The questioner must know the answer(s) expected of the reasoner before asking the question.

Having said this, however, I hasten to point out that we must always remain open to the possibility that our students might outthink us! They may come up

Reasoning	Illustration
Analysis	Of the four laboratory apparatus setups illustrated below, which will permit the user to carry out a distillation? (Offer four diagrams, one of which is correct.)
Synthesis	If we combine what we know about the likely impact of strong differences in barometric pressure and in temperature, what weather prediction would you make from this map? (Accompany the exercise with a map and several predictions, one of which is most likely.)
Comparison	What is one important difference between igneous and sedimentary rocks? (Offer several differences, only one of which is correct.)
Classification	Given what you know about animal life of the arid, temperate, and arctic regions, if you found an animal with the following characteristics, in which region would you expect it to live? (Describe the case and offer regions as choices.)
Inference	From the evidence provided to you in the graph, if water temperature were to go up, what would happen to the oxygen content of that water? (Provide a graph depicting the relationship between the two and offer conclusions as choices.)

Figure 9.10
Sample selected response exercises that require reasoning

To Tap	Begin the Question with...
Analysis	How do the parts of a _____ work together? How does _____ break down into its parts? What are the components of _____ ? What are the active ingredients in _____ ?

Synthesis	Given what you know about _____ and _____,
	    what would happen if you _____ ?
	What two sources of knowledge do you need to
	    combine to solve this problem?
	What do _____ and _____ have in common?

Comparison	How are these alike? different? Define the similarities between . . . (differences)? How does this correspond to that?
Classification	Into which category does each of the following fit? Group the following and label each category. Match each entry below with its classification.
Induction & Deduction	If this were to happen, then what would result? Using what you know about _____, solve this problem. What would be the consequences of _____? The central idea or theme of the story is what?
Evaluation	State your position on this issue and defend it. Is this a good quality piece of work, in your opinion? Why? Argue in favor of or against _____.

Figure 9.11
Triggers for test questions

with solidly defensible inferences that we had not considered. When this happens, we should give them credit for their insight.

In any event, evaluation of the quality of student reasoning is based on the correctness of their answers. If the exercise is well constructed and respondents reason well, they answer correctly. In the context of assessing reasoning, the strengths of selected response assessment are the same as those of all applications of this method: tight control over the reasoning sampled within test items, the possibility of obtaining comparable results across multiple students, and great efficiency in doing so. We can administer a large number of test items per unit of testing time, permitting us to sample broadly. But always remember, if they are to tap reasoning proficiency, our exercises must offer new challenges.

The major limitation of this format is its inability to tap multistage, complex reasoning, requiring the synthesis of various information sources, completed over a period of time. Another limitation is that this kind of assessment exercise doesn't help us identify and help misinformed students who select an incorrect response but rely on sound reasoning. Also, selected response questions assess skills in isolation; we also want to know if students know *when* to use each skill and how to use them in concert to solve complex problems.

Essay

We can pose essay exercises that ask students to convey the nature and quality of their reasoning in brief written responses. For instance, we might ask them to figure out this analytical problem:

> *Break air pollution down into its different sources, detailing how they can combine with each other to lead to an air stagnation alert.*

Or, we could investigate reasoning in the context of evaluative probes:

> *Some argue for and some against irrigating deserts to grow food. Take a position on this issue and defend it. Make explicit the criteria you are using as the basis for your position and be sure to apply them logically.*

We may use similar probes to determine if students can use their reasoning proficiencies to compare, classify, or reason inductively or deductively.

However, in this case, our evaluation of the quality of student response is not quite as straightforward as it was with selected response. We have entered the realm of subjective assessment and so must devise appropriate scoring schemes. See Figure 9.9, for example.

Clearly, the strength of this method for assessing reasoning is the richness of insight it can offer, provided respondents are proficient writers. Not only can we determine if the requisite knowledge and understanding are present, but also, we can determine if students have reasoned well. The major drawbacks are the complexity and time demands of scoring.

> Remember, if students aren't proficient writers, essay assessment of reasoning will not be valid or reliable. They may be able to reason and not be able to let you know it.
>
> TECHNICAL NOTE

Performance Assessment

In this case, exercises must ask students to reveal their proficiency either by (1) reasoning in some publicly visible manner so the nature and quality of their thought processes are apparent for all to see, or by (2) creating a tangible product that contains within it evidence of the reasoning that led to its creation. One way to accomplish option two is to ask for a public display reflecting the embedded reasoning. Marzano, Pickering, and McTighe (1993) offer an example:

You have volunteered to help out at your local library with their literacy program. Once a week after school, you help people learn how to read. To encourage your student to learn, you tell her about the different kinds of literature you have read, including poems, biographies, mysteries, tall tales, fables, and historical novels. Select three types of literature and compare them using general characteristics of literature that you think will help your student see the similarities and differences. Prepare a visual display of the comparison. (p. 98)

Or, by simply changing the display of reasoning prowess from a visual presentation to a speech detailing the comparison, we switch to option one. Those familiar with science fairs will recognize that they require a combination of a public display of the reasoning carried out and public commentary on that thinking.

However, a completely different approach to conducting a skill-based performance assessment of reasoning might be to pose a problem, such as a science challenge, and observe students as they set about solving it. A science teacher friend of mine presents students with two seemingly identical glasses of soda, but one is the diet version. Their task is to identify which is which. She observes carefully as they proceed, specific performance criteria in hand.

Her product-based performance assessment version of this exercise asks students to prepare a written report detailing how they solved the problem, including (1) the steps they completed to solve the problem, (2) the results of each step, and (3) how they decided on each succeeding step. She sees their analytical, comparative, inductive, deductive, and other forms of reasoning come alive in these reports. It's important to note that we draw a distinction here between a brief response to an essay assessment exercise and a long written product, such as a term paper or product. I feel more comfortable classifying the latter as a product-based performance assessment.

In the early grades, before students develop reading and writing skills, only two assessment methods can reflect their reasoning: **PERFORMANCE ASSESSMENT** (watch them) and **PERSONAL COMMUNICATION** (talk to them). Thus, these are the only potentially valid assessments at that level.

In all of these cases, the key to assessment success is to apply performance criteria that reflect the quality of reasoning demonstrated.

Personal Communication

This assessment option is labor intensive because of the need to conduct direct interactions with students; nevertheless, many contend that it provides the clearest window into student reasoning. To begin with, it allows us to ask those follow-up questions that probe more deeply into student reasoning. We can ask why they responded or thought as they did. When we ask focused questions, exploring the depths of student responses, we can both highlight good thinking and uncover misconceptions and inadequate reasoning.

In another form, this kind of assessment permits us to listen to students "think aloud" as they solve the problems we pose. Math teachers often report that the easiest way to see and understand the mistakes their students are making in solving problems is to have them talk about their reasoning as they do it. Many reading teachers ask students to retell the story in their own words. By interspersing strategic questioning, these teachers generate insights into analytical, comparative, or other forms of reasoning.

A great advantage of this option is that we can tap reasoning proficiency with students one on one or through group discussions. Just remember, to assess reasoning skills, the questions we pose during these interchanges must require that students address novel problems.

With personal communication-based assessments, sometimes our questions might have right answers. If students reason effectively, they will get them right. Other times, reasoning proficiency is reflected in extended, more complex discussions. In these cases, we face the challenge of subjectively applying more complex evaluative criteria like those that characterize essays or performance assessments.

Time for Reflection

A comparative reasoning exercise: As you look back over these applications of our four basic assessment methods for assessing reasoning proficiency, what do you see that these applications have in common? What are the most prominent differences among them?

Involving Students in Assessing Reasoning

Our ultimate goal is to teach students to understand, organize, and monitor their own reasoning. They come to us already thinking. It's wired in, so to speak. Our job is to point out how they can use those natural thinking processes to advantage to reason and solve problems both in school and beyond. The way to do this is to provide them with (1) an understanding of their reasoning processes, (2) a vocabulary with which to communicate about those processes, and (3) the insights they need to evaluate their own reasoning.

But perhaps most important, as Norris and Ennis (1989) have shown us, we must help them to take charge of their own reasoning and problem-solving proficiencies, to have a "critical spirit." Those with a critical spirit demand sound thinking from themselves and from those around them. They strive to stay well informed from the most credible sources, remain open minded, and take personal pleasure in dealing as completely as possible with complex problems. To help them attain this level of competence we must help them become confident in this performance domain. That calls for involving students in assessing their own reasoning using strategies such as those listed in Figure 9.12.

To reiterate, remember that assessing students' abilities to reason and solve significant problems requires the presentation of novel challenges at assessment time. This means we must set students up for success by being sure they have access to essential knowledge via memory or reference materials and by providing practice with essential reasoning processes. Then, at assessment time, we must present brand-new exercises, so they can put their reasoning tools to work.

- Have students think aloud or write out steps when problem solving. This allows them to hear or see their thought processes, and makes those processes easier to think and talk about.
- Be sure your students learn to label and understand the various ways in which they reason. This provides a language to use in self-reflection and in communication about reasoning. As a matter of classroom routine, constantly and explicitly model, label, and explain your reasoning, using the specific labels *analyze, compare, evaluate,* etc.
- Ask students to challenge each other's reasoning. The process of searching for the proper challenge to a classmate's reasoning helps students understand the attributes of sound reasoning more completely.
- Offer students repeated opportunities to participate in developing assessment exercises that tap different kinds of reasoning, and to interpret assessment results in terms of the information they provide about performance in different problem-solving contexts.
- When asking questions that require reflection and thought, be sure to wait for a response. Reasoning takes time.
- Avoid questions during instruction that call for yes or no answers. Pose questions that require more complete thought and communication.
- Use "concept mapping" (Novak & Gowin, 1984) to assess analytical reasoning proficiency. In this approach, students create bursting diagrams to convey their understanding of concept relationships. Figure 9.3 shows a sample concept map about assessment as we are studying it.
- Have students develop and apply scoring criteria to evaluate strong and weak responses to reasoning exercises, and then to their own responses. This represents practice in evaluative reasoning of critical thinking.
- Keep the whole class involved in the reasoning process during instruction by calling on non-volunteers, by asking students to paraphrase each other's responses, and by asking them to add to each other's responses.
- Have students keep journals in which they describe the effectiveness of their reasoning and problem solving. This provides experience using the language of reasoning and in being reflective.
- Have students build portfolios of examples of their own reasoning that provide evidence that they are becoming more and more proficient in terms of the nature and complexity of the reasoning they can carry out and the problems they can solve.
- Have students analyze the patterns of reasoning required to solve complex problems.
- Involve students in the process of analyzing incorrect answers to multiple choice items by identifying the flawed reasoning that makes each incorrect.

Figure 9.12
Ideas for student-involved assessment

Summary: Finding the Path to Reasoning Power

If students are to hit important reasoning and problem-solving targets, if they are to become enthusiastic, confident, and competent users of their own reasoning power, they must be in touch with their own capabilities in this critical performance arena. We need not teach them to think, but we must help them understand, clean up, and organize their thinking so they can use it to maximum advantage. We must remember that the human mind does not come with a user's guide. Part of our job as teachers is to provide that guidance.

If we are to assist students, each of us must establish with our colleagues that vision of the proficient problem solver that will guide instruction in our classroom. In effect, we must become comfortable with ourselves as thinkers. To the extent that we can agree across classrooms and grade levels about what it means to succeed at this, we maximize the chances of developing ever more advanced levels of student proficiency over time.

You need a conceptual scheme of reasoning that you are willing to master completely, so completely that it becomes second nature to you in teaching and in assessing. Your vision needs to make sense in the real world. You will need many examples to share with your students of ways to address real-world problems using whatever ways of thinking you choose. It

is only through these applications that you can help your students to both see the relevance of becoming more capable problem solvers, and take responsibility for their own reasoning and problem solving.

Your vision must be one that you can bring to life for your students. It must be made up of component parts that students can understand, translated into a vocabulary they can use in conversation with you and with each other. One excellent way to share the meaning of success with students is to teach them to reflect on, understand, and evaluate their own reasoning.

Our professional development challenge in preparing to assess reasoning is to understand how to translate the reasoning models we value into appropriate forms of assessment. All four basic methods (selected response, essay, performance assessment, and personal communication) can reflect valuable kinds of reasoning if users understand and adhere to the key attributes of sound assessments. Start with a complete vision of the pattern(s) of reasoning you are assessing, select an appropriate method, sample student reasoning with enough exercises to give you confidence in your results, and use it in ways that control for all those sources of bias (as discussed in earlier chapters).

Exercises for Self-Assessment

1. Make a chart identifying the key characteristics of each pattern of reasoning discussed in this chapter.

2. Write a brief essay or create a simple diagram demonstrating that you understand the relationships that exist among the six

ways of reasoning described at the beginning of the chapter.

3. In your own words and referring back to the text as needed, briefly describe the five key principles offered in this chapter to guide your assessment of reasoning.

4. List the strengths and weaknesses of each of the four basic assessment methods when applied to the assessment of reasoning.

5. List as many different ways as you can to integrate assessing reasoning into day-to-day classroom teaching and learning.

6. Select a content area of interest to you in which you have developed a strong background. Within that context, develop three exercises that tap reasoning as discussed in this chapter.

7. Throughout this chapter, I have argued that access to knowledge and understanding are essential components of sound reasoning. Do you agree or disagree? Why?

8. It has been common in schools in the past to make "higher-order reasoning" a special emphasis of talented and gifted programs. At the same time, it has rarely been a special thrust of remedial programs. Do you think such differentiation across program lines is appropriate? Why?

 You may go to the Companion Website at www.prenhall.com/stiggins and answer these questions in the Self-Assessment module.

Final Chapter Reflection

1. *What are the three most important new insights to come to you as a result of your study of this chapter?*
2. *Which of your previous questions about assessment can you now answer based on your study of this chapter?*
3. *What new questions have come to mind as a result of your study of this chapter that you hope to have answered as your study continues?*
4. **For practicing teachers only:** *What do you plan to do differently in assessment in your classroom as a result of your study of this book so far?*

For those in preservice study only: As you think about the classroom assessment environment that you hope to create for your students, how has your thinking changed as a result of your study of this book so far?

Workbook Activities

Those of you using the workbook, *Practice with Student-Involved Classroom Assessment*, as part of your study of this material will find the following activities and others included for Chapter 9:

- *Compare the Text's Classification Scheme to Those You Use Now.* A key part of Chapter 9 is the discussion of the many interrelated parts of the reasoning process. This activity gives you the opportunity to compare Rick's classification scheme for reasoning with others you might already be using.

- *Real-World Examples.* This activity helps you to internalize the reasoning patterns discussed in the chapter by finding examples of reasoning in action in the real world.

- *Key Words.* You can use a variety of methods to assess the quality of student reasoning. This activity asks you to generate key words that trigger different thinking patterns and convert the list into questions that you could ask.

- *Convert Patterns of Reasoning into Student-Friendly Language.* If *reasoning* is an important learning target for students, they need to understand the target they are to hit. This activity gives you the opportunity to translate the patterns of reasoning in Chapter 9 into student-friendly language and then see what students have to say about it.

Video Support

The ATI interactive video training package, *Assessing Reasoning in the Classroom*, carefully analyzes the various patterns of reasoning and provides more practice in applying them. Brief videos segments alternate with hands-on activities to bring the power of student-involved assessment to the fore.

10

Performance Assessment of Skills and Products

CHAPTER FOCUS

This chapter answers the following guiding question:

How can I devise assessments that help my students know that they are confident, competent masters of the performance skills and product development capabilities that I expect of them?

From studying this chapter you will come to understand the following general principles:

1. Performance assessment scoring criteria must be sharply focused on the right achievement targets, including all of the active ingredients needed for success.

2. Performance tasks must engage students in interesting tasks that afford them the opportunity to demonstrate mastery of all key elements of skill and product achievement.

3. The heart of academic competence resides in students' ability to use their own knowledge and understanding to continuously improve their performance until they achieve success. Therefore, there is a direct link between performance criteria and student involvement.

As you read this chapter, continue to keep in mind the big classroom assessment picture. The shaded areas of Figure 10.1 indicate the relevant achievement targets and assessment methods.

	SELECTED RESPONSE	ESSAY	PERFORMANCE ASSESSMENT	PERSONAL COMMUNICATION
Know				
Reason				
Skills				
Products				
Dispositions				

Figure 10.1
Aligning achievement targets and assessment methods

Quality Control Guidelines with Examples, Examples, Examples

As you know, this is our second chapter on performance assessment. The first was Chapter 7, where we introduced the basic structure of a performance assessment and aligned it with the achievement targets. Now that you understand how this method fits into the big classroom assessment picture, let's begin the process of fine tuning your ability to develop good assessments.

To accomplish this, we will rely on two learning aids. The first is a set of standards by which to judge the quality of performance assessment scoring criteria, and the second is a parallel set of standards for evaluating performance exercises or tasks. Each set is analytical in that it includes several key dimensions of quality. Within each dimension, we define attributes of performance assessments that we believe are "ready to use." Any assessment that does not meet those standards of excellence needs revision.

To help you understand and learn to apply these standards of performance assessment quality, we will examine a variety of examples that illustrate different levels of quality. I have selected these examples to reveal the diversity of possible applications of this rich form of assessment. They cross grade levels from primary through high school, include disciplines ranging from language arts to math and science, and cover such scoring options as rating scales and checklists of individual and group performance scored holistically and analytically. Each example, strong or weak, teaches important lessons about how to develop and use performance assessments.

As our journey spirals once again through the domain of performance assessment, it is important that we revisit lessons learned earlier. In Chapter 7, you will recall, we developed a three-part performance assessment design framework. We begin by defining the *reason for the assessment*. Then we *define the performance* to be evaluated. And finally we *devise exercises* to elicit instances of that performance.

Because it may have been a while since you studied the basic design structure in Chapter 7, I recommend that you return to the section titled, "Developing Performance Assessments" to refresh your understanding. Keep the basic performance assessment design framework presented in Figure 7.2 in mind as you proceed through this chapter on developing sound performance criteria and performance tasks.

Keeping Perspective

Remember, the assessment examples presented here are intended to serve only as illustrations. They are meant to trigger your imagination, stimulate your curiosity, and encourage you to learn more about this methodology. In that regard, you should not simply read through this chapter and move on. Rather, reflect on the examples as a means of widening your perspectives about performance assessment. If you are teaching, consider adapting some of the samples for experimental use in your classroom.

Further, while several examples appear to be highly refined applications, still think of them as works in progress. One of the great lessons we are learning from our experiences in designing and developing performance assessments is that the very process of devising exercises and performance criteria helps us to refine our vision of the meaning of academic success. As a result, *it is best to think of any set of performance criteria as the "latest version" of an ever-sharpening portrait of that success.*

As you use these assessments, remember your students. It is very important that they develop a sense of both understanding and ownership of the performance criteria. This argues against the wholesale installation of other people's criteria in the classroom. Rather, even when using criteria developed by others, it is wise to "lead" students to your adopted standards of quality by using the student-involved performance assessment development procedures specified in the subsection in Chapter 7 titled, "Developing Your Own Performance Criteria." Keep in mind what that experience was like from Emily's point of view. Also, review the ideas found in Figure 7.7 in that chapter titled "Ideas for Student-Involved Performance Assessment."

In addition, remember that an appropriately focused set of performance criteria, although certainly necessary for quality performance assessment, is far from sufficient. The key to the effective application of those criteria in the classroom is carefully prepared observers/raters. Skillful performance assessors are trained, not born. And training them is important, whether they're Olympic figure skating judges, assessors of student writing, evaluators of learning disabled students, or students preparing to evaluate their own performance. Aspiring performance assessors must remain open minded and willing to learn as they strive to master achievement standards. Unless we invest in thoughtful preparation, we cannot expect our observations of and judgments about student performance to be dependable, regardless of the quality of the performance criteria we start with.

And finally, remember to maintain balance. Performance assessment represents just one of four viable methods of assessment that we have at our disposal. We can use selected response, essay, and personal communication formats to tap student mastery of many of the important dimensions of knowledge and reasoning prerequisite to becoming skillful in performance. In addition, we can use the essay format to approximate some very sophisticated forms of performance. Classroom teachers faced with growing assessment challenges and shrinking assessment resources cannot overlook these options.

Achieving Excellence in Performance Criteria

A performance assessment scoring guide is made up of performance criteria that frame the standards of excellence to be used to judge student work. But how do we know if the performance criteria are any good? We know our criteria are good when they are "on target"; that is, when they cover the right ingredients of performance and do it in the right way. We also know our criteria are sound when they're "practical." In other words, they're precisely focused in a manner that makes them helpful to teachers and students in real classroom settings. In this section, your learning goals are to understand what "on target" and "practical" mean, why each is important, and how each plays out in strong and weak performance criteria.

Be advised that the terms *performance criteria, scoring criteria*, and *rubrics* are synonymous in this chapter. They all refer to achievement expectations spelled out in a form that allows us to compare student performance to different levels of quality to judge where each student is improving.

Also be advised that the standards of quality discussed here were developed for use with classroom assessments, not large-scale assessments. As you know by now, the distinction is important. The classroom context places a premium on detail, instructional relevance, and practicality that might not be required for a once-a-year standardized performance assessment.

To simplify some relatively complex concepts I have chosen to rely on a checklist of attributes of scoring criteria. Experience has shown that a simplified version is more accessible to new learners. Each ingredient on the checklist defines the high-quality end of a continuum of quality. Your goal is to learn to develop or select criteria that come as close to these standards of excellence as possible.

First read about the standards of performance criteria quality, and then we'll apply them to some examples of varying quality.

Quality Standard 1: Performance Criteria Must Be "On Target"

Performance criteria can be considered to be "on target" when they clearly define attributes of the achievement target we wish to evaluate, center on the real keys to good performance, and include all of the active ingredients of good performance. In other words, they are *clear, complete*, and *compelling*.

Clear.   The following four attributes indicate clarity in performance criteria:

First, each performance criterion is vividly and understandably described. That is, the terms used to define the criterion and to describe levels of performance, from poor to outstanding quality, are specific and accurate. Those knowledgeable about the field of study would agree on the meaning of each entry in the scoring guide.

Second, a high-quality set of performance criteria is well organized. The order of presentation of the criteria makes sense and levels of proficiency progress comfortably from weak to strong (or unsophisticated to sophisticated, or from beginning to mastery).

Third, performance criteria are "clear" only when—and this is crucial—we have uncovered samples of student work to illustrate each level of quality. *Our objective in devising sound performance criteria is to describe levels of quality, not merely judge them.* We describe in two ways: first by using descriptive language and second by providing examples to illustrate each level. Given verbal descriptions and examples, students can find where any piece of their own work lies on the continuum and understand what they have yet to achieve.

Fourth, clear criteria yield consistent ratings—the performance criteria are sufficiently well defined to permit two evaluators judging the same work independently to agree on the level of proficiency demonstrated. We might investigate the degree of agreement among raters by comparing the judgments of two qualified teachers or two students who have been carefully trained to apply the criteria. For now, just realize that, if two teachers judge the same piece of student work to be of different levels of quality, then those ratings aren't a function of real quality but rather of who does the judging. Rater bias is evident. That's not fair. So we need to aspire to sufficient clarity in our criteria that those who are to be judges can learn to apply them consistently.

> We've discussed this before: Inter-rater reliability must be high.

Complete and Compelling.   When we speak of performance criteria as being *complete and compelling*, we refer to the extent to which we are convinced of their importance in differentiating levels of quality in student work. The criteria do the following:

1. Center on what experts in the field would consider important aspects of the right target. They are not merely matters of local opinion; rather, they are based on the best current thinking of the field of study.

2. Include all key facets of performance; nothing that experts in the field would regard as important has been left out.

3. Have a ring of truth about them. It's clear why each ingredient is included.

4. Leave out trivial, tangential, or unrelated aspects of performance.

5. Are balanced—the most important aspects of performance are weighed more heavily.

Quality Standard 2: Performance Criteria Must Be "Practical"

Practicality means usefulness. Can people use the criteria easily? Do the criteria have clear implications for instruction? Can students use them to self-assess? Consider three aspects of practicality: Are the criteria focused at a useable level of *precision*, useful to *teachers*, and useful to *students*?

Precise.   The matter of precision plays out in a number of important ways. The following are indicators of precision:

First, you will recall from Chapter 7 that scoring guides can be devised to provide one overall judgment of performance (holistic scoring) or to break performance down into its component parts (analytical scoring). Each is useful in certain contexts, for various uses. When we need to diagnose student strengths and weaknesses on a complex skill, for example, only the greater precision of analytical score scales will suffice. On other occasions, the general scores derived from holistic scoring will do, such as when scoring large-scale assessments or when the skill being assessed is less complex. Thus, among the standards of excellence we must apply when evaluating performance assessment criteria is whether the level of precision woven into the scoring guide *meets the requirement of the context* within which we will use it.

We also must know whether the criteria are sufficiently sharp in their focus to be *applicable to student responses to a variety of similar performance tasks*. We encourage the development of generalizable, rather than task-specific, scoring criteria for classroom use. When the criteria can be used repeatedly across similar exercises over time, we can use them to help students see and understand improvements in their own performance.

Finally, we must aspire to sufficient precision in our descriptions of quality student performance that, when we apply our criteria, all *students receive fair evaluations* based on the attributes of their work and not on matters independent of quality, such as ethnicity or socioeconomic status. That is, criteria must be so precise in their focus that they accommodate cultural differences among students. To investigate such matters, we might have members of different ethnic groups review the criteria to be sure students are not placed at some obvious disadvantage due to their cultural experiences.

Teacher Friendly.   Obviously, practicality also refers to the usefulness of the scoring guide to teachers. Indicators of usefulness to teachers include the following:

The practical value of performance criteria to teachers is indicated by the extent to which they can quickly learn, through guided practice, to apply the criteria dependably. Teachers are more likely to actually *use* those criteria they can master quickly.

Another important aspect of practicality is the extent to which teachers report that performance ratings provide them with useful information. The most valuable criteria are going to be those that provide information about what to do next to help students improve, that dependably track student progress toward important learning targets, and/or that help teachers communicate effectively with others.

So, usefulness to teachers means that the time needed to learn the rubric is worth it in terms of the information obtained and the perceived instructional value for students.

Student Friendly.   Last, but by no means least, the practicality of performance criteria is determined by the extent to which students can be partners in applying them. Criteria are:

- student friendly when they address dimensions of quality that students can come to understand with training and practice—these are the criteria that permit students to go on internal control and manage their own improvement.

- practical for student use when their developers have taken the time to translate them into student-friendly language. Often, this requires simplifying language and syntactic structure.

- practical for student use when students are successful in locating examples of work that illustrate different levels of proficiency. They may not yet be able to produce high-quality work, but they can identify it. This sets them on the road to success.

Figure 10.2 summarizes the attributes of sound performance criteria.

Illustrations of Rubric Quality

Criteria That Are "On Target"

Ready to Use

Example 1: Six-Trait Model in Writing.   The sample writing assessment criteria detailed in Figure 10.3 (Spandel, in press) model strong standards for completeness and clarity. Please note that the Six-Trait Model for assessing writing is *an analytical model* having six dimensions. It is also a *generalizable* rubric because it can be used across all types of writing and for all writing assignments.

The traits shown in Figure 10.3 represent just three (organization, voice, and conventions) of the six dimensions that are part of the model. The other traits are ideas, word choice, and sentence fluency. All six were presented in their student-friendly version in Figure 7.3 in Chapter 7. The model has been under refinement for 15 years—we are continually attempting to refine the descriptions of what we

On-Target Criteria Are

A. *Clear*

- Each element to be scored is vividly and understandably described; all language is specific and accurate.
- The scoring guide is well organized both within and across rating scales.
- Examples of student work are provided, or can be easily found, to illustrate each level of quality.
- There is evidence that two teachers or two students evaluating the same piece of work independently rate it the same.

B. *Complete and Compelling*

- The criteria center on what experts in the field would consider the most important or telling aspects of quality.
- All key facets of performance are reflected in the criteria; nothing of importance is left out.
- They have a ring of truth about them—it is clear why each ingredient is included and the balance seems right.
- The criteria are couched in the best current thinking of the academic field.
- The criteria leave out trivial, tangential, or unrelated aspects of performance.

Practical Criteria Are

A. *Precise*

- The level of detail and precision in ratings (holistic or analytical) fits the use.
- The criteria can be applied to student responses to a variety of similar performance tasks; that is, they are generalizable across exercises.
- The criteria lead to fair evaluations for all students, regardless of ethnicity, socioeconomic status, or any factors other than achievement.

B. *Teacher Friendly*

- Teachers feel that the time required to learn to use the rubric dependably is worth it in terms of the usefulness of the information obtained and the perceived instructional value for students. Usefulness of information includes planning instruction, tracking student progress, and communicating with others.

C. *Student Friendly*

- The criteria address aspects of performance that students can understand.
- The criteria have been translated into language that students understand and can apply.
- All levels of performance can be illustrated with examples students themselves can find.

Figure 10.2
A quality control checklist for performance criteria

mean when we say "good writing." Through this refinement, the content of each trait has gained a "ring of truth." Nothing major is left out. Definitions are correct. Relative emphasis is good. The developers have been selective, yet complete. You are left with few questions. The rubric is insightful. Thus, the rubric is complete and compelling.

Likewise, the rubric not only looks clear, but also has been shown to result in consistent scoring. Raters, both in large-scale assessment and teachers in the classroom, have been easily trained to be consistent in scoring. Two experienced raters typically attain at least a 60 percent exact match in the ratings they assign to student papers, with 98 percent of their ratings falling within one point of one another.[1] Thus, evidence of a history of dependable applications is available. The words and phrases used to describe the quality of student papers are clear and compelling. All key dimensions of performance are defined, as are score points. The developers seem to have a sense of that which is most telling. Scored examples of student work have been assembled for all dimensions and score points across a range of grade levels.

> Here we see an index of inter-rater reliability, the degree of agreement among raters scoring the same work.

Example 2: ACTFL Oral Proficiency Interview.   The Oral Proficiency Interview (ACTFL, 1989), developed by the American Council on the Teaching of Foreign Languages (ACTFL), is a standardized procedure for the global assessment of speaking ability that relies on a trained examiner to carry on a conversation with the examinee and rate oral proficiency during the interaction, as well as afterward, via audiotape recording.

ACTFL currently offers training in applying the criteria in eleven languages: Arabic, Chinese, English as a second language, French, German, Hindi, Italian, Japanese, Portuguese, Russian, and Spanish. Thus, scored samples of student speaking that illustrate the criteria are available.

Another useful feature of the ACTFL rating system is that it begins with four major levels of proficiency and then further subdivides and defines each level in a straightforward manner, as seen in Figure 10.4. The result is a nine-level rating scale that teachers can use to track student progress over several years. But even more exciting is the possibility of students tracking their own development over time. Therefore, this rubric is *holistic and developmental*—users can track progress in learning a new language over the long haul.

The rubric also is *generalizable* because it can be used for all languages and across communication settings.

Although foreign language proficiency is a complex achievement target, the criteria levels capture that complexity with thoughtful, clearly descriptive language that describes the most telling aspects of performance. The criteria have the ring of

---

[1] Based on 1998 Northwest Regional Educational Laboratory analysis of rater consistency in scoring 12,000 student papers for the Seattle, Washington, Public Schools.

ORGANIZATION

5 *The organization enhances and showcases the central idea or theme. The order, structure, or presentation of information is compelling and moves the reader through the text.*

- A. An **inviting introduction** draws the reader in; a **satisfying conclusion** leaves the reader with a sense of closure and resolution.
- B. **Thoughtful transitions** clearly show how ideas connect.
- C. Details seem to fit where they're placed; **sequencing is logical** and **effective**.
- D. **Pacing is well controlled;** the writer knows when to slow down and elaborate, and when to pick up the pace and move on.
- E. The **title,** if desired, is **original** and captures the central theme of the piece.
- F. Organization **flows so smoothly** the reader hardly thinks about it; the choice of structure matches the **purpose** and **audience**.

3 *The organizational structure is strong enough to move the reader through the text without too much confusion.*

- A. The paper has a **recognizable introduction and conclusion.** The introduction may not create a strong sense of anticipation; the conclusion may not tie up all loose ends.
- B. **Transitions often work well**; at other times, connections between ideas are fuzzy.
- C. **Sequencing** shows **some logic**, but not under control enough that it consistently supports the ideas. In fact, sometimes it is so predictable and rehearsed that the **structure takes attention away from the content.**
- D. **Pacing is fairly well controlled,** though the writer sometimes lunges ahead too quickly or spends too much time on details that do not matter.
- E. **A title (if desired) is present,** although it may be uninspired or an obvious restatement of the prompt or topic.
- F. The **organization sometimes supports the main point or storyline;** at other times, the reader feels an urge to slip in a transition or move things around.

1 *The writing lacks a clear sense of direction. Ideas, details, or events seem strung together in a loose or random fashion; there is no identifiable internal structure. The writing reflects more than one of these problems:*

- A. There is **no real lead** to set up what follows, **no real conclusion** to wrap things up.
- B. Connections between ideas are **confusing** or not even present.
- C. **Sequencing needs** lots and lots of **work.**
- D. **Pacing feels awkward;** the writer slows to a crawl when the reader wants to get on with it, and vice versa.
- E. **No title is present** (if requested), or if present, **does not match** well with the content.
- F. Problems with organization make it **hard for the reader to get a grip** on the main point or story line.

Figure 10.3
Writing assessment criteria
Source: Spandel, Vicki (in press). *Creating writers.* Reading, MA: Addison-Wesley Longman. Reprinted by permission.

VOICE

5 *The writer speaks directly to the reader in a way that is individual, compelling and engaging. The writer "aches with caring," yet is aware and respectful of the audience and the purpose for writing.*

A. The reader feels a **strong interaction** with the writer, sensing the **person behind the words.**

B. The writer **takes a risk** by revealing who he or she is and what he or she thinks.

C. The tone and voice give **flavor and texture** to the message and are **appropriate for the purpose and audience.**

D. **Narrative** writing seems **honest, personal,** and written **from the heart. Expository or persuasive** writing reflects a **strong commitment** to the topic by showing **why** the **reader needs to know this** and why he or she should care.

E. This piece **screams to be read aloud, shared, and talked about.** The writing makes you think about and react to the author's point of view.

3 *The writer seems sincere, but not fully engaged or involved. The result is pleasant or even personable, but not compelling.*

A. The writing communicates in an **earnest, pleasing** manner.

B. Only **one or two moments here or there** surprise, delight, or move the reader.

C. The writer seems aware of an audience but **weighs ideas carefully** and discards personal insights in favor of **safe generalities.**

D. **Narrative writing seems sincere,** but not passionate; expository or persuasive writing **lacks consistent engagement** with the topic to build credibility.

E. The writer's willingness to share his/her point of view may **emerge strongly in some places,** but is often obscured behind **vague generalities.**

1 *The writer seems indifferent, uninvolved, or distanced from the topic and/or the audience. As a result, the paper reflects more than one of the following problems:*

A. The writer speaks in a kind of **monotone** that flattens all potential highs or lows of the message.

B. The writing is **humdrum and "risk-free."**

C. The writer **is not concerned with the audience,** or the writer's style is a **complete mismatch** for the intended reader.

D. The writing is **lifeless or mechanical;** depending on the topic, it may be overly technical or jargonistic.

E. **No point of view** is reflected in the writing—zip, zero, zilch, nada.

continued

CONVENTIONS

5 *The writer demonstrates a good grasp of standard writing conventions (e.g., spelling, punctuation, capitalization, grammar, usage, paragraphing) and uses conventions effectively to enhance readability. Errors tend to be so few that just minor touch-ups would get this piece ready to publish.*

A. **Spelling is generally correct,** even on more difficult words.

B. The **punctuation is accurate,** even creative, and guides the reader through the text.

C. A thorough understanding and consistent application of **capitalization** skills are present.

D. **Grammar and usage are correct** and contribute to clarity and style.

E. **Paragraphing tends to be sound** and reinforces the organizational structure.

F. The writer **may manipulate conventions** for stylistic effect—and it works! The piece is very close to being **ready to publish**.

GRADES 7 AND UP ONLY: The writing is sufficiently complex to allow the writer to show skill in using a wide range of conventions. For writers of younger ages, the writing shows control over those conventions that are grade/age appropriate.

3 The writer shows reasonable control over a limited range of standard writing conventions. Conventions are sometimes handled well and enhance readability; at other times, errors are distracting and impair readability.

A. **Spelling** is usually **correct or reasonably phonetic on common words,** but more difficult words are problematic.

B. **End-punctuation is usually correct;** internal punctuation (commas, apostrophes, semi-colons, dashes, colons, parentheses) is sometimes missing/wrong.

C. **Most words are capitalized correctly;** control over more sophisticated capitalization skills may be spotty.

D. **Paragraphing is attempted** but may run together or begin in the wrong places.

E. **Problems with grammar or usage are not serious** enough to distort meaning but may not be correct or accurately applied all of the time.

F. **Moderate** (a little of this, a little of that) **editing** would be required to polish the text for publication.

1 Errors in spelling, punctuation, capitalization, usage and grammar and/or paragraphing repeatedly distract the reader and make the text difficult to read. The writing reflects more than one of these problems:

A. **Spelling errors are frequent,** even on common words.

B. **Punctuation** (including terminal punctuation) is often **missing or incorrect.**

C. **Capitalization** is **random** and only the easiest rules show awareness of correct use.

D. **Errors in grammar or usage are very noticeable,** frequent, and affect meaning.

E. **Paragraphing is missing, irregular, or so frequent** (every sentence) that it has no relationship to the organizational structure of the text.

F. The reader must **read once to decode,** then again for meaning. **Extensive editing** (virtually every line) would be required to polish the text for publication.

Figure 10.3
continued

Novice	*The Novice level is characterized by the ability to communicate minimally with learned material.*
Novice-Low	Oral production consists of isolated words and perhaps a few high-frequency phrases. Essentially no functional communicative ability.
Novice-Mid	Oral production continues to consist of isolated words and learned phrases within very predictable areas of need, although quality is increased. Vocabulary is sufficient only for handling simple, elementary needs and expressing basic courtesies. Utterances rarely consist of more than two or three words and show frequent long pauses and repetition of interlocutor's words. Speaker may have some difficulty producing even the simplest utterances. Some Novice-Mid speakers will be understood only with great difficulty.
Novice-High	Able to satisfy partially the requirements of basic communicative exchanges by relying heavily on learned utterances but occasionally expanding these through simple recombinations of their elements. Can ask questions or make statements involving learned material. Shows signs of spontaneity although this falls short of real autonomy of expression. Speech continues to consist of learned utterances rather than of personalized, situationally adapted ones. Vocabulary centers on areas such as basic objects, places, and most common kinship terms. Pronunciation may still be strongly influenced by first language. Errors are frequent and, in spite of repetition, some Novice-High speakers will have difficulty being understood even by sympathetic interlocutors.
Intermediate	*The Intermediate level is characterized by the speaker's ability to:* • *create with the language by combining and recombining learned elements, though primarily in a reactive mode;* • *initiate, minimally sustain, and close in a simple way basic communicative tasks; and* • *ask and answer questions.*
Intermediate-Low	Able to handle successfully a limited number of interactive, task-oriented and social situations. Can ask and answer questions, initiate and respond to simple statements and maintain face-to-face conversation, although in a highly restricted manner and with much linguistic inaccuracy. Within these limitations, can perform such tasks as introducing self, ordering a meal, asking directions, and making purchases. Vocabulary is adequate to express only the most elementary needs. Strong interference from native language may occur. Misunderstandings frequently arise, but with repetition, the Intermediate-Low speaker can generally be understood by sympathetic interlocutors.

Figure 10.4
ACTFL foreign language proficiency guidelines for speaking
Source: Reprinted from *Oral Proficiency Interviews: Tester Training Manual* (n.p.) by the American Council on the Teaching of Foreign Languages, 1989, Yonkers, NY: Author. Reprinted by permission.

Intermediate-Mid	Able to handle successfully a variety of uncomplicated, basic and communicative tasks and social situations. Can talk simply about self and family members. Can ask and answer questions and participate in simple conversations on topics beyond the most immediate needs; e.g., personal history and leisure time activities. Utterance length increases slightly, but speech may continue to be characterized by frequent long pauses, since the smooth incorporation of even basic conversational strategies is often hindered as the speaker struggles to create appropriate language forms. Pronunciation may continue to be strongly influenced by first language and fluency may still be strained. Although misunderstandings still arise, the Intermediate-Mid speaker can generally be understood by sympathetic interlocutors.
Intermediate-High	Able to handle successfully most uncomplicated communicative tasks and social situations. Can initiate, sustain, and close a general conversation with a number of strategies appropriate to a range of circumstances and topics, but errors are evident. Limited vocabulary still necessitates hesitation and may bring about slightly unexpected circumlocution. There is emerging evidence of connected discourse, particularly for simple narration and/or description. The Intermediate-High speaker can generally be understood even by interlocutors not accustomed to dealing with speakers at this level, but repetition may still be required.
Advanced	*The Advanced level is characterized by the speaker's ability to:* • *converse in a clearly participatory fashion;* • *initiate, sustain, and bring to closure a wide variety of communicative tasks, including those that require an increased ability to convey meaning with diverse language strategies due to a complication or an unforeseen turn of events;* • *satisfy the requirements of school and work situations; and* • *narrate and describe with paragraph-length connected discourse.*
Advanced	Able to satisfy the requirements of everyday situations and routine school and work requirements. Can handle with confidence but not with facility complicated tasks and social situations, such as elaborating, complaining, and apologizing. Can narrate and describe with some details, linking sentences together smoothly. Can communicate facts and talk casually about topics of current public and personal interest, using general vocabulary. Shortcomings can often be smoothed over by communicative strategies, such as pause fillers, stalling devices, and different rates of speech. Circumlocution which arises from vocabulary

Figure 10.4
continued

	or syntactic limitations very often is quite successful, though some groping for words may still be evident. The Advanced-level speaker can be understood without difficulty by native interlocutors.
Advanced-Plus	Able to satisfy the requirements of a broad variety of everyday, school, and work situations. Can discuss concrete topics relating to particular interests and special fields of competence. There is emerging evidence of ability to support opinions, explain in detail, and hypothesize. The Advanced-Plus speaker often shows a well-developed ability to compensate for an imperfect grasp of some forms with confident use of communicative strategies, such as paraphrasing and circumlocution. Differentiated vocabulary and intonation are effectively used to communicate fine shades of meaning. The Advanced-Plus speaker often shows remarkable fluency and ease of speech but under the demands of Superior-level, complex tasks, language may break down or prove inadequate.
Superior	*The Superior level is characterized by the speaker's ability to:* • *participate effectively in most formal and informal conversations on practical, social, professional, and abstract topics; and* • *support opinions and hypothesize using native-like discourse strategies.*
Superior	Able to speak the language with sufficient accuracy to participate effectively in most formal and informal conversations on practical, social, professional, and abstract topics. Can discuss special fields of competence and interest with ease. Can support opinions and hypothesize, but may not be able to tailor language to audience or discuss in depth highly abstract or unfamiliar topics. Usually the Superior-level speaker is only partially familiar with regional or other dialectical variants. The Superior-level speaker commands a wide variety of interactive strategies and shows good awareness of discourse strategies. The latter involves the ability to distinguish main ideas from supporting information through syntactic, lexical, and suprasegmental features (pitch, stress, intonation). Sporadic errors may occur, particularly in low-frequency structures and some complex high-frequency structures more common to formal writing, but no patterns of error are evident. Errors do not disturb the native speaker or interfere with communication.

continued

truth. Because ACTFL provides training, there are many samples of speaking tied to the various languages. These kinds of criteria represent far more than rating scales. They represent the basis for communication and shared meaning about assessment between teacher and student.

Criteria Close to Being "On Target."   There is much to like about each of the following rubrics. Each of them has some strengths, but each also has some aspects that could be tightened up. Therefore, each has a balance of strengths and weaknesses and so is midway on the "on target" scale. Each also exhibits different strengths and weaknesses ranging from important aspects of performance being left out to some poorly defined terms to nonexisting definition of performance levels.

Example 1: Oral Presentation Performance Criteria.   These criteria for evaluating oral presentations (Figure 10.5) need some work in completeness and clarity. This rubric contains much that is relevant, but leaves out an entire essential trait—content. Further, the descriptions under each of the score points leave out important indicators. Additionally, why are "4" and "3" grouped together? How are they alike or different? Do they need to be (indeed, can they be) differentiated? Likewise for "2" and "1." These problems can reduce practicality for students and teachers (see the trait of "Practicality" following). In its favor, the developer created samples of student oral presentations that illustrate the score points and collected evidence that raters can be trained to be consistent in scoring.

Please note that these criteria are an *analytical* model having three traits or dimensions that describe quality. (A fourth trait, content, could profitably be added.) These criteria are also generalizable—they can be used for a variety of oral presentations.

Example 2: The Rubric for Application Letter.   This rubric (Figure 10.6) offers much relevant content. But some important things have been left out, like organization. Also, some criteria are limiting—for example, the criteria only allow two possible openings for the letter. What happens if another opening would work better for a particular job or audience?

This rubric is *analytical*; look at the number of things to be rated! Because this list is long, it is critical that it be highly organized. All the items listed here could be nicely organized into four categories (analytical traits): content, style, format/presentation, and mechanics/conventions. Additionally, the content of attributes, as stated, is somewhat out of balance, placing much emphasis on format and not on organization, style, and conventions. Reorganizing the rubric into four traits would restore balance and make the rubric more practical to use (see the trait of "Practicality" following).

Much of the rubric for the application letter is very clear. We must be constantly vigilant that the words and phrases we use are likely to have the same meaning for teachers. For example, would all teachers agree on what "highlights the best items from applicant's background" means?

Score	Language	Delivery	Organization
A = 5	Correct grammar and pronunciation are used. Word choice is interesting and appropriate. Unfamiliar terms are defined in the context of the speech.	The voice demonstrated control with few distractions. The presentation holds the listener's attention. The volume and rate are at acceptable levels. Eye contact with the audience is maintained.	The message is organized. The speaker sticks to the topic. The main points are developed. It is easy to summarize the content of the speech.
B = 4 C = 3	Correct grammar and pronunciation are used. Word choice is adequate and understandable. Unfamiliar terms are not explained in the context of the speech. There is a heavy reliance on the listener's prior knowledge.	The voice is generally under control. The speaker can be heard and understood. The speaker generally maintains eye contact with the audience.	The organization is understandable. Main points may be underdeveloped. The speaker may shift unexpectedly from one point to another, but the message remains comprehensible. The speech can be summarized.
D = 2 F = 1	Errors in grammar and pronunciation occur. Word choice lacks clarity. The speaker puts the responsibility for understanding on the listener.	The student's voice is poor. The volume may be too low and the rate too fast. There may be frequent pauses. Nonverbal behaviors tend to interfere with the message.	Ideas are listed without logical sequence. The relationships between ideas are not clear. The student strays from the stated topic. It is difficult to summarize the speech.

Figure 10.5

Oral presentation performance criteria

Source: Reprinted from Toolkit98: Chapter 3, Activity 3.3—Performance Criteria, Keys to Success. Reprinted by permission of Northwest Regional Educational Laboratory, Portland, Oregon.

Example 3: Mechanized Vehicle.   This rubric was developed for use in a high school physics class—students were to build a mechanized vehicle that could move in at least two directions (e.g., an oscillating fan or a dump truck). This was a culminating project in which students were to demonstrate not only their understanding of physics, but other valued skills such as working in a group, oral presentation, and written presentation. The rubric is presented in Figure 10.7.

The list of things to be assessed seems to cover the important outcomes for a semester's work; therefore, the rubric seems complete and compelling. However, there are problems with clarity. Major headings are defined, but there is little detail to assist the rater to choose the proper score points. There is some attempt to define terms and include descriptors, but it doesn't go far enough. There is likely to

Name_____

Period_____

Row_____

RUBRIC FOR APPLICATION LETTER

Letter includes applicant's

    Street address

    City, State, Zip

    Date written out

    Followed by 3 blank lines

    Full name of person to receive letter

    Title of person, if known

    Name of company

    Address

    City, State, Zip

    Followed by a double space

    Salutation including addressee's name

    Followed by a :

    Followed by a double space

Letter:

    Opens with a strong, positive statement about applicant or his qualifications

    or

    Opens with a statement naming a person known by the addressee who advised the applicant of available position

    Highlights the best items from applicant's background which directly qualifies him for the job

    States why applicant wants to work for this organization

    Requests an interview

    Suggests how applicant will follow-up or where he can be reached to schedule an interview

    Includes a proper closing followed by a comma

    Closing followed by four hard returns

    Applicant's full real name is typed below closing

    Applicant signed letter in ink between the closing and his name

    Letter is one page

    Sentences and paragraphs are short and easy to read

    No misspelled words or grammar errors

    Printed on high-quality paper

Figure 10.6

Rubric for application letter

Source: From Anna Lipski's entry in the 1997 NCME Classroom Assessment Recognition Program. Reprinted by permission.

Thinking Skills	Communication/Presentation Skills	Work Management/Interpersonal Skills
UNDERSTANDING	**CLARITY AND COHERENCE OF PRESENTATION:**	**TEAMWORK (FOR GROUP WORK ONLY):**
☐ Understands relationships between variables and topics covered.	☐ Uses visual aids to make explanations clear.	☐ Group members show interest in project/evidence that all members played a part in work.
☐ Locates pertinent information to solve problems. Makes observations about the work.	☐ Explains calculations and reviews components of final product.	☐ Labor is divided equally, or an obvious attempt to do so is made.
☐ Explains known principles/concepts/theories and how they fit into work: uses examples to demonstrate knowledge—uses relevant terminology—applies formulas accurately and appropriately—uses diagrams, and graphs appropriately.	☐ Uses clear and concise language.	**THOROUGHNESS/EFFORT:**
	☐ Organizes materials systematically.	☐ Completes work and meets requirements of task.
	☐ Uses conventions that make student's train of thought evident.	☐ Shows evidence of hard work in quality of final product or in explanations about work.
CRITICAL THINKING/INQUIRY:	**PRESENTATION AESTHETICS:**	☐ Adds aspects that go beyond what is required in original assignment.
☐ Identifies the problem.	*Written Work*	☐ Plans work, reports on activities.
☐ Justifies decisions made (thinking process evident).	☐ Work is legible and neat; shows pride in work.	**REFLECTIVENESS:**
☐ Makes analysis/inferences/predictions based on the work.	☐ Pays attention to details.	☐ Includes individual or group opinion about process (steps involved in completing work)
☐ Responds appropriately to unanticipated problems.	☐ Grammar and spelling.	☐ Personal Voice: Explains the origins of her/his ideas—indicates originality and ownership of work.
☐ Asks informed questions about the work/curiosity.	*Presentations and Oral Work*	☐ Reflects on interpersonal relations within the group (when working in groups).
☐ Uses resources creatively.	☐ Body language and poise—addresses audience/eye contact.	☐ Reflects on own limitations and strengths as learner.
☐☐ Has innovative ideas.	☐ Is confident with/has ownership of material.	☐ Points out significance of work for own learning.
	☐ Has rehearsed and/or smooth delivery.	☐ Puts work in a larger context or relates work to real-life.
	☐ Craftsmanship—puts components of product together well.	
	☐ Uses appropriate medium or materials to convey ideas.	
	☐ Pays attention to details.	

Figure 10.7

Mechanized vehicle criteria

Source: Center for Technologies. Bank Street College. New York.

be disagreements in ratings either between teachers or with the same teacher over students or assignments.

Criteria That Are Not "On Target"

Example 1: Informal Writing Assessment.   The writing criteria presented in Figure 10.8 (fictional, but designed to illustrate a common problem) need substantial revision. This rubric covers almost nothing that defines a piece of quality writing; all that is covered is grammar. "Why should *this* count?" is a dominant question. The rubric doesn't represent the best thinking in the field with respect to the qualities that constitute good writing—it doesn't align with the target it's supposed to assess. Also, the rubric is not clear; for example, what does "disrupting communication" mean?

Just for completeness, this rubric is *holistic* (based on one, overall calculation of quality) and *generalizable* (it could be used for any piece of writing).

Example 2: Skimpy Criteria in Math.   Study the math problem-solving criteria shown in Figure 10.9. (This rubric is fabricated to illustrate a common problem.) The major problem here is clarity, rather than completeness. This rubric is little more than a list of categories of things to rate. There is no definition of terms or descriptors for levels of performance. The language is so vague that there could be many interpretations. Teachers are unlikely to agree on ratings. (In fact, there is data to show that teachers, using a very similar real version of the rubric, in fact did not agree.) The only way that levels are distinguished are with the terms "frequently," "occasionally," and so on. A common response is, "What do they mean by this?"

Again, for completeness, this rubric is *analytical* (there is more than one score for a performance) and *generalizable* (the rubric could be used for any math problem).

Example 3: Poor Quality Math Rubric.   Figure 10.10 is another fabricated example that we created to illustrate common problems with rubrics. In this case the

Figure 10.8
Informal writing assessment

Informal Writing Assessment

The Informal Writing Assessment asks young students to respond to a picture—what is happening in the picture, what preceded the picture, what will happen next, etc. To score the essay, the rater first counts up the total number of grammatical errors. Then the rater counts up the number of "fatal" grammatical errors—those that are so confusing that meaning is lost. The number of fatal errors is divided by the total number of errors to get the error index. An error index of greater than 75% indicates the need for remediation.

	Frequently	Occasionally	Sometimes	Never
Understanding the problem	4	3	2	1
Appropriate use of math	4	3	2	1
Clearly focused, good reasoning	4	3	2	1
Effective communication	4	3	2	1

Figure 10.9
Skimpy math criteria

rubric is neither complete nor clear. No terms are defined or described. One can't tell if it centers on the best thinking in the field—there isn't enough there to go on. Such skimpy criteria are quite common. In fact, they give criteria and rubrics a bad name. I recently read a newspaper article that questioned the competence of a school district for using a rubric such as this. Just to complete the picture, this rubric is generalizable and holistic.

Criteria that are "Practical"

Ready to Use
Example 1: Six-Trait Writing Assessment Criteria.   The intended use of the Six-Trait Writing Assessment Criteria (see Figure 10.3) is instruction, therefore the rubric is both *analytical* and *generalizable* (able to be applied to a variety of student writing).

Teachers across the country report that ratings on these criteria help them become better teachers and their students become more competent, confident writers. There is also research evidence to support these anecdotal stories (contact Write Traits, Portland, Oregon, 800-825-1739). Teachers find the rubric manageable. It takes a while to learn, but there is unanimous consensus that the payoff is worth the time. It is clear how to translate results into instruction. The descriptive

1 Point: Shows no understanding of the requirements of the problem.
2 Points: Shows a little understanding of the requirements of the problem.
3 Points: Shows partial understanding of the requirements of the problem.
4 Points: Shows considerable understanding of the requirements of the problem.
5 Points: Shows complete understanding of the requirements of the problem.

Figure 10.10
Poor quality math rubric

detail in the rubric relieves teachers of having to write comments on each piece of student writing. Once students learn the rubric, they know what the shorthand "scores" mean and what to do about any weaknesses found.

The rubric is also manageable for students. There are visually appealing student-friendly versions for primary, elementary, and secondary students. The rubric is so clear that a student doing poorly would know exactly what to do to improve. Much material is available to help teachers teach students to be self-assessors and revisers of writing (contact Write Traits). Evidence abounds that students can use the Six-Trait Model to assess their own work.

Example 2: Central Kitsap (WA) Math Problem-Solving Criteria.   Once again the rubric, shown in Figure 10.11 is *analytical* (a performance is scored on several dimensions) and *generalizable* (can be applied across problems) and lends itself nicely to classroom uses—diagnosing student strengths and weaknesses, planning instruction, tracking student progress, communicating with others, and using with students to help them understand the nature of quality problem solving.

Teachers report that this rubric has the same benefits to assessment and instruction that are reported for the Six-Trait Model in writing. The rubric is worded in a manner that obviously welcomes students into the process of monitoring their own progress.

Criteria Close to Being "Practical."   Once again, these rubrics have many good features we can successfully build on. They represented a balance of strengths and weaknesses on the trait of "practical."

Example 1: Task-Specific Criteria in Math.   I have not spoken much thus far about task-specific rubrics. I present here two rubrics for the same task (Figure 10.12) so that we can discuss their use. On the surface, task-specific criteria look easy to use—after all, the rubric tells you exactly what "counts" in the response. We should score work quickly and scoring should be consistent across students. The rubric might even provide relevant information on how good students are as problem solvers.

But, here's the rub. After getting an overall point value using either of the rubrics in Figure 10.12, it is not clear exactly what we would need to teach differently in problem solving in order to improve student achievement. Also, these rubrics don't help define quality problem solving so that teachers and students can clearly see the target. They define what good-quality problem solving might look like on *this* problem, but what about the next? Would we need a new rubric? Task-specific criteria can't be shared with students ahead of time because they give away the answer. If the goal is for students to understand the nature of quality so that they can apply what they learned from one problem to the next, then generalizable criteria are better.

So the problem with task-specific rubrics is not that they aren't easy to use—they *are* easy to use if our only goal is assessment. But if our goal is instruction and student-involvement they offer fewer advantages. One solution, frequently

Mathematical Concepts and Procedures

5   **I completely understand the appropriate mathematical operation and use it correctly.**

- I understand which math operations are needed.
- I have used all of the important information.
- I did all of my calculations correctly.

3   **I think I understand most of the mathematical operations and how to use them.**

- I know which operations to use for some of the problem, but not for all of it.
- I have an idea about where to start.
- I know what operations I need to use, but I'm not sure where the numbers go.
- I picked out some of the important information, but I might have missed some.
- I did the simple calculations right, but I had trouble with the tougher ones.

1   **I wasn't sure which mathematical operation(s) to use or how to use the ones I picked.**

- I don't know where to start.
- I'm not sure which information to use.
- I don't know which operations would help me solve the problem.
- I don't think my calculations are correct.

Figure 10.11
Central Kitsap School District's student-friendly math problem-solving criteria
Source: From Central Kitsap School District, Silverdale, Washington. Reprinted by permission.

Problem Solving

5   I came up with and used a strategy that really fits and makes it easy to solve this problem.

- I knew what to do to set up and solve this problem.
- I knew what math operations to use.
- I followed through with my strategy from beginning to end.
- The way I worked the problem makes sense and is easy to follow.
- I may have shown more than one way to solve the problem.
- I checked to make sure my solution makes sense in the original problem.

3   I came up with and used a strategy, but it doesn't seem to fit the problem as well as it should.

- I think I know what the problem is about, but I might have a hard time explaining it.
- I arrived at a solution even though I had problems with my strategy at some point.
- My strategy seemed to work at the beginning, but did not work well for the whole problem.
- I checked my solution and it seems to fit the problem.

1   I didn't have a plan that worked.

- I tried several things, but didn't get anywhere.
- I didn't know which strategy to use.
- I didn't know how to begin.
- I didn't check to see if my solution makes sense.
- I'm not sure what the problem asks me to do.
- I'm not sure I have enough information to solve the problem.

Figure 10.11
continued

318

Communication

5	I clearly explained the process I used and my solution to the problem using numbers, words, pictures, or diagrams.

- My explanation makes sense.
- I used mathematical terms correctly.
- My work shows what I did and what I was thinking while I worked the problem.
- I've explained why my answer makes sense.
- I used pictures, symbols, and/or diagrams when they made my explanation clearer.
- My explanation was clear and organized.
- My explanation includes just the right amount of detail—not too much or too little.

3	I explained part of the process I used, or I only explained my answer.

- I explained some of my steps in solving the problem.
- Someone might have to add some information for my explanation to be easy to follow.
- Some of the mathematical terms I use make sense and help in my explanation.
- I explained my answer, but not my thinking.
- My explanation started out well, but bogged down in the middle.
- When I used pictures, symbols, and/or diagrams, they were incomplete or only helped my explanation a little bit.
- I'm not sure how much detail I need in order to help someone understand what I did.

1	I did not explain my thinking or my answer, or I am confused about how my explanation relates to the problem.

- I don't know what to write.
- I can't figure out how to get my ideas in order.
- I'm not sure I used math terms correctly.
- My explanation is mostly copying the original problem.
- The pictures, symbols, and/or diagrams I used would not help someone understand what I did.

Figure 10.11
continued

Going To School

Jane, Graham, Susan, Paul, and Peter all travel to school along the same country road every morning. Peter goes in his dad's car, Jane rides her bicycle and Susan walks. The other two children vary how they travel from day to day—sometimes walking, sometimes bicycling, and sometimes going in a car. The map shows where each person lives.

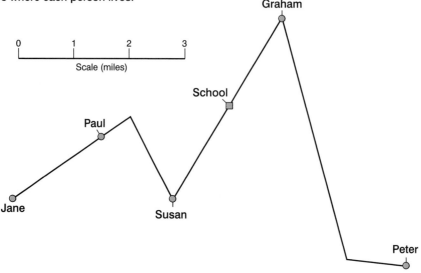

This graph describes each pupil's journey to school last Monday.

1. Label each point on the graph with the name of the person it represents.

2. How do you think Paul and Graham traveled to school on Monday–walking, bicycle, or car?

3. Describe how you decided on your answer in question 2.

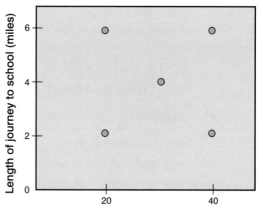

Figure 10.12
Going to school

Source: From Toolkit98: Chapter 1, Activity 1.9—Going to School. Reprinted by permission of Northwest Regional Educational Laboratory, Portland, Oregon.

1 Point: Show no understanding of the requirements of the problem. Is unable to label the graph or give a reasonable answer about how Graham and Paul travel to school.

2 Points: Labels one or two points on the graph correctly. Provides an answer to the type of transportation taken by Graham and/or Paul, although it may be incorrect. Provides some sort of rationale for the answer, although it might include faulty reasoning. For example: "Paul lives between Susan and Jane so he probably rides a bike since Jane does," or "Graham lives the same ways away as Susan so he walks."

3 Points: Has three points on the graph labeled correctly. Has identified "bicycle" as the means of transportation for either Graham or Paul. Provides a reasonable rationale for the choice of answer, although it may not be complete. For example, "Graham is faster than Susan so he takes a bike."

4 Points: Has all or most of the graph labeled correctly (4 out of 5). Has identified "bicycle" as the means of transportation of Graham and Paul. Has an explanation for choice of "bicycle" that shows understanding, but requires some interpretation on the part of the rater. For example, "Paul was in the middle and it took him about 30 minutes. Cars are faster and walking is slower."

5 Points: Has labeled the graph correctly. Has identified "bicycle" as the means of transportation for Graham and Paul and is able to explain how the answer was determined. An example of an excellent explanation is: "Susan lives the same distance away as Graham, and Susan walks. If Graham walked, it would probably take about the same time. Since it doesn't take as long, he probably rides a bike or in a car. Peter takes a car, but goes a lot further in the same amount of time. Therefore, Graham probably doesn't take a car. So, he takes a bike." The response doesn't necessarily have to have this level of detail to be a "5", but the general line of reasoning needs to be there.

Task-Specific Scoring Guide #2 for "Going to School"
Points for Various Features

Graph: 1 point for each labeled correctly (5 points possible)

Graham and Paul: 1 point for correctly identifying that each ride their bike (2 points possible)

Rationale: (4 points possible)

    4 points: Excellent rationale—includes accurate comparison to other students

    3 points: Good rationale— includes comparison to other students, but some parts might be hard to follow or incorrect

    2 points: Fair rationale—provides a rationale, but includes fairly faulty reasoning

    1 point: Poor rationale—shows no understanding of the problem

Figure 10.12
continued

embraced by teachers who want students involved is to have a generalized rubric that they (and their students) can translate into task-specific versions for individual tasks.

Example 2: Rubric for Application Letter.   The rubric for an application letter (see Figure 10.6) has strengths to build on. It is *analytic* and *generalizable* (can be applied to any application letter) so it is useful for instruction. It is only partially teacher friendly—the main reaction to it is, "There's so much to rate; when will I find time?" Reorganizing the rubric into four traits, as indicated previously, would make it much more usable.

As for students, much of it is already written at a level that students could understand. Reorganizing the rubric into traits would also help students and would make the rubric even more generalizable. Adding samples of letters that illustrate levels of performance would help students even more.

Criteria That Are Not "Practical"
Example 1: Informal Writing Criteria.   Refer again to Figure 10.8. This rubric is not easy to use for either teachers or students and provides little assistance to teachers in planning instruction. The goal seems to be "quick and dirty" screening rather than usefulness for instruction. It would not help students understand the nature of quality. It is not written at students' level and only superficially covers essential ingredients for quality.

Example 2: Skimpy Criteria in Math.   Refer again to Figure 10.9. To be clear, my point is not that these are inappropriate criteria. They may well reflect key dimensions of good math problem solving. But they do not teach understandable lessons. This rubric would not be useful to students because it does not communicate what unsuccessful students would need to do differently on the next assignment to improve. Students wouldn't understand the terminology.

Now please study Figure 10.3 again for a brief summary review.

Developing Performance Tasks That Work

Next, let's turn to standards of excellence for evaluating the quality of performance exercises—the tasks or assignments we give students to complete.

Obviously, a good task must elicit the intended performance, so that we may observe and evaluate it. Tasks can include simulations, work samples, games, projects, or naturally occurring events in the classroom, such as reading aloud, working in a group, or giving an oral presentation. Because many targets evaluated with a performance assessment are complex, performance tasks tend to be complex as well. For example, to evaluate students' understanding of how to convert energy into motion, we might ask them to develop a mousetrap car. This exercise asks students to build a vehicle that can travel as far as possible using the energy created by one snap of a mousetrap.

However, tasks don't have to be complex. Consider, for example, reading rate. The task is very simple: ask students to read aloud and calculate the number of words read per minute. Now to be sure, one would want other assessments of reading proficiency besides rate. But, especially at the lower grade levels, reading rate represents a dimension of fluency that is a legitimate instructional target that many teachers wish to assess.

The attributes that describe sound performance tasks carry the same labels as those we used for performance criteria: tasks must be "on target" and "practical." Further, just like criteria, exercises that are "on target" are clear, compelling, and complete. The dimensions of "practicality" to consider are appropriateness for the age group of students, feasibility given the resources of the classroom, fairness, and accuracy. Let's consider each in greater depth.

Tasks That Are "On Target"

Clear.   Obviously, high-quality tasks provide a clear description of the assignment—that is, what students are to do or create.

A clear task provides *enough scaffolding and specific instructions* about what students are to do to ensure their complete understanding of what is required on reading the instructions or hearing you speak them.

Further, a clearly described assignment spells out for students the *conditions under which they are to complete the work*. That is, it includes time limits or other constraints, resources and help you will provide, and resources students must supply.

All *key terms* used in the task description are either *familiar to students* from prior learning or are defined in sufficient detail to ensure understanding.

The task description should include a *brief reminder* to students of the *scoring criteria* used to judge performance. (You should never give students any assignment for which they have not had the opportunity to learn to meet the criteria. So this reminder just reaffirms for them what they already know.)

The only way to be sure students understand what is required is to check with them as they begin, to be sure that they know where they are headed.

Compelling.   It should be clear to both you and your students that the *task is worth doing*. That is, the assignment should relate directly to an important achievement target—one you are certain you want students to be able to do.

A compelling task promises to elicit the intended skill or product. Obviously, if you want to assess students' group discussion skills, the students need to discuss something in a group so that you can observe.

Prior instruction should have established the importance of the skill or product to be produced and it should have provided students with enough guided practice in hitting the target that you are certain they have had the opportunity to learn to be successful at what the performance task requires.

Complete.   Further, the task should be an episode of learning in and of itself. It should communicate to students in the assignment what is important for them to know and be able to do.

A good task is one of a number of such tasks that tap the same kind of achievement. This is important because such parallel tasks can be used over time with the scoring criteria held constant in order to help students witness their own growth.

Another key aspect of this standard is that a complete performance assessment must consist of a set of exercises that, taken together, cover an appropriate range of relevant applications of the proficiency being evaluated. That is, they must sample performance appropriately. This can occur with a series of short tasks or with a longer, novel task that captures the essence of the skills to be assessed.

Tasks That Are "Practical"

Tasks that are "practical" are appropriate, feasible, fair, and accurate.

- *Appropriate:* The task is appropriate for the grade level and mental capabilities of the students who are expected to complete it.
- *Feasible:* The task poses a realistic challenge for students; that is the work can be done within the constraints of the time, facilities and equipment available to do it.
- *Fair:* The task poses a problem that can be completed by both genders, students of different cultural and ethnic backgrounds, students with disabilities, learning styles, personality, language proficiency, etc. No student or group is placed at a disadvantage in completing the task because of factors unrelated to achievement.
- *Accurate:* A good task avoids sources of bias and distortion, such as assessing individuals in the context of a group project or attempting to assess more than a rater can attend to in a session.

Figure 10.13 summarizes this information in the form of a quality control checklist for performance tasks.

Illustrations of Exercise Standards

All of the sample performance tasks referred to in this section are shown in Figure 10.14 in the order in which we discuss them.

Tasks That Are "On Target"

Ready to Use
Example 1: Exhibition of Mastery.   Students are expected to participate actively in a seminar discussion, in this case, demonstrating the ability to analyze texts, reason comparatively, and synthesize information to draw conclusions and support them. The task represents important, core aspects of the reasoning curriculum. The task is worth the time spent on it. It supports appropriate instruction and com-

On-Target Tasks Are

A. *Clear*

- The assignment clearly describes what students are to do or create—the instructions (assignment) given provide sufficient depth to assure that each student understands them.
- The conditions under which students are to perform (time limits, available resources) are spelled out.
- Key terms are either familiar to students or are defined.
- The task description includes a reminder to students of the criteria that will be applied in evaluating the work.
- The teacher has verified that each student understands the task.

B. *Compelling and Complete*

- The task reflects the heart of the discipline—it seems, to both teachers and students, worth doing.
- The task is engaging to students.
- The task relates directly to the important achievement target it is supposed to reflect; it will elicit the intended skill or product.
- There is a specific time during instruction when students have the opportunity to learn to do it well.
- The task is an episode of learning and it communicates to students what is important to know and be able to do.
- The task is one of a class of such tasks that can be used over time with the same criteria, so students can witness their own growth.
- The set of exercises that comprise an assessment, taken together, sample an appropriate range of relevant applications of the proficiency being evaluated.

Practical Performance Tasks Are

- *Appropriate.* The task is appropriate for the age and mental faculties of the students being evaluated.
- *Feasible.* The work can be done within available time and resources. It is safe.
- *Fair.* The task accommodates differences in gender, ethnicity, learning style, cultural background, language proficiency, physical capabilities, etc. of the students being evaluated.
- *Accurate.* The task avoids other sources of bias and distortion, such as assessing individual students in the context of a group project, or too much for a rater to attend to all at once.

Figure 10.13
A quality control checklist for performance tasks

1. Exhibition of Mastery: Students in Action—High School

As a requirement of graduation, . . . each senior will participate in a seminar and turn in a paper on that seminar. . . . There will be no more than ten seniors and two seminar leaders in each seminar. . . . In a Socratic seminar, the students and teacher examine a text as partners. . . . The reading examined in a Socratic seminar is from a primary source. . . . The discussion in a Socratic seminar begins with a question. . . . Subsequent questions [that follow] arise from the discussion of the opening question . . .

Sample seminar focus:

Read *Good and Evil Reconsidered* by Friedrich Nietzsche and *The Greatest Man in the World* by James Thurber. The Exhibition begins with these opening questions:

1. Based on the dichotomy (overlords vs. peasant moralities) in Nietzsche's work, where would you put the main character in the Thurber piece?

2. Nietzsche is writing about a very structured society. Thurber is writing about a classless society. Does Nietzsche's dichotomy apply to the characters in the Thurber piece?

Your performance in the discussion will be judged using the group discussion rubric you've practiced since the beginning of high school. Remember the traits:

- *Interaction:* The student is attentive, open-minded, courteous, and sensitive to the ideas, tone, and purpose of the activity. The student confidently shares ideas and feelings and actively builds on the ideas of others.

- *Conceptual Understanding:* The student's discussion is perceptive, thorough, and insightful. Support is substantial and logical. The student shows perception while actively developing understanding of themes, main ideas, and supporting details. The student selects details from the readings to support interpretations and revises interpretations to accommodate all details in the text. The student has a clear idea of the shape of the task and sustains inquiry until the task is thoroughly completed.

- *Language Use:* The student uses precise vocabulary and language that is appropriate for the others in the group.

Source: From Sullivan High School, Chicago, Illinois. Reprinted by permission.

2. Motorized Vehicle—High School

This is a problem in applied physics. Design and construct a motorized vehicle that can produce at least two simultaneous motions in different directions to accomplish an action. When your work is done, you will demonstrate your device and explain how it works. In addition, you will be asked why you made certain design decisions, relying on your understanding of physics concepts. Finally, you will also be asked how well your device worked and to explain how you might modify your vehicle to make it better. The rubric shown in Figure 10.7 will be used to judge the quality of your work.

Source: Bank Street College of Education Center for Technology in Education, New York, NY. Reprinted by permission.

Figure 10.14

Examples of performance exercises

Source: From Sullivan High School, Chicago, Illinois. Reprinted by permission.

3. The Car Problem—High School

From the classified section of a newspaper, select one particular brand and model of automobile that appears several times. Collect data on the age (number of years old) of the vehicle versus the asking price. You should have at least 8 points.

a. Plot the data you have gathered. Carefully label your graph.

b. Draw an "eyeball fit" line through the data. (Your next task will be easier if the line goes through two of the data points.)

c. Write an algebraic linear model to describe the line you have drawn.

d. Interpret the meaning of the slope in your model.

e. Interpret the meaning of the vertical-intercept of your model. (Include the numerical value and the units.)

f. If there are other data points that do not seem to fit the overall linear pattern of the other data, try to explain why.

Source: Mount Hood Community College, Math Department, Gresham, OR. Reprinted by permission.

4. Camping Trip—Grade 5

A group of 8 people are all going camping for 3 days and need to carry their own water. They read in a guide book that 12.5 liters are needed for a party of 5 people for 1 day. Based on the guidebook, what is the minimum amount of water the 8 people should carry all together? Explain your answer.

Source: Used in several assessments including Lewiston, Idaho, and the Oregon state assessment.

5. Sow Bugs—Grade 4

Students receive five sow bugs, a round dish to contain them, a bright light and strips of dark cardboard to create regions of light and dark, filter paper, a spray bottle for creating damp regions, and a stopwatch. The students are to answer the following questions:

1. Do sow bugs prefer light or dark environments?

2. Do sow bugs prefer damp or dry environments?

3. Do dampness and amount of light in combination make a difference in sow bug preferences?

Scoring is procedure based. For each experiment, observers focus on the method used to solve the problem, the adequacy with which conditions are manipulated, the measurement strategies used to determine the results, and the correctness of the solution generated.

Source: Assessments for Hands-on Science Curriculum (1992). University of California-Santa Barbara, Graduate School of Education.

6. Create a Flag—Middle School

You have been asked to submit a design for the flag of a new South Pacific island nation. The inhabitants of this new nation have migrated over time from the outer islands of three surrounding island nations after a series of typhoons. Traditional chiefs have formed a governing body and share a vision of unity among the people upheld by extended family relationships. The hope to carefully expand their economy around ecotourism.

Using what you know about the islands of the Pacific, the information provided above, and your creativity, design a flag that can serve as a visual symbol of national unity. You will need to prepare to exhibit your design to the council of chiefs and explain how each element of the flag contributes to the identity of the nation.

Source: Pacific Resources for Education and Learning. Reprinted by permission.

continued

7. Tall Tales and Fables—Grade 2

Concepts/Skills Introduced or Reinforced:

Language arts	Writing
Reading	Spelling

Duration: 2 Weeks

Activity List:

Read a tall tale or fable.	Watch a video of a tall tale or fable.
Listen as a teacher reads a tall tale or fable.	Retell the tall tale or fable. List exaggerations found in the story.
Describe a character in a tall tale or fable.	Look through magazines and find pictures related to the story.

Alternative Assessments Used: Product

Unit Assessment List: Writing or retelling a tall tale or fable

Activity/Assessment Descriptions and Rubrics: Develop and write a tall tale or fable.

Criteria: Handwriting or word processing is neat and legible.
Spelling of all core words is correct, and most other words are correct.
Students use complete sentences.
Capital letters are used appropriately to begin sentences and for proper names.
Punctuation is used correctly.
Students demonstrate understanding of the exaggeration and fictitious characters found in tall tales or fables.

Rubric:

• Distinguished—Writing shows creativity in plot and character development. Tall tale or fable uses exaggeration appropriately. Writing is correct in all mechanics.

• Proficient—Tall tale or fable correctly uses plot and exaggeration. Characters may not be well developed. Few errors in mechanics are apparent.

• Apprentice—Tall tale or fable does not show exaggeration or fictitious characters. Errors in mechanics are common.

• Novice—Tall tale or fable is begun but not concluded. Writing shows lack of understanding of exaggeration. Several errors in mechanics are found.

Source: Interdisciplinary Alternative Assessments (1995). Virginia Education Association.

8. Three-Minute Persuasive Speech—Post High School

In five minutes, you will be asked to stand at the front of the room and give a three-minute persuasive talk on a topic of your choice. You may choose any topic you wish, perhaps something with which you are familiar, or you may choose a topic from the list provided below. You have five minutes to think about what you will say before your speech begins. If you desire you may make some notes for yourself to use during the speech.

(Portion of the list offered):

Gun Control	Women's Equal Rights
The Race to Space	Nuclear Disarmament
National Health Insurance	
(etc. as developed)	

Source: Communication Competence Assessment Instrument. Speech Communication Association. Annadale, Virginia.

Figure 10.14 *continued*

municates to students what is important to know and be able to do. Students have practiced doing similar tasks; this is, in fact a culminating chance for students to show what they can do. The task itself is an episode of learning. The task is clearly described and the criteria for success are included.

The only potential flaw in this task is sampling. Although the single task is a complex, good instance of the skills to be learned, the assessment could be improved by providing students more than one opportunity to perform, with different texts and peers.

Example 2: Motorized Vehicle.   With the motorized vehicle task, the teacher was attempting to assess conceptual understanding of certain physics concepts, reasoning, ability to work in a group, and communication skills. This activity fits the targets to be assessed, represents core aspects of the course, sends appropriate messages, is developmentally appropriate, and will motivate students. Students will also learn something from the task. The task is clearly described and the criteria for success are provided. Once again, the only major potential flaw in this task is sampling, although the task to be performed is a good, complex, instance of the skills to be demonstrated.

Tasks Close to Being "On Target."   These examples have potential and demonstrate a balance of strengths and weaknesses on the trait of "on target."

Example 3: The Car Problem.   The car problem presents a very interesting and engaging challenge. But it's not clear what this problem is supposed to assess— ability to follow the prescribed steps, knowing how to apply specific algebraic concepts, some other kind of problem solving? If it's the latter, it is too prescriptive— the task reveals its own solution procedures and therefore wouldn't elicit the right performance from students. To assess either problem solving or the ability to apply specific algebraic concepts, the question might be better stated as follows: "From the classified section of a newspaper, select one particular brand and model of used car that appears several times. Use the information provided to determine which listings give the buyer the best deal." No performance criteria are referenced to assist students to understand circumstances for successful performance.

Example 4: Camping Trip.   The problem itself is clear. However, "Explain your answer," is not. From having used this problem many times in workshop settings, participants will frequently say, "If I had known what 'explain' meant, I could have done it better." This is made worse because the criteria by which the work will be judged are not included. Including the rubric would have made it clear that the response would be judged on understanding the problem, strategies, computation, and communication. The rubric would especially have made it clear what is meant by "explain your answer"—communication. Additionally, basing the judgment of ability to solve math problems on one short sample is not enough. Hopefully, this problem is part of a larger set of problems that samples math content for grade 5.

Example 5: Sow Bugs.   In the sow bugs task, students are assessed on their ability to design an experiment by actually designing one—demonstrating the ability to reason within the discipline. The task supports appropriate instruction and communicates to students what is important to know and be able to do. The task itself is an episode of learning. The task is engaging, and is clearly described. While it is true that this task only provides the students one opportunity to design and conduct an experiment, it is a good opportunity that is developmentally appropriate. However, the assessment could be improved by better sampling.

Students, however, do not know the criteria for a successful performance—is it getting the right answer? efficiency? soundness of technique? particular features of technique? how well the equipment is handled? The observers knew what they were looking for, but the students don't know. The problem could be solved by informing students of the criteria.

Tasks That Are Not "On Target"

Example 6: Create a Flag.   It is reasonably clear what students are supposed to do in the create a flag task; and the task might be motivating for students. The big issue here is that it's not clear what this task is supposed to assess. Is the task worth the time devoted to it? We don't know. This issue is worsened by the lack of a performance criteria reminder. This might be solved by providing such criteria. But, the developers would still need to demonstrate that the task really does get at the heart of the discipline, will adequately elicit the reasoning or performance in the criteria, and provides an adequate sample of the core skills to be mastered.

Example 7: Tall Tales and Fables.   This task is simply unclear. Under "Unit Assessment List" the task is stated as: "Writing or retelling a tall tale or fable." However, under "Activity/Assessment Descriptions and Rubrics" is listed: "Develop and write a tall tale or fable." So which is it? Can students write or orally tell a tall tale or fable or not? Can they retell one, or do they have to develop it (make it up)? Further confusion comes from the mismatch between the criteria and the task. The criteria emphasize writing mechanics; only one part relates to content. Unfortunately, the content that counts in the criteria is "exaggeration" in one place and "creativity in plot and character development" in another. Further confusion comes from the mismatch between the assessment and the instructional plan—What are students really supposed to know and be able to do at the end of this two-week unit? Is this worth the time devoted to it?

Example 8: Three-Minute Speech.   It is hard to see how this task would give one an adequate picture of student ability to do an oral persuasive presentation. Students are given five minutes to prepare a three-minute speech—reading and understanding the task alone might take a substantial part of that time. There are no criteria by which students can target their performance. Given the content of the task and problems with sampling, this task is not worth the time devoted to it.

Tasks That Are "Practical"

Tasks that are practical are appropriate, feasible, fair, and accurate.

Ready to Use

Example 1: Exhibition of Mastery.   Although requiring real-time observation, this assessment can still be done in a large group with one or more observers. It is easy to obtain all the materials that are necessary, and it is safe. It also provides two ways to respond—orally and in writing—thus allowing for differences in personality and so on.

Tasks Close to Being "Practical".   Again, there is much to like in these tasks. They are balanced in their strengths and weaknesses. It is easy to see how they can be fixed.

Example 2: Motorized Vehicle.   The task is safe. Students acquire their own materials and have several weeks to complete the project. Observation is real time, but is done with groups of students, so it is efficient. It also provides two ways to respond—orally and in writing—thus allowing for differences in personality and so on. The biggest issue here is the assessment of individual students in the context of a group project. How do you know that the products are representative of the knowledge of an individual student?

Example 4: Camping Trip.   This task is feasible: It is done in a large-group setting. It takes about 15 minutes. All responses are written, so that they can be taken away and scored. No special materials are required. Further, the task is appropriate for students' age.

   The main issue with this task is that all responses must be written—what about students who can do the math, but don't have enough written English skills to write an answer that reflects their ability? Not all groups of students with equal ability in math problem solving have an equal chance to shine. This problem could be fixed by allowing oral responses.

Tasks That Are Not "Practical"

Example 5: Sow Bugs.   Although a great task in terms of content, sow bugs is not very feasible. It requires specialized equipment and live animals (sow bugs) and must be reset for each student. Students are observed one on one for the entire duration of their experiment, which could take up to 30 minutes. There is an extensive rating system to learn.

Example 6: Create a Flag.   Depending on the circumstances, this might not be a good task. This exercise was originally developed for use in a particular cultural context, where students live and learn in small Pacific island nations. In this context, new nations have emerged relatively recently. So this task has social relevance. But students who live in long-established stable nations may lack a social reference for seeing the relevance of the task. However, because it is not clear what skills the task is assessing, it is hard to tell where the sources of bias and distortion might lie.

Now return to Figure 10.13 for a brief review.

More on Appropriate Sampling

If we wish to know "how well a student can write a story," then we would need to evaluate a story that the student wrote to make a confident judgment. If, however, the achievement target is "how well students write for various audiences and purposes" then our sampling challenge is greater. We would have to ask students to write for a variety of audiences and purposes in order to generate a representative sample and draw confident conclusions.

The essential question is, What conclusion do we wish to draw about student performance? Do we wish to know how well students can do on this task? This takes just one task. Or do we want to draw conclusions about how well students can do on tasks *like* these? This takes a set of tasks that cluster around the same set of skills. These questions frame the classroom assessment sampling challenge. How many times do we need to see students do it to be confident in our conclusions?

We have a good chance of sampling well when the following are true:

- The target product or skill is defined well enough that one can judge the degree to which any given task represents one relevant application—it is easy to see how a single task fits into the "big picture" of assessing overall skill.
- The tasks sample appropriately from the possible breadth and depth of the skill or body of knowledge to be applied.

We need to reevaluate our sample when the following are true:

- It seems like the given set of tasks is representative, but the target product or skill needs to be a little better defined to be sure.
- The task represents an important part of the achievement to be measured, but there needs to be an explanation of what is left out and why.
- The task or set of tasks represents a somewhat restrictive view of the target, but it is fairly easy to see how they could be amended.

We face real sampling challenges when the following are true:

- It is difficult to know how well the task samples the target because the target is not very well defined to begin with.
- The task represents only a very small portion of the achievement target. One would be ill advised to draw any sweeping generalization about student achievement based on this thin sample of performance.
- You find yourself asking, "Why did they choose to assess that target using this task; it represents a pretty narrow definition of the target?"

Summary: Performance Assessment, a Diverse and Powerful Tool

The examples in this chapter, combined with those presented in Chapter 7, reveal the immense flexibility and potential of performance assessment. They remind us, too, of the great depth of information we can generate about student attainment of complex skill and product achievement targets.

They also lead us to a few conclusions about effectively using performance assessment:

- Start with a sharply focused vision of the meaning of academic success. A thorough understanding is essential. Imagine what it would be like to try to develop performance criteria to evaluate a skill or product you knew nothing about.

- Use precise language to label and define all key dimensions of performance before trying to devise a scoring scheme.

- Develop scoring schemes that describe performance at all points along the continuum, from "beginner" to "competent." This is how you can help students see themselves becoming more proficient. They will feel in control and their confidence will grow, too.

- Devise performance tasks that ask respondents to prove they can use what they know. Be sure to remind them of the scoring criteria you will apply to each performance, with no surprises.

- Even when relying on holistic scoring, you must develop a complete set of performance criteria. What are the elements of performance to be combined into the overall judgment? Don't let holistic scoring be a license to be sloppy.

- You can also focus your performance assessments on group performance. In real life, people are team members much of the time.

- Invest in thorough rater training (whether those assessors be teachers or students). Remember, your goal is high inter-rater agreement. You want two independent observers to agree on the level of proficiency demonstrated.

Remember that our professional literature is offering more and more examples of performance assessments, including descriptions of tasks and performance criteria. Thus, very often, if you wish to assess performance you need not start from scratch. Further, colleagues and associates may already have designed exercises and devised scoring criteria. Tap these sources. But be a critical consumer. Never assume that they are of high quality. Apply the checklists provided in this chapter as a matter of routine.

Finally and most important, remember that your students can be full partners in designing, developing, and using performance assessments in your classroom. And when they do play key roles in assessment, they will think of creative and engaging exercises and will define performance criteria that have value for them. They will need your guidance and leadership. But with that help, they can contribute, learn a great deal, and enjoy doing so. For examples of science performance assessments, go online to http://pals.sri.com

Exercises for Self-Assessment

1. Review all of the examples of performance assessments provided in Chapters 7 and 10 and analyze them according to the following:

   - List all of the achievement targets covered.
   - How many assess skills? How many products?
   - How many cover individual performance? group performance?
   - How many focus on structured assignments? naturally occurring events?
   - How many yield holistic scores? analytical scores?
   - How many transform results into rating scales? checklists?

   - How many rely on criteria that students could learn to apply? If it depends, what does it depend on?

   What generalizations can you make about performance assessment from these analyses?

2. Some have argued that performance assessments are too subjective and potentially biased to justify the attention they are receiving these days. Now that you have studied the methodology itself and many examples of its application for classroom use, do you think it is possible to devise assessments that minimize bias? How might you convince skeptics?

You may go to the Companion Website at www.prenhall.com/stiggins and answer these questions in the Self-Assessment module.

Final Chapter Reflection

1. *What are the three most important new insights to come to you as a result of your study of this chapter?*
2. *Which of your previous questions about assessment can you now answer based on your study of this chapter?*
3. *What new questions have come to mind as a result of your study of this chapter that you hope to have answered as your study continues?*
4. *For practicing teachers only: What do you plan to do differently in assessment in your classroom as a result of your study of this book so far?*

   For those in preservice study only: As you think about the classroom assessment environment that you hope to create for your students, how has your thinking changed as a result of your study of this book so far?

Workbook Activities

Those of you using the workbook, *Practice with Student-Involved Classroom Assessment*, as part of your study of this material will find the following activities and others included for Chapter 10:

- *Types of Rubrics and When to Use Them*.   This activity highlights the differences between holistic and analytical trait rubrics—why the distinction is important and when to use the two types.
- *Expanding a Checklist Into a Rubric*.   Any rubric, scoring guide or set of performance criteria should be considered a work in progress. This is also true of the "A Quality Control Checklist for Performance Criteria" presented in the chapter. This activity models a procedure for "filling-out" rubrics when starting with a checklist.

- How many transform results into rat-*Analyze Sample Performance Criteria for Quality*.   In this activity you use the "Quality Control Checklist for Performance Criteria" to analyze the strengths and weaknesses of real rubrics. Practice!
- How many transform results into rat-*Analyze Sample Performance Tasks for Quality*.   In this activity you use the "Quality Control Checklist for Performance Tasks" to analyze the strengths and weaknesses of performance tasks from real performance assessments.

Assessing Dispositions

CHAPTER FOCUS

This chapter answers the following guiding question:

> Why, when, and how should I assess the motivational dispositions of my students?

From your study of this chapter you will come to understand the following important principles:

1. Students' dispositions are motivations, feelings, and desires that inevitably underpin their academic achievement, so considering them carefully can help us maximize student success.

2. As with achievement, we must carefully define affective student characteristics in order to assess them accurately. This also means that we must clearly understand cultural differences in students' expression of affect.

3. Dispositions vary in focus, direction, and intensity, and are assessable in these terms in the classroom.

As we start this part of our journey, keep our big picture in mind. Refer to Figure 11.1. In this chapter, we will be dealing in depth with the shaded areas.

School Is Not Just About Academic Achievement

From the beginning, I have contended that we can succeed as teachers only if we help our students *want* to learn. Motivation and desire represent the very foundations of learning. If students don't want to learn, there will be no learning. If they

	SELECTED RESPONSE	ESSAY	PERFORMANCE ASSESSMENT	PERSONAL COMMUNICATION
Know				
Reason				
Skills				
Products				
Dispositions				

Figure 11.1
Aligning achievement targets and assessment methods

feel unable to learn, there will be no learning. We must be clear about who's in charge of the learning in schools. It is not teachers. *Our students control their own success.* Thus, a critically important part of our job is to instill in them that desire to learn.

Desire and motivation are not academic achievement characteristics. They are *affective* characteristics. Feelings. Emotions. Nevertheless, from time to time, it will be to both our and our students' advantage if we assess them.

When we assess mastery of subject matter knowledge, we seek to know how much of the material students have learned. When we assess reasoning, we seek to know how effectively students can use that knowledge to solve problems. When we assess skills, we evaluate what students can do. When we assess products, we evaluate the quality of the things students create.

We now turn to the fifth target: student dispositions, the feeling dimensions of students in school, the inner motivations or desires that influence their thoughts and their actions. In this case, we center not on what students know and can do, but on what they feel about key aspects of their schooling; the attitudes, motivations, and interests that predispose students to behave in academically productive ways.

We do little good to teach students to be competent writers if, in the end, they do not see themselves as competent, or worse, if they don't like to write. If they fail to see the value of writing, they will not be disposed to use the skills they have acquired. Similarly, we fall short of our goal of developing competent readers if we fail to impart the great joy and power of reading. If those feelings are missing, students will not be disposed to weave reading into their lives. Indeed, we can do great harm if school leaves students feeling as though they are incapable of learning. Regardless of their actual ability to learn, if they don't perceive themselves as in charge of their own academic well-being, they will not be predisposed to become the lifelong learners they will need to be in the twenty-first century. Attitudes about writing, reading, and other academic domains, as well as academic self-concept, are important targets of classroom instruction.

Thus, in this chapter we deal with the emotional or affective dimension of students in school. Like achievement, affect is a multidimensional human characteristic, including such subcategories as attitudes, motivations, and interests. We will discuss the assessment of student affect about many ingredients of school: teachers, classmates, school subjects, extracurricular activities, instructional methods, themselves as learners, and others.

I hope you will be pleased to learn that our assessment challenge in this case is quite easy to understand. Feelings about school vary both in their direction (from positive through neutral to negative) and intensity (from very strong to moderate to very weak). Our assessment task is to tap both direction and intensity.

With these two features in mind, I can share why I have adopted the label *dispositions* in this chapter. Our instructional goals for developing student affect are not value neutral. Often, we hope for strong, positive or negative feelings in students when it comes to learning. We strive to develop learners predisposed to behave in certain academically productive ways in school. Often, we seek a strong work ethic, positive motivation, intense interests, positive attitudes, and a positive academic self-concept, that is, a strong sense of internal control over one's own academic success. But sometimes we seek to develop strong negative dispositions that influence students to behave in certain ways, such as the disposition not to use drugs or to engage in other unhealthy, unsafe, or inconsiderate behaviors. We can know if we are succeeding only if we are ready to assess student dispositions or affect within the context of our own schools and classrooms.

Why Should We Care About Student Dispositions?

There are those who contend that school should be only about academic achievement, that student feelings or dispositions should be off limits. They feel that attitudes and interests are the responsibility of family, church, and community. In a sense, I must agree. Families and communities differ widely regarding the "proper" attitudes and values to hold. Given those differences of opinion, it becomes very difficult for school leaders to decide which ones to factor into the school curriculum.

One approach to resolving such a dilemma would be to leave the matter of values, attitudes, and such out of the educational equation altogether. Render those unto the family, community, and religious institutions.

But there are at least two compelling reasons why, as teachers, we cannot do that—why we absolutely must address dispositions in the classroom. The first is that motivational predispositions go a long way toward determining whether any given student will or can achieve academically. But in addition, at the time of this writing, students with destructive dispositions are exploding in their schools, resulting in tragedy. If we are to set our students up for academic success and prevent such dangerous explosions, we must remain in touch with the dispositions evolving within them.

Dispositions as a Means to an End

We cannot separate affect and achievement from one another in the classroom. As teachers, we must know how to help students develop academically empowering dispositions and must be ready to teach them how to use those dispositions to promote their own success.

Students who have positive attitudes about the things they are learning, and feel a sense of internal control of their own academic well-being are more likely to achieve at high levels than those who are negative, lack desire, and see themselves as victims of a hostile school world. Very often, students fail not because they cannot achieve, but because they *choose* not to achieve. Often, they have given up and are not motivated to learn. Why? There may be many reasons: They don't understand the work, find it too hard to do, lack prerequisite achievement, and so on. And so they fail, which in turn robs them of (1) the prerequisites for the next learning and (2) a sense that they could succeed if they tried. This can become a vicious cycle, a self-fulfilling prophecy. They feel academically powerless and thus become powerless. This negative academic self-concept drives out of students any motivation to try. This downward spiral can result from the complex interaction between achievement and affect. These students become predisposed to fail.

Remember, however, that this spiral also has a positive version. Right from the time students arrive at school, they look to us, their teachers, for evidence of the extent to which they are succeeding in this place called school. If that early evidence (from our classroom assessments) suggests that they are succeeding, what can begin to grow in them is a sense of hope for the future and expectation of further success down the road. This, in turn, fuels their motivation to strive for excellence, which spawns more success and results in the upward spiral of positive dispositions and academic achievement that every parent and teacher dreams of for their children. These students become predisposed to succeed.

Clearly, many forces in a student's life exert great influence on attitudes, values, interests, self-concept, and indeed on dispositions to try to achieve excellence. Chief among these are family, peer group, church, and community. But schools are prominent on this list of contributors, too, especially when it comes to dispositions to invest the energy required to learn. To the extent that we wish to help students to take advantage of affect as a driving force toward greater achievement, it will be important for us to know how to define and assess it well.

In a very real sense, the theme of this book is that *students' willingness to take responsibility for their own learning and their ultimate academic success go hand in hand.* We can use assessment to engender in our students strong motivation to try by using it to do the following:

- Reveal achievement targets to them in rich detail
- Show students how to get there from here
- Provide focused practice
- Permit students to monitor their progress along the way

Thus, student-involved assessment can fuel a strong sense of hope for success on every student's part, predisposing them to pursue academic excellence.

Time for Reflection

From a personal point of view, which of your school-related feelings (positive or negative) seem to have been most closely associated with your achievement successes in school? Were there subjects you liked or disliked? Instructors who motivated or failed to motivate? Positive or negative values that you held? How have your dispositions toward school related to your achievement?

Dispositions and the Mental Health of Schools

Recently, a number of tragic incidents have occurred in schools across the country in which individual students or groups of students have come to school armed with powerful weapons and the intent to kill classmates and teachers. Sometimes, they have even been intent on ending their own lives in the process. These students have come to such a place of personal hopelessness or rage that they felt justified in expressing their feelings in such horrific ways. And perhaps most startling, either no one in school knew these emotional explosions were coming or they failed to regard the seriousness of the dispositions these students harbored.

These events represent the most blatant manifestations of student characteristics that are as important as writing or reading proficiency. Undercurrents of important feelings may be arising within students that are not nearly as dramatic as these but which can be every bit as critical to their academic and personal health. Sometimes, students' academic records do not tell the complete or even the most important story. We must strive to understand the dispositions that can lead to such behavior. As teachers, we must do everything in our power to know how our children are growing both academically and emotionally, remaining mindful of the ground rules for dealing with student affect spelled out later in the chapter.

Remain Mindful of Standards of Assessment Quality

During the course of my decades of classroom assessment research, and as I offer workshops across the country on classroom assessment topics, I find a pervasive tendency to take lightly the responsibility to accurately assess affect. Many seem to assume that, because it is not achievement ("It's only affect"), we don't have to plan for or conduct rigorous assessments. As a result, many fail to attend carefully to standards of assessment quality in this endeavor. If your assessments of student dispositions are to be useful, they too must arise from clear targets and reflect those targets with proper methods. In fact, as you shall see, everything you have learned about quality assessment up to this point remains relevant in assessing student dispositions:

- Start with a clear vision of the affective target. What dispositions will you assess? Have you defined them clearly?

- Establish a clear reason for assessing. How will you use the results?

- Rely on proper assessment methods. Which method provides the most accurate reflection?

- Sample appropriately. How can you gather sufficient information to make dependable inferences about student dispositions?

- Control for relevant sources of bias. What factors could bias or distort results and how do you prevent these problems?

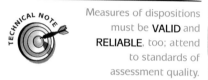

Measures of dispositions must be **VALID** and **RELIABLE**, too; attend to standards of assessment quality.

The range of available assessment methods is the same as it is for achievement targets. You can opt for paper and pencil methods (selected response or essay), performance assessments, and/or personal communication. While the assessments themselves may look different in format, the basic methodology remains constant, as do the attributes of sound assessment.

But There Is One Critical Difference

There is, however, one very important difference between student achievement and student affect that bears directly on differences in the manner in which we *use* assessment. That difference has to do with the reasons for assessing.

It is perfectly acceptable to hold students accountable for mastery of knowledge, reasoning, skill, and/or product targets. In this context, we assess to verify that students have met our academic achievement expectations. However, it is *not* acceptable to hold students accountable in the same sense for their dispositions. It is never acceptable, for example, to lower a student's grade because of an attitude that we regard as negative or because a student has a poor academic self-concept. Nor, conversely, is it acceptable to raise a student's grade just because of a positive attitude, regardless of achievement.

Rather, we assess dispositions in the hope of finding positive, productive attitudes, values, and sense of academic self; strong positive academic values and attitudes about particular subjects; strong interests in particular topics; and things students say they like to do and can do well so we can take advantage of these to promote greater achievement gains.

But if our assessments reveal negative affect, then we are obliged to plan educational experiences that will result in the positive dispositions we hope for. In fact, such experiences may or may not succeed in producing the positive motivational predisposition we desire. But if we do not succeed in this endeavor, we cannot place sanctions on students with negative affect in the same way we can for those who fail to achieve academically. We cannot hold them accountable for positive affect in the same way we do for positive achievement.

On the contrary, I think *responsibility for school-related affect should rest with us educators.* As a teacher, I hold myself accountable for the dispositions of my students. If I don't turn you on to the critical importance of quality assessment, if you don't leave my classes or complete this book feeling a strong sense of responsibility to learn about and create quality assessments, then *I regard that as my fault.* I must strive to find better ways to motivate my students to act responsibly with respect to the quality of their classroom assessments. I believe you have that same responsibility with your students.

Three Very Important Ground Rules

Before we define and discuss ways to assess dispositions, let's pause briefly and agree on three critically important ground rules for dealing with affect in the classroom.

Ground Rule 1: Remember, This *Is* Personal

Always remain keenly aware of the sensitive interpersonal nature of student feelings and strive to promote appropriate dispositions through your assessment of them. Assessing feelings of any sort yields vulnerability on both sides. When you assess, you ask students to risk being honest in an environment where honesty on their part has not always been held at a premium. They may be reticent to express honest feelings because of a lack of experience in doing so and because of the risk that you may somehow use the results against them. It takes a teacher who is a master of human relations to break through these barriers and promote honest expression of feelings in classrooms. One way I have done this is to permit respondents to my queries to remain anonymous. More about this later.

For your part, you risk asking for honesty in a place where the honest response just may not turn out to be the one you had hoped to hear. Negative feedback is never easy to hear and act on. Many avoid this danger by simply not asking. If you ask how students are feeling about things in your classroom, listen thoughtfully to the answers, and act on the results in good faith—the reward will be worth the risk you take. The result will be a more productive student-teacher relationship, a working partnership characterized by greater trust.

Time for Reflection

Under the best of circumstances, teachers become anxious when the time comes to ask students what they think about their teaching. Can you think of specific actions you might take to minimize your personal risk when prepar-

ing for, conducting, and interpreting the results of such an assessment? List as many ideas as you can.

Ground Rule 2: Stay in Bounds

Know your limits when dealing with affective dimensions of instruction. There are two important interrelated limits you should be aware of. First, as you come to understand and assess affect, you will occasionally encounter students who are deeply troubled, personally and/or socially. Be caring but cautious in these instances. These are not occasions for you to become an amateur psychologist. *If you find yourself in a situation where you feel uneasy with what you are learning about a student or about your ability to help that student deal productively with feelings or circumstances, you may well be reaching the limits of your professional expertise. Listen to your instincts and get help.*

The most caring and responsible teachers are those who know when it is time to contact the principal, a counselor, a school psychologist, or a physician to find competent counseling services for students. Do not venture into personal territory for which you are not trained. You can do great harm if you fail to respond appropriately, even with the most positive intentions.

The second set of limits is a corollary to the first. I urge you to focus your attention on those classroom-level dispositions over which you are likely to (and in fact should) have some influence. When assessing and evaluating student feelings, stick with those feelings as they relate to specific school-related objects: dispositions toward subjects or classroom activities, interests students would like to pursue, personal dispositions as learners in an academic setting, and so on. These have a decidedly school-oriented bent, and they represent values families and school communities are likely to agree are important as parts of the schooling experience.

I urge you to avoid those aspects of personal circumstance or personality that stretch beyond the classroom, such as family values, anxiety, or personal self-concept. These can either take you beyond your capacity as a professional, or take you into value arenas that your students' families or communities may regard as out of bounds for school personnel.

Please understand this: You need not go too far over those classroom-related limits before members of your community may begin to see your actions on behalf of positive, productive affect as invading their turf. Some families and communities are very protective of their responsibility to promote the development of certain strongly held values and will not countenance interference from schools. This is their right.

You must decide how to deal with these limits within your community. Just be advised that the conservative approach is to focus in your classroom on those dimensions of affect that we all agree are the legitimate purview of the teacher, dispositions toward school-related matters. As the chapter progresses, you will attain a clearer sense of what this means.

Time for Reflection

How might a teacher, or even an entire school, work with the community to establish parameters for dealing with affective targets, to divide responsibility for ensuring positive student feelings about school and school-related topics without stepping out of bounds? What specific strategies come to mind for heading off problems?

Ground Rule 3: If You Ask, Do Something with the Results

If you care enough to invest in understanding affect and in developing quality assessments in this arena, then care enough to take the results seriously and change your instruction when they suggest a need for change. In other words, don't ask how students are feeling about things just to appear to care. The more you act on these assessment results, the greater the potential that students will share feelings in the future that will allow you to improve the nature and quality of your learning environment. When done well, assessment of school-related dispositions can be a productive classroom activity for students and teachers. It can lead to specific actions on the part of both that promote constructive learning and maximum achievement.

Defining Affect as It Relates to Dispositions

To help you make sense of the range of relevant student dispositions, I will follow Anderson and Bourke (2000) and share several kinds of affect that can come into play in the school setting:

- attitudes
- school-related values
- academic self-concept
- locus of control
- self-efficacy
- interests
- academic aspirations
- anxiety

These represent significant dimensions of classroom affect that bear directly on students' motivation to learn. They represent students' attributes that predispose them to behave in academically and socially productive ways. In addition, each has been clearly defined in the professional literature, is relatively easy to understand, and can be assessed in the classroom using relatively straightforward procedures.

Attitudes

Citing the work of Fishbein and Ajzen (1975), Anderson and Bourke (2000) define *attitude* as "a learned predisposition to respond in a consistent favorable or unfavorable manner with respect to a given object" (p. 31). One does not learn the feeling, but learns rather the association between the feeling and a particular focus. And once ingrained, the feeling is consistently experienced in the presence of that object. The focus might be a person, a school subject, or a particular method of instruction. Attitudes vary in direction (favorable to unfavorable) and intensity (strong to weak). The stronger the favorable or unfavorable attitudes, the greater is the likelihood that they will influence behavior.

Obviously, the range of attitudes within any individual is as broad as the array of experiences or objects to which that person reacts emotionally. In schools, students might have favorable or unfavorable attitudes about each other, teachers, administrators, math, science, reading, writing, instructional activities, and so on. It is our hope as educators that success breeds positive attitudes, which then fuel the desire for greater achievement, which in turn breeds more positive attitudes. Thus, certain attitudes predispose students to academic success.

School-Related Values

Anderson and Bourke (2000) thoughtfully define these feelings: "First, values are beliefs about what should be desired, what is important or cherished, and what standards of conduct are . . . acceptable. Second, values influence or guide behavior, interests, attitudes, and satisfactions. Third, values are enduring. That is, they tend to remain stable over fairly long periods of time" (pp. 32). Values also are learned, tend to be of high intensity and tend to focus on ideas. They seem to find anchor points deep in our beings.

The following are among those values related to academic success:

- Belief in the value of education as a foundation for a productive life
- Belief in the benefits of strong effort in school
- A strong sense of the need for ethical behavior at testing time (no cheating)
- The belief that a healthy lifestyle (for example, no drugs) underpins academic success

These, then, are among the values that predispose students to succeed in school.

Academic Self-Concept

No affective characteristic is more school related than this one. It is the sum of all evaluative judgments one makes about one's possibility of success and/or productivity in an academic context. In essence, it is an attitude (favorable or unfavorable) about one's self when viewed in a classroom setting. Academic self-concept, write

Anderson and Bourke (2000), is a learned vision that results largely from evaluations of self by others over time. Quite simply, those who see themselves as capable learners are predisposed to be capable learners.

This speaks to the bond between assessment and student confidence that we began with in Chapter 1. Students who experience success build the capacity to keep trying. Each success breeds greater confidence.

Locus of Control

This represents a sufficiently important part of one's academic self-concept to justify its separate consideration. In this case, the characteristic of interest is students' attributions or beliefs about the reasons for academic success or failure. One kind of attribution is defined as *internal*: "I succeeded because I tried hard." Another possible attribution is *external*, where chance rules: "I sure was lucky to receive that A!" Yet another external attribution assigns cause to some other person or factor: "I performed well because I had a good teacher." At issue here are students' perceptions of the underlying reasons for the results they are experiencing. This, too, is a learned self-perception arising from their sense of the connection of effort to academic success.

In school, our aspiration must be to help students see the connection between their efforts and their levels of academic success. Those who perceive themselves as being in control of their own academic destiny, and who at the same time see the goal as being within their grasp, are predisposed to succeed. In short, we seek to imbue students with an internal locus of control.

Students who attribute their academic success to their own strong effort tap internal sources of motivation. This effort/achievement connection leaves them able to operate independently of external rewards. The result can be their greater achievement.

But this can be tricky, too. There is a danger that students who attribute a particular failure to low ability to learn (rather than a lack of effort) will give up in hopelessness. They can come to see themselves as "just too dumb to learn it." This is precisely the kind of attribution that we hope to stop by involving students in assessment, record keeping, and communication.

By the way, teachers also have to believe that student effort *can* improve their performance and their achievement is *not* totally determined by what they walk in the door with. If *we* don't believe it, our students won't either.

Self-Efficacy

This, too, represents a subpart of academic self-concept. According to Anderson and Bourke (2000), "The target of self-efficacy is a task, a [school] subject, an instructional objective and the like. The direction is best captured by 'I can' versus 'I can't.' Like the majority of affective characteristics, self efficacy is learned. The learning takes place over time as the student experiences a series of successes or failures" (p. 35).

Its importance in the realm of classroom assessment should be self-evident. Anderson and Bourke (2000) remind us that "a 'can't do' attitude lies at the heart of a concept known as 'learned helplessness.' The symptoms . . . include a lack of persistence in the face of failure, negative affect, and negative expectations about the future" (p. 11). At the risk of being repetitive, once again I say that through their involvement in assessment, record keeping, and communication, we hope to help students develop a "can do" perspective in the classroom.

Interests

Citing the work of Getzels (1966), Anderson and Bourke (2000) define an *interest* as a "disposition organized through experience which impels an individual to seek out particular objects, activities, understandings, skills or goals for attention or acquisition" (p. 35). These represent feelings that can range from a high level of excitement to no excitement at all at the prospect of engaging in, or while engaged in, some particular activity. Once again, the relationship between the object and level of interest is learned.

A student might be very interested in drama, but completely disinterested in geography. Strong interests, like positive attitudes, can link students to the greater potential for success. In this sense, they too relate to student dispositions. Students learn most effectively and efficiently when they are interested in that which they are expected to learn.

Academic Aspirations

In this case, we refer to the desire to learn more—the intent to seek out and participate in additional education experiences. Thus, Anderson and Bourke (2000) tell us, "we would suggest that aspirations are moderately high intensity affective characteristics . . . the direction of which is 'more' or 'no more'" (p. 30). Aspirations emerge from students' history of academic success or the lack thereof, feelings of self-efficacy or control over that level of success, interests in the topic(s) they are studying, and attitudes about school.

Anxiety

Hall and Lindsay (1970) define *anxiety* as "the experience of [emotional] tension that results from real or imagined threats to one's security" (p. 145). This feeling varies from a sense of relaxed safety on one end to extreme tension on the other.

In the classroom, we can conceive of two ways in which anxiety can affect students. One is as a driving force. It can supply positive energy, motivating students to work hard, or serve as a source of debilitation, fear, and frustration, causing them to give up in hopelessness or cynicism. Anxiety also can be a source of feelings of personal safety and well-being or a source of vulnerability, leading students to feel at risk of harm from someone. Both can exert great influence on student behavior and success in school.

Dispositions and Student Confidence

Through the preceding chapters I have suggested that ongoing student involvement in assessment can build their confidence in themselves as learners. Students' confidence builds when evidence of achievement derived from classroom assessment reinforces their belief that they are improving.

Confidence certainly is an affective characteristic. But I do not describe it separately in this chapter because I think it represents a constellation of the others listed. Let's consider the positive instance first—the confident learner who anchors one end of a continuum.

The Confident Student.   Students who are succeeding typically start with and further develop positive attitudes about what they are learning and about those who are teaching them. Success deepens the value students are likely to attach to education and to its institutions. Successful students with positive attitudes and strong values are very likely to be confident learners.

Their academic self-concept has its foundations in expectation of future success. They see the relationship between their efforts and their achievement and thus feel in control. They spiral upward from success to success with a "can do" attitude. They are confident enough to take the risks associated with trying new things, because they know that they have the reserves to bounce back if they fail (a rare occurrence for them). They are confident.

As a result, their educational aspirations are high and their anxiety stays at levels that allow them to maintain whatever level of effort they require to succeed.

The Student Who Lacks Confidence.   Now let's consider the other end of the confidence continuum. Psychologists who study motivation tell us that students can fall into a classification that they call "failure acceptors" (Covington, 1992). Typically, these students have experienced sufficient failure in the classroom to infer either that they are too dumb to get it or that getting it is just not worth the effort. They took the risk of trying to learn early in their academic lives, did not succeed, were punished for it, lost confidence, and do not want to risk such pain again.

Typically their attitudes about school, school subjects, and their teachers are unfavorable. They place little value in learning. Their academic self-concept is in the gutter. Often they blame their teachers for their lack of success. When they do succeed, they tend to attribute it to luck. Their school life depicts a "can't do" soap opera. Their interests may be strong, but not for participating in academic activities. They aspire to nothing more by way of schooling. Additionally, their level of concern or anxiety about it all appears to be very low. These students are not confident learners.

Between the Extremes, a Chance to Help.   Between these two anchor points we find students whose disposition profiles vary widely. They may be academically positive and productive at some tasks or subjects, while remaining in the doldrums on others. But we know one thing for sure: If our objective is maximum achievement, our goal must always be to move all students in the direction of becoming more confident learners. Anything we do to set goals, instruct, and assess student achievement that has the effect of destroying confidence is, by definition, counterproductive.

We can encourage students to develop confidence by sharing with them appropriate rewards for success. But I am now convinced that *we cannot turn a weak student into a high achiever through the use of coercion or intimidation*. They are so lacking in inner reserves that the threat of pending punishment will cause them to give up in hopelessness and frustration.

As a teacher, I think our challenge regarding dispositions comes in two parts. *The first is to strive to know the dispositions of our students. The second is to implement confidence-building interventions.* We can do this with student-involved assessments, record keeping, and communication. The trick to using assessment to build confidence is to use it in ways that keep students believing that the target is within reach for them; that is, to instill hope. Then we must help our students succeed as learners. Only then can their confidence begin to grow.

Variations in Dispositions

As mentioned earlier, the various kinds of affect vary along some important dimensions: focus, direction, and intensity. They focus on our feelings about specific aspects of the world around us. Some, like attitudes and values, can focus outside of ourselves. Others, like academic self-concept and locus of control, focus on our inner views.

Affect also can vary in direction, stretching from a neutral point outward in both directions along a continuum to differing anchor points. Table 11.1 lists those end points.

And finally, feelings vary in their intensity, from strong to moderate to weak. As you visualize the continuum for each type of affect, as you move further and further away from neutral, think of feelings as increasing in intensity. In the extremes, feelings become strong.

Bear in mind also that some feelings can be very volatile, especially among the young. Student dispositions, like attitudes, interests, and anxiety, can quickly change both in direction and intensity for a large number of reasons, only some of which are rational or understandable to adults. On the other hand, values, self-concept dimensions, and aspirations may be more enduring. I mention this to point out that it may be important to sample volatile dispositions repeatedly over time to keep track of them. The results of any one assessment may have a very short half-life.

Given our discussion so far, I'm sure you can understand why our assessment challenge is to gather information on the direction and intensity of school-related feelings. We capture the essence of student dispositions about success in school when we focus on the right-hand column of Table 11.1. It is quite possible to determine how closely students approximate these desired feelings, if we understand and apply some relatively straightforward assessment strategies.

Table 11.1
The range of dispositions

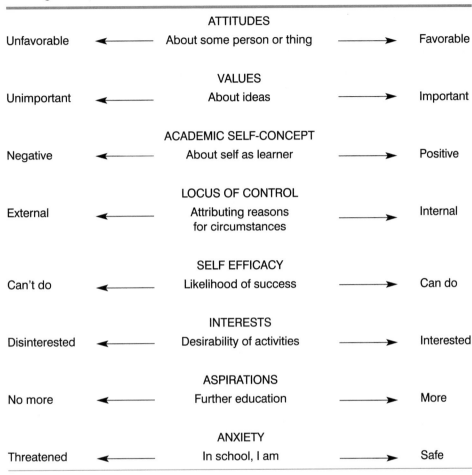

ATTITUDES
Unfavorable ← About some person or thing → Favorable

VALUES
Unimportant ← About ideas → Important

ACADEMIC SELF-CONCEPT
Negative ← About self as learner → Positive

LOCUS OF CONTROL
External ← Attributing reasons for circumstances → Internal

SELF EFFICACY
Can't do ← Likelihood of success → Can do

INTERESTS
Disinterested ← Desirability of activities → Interested

ASPIRATIONS
No more ← Further education → More

ANXIETY
Threatened ← In school, I am → Safe

Source: From *Assessing Affective Characteristics in Schools*, 2d ed. (p. 38) by L. W. Anderson, & S. F. Bourke, 2000, Mahwah, NJ: Lawrence Erlbaum & Associates. Copyright 2000 by Lawrence Erlbaum & Associates. Adapted by permission.

Time for Reflection

Read through Table 11.1. For each line, think of some current aspect of your life that comes close to each end of that continuum. That is, identify something you have a very positive attitude about and something about which your attitude is very negative. Think of something that you value and something that you do not, and so on, all the way to the bottom. Your students have feelings too, just as strong as yours. The key question is, How can you tap those feelings to improve achievement and student confidence?

Exploring the Assessment Options

So how do we assess the focus, direction, and intensity of feelings about school-related things? Just as with achievement, we rely on standard forms of assessment: selected response, open-ended written response (essay), performance assessment, and personal communication with students.

In this case, let's group selected response and essay into a single paper and pencil assessment form because the two options represent different ways that questions can appear on a basic affective assessment tool: the *questionnaire*. We can ask students questions about their feelings on a questionnaire and either offer them a few response options to select from, or we can ask them open-ended questions and request brief or extended written responses. If we focus the questions on affect, we can interpret responses in terms of both the direction and intensity of feelings. Examples are coming right up. But first, let's see the other options.

Performance assessment of affective targets is like performance assessment of achievement targets. We conduct systematic *observations* of student behavior and/or products with clear criteria in mind and from them infer the direction and intensity of students' dispositions. So, once again as with open-ended questionnaires, professional judgments form the basis of our affective assessment.

Assessments of dispositions via personal communication typically take the form of *interviews*, either with students alone or in groups. In addition, we can interview others who know the students. These can be highly structured or very casual, as in discussions or conversations with students. The questions we ask and the things we talk about reveal the direction and intensity of feelings.

The remainder of this chapter examines each of these basic assessment options and explores how each can help tap the various kinds of affective targets defined previously.

Matching Method to Target

Each method for tapping student affect can be cast in many forms and each carries with it specific advantages, limitations, keys to success, and pitfalls to avoid. Let's examine these, then review a few tips for your effective development and use of each. As we go, I will try to illustrate how you can use the various forms of questionnaires, performance assessment, and personal communication to tap the eight defined kinds of affect.

Table 11.2 presents an overview of affective assessment methods. As you can see, each method offers its own special set of strengths. These can help you fit each into your context as needed. Notice also that the keys to success and potential pitfalls are consistent across the bottom part of the table. Students who fail to understand and appreciate the purpose for the assessment and/or are feeling vulnerable are less likely to communicate feelings honestly. By the same token, it is

Table 11.2
Tools for assessing dispositions and affect

	Selected Response (Structured) Questionnaire	Open-ended (Nonstructured) Questionnaire	Performance Assessment	Personal Communication
Strengths	Can be sharply focused Easy to administer Easy to summarize results Results comparable across respondents Can be anonymous Can repeat over time to see change	Focus can be sharp Relatively easy to develop Relatively easy to administer Reasons for feeling can be probed Can be anonymous Can repeat over time to see change	Inferences can be drawn by observing behavior or products Can focus on nonverbal cues Can be unobtrusive Can observe groups or individuals	Can be highly focused Can be casual, nonthreatening Can be highly structured or not Can attend to verbal and nonverbal cues Can ask follow-up probes Respondents like attention Can produce greater depth
Limitations	No follow-up probes Reasons for feelings may not be apparent Reading proficiency required	No follow-up probes Labor-intensive processing of results Scorer can misinterpret Reading proficiency required Writing proficiency required	Can unwittingly observe atypical behavior (i.e., nonrepresentative sample) Sometimes may not be anonymous Can misinterpret cause of behaviors seen Can be time consuming	Shy student may not communicate Interviewer can misinterpret Cannot be anonymous Can be time consuming
Best Results When	Purpose is clear Affective target defined Students understand and value the purpose Administration is relaxed Instructions are clear Questions worded clearly Students can read	Purpose is clear Affective target defined Students understand and value the purpose Administration is relaxed Instructions are clear Questions worded clearly Students are proficient writers	Purpose is clear Criteria are clear and appropriate Multiple observations are made Students understand and value the purpose Instructions are clear	Purpose is clear Affective target defined Students understand and value the purpose Interaction is relaxed Instructions are clear Questions worded clearly
Pitfalls to Avoid	Students don't take it seriously or feel threatened Students offer socially desirable response Too long Ambiguous questions Leading questions	Students don't take it seriously or feel threatened Students offer socially desirable response Too long Ambiguous questions Leading questions	Unclear criteria Too few observations Assessment triggers socially desirable behaviors that misrepresent dispositions	Students don't take it seriously or feel threatened Students offer socially desirable response Too long Ambiguous questions Leading questions

SOCIAL DESIRABILITY is a source of biased assessment if the student's attempt to please leads to a misrepresentation of real dispositions.

critical that they understand that their task is not to create responses to please their teacher. There are no "right" answers, only honest answers. This can be a surprisingly difficult concept to get across to students whose only experience has been to strive to be correct, to try to please the teacher.

Time for Reflection

As a teacher, what specific actions can you take to help students understand the meaning of a "socially desirable response"? This is when students give you the answer they think you want to hear or will be comfortable with, regardless of how they really feel. How can you help them see why truly honest answers are more appropriate under some circumstances?

In addition, your assessment should not be so long that motivation lags among respondents. And it should not include questions that "lead" them to the response you want to receive. Here are two out-of-balance items that lead respondents:

You really do like math, don't you?

Which response best reflects your attitude toward math?
    a. I love it
    b. I like it a lot
    c. I find it very challenging
    d. I really enjoy it

By leading the respondent you bias results, leading to undependable assessment.

You should instead ask focused, value-neutral questions:

How confident are you that you can solve this kind of math problem appropriately: (fill in some math problem-solving challenge)?

And, you should offer response options that combine direction and intensity:

    a.   Very confident
    b.   Quite confident
    c.   Somewhat confident
    d.   Not confident at all

We will now consider procedural guidelines that can enhance the quality of questionnaire, performance assessment, and interview planning and design.

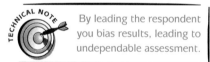

Questionnaires

Questionnaires represent one of the most convenient means of tapping important student dispositions. And yet, in all of my years involved in classroom assessment research, I cannot remember more than a handful of teachers who used this method in their classrooms. There are many possible reasons. Perhaps for some the risk of tapping student feelings within the learning environment is too high. Others may lack confidence in questionnaire development. Still others may think of achievement as so important that they give no attention to affect. Some may simply feel that students won't take it seriously.

The best way I know to get students to take questionnaires seriously (i.e., to provide complete and honest responses) is to let them know that they have everything to gain and nothing to lose by being honest. That means focusing on topics that students care about and establishing a reputation for acting on results in ways that benefit them.

Within the questionnaire itself, we must strive to ask questions that are relevant, about which students are likely to have an informed opinion. We must avoid ambiguity; ask brief, precise, complete questions; and offer response options that make sense.

Whenever I develop a questionnaire, I strive to combine all of these ideas in a way that enlists respondents as allies, as partners in generating useful information, information that promises to help us all. Sometimes that means permitting responses to be offered anonymously, to reduce the risk to respondents. Sometimes it means promising to share results or promising to act purposefully and quickly based on those results. Sometimes it just means urging them to take the questionnaire seriously, to care as I do about the value of the results for making things better for all. In any event, I try to break down the barriers between us.

Time for Reflection

What ways can you think of to develop and use questionnaires in the classroom to (1) encourage students to become partners in the process and (2) to use the results to create a better classroom for all?

Selected Response Formats.   We have a variety of formats to choose from as we design questionnaires. For example, we can ask students if they agree with specific statements, how important they regard specific things, how they would judge the quality of an object of interest, or how frequently an event occurs. The following examples demonstrate possible response options for these kinds of scales. Note that each scale represents both direction and intensity of feelings. Let's see how they apply to our defined kinds of affect.

We might wish to assess student attitudes toward a specific instructional strategy. One way to do this is to present a positive statement and ask if respondents agree:

> The group project we did in class yesterday helped me learn more about my leadership skills.
> a.   Strongly agree
> b.   Agree
> c.   Undecided
> d.   Disagree
> e.   Strongly disagree

Or, we might assess student interest in participating in certain activities with two questions:

How important are such projects to you?

Would you like to do more collaborative group projects in the future?
   a.   Yes
   b.   Undecided
   c.   No

How important are such projects to you?
   a.   Very important
   b.   Important
   c.   Undecided
   d.   Unimportant
   e.   Very unimportant

Other such selected response scales tap the perceived quality of some object or activity:

How would you judge your performance in preparing your term paper?
   a.   Excellent
   b.   Good
   c.   Fair
   d.   Poor
   e.   Very poor

You might supplement the information derived from the rating by asking students to write a brief paragraph explaining why they selected that rating.

Some questions may determine perceived frequency of occurrence of a particular event:

How frequently do you feel you understand and can do the math homework assignments you receive in this class?
   a.   Always
   b.   Frequently
   c.   Occasionally
   d.   Rarely
   e.   Never

One of the most common forms of selected response questionnaire items asks students to choose between or among some forced choices. The following examples are designed to help us understand students' locus of control:

If I do well on a test, it is typically because
   a.   My teacher taught me well.
   b.   I was lucky.
   c.   I studied hard.

Or

I failed to master that particular skill because
   a.   I didn't try hard enough.
   b.   My teacher didn't show me how.
   c.   I was unlucky.

Yet another kind of selected response format, one that I use extensively, is a scale anchored at each end by polar adjectives and offering direction and intensity options in between. Here's an example focused on student interest and motivation:

Use the scales provided below to describe your interest in learning the school subjects listed. Place an X on the line that best reflects your feelings:

Mathematics

Very Interested   ___ ___ ___ ___ ___   Completely Uninterested
Very Motivated   ___ ___ ___ ___ ___   Completely Unmotivated

Science

Very Interested   ___ ___ ___ ___ ___   Completely Uninterested
Very Motivated   ___ ___ ___ ___ ___   Completely Unmotivated

Time for Reflection

Let's say you want to tap the attitudes of your students about the textbook you are using. Your task is to gather information about the direction and intensity of their most important feelings about this book. Create 5 to 10 bipolar scales like those shown that reflect key elements of a textbook. Once gathered, how might you use such information to advantage?

An easy adaptation of the selected response format can provide a means of tapping the attitudes of very young students. Rather than using words to describe feeling states, we can use simple pictures:

Given school-related events or activities about which to express their feelings, such as free reading time, for example, you would instruct the students to circle the face that tells how they feel about it.

Using these kinds of scales, students can easily reveal their attitudes, interests, school-related values, academic self-concept, and the like. Further, it is usually easy to summarize results across respondents. The pattern of responses, and therefore the feelings, of a group of students is easily seen by tallying the number and percent of students who select each response option. This can lead to a straightforward summary of results.

Open-Ended Written Response.   Another way to assess affect is to offer open-ended questions, to which respondents are free to write their responses. If we ask specific questions eliciting direction and intensity of dispositions about specific school-related issues, we may readily interpret responses:

> Write a brief paragraph describing your reaction to our guest speaker today. Please comment on your level of interest in the presentation, how well informed you thought the speaker was, and how provocative you found the message to be. As you write, be sure to tell me how strong your positive or negative feelings are. I will use your reactions to plan our future guest speakers.

Or here's an interesting option—consider combining assessment of affect with practice in evaluative reasoning:

> As you think about the readings we did this month, which three did you find most worthwhile? For each choice, specify why you found it worthwhile.

A thoughtful reading of the responses to these kinds of questions will reveal similarities or differences in students' opinions and can help you plan future instruction.

Additional Thoughts about Questionnaires.   To maximize the efficiency and value of the results obtained, always connect your questions to direct action. By this, I mean ask only those questions that will provide you with the specific and significant information you need to make your decisions. For each question you pose, you should be able to anticipate the course of action you will take given each possible response: "If my students respond this way, I will do. . . . If they respond the other way, I should instead do. . . . " Discard any query that leaves you wondering what you'll do with the results.

I have one more critical piece of advice: *If you promise respondents that you will gather information anonymously, stick with that promise under all circumstances.* Never try to subvert such a promise with invisible coding or other identification systems. Students need to be caught in that trap only once to come to believe they can trust neither teachers nor administrators. We face a hard enough challenge establishing open channels of communication without having to overcome this kind of obstacle as well.

Remember too, if you plan your selected response questionnaire carefully and coordinate the response modes with a mark-sensing optical-scan response sheet, you can use scanning technology to save time and effort in summarizing the questionnaire results for you. Very often, these machines can produce frequency-of-response tallies in record time, making your job much easier. If there is one mistake I see inexperienced questionnaire designers make, it is failing to comprehend the time it will take to summarize the results. Check with your district computer personnel to see if this technology is available.

Observations as Assessments of Dispositions

In one sense, using observations and judgments as the basis for evaluating student dispositions is a practice that is as old as humankind. In another sense, it is an idea that has barely been tried.

The sense in which performance assessment has been a standard indicator of dispositions has to do with the inferences we tend to draw when we see students doing certain things. Adhering to classroom rules, for example, is often cited as evidence of a "positive attitude." Tardiness is seen as evidence of a lack of respect for school or as evidence of poor attitude. It has been almost a matter of tradition that teachers observe and reflect on their interactions with students, such as when students appear not to be trying or when they just don't seem to care. Our almost automatic inference is that they are "unmotivated" and "have a bad attitude."

While these inferences may be correct, they also can be dangerous. What if our casual observations and intuitive conclusions about the underlying causes of the behavior you see are wrong? What if adhering to the rules comes from a sense of personal vulnerability and reflects a low willingness to take risks? What if tardiness is due to some factor at home that is beyond the student's control, or the apparent lack of motivation is not a result of low self-esteem, but rather an indication that we were not clear in helping that student understand the task to be completed? If our inferences are wrong, we may well plan and carry out remedies that completely miss the point.

This leads me to a very important note of caution: The cavalier manner in which some observe and draw inferences about student attitudes, values, interests, and the like very often reflects a lack of regard for the basic principles of sound assessment. The rules of evidence for observing and judging don't change just because the nature of the target changes. Vague targets, inappropriately cast into the wrong methods, that fail to sample or control for bias lead to incorrect assessments of dispositions just as they lead to incorrect inferences about achievement. The rules of evidence for sound assessment are never negotiable.

Remember, biased assessments are invalid and unreliable; misleading results lead to bad decisions.

For this reason, developing performance assessments of affect requires that you follow exactly the same basic design sequence used for performance assessment of achievement. You must specify the performance you will evaluate, devise scoring criteria, select a context and task within which to observe, and record and store results dependably.

This does not mean spontaneous observations and judgments are unacceptable. But you must remain vigilant, for many things can go wrong with such on-the-spot assessments. That awareness can serve to make you appropriately cautious about making snap judgments.

Time for Reflection

Have you ever been the victim of a performance assessment in which a teacher's observation and judgment of your actions led to an incorrect inference about your affect? What were the circumstances? What impact did this mismeasurement have on you?

As developers of affective performance assessments, we face the same design decisions that we spelled out in detail in Chapters 7 and 10. They are translated into design questions for the assessment of affect in Figure 11.2.

I know this list of design questions looks imposing in this context. You might read it and ask, Why be so formal? It's not as if we're conducting an assessment for a final grade or something! In fact, many regard it as instinctive for teachers to observe some behavior and infer almost intuitively about student attitudes, motivations, school-related values, and so on.

But this is exactly my point. We often think that, just because this is "only affect," we can disregard all of the requirements of sound assessment. I promise you, *if you disregard the rules of evidence in conducting assessments based on observation and judgment whether assessing attitude or writing proficiency,*

---

1. How shall we define the disposition to be assessed?
   What shall we focus on to evaluate student feelings?
   - A behavior exhibited by the student?
   - A product created by the student?

   Who will our assessment focus on?
   - Individual students?
   - Students in groups?

   What specific performance criteria will guide our observations and inferences about student affect?

2. How shall we elicit performance to be evaluated in terms of the disposition it reflects?
   Which format will we use?
   - Structured exercises?
   - Observe students during naturally occurring classroom events?

   How many instances of performance will we need to observe to make confident generalizations about student feelings?
   If we use structured exercises, what will we tell students to do under what conditions, according to what standards of performance?

3. What method will we use to record results of our observations?
   Which do we wish to obtain?
   - A single holistic judgment about student affect?
   - Are there specific aspects of their feelings we wish to analyze?

   What record will we create of student affect?
   - Checklist?
   - Rating scale?
   - Anecdotal record?

   Who will observe and judge?
   - The teacher?
   - Students themselves?

Figure 11.2
Designing performance assessments of dispositions

your assessment will almost always produce undependable results. For this reason, it is always important to strive for quality assessment.

A Useful Classroom Application.   Here is an example of a productive performance assessment of student dispositions in the classroom: Let's say we want to assess students' motivational predispositions to apply their best critical reasoning proficiencies when they are needed. Norris and Ennis (1989) help us expand our understanding of the relevance of this by pointing out that the truly proficient critical thinker also develops a "critical spirit," or a propensity to use their reasoning powers. How might one assess the direction and intensity of this affective characteristic?

To conduct this assessment, we might plan to focus on individual student performance in a team problem-solving context. To make the assessment as efficient as possible, we randomly select a few students to observe each day.

Further, let's say that we know from prior assessments that the students have mastered critical thinking proficiencies and that they know how and when to bring these proficiencies into play in group work contexts. So the essential procedural knowledge is in place. Now the question is, Will they demonstrate a critical spirit when appropriate? If they do, we will assume that students have a positive attitude about critical thinking, that they value it, that they are confident in using their reasoning proficiencies.

Our primary source of evidence will be student interaction behaviors. That is, when students work in groups, do they exhibit proper critical thinking skills at appropriate times? If so, we can infer that they are, in fact, motivated to display the desired "critical spirit."

Our performance criteria, therefore, will list group interaction indicators of critical reasoning. We will look for their application during teamwork time. And so, in this case, just as with performance assessment of achievement, we must know in advance how a high-level performer differs from a low-level performer. If we cannot specify that difference, we cannot dependably assess the desired dispositions.

Because we want to observe performance under normal conditions, we will conduct our assessment unobtrusively by watching and evaluating interaction skills during our regularly scheduled teamwork time. Thus, we will rely on naturally occurring events to trigger performance.

Our record-keeping method will be a simple checklist of attributes of those who demonstrate "critical spirit" behaviors, as shown in Figure 11.3. We will randomly select several students and watch their interactions. Every time a certain skill should have come into play, we check that skill. If the student comes through and delivers as needed, we check that, too. The question is, What proportion of invitations to exhibit specific critical thinking skills actually elicits the required skill? The higher the proportion, the stronger the "critical spirit." But remember, all of this is contingent on verifying in advance that students know how and when to behave as critical thinkers. If that knowledge base is not in place, performance becomes moot.

This example of performance assessment of affect reveals the subtlety of this evaluation process: We observe behaviors or examine products to infer student attitudes, values, interests, and so on. Thus, we analyze performance for signs of

Figure 11.3
Checklist for evaluating critical spirit

Source: Adapted from *Evaluating Critical Thinking* (Chapter 1) by S. Norris and R. Ennis, 1989, Pacific Grove, CA: Critical Thinking Books & Software. Copyright 1989 by Critical Thinking Books & Software. Adapted by permission of the publisher.

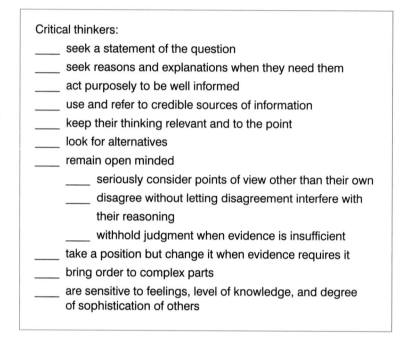

Critical thinkers:

_____ seek a statement of the question

_____ seek reasons and explanations when they need them

_____ act purposely to be well informed

_____ use and refer to credible sources of information

_____ keep their thinking relevant and to the point

_____ look for alternatives

_____ remain open minded

    _____ seriously consider points of view other than their own

    _____ disagree without letting disagreement interfere with their reasoning

    _____ withhold judgment when evidence is insufficient

_____ take a position but change it when evidence requires it

_____ bring order to complex parts

_____ are sensitive to feelings, level of knowledge, and degree of sophistication of others

the direction and intensity of attitude, interest, school-related values, or self-concept. In this sense, it is an indirect assessment method. We rely on external indicators to infer internal states of mind. When we use questionnaires or interviews, we ask students direct questions about their feelings. This typically is not the case with performance assessment. That means we could easily draw incorrect inferences if we do not plan carefully and carry out a thoughtful assessment, according to the rules of performance assessment evidence described earlier in this text. Beware here, danger lurks if you violate our standards of assessment quality.

Personal Communication as a Window to Student Feelings

Most regard direct communication as an excellent path to understanding student feelings about school-related topics. We can interview students individually or in groups, conduct discussions with them, or even rely on casual discussions to gain insight about their attitudes, values, and aspirations. In addition, if we establish a trusting relationship with students that permits them to be honest with us, we can understand their sense of self efficacy and even the levels of anxiety that they are feeling.

This method offers much. Unlike questionnaires, we can establish personal contact with respondents, and can ask follow-up questions. This allows us to more completely understand students' feelings. Unlike performance assessment, we can gather our information directly, avoiding the danger of drawing incorrect inferences. This assures a higher level of accuracy and confidence in our assessment results.

Keys to Success.   One key to success in tapping true student dispositions is trust. I cannot overemphasize its critical importance. Respondents must be comfortable honestly expressing the direction and intensity of their feelings. Respondents who lack trust will either tell us what they think we want to hear (i.e., give the socially desirable response) or they will shut us out altogether. For many students, it is difficult to communicate honest feelings in an interview setting with the real power sitting on the other side of the table, because all hope of anonymity evaporates. This can seem risky to them.

Another key to success is to have adequate time to plan and conduct high-quality assessments. This is a labor-intensive means of soliciting information.

In many ways, the remaining keys to success in an interview setting are the same as those for questionnaires:

- Prepare carefully.
- Make sure respondents know why you are gathering this information.
- Ask focused, clear, brief questions that get at the direction and intensity of feelings about specific school-related topics.
- Act on results in ways that serve students' best interests.

In other ways, this assessment format brings with it some unique challenges. Figure 11.4 offers guidelines to help you meet those challenges.

- *Don't overlook the power of group interview.* Marketing people call these *focus groups*. Sometimes students' feelings become clear to them and to you by bouncing them off or comparing them to others. Besides, there can be a feeling of safety in numbers, allowing respondents to open up a bit more.

- *Rely on students as interviewers or discussion leaders.* Often, they know how to probe the real and important feelings of their classmates. Besides, they have credibility in places where you may not.

- *Become an attentive listener.* Ask focused questions about the direction and intensity of feelings and then listen attentively for evidence of the same. Sometimes interviewers come off looking and acting like robots. Sometimes just a bit of interpersonal warmth will open things up.

- *Be prepared to record results in some way.* Often we use tape recorders in interview contexts, but this is certainly not the only way to capture student responses. For example, you could create a written questionnaire form but ask the questions personally and complete the questionnaire as you go. Or, you could just take notes and transcribe them into a more complete record later. In any event, students will appreciate that you asked how they felt, but only if you seem to remember what they said and take it into consideration in your instructional planning.

Figure 11.4
Guidelines for conducting interviews to assess dispositions

Summary: Dispositions, a Path to Higher Achievement

Our fifth and final aspiration for students is that they develop positive dispositions about learning and negative dispositions about those things that interfere with it. Our assessment questions are these:

- Are students developing the positive attitudes, strong interests, positive motivations, positive school values, positive academic self-concept, and the "can do" sense of internal locus of control needed to succeed in school and beyond?

- Are students feeling safe in school and are they experiencing levels of anxiety appropriate to fuel productive learning but not so high as to be debilitating?

These are affective targets influencing student tendencies to behave in academically productive ways. They vary both in intensity and direction, ranging from strongly positive to strongly negative. Our assessment challenge is to track their intensity and direction.

There are two basic reasons why we should care about student dispositions. First, they have value in their own right. They represent personal characteristics that we value as a society. We want all citizens to feel as though they are in control of their own destinies. Second, student attitudes, motivation, interests, and preferences are closely related to achievement. Those who experience academic success are far more likely to develop appropriate attitudes and values which, in turn, provide the impetus to take the risks associated with seeking further academic success. Thus, we know that affect and achievement support each other in important ways.

Our assessment options in this case are the same as those we use to track student achievement: selected response, open-ended written response, performance assessment, and personal communication. Selected response and open-ended written alternatives take the form of questionnaires. We reviewed several different question formats for use in these instruments. Performance assessments have us observing student behaviors and/or products and inferring affective states. Careful development of these observation-based assessments may help us draw strong inferences about dispositions. Personal communication using interviews, discussions, and conversations can clarify student attitudes and often give us the clearest insights.

We began the chapter with three specific ground rules intended to prevent misuse of assessment in this arena. They bear repeating as final thoughts on this topic.

1. Always remain keenly aware of the sensitive interpersonal nature of student feelings and strive to promote productive dispositions through your assessment of these outcomes.

2. Know your limits when dealing with student affect. Assess school-related dispositions only and get help when you need it.

3. If you care enough to learn about these affective student characteristics and to develop quality assessments of them, then care enough to take the results seriously and change your instruction when needed.

Exercises for Self-Assessment

1. Explain in your own words two specific reasons why all teachers should attend to student feelings in their classrooms.

2. Without referring to the text, describe the key attributes of quality assessment of student dispositions.

3. Referring to the text, describe the essential differences between classroom assessment of achievement and assessment of dispositions.

4. Learn the three ground rules for dealing with assessing student feelings in the classroom so you can repeat them without referring to the text. In your own words, state why each is important.

5. Referring to the text as needed, list and define the specific kinds of affect discussed in this chapter.

6. Create your own personal version of a chart identifying alternative methods of assessing those targets. In your own words, detail strengths, limitations, and keys to effective use of each method.

 You may go to the Companion Website at www.prenhall.com/stiggins and answer these questions in the Self-Assessment module.

Final Chapter Reflection

1. *What are the three most important new insights to come to you as a result of your study of this chapter?*
2. *Which of your previous questions about assessment can you now answer based on your study of this chapter?*
3. *What new questions have come to mind as a result of your study of this chapter that you hope to have answered as your study continues?*
4. *For practicing teachers only: What do you plan to do differently in assessment in your classroom as a result of your study of this book so far?*

   For those in preservice study only: As you think about the classroom assessment environment that you hope to create for your students, how has your thinking changed as a result of your study of this book so far?

Workbook Activities

Those of you using the workbook, *Practice with Student-Involved Classroom Assessment*, as part of your study of this material will find the following activities and others included for Chapter 11:

- *What's Appropriate?* We all have questions in our minds regarding the appropriateness of assessment affect—academic self-concept, attitude toward school and learning, anxiety, etc. This activity gives you a chance to think through the types of affective targets that would be useful and appropriate to assess in your local context

- *Analyze Sample Surveys for Quality.* Using the quality criteria for affective assessment presented in the chapter, this activity asks you to analyze the strengths and weaknesses of the Teacher Confidence Survey offered in the Workbook.

- *Look for the Unexpected.* As the text points out, making judgments about students based on observation can be tricky because of all the possible, subtle and unconscious sources of bias and distortion that can creep in. This activity gives you the chance to consciously look for evidence that contradicts a judgment that you might have already made about a student.

- *Evaluate then Try the "Critical Spirit Checklist."* You begin by analyzing this assessment of dispositions for quality using guidelines offered in the text. Then, you self-assess your own critical spirit. Finally, if possible, you try out the Checklist with students.

- *Build, Administer and Interpret a Measure of Dispositions.* This activity gives you step-by-step practice in building, administering, and interpreting a measure of student dispositions.

Workbook Activities for the End of Part III

The following activities are included to consolidate your learning in Part III of this text.

- *Show What You Know.* This activity provides several different options for personal reflection on the material covered in the third section of the textbook—a concept map, drawing pictures, writing a letter, outlining the major learnings in Part III, or preparing a workshop agenda.

- *Building Your Portfolio.* Here's where you get to make the fourth set of choices from your working folder to your classroom assessment growth portfolio. Instructions are included for (1) analyzing your portfolio for the patterns of reasoning you used in producing specific portfolio entries, and (2) additional self-reflection.

Effective Communication about Student Achievement

This final part of our journey through the realm of classroom assessment requires more of an introduction than did the first three parts. To a great extent, Part IV represents a review of our journey to date. But it also adds critical new dimensions to your understanding of how to meet the challenges of classroom assessment.

One goal of Part IV is to consolidate the notion that accurate information derived from quality assessments is an essential prerequisite of effective communication. And effective communication about achievement, of course, is essential for good teaching and learning. Another goal is to expand our discussion of student-involved classroom assessment to include the consideration of student-involved communication of assessment results. As you know from Parts I, II, and III, involving students in assessment development helps them understand the terms of their own success. If we involve students in repeated assessment of their own achievement over time, we provide them with the opportunity to see themselves growing and to feel in control of their own success. This can motivate them to strive for excellence.

So it is with student-involved communication. We seek to involve students in the process of presenting evidence of their own success in order to generate within them the expectation that they can and will succeed. For this reason, in Part IV we will analyze the relationship between communication and student motivation.

To communicate effectively, regardless of method, we must satisfy certain conditions. I will outline them here. Then, in the chapters of Part IV, we will examine how to satisfy these conditions when communicating by means of standardized tests, report card grades, portfolios, and conferences.

The Conditions Underpinning Effective Communication

Agree on What to Communicate About

If we are to communicate effectively about student achievement, we must first identify the targets we wish to communicate about. Both message sender and message receiver must be aware of these achievement expectations. If we can't agree on the targets that are to be the focus of our assessment and communication systems, we're sure to have difficulty arriving at a mutually agreeable set of symbols to convey information about student success. If message receivers don't know what knowledge, reasoning, skill, product, or dispositional targets underpin our assessments, then grades based on those assessments will be devoid of meaning for them.

Accurate Assessments

Given a common vision, to communicate effectively, we must transform our targets into quality assessments, assessments capable of producing accurate information about student achievement. As you know, sometimes those assessments may take the form of assignments, projects, tests, or any classroom event that provides evidence of achievement. They might be selected response, essay assessments, performance assessments, or assessments based on personal communication, depending on which option best matches with the target and with available resources. Also, as you know, each assessment must do the following:

- Rely on a proper method
- Sample achievement appropriately
- Control for all relevant sources of bias and distortion

We can communicate effectively only if we can depend on our assessment results to accurately reflect student achievement. This requires high-quality design and development of every assessment created to contribute information to our communication system.

The result of our administration and scoring of these high-quality assessments will be a reservoir of accurate information about the extent to which each individual student has met established achievement expectations. If the time over which we gather information is relatively brief and the target relatively narrow,

this reservoir may include just one or two tests or projects. But if it spans a longer period covering broader targets, such as a quarter, semester, or full year, our record may include numerous pieces of information we must collate to draw our conclusions. It is this accumulated academic record of student success that we must summarize and share with those who must consider it in their decision making.

In short, when we agree on the meaning of academic success, develop quality assessments of those expectations, and carefully accumulate, store, and summarize appropriate information about student achievement, we build a support structure that underpins effective communication. On the other hand, if we are vague about our targets, inept in our use of assessments, and sloppy in our record keeping, then effective communication about student achievement will remain beyond our reach. It is only when we have satisfied these necessary conditions that we can begin to discuss how to communicate effectively.

Proper Interpersonal Communication Environment

While we are developing the underlying structure of quality assessment and information storage, we must also thoughtfully manage the interpersonal communication environment. Message sender and message receiver(s) must be ready to share information in an environment conducive to hearing and understanding each other. Such an environment is characterized by the elements discussed in the following subsections.

Clear Reasons for Sharing Information.   Message sender and message receiver(s) must understand and agree on the expected consequences of communicating. If communication is to "work" in the desired ways, we must know what this means both from the sender's and receiver's points of view. What motivates the message sender to share the achievement information? What do the receivers expect to do with the assessment results? We must think through these questions in advance for communication to be effective.

But the questions don't stop there. What motivates the message receivers? Are their motivations likely to leave them open to hearing the message being sent? Do the receivers regard the sender as a credible source of information? Are all users clear about how to use the information most productively? Take these issues for granted and we risk miscommunication. Take time to clarify them and we build a foundation of accurate communication.

A Shared Language.   Effective communication is possible only if all participants assign the same meanings to the symbols used to convey information, whether words, pictures, examples, grades, scores, graphs, charts, or something else. We address part of this requirement when we agree in advance on the forms of academic achievement we will communicate about. But that's not enough. When we transform those expectations into assessments, then transform the assessments into scores or other indicators, and then transform the results into evaluative judgments about proficiency (such as grades), there is ample opportunity along the way for the true meaning of achievement to be lost. Accurate communication about levels of achievement is possible only if we prevent a loss of meaning by (1) carefully explaining the nature of all transformations to users, and (2) making sure message receivers understand the intended meaning of the symbols we use to communicate before we ever use them.

An Opportunity to Share.   If we are to effectively communicate messages about student achievement, there must be a designated time, place, and set of circumstances where message sender and message receiver(s) attend, without distraction, to the information being

shared. This might take the form of a conference between sender and receiver, a written report of achievement, a public presentation of achievement information, the delivery of an anticipated report card, or other communication method. To work effectively, these opportunities must permit a time when all involved can suspend other activities and attend to the information. To be most effective, they also should include time to interpret the meaning of the message, check for understanding, and devise action plans if needed.

Check for Understanding.   But our list of keys to effective communication is not complete until we have considered another key question: How will we know if receivers understand the communication? How shall we know if it serves its intended purpose?

Violations of this standard are common, sometimes occurring in the midst of games we play in the service of trying to look like we are checking. We place letter grades on report cards and send them home with the request that parents sign the back of the cards as evidence of having seen them. But we rarely ask them to explain back to us what the grades mean to see if they understand the message being sent. We virtually never check to see if parents know what to do about the grades reported. We just assume . . .

Understanding the Barriers to Effective Communication

As you can see, there is a great deal of work associated with preparing to communicate effectively about classroom assessment results. Nevertheless, given the critical role of accurate information about student achievement, it is clear that the work must be done. Student well-being depends on our willingness to devote the time and energy needed to do a good job.

By the same token, we would be naïve if we assumed that this kind of careful analysis of the keys to success has driven the design of our grading and other communication systems in the past. The fact is, schools have been reticent to establish truly effective communication. There are several reasons for this.

The Risk of Accountability

For example, educators might risk being judged on the basis of student success. If students succeed, everyone wins. But what if student performance is very low? And what if students fail, not as a result of teacher action, but as a result of problems that are beyond the control of schools? Then as an educator, I might be unfairly blamed. If I'm clear and public about my expectations and rigorous and public about my assessments, my own evidence might be used against me. As a teacher, I have a great deal on the line here.

To keep from being unfairly victimized by this, I may conclude that it is safer for me to remain vague about achievement expectations. I might cloak my assessments of student success in the mysteries of highly complex and technical testing practices and grading procedures. Because few educators or citizens understand what those test scores mean anyway, and no one will ever be able to check my gradebook or know my real underlying report card grading practices, the fact is that I can put forth a very convincing case for having taught well, regardless of the underlying reality. Thus, teachers can escape any real accountability for student learning, if they wish, and minimize their risk by hiding behind a smoke screen of assessment and grading complexity.

Why, you might ask, would a teacher think this way? Consider the practicalities. Teachers who are clear and public about their achievement targets, rigorous and public about the results of their assessments of student performance, and completely honest in their communication of those results open themselves to criticism on several fronts. For instance, some parents or taxpayers out there may disagree with and want to challenge their vision of the meaning of academic success. If I want to avoid that discussion, I remain vague about their expectations. Worse yet, what if classroom assessments consistently reveal a lack of achievement? If I am that teacher, my own students and their families might turn on me, portfolios in hand, demanding that I provide them with more effective help. In short, I stand to lose control, to lose power, to lose my sense of personal professional safety. If I feel vulnerable about any of this, why go through it when I can just hide in my gradebook with no one the wiser?

But on the other hand, if I am a confident teacher whose goal is to help the highest possible proportion of my students attain the highest possible levels of academic achievement, my reasoning might be somewhat different. The reason why I would communicate openly would be clear. I cannot reach my teaching goals unless I take this risk. Consider, for example, which students are more likely to succeed academically:

- Those striving to hit clearly defined standards of excellence, or those for whom those standards remain a mystery?

- Those who see a clear path to success, or those for whom that path remains a mystery?

- Those who get to take advantage of effective communication to watch their work improving, or those who are forced to remain in the dark about their learning due to absence of feedback or inability to interpret the feedback they receive?

As a teacher working for student success, I must risk being open to public review of my success in teaching.

One final point about this issue. Let's not be so naïve as to think that only teachers face this kind of risk. It reaches all levels of educational responsibility. If I am a superintendent who is unclear about the mission of my schools, unclear about valued achievement targets, fearful that teachers might not be successfully promoting student learning, and know little about assessment, I might feel insecure about developing and implementing an assessment management and communication system that ensures the public will learn the truth about student achievement. The results might be very good or very bad. If I sense that the risks of the latter occurring are too high, I might opt to keep achievement expectations vague and to put forth the appearance of rigorous assessment more than the reality of rigor. When the public doesn't understand assessment, it is very easy to project the image that all is well. Often, it appears to be the politically smart thing to do.

The Challenge of Too Little Time

Perhaps the most prominent internal barrier to best practice from the teacher's point of view is the lack of time to communicate well. As a teacher, several specific time issues might trouble me deeply. For instance, the past decade has seen an explosion in the scope of the school curriculum, with new targets being added and the old targets acquiring greater complexity. This broadening of the curriculum means I have more to assess and more to communicate about. I might simply feel that I don't have time to communicate about everything.

Further, many of the new communication methods advocated these days, such as portfolios, conferences, and narrative reports, seem very labor intensive. And to top this off, whenever student achievement is being assessed and communicated about, I am the only laborer in this classroom and must do all the work.

The bottom line might be that all of this talk about effective communication can leave teachers frustrated about the apparent lack of concern for their workload. Better to keep it simple, even if the results might be imperfect.

What If the Message Receiver Can't or Won't Listen?

Another troubling barrier to effective communication can be the lack of willingness or ability of the message receiver(s) to hear or accept the message being delivered. Obviously, this is rarely a problem when the message is positive, when grades or test scores are high, or when sincerely felt words of praise are flowing forth. But it is a problem when the message is about disappointing student achievement. For example, students may simply avoid or dismiss the feedback or parents may simply not show up for parent-teacher conferences. The "turn off" can happen for any of a number of reasons, most of which have to do with the receiver's self-concept or view of the message sender.

Sometimes it's difficult to remain mindful of the conditions under which individuals may actually listen to and accept negative information about themselves. For instance, students may need to hold certain attitudes and perspectives to be able to receive and act on such messages. They may need to see themselves as key players in the search for information about their own achievement. They may need assistance in developing a sufficiently strong academic self-concept so they can acknowledge their shortcomings and not feel defeated. Further, students must see the person who provides the feedback as credible, honest, and helpful. And finally, they must come to see the benefits of the message very quickly, so they can muster the resources needed to act purposefully. These are very challenging standards to meet.

From the other point of view, as the givers of the feedback, we must be able to present it constructively, delivering a clear, focused, and understandable message. We must be able to communicate acceptance of the students while critiquing their achievement. Even more importantly, we must help students understand that we share a common mission: greater achievement for them.

Clearly, it is no simple task to communicate to students that they have missed the target but still have the hope of success and reason to stay motivated. But as teachers and communicators, that is exactly what we must do.

So Risk We Must

The bottom line is that classrooms and schools cannot function effectively unless decision makers (students, teachers, parents, etc.) can count on ongoing access to accurate information about student achievement. Further, we can do this only by relying on open, student-involved forms of communication—only by becoming confident, competent assessors prepared to do the following:

- Help our communities understand the differences between sound and unsound communication practices.

- Become skillful in delivering tough messages in ways that leave students able to respond.

- Find smarter ways to communicate in order to overcome time barriers.

- Make a commitment to communicate effectively in the service of greater student achievement.

We either communicate effectively or we fail at our mission.

Understanding Student-Involved Communication

As we visualize lines of communication in school settings, it is tempting to see the teacher at the head of the communication network, conducting assessments, entering the results in a gradebook, and delivering information to those who need it—most often students and their parents. Our habit of mind is to think of teachers as message senders and others as message receivers. And to be sure, if we follow the guidelines for effective communication described above, this can be an effective way to share achievement information.

However, we make a mistake if we assume that this represents the only or even the most effective way to deliver messages about student success. We have an array of additional communication options at our disposal, many of which can be distinctly more productive, depending on the context.

For example, it has become the custom in our most visible communication systems, such as report cards and test score reports, to define our achievement targets very simply, using such one-word labels as *reading, mathematics, spelling, science*, and so on, with no accompanying information about underlying meaning. Typically, we have assumed that both message senders and receivers understand and agree on the meaning of each label. But what if this is an invalid assumption? The message is lost.

There is a way to avoid this risk. We can devise more inclusive communication systems that still value reading, math, spelling, science, and other domains of achievement but that describe them in richer detail, permitting us to share more precise information about student success. For instance, reading can be more than a generic label. The word actually refers to a process made up of component parts, all of which must come together for readers to construct meaning from the text. In this context, relevant assessment questions would include the following: Are readers able to use context to determine word meaning? To comprehend and monitor their own understanding? To alter reading strategies to fit the material? We can assess to gather answers to such questions, and we can devise information management systems to reflect the extent to which students have demonstrated the component proficiencies in each academic subject area, if we wish. Such systems are likely to be far more useful than simple labels and associated grades to teachers helping students to achieve ever-higher levels of proficiency.

Further, our traditions have assigned textbook authors, standardized test publishers, and teachers the role of "keepers of the flame," placing them in charge of defining the meaning of academic success, and of deciding if, when, and with whom to share that meaning. If they fail to share with students, or do it poorly, students will not see or understand the target. In this context, any information shared about student success will be devoid of meaning for students.

The alternative is to open lines of communication so all participants, students, teachers, and (to the extent possible) parents, share a common understanding of the relevant vision of success. Only when all individuals involved actually understand that vision can they communicate about its attainment. Further, if students can play even a small role in setting the target (under the teacher's leadership), we can gain considerable motivational, and therefore achievement, benefits.

Our traditional communication systems have relied on test publishers and teachers to be the assessors. In open, inclusive systems, all share responsibility for assessing and interpreting results, again under the teacher's leadership. All three key players in the classroom assessment process—students, teachers, and parents—understand the meaning of academic success, the standards to meet, and the meaning of assessment results.

Our traditions also have made teachers directors of communication, with all information emanating from them and going to students and parents. In more inclusive communication, teachers, students, and parents trade responsibility for delivering information to others. Sometimes students take charge, sending information to teachers and parents. Sometimes parents deliver information to students and teachers. Still other times, teachers run the show. Sometimes, members of the network team up to inform the other. Information about student achievement can pass in all directions.

Our primary communication symbols traditionally have been grades and test scores. Inclusive systems might rely on these, too, but in a context of deeper mutual understanding of what they mean. More importantly, participants also use other forms of communication, such as descriptions, pictures, and examples conveyed in narratives, lists of goals attained, and so on.

Finally, our traditions have us relying on report cards, test score reports, and parent-teacher conferences as primary vehicles for sharing achievement information. To be sure, when used appropriately, such vehicles can help us convey meaningful information. But, again, we have choices. We also can rely on more complete written reports, conferences that involve students, and portfolios as treasure troves of information about and reflections on student achievement. In the remaining chapters of this book, we will explore both traditional and more inclusive communication.

Chapter 12 explains communication by means of standardized test scores. Chapter 13 addresses report card grades. Chapter 14 explores portfolios as communication. Chapter 15 unravels the mysteries of student-involved conferences, a practice that I believe represents the biggest breakthrough in communicating about student achievement in the past century.

If you are ready, then, let's move into the final leg of our journey.

Classroom Perspectives on Standardized Testing

CHAPTER FOCUS

This chapter answers the following guiding question:

> What role should periodic large-scale standardized tests play in communicating about student achievement?

The following important principles guide this part of our journey through the realm of classroom assessment:

1. Historically, standardized tests have played a major role at several levels of the evolution of schools.

2. The scores they produce can provide valuable information to some very important decision makers although they are of limited value day to day in the classroom.

3. As professional educators, it is our responsibility to see that standardized tests are administered and used appropriately.

As you read this chapter, continue to keep in mind our big classroom assessment picture. Standardized tests represent one way to gather and communicate information about student achievement to some assessment users. Typically, they meet the once-a-year information needs of policy makers and curriculum and program planners.

Tests That Produce Comparable Results

Thus far, our journey through the realm of assessment has focused exclusively on assessments teachers develop or select for use in their particular classrooms. In this chapter, however, we will veer away from that track to explore the world of large-scale standardized achievement tests. We will study their purposes, the complex array of assessment forms used, and how to interpret and use test results. We will consider the techniques test developers use to create quality assessments, and we'll compile a list of responsibilities that teachers and administrators who administer, interpret, and use standardized testing must fulfill.

I suggested in Chapter 2 that these once-a-year tests are not likely to be of much specific value to classroom teachers. They are too infrequent, broad in focus, and slow in returning results to inform the ongoing array of day-to-day decisions. But here is the critical point: This does not mean that these tests are without value in improving schools. They can communicate valuable information to decision makers at other levels. So I have included this chapter in Part IV specifically to address the classroom teacher's primary standardized testing question: What should I, as a conscientious teacher, do in response to unrelenting demand from school administration and the community to "raise those test scores?"

The purposes of this chapter are to provide you with enough background information about large-scale standardized assessment to permit you to understand how such assessments fit into the big assessment picture in general and into your classroom in particular.

A Quick Overview

First, it is important to understand that the educational system in the United States has included a strong standardized test tradition for the better part of a century. The idea in standardized testing is to have large numbers of students respond to the same or similar sets of exercises under approximately the same conditions. Thus, test exercises, conditions of test administration, scoring procedures, and test score interpretation are "standardized" across all examinees. As a result, users can interpret the scores to mean the same for all examinees and thus can compare them across students and classrooms.

Precisely comparable scores can inform some important decisions. For example, special education teachers can use them to identify relatively strong or weak students, so limited special education resources can be channeled to them. Scores on standardized tests averaged across students within schools or districts communicate about strong and weak programs. Here again, the objective is to funnel resources to those places where they will do the most good.

Standardized tests are developed and published to assess both students' achievement and their aptitude or intelligence. This chapter is limited to the consideration of achievement tests only. Fundamental and deep-seated disagreements among learned scholars about the definition of intelligence, as well as their concern over the dangers of intelligence testing, cause me to exclude them from this book. *If you wish to accommodate individual differences in student learning, I recommend individualizing on the basis of prior achievement, not intelligence.*

Often, school districts participate in several layers of standardized achievement testing, from districtwide testing to statewide to national and sometimes even international programs. Some districts may administer a dozen or more different standardized testing programs in a given year for different purposes involving different students. Some districts test every pupil at every grade, while others sample students or grade levels.

Some standardized tests produce scores that are *norm referenced*; they communicate in a manner that permits us to compare a student's achievement to that of other students who took the same test under like conditions. Scores on these tests can communicate information about how students rank in achievement.

> This is a critical technical distinction that filters through all assessment applications in schools. So be sure you study it carefully as it plays out through this chapter.
>
> *TECHNICAL NOTE*

Some standardized tests yield scores that are *criterion referenced*; they communicate how each student's test score compares, not to other students, but to a preset standard of acceptable performance. These kinds of scores permit us to detect which specific achievement standards students have and have not met; that is, to determine individual strengths and weaknesses in achievement.

Professional test publishers typically develop standardized tests, either to sell directly to schools or under contract for a local, state, or national educational agency. Tests are available to cover virtually all school subjects across all grade levels. Further, they can involve the use of any of our four basic forms of assessment, although historically most have relied on selected response formats because they can be automatically scanned and scored with great efficiency. This permits relatively inexpensive scoring of very large numbers of tests. Recently, we have seen a major increase in reliance on essay and performance assessment formats too, as test publishers strive to align their tests with more complex forms of achievement targets. This is a healthy development.

A Brief History Lesson

To set the stage for you, let's travel back to the United States in the early 1900s, when we first began to rely on these comprehensive achievement testing programs. By examining cultural and educational forces at work in our society at that time, we can gain important insights into the emergence of educational assessment as a prominent part of school life.

In the Beginning

In those days, the United States was built on an agricultural economy, with some heavy industry emerging in the northeast. In that context, Americans could secure economic well-being without a great deal of formal education. School dropout rates in those days were three times those of today. However, those leaving the educational system were not labeled "at-risk youth" as they are today, because our society and economy offered them diverse opportunities to contribute and succeed.

During the 1920s and 1930s, the post–World War I era, our population was becoming increasingly diverse, as immigrants from the world's cultures arrived at all borders in huge numbers. It became popular in those days to conceive of the United States as the great "melting pot." We aspired to a common language, culture, national experience, and heritage. To achieve this end, we needed a homogenizing experience. Schools were able to serve that function. So we conceived of the standard curriculum for all students, and we sent out word by means of compulsory school attendance laws that everyone would have to come to school and be educated.

And so, to school they came, in numbers unprecedented in the history of humankind, thus presenting educators of those times with the immense challenge of schooling the masses with very limited resources. To meet this challenge, we conceived of what amounted to "assembly line schools," schools in which young children entered the system and stopped at the first point on the assembly line. We allowed a fixed amount of time, one year, for students to master the required standard curriculum. Because students learn at different rates, at the end of one year, some students would have learned a great deal, some not very much.

Nevertheless, they all moved on to stop two—second grade. By the time they reached the end of their time at stop two, those who mastered a great deal at stop one on the assembly line would have learned much more. Those who learned little at stop one would have learned a little more at stop two. The amount of variation in achievement among students increased. And so it would go through several years of public school education. The range of student achievement at any single grade level would continue to expand. Some students would find success and redouble their efforts. Others would be overwhelmed with failure and give up in hopelessness.

This kind of sorting, society decided, would be an important social function of schools. By spreading students out along a continuum of achievement, schools could help merge them into the various segments of the economic and social structure. In effect, this sorting function formed the foundation for the era of assessment that was about to begin in the 1930s and would extend into the 1990s.

Juxtaposed with this evolution of schools was another revolutionary change that brought educational assessment into the forefront of schooling. As it happened, at precisely this same time, there appeared on the educational scene a new kind of achievement test, a format that appeared to fill several critical needs.

A "New" Kind of Test Appears on the Scene

Educators writing in the professional literature referred to this new kind of test as "scientific" (Scates, 1943), giving it immense credibility. It was capable of controlling for inherent biases and idiosyncrasies of teachers' subjective judgments, which prior to this time had formed the basis for assessment in schools. Also, advocates pointed out, this new kind of test could be mass produced, mass administered, and mass scored very efficiently, and efficiency was seen as essential in those times of rapid growth in education.

This test also brought with it an even more important advantage: It was able to produce an objective and easy-to-use sorting mechanism in the form of a score that had (presumably) exactly the same meaning for every student who took the same test. It offered concrete, apparently "scientific" support for the sorting function of schools.

This new entry in the assessment arena was, as you may have deduced, the objectively scored multiple-choice paper and pencil test. The "old" kind of test was the essay exam, often accompanied by teacher-conducted oral exams. Because of its greater efficiency, apparent precision, and comparable scores, selected response assessment became so popular that it dominated our conception of the very meaning of educational assessment for 60 years.

A Time of Disconnected Efforts

The era of assessment that began in the late 1930s can be characterized in terms of three important patterns of professional practice, one involving teachers, another involving assessment personnel, and a third involving administrators and policy makers.

First, very early in this era, educators separated two critical functions. On one hand, teachers would have responsibility for teaching. Their challenge would be to master and apply the technology of instruction. On the other hand, professional assessment experts would assess. Their professional challenge and role would be to master and apply the rapidly emerging technology of testing.

In effect, local educators entrusted responsibility for assessment to the measurement community, thus in effect separating assessment and instruction and assigning them to different parties. This amounted to saying, "Teachers, you teach and you don't need to know anything about assessment. And assessors, you test and you need not know anything about teaching." Training programs, certification requirements, and job responsibilities were defined according to this difference in function.

This led to the second important pattern of professional practice that characterized this era. Once in charge, the assessment community launched a decades-long program of psychometric research and development that had some very important characteristics. Assessors began to define *assessment* as the quantification of student achievement. This permitted them to introduce and use sophisticated mathematical models to describe student achievement and to summarize achievement information. As a result, the world of testing quickly became complex and highly technical in its concepts, practices, and vocabulary, which made communication among assessment specialists very efficient and effective. However, few outside the field could understand them. As a result, assessment experts could communicate clearly among themselves, but outsiders (teachers, administrators, policy makers) were left out of the discussion. In effect, an impenetrable wall was constructed between assessment and instruction due to a lack of common understanding, and that wall grew very high very quickly.

The Various Layers of Standardized Testing

Once school officials began to understand the great efficiency of these new objectively scored selected response tests, they took the first steps in what also turned out to be a 60-year march toward ever-more centralized assessment of student achievement, which resulted in the layers of standardized testing programs that we see in place today.

College Admissions Testing.   This march began modestly in the 1920s and 1930s with a few local scholarship testing programs, which relied on essay tests to select winners. Thus, right from the outset, quality tests were those that could differentiate among levels of student achievement. These differences would serve to rank examinees for the award of scholarships.

These local applications were so effective that they gave rise to our first national college admissions testing programs, the College Boards (also known as the SAT). While the earliest of tests relied on essay assessment, in the 1930s the huge volume of national testing soon forced a change as the College Board turned to multiple-choice testing technology as a more efficient format. With this change dawned the era of selected response testing for sorting purposes. Then in the 1940s, the second college admissions test appeared on the scene, the ACT Assessment Program. It relied on the same technology for the same sorting and selecting purposes.

Districtwide Testing.   By the 1940s, several test publishers were selling standardized versions of selected response tests to schools for use at all grade levels. The test user guides were careful to point out that scores on these tests were intended to serve as one additional piece of information for teachers to use *to supplement their classroom assessments* and help sort students into proper instructional treatments. Remember this purpose; it is a critical issue in the whole historical picture.

The most commonly used form of assessment in districtwide programs is the commercially published, norm-referenced, standardized achievement test battery. Test publishers design, develop, and distribute these tests for purchase by local users. Each battery covers a variety of school subjects, offering several test forms tailored for use at different grade levels. Users purchase test booklets, answer sheets, and test administration materials, as well as scoring and reporting services. It is not uncommon these days for districts with their own response sheet scanning technology to also purchase test scoring software from the publisher to analyze their own results.

The unique feature of these tests is the fact that they are nationally "normed" to facilitate test score interpretation. This simply means that the designers administered the tests to large numbers of students before making them available for general purchase. Test results from this preliminary administration provide the basis for comparing each subsequent examinee's score. In addition, most test publishers now report at least some criterion-referenced information on score reports. Items in the battery that test the same skill or objective are collected into a small test within a test, allowing the publisher to generate a score for that specific objective. As this chapter unfolds, you will come to understand what all of this means.

Table 12.1 lists some of the currently available multisubject standardized achievement test batteries. Test publishers also develop and distribute a variety of single-subject tests designed for use at various grade levels. They all provide catalogues of their products on request.

Statewide Testing.   In the 1950s and 1960s, society began to raise serious questions about the effectiveness of U.S. schools. With the former Soviet Union first into space, for example, our society began to question the quality of math and science education in schools. In addition, the upheavals surrounding the Vietnam War, the Civil Rights Movement, student protests, and the like gave rise to and fueled an environment of questioning and challenge. Many social institutions came under scrutiny, including schools. This general reexamination of our social priorities and institutions gave birth to the sense that schools (and the educators who run them) might need to be held accountable for more than just providing quality opportunities to learn, for more than just sorting students according to achievement. Rather, they might also be held responsible for producing real student learning and for ensuring that all students attain certain specified levels of achievement.

In response to the challenge that schools might not be "working," to evaluate their programs, administrators were forced to turn to their only source of believable student achievement data: scores from commercially available standardized objective paper and pencil achievement tests.

This represented a profoundly important shift in society's perceptions of these tests. They would no longer be seen as just one more piece of information for

Table 12.1

Examples of standardized achievement test batteries

Test	Tests available for grades:	Publisher
California Achievement Test & Terra Nova	K–12	CTB McGraw-Hill 20 Ryan Ranch Rd. Monterey, CA 93940
Iowa Test of Basic Skills & Iowa Test of Educational Development	K–12	Riverside Publishing 8420 Bryn Mawr Ave. Chicago, IL 60631
Metropolitan Achievement Test & Stanford Achievement Test	K–12	Harcourt Educational Measurement 555 Academic Ct. San Antonio, TX 78204

teachers. Now they would be seen as standards of educational excellence. Understand that the underlying testing technology did not change. These were still tests designed to sort students based on assessments of very broad domains of content. All that changed was our sense of how the tests should be used. They came to be seen as the guardians of our highest academic expectations, a use their original developers had never intended.

Educational policy makers across the land began to believe that society could achieve major improvements in school effectiveness if we broadened the scope of our application of standardized tests. We moved rapidly beyond just districtwide testing to statewide testing applications.

We began the decade of the 1970s with just three or four such tests and ended with nearly 40 states conducting their own testing programs. As of this writing, there are 48. Significantly, many states opted to develop their own tests to be sure they focused on important educational outcomes in that state. They tended to move from tests designed to sort to tests reflecting student attainment of specific achievement targets (from norm-referenced to criterion-referenced tests).

Because these tests often are created to see if students are meeting state standards of educational attainment, many statewide tests include criterion-referenced components. Norm-referenced tests also continue in use, however, as the summary of current testing programs in Figure 12.1 shows.

National Assessment.   Beginning in the late 1970s and extending into the 1980s and 1990s, we added the National Assessment of Educational Progress (NAEP), along with international testing programs, in the hope that testing achievement at ever more centralized levels would somehow lead to school improvement in ways that other tests had not. NAEP is a federally funded testing program that periodically samples student achievement across the nation to track the pulse of changing achievement patterns. These biannual assessments gauge the performance of national samples of 9-, 13-, and 17-year-olds, as well as young adults, reporting results by geographic region, gender, and ethnic background. Results are intended for use by policy makers to inform decisions. Since its first test administration in 1969, NAEP has conducted criterion-referenced assessments of valued outcomes in reading, writing, math, science, citizenship, literature, social studies, career development, art, music, history, geography, computers, life skills, health, and energy. NAEP assessment procedures have used all four assessment methods, with selected response methods dominating.

International Assessment.   Periodically, the United States, Canada, and other nations around the world collaborate in competitive assessments specifically designed to determine the relative standing of nations with respect to student achievement. Content and assessment experts from around the world meet for the following purposes:

● Define achievement targets common to the participating nations' collective curricula.

	Number of States Conducting
Statewide testing programs	48
Tests in Subjects:	
English/Language Arts	48
Mathematics	47
Writing	42
Science	36
History/Social Studies	33
Using these Methods:	
Writing Assessment	42
Performance Assessment	34
Multiple Choice Only	13
Portfolio	2
Permitting Interpretation that is:	
Criterion Referenced	42
Norm Referenced	29

Grade Levels Tested	Number of States Using Multiple Choice	Number of States Using Performance Exercises
1	1	1
2	5	2
3	17	11
4	18	27
5	16	19
6	13	11
7	16	11
8	20	33
9	13	8
10	14	24
11	16	15
12	1	4

Figure 12.1
1999 Summary of state testing programs
Note: Adapted from "Quality Counts '99". Copyright 1999 by *Education Week,* Bethesda, MD.

- Design exercises that pose problems that make sense in all particular cultures.
- Translate those exercises into a broad range of languages.
- Devise scoring criteria reflecting differing levels of proficiency.

Given the cultural and linguistic diversity of the world, surely you can anticipate the challenges in conducting such an assessment.

The most recent of these was the TIMSS, or Third International Mathematics and Science Study. Five hundred thousand fourth, eighth, and twelfth graders from 41 nations participated. The result was a rank order of nations by subject and grade level.

The Result? Layer upon Layer of Tests.   You can see the pattern of practice that has emerged since the 1930s. The conventional wisdom has held that, if we just find the right level at which to test, schools will improve. To illustrate the strength of this view, as we moved into the 1990s as concerned as ever about the quality of schools, we were poised to repeat the same behavior as we faced the prospect of the mother of all centralized, standardized tests: the national every-pupil examination. At the time of this writing, it is being described as a "voluntary national test." It is as though over the decades, policy makers invested more and more deeply in the belief that, if we just test it, it will improve.

Troubling Contradictions

Throughout this evolution, standardized testing has been troubled with apparent contradictions arising out of a general lack of understanding of these tests, both within and around our school culture. Let me illustrate.

As a society, we have placed great value on standardized tests. We assign great political visibility and power to the results they produce at local, state, national, and international levels. The paradox is that, as a society (both within and outside schools), we seem to have been operating on blind faith that educators are using them appropriately. As a society, almost to a person, we actually know very little about college admission testing, national assessment, state testing, or local assessment programs. It has been so for decades. This blind faith has prevented us from understanding either the strengths or the important limitations of standardized tests. *As a result, the discrepancy is immense between what most educators and the public think these tests can do and what they actually are capable of delivering.*

We have tended to ascribe a level of precision to test scores that belies the underlying reality. Many believe we can use standardized test scores to track student acquisition of new knowledge and skills so precisely as to detect deviations from month-to-month norms; so precisely that we can use them to predict success at the next grade level, in college, or in life after school. But standardized tests typically are not the precision tools or accurate predictors most think they are. They do not produce high-resolution portraits of student achievement. Rather, they are designed to produce broad general indicators of that achievement. This is their often misunderstood heritage.

In addition, because we have tended to grant such power to these once-a-year tests and to the scores they produce, we have been relentless in our attempts to make them powerful instructional tools that are relevant in the classroom. The problem here is that they tend to provide little information of value for day-to-day instruction. There are several reasons for this. First, the tests often are so broad in their coverage that the information they provide is too imprecise for teachers' use. Second, the delay between testing and score reporting is often weeks or even months. By the time scores return, they may no longer reflect the current achievement of ever-growing learners. Third, these tests are administered (normally) only once a year, while teachers must make instructional decisions every three to four minutes. For these reasons, standardized tests typically are of little value at the instructional level. But, of course, this does not preclude their use at instructional support and policy levels of decision making.

Over the decades, some have noticed these problems and concluded that we should do away with standardized tests, arguing that the problems meant that the tests were of poor quality. In fact, *standardized tests generally do a good job of assessing the characteristics they are intended to measure*. They are designed to sample student achievement in broad classifications of content and to tap specific kinds of reasoning and problem solving. Typically, a careful analysis by an assessment literate educator will reveal that a quality standardized test does this very well.

Our long-term societal habits of assigning great power to standardized tests, ascribing unwarranted precision to the scores they produce, striving to make them instructionally relevant, and generally misunderstanding them even while attacking them have conspired to create a major dilemma in education today. We have permitted these tests to form the basis of a school accountability system that is incapable of contributing to much-needed school improvement efforts. Sadly, our general lack of understanding of these tests has prevented us from achieving the real accountability that we all desire.

Addressing the Contradictions: A Guiding Philosophy

One challenge we face as a school culture and as a larger society is to keep these standardized tests in perspective in terms of their potential impact on student learning. They do inform policy and program level users once a year in productive ways. But the plain and simple fact is that *large-scale assessment results have much less impact on student learning than do classroom assessments*. Yet our allocation of resources, media attention to scores, and political emphasis on standardized tests would lead one to believe just the opposite is true. In this regard, our priorities have been grossly out of balance.

If we are to establish a more balanced set of assessment priorities, we must give far greater attention to (1) achieving sufficient general understanding of standardized tests to ensure their proper use, and (2) establishing and maintaining the quality of classroom assessments. A balanced perspective encourages effective use of all assessment tools we have at our disposal. This includes standardized tests. In the hands of informed users who know and understand both the strengths and limitations of these tests, they can contribute useful information to educational decision making. Besides, they are so deeply ingrained in our educational fabric that our communities have come to expect periodically to see scores from these tests.

For these reasons, I believe that districts that abandon this kind of testing altogether make a serious mistake. The reason is that the vast majority of districts currently are unable to develop and implement the kinds of sound assessment alternatives needed to provide quality information for policy-level decision making.

Therefore, I think sound practice is conveyed through procedures such as those recounted in the story of Emily in Chapter 1, in which the school district did the following:

- Continued to use its traditional standardized testing program, but
- Changed from testing every pupil to sampling methods that reduced the number of students tested, and thus reduced testing costs, and
- Used the savings to establish the professional development needed to begin assessing specific aspects of student achievement not currently measured.

This is the kind of plan that can permit us to introduce the full array of assessments needed to profile the full set of achievement targets we expect of students. But, we need to complete a solid program of professional development and intense local assessment planning to achieve this goal. So, as a nation, we had better get started. In the meantime, most of our communities will demand that we continue with some form of standardized test results.

This leads me to the following statement of beliefs: *We should continue the limited use of standardized tests where relevant to inform instructional support and policy decisions. At the same time, we must be absolutely certain each and every user of assessment results (from the classroom to the living room to the boardroom to the legislature) is thoroughly schooled in the meaning and limitations of the scores.* Ill-prepared users misunderstand, misinterpret, and misuse test results. From the perspectives of student well-being, sound public policy, and effective instructional practice, this is unacceptable.

Understanding the Purposes for Large-Scale Assessment

Standardized testing, as noted, can serve the purpose of sorting students along a continuum of achievement. Tests designed to serve these sorting functions highlight achievement differences between and among students to produce a dependable rank order of achievers from lowest to highest. As you will recall, this is called *norm-referenced* test interpretation. These kinds of tests also are used to rank schools, districts, and states in terms of average test scores.

Time for Reflection

What are some instructional support and policy decisions we make that necessitate ranking students (individually or in groups) so as to compare them? Who makes these decisions?

But sometimes standardized tests serve a different purpose. These days they serve to verify student mastery of specific educational standards. Rather than referring scores to a norm group for comparative interpretation, each student's score is compared with a preset standard of acceptable performance, or a *criterion*. Assessments interpreted in this way are said to be *criterion referenced*. Assessments of this kind help us identify learners' strengths and weaknesses.

> Remember, the validity of an assessment is in part, a function of its ability to serve its intended purpose. To select a good standardized test, start with a clear sense of purpose.

In any standardized testing context, therefore, it is critical that assessors understand which kind of interpretation of test scores will serve the desired purpose. Who will be the users and what decisions will they be making?

Time for Reflection

What are some of the kinds of decisions that require a criterion-referenced interpretation of test results? Who makes these decisions?

Revisiting Users and Uses

In Chapter 2, you may recall, we analyzed the users and uses of assessment at three levels: instruction, instructional leadership, and policy. We revisit those now, to establish a context for this chapter. Consider the key differences among assessment users in information needs as depicted in Tables 2.1, 2.2, and 2.3 in Chapter 2. Clearly, large-scale standardized tests are tools for instructional support and policy, where decisions require information summarized over large numbers of students. They do not serve classroom-level decision makers well, because of their relative infrequency and the low-resolution picture of student achievement they convey.

Standardized Test Development

While standardized tests may differ in coverage from publisher to publisher, they all rely on the same basic test development process. Understand that process, to appreciate how much work must be done, and how dedicated to quality local, state, and national large-scale test developers must be.

> As you read on, notice how test publishers attend to our agreed-on standards of quality: (1) clear targets, (2) clear purposes, (3) proper method, (4) sound sampling, and (5) bias control

Clarifying Targets

Typically, standardized test developers begin with the thoughtful study of the valued achievement targets they wish to assess—mastery of content knowledge and the ability to use that knowledge to reason and solve specified kinds of problems, as well as performance skills and products. Test development typically begins with comprehensive studies to identify such achievement target priorities using curriculum materials, commonly used textbooks, practicing teachers, and experts in the academic disciplines being tested.

In terms of our five attributes of sound assessment, therefore, these tests typically arise from very clear targets. But most users don't realize that these targets are very broad in scope, often including several grades' worth of content in a single 40-item test. That means the coverage of any single topic may be very shallow, including no more than a few items to cover a year's worth of material. Indeed, given this constraint, you can see why the vast majority of material covered in any textbook or local curriculum will not be tested. But these tests cannot be made too long, or they will take up too much instructional time.

Time for Reflection

In what way could this limited content coverage become a problem for test publishers? On the surface, it appears to be the user's problem, demanding cautious test score interpretation. From what perspective(s) is it (1) a test construction problem and (2) a marketing problem for test publishers?

Translating Targets into Assessments

Developers of large-scale standardized tests typically know how to match their target with a proper assessment method. In the past, they have relied on selected response formats because these have allowed them to easily tap their valued knowledge and reasoning targets. Now, however, these same test publishers are beginning to turn also to performance assessments, to tap more complex skill and product targets.

Selected Response.   The most popular mode of assessment in this context is and always has been selected response. It is relatively easy to develop, administer, and score in large numbers. When the achievement targets are content mastery and/or certain kinds of thinking and problem solving, its great efficiency makes this the method of choice for large-scale test developers. Its major drawback, as you know, is the limited range of targets test developers can translate into these formats.

Essay.   The essay mode, a dominant form of assessment in European testing tradition, has been infrequently used in standardized testing in the United States. Recently, however, this has begun to change. Short answer essays have begun to appear in the content area exams, such as science and social studies, of state assessments. This popularity arises directly from the fact that, these days, state proficiency standards typically include reasoning and problem-solving targets. Document scanning technology and computer-driven paper management systems have permitted test scoring services to evaluate written work with great dependability and efficiency. Test scoring services have developed the ability to scan student essays, train raters to score them dependably, and present those scorers with student essays online for rating. The result is a powerful new test scoring technology.

Performance Assessment.   This option is the focus of much current discussion and exploration in large-scale assessment. The assessment research and development community is exploring applications in writing, mathematics problem solving, science, reading, foreign languages, the arts, interdisciplinary programs, and other performance areas. The great strength of this methodology is its ability to capture useful information about student performance on complex targets. Its limitations are the cost of sampling and scoring. This is a labor-intensive option when large numbers of examinees are involved.

One very promising application of computer technology to help with efficiency has been developed by NCS of Eden Prairie, Minnesota, in its *Mentor* software. This CD-ROM technology permits users to scan in samples of student writing selected to represent different levels of proficiency, along with the performance criteria used to rate that work. Teachers (raters-in-training) read student papers onscreen, evaluate them, and enter their scores into the system. The computer compares those scores with those assigned by highly proficient raters using the performance criteria. This process repeats until the teachers learn to apply the scoring criteria consistently and accurately, too. From then on, these teachers are qualified raters of student writing in terms of the criteria they have been trained to apply.

In a very creative twist, some teachers are taking this technology right into their classrooms and are using it to train their students to apply writing assessment criteria. Students who become dependable critics of writing become better writers. In fact, I know of one school in which a teacher trained some sixth graders to evaluate student performance dependably. Then those sixth graders trained fifth and fourth graders to apply those same criteria. *That's student-involved assessment!*

Personal Communication.   The role of personal communication in large-scale assessment is beginning to change as well, as researchers begin to discover the strengths of interviews as a method of data collection. By having students "think aloud" about what they have read, reading specialists gain insight into student comprehension. Math and science assessments also can take advantage of this idea. By having students reason out loud as they solve complex problems and respond to carefully crafted questions, assessors can gain insight into students' reasoning and into their ability to communicate effectively. Of course, the drawback of this labor-intensive assessment method is the time required to interview large numbers of students. For this reason this method will be most attractive when assessing relatively small samples of students. But it is an idea with great potential.

Test Development

When assessment plans are ready, test construction begins. Some developers use their own in-house staff of item writers; others recruit qualified practicing teachers to create exercises. In either case, item writers are trained in the basic principles of sound item construction. Further, once trained, item writers must demonstrate an appropriate level of proficiency on a screening test before being asked to contribute to test development.

Typically, test publishers write two or three times more test exercises than will appear on the final test. In doing so, they are guided by a sampling plan or test blueprint that assures sound sampling of the intended targets.

Attention to Sound Sampling and Control of Bias

Once items have been written, qualified test-development experts, content-area experts, and members of minority groups review the exercises for accuracy, appropriateness, and bias. Poor-quality or biased exercises are replaced. This review and evaluation removes possible extraneous sources of bias and distortion.

To uncover and eliminate other potential problems, the next step in test development is to pretest or pilot-test the items. Developers recruit classrooms, schools, or districts to administer the exercises under conditions as similar as possible to those in which the final test will be used. Their objectives are to find out if respondents interpret exercises as the authors intended and to see how well the exercises "function." Test developers also want to know how difficult the items are and how well they differentiate between those who know and do not know the material. All of this helps them retain only the most appropriate exercises for the final test.

Then, yet another external review takes place. Test item development experts, content-area experts, and representatives from various minority groups examine the final collection of test items again to ensure quality, equity, and appropriateness.

Test Norming

The result of this creation, selection, and review of items is a broadly focused, high-quality new test. But the work doesn't stop there. Many test development plans call for administering the final test as a whole for further quality control analysis and, in the case of norm-referenced tests, to establish norms for score interpretation.

As soon as a test is ready, the publisher launches a national campaign to recruit school districts to be part of the "norming sample." The aim is to involve large and small, urban and rural districts in all geographic regions, striving to balance gender and ethnicity; in short, to generate a cross-section of the student population in the United States.

Even though thousands of students may be involved, these norm groups are volunteers. For this reason, they cannot be regarded as systematically representative of the national student population. Thus, when we compare a student's score with national norms, we are *not* comparing them with the actual national student population, but rather to the norm group recruited by that test publisher for that particular test.

Because of the voluntary nature of norm group selection, different test publishers end up recruiting different districts to norm their particular tests. Because none is necessarily equivalent to the national student population nor to any norm group used by another publisher, norm-referenced scores attained on different test batteries cannot be meaningfully compared to one another.

Norm-referenced standardized tests are revised and renormed regularly to keep them up to date in terms of content priorities, and to adjust the score scale. This is necessary because, as the test remains on the market, districts align their curricula to the material covered. This is how they meet the accountability challenge of producing high scores. Over time, more and more students will score higher on the test. To adjust for this effect and to accommodate changes in the student populations, test publishers renorm their tests to adjust the score scale downward.

Setting Standards of Acceptable Performance

As states have established statewide achievement standards and transformed them into criterion-referenced state assessments, an important issue has come to the fore: How do we decide if a student's score is "high enough" to be judged competent? This is a critically important issue when decisions such as grade-level promotion, high school graduation, or the award of certificates of mastery hang in the balance.

Typically, these "cutoff scores" are established by pooling the collective opinions of teachers, administrators, parents, representatives of the business community—a cross-section of society within that state. The processes employed to accomplish this are too complex to describe here. But suffice it to say that this test scoring technology is very well developed and is very precise when carried out by experts.

Once those cutoff scores or standards are established, then each new test developed for use in subsequent years can be "equated" to the original to assure comparability of score meaning, even though it might use different test items. This is important to ensure equity of opportunity for students regardless of the year when they happen to be tested. Again, for our purposes, it's not important that you know how this is done. I just want you to know that it *is* done.

Interpretation of Commonly Used Test Scores

Standardized tests that rely on selected response items can report any of a variety of kinds of scores. We will review the five most common of these in this section by explaining how each score is derived and suggesting how educators may use each score to understand and interpret test performance: raw scores, percent correct, percentile ranks, stanines, and grade equivalent scores.

While these do not represent the only scores you will confront as a test user, they are the ones you are most likely to use and have to interpret for others. You must be conversant with these scores to interpret and use them appropriately.

Raw Score

This is the easiest score to explain and understand. When students take a test, the number of items they answer right is called their *raw score*. In the standardized test context, this forms the basis of all the other scores. In other words, all other scores are derived from it, as you will see. It is the foundation of any communication arising from a standardized test.

Percent Correct

This score is as familiar and easy to understand as the raw score. *Percent correct* reflects the percent of test items the examinee answered correctly: raw score divided by total test items. This is the kind of score we use in the classroom to promote a common understanding and interpretation of performance on classroom tests. As the total number of items changes from test to test, we can always convert raw scores to percent correct and obtain a relatively standard index of performance.

There are two reasons why this kind of score is important in the context of standardized tests. First, this is the kind of score large-scale test developers use to determine mastery of objectives for a criterion-referenced score report. Score reports often label these *objective mastery scores* or something similar. Examinees are judged to have mastered the objective if they answer correctly a certain percentage of the items covering that objective. The exact cutoff varies at around 70 to 80 percent correct across standardized tests.

The second reason for addressing this kind of score is to differentiate it from percentile score or percentile rank. Very often, test users confuse percent correct with percentile scores. *They are fundamentally different kinds of scores bringing completely different interpretations to the meaning of test performance.* To understand the differences, we must first understand each.

Percentile Score

The *percentile score* (or *percentile rank*) represents the essence of a norm-referenced test score. This score tells us what percent of the norm group a student with any given raw score outscored. A student with a percentile rank of 85 outscored (scored higher than) 85 percent of the examinees in that test's original norm group. They allow us to see how each student's score ranked among others who have taken the same test under the same conditions. Did the student score higher than most? Lower? Somewhere in the middle?

Table 12.2 shows you how a student's raw score can be converted to a percentile score. It describes the performance of our norm group on a new test. We will study this table column by column to describe this conversion.

Column one tells us we will be analyzing student performance on a 30-item test. The maximum number correct is 30 and is the score at the top of the column. Possible raw scores range from 0 to 30. If the test is a four-choice multiple-choice test students, scoring 7 or 8 may have been guessing (therefore there are no percentiles reported for scores under 7).

Column two tells us how many students in our 1,500-person norm group (see "Total" at the bottom of the column) actually got each raw score. For instance, 20 students scored 25 on the test, 70 scored 13, and so on.

Table 12.2
Understanding percentile scores

(1) Raw Score	(2) Number of Students	(3) Percent of Students	(4) Cumulative Percent	(5) Percentile Score
30	10	0.5	99.5	99
29	10	0.5	99.0	98
28	20	1.5	98.5	97
27	20	1.5	97.0	96
26	30	2.0	95.5	94
25	20	1.5	93.5	92
24	40	2.5	92.0	90
23	60	4.0	89.5	86
22	80	5.5	85.5	80
21	120	8.0	80.0	72
20	150	10.0	72.0	62
19	180	12.0	62.0	50
18	170	11.5	50.0	39
17	130	8.5	38.5	30
16	120	8.0	30.0	22
15	90	6.0	22.0	16
14	80	5.5	16.0	11
13	70	4.5	10.5	6
12	40	2.5	6.0	4
11	20	1.5	3.5	2
10	10	0.5	2.0	2
9	10	0.5	1.5	1
8	10	0.5	1.0	1
7 (Chance)	10	0.5	0.5	0
6				
5				
4				
3				
2				
1				
Total	1,500	100		

Column three presents the percentage of students who got each raw score. Look at raw score 20. One hundred and fifty students actually achieved this score, which represents 10 percent of the total of 1,500 examinees in the norm group.

Column four is where it begins to get tricky. This column presents the percentage of students who scored at or below each raw score. Start at the bottom of the column. What percent of students attained a raw score of 7 or lower? One-half of one percent. Move up the column. What percent of students attained a raw score of 17 or lower? 38.5 percent—the sum of all the percentages for raw scores 0–17:

.5 + .5 + .5 +.5 + 1.5 + 2.5 + 4.5 + 5.5 + 6 + 8 + 8.5 = 38.5. So, a student who attains a raw score of 17 scored equal to or higher than 38.5 percent of those in the norm group.

Now on to percentile scores—see column 5. For each raw score, by definition we need to know *what percentage of those who took the test scored lower than that score.* Look at raw score 26. These students outscored everyone with scores of 25 or lower. We see that 93.5 percent of examinees attained a score of 25 or lower. If we round to whole numbers, then the percentile score for a raw score of 26 is 94. Anyone attaining a raw score of 26 outscored 94 percent of those in the norm group; thus, a raw score of 26 converts to a percentile score of 94.

Test publishers calculate each of these conversions and then place them in the computer. From that point on, all students who get a certain raw score have its corresponding percentile score printed on their score report. So, for example a raw score of 29 reflects a level of achievement on this test that is higher than 98 percent of the examinees in the norm group. This will remain true as long as this test is in use.

When test publishers norm a test, they create conversion tables for their national norm group, and typically also offer percentile conversions based on geographic region, gender, race/ethnicity, and local performance only. This means that exactly the same kind of conversion table is generated for students who are like one another in these particular ways.

You can see why the percentile is a norm-referenced score. It provides a straightforward comparison of student-to-student performance as the basis for score interpretation.

It also should be clear how percent correct and percentile differ. The former refers scores back to the number of items on the test for interpretation, while the latter compares the score to those of other examinees for interpretation. Their points of reference are fundamentally different.

Stanine

A student may also be assigned a stanine score based on percentile rank. *Stanine* simply represents a less precise score scale, each point of which can be interpreted quite easily (Table 12.3). In this case, the percentile scale is divided up into 9 segments, each of which represents a "standard nine" or, abbreviated, stanine. When interpreted in terms of the general descriptors listed in the right-hand column on Table 12.3, this score is easy to understand. A student who attains a stanine of 3 on a test is interpreted to have scored below average in terms of the performance of the norm group.

Grade Equivalent Scores

This score scale represents yet another way to describe the performance of a student in relation to that of other students. The basis of the comparison in this case is students in the norm group at specified grade levels.

Table 12.3
Understanding stanines

Stanine	Percent of scores	Percentile range	Descriptor
9	4	96–99	well above average
8	7	89–95	above average
7	12	77–88	
6	17	60–76	
5	20	40–59	average
4	17	23–39	
3	12	11–22	below average
2	7	4–10	
1	4	1–3	well below average

Let's say a test publisher is norming a newly developed 40-item test of fifth- and sixth-grade math. It administers its test to large numbers of students in those two grades at the very beginning of the school year. Each student receives a raw score ranging from 10 to 40. On further analysis of test results, let's say that the average score for fifth graders is 23, while sixth graders score an average of 28 correct. With this information, as represented graphically in Figure 12.2, graph A, we can begin to create our conversion table. The first two conversions from raw to grade equivalent scores are those for the average raw scores. Because 23 was the average score for fifth graders, we assign that raw score a grade equivalent of 5.0. Because 28 was the average raw score of sixth graders when we administered our test, it is assigned a grade equivalent of 6.0. That accounts for 2 of the 30 raw score points to be converted. What about the rest?

Under ideal circumstances, the best way to convert the rest would be to administer our new test to students each month, so we could compute averages for them and complete more of our conversion table. Unfortunately, however, real schools will never permit that much test administration. Besides, the cost would be astronomical.

So, as an alternative, we can simply assume that students grow academically at a steady and predictable rate between grade levels. By connecting the two dots (averages) with a straight line that depicts that steady rate of growth, we create a mathematical equation that allows us to convert the scores between 23 and 28 to grade equivalents, as in Figure 12.3, graph B. By projecting each raw score point over to the straight line on the graph and then down to the corresponding point on the grade scale, we find the grade equivalent to assign to each raw score.

But what about scores above and below this grade level? How shall we convert these? We have two choices: (1) Administer the new test to students at higher and

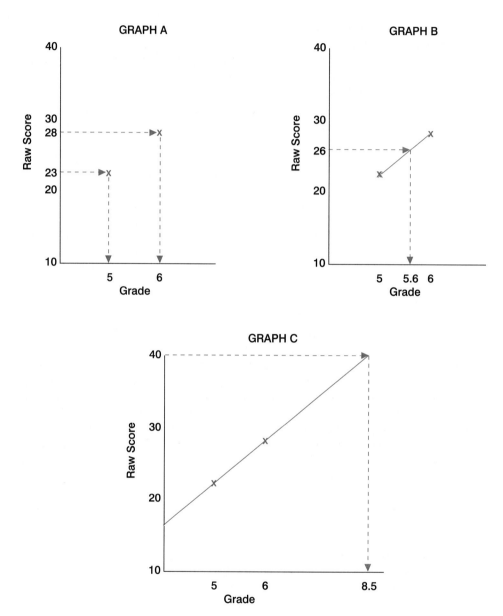

Figure 12.2
The derivation of grade equivalents

lower grade levels, compute averages, and complete the table, or (2) rely on our assumption that students grow at a predictable rate and simply extend our line down from 23 and up from 28. Option 2 is depicted in Figure 12.3, graph C, where a raw score of 40 converts to a grade equivalent of 8.5.

Once the conversion table is completed and read into the computer, hence-forth, any student who attains a given raw score will be assigned its corresponding grade equivalent. Thus, the grade equivalent score reflects the approximate grade level of students in the norm group who attained that raw score.

The strength of this kind of score is its apparent ease of interpretation. But this very strength also turns out to be its major flaw. Grade equivalent scores are easily misinterpreted. They don't mean what most people think they mean. Here is an example of what can go wrong:

Let's say a very capable fifth-grade student scores a perfect raw score of 40 on our new math test. As you can see from Figure 12.3, graph C, this will convert to a very high grade equivalent score. For the sake of illustration, that score is 8.5. An uninformed person might see that and say "We must start this fifth grader using the eighth-grade math book at once!"

This is an incorrect conclusion for two reasons. First of all, no information whatever was gathered about this student's ability to do seventh- or eighth-grade math. All that was tested was fifth- and sixth-grade math. No inference can be made about the student's proficiency at higher-level work. Second, eighth graders have probably never taken the test. The score represents an extrapolation on the part of the test score analyst as to how eighth graders would be likely to score if they had taken the test of fifth- and sixth-grade math. Thus, again no reliable con-clusion can be drawn about any connections to eighth-grade math.

The bottom line is that grade equivalent scores are not criterion-referenced scores. There is no sense in which the grade equivalent score is anchored to any body of defined content knowledge or skill mastery. It is only a comparative score referring a student's performance back to the typical performance of students at particular grade levels in the norm group. Our fifth grader is just very good at fifth- and sixth-grade math—probably a whole lot better than most fifth and sixth graders.

Table 12.4 provides a concise summary of the various kinds of scores we have discussed.

Real-World Test Score Interpretation

Now let's apply these definitions to interpreting a real score report. Refer to Figure 12.3, an individual student score profile for *Terra Nova*, a standardized test prod-uct of CTB McGraw Hill of Monterey, California. Note that it reports both norm-ref-erenced scores (at the top) and criterion-referenced information on student perfor-mance on objectives (at the bottom).

In the top section, we see the headings "Grade Equivalent," "National Stanine," "National Percentile," and "Range." (For our purposes, we can disregard the first column, "Scale Score." This is a technical score not useful in the classroom.) So in the top section, in Reading, Mary Brown, a seventh grader, demonstrated a grade equivalent score of eighth grade, fifth month and a national stanine of 6. In the per-centile column, we see that Mary outscored 65 percent of the students who took the test during norming. Further, see the "Range". If Mary took this test lots of

Table 12.4
Test score summary

Score	Meaning	Strength	Caution
Raw	Number of items answered correctly; range=0 to number of items (points) on the test	Provides the basis of all other scores	Difficult to interpret by themselves; can't be used to compare scores across tests
Percent correct	Percent of total test items answered correctly; range= 0% to 100%	Easy to understand; can communicate mastery of specific objectives	Sensitive to test length— short tests yield huge % jumps between scores
Percentile	Percent of students in norm group that the nominee outscored; range=0 to 99 percentile	Permits clear comparison to other similar students; can serve to compare scores across tests in same battery	Often confused with percent correct; cannot be averaged
Stanine	Divides scores into 9 broad categories	Permits a broad grouping of students by score	Too imprecise to detect small differences in achievement; cannot be averaged
Grade equivalent	Compares performance on the test to that of students at various grade levels who took the same test	Provides interpretive reference to grade levels	Often misinterpreted; does not refer to grade level competencies

times, we would expect her score to vary up or down slightly, to fluctuate between the 55th and 75th percentile—due to errors of measurement—those factors that come up day to day that make all test scores slightly unstable.

The reference to "National" for these scores is important, because it means that the norms were based on the performance of all students from across the nation who participated in test administration during norming. Sometime score reports will list "State" percentiles. That simply means that we interpret each student's score in terms of those who took the test within our state during norming. In addition, school districts also can request norm-referenced scores comparing each student's performance to their classmates within their own community. These are called "Local" norms. Neither state nor local norms appear on the report in Figure 12.3.

The "Performance on Objectives" section of the profile tells us what objectives Mary was judged to have mastered based on her performance in individual items. Here's how to interpret these scores, according *Terra Nova's* guidelines for teachers:

Each objective is measured by a minimum of four items. The Objective Performance Index provides an estimate of the number of items that a student could be expected to

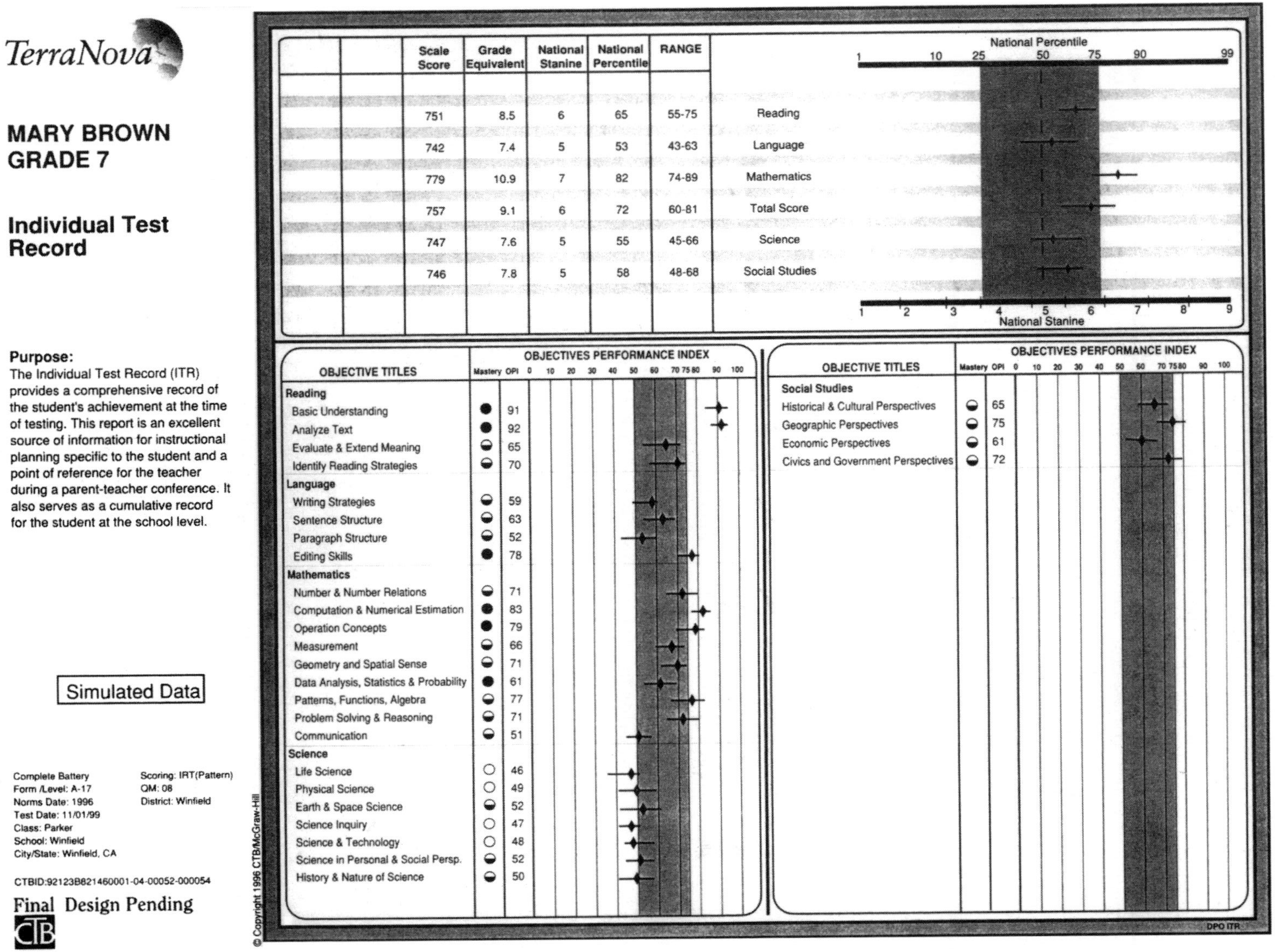

TerraNova

MARY BROWN
GRADE 7

Individual Test Record

Purpose:
The Individual Test Record (ITR) provides a comprehensive record of the student's achievement at the time of testing. This report is an excellent source of information for instructional planning specific to the student and a point of reference for the teacher during a parent-teacher conference. It also serves as a cumulative record for the student at the school level.

Simulated Data

Complete Battery
Form /Level: A-17
Norms Date: 1996
Test Date: 11/01/99
Class: Parker
School: Winfield
City/State: Winfield, CA

Scoring: IRT(Pattern)
QM: 08
District: Winfield

CTBID:92123B821460001-04-00052-000054

Final Design Pending

CTB

	Scale Score	Grade Equivalent	National Stanine	National Percentile	RANGE
Reading	751	8.5	6	65	55-75
Language	742	7.4	5	53	43-63
Mathematics	779	10.9	7	82	74-89
Total Score	757	9.1	6	72	60-81
Science	747	7.6	5	55	45-66
Social Studies	746	7.8	5	58	48-68

OBJECTIVES PERFORMANCE INDEX

OBJECTIVE TITLES	Mastery	OPI
Reading		
Basic Understanding	●	91
Analyze Text	●	92
Evaluate & Extend Meaning	◒	65
Identify Reading Strategies	◒	70
Language		
Writing Strategies	◒	59
Sentence Structure	◒	63
Paragraph Structure	◒	52
Editing Skills	●	78
Mathematics		
Number & Number Relations	◒	71
Computation & Numerical Estimation	●	83
Operation Concepts	●	79
Measurement	◒	66
Geometry and Spatial Sense	◒	71
Data Analysis, Statistics & Probability	●	61
Patterns, Functions, Algebra	◒	77
Problem Solving & Reasoning	◒	71
Communication	◒	51
Science		
Life Science	○	46
Physical Science	○	49
Earth & Space Science	◒	52
Science Inquiry	○	47
Science & Technology	○	48
Science in Personal & Social Persp.	◒	52
History & Nature of Science	◒	50

OBJECTIVES PERFORMANCE INDEX

OBJECTIVE TITLES	Mastery	OPI
Social Studies		
Historical & Cultural Perspectives	◒	65
Geographic Perspectives	◒	75
Economic Perspectives	◒	61
Civics and Government Perspectives	◒	72

Figure 12.3
Sample score report

answer correctly if there had been 100 items for that objective. The OPI is used to indi-cate mastery of each objective. An OPI of 75 and above characterizes Mastery. An OPI between 50 and 74 indicates Partial Mastery, and an OPI below 50 indicates Non-Mas-tery. The two-digit number preceding the objective title identifies the objective, which is fully described in the Teacher's Guide to *Terra Nova*. The bands on either side of the diamonds indicate the range within which the student's test score would fall if the stu-dent were tested numerous times. (CTB/McGraw-Hill, 1996, p. 2)

Implications for Teachers

So what does all of this mean for those concerned primarily with classroom assess-ment? For you as a teacher, it means understanding that you have a three-part responsibility with respect to standardized tests.

Responsibility 1: Protect the Well-Being of Your Students!

Your first and foremost responsibility is to keep your students free from harm. First, make sure they have the opportunity to learn to hit the achievement targets reflected in whatever standardized tests they will take. Second, ensure that the scores reported for your students are accurate—that they reflect each student's real level of achievement. Third, you must do everything you can to be sure all students come out of large-scale assessment experiences with their academic self-concepts intact. You can do several specific things to fulfill these professional obligations.

Opportunity to Learn.   Do all in your power to gather information about and to understand the achievement targets to be assessed in upcoming standardized tests. If a state assessment is pending that reflects state standards, it is your job to know what those standards are and how they apply to your students. If a published test is to be administered, consult the teacher's guide or the user's materials for that test to know precisely what knowledge, reasoning, performance skill, or product targets it will be assessing.

Once you understand the lay of the land, be sure you yourself are a master of the achievement targets your students will be expected to master.

Be sure your instructional program sets students up for maximum achieve-ment. Make sure you cover the areas to be tested. But keep this in perspective. If the standardized tests represent only a fraction of your total curriculum, allocate a relative fraction of your instructional time to its particular targets. To do otherwise is to permit the standardized test to inappropriately narrow your instructional pro-gram. Make sure everyone knows what proportion of your curriculum is covered so they can keep these tests in perspective!

Maximizing Accuracy.   The key decision in ensuring the accuracy of test scores is that of finding the achievement test battery that aligns most closely to the user's local curriculum. To maximize this match, a district must compare coverage of the various available tests with its local curriculum priorities at the grade level(s) at which they wish to use the test. The user's guide for each test will present detailed test specifications representing the specific content knowledge, patterns of reasoning, and skill and product targets tapped by every test in the battery. That coverage will vary greatly for the same grade levels across test batteries. Test publishers test different content under the same subject label aimed at the same grade levels. For this reason, each district must compare and decide which test battery most closely aligns with its curriculum. Only this kind of analysis can assure sound sampling of student achievement and scores that accurately reflect student achievement.

It is interesting to speculate on the implications for student well-being and school improvement when school districts fail to examine the degree of match between their curriculum and the particular test battery they have chosen to administer.

Participate in standardized test selection within your district whenever possible. Be sure to bring your knowledge of the attributes of sound assessments to the table. You know the standards of quality. Table 12.5 translates those standards into critical consumer questions you can ask. Demand quality. Your students and their families are counting on you.

When asked to administer standardized tests, take the responsibility seriously and follow the prescribed instructions. This, too, contributes to accuracy. You must

Table 12.5
Key questions to ask in standardized test selection

Standard of Quality	Critical Questions
Tests arise from clear and appropriate achievement targets	Which of the tests under consideration most closely approximates local curriculum priorities? What percent of the items to be used at a given grade level actually test material our district teaches at that level?
Assessments serve clear and appropriate purposes	What are our specific purposes for standardized testing—who are the users and what information do they need? Which of the tests under consideration is most capable of providing the needed information, in understandable terms and in a timely manner?
Method accurately reflects the valued outcomes	What are all of our valued school and/or district targets? Which of these targets require the use of which methods of assessment? Which of the standardized tests under consideration rely on proper methods for our targets and purposes?
Assessments sample achievement appropriately	How does each test under consideration sample student achievement and how does each sampling plan relate to our local achievement targets? Which test samples our curriculum most completely?
Assessments control for bias and distortion	What sources of interference present potential problems, given our standardized testing context? Which of the tests under consideration allow us to control for the most sources of potential problems?

follow accepted standards of ethical practice. Anything you may do to cause students to misrepresent their real levels of achievement has the potential of doing harm to them, to you as a professional, and to the integrity of the educational community as a whole. *If you are opposed to a particular set of standardized testing practices, bring all of your assessment literacy tools to bear during the debate. That is your right and your responsibility. But when assessment begins, adhere to prescribed procedures so users can accurately interpret the results.*

Sometimes ensuring accuracy demands more than merely following prescribed test administration procedures. Some students bring physical or intellectual handicaps to the testing environment that require you to adjust test administration procedures to obtain accurate scores for them. Most often these days, test publishers or state testing agencies will issue guidelines for such accommodations. One such list is presented in Figure 12.4. Note that adjustments can be made in setting, timing, scheduling, presentation, and response. As a general rule of thumb, accommodations allowed at testing time are the same as accommodations made during instruction as listed in the student's individualized education program (IEP).

Is it clear to you why such adjustments are necessary in some cases? If some students take the test under standard conditions, the result may well be a score that misrepresents what they know and can do. These accommodations permit us to get past those physical or intellectual challenges to use their strengths to permit us to see students' real achievement more clearly. But we have to be sure that such accommodations don't alter the target being assessed, thus leading to inaccurate measurement.

Whenever standardized test results are being reviewed, discussed, or used in a decision-making context, urge complete understanding and proper interpretation and use of those results. If you determine that users do not understand the meaning and/or limitations of the scores in question, strive to explain them, or, if necessary, urge that users seek professional assessment expertise. Be diplomatic in this effort, but assertive. Do not permit misinterpretation. Your students' well-being hangs in the balance.

Student Self-Confidence.   Prepare your students to participate productively and as comfortably as possible in large-scale testing programs. Take time to be sure they understand why they are taking these tests and how the results will be used. Be sure they know what the scores mean and do not mean. Provide practice with the kinds of test items they will confront, so they know how to deal with those formats. This includes practice with accommodations in place for special education students.

Communicate with parents about the importance of a settled home environment during the times of standardized testing. Be sure they, too, are advised on how to keep these tests in perspective. Be sure they know the meaning of the scores. And above all, be positive and encouraging to all before, during, and after these assessments and encourage parents to do the same. All of these steps help students become "test wise." Positive talk can send students into uncomfortable testing circumstances knowing that you are on their side—and that helps.

Examples of Setting Accommodations	
Conditions of Setting	**Location**
Minimal distractive elements (e.g., books, artwork, window views)	Study carrel
Special lighting	Separate room (including special education classroom)
Special acoustics	Seat closest to test administrator (teacher, proctor, etc.)
Adaptive or special furniture	Home
Individual student or small group of students rather than large group	Hospital
	Correctional institution

Examples of Timing Accommodations	
Duration	**Organization**
Changes in duration can be applied to selected subtests of an assessment or to the assessment overall.	Frequent breaks, even during parts of the assessment (e.g., during subtests)
Extended time (i.e., extra time)	Extended breaks between parts of the assessment (e.g., between subtests) so that assessment is actually administered in several sessions
Unlimited time	

Examples of Scheduling Accommodations	
Time	**Organization**
Specific time of day (e.g., morning, midday, afternoon, after ingestion of medication)	In a different order from that used for most students (e.g., longer subtest first, shorter later, math first, English later)
Specific day of week	Omit questions that cannot be adjusted for an accommodation (e.g., graph reading for student using Braille) and adjust for missing scores
Over several days	

Figure 12.4

Example of assessment accommodations to meet special needs

Source: Adapted from *Testing Students with Disabilities*, pp. 47–58, by M. L. Thurlow, J. L. Elliott, and J. E. Ysseldyke, 1998, Thousand Oaks, CA: Corwin Press. Copyright 1998. Adapted by permission of Corwin Press.

Examples of Presentation Accommodations

Format Alterations	Procedure Changes	Assistive Devices
Braille edition Large-print version Larger bubbles on answer sheet One complete sentence per line in reading passages Bubbles to side of choices in multiple-choice exams Key words or phrases highlighted Increased spacing between lines Fewer number of items per page Cues on answer form (e.g., arrows, stop signs)	Use sign language to give directions to student Reread directions Write helpful verbs in directions on board or on separate piece of paper Simplify language, clarify or explain directions Provide extra examples Prompt student to stay focused on test, move ahead, read entire item Explain directions to student anytime during test Answer questions about items anytime during test without giving answers	Audiotape of directions Computer reads directions and/or items Magnification device Amplification device (e.g., hearing aid) Noise buffer Templates to reduce visible print Markers or masks to maintain place Dark or raised lines Pencil grips Magnets or tape to secure papers to work area

Examples of Response Accommodations

Format Alterations	Procedure Changes	Assistive Devices
Mark responses in test booklet rather than on separate page Respond on different paper, such as graph paper, wide-lined paper, paper with wide margins	Use reference materials (e.g., dictionary, arithmetic tables) Give response in different mode (e.g., pointing, oral response to tape recorder, sign language)	Word processor or computer to record responses Amanuensis (proctor/scribe writes student responses) Slantboard or wedge Calculator or abacus Brailler Other communication device (e.g., symbol board)

Figure 12.4
continued

Responsibility 2: Community Awareness

Promote understanding within your community of the role of standardized testing and the meaning of test results. Members of the school board, parents, citizens, and members of the news media may need basic assessment literacy training to participate productively in the proper use of results. Only when they, too, understand the meaning of sound assessment will they be in a position to promote the wise use of these tests.

Responsibility 3: Maintain Perspective

Be constantly mindful of when standardized tests are likely to contribute useful information and when they are not. You can do this only if you understand the meaning of test results and how that meaning relates to the reasons for testing. In my opinion, we have entirely too much standardized testing being conducted merely as a matter of tradition, with no sense of purpose. Always insist on attention to purpose: What are the specific decisions to be made, by whom, and what kind(s) of information do they need? Will the test provide useful information?

We must all constantly urge those who support, design, and conduct standardized testing programs to keep these tests in perspective in terms of their relative importance in the larger world of educational assessment. We must constantly remind ourselves and others that these tests represent but a tiny fraction of the assessments in which students participate and that they have relatively little influence on day-to-day instruction. *While standardized tests should continue to command resources, we must begin to move rapidly toward a more balanced expenditure of those very limited resources so as to support quality classroom assessment as well.*

Summary: Meeting the Challenges of Standardized Testing

Our purpose in this chapter has been to understand and learn to negotiate the challenges presented by standardized testing to teachers and those in positions of instructional support.

We reviewed the array of assessment purposes introduced in Chapter 2, emphasizing again the place of standardized testing in the larger context of educational assessment. These tests serve both policy and instructional support functions. They tend to be of little specific value to teachers, because classroom demands require greater frequency of assessment and higher resolution pictures of student achieve-

ment than the typical standardized test can generate. The one part of the score report teachers are likely to find useful are the criterion-referenced scores reflecting student mastery of specific objectives. While once a year is not frequent enough to be comprehensive, at least teachers get some detail with these scores.

We studied the various levels of standardized testing, from local to state to national to college admission testing, pointing out that all four assessment methods are used at various levels. We discussed their history, and the mechanics of their development.

Next, our attention turned to understanding and interpreting commonly used standardized test scores: raw scores, percent correct, percentile, stanine, and grade equivalent. These and other such scores are safe and easy to use when users understand them. But, by the same token, they can be easily distorted by the uninformed. Your challenge is to become informed.

We ended with a quick summary of your professional responsibilities, emphasizing that your concern first and foremost should be for the well-being of your students. Under all circumstances, we must demand accurate assessment of the local curricula. Each of us should strive to be an activist with a voice of reason in this arena. Only then will we be able to use this form of assessment productively.

In the introduction to Part IV, we established certain conditions that must be satisfied to achieve effective communication: a mutual understanding of the targets tested, accurate scores, and an interpersonal communication environment amenable to productive sharing. When using standardized tests as the means of gathering information and communicating about learning, we maximize the chances of success if all of the following is true:

1. Both message sender and receiver understand the nature of the achievement targets reflected in the exercises of the test; they know and understand what was and what was not tested.

2. The tests are developed by professionals who have the technical credentials to create tests that provide dependable information; tests developed in the absence of this expertise are likely to be of inferior quality.

3. The interpersonal communication environment is open to good communication:

   a. Everyone involved knows what the scores can and cannot be used for, and use them accordingly.

   b. Message sender(s) and receiver(s) share a common language; in this case, meaning that both know what the scores mean and how to interpret them correctly.

   c. Opportunity is created by message senders where they and all receivers are compelled to attend to the test scores being shared.

   d. During this time message senders ask receivers to restate in their own words what the scores mean and what their implications are.

Exercises for Self-Assessment

1. Based on your review of material presented in Chapter 2 and reexamined in this chapter, list the decisions informed by standardized test results and identify the various decision makers who use these results.

2. List the various steps in standardized test development, explaining how test publishers attend to issues of test quality at each step.

3. After studying the section in this chapter on score interpretation, identify and define the kinds of standardized test scores discussed.

4. Commit to memory the classroom teacher's basic standardized testing responsibilities.

5. Turn to the section in this chapter titled, "Troubling Contradictions." List each of the contradictions, and explain why it represents a potential problem in our effective use of standardized tests in schools.

6. Assume that your careful analysis of commercially available standardized tests reveals that only one-half of the items in

any subtest covers material specified in your curriculum at the specified grade levels you had planned to test. That is, the best overlap you can get between what you want to test and any available test is 50 percent. This means that you will not have taught one-half of the material tested during the year you test it. Yet your school board and administration compel you to choose and administer a test anyway. How should you proceed? What should you do to maximize the value of this assessment and minimize harm to students?

7. Compare and contrast *norm-referenced* and *criterion-referenced* interpretations of test scores.

8. Compare and contrast *percent correct* and *percentile rank* scores.

 You may go to the Companion Website at www.prenhall.com/stiggins and answer these questions in the Self-Assessment module.

Final Chapter Reflection

1. *What are the three most important new insights to come to you as a result of your study of this chapter?*
2. *Which of your previous questions about assessment can you now answer based on your study of this chapter?*
3. *What new questions have come to mind as a result of your study of this chapter that you hope to have answered as your study continues?*
4. *For practicing teachers only: What do you plan to do differently in assessment in your classroom as a result of your study of this book so far?*

   For those in preservice study only: As you think about the classroom assessment environment that you hope to create for your students, how has your thinking changed as a result of your study of this book so far?

 ## Workbook Activities

Those of you using the workbook, *Practice with Student-Involved Classroom Assessment*, as part of your study of this material will find the following activities and others included for Chapter 12:

- *Visualizing Invisible Targets/Analyzing Standardized Tests.* Part A prepares you to think about standardized testing by considering the achievement targets such tests can and cannot assess well. Part B asks you to take this brainstorm list into the realm of reality by actually analyzing a standardized test for its match to what the developers say it measures.

- *Interpreting Standardized Test Score Reports.*   Everyone needs to know how to interpret and use the scores found on standardized tests. This activity gives you practice in doing that. Part A covers test score meanings; Part B asks you to find information on your local test score report and discuss implications for instruction; Part C gives you a chance to practice describing test scores and results in student and parent-friendly language.

- *Panel Hears Exam Horrors.*   "The board of education will hold further hearings today on the high school graduation test. . . . " How might have the situation presented in the case been avoided?

- *If the Targets Stay the Same Can We Change the Context?*   Classrooms are becoming increasingly diverse. With this diversity come a multitude of questions about assessment—Do we hold all students to the same standard? Does "fair" mean "everyone has to take exactly the same time" or does it mean, "everyone has to take a test that measures the same competencies even though the tasks might be slightly different?" This activity examines the factors on tests that fool us into mismeasuring students and parallel versions of the same tests that measure the same thing while honoring diversity.

13

Report Cards

CHAPTER FOCUS

This chapter answers the following guiding question:

> How can I communicate about student achievement using report cards in a manner that helps my students find success?

After studying this chapter you will understand the following important principles:

1. Historically, we have assigned report card grades based on evidence and teacher judgment about student ability, achievement, effort, compliance, and attitude. This practice has done far more harm than good in building effective lines of communication.

2. There is one best way to develop report card grades. In fact, in a standards-driven educational environment, there is only one acceptable way.

3. As professional educators, it is our ethical and pedagogical responsibility to understand and apply only acceptable grading practices.

4. Grades represent just one of several ways to communicate using report cards. Other options include lists of competencies, narrative reporting, and continuous progress reporting.

Report Card Grading

We can begin our exploration of report cards nowhere but with a comprehensive treatment of grading issues. The key issues revolve around the following:

- What student characteristics to factor into a report card.
- What sources of evidence to tap in determining a student's grade.
- How to combine evidence gathered over time into the composite index that will form the basis of the grade.
- How to convert that composite picture into a grade.

Each hides troubling dilemmas for teachers within it, and thus poses grave dangers to student confidence and to their ultimate academic success.

But before we begin that journey, let me remind you that grades are by no means the only way to share information about student achievement using report cards. Some report card designs convey much greater detail about student achievement to message receivers. Sometimes that detail is crucial to sound decision making. So, after we address grades, I will share examples of useful alternatives.

Grading, What's a Teacher to Do?

As a teacher for many years, I experienced great anxiety about the appropriateness of my grading practices. I wondered whether there is a right way and whether I was grading my students that way. I constantly questioned myself:

- Why do I have to assign grades? What's the purpose?
- Exactly what distribution of grades am I to assign? How many As, Bs, and so on?
- Should I grade on a curve (comparing students to each other) or use preset cutoff scores (everyone with a 90% average or above gets an A)?
- Should my grades reflect absolute achievement at one point in time or improvement over time?
- How do I grade students who already know all the material at the beginning of the term?
- Should I hold all students to the same standard or can I adjust my grading expectations for special needs students?
- Should I grade just on ability and achievement or should I consider effort and attitude as well?
- How am I supposed to keep records of all this achievement information for all these students?
- What should I do if my tests are too hard and everyone fails? What grades do I assign?
- Are my grades supposed to mean the same thing as those of others who teach the same courses? How can we ensure that this is true?
- If we all reflect different expectations and standards in our grades, how can anyone interpret our grades accurately? How do we make any of this make sense?

school effectiveness. The demand for higher levels of competence for larger proportions of our students brought about a demand for schools driven by expectations of high achievement, not merely a rank order.

This change in mission carries implications for our grading practices. For decades in the American educational system, we have been demonstrating how it is possible to rank students dependably without knowing much about the quality of the assessments or sound grading practices. This is evidenced by the historic lack of teacher training in assessment and grading. The ritual sorting of students connects to society's need to have a range of achievement emerge from high schools in order to meet the needs of a diverse workplace. As long as students were ranked, no one was concerned about the underlying dangers of mismeasurement and/or unsound grading practices.

The troubling fact is that *it is possible to obtain a dependable rank order of students at the end of high school, even if the accumulated assessments and grades are individually undependable*. Here's how this can happen: Over four years and many courses, if classroom assessments are unreliable, some teachers will overestimate real student achievement, while others will underestimate it. When these inaccuracies are averaged into a composite grade point average at the end of four years, these errors of measurement (some too high and some too low) will tend to cancel each other out and the result will be a dependable estimate of each student's overall achievement. Thus a class rank based on this four-year composite will, in fact, sort accurately according to achievement. Few cared that meaningful comparison and interpretation of grades across classrooms, schools, or districts was impossible. The actual information about student achievement contained within an individual grade wasn't considered very important. As long as the symbols (grades and grade point averages) appeared to be based in academic rigor, students were assumed to be learning different amounts, as society expected.

But this changed in the 1980s and 1990s, as society began to realize the limitations of schools that merely rank students. We have come to understand that, *while we can assign grades and sort students dependably without quality assessments and sound grading practices, we cannot ensure the highest level of competence for all students without them*. Here's why: As students ascend through ever-higher levels of competence, seeking ultimately to meet graduation standards, each unit and course of study provides prerequisites for those that follow. If the individual assessments and grades assigned along the way are undependable, both teachers and students are likely to fall victim in their decision making to the resulting misinformation. Teachers, for instance, may misdiagnose student needs, fail to discover ineffective teaching practices, and misinform subsequent teachers about a student's current level of competence. Misinformed students may not allocate study time and energy appropriately, lose confidence in themselves, or make inappropriate educational or vocational plans.

In short, when schools are driven by a desire for competence for all students, the ongoing mismeasurement of student achievement (which was no problem with

> Here we see a series of unreliable assessments producing a reliable rank order of students.

a rank-order mission) becomes a formula for disaster. Thus, with a mission of ensuring competence, we are forced to assess and grade accurately. We realize that, if we are to take students to the highest levels of competence, everyone must have access to dependable information about their current achievement status. We have also realized that teachers must communicate with each other, with families, and with students themselves about the specifics of student achievement if we are to support the continuous progress of students. It is within this change of mission that we address grading practices in this chapter.

4. Evolving Achievement Targets.   We also are experiencing rapid changes in our collective vision of the meaning of academic success. Two facets of our evolving expectations are important from a grading point of view. First, our range of expectations is expanding with the addition of technology, health-related, and teamwork achievement targets, among others. Second, the complexity of our expectations is increasing as researchers help us understand more clearly what it means to be a good reader, writer, math problem solver, computer user, and team member, to mention a few. These changes make it necessary for teachers to gather, store, retrieve, summarize, grade, and otherwise communicate about far more achievement targets today than ever before. In short, the information-processing challenges faced by the typical classroom teacher are immense. This means that we must also address grading practices from a perspective of efficiency.

5. Changing Student Needs.   In addition, we must deal with the grading implications of mainstreaming special needs students. The typical teacher is facing a much broader range of academic abilities than ever before. As our society becomes more ethnically diverse, this challenge intensifies. We must plan and conduct assessments and assign grades in classrooms where individual students are working toward attaining fundamentally different achievement targets. If each student succeeds at a personally appropriate level, each deserves an "A." But how do we communicate the differences among those As? Is it even conceivable to individualize these communication systems to promote understanding and sound decision making? This reality places immense pressure on our traditional report card grading practices. We must deal with them. I will explain how in this chapter.

The Meaning of Effective Communication

As we discuss grading practices within this evolving environment, we must bear in mind four of the conditions underpinning effective communication discussed in the Part IV introduction. If we are to communicate effectively via grades, we must start with the following:

- Clearly articulated and appropriate expectations. Message senders and receivers must agree on what we seek to communicate about.

- Quality assessments capable of accurately reflecting student proficiency. We need accurate information if we are to communicate effectively.

- A shared language for message senders and receivers to use in passing information. If the symbols used to convey information mean different things to senders and receivers, miscommunication is assured.

- An opportunity to communicate—a time, place, and set of circumstances when message senders and receivers can set other concerns aside, attend to the information being shared, and check for understanding.

In the outline of sound grading practices that follows, we address all of these standards in various ways.

Time for Reflection

Before we proceed, please take time to reflect about the grading process in your school world. If you are (or were) a teacher, to what extent do (did) your grading practices meet each of these four standards of effective communication? If you are a student preparing to teach, to what extent do your professors' grading practices satisfy these criteria?

Communicate about What?

If we are to devise report card grading approaches that meet our communication needs in achievement-driven schools and that contribute to a supportive, productive, and motivating environment, the first issue we must confront is, What do we wish to communicate about? We must decide which student characteristics should be factored into report card grades.

Traditionally, most teachers have considered several factors, among them the following:

- *Achievement*—Those who learn more receive higher grades than those who learn less.

- *Aptitude*—Those who "overachieve" in relation to their aptitude, intelligence, or ability receive higher grades than those who fail to work up to their potential.

- *Effort*—Those who try harder receive higher grades.

- *Compliance*—Those who follow the rules receive higher grades than those who don't.

- *Attitude*—Those who demonstrate more positive attitudes receive higher grades than those with negative attitudes.

It is likely that teachers will define these in different terms, assess them in different ways, or give them different relative weights in assigning grades. It is interesting to speculate on the interpretability of a single letter grade when the message receivers and interpreters don't know (1) which of these elements the grader deemed important, (2) how they defined each, (3) how or how well they assessed each, and (4) what weight they gave each factor in grade computation. If we expect to communicate effectively about student achievement via grades, we must regard all of these unknowns as deeply troubling. But this is just the tip of the iceberg when it comes to describing the challenge of communicating through grades.

To illustrate what I mean, join me now in a wide-ranging and thoughtful analysis of the role in the grading process of each of the five listed factors. Here are the issues in a nutshell:

- Should *achievement* be a factor in grading? That is, if two students have demonstrated fundamentally different levels of attainment of your achievement expectations, should you assign them different grades?

- Should you consider students' *aptitude, intelligence*, or *ability* when grading? That is, let's say two students have demonstrated exactly the same level of achievement, and let's say that level is right on the line between two letter grades. But you regard one as an overachiever in relation to ability and the other an underachiever, not having worked up to potential. Is it appropriate to assign them different grades?

- Is it appropriate to consider a student's level of *effort*, seriousness of purpose, or motivation in the grading process? That is, let's say two students have demonstrated exactly the same level of achievement and, again, that level is right on the line between two letter grades, but you regard one as having tried very hard while the other has not tried hard at all. Is it appropriate to assign them different grades?

- If we establish rules and deadlines with which students are expected to *comply*, should students who violate them be assigned lower grades? For instance, if we have two students both of whom demonstrate the highest level of achievement on major tests and assignments, but one is, say, delinquent in completing work, should that student's grade suffer?

- Is it proper to factor students' *attitudes* into the grade? Again, given two students equal in actual achievement and on a grade borderline, one of whom has exhibited a positive attitude in class and one a distinctly negative attitude, is it appropriate to assign them different grades?

Time for Reflection

NOTE: The reflections requested in this chapter represent particularly critical aspects of your learning. I am going to make some very provocative assertions in the following discussion. They are intended to elicit a response from you. You need to be a critical consumer of the ideas that I offer. This chapter's "Times for Reflection" will help you in this regard. Please take time to think them through. *Before reading on, think about and take a personal position on each of the five questions listed above. If possible, discuss your views with colleagues or classmates. Continue only after you have answered each of the five questions above with a yes or no.*

To figure out the best answers to these questions, we need to conduct a thoughtful analysis of arguments for and against weaving each of these factors into a grade. Then we must compare these two sets of arguments to draw conclusions regarding which should win out, arguments for or against, given that our purpose is to communicate effectively.

Achievement as a Grading Factor.   If we use achievement as one basis for determining students' report card grades, in effect, our contract with students says that those who learn more (that is, master a larger amount of the required material, hit a larger proportion of the valued targets, progress further, or produce higher-quality work) will receive higher grades than those who learn less. This has long represented the foundation of grading.

Arguments For.   One obvious reason this factor has been so prominent in grading is that schools exist to promote student achievement. In that sense, it is the most valued result of schooling. If students achieve, schools are seen as working effectively. Grades are supposed to reflect students' success in learning the required material.

Besides, students are expected to achieve in life after school. School is an excellent place to learn about this fundamental societal expectation.

In addition, achievement in most academic disciplines can be clearly defined and translated into sound assessments. We can build a strong basis for grading achievement in our assessments. In short, it can be done well, given currently available technology.

These are all compelling reasons why we traditionally have factored achievement into the report card grade, most often as the most prominent factor. Who would question the wisdom of grading in this way? Are there reasons not to factor in achievement?

Arguments Against.   Not really. Given that achievement is the mission of school, we must communicate about it and grades represent one possible vehicle.

But to be sure, some dangers deserve our attention, if only to remind us of our assessment responsibilities. For example, what if we define achievement in complex terms that are difficult to assess well, and we inadvertently mismeasure it? Or, what if we grade student performance based on a very important term-length homework assignment that a student, in fact, did not do but rather was done by a well-meaning parent instead? In both cases the grade will misrepresent real student achievement. Those who read the grade later would draw incorrect inferences about student achievement and would make inappropriate decisions.

Or, what if we lack sufficient assessment expertise in the valued target to adequately evaluate student achievement of it? Again, mismeasurement is likely and the grade might not reflect real achievement.

Or, in a more serious and more likely dilemma, what if each teacher has a different definition of the meaning of successful achievement, assesses it differently, and assigns it a different weight in the grade computation? Now our attempts to communicate about achievement are full of noise and static, not clear, meaningful signals. When this happens, grades become uninterpretable.

Besides, if we factor in achievement, isn't there a danger that perennial low achievers will never experience success in the form of high grades? For them, factoring achievement into the grade simply means more failure and an inevitable loss of confidence as a learner. Those who stop believing in themselves stop trying and thus stop learning.

But these do not represent arguments against grading on achievement. Rather they tell us that we had better know what we are doing when we do so.

Resolution.   In this case, the decision is straightforward. In effect, *there are no compelling arguments against factoring achievement into report card grades.* But we must confront the dangers and eliminate all of them.

If there is a danger of mismeasurement due to the complexity of targets, we can either simplify them, or we can participate in professional development to help us to (1) refine our vision of the target to capture its complexity, and (2) devise more accurate assessments. These actions can help us prevent inadvertent mismeasurement of achievement.

If the problem is a lack of assessment expertise on the part of teachers responsible for grading, this may be alleviated by providing professional development in assessment so all teachers may attain essential expertise. Or, we can work with qualified colleagues, supervisory staff, or higher-education faculty to devise sound assessments.

If problems arise because some teachers hold different definitions of achievement, we can meet to compare definitions. By airing differences of professional opinion, we can find the common ground on which to build sound grading practices.

If the problem is inevitable failure for the perennial low achiever, we can establish individual achievement targets that are within the grasp of each individual student, grading students in terms of standards that hold the promise of success for each and communicating individualized results. In this case, we would base grades on the expectations framed in each student's individualized education program (IEP). More about this later.

Thus, if we act purposefully to develop and implement practices that remove objections by setting clear and specific targets that are within all students' reach, and using sound assessments, we can find ample justification for including achievement in report card grades.

Aptitude as a Grading Factor.   Remember the issues here: Assume two students demonstrate exactly the same level of achievement, and that level happens to be right at the cutoff between two grades. If you judge one student to be an overachiever in relation to ability, aptitude, or intelligence, and judge the other to be an underachiever, is it appropriate to assign them different grades? In other words, is it appropriate to factor a judgment about students' aptitude into the grading equation?

Arguments For.   If we consider intelligence, ability, or aptitude in the grading equation, we hold out the promise of success for every student. This is encouraging to students. As they gain a sense of their own efficacy, we hope they will be motivated to try harder. What teacher is not energized by the promise of individualized achievement targets set to match the capabilities of individual students, thus ensuring each student at least the chance of academic success?

Besides, if we can identify those underachievers, we can plan the special motivational activities they need to begin to work up to their fullest potential. And we do so with no grading penalty to the perennial low achiever. This is a win-win proposition!

These are compelling arguments indeed. Factoring aptitude or ability into the grading process makes perfect sense. Who could argue against it?

Arguments Against.   In this case, there are important counterarguments. For example, the definition of this thing called *aptitude* or *intelligence* is far from clear. Scholars who have devoted their careers to the study of intelligence and its relationship to achievement do not agree among themselves as to whether each of us has one of these or many, whether this is a stable or volatile human characteristic, or whether it is stable at some points in our lives and unstable at others. Not only do they disagree fundamentally about the definition of these characteristics, but they also are at odds regarding how to assess them (Gardner, 1993; Sternberg, 1996).

Given these uncertainties among experts, how can we, who have no background whatever in the study of intelligence, presume to know any student's aptitude or intelligence? That is not to say that all students come to school with the same intellectual tools. We know they do not. But it is one thing to sense this to be true and quite another matter to assume that we possess enough refined wisdom about intelligence to be able to measure it dependably, turn it into a single quantitative index, and then factor it in when computing report card grades.

Given the absence of training in aptitude assessment, if teachers were to come up with a dependable definition (which is not possible), they would face the severe difficulty of generating the classroom-level data needed to classify students according to their aptitude. Remember the key attributes of a sound assessment? Clear targets, proper method, representative sampling, control of bias. Each would have to be met for an attribute called *aptitude*, separately from achievement!

And then, if we were able to resolve those problems (which we cannot), we would face another insurmountable dilemma. How do we determine the amount of over- or underachievement? Specifically, each teacher would need a formula for deciding precisely how many units of achievement are needed per unit of aptitude to be labeled an over- or underachiever, and that formula would have to treat each and every student in exactly the same manner to assure fairness. *We do not possess the conceptual understanding and classroom assessment sophistication to enable us to do this.*

A brief comment is in order about this issue of aptitude as something separate from achievement. It is tempting to use students' records of prior achievement as a basis from which to infer ability, intelligence, or aptitude. But achievement and aptitude are not the same. Many things other than intellectual ability influence achievement, such as home environment, school environment, and dispositions. *Inferring level of ability from prior achievement is very risky. Resist this temptation.*

Besides, what if you label a student as an underachiever on the record and you are wrong? That student may be misclassified for years and suffer dire consequences. Such a wrong label may well become a self-fulfilling prophecy.

Even if the label was justified, is there not a danger of backlash from the student labeled as being a bright high achiever? At some point, might this student ask, How come I always have to strive for a higher standard to get the same grade as others who have to do less? Consider the motivational implications of this!

And then there is the possibility, if we consider aptitude when grading, that the same level of achievement attained by two students in the same class could deserve different grades, especially in borderline cases. I know of no one who wants to try to explain *this* one to those students or their parents.

And finally there is the same "signal-noise" dilemma we faced with achievement. To the extent that different teachers define intelligence or ability or aptitude differently, assess it differently, and factor it into the grade computation equation differently, those who try to interpret the resulting grade later cannot hope to sort out those teachers' intended messages. This adds only noise to our communication system.

Resolution.   There are compelling arguments for and against factoring this student characteristic called *aptitude* into report card grades. Which shall win?

Time for Reflection

How do you sort out the arguments for and against? Take a position and articulate your defense before reading on.

The standards by which we judge the appropriateness of factoring intelligence into grades are the same as those we used for achievement. To justify incorporating it, we must be able to take action to overcome all arguments against it. Can we devise a definition of aptitude that translates into sound assessment that promises to treat each student equitably? Perhaps someday, but not today. We lack a defensible definition and the measurement tools needed to know students' intelligence. We can't even say for sure whether it's a stable human characteristic. There is no place for aptitude, ability, or intelligence in the report card grading equation. For now, these problems are insurmountable.

But, you might ask, what about all of those compelling arguments in favor of this practice? What about our desire to individualize so students and teachers can be motivated by the potential of success? What about the hope this practice seems to offer to perennial low achievers? Must we simply abandon these hopes and desires?

The answer is a clear and definite, No! But we must individualize on the basis of a student characteristic that we can define clearly, assess dependably, and link effectively to learning. I submit a far better candidate, a candidate that meets all requirements while not falling prey to the problems we experience in struggling with aptitude or intelligence. That individualizing factor is students' *prior achievement*.

Think of it this way: If we know where a student stands along the continuum of ascending levels of competence, then we know from our carefully planned continuous progress curriculum what comes next for that student. Thus, we can tailor instruction to help that student move on to that next step in mastery of knowledge, demonstrated reasoning proficiency, performance of required skills, and/or creation of required products. Each student's success in hitting those next targets, then, becomes the basis for our assignment of report card grades. Think of it as a contract between teacher and student where all agree on targets at the outset and then monitor progress continually together, until success is achieved.

Effort as a Grading Factor.   Remember that, in this case, the issue is framed as follows: Assume two students demonstrate exactly the same level of achievement, and that level happens to be right on the borderline between two grades. If one student obviously tried harder to learn, demonstrated more seriousness of purpose, or exhibited a higher level of motivation than did the other, is it appropriate to assign them different grades? Does level of effort have a place in the report card grading equation?

Arguments For.   Many teachers factor effort into their grading for a variety of apparently sound reasons. They see effort as being related to achievement: Those who try harder learn more. So by grading on effort, in effect, they believe that they are driving students toward greater achievement.

Besides, as a society, we value effort in its own right. Those who strive harder contribute more to our collective well-being. School seems an excellent place to begin teaching what is, after all, one of life's important lessons.

A subtle but related reason for factoring effort into the grade is that it appears to encourage risk taking, another characteristic we value in our society. A creative and energetic attempt to reach for something new and better should be rewarded, even if the striving student falls short of actual achievement success. And so, some think, it should be with risky attempts at achievement in school.

This may be especially important for perennial low achievers, who may not possess all of the intellectual tools and therefore may not have mastered all of the prerequisite knowledge needed to achieve. But the one thing within their control is how hard they try. So even if students are trapped in a tangle of inevitable failure because of their intellectual and academic history, at least they can derive some rewards for trying.

Thus, there are compelling reasons, indeed, for using effort as one basis for grades. Could anyone argue against such a practice?

Arguments Against.   In fact, we can. One such argument is that definitions of what it means to try hard vary greatly from teacher to teacher. Some definitions are relatively easy to translate into sound assessments: Those who complete all homework put forth effort. But other definitions are not: Trying hard means making positive contributions to the quality of the learning environment in our classroom. To the extent that teachers differ in their definition, assessment, and manner of integrating information about effort into the grading equation, we add noise to our grade interpretation. Message receivers simply have no way to uncover the subtleties of the teacher's intended message.

Besides, some teachers may say they want students to participate in class as a sign of their level of effort. But who most often controls who gets to contribute in class? The teacher. How, then, do we justify holding students accountable for participating when they don't control this factor?

Further, students can manipulate their apparent level of effort to mislead us. If, as a student, I know you grade in part on the basis of my level of effort and I care what grade I receive, I promise that I can behave in ways that make you believe that I am trying hard, whether I am or not. How can you know if I'm being honest?

From a different perspective, effort often translates into assertiveness in the learning environment. Those who assertively seek teacher attention and participate aggressively in learning activities are judged to be motivated. But what of naturally quieter or more timid students? Effort is less likely to be visible in their behavior regardless of its level. And this may carry with it gender and/or cultural differences, yielding the potential of systematic bias in grades as a function of factors unrelated to achievement. Members of some groups are enculturated to avoid competition. Gender, ethnicity, and personality traits have no place in the report card grading equation.

And finally, factoring effort into the grade may send the wrong message to students. In real life, just trying hard to do a good job is virtually never enough. If we don't deliver relevant, practical results, we will not be deemed successful, regardless of how hard we try.

Besides, from the perspective of basic school philosophy, What is it we really value, achieving, or achieving and knowing how to make it look like we tried hard? What if it was easy?!

Resolution.   The balance scale tips in favor of including effort in the computation of report card grades only if we can eliminate all arguments against including it.

Time for Reflection

Given the arguments of both sides, how do you come down on this one? How does the scale tip and why?

First, as a matter of general principle, we must decide what we value. If we value learning, then we must define it and build our reporting systems to share information about student success in learning. If we value effort too, then again we must arrive at a mutually acceptable definition and must devise appropriate assessment tools and procedures. If we value both, why must we combine them into the same grading equation? It's not complicated to devise reporting systems that present separate information on each.

Continuing the theme of what we value, what do we care about, learning, or learning and making it look hard? What if, as a student, it's easy for me? What if I don't need to put forth much effort to succeed? What if I don't have to practice? What if I can demonstrate mastery without doing hours of homework assignments? Am I to be penalized for this? *However we define and assess effort, there can be no penalty for those who need little effort to learn.*

Let's examine the other side as well. Let's say, as a student, I do need to practice a lot to learn and I don't take responsibility for doing so. Will that fact (my lack of effort) not be reflected in my lack of achievement? Certainly it will. I won't learn much. So if you factor my level of effort into the report card grade in addition to achievement, are you not in effect counting effort twice?

Then, after we define effort, we must assess it well. As we have established, the assessment must arise from a clear target, rely on a proper method of assessment, sample effort in a systematically representative manner, and control for all relevant sources of bias that can distort our assessment and mislead us. But if we use behavioral indicators of students' level of effort and most of the "trying hard" behaviors take place outside of our presence (i.e., at home) how can we know that we are sampling well or controlling for bias?

For example, here's one form of bias that is hard to overcome: When students set out purposely to mislead us with respect to their real level of effort, they can seriously bias our assessment. This may be impossible to eliminate as a problem. If we see 30 students per day all day for a year and some are misleading us about their real level of effort, we may well see through it. But as the number approaches and exceeds 150 students for one hour a day and sometimes only for a few months, as it does for many middle and high school teachers, there is no way to confidently and dependably determine how hard each student is trying.

Think about the implications of these problems for student motivation. Let's say that you gather undependable evidence and conclude that a student is not trying hard and, in fact, this is incorrect. That is, in the truth of the world, that student is giving maximum effort but you contend the opposite. What message does that send to the student? What effect is this turn of events likely to have on that student's desire to try hard and learn? Also consider the other error. What if you say that a student is trying hard and, in fact, he is not? What message does this send and what impact is that message likely to have?

Moreover, if effort influences the grades of some, equity demands that it have the same influence on all. The assessment and record-keeping challenges required to meet this standard are immense, to say the least.

But a more serious challenge again arises from the personality issue. Less aggressive people are not necessarily trying less hard. Quiet effort can be diligent and productive. As teachers, we really do have difficulty knowing how much effort most students are putting forth. And we have few ways of overcoming this problem, especially when most of the effort is expended outside the classroom.

If you can define effort clearly, treat all students consistently, and meet the standards of sound assessment, then gather your data and draw your inferences about each student's level of effort. Just be very careful how you use those results at report card grading time. This is a minefield that becomes even more dangerous when you combine effort and achievement data in the same grade. *I urge you to report them separately*, if you report effort outcomes at all.

Finding Better Ways to Motivate.   We grade on effort to motivate students to try hard. We feel that if they try hard, they will learn more. For those students who care about their grades, this may work. But if we are to understand other ways to motivate, we must also consider those cases in which our leverage has lost its power. We discussed this in Chapter 2. How shall we motivate those students who could not care less what grade we assign them, those who have given up and who are just biding their time until they can get out? For them, grades have lost all motivational value. If you think they are going to respond to our admonitions that they try harder so they can raise their grade, you are being naïve.

Consider this hypothetical situation: What would you do to encourage students to come to school and participate with you in the learning experiences you had designed for them if you could no longer use grades and report cards as a source of reward and punishment to control them?

Now consider these options: You might strive to learn students' needs and interests and align instruction to those. You might work with students to establish clear and specific targets so they would know that they were succeeding. In short, you could try to take the mystery out of succeeding in school.

You could be sure instructional activities were interesting and provocative, keeping the action moving, always keeping agreed targets in mind. You would share decision-making power to bring them into their learning as full partners, teaching them how to gauge their own success. In short, you would strive to establish in your students an internal locus of control over their own academic well-being. If they participate, they benefit, and they know this going in.

These ideas will work better as motivators than saying to students, "If you make it look too easy, I will lower your final grade," or, "If you convince me you are trying hard, I will raise your grade." The message we must send is "Hard work leads to higher achievement. Higher achievement leads to good grades." This is a tough love message. In effect it says, "Trying hard may or may not be important for you, but either way it's never good enough. Just doing the work does not get good grades. The only thing that gets good grades is the *learning* that comes from doing the work." Achievement standards never merely ask that students "try hard to become good writers." They always demand that students "become good writers." In a standards-driven environment, it's achievement that counts.

Compliance as a Grading Factor.   The issue in this case is, what role should adherence to school and classroom rules play in determining students' report card grades? If two students have demonstrated exactly the same level of achievement, but one disobeys the rules, should that student's grade be lowered?

Arguments For.   Of course it should. Consider the kinds of compliance that we absolutely must demand. What if students fail to come to school? The law says they must attend. If they're not in school, how can they learn? The threat of reduced or failing grades can compel attendance, as well as punctuality. Students are expected to learn important lessons of personal responsibility. Fail to show up on the job after school and you get fired. We can use grades to teach this lesson.

Another problematic behavior that we can control with the threat of grade reduction is cheating. If you cheat on a test, you get a zero. When averaged in at the end of the term, this will have the effect of radically reducing the final average and grade. This kind of punishment will deter cheating and, again, teach another important life lesson.

Besides, without factoring compliance into grading, how do we manage the classroom? Deadlines would mean nothing. If students thought they didn't have to get homework in on time, they'd never do it. Then we'd have no evidence on which to base their grade. Or they'd hand it in late all at once and the teacher's grading workload would become overwhelming. If we can't issue sanctions for misbehavior by connecting compliance with the rules to their grade, students would be out of control. We're talking about one of the teacher's most powerful classroom management tools here.

In real life, society expects us to follow the rules—to obey our agreed-on laws. It's the way we preserve the social order. Schools are supposed to be conveying to young people the lessons of behavior in a civil culture. Connecting grades to behavior helps us in that effort.

Compliance with the rules leads to greater student learning in at least two ways. First, as the teacher, I know better than my students do what is best for them. Learning is maximized when they follow my plan—comply with my wishes. If they deviate, learning suffers. Second, a well managed, compliant class permits everyone to benefit the most. If one or two students fail to follow the rules, everyone's learning suffers. We should not permit that to happen. It's not fair to the others.

Finally, while students are not in control of the academic ability that they bring to school, they are in complete control of whether they follow the rules and meet deadlines. So if they wish to influence the grades they receive, this is one concrete way for them to do it.

Arguments Against.   Before citing the counterarguments, I need to establish one key point. *It is very important for students to obey school and classroom rules.* Not only can those rules impact student learning, but they can protect their safety and well being.

But surprising as it may seem, that's not the issue in this case. When behaviors like truancy, tardiness, cheating and the like come up, as they did above, they inflame the rhetoric. I mentioned them in citing "arguments for" for just that reason. I wanted to show you how easy it is to draw your attention away from the essential issue. These behaviors are counterproductive and need to be addressed. But the question is how? If our desire is to punish them in the hope that we can extinguish the undesirable behaviors, then what is the most appropriate way to punish? Is the lowering of one's report card grade the best way?

If we do issue sanctions in the form of lowered grades, then the accuracy of the information about student achievement contained within the grade suffers and miscommunication is assured. Let me explain how. Let's say a student had taken four of five exams during a grading period and averaged 93% across all of them. Then this student is accused of cheating on the fifth exam and is given a zero in the grade book. To add to the intrigue of this case, let's say that, in the truth of the world, this student had in fact mastered the material of that last exam and could have attained another very high score. So if we wanted to communicate accurately about the achievement of this student we would assign an A on the report card to deliver a message to all message receivers of almost total mastery of the material.

However, when we factor the zero into the average, the result is 74% (93 times 4 on the first four exams plus zero on the fifth exam equals 374 divided by 5 equals 74) or a C on the report card. The effect is a complete misrepresentation of the student's level of achievement. Miscommunication. We have no way to let the various message receivers know the subtle message hidden in this grade. Is it wise to completely sacrifice any hope of accurate communication in order to punish the alleged dishonest behavior? Are there no other punishment options that don't result in such profound communication breakdown?

Besides, once again we must consider the noise that is introduced into our communication system if every teacher defines standards of compliance differently, gathers evidence of different sorts and gives compliance issues different weight in the determination of their particular grades. The message receiver will always have difficulty determining what the report card grade is supposed to mean. Miscommunication will result.

Finally, we have to be very careful about the messages our grading practices send to our students. Sometimes adult life presents us with situations where it might be wise to challenge established rules. While I would never advocate violation of accepted codes of behavior, if our nation's forefathers and mothers had merely obeyed the prescribed rules, where would our country be today? Obviously, I am not encouraging rebellion. But we must help our students keep perspective regarding the meaning and role of compliance.

Time for Reflection

How do you sort out these arguments for and against? Take a position and articulate your defense before reading on.

Resolution.   To be sure, as mentioned previously, violation of some school or classroom rules unacceptable. Sometimes, stiff penalties should be imposed.

However, I believe that the decisions that will be made based on the achievement information contained in report card grades are too important to permit its accuracy to be sacrificed by permitting grades to be lowered as punishment for behaviors unrelated to actual achievement. Besides, there is strong legal precedent for this perspective. The courts have consistently disallowed grading policies that, for example, permit grade reduction for poor attendance. When the use of grade reduction as punishment has the effect of distorting the student's academic record, we violate the student's constitutional guarantees to equal access to future educational opportunities. By factoring things other than achievement into a report card grade, like compliance with the rules, we distort and thus misrepresent the student's true academic record. According to the rulings of several federal district courts, this is unjust (Bartlett, 1987).

Let me hasten to add that the courts also have upheld the school's right to administer punishment for violating the rules. It's just that the punishment cannot lead to a distortion of the student's record of achievement. The courts compel us to separate the punishment, whatever that is, from our grading practices.

So in the case of cheating cited above, the school is justified in administering fair punishment. But that punishment cannot have the effect of reducing the student's grade. The only acceptable course of action is to administer another fifth exam, average the resulting score with the other four, and assign the grade indicated by that average.

We have plenty of appropriate punishment options at our disposal that don't distort the record and violate student rights, like detention, limiting access to desirable activities, community service, and so on. There is no need to sacrifice the accuracy of our communication.

Attitude as a Grading Factor.   You understand the problem: Two students attain exactly the same level of achievement. Their semester academic average is on the cutoff between two letter grades. One has constantly exhibited a positive attitude, while the other has been consistently negative. Are you justified if you assign them different grades?

Arguments For.   A positive attitude is a valued outcome of school. Anything we can do to promote it is an effective practice. People with positive attitudes tend to secure more of life's rewards. School is an excellent place to begin to teach this lesson.

Besides, this just may be the most effective classroom management tool we teachers have at our disposal. If we define *positive attitude* as treating others well, listening to the teacher, interacting appropriately with classmates, and the like, then we can use the controlling leverage of the grade to maintain a quiet, orderly learning environment.

And, once again, this represents a way for us to channel at least some classroom rewards to perennial low achievers. As with effort, attitude is within students' control. If they're "good," they can experience some success. Sounds good, let's make it part of the grading equation!

Arguments Against.   It is seldom clear exactly which attitudes are supposed to be positive. Are students supposed to be positive about fellow students, the teacher, school subjects, school in general, or some combination of these? Must all be positive or just some? What combinations are acceptable?

How shall we define a positive attitude? As teachers, we value different human characteristics. Is it positive to accept an injustice in the classroom compliantly, or is it positive to stand up for what you think is right? What is the important value here? Is it positive to act as if you like story problems in math, when in fact you're frustrated because you don't understand them? The definition of "positive attitude" is not always clear.

Further, if students can manipulate their apparent effort, so can they manipulate their apparent attitude. Regardless of my real feelings, if I think you want me to be positive and if I care about that grade, you can bet that I will exhibit whatever behavior you wish. Is dishonest game-playing a valued outcome of education?

Assessment also can be a source of difficulty in this case. It takes a special understanding of paper and pencil assessment methodology, performance assessment methods, and personal communication to evaluate affective outcomes such as attitudes, as you saw in Chapter 11. The rules of evidence for quality assessment are challenging, as you will recall from our earlier discussion of the assessment of affect. So mismeasurement is a very real danger.

Oh, and as usual, to the extent that different teachers hold different values about which attitudes are supposed to be positive, devise different definitions of positive, assess attitudes more or less well, and assign them different weights in the grading equation, we factor even more noise into our communication system.

Some pretty tough problems . . .

Time for Reflection

Once again, are you for or against? Make your stand and then read on.

Resolution.   To decide which side of the balance sheet wins out here, we must determine which use of attitude information produces the greatest good *for students*. Let's say we encounter an extremely negative attitude on the part of one student about a particular school subject. Which use serves that student better: Citing your evidence of the attitude problem (gathered through a good assessment) and telling that student she or he had better turn it around before the end of the grading period or their grade will be lowered? Or, accepting the attitude as real and talking with the student honestly and openly about the attitude and its origins (using high-quality assessment of this disposition through personal communication) in an honest attempt to separate it from achievement and deal with it in an informed manner?

The power of attitude data lies, not in its potential to help us control behavior, but in helping us promote more positive learners and learning environments. If we go through the difficulty of

1. Defining the attitudes we want to be positive (and this can be done),

2. Devising systematic, high-quality assessments of those attitudes (which can be done, too), and

3. Collecting representative samples of student attitudes (an eminently achievable goal),

and then we fail to use the results to inform instructional design, choosing only to factor the results into grades, we have wasted an immense opportunity to help students.

If we enlist students as partners, they are likely to be even more honest with us about how they feel about their learning environment, thus providing us with even more ammunition for improving instruction. But if you think for one moment students are likely to be honest with us in communicating attitudes if they think the results might be used against them at grading time, you are being naïve.

Although we might be able to overcome the difficulties associated with defining attitudes for grading purposes, and can overcome the assessment difficulties attendant to these kinds of outcomes, I personally think it is bad practice to factor attitudes into report card grades.

Summary of Grading Factors

In an era of standards-driven schools, if report card grades are to serve decision makers, they must reflect student attainment of specific achievement targets. Only then can we teachers, for example, know where students are now in relation to where we want to take them. For this reason, grading systems must include indicators of student achievement unencumbered by other student characteristics, such as aptitude, effort, compliance, or attitude. This is not to say that we should not report information about nonachievement factors, if definition and assessment difficulties can be overcome, which is no small challenge. But under any circumstances, aptitude or intelligence or ability have no place in grade reporting.

Grades can help us communicate effectively about student success in meeting our achievement expectations only if we clearly define these expectations in each grading context for a given grading period, develop sound assessments for those outcomes, and keep careful records of student attainment of the achievement expectations over the grading period. In the next section, we explore these procedures in detail.

Gathering Achievement Information for Grading Purposes

If report card grades are to inform students, parents, other teachers, administrators, and others about student achievement, then we must clearly and completely articulate and assess the actual achievement underpinning each grade. To be effective, we must spell out the valued targets before the grading period begins. Further, we must lay out in advance an assessment plan to systematically sample those targets. While it sounds like a great deal of preparation to complete before teaching begins, it saves a great deal of assessment work during instruction.

Remember the great benefits of being clear about your achievement targets:

- *They set limits on teacher accountability*—you know the limits of your teaching responsibility. When the target is clear and appropriate and all of your students can hit it, you are successful as a teacher.

- *They set limits on student accountability*—they know the limits of their learning responsibility. When they can hit the valued target, they are successful as students. And the less mysterious that target is, the more serious they will be about striving to hit it.

- *Clear targets allow students to share in a great deal of the assessment work,* thus turning assessment time into valuable teaching and learning time.

Let's look at an effective and efficient five-step plan for gathering sound and appropriate achievement information for grading purposes. Figure 13.1 summarizes the key steps.

Step 1: Spelling out the Big Achievement Picture

To complete a picture of the valued achievement targets for a given subject over a grading period, gather together all relevant curricular and text materials and ask four questions (they will sound very familiar!):

- What is the subject matter *knowledge* that students are to master? Outline the big ideas and essential concepts that you want students to know and understand. Write them out.

- What patterns of *reasoning* and problem-solving are they to master? Specify each of them in writing.

- What *performance skills,* if any, are students to demonstrate? What things do they need to be able to do? List them.

- What *products,* if any, are they to create and what are the attributes of a good one? Outline them.

Figure 13.1
Steps in report card grading

1. Begin the grading period with a comprehensive set of achievement expectations.
2. Transform that "big picture" into an assessment plan describing evidence-gathering tactics.
3. Develop and administer the specific assessments as instruction unfolds.
4. Summarize assessment results into a composite index of achievement for each student.
5. Convert the composite into a grade.

Further, if you have a sense of the relative importance of these four kinds of targets in your overall instructional plan, write down those priorities, with relative emphasis in the form of percentages that add to 100.

By the way, I do not list disposition targets here, not because they are unimportant, but because, as discussed, they should not play a role in report card grading decisions.

The targets you select for students obviously will form the basis of your actual assessments and instruction. For now, simply create a general outline of the important elements of your big assessment picture, spelled out in your own words. In short, immerse yourself in this and force yourself to set priorities within and to impose limits on it.

As you do this, if any part of this picture remains unclear, you have several places to turn for help: state or local content or performance standards, curriculum goals and objectives, your text and its support materials, your principal, department chair, or colleagues, and your professional library.

Here is another productive way to think about this planning (we have discussed this idea before): States or districts that adopt an achievement-driven mission for their schools typically begin by working with their communities to agree on a set of achievement expectations for students in their school system. From that start, then, it is up to educators, working across all grade levels, to back those expectations down into the curriculum and divide up responsibility for helping students progress smoothly through the various levels of competence. Teachers from kindergarten through twelfth grade must collaborate with one another to plan this integrated and articulated instructional program. Only then can the progression of students' growth be coordinated over their years of schooling. The purpose of this planning is to be sure that you and each of your colleagues understand how your contribution will contribute to the long-term evolution of student competence. From that process you must derive a clear sense of the knowledge, reasoning, skills, and product development capabilities that are your instructional responsibility.

As you prepare to present each unit of instruction, you will need to provide your students with the opportunity to learn to hit each of the kinds of achievement targets you have set out for them. There should be one-to-one correspondence between targets and instruction. For each target, you should be able to point to its coverage in your instructional plans.

Step 2: Turning Your Big Picture into an Assessment Plan

Once you are clear about your targets, your assessment and report card grading challenge is clearly drawn. The next question is, How will you assess to accumulate evidence of each student's attainment of those targets? Taken together, the assessments that you use over time must help you determine, with confidence, what proportion of the total array of achievement expectations each student has met. In other words, what specific assessments (selected response, essay, performance, personal communication) will provide you with an accurate estimate of how much of the required material each student has mastered? You need an assessment plan to determine this.

A series of valid and reliable assessments assemble into a dependable portrait of total achievement for each student.

You don't need the assessments themselves, not yet. Those come later, as each unit of instruction unfolds. But you do need to know how you will take students down the assessment road, from "Here are my expectations" to "Here is your grade," making sure both you and they know how they are progressing all along that road. The assessment plan that you start the grading period with needs to satisfy certain conditions:

- It must list each assessment you will conduct during the grading period, detailing the expected achievement target focus of each, approximately when you expect the assessment to take place, what assessment method(s) you will use.

- Each assessment listed in the plan needs to supply an important piece of the puzzle with respect to the priority targets of the unit and grading period within which it occurs.

- Each assessment must accurately represent the particular targets(s) it is supposed to depict (i.e., each must be a sound assessment according to our five quality standards).

- The full array of assessments conducted over the entire grading period must accurately determine the proportion of your expectations that each student has attained.

- The entire assessment plan must involve a reasonable assessment workload for both you and your students.

A Reality Check.   These conditions may be easier to meet than you think. The report card grading challenge is to gather just enough information to make confident grading decisions and no more. Ask yourself: How can I gather the fewest possible assessments for grading and still generate an accurate estimate of performance? I believe that most teachers spend entirely too much time gathering and grading too many assessments. Some feel they must grade virtually everything students do and enter each piece of work into the record to assign accurate report card grades. This is simply not true. With planned, strategic assessments, you can generate accurate estimates of performance very economically.

I also see many teachers operating on the shotgun principle of grading: Just gather a huge array of graded student work over the course of the grading period, and surely somewhere, somehow, some of it will reflect some of the valued targets. While this may be true in part, this approach is at best inefficient. Why not plan ahead and minimize your assessment work?

If you can zero in on the key targets and draw dependable inferences about student mastery of big picture targets with a few unit assessments and a final exam or project assignment, that's all you need to produce report card grades that reflect student achievement.

Assessments for Learning, But Not for Grading.   Let's be sure to remember that we don't assess in the classroom merely for the purpose of assigning grades. We established that fact very early in Chapters 1 and 2. We also assess to diagnose student needs, provide students with practice performing or evaluate their performance, and track student growth as a result of instruction. In fact, sometimes we assess just to boost student confidence or to help them focus their studies.

For example, I give my students assignments every class and inform them that practice is critical for performing well on the final essay exam. Our agreement is that if they wish to hand in practice assignments for feedback, I'll be pleased to provide it. Some take advantage of this opportunity. Some don't. But there is no grade involved in this "homework for practice" process.

Generally, it's a bad idea to factor into the report card grade student performance on assessments used for purposes other than grading. Self-assessment is used for diagnosing needs. We don't grade students when they are evaluating their own needs. Practice assessments are for polishing skills, overcoming problems, and fine tuning performance. We shouldn't grade students when they are trying to learn from their mistakes. Students need time simply to muck around with new learnings, time to discover through risk-free experimentation, time to fail and learn from it without the shadow of evaluative judgment.

Experienced teachers who read this might say, "If I don't assign a grade and have it count toward the report card grade, students won't take it seriously, they won't do it!" Trust me. Once students come to understand that practice helps, but performance on subsequent assessments is what counts for the grade, they will learn to practice, if they need to. They must take responsibility for developing their own sense of control over their success. This is exactly the point Covington (1992) made, as discussed in Chapter 2, when we spoke of developing an internal sense of responsibility for one's own success.

While it might take some time to break old dependencies, *once our students come to understand that good grades are not the rewards for doing work but are rather a signal of their success at achieving through studying effectively, I think they will practice as needed*, especially if that practice can take place in a supportive, success-oriented classroom.

Academic success requires a collaborative partnership, with both partners fulfilling their part of the bargain. Has that occurred? As a teacher, you can provide the supportive environment, opportunity, and means to learn. But you cannot do the learning for your students. As a teacher, you must set limits on your contribution. All you can do is be sure students see the relationship between practice and successful performance on the assessments that contribute to their grades.

But, let's say a student fails to practice on interim assignments and performs poorly on the assessment that counts for the grade. As a teacher, how do you respond? One option is to say, "I told you so," and let it go so you can move on to the new stuff. Another response is, "I guess you found out how important practice is, didn't you? Nevertheless, I value your learning whenever it occurs. Do you want to practice now and redo the assessment? If you do, I will reevaluate your performance, no penalties. But that reevaluation will need to fit into my schedule."

Incidentally, you can prepare for such retest eventualities by developing more than one form of your graded assessments. That may mean creating more than one set of items reflecting your tables of test specifications or more than one sample of tasks for your performance assessments. Remember, in the latter case, the performance criteria would be held constant. Just be sure these alternate forms are parallel, that they sample exactly the same achievement targets.

Your job as a teacher is to set appropriate targets that reflect your assigned teaching responsibilities. Then agree with your students and your supervisor that you will do everything ethical within your power to maximize student success in hitting those targets.

That means *there is no artificial scarcity of high grades*. If you want to see students rapidly become hopeless failure acceptors, just set up an environment in which they actually learn a great deal but receive low grades. In a healthy, success-oriented classroom, if everyone succeeds, everyone receives a high grade. The more students believe they can succeed, the more seriously they will practice in preparation for the assessments that contribute to their grades. You need conduct only enough assessments during a grading period to identify when that learning has happened.

Step 3: From a Plan to Actual Assessments

So you begin the grading period with your assessment plan in hand. What next? You then need to devise or select the actual assessments for each unit, being sure to follow the assessment development guidelines specified in Chapters 5 through 8. You will need to create and conduct each assessment, evaluating and recording the results as you go.

In each case where you have knowledge and reasoning targets to assess via selected response or essay assessments, you need to devise those specific assessments around precisely defined categories of knowledge and kinds of reasoning. You can capture these in lists of objectives, tables of specification, propositions, and finally the test exercises themselves, which you may assemble into assignments, quizzes, and tests.

When assessing skill and product outcomes, you need to assemble performance criteria, tasks to elicit performance, and rating scales or checklists. Each component assessment fills in part of your big picture.

All assessments should also align exactly with your vision of student competence. Although you may develop some in advance, to save time later, you may develop others during instruction and involve students in the process. I know this sounds like a great deal of work, but remember six important facts:

1. This grading approach is not nearly as much work as the shotgun approach.

2. It affords the conscientious teacher a great deal more peace of mind. When your students succeed, you will know that you have been successful.

3. Students can play key roles in specific ways spelled out earlier, thus turning nearly all of this assessment time and energy into productive learning time and energy.

4. Student motivation to learn is likely to increase; "no surprises, no excuses" leads to a success orientation.

5. Your plan remains intact for you to use or adapt the next time you teach the same material, and the time after that. Thus, development costs are spread out over the useful life of your plan and its associated assessments.

6. Assess a lot, with student help, but don't grade everything—make time for practice.

A Comment on Assigning Grades to Individual Assessments and Assignments. Because it is common practice to assign grades to the component assessments, such as assignments, during the grading period, not just at report card time, we need to reflect for a moment on this meaning of "grading." Think of your big picture of achievement expectations as a mosaic, with small tiles (each component assessment) coming together to tell the overall story. In fact, each component assessment represents its own small mosaic in the sense that it too is made up of its own small tiles, the exercises (e.g., test items) used to sample student achievement. If in the end you wish to draw conclusions about the proportion of your overall set of expectations each student has met, then each component assessment must help you see what proportion of its targets each student has mastered. When you combine all of these component assessment results at grade computation time (i.e., combine all of the tiles in the form of individual assessment grades into the mosaic) you create the overall picture of student achievement you need. I'll share an example later in the chapter to illustrate.

Given the mosaic metaphor, it should be clear to you why step two, building an assessment plan, is so critical. How do you plan instruction to help students master the mosaic if you don't know, in advance, how the overall picture comes together? Or even more importantly, how do you help them practice hitting targets not yet specified? This has been our theme throughout our journey together. It is relevant in the grading process, too. At no point during the grading period should either you or your students have any question about what grade students are achieving at that point in time. Both you and they should know how much of the big picture has been covered as well as how much they have mastered, based on component grades.

Further, at no point should students feel that they can no longer influence the grade they receive. At one point in high school, a student I know informed her parents that her algebra teacher told her two weeks before the end of the semester that she was going to get a C on her report card regardless of how she did on the final exam. Would you care to speculate how much algebra she learned after that announcement? Only students who possess some hope of succeeding are likely to succeed.

As you carry out your plan, developing and administering your assessments when appropriate as the grading period progresses, you will need to keep good records. Here are a few guidelines to follow:

- Maintain written records. Remember the fallibility of the human mind; no mental record keeping.

- Include as much detail in the accumulated records as you can. If scores result, record them as is. Don't convert them to a grade and record the grade, thus unnecessarily sacrificing information that could be useful later. Or, if a profile of performance ratings results, such as when you use a performance assessment with several rating scales, record the profile. Again, don't convert the information to a grade and lose valuable detail. Instead, record percent correct in the first case or actual profiles of ratings in the second.

- If you are going to weigh scores differently later to compute a composite index of achievement (i.e., you regard some assessments as more important than others because they reflect attainment of critical material, or just cover more material) record those scores in the same units, such as percent of total available points. This is illustrated in step 5 later in the chapter.

When you have carried out your assessment plan and collected the records, the time has come to generate a composite index of achievement for conversion to a grade. Incidentally, teachers have discovered that they can easily store, retrieve, and summarize grading records and convert them to actual grades using their personal computers. Software packages are available that can serve as your gradebook and much more. More about this later in the chapter.

Step 4: Summarizing the Resulting Information

At the end of the grading period, your recording will result in a range of information indicating students' performance on each of the components in your strategic assessment plan. This constitutes a portrait of how well each student mastered the targets that made up your big picture. The question is, how do you get a grade out of all of this information?

I urge you to rely on a consistent computational sequence for all students that you can reproduce later should you need to explain the process or revise a grade. Such a sequence helps to control for your personal biases, which may either inappropriately inflate or deflate a grade for reasons unrelated to actual achievement.

Please note that I am not opposed to a role for professional judgment in grading. As we established in earlier chapters, that role comes in the design and administration of the assessments used to gather information about student achievement. We need to minimize subjectivity when combining indicators of achievement for grading purposes. Let the evidence speak for itself.

Combining Achievement Information.   To derive a meaningful grade from several records of achievement, again, *each piece of information gathered should indicate the proportion of the targets each student has mastered*. So, if we combine them all, we should obtain an estimate of the proportion mastered for the total grading period. Remember the mosaic? Two relatively simple ways to achieve it are the percent method and the total points method.

Percent Method.   Convert each student's performance on each contributing assessment into a percent of total possible points. If you convert everything to the same percent scale, then both recordkeeping and later averaging become much simpler. For instance, if a selected response test has 40 items, and a student answers 30 correct, enter 75 percent in the record. But be careful with performance assessment. If a student scores all 4s on six 5-point performance assessment rating scales, that totals 24 of 30 possible points, or 80 percent. However, for reasons explained later in the chapter, I recommend against this grade computation practice. While several analytical scales can be combined in this manner, I recommend treating them differently in grading.

Beware of holistic ratings too. Let's say you are rating student performance on a single 4-point holistic scale. Only five percentage scores are available for conversion: 100 percent (4 of 4), 75 (3 of 4), 50, 25, or 0. There is simply not enough precision in such a scale to permit meaningful conversion to percents or grades.

Time for Reflection

Think about the assumption being made here. If those 40 test items have been carefully selected during test development to sample a defined domain of content, then we can confidently conclude that this student probably mastered about 75 percent of that domain. Under what specific conditions is this an acceptable conclusion? What could cause such a conclusion to be wrong?

If the individual assessment results recorded as percentages are averaged across all assessments for a whole grading period, then the result should indicate the proportion of the total array of expectations for that grading period that each student has mastered. In effect, translating each score to a percent places all on the same scale for averaging purposes and permits you to combine them in an easily interpreted manner, in terms of intended targets.

With this procedure, if you wish to give greater weight to some assessment results than to others, you can accomplish this by multiplying those scores by their weight before adding them into the overall computation. For instance, if some are to count twice as much as others, simply multiply their percentages by two before summing to arrive at an average. Here's an example: Let's say you administer three tests during a grading period, all of which contribute to the grade. But one test (number 3) covers a much broader segment of the curriculum than do the other two. So you weigh it at twice the value of the other tests. The result is a higher grade that is more reflective of student mastery of the big picture of achievement expectations, as shown in the following table.

Test	% Coverage	Student Score %	Unweighted Average	Weighted Grades
1	25	60	60	60
2	25	80	80	80
3	50	90	90	180 (counted twice, as covers more)
Average			$230 \div 3 = 77$	$320 \div 4 = 80$
Grade assigned			C	B

Time for Reflection

Under what conditions might you assign some assessment results a higher weight than others in your grading?

With this system of record keeping and grade computation based on percents, everyone involved can know at any particular point in time how their scores, to that date, relate to expectations to date. This permits students to remain aware of and in control of their success. Some teachers also ask students to assign their own grade as a means of promoting student self-evaluation. If information gathering, storage, and retrieval systems are working effectively, there should be total agreement between teacher and students at all times about what grade students are earning.

Total Points Method.   Another way to combine information is to define the target for a grading period in terms of a total number of points. Students who earn all or most of the points demonstrate mastery of all or most of the valued targets and earn a high grade.

In this case, each individual assessment contributes a certain number of points to the total. If you carefully plan this so the points earned on each assessment reflect their fair share of the big picture, then at the end of the grading period you can simply add up each student's points and determine what percentage of the total each student earned. That percentage of total points, then, represents the proportion of valued targets attained. Just remember that the assessments that result in the largest number of points will contribute the most to the determination of the final grade.

This fact makes differential weighting possible. Just be sure that you assign a large number of points to those assessments (such as final exams or large projects) that cover the largest proportions of the valued targets and fewer points to the assessments (such as daily assignments) that are narrower in focus.

Either of these options provides an acceptable basis for clearly communicating via report card grades about student achievement. But be careful, difficulties can arise! We discuss next some of these difficulties, and offer ways to handle them.

Some Practical Advice.   Unless you carefully develop and summarize assessments, the result may be misleading about the proportion of the total achievement picture that students have mastered. Let me illustrate.

Using the Most Current Information.   Let's say your strategic assessment plan includes five unit assessments and a comprehensive final exam that covers the entire set of targets for the grading period. And, say a particular student starts slowly, scoring very low on the first two unit assessments, but gains momentum and attains a perfect score on the comprehensive final exam, revealing, in effect, subsequent mastery of the material covered in those first two unit assessments.

The key grading question is this: Which piece of information provides the most accurate depiction of that student's real achievement at the end of the grading period, the final exam score or that score averaged with all five unit tests? If the final is truly comprehensive, averaging it with those first two unit assessments will result in misleading information.

If students demonstrate achievement at any time that, in effect, renders past assessment information invalid, then you must drop the former assessment from the record and replace it with the new—even if the new information reflects a lower level of achievement. To do otherwise is to misrepresent that achievement.

Grading on Status versus Improvement.   An issue many teachers struggle with is whether a grade should reflect a student's achievement status at the end of the grading period or improvement over time. The resolution of this important issue lies in understanding the immense difficulties we face in dealing with the concept of improvement.

If *improvement* means that those who gain more over time get higher grades, students who happen to arrive knowing less have an advantage. Is that fair to those who arrive knowing more? Besides, to grade on improvement, you need to establish a baseline by conducting a comprehensive preassessment of students on all relevant outcomes for that grading period. We are seldom able to preassess in this manner. And even if you could, you would face challenging statistical problems in dealing effectively with the undependable "gain scores" that would result.

Then, over and above these problems, how do you deal with academically challenged students who might grow at a much slower rate than others? Shall they be penalized because of factors beyond their control? Regardless of their rate of improvement, however, if they meet the objectives framed for them in their IEP, then they deserve recognition for success.

For all of these reasons, grades should reflect each student's end status in attaining the prespecified targets in that classroom during the grading period just completed.

Time for Reflection

Given this guideline, if a special education student is "mainstreamed" into a regular classroom, is it possible for that student to receive an A on the report card—even though other students are hitting much higher targets? Collect your thoughts on this and we will return to it later.

What about Borderline Cases?   Another common problem arises when a particular student's academic average is literally right on the borderline between two grades and you just don't know which way to go. Some teachers allow factors unrelated to achievement to push the grade one way or the other. We addressed the unacceptability of that approach previously. A better way to determine such grades is to collect one or two significant pieces of achievement data during grading that overlap other assessments, thus double checking previous information about achievement. Hold these assessments in reserve, don't factor them into your grades. Then, if you need "swing votes," use them to help you decide which grade to assign. This keeps unrelated factors out of both the grading decision and the communication system.

Grading in a Cooperative Learning Context.   With the increasing popularity of cooperative learning environments, questions often arise about how to treat grading. If students achieve together, how does that get factored into the grade? The simple rule is this: Grades to be assigned and communicated on report cards need to provide dependable information about the actual achievement of the *individual students* graded. This means that grading in a cooperative environment must include procedures that permit individual students to demonstrate their attainment of the prescribed targets. If there is any doubt that a score on a group performance reflects the achievement of any group member, then it has no place in grade computation for that student.

Dealing with Cheating.   Let me address this one more time: A student cheats on a test and, as punishment, is given a zero in the gradebook, to be averaged with other assessments to determine the semester grade.

The problem in this instance is that the zero may systematically misrepresent that student's real achievement. *This is not acceptable under any circumstances.* Consequently, you must separate the grade and the discipline for cheating. You should retest the student to determine real levels of achievement and enter that retest score into your gradebook. Cheating should not be punished via grade reduction if you are to communicate accurately.

Awarding "Extra Credit."   Some teachers try to encourage extra effort on the part of their students by offering extra credit opportunities. You must be very careful of the message you send here. If grades are to reflect achievement, you must deliver the consistent message that *the more you learn, the better your grade.* If extra credit work is specifically designed to provide dependable information that students have learned more, then it should influence the grade assigned. But if students come to believe that merely doing the work, whether or not it results in greater learning, is sufficient to attain a higher grade, then it is counterproductive. To communicate effectively, grades must reflect the amount learned—not how much work was done to accomplish the learning.

The Matter of Unsound Grading Policies.   Sometimes, district policy can cause serious grading problems. For instance, some districts link grades to attendance. A policy might specify that more than five unexcused absences in a given grading period must result in an F for the student, regardless of actual achievement. In the case in which a student has mastered enough of the material to receive a higher grade, this policy leads to the purposeful misrepresentation of actual student achievement, and is unacceptable. Administrative policies that mislead anyone about academic achievement and that interfere with report card grading must be avoided if we are to communicate accurately about student attainment.

Advance Notice.   Another critically important guideline to follow is to be sure all students know and understand in advance the procedures you will use to compute their grades. What assessments will you conduct, when, and how will you factor each into your grading? What are students' timelines, deadlines, and important responsibilities? *If students know their responsibilities up front, they have a good chance of succeeding.*

Grades and Heterogeneous Grouping.   There is just one more very difficult challenge to address: How do we grade different students in the same classroom who are striving to attain fundamentally different targets? As we try to mainstream special needs students and students from diverse cultural and linguistic backgrounds, this becomes a critical issue. It is critical because I think I just described *every* classroom.

In a classroom of mixed ability, for instance, one student might be working on basic math concepts, while another is moving toward prealgebra. If both hit their respective targets, each deserves an A. But those A's mean fundamentally different things. How is someone reading the report cards of these two students to be made aware of this critical difference?

If we report the grade alone, they cannot. We are doomed to miscommunicate. In my opinion, this single problem renders simple letter grade-based communication systems inadequate to meet our communication needs in a standards-driven educational environment. The only solution I can find for this problem is to add greater detail to the reporting system, by identifying the achievement targets covered by the grade reported. Without that detail, we cannot communicate about individual differences in the grades assigned within the same classroom.

The Bottom Line.   In developing sound grading practices for use in communicating about achievement, logic dictates that you start with a clear vision of targets, translate it into quality assessments, and always remain mindful of that big achievement picture for a given grading period. Then you must follow this simple rule (another part of the art of classroom assessment): *Grades must convey as accurate a picture of a student's real achievement as possible. Any practice that has the effect of misrepresenting real achievement is unacceptable.* Figure 13.2 presents a summary of guidelines for avoiding the problems we have discussed here.

> When we try to pack a wide variety of student characteristics into one grade, that grade is not a valid reflection of any one of them.
>
> TECHNICAL NOTE

Step 5: Converting Composite Achievement Scores to a Grade

Once you have attained an average or total set of points or some other overall index of student achievement for the grading period, you face the final and in some ways most difficult decision in your grading: What grade do you report?

- Grade on achievement of prespecified targets only, not intelligence, effort, attitude, or personality.
- Always rely on the most current information available about student achievement.
- Devise grades that reflect achievement status with respect to preset targets rather than improvement.
- Decide borderline cases with additional information on achievement.
- Keep grading procedures separate from punishment.
- Change all policies that lead to miscommunication about achievement.
- Advise students of grading practices in advance.
- Add further detail to grade report when needed.
- Expect individual accountability for learning even in cooperative environments.
- Give credit for evidence of extra learning—not for doing extra work if it fails to result in extra learning.

Figure 13.2
Practical guidelines for avoiding common grading problems

Over the years, some districts and schools have opted simply to report that final achievement average in the form of a percentage score. This has the benefit of permitting the record to convey the maximum amount of available information about a student's achievement. In doing so, no useful information is sacrificed by converting it to another scale. That's good.

But most districts require teachers to convert the academic achievement average or point total to a letter or number grade, from A to F or from 4.0 to 0. This has the effect of sacrificing a great deal of available information. For instance, a range of scores, say the ten points between 90 to 100 percent, are all transformed into just one point on the grade scale, and in effect, are made equal.

The key question is, How do you convert a composite index of student achievement into an accurate report card grade? Traditionally, we have accomplished this in one of the following ways:

- Grading in terms of preset performance standards
- Assigning students grades according to their place in the rank order of class members

In an era of achievement or performance-driven education, only the first option makes sense. Let's explore each and see why.

Grading with Preset Standards.   Grading in terms of preset standards says, Here are the assessments that represent the achievement targets; score at this level on them and this is the grade you will receive. A set of percentage cutoff scores is set and all who score within certain ranges receive that designated grade:

90–100 = A
80–89 = B
70–79 = C
etc.

Time for Reflection

Before you read on, please take just a minute to think about this kind of conversion plan. What do you think are both the strengths and weaknesses of this method?

If two important conditions are met, this method maximizes the opportunity for success for students. Those conditions are (1) that students possess the prerequisites to master the required material, and (2) that assessments accurately represent the targets on which you will base the grade.

One advantage of this system is that the meaning of the grade is clearly couched in the attainment of intended achievement targets. Another is that it is computationally simple; you need only know how to compute percentages and averages. Still another strength is that grades can work effectively in the context of a continuous progress curriculum. As students master prerequisites for later, more advanced work, as indicated by high grades, teachers can know that they are ready for the next stage. A fourth advantage is that grading in terms of preset standards increases the possibility that all students can succeed, if they achieve. And finally, from your perspective, if you as a teacher become more effective over time, greater student success will be reflected in a greater proportion of higher grades.

However, grading in terms of predetermined percentage cutoff scores is not without its limitations. For instance, the cutoff scores themselves are arbitrary. There is no substantive or scientific reason why 90 to 100 percent should be considered an A. This cutoff, and those used to assign other grades, represent social conventions adopted over decades. As a result, cutoffs vary from district to district, school to school, and even teacher to teacher. The range for an A in some places may be 94 to 100 percent, for example. Although these differences cannot be eliminated, we can acknowledge the lack of precision they imply. Just be sure everyone knows what conventions of communication (cutoff scores) you are using.

Grading on a Curve.   The tactic of assigning grades based on students' place in the rank order of achievement scores within a class is commonly referred to as "grading on a curve." In its classic application, the teacher uses the composite index of achievement for each student to rank students from the highest to the lowest score. Then, counting from the top, the teacher counts off 7 percent of the students on the list. These students receive As. Then the next 24 percent receive Bs, and so on down to the bottom 7 percent of students, who are assigned Fs.

Another variation on this method is to tally how many students attained each score and then to graph that distribution to find natural gaps between groups of scores that appear to permit division into groups of students to whom you can then assign different grades.

These ranking methods have the strength of yielding a grade that is interpreted in terms of group performance. They also have the effect of promoting competition among students: Students will know that their challenge is to outscore the others.

But in a context in which high achievement is the goal, the limitations of such a system become far more prominent than the strengths. The percentage of students receiving each grade is not a matter of science. Again, the cutoffs are arbitrary, and once grades are assigned and recorded on the transcript, no user of that grade information will necessarily know or understand the system of cutoffs used by the grader.

Besides, it's not clear what group should be ranked for grading purposes. Is it all students in the same class at the same time? In the same school? District? In the same semester or year? Over the years? The answers to these questions can have major implications for the grade a student receives. For instance, if a student happens to fall into an extremely capable cohort, the results might be vastly different from how they would be if that same student just happens to be part of a generally lower-achieving group. So issues of fairness come into play.

Further, this system produces grades that are unrelated to real achievement. A class could, in fact, learn very little but the grade distribution could still convey the appearance that all had performed as expected. In other words, in a high-achieving group, some who actually learned a great deal but scored below the highest achievers might be doomed to receive a low grade.

And again, from your point of view as a teacher, even if your instruction improves markedly over the years, and helps more and more students master the important material, the distribution of grades will appear unchanged. That would frustrate anyone!

Teachers who develop success-oriented partnerships with students have no use for grading on a curve. They know they are not the best teacher they can be until every student attains an A by demonstrating the highest possible achievement on rigorous, high-quality assessments.

An Illustration

To tie all of these procedures together, let's work through a hypothetical example of a fifth-grade teacher developing grading procedures in science. The context is a self-contained classroom of 32 students.

Step 1: Specify Targets.   This teacher's comprehensive picture for this particular 10-week grading period includes knowledge, reasoning, skill, and product outcomes for three 3-week units of instruction:

- An ecology unit on wetlands
- A biology unit on amphibians
- A chemistry unit on biodegradable substances

Our teacher lists the priority achievement targets for each unit: science knowledge students are to understand, specific reasoning patterns they are to apply, performance skills, and products they are to create. These include the following

Knowledge

Ecology

Biology

Chemistry

} *List facts, concepts and general principles to be mastered by students*

Reasoning

Specific patterns students are to master.

Types of problems students are to solve.

Performance Skills

Field study and laboratory skills students are to demonstrate.

Oral presentations expected and attributes of quality.

Product Development Capabilities

Attributes of models or displays students are to build, extended written reports they are to prepare, and/or other products expected.

Step 2: Assessment Plan.   The instructor decides to sample student mastery of content and most reasoning targets with three weekly quizzes in each unit and a culminating unit test, each combining selected response and essay formats.

In addition, each student will produce a brief written report in a combined performance assessment for the ecology and amphibian units, to tap scientific process achievement targets. The combination of nine quizzes, backed up with three unit tests and the report, our teacher reasons, will provide an excellent portrait of student achievement for end-of-term report card grading.

Step 3: Gathering Evidence.   Our teacher translates content and reasoning outcomes into tables of specifications for the short quizzes and the unit tests, making sure to include each relevant content category both on a quiz and on a subsequent unit test. She drafts lists of propositions reflecting important content to test, ensures their importance, then writes the required test items. As an ungraded exercise, the teacher also asks students to write some practice test questions to ask each other.

Students also prepare for the written performance assessment by reading samples of previous reports of varying quality and trying to figure out what makes a really good report. With the teacher's guidance, they then devise a solid set of performance criteria. The teacher develops the performance task that spells out each student's research reporting responsibilities.

During the grading period, the teacher administers the various assessments. Some of the tests and quizzes are open book, and call for students to know how to retrieve information; others require them to learn information outright. Some occur in class, others students take home.

The performance assessment takes place as planned, including distributing the exercise and developing the performance criteria in class, with teacher and students working together to define success. Students then draft their reports and share them in their collaborative teams with classmates. Each student gets focused feedback from teammates using the agreed-on performance criteria. They then complete the final product.

As each assessment is completed, the teacher enters information into her gradebook (installed on a personal computer), regarding students' performance in terms of the percentage of total possible points on each test and quiz.

Students who score low have 2 days to study and take advantage of the regular "afterschool retake," which is another version of the test or quiz that covers the same required material with different exercises. If they score higher, the new scores replace the old ones in the gradebook. If they score lower, student and teacher meet to discuss why and plan further assessments together. Students who miss a test or quiz may use the afterschool option to make it up.

The students' research reports are evaluated by three previously trained raters: the teacher, a high school student who volunteered to help the fifth graders conduct the wetlands study, and a member of the school's community advisory committee who works in the area of environmental science. Each applies the five 5-point rating scales.

Students receive detailed feedback in the form of profiles of ratings on each criterion used and written comments about their products. The gradebook gets an entry for each student: the combined total of ratings converted to a percentage of the maximum possible score of 75 points (five scales, 5 points, three raters). Students disappointed with their ratings have one week to redo the work and resubmit. The teacher will reevaluate the work and enter the new score in the record. Otherwise, the old score stands.

Step 4: Combining into a Composite.   The teacher has devised a specific strategy for combining all of these percentages to a composite that reflects student mastery of all relevant outcomes: Each of the nine quizzes receives a weight of 1, unit tests count as 2, and the performance assessment counts 5 times. That means the teacher will average 20 scores—9 quiz scores, 6 test scores (3 test scores each counted twice), and the performance assessment grade counted 5 times—to determine an overall percentage. The teacher generates composite scores using the gradebook computer, and prints summaries for each student, who checks the record of scores and the composite for any errors.

Step 5: Assigning Grades.   Our instructor transforms these composites into grades for the report card by applying a previously announced set of standards: 90 to 100 percent equals an A, and so on.

Time for Reflection

Assume you are the teacher in this illustration. You have set specific percentage cutoff scores to be used in grade determination and made them public from the beginning of the grading period. A student who scores 90 to 100 percent receives an A. One of your students ends up with an average of 89.5 percent. What grade do you assign and why?

An Illustration Using Performance Assessment

In contexts where all assessments convert neatly into percent correct, assigning grades by means of traditional grading rules is relatively easy. But these days, with many teachers assessing with performance assessments that result in profiles of ratings rather than single scores, conversion to grades can be somewhat more complicated. So to avoid confusion, let's consider an example of this.

It's important not to equate ratings on a rubric directly with a letter grade in a summative sense. Although a "5" on a 5-point scale means the work is very good, it doesn't necessarily mean that 5 = A. On some occasions and in some contexts, the description of a "4" performance might come closer to what you think of as "A-quality work." Likewise, "3" might not mean average work equivalent to a "C," and a "1" is not necessarily a signal for "failure." It might mean that the student is just beginning to learn how to perform well. Rather, most of the time, I think of scores on a set of rating scales as signs of strengths and weaknesses in student work that can serve to promote improvement; most often, they should be diagnostic and thus formative.

But, at some point, you must assign a grade for the report card. When that time arrives, you have a number of choices available for determining what grade to assign.

To see how these work out, consider the example of Emily's record of achievement in writing over an entire grading period, depicted in Table 13.1. She has completed a total of 13 assignments, some of which were rated on all six analytical score scales, and some of which were only partially rated. Following are some ways to summarize all of this for conversion to a grade that represents applications of ideas offered in this chapter.

The Composite Profile Method.   This method simply stipulates that, at the end of the grading period, the pattern of analytical ratings the student has received across

Table 13.1
Emily's writing assessment record

Student's Name   **Emily**

	Ideas and Content	Organization	Voice	Word Choice	Sentence Fluency	Conventions
Public Lab	1 2 3 4 5	1 2 3 4 5	1 2 3 4 5	1 2 3 4 5	1 2 3 (4) 5	1 2 3 4 5
Reports #5 & 6	1 2 3 4 5	1 2 3 4 5	1 2 3 4 5	1 2 3 4 5	1 2 3 4 5	1 2 3 4 (5)
Writing assessment #1	1 2 3 (4) 5	1 2 (3) 4 5	1 2 3 (4) 5	1 2 3 (4) 5	1 2 (3) 4 5	1 2 (3) 4 5
Computers	1 2 3 4 5	1 2 3 4 5	1 2 3 4 5	1 2 3 4 5	1 2 3 4 (5)	1 2 3 4 5
Amazing Ride	1 2 3 4 (5)	1 2 3 4 (5)	1 2 3 4 (5)	1 2 3 4 (5)	1 2 3 (4) 5	1 2 (3) 4 5
Baseball	1 2 3 4 5	1 2 3 4 5	1 2 3 4 5	1 2 3 4 5	1 2 3 (4) 5	1 2 3 4 5
Autobiography	1 2 3 4 5	1 2 3 4 5	1 2 3 4 (5)	1 2 3 4 5	1 2 3 4 (5)	1 2 3 4 5
Poster	1 2 3 4 5	1 2 3 4 5	1 2 3 4 5	1 2 3 4 5	1 2 3 4 5	1 2 3 4 (5)
Pet Essays	1 2 3 4 5	1 2 3 4 5	1 2 3 4 5	1 2 3 4 (5)	1 2 3 4 5	1 2 3 4 (5)
Social Studies Research	1 2 3 (4) 5	1 2 (3) 4 5	1 2 3 (4) 5	1 2 3 (4) 5	1 2 (3) 4 5	1 2 3 4 (5)
Science Research	1 2 3 (4) 5	1 2 3 (4) 5	1 2 3 (4) 5	1 2 3 (4) 5	1 2 3 (4) 5	1 2 3 (4) 5
TV Preview	1 2 3 4 5	1 2 3 4 5	1 2 3 4 (5)	1 2 3 4 5	1 2 3 4 5	1 2 3 4 5
Space Report	1 2 3 (4) 5	1 2 3 (4) 5	1 2 3 (4) 5	1 2 3 (4) 5	1 2 3 (4) 5	1 2 3 (4) 5
	1 2 3 4 5	1 2 3 4 5	1 2 3 4 5	1 2 3 4 5	1 2 3 4 5	1 2 3 4 5
Rating Totals	4,1	2,2,1	4,3	4,2	2,5,2	2,2,4

all assessments must take a certain form to attain a certain grade. For instance, you might stipulate that a student needs to have attained 90 percent 4s and 5s to earn an A, and 25 percent 4s and 5s with 90 percent above 3 to get a B. Figure 13.3 presents examples of possible decision rules. Referring to Table 13.1, Emily received 34 4s and 5s out of 40 scores, or 85 percent. So she has earned a B.

The decision rules that you use for converting ratings to grades need to make sense in terms of quality. Consider involving your students in the process of establishing these rules. Be sure that everyone involved knows and understands your conversion rules from the outset. No surprises, no excuses.

The Final Profile Method.   This method of grade determination holds that competence at the end of the grading period is more important than competence at the

Grade	Sample Rule	Interpreting Emily's Record from Table 13.1
A	90% 4s and 5s	Emily's ratings are not this high
B	At least 25% 4s and 5s, with 90% 3s or better	Emily meets both criterion with 85% 4s and 5s and 100% 3s or above; she earns a B
C	At least 75% 3s or better	Emily's work exceeds this level
D	25% 3 and above	Emily's work is at a higher level
F	10% 3s and above	Emily is way above this

Figure 13.3
Sample decision rules for converting rating profiles to grades

beginning. You might still have a record of performance over time, as above, but past performance is not considered. If the student produces consistent evidence of one level of proficiency at the end, all previous records of writing achievement are deemed out of date. They no longer reflect the student's reality. The student's goal, therefore, is to be constantly striving to establish and maintain evidence of a new high level of proficiency. Student profiles can decline, too, if they fail to maintain or demonstrate competence.

Referring to Table 13.1, if we were to apply this standard to Emily, only the last few assignments would count toward the grade. Use enough to provide a representative sample of the final level of achievement attained. On the final few assessments, Emily's ratings are right at 90 percent 4s and 5s and so she might well be assigned an A.

Understand that the profiles of analytical scale ratings established to represent each letter grade, once again, are completely up to you. They merely represent conventions of understanding between you and your students. But they must reflect clear differences in performance and everyone must know them in advance (no moving targets!). This represents the best internal control grading option. At any time, students can aim as high as they wish.

Variations of These Methods.   As always, I advise using systems that permit students to be in control of their own ultimate level of success. So consider using the systems described above but give students the opportunity to improve their work and thus their grade. Allow them to revise any papers with ratings of 3 or below, using feedback from you or their peers, for reevaluation and regrading. If they attain a new level of proficiency, that grade replaces the previous (now outdated) one.

Or consider weaving the above ideas into contracts with students. This will be helpful in motivating special needs students. Conduct a preassessment to determine a student's starting level of proficiency and then conduct a student-led parent/teacher conference to agree on a profile of subsequent ratings that represents a reachable but demanding goal for the student. In contract terms, agree that attainment of that level will represent an A. Then back down from that to set decision rules for other letter grades. Place this set of expectations into the student's IEP and set about helping that student succeed in those concrete terms.

These systems for record keeping and grade computation allow everyone involved to know at any particular time how their performance relates to expectations. This permits students to remain aware and in control of their success. Some teachers also ask students to assign their own grades, as a means of promoting student self-evaluation. But they must be ready to justify their grade with specific evidence. If information gathering, storage, and retrieval are working effectively in a manner that involves students, there should be absolute agreement between student and teacher at all times as to the grades being earned.

Each of these options provides an acceptable basis for communicating via report card grades about student achievement as reflected in performance assessments.

A Final Time-Saving Thought

It troubles me deeply that so many teachers beginning this new century still maintain grade records the way teachers did at the turn of the old century. They rely on Fred Flintstone technology, a gradebook with one line per student containing all of the test scores and assignment grades for the grading period. There is a better way. Many software producers have developed gradebook packages specifically designed for teachers to use on their personal computers. They permit easy entry, long-term accurate storage, efficient retrieval, and convenient summary functions for interim or final reporting. In the hands of proficient users, these software programs can save immense amounts of time. For further information on these programs, go to www.wested.org/acwt on the Internet.

Report Cards That Deliver the Details

The reporting alternatives I describe in this section permit us to maintain and share more detailed messages about student achievement than do grades. The examples provided cross grade levels, from primary to elementary to junior high and high school. Each offers special features worthy of your consideration.

Reporting with Lists of Competencies

One currently popular way to report greater detail about student achievement in preparation for conferences is to assemble an extended list of specific competencies and to indicate the extent to which students have mastered each. An example from Lincoln Elementary School, Madison, Wisconsin, appears in Figure 13.4. Note

LINCOLN ELEMENTARY SCHOOL—GRADE 5

Student _____   Teacher _____   Principal _____   Quarter 2 3 4

E = Excellent   S = Satisfactory   P = Making Progress   N = Needs Improvement

READING PROGRAM

Materials Used: _____

___ Reads with understanding
___ Is able to write about what is read
___ Completes reading group work accurately and on time
___ Shows interest in reading

Reading Skills
___ Decodes new words
___ Understands new words

Independent Reading Level:
Below   At Grade Level   Above

LANGUAGE ARTS
___ Uses oral language effectively
___ Listens carefully
___ Masters weekly spelling

Writing skills
___ Understands writing as process
___ Creates a rough draft
___ Makes meaningful revisions
___ Creates edited, legible final draft

Editing skills
___ Capitalizes
___ Punctuates
___ Uses complete sentences
___ Uses paragraphs
___ Demonstrates dictionary skills

Writing skill level:
Below   At Grade Level   Above

MATHEMATICS

Problem Solving
___ Solves teacher-generated problems
___ Solves Self/Student-generated problems
___ Can create story problems

Interpreting Problems
___ Uses appropriate strategies
___ Can use more than one strategy
___ Can explain strategies in written form
___ Can explain strategies orally

Math Concepts
  Understands Base Ten
Beginning Developing Sophisticated
  Multiplication, Basic facts
Beginning Developing Sophisticated
  2 digit Multiplication
Beginning Developing Sophisticated
  Division
Beginning Developing Sophisticated
  Geometry
Beginning Developing Sophisticated

Overall Math Skill Level:
Beginning Developing Sophisticated

Attitude/Work Skills
___ Welcomes a challenge
___ Persistence
___ Takes advantage of learning from others
___ Listens to others
___ Participates in discussion

It Figures
Is working on: _____

Goal:
Is working on achieving goal: _____

SOCIAL STUDIES
___ Understands subject matter
___ Shows curiosity and enthusiasm
___ Contributes to class discussions
___ Uses map skills
___ Demonstrates control of reading skills by interpreting text

Topics covered: Individual cultures, Columbus–first English colonies

SCIENCE
___ Shows curiosity about scientific subject matter
___ Asks good scientific questions
___ Shows knowledge of scientific method
___ Uses knowledge of scientific method to help set up and run experiment(s)
___ Makes good scientific observations
___ Has researched scientific topic(s)
    Topic(s) _____

I Wonder
Is currently working on _____

WORKING SKILLS
___ Listens carefully
___ Follows directions
___ Works neatly and carefully
___ Checks work
___ Completes work on time
___ Uses time wisely
___ Works well independently
___ Works well in a group
___ Takes risks in learning
___ Welcomes a challenge

HOMEWORK
___ Self-selects homework
___ Completes work accurately
___ Completes work on time

PRESENTATIONS/PROJECTS

HUMAN RELATIONS
___ Shows courtesy
___ Respects rights of others
___ Shows self-control
___ Interacts well with peers
___ Shows a cooperative and positive attitude in class
___ Shows a cooperative attitude when asked to work with other students
___ Is willing to help other students
___ Works well with other adults (subs, student teacher, parents, etc.)

ATTENDANCE

	1st	2nd	3rd	4th
Present				
Absent				
Tardy				

Placement for next year: _____

Figure 13.4

Reporting specific competencies attained

Source: From *ASCD Yearbook: Communicating Student Learning* (p. 104) by T. Guskey (ed.), 1996. Alexandria, VA: Association for Supervision and Curriculum. Copyright 1996 by ASCD. Reprinted by permission of the publisher.

that each academic discipline is allocated one section of the report. Then each of these is subdivided into statements about student work. The teacher rates each, from "Excellent" to "Needs Improvement." This form presents over 80 different pieces of information about student achievement.

Another commonly used way of sharing greater detail about student achievement is to devise performance continua along which student achievement might vary. For example, part of the Juneau, Alaska, School District primary grade reporting system is depicted in Figure 13.5, detailing the reading continuum. Similar rating scales are available for writing targets. Note once again that specific proficiencies are listed. Then various levels of performance are described. It is along these continua that student achievement is profiled. One interesting feature of this kind of reporting is the progress that can be reported during the year. This kind of reporting, backed up by a writing portfolio, can provide an excellent basis for student, parent, and/or teacher discussion at a conference.

Time for Reflection

Based on what you have seen of this communication system, what do you anticipate would be its biggest limitations? Can you see any way(s) around the potential problems you identify?

Dealing with the Practicalities.   As you consider these options, remember that their successful implementation requires that teachers collaborate in developing the achievement targets, creating the performance rating system, and implementing the communication system. It must represent the collective wisdom and teamwork of many experienced professionals. This kind of backing and commitment is required to make such a system work.

Another important key to successfully using this kind of communication system is that teachers must be trained to make dependable ratings of student performance. This training takes time and effort. Resources must be allocated to make it possible. However, these costs are minimized to the extent that the teachers who are to use the system play a role in its development.

This system provides a high level of detail about student achievement. Although users report that the performance criteria become second nature and easy to rate with practice and experience, we would be naïve to think such records are easy to create and deliver at conference time. Because the report is detailed, communicating results can be time consuming.

Narrative Reporting

Another way to forge a stronger communication link between school and home is to use narrative descriptions of student learning. Rather than grades, to convey meaning, Catlin Gabel School in Portland, Oregon, uses this method in its elementary and middle school. The philosophy that guides the evaluation system is effectively summarized in the school's policy statement:

We maintain that the student is the unit of consideration, and that our commitment is to create conditions within our school that serve to develop each student's fullest powers as an individual and as a group member. Further, we hold that any system of evaluation ought to:

1. enhance intrinsic motivation for learning.
2. help students take increasing responsibility for their own learning and be active partners in the learning process through continual self-evaluation.
3. serve as a means for direct, sensitive communication between the teacher and student and the teacher and family.
4. focus on the specific strengths and weaknesses of individual students and provide prescriptive as well as descriptive information. (Catlin Gabel School, n.d., p. 18)

This philosophy, as the following illustrates, is intrinsic to the way Catlin Gabel staff communicate about student achievement with parents:

The [elementary school faculty] chooses to write narrative reports rather than issue letter grades because it enables faculty to convey specific information about a child's strengths, weaknesses, progress and problems, as well as suggest strategies for improvement and enhancement. In addition, it provides a vehicle to impart information about a child's motivation, attitudes toward learning, special interests, socialization skills, and emotional tone. The written evaluation also allows the teacher to describe facets of an individual's intellectual and emotional development and compare children to themselves rather than to their peers. Finally, it provides content for conferences, which promotes dialogue between home and school and contributes to the sense of partnership that we seek to develop between student and teacher. (Catlin Gabel School, n.d., p. 28)

The nature and quality of the communication that results is clearly seen in the sample Catlin Gabel narrative report presented in Figure 13.6, a description of a hypothetical fourth-grade student.

This carefully crafted description reflects a clear vision of achievement, clear criteria and standards, and a vivid sense of how this student relates to those expectations. This report demonstrates how we can use written descriptions and samples of student work, in addition to grades and scores, to communicate about student achievement.

However, the potential value of narrative reporting doesn't stop here. While I find few teachers doing it, we also can deliver very engaging and highly motivating narratives to our students. Figure 13.7 illustrates.

Time for Reflection

What are some of the potential limitations of written narrative description? As you identify problems, see if you can identify possible remedies.

Dealing with the Practicalities.   The major drawback of these kinds of reports, obviously, is the time required to prepare them. High student-teacher ratios may render this option impractical for many teachers. However, if the narrative is

	Emergent	Beginning	Developing
Comprehension	• Relies on memory for reading • Responds to stories • May label pictures • May tell a story from pictures using oral language • May pretend to read • May invent text with book language • Focuses on pictures for meaning rather than print	• Reads simple books in which text is repeated; (illustrations provide a lot of support) and demonstrates understanding in the following ways: - Recalls random details - Recognizes when the reading isn't making sense - Shows understanding that print carries meaning	• Reads books with varied sentence patterns; (illustrations provide a moderate amount of support) and demonstrates understanding in a few of the following ways: - Recounts sequence of events - Summarizes story - Predicts what will happen next - Backs up statements with proof from reading - Connects experiences with reading
Skills/Strategies	• Identifies own name on print • Understands "how" books work, e.g., top and bottom and front to back	• Recognizes that letters carry sounds • Begins to use context, grammatical, and/or phonics cues and cross checks with pictures • Matches words spoken to words in print • Locates a known word • Understands concepts about print, e.g. directionality, sentence, word, letter, space, beginning, end	• Increases and refines use of context, language, and/or phonics cues, and begins to use cross checking to self correct • Begins to pause at appropriate places when reading orally • Knows the meaning of a period, question mark, and exclamation mark • Follows single step written instructions
Attitudes/ Behavior	• Shows curiosity about print in environment • Participates in the oral reading of familiar stories	• Is willing to read • Focuses on print, supported by pictures • Reading is vocal	• Selects books independently • Shows familiarity with titles and authors • Is beginning to read silently

Select the column(s) that best describe how a child habitually and naturally reads from a variety of materials at his/her instructional reading level. (Instructional Level Material that is challenging but not frustrating with normal classroom instruction and support.)

Figure 13.5
Juneau primary reading continuum
Note: From The Juneau, Alaska, School District. Reprinted by permission.

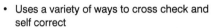

Expanding	Transitional
• Reads books with long descriptions, challenging vocabulary; (illustrations provide low support) and demonstrates understanding in several of the following ways:	• Reads books with long descriptions, challenging vocabulary (illustrations provide very little or no support) and demonstrates understanding in most of the following ways:
- Remembers sequence of events	- Remembers sequence of events
- Summarizes story	- Summarizes story
- Predicts what will happen next	- Predicts what will happen next
- Backs up statements with proof from reading	- Backs up statements with proof from reading
- Connects and builds to draw conclusions	- Connects and builds to draw conclusions
- Uses prior knowledge with relevant information from the story to form an opinion	- Uses prior knowledge to form an opinion
- Connects experiences with reading	- Connects experiences with reading
	- Evaluates/judges character, authors, books
	• Verbally responds to literature in depth and is beginning to shift this ability to writing

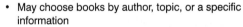

Expanding	Transitional
• Uses a variety of ways to cross check and self correct	• Self corrects automatically
• Begins to read orally with expression and with appropriate pauses	• Confidently reads a story with appropriate expression
• Knows the meaning of quotation marks and commas	• Follows written multi-step directions
• Follows two step written directions	• Begins to ask questions about the structure of language

Expanding	Transitional
• Chooses appropriate books to read for pleasure	• Chooses to read a variety of materials for a variety of purposes
• May choose books by author, topic, or a specific information	• Often chooses reading over other activities
• Usually reads silently for an extended period of time, sometimes vocalizing when text is difficult	• Reads silently for extended periods of time
• Reads lengthier material	• Recommends books to others

continued

ABC Lower School
June 1990
Fourth Grade
Teacher's Name   Joan Student

Joan is determination and strength presented in a lively package. This strong-willed student has contributed much to her peers in her fourth-grade year. From her they have learned the importance of fighting for one's point of view. Joan is never wanting for an opinion on any subject. It is easy for her to express her viewpoint. On occasion she takes the opposite point of view solely for the pleasure of differing from the group consensus. Where she has made considerable growth this year is in her willingness to consider the ideas of others. She has learned to back away from a stance when she sees that it is unreasonable or in error. This has helped Joan progress academically because she has become more open to the learning process—the give and take of ideas. Joan is a motivated and independent student who cares deeply that the work she pursues is meaningful. She has grown in her ability to engage fully in an assignment, and has learned that revising an idea only enhances its content.

"I am the Emperor's garden/With a plum tree by my side/The blossoms bloom in the sunlight/while the fragrance is carried by a gentle breeze . . . " Joan has the soul of a poet. She creates strong vivid images of lovers willing to die for their love, souls tortured by war or gentle gardens peaceful in the sunlight. She allows whole worlds to come alive with her writing. As the year has progressed she has learned how to return to her writing and flesh out her images to make them even more dramatic. Joan has shown great tenaciousness in her willingness to revise a piece, searching for the exact words to make the images strong. She is developing the writer's gift of seeing detail, recognizing its significance, and then understanding how to weave all that she envisions into a finely crafted piece of writing.

Joan has broadened her vocabulary and added many new concepts and words to her knowledge base. This has helped her comprehension improve as the year has progressed. She has taken on increasingly difficult books and relishes the specific details. Joan prefers to read books that are challenging in their content and possess valuable issues with which to grapple. However, she still struggles with jumping to conclusions on first glance of a passage. It is the subtler levels of comprehension that still present her with a challenge. If her interpretation of the information is incorrect, as it sometimes is, she finds it difficult to backtrack and clarify her ideas. The format of reading group, where the content of a book is carefully analyzed, has helped

Figure 13.6
Sample narrative report
Source: From "Sample School Report" (n.p.) by Catlin Gable School, 1990, Portland, OR: Author. Copyright 1990 by Catlin Gabel School. Reprinted by permission

her to see when she needs to readjust her ideas. There were many incidents where Joan discovered that what she thought was occurring was in error. The growth has occurred in her willingness to accept this and go back to the book to discover where she made the misinterpretation. She needs continued encouragement to ask herself if what she is interpreting from the reading makes sense with what she knows of the details of the book. It would help her to continue reading over the summer with the opportunity to discuss with an adult the content of the books. It would be helpful if she could even take a reading course over the summer.

It was a challenge for Joan to work cooperatively on the Japanese research. Being paired with another strong-willed student gave her both frustration and rewards. Together they explored the topic of Kabuki theater, and they designed a well organized presentation that thoroughly covered the topic. Joan was a very captivated audience during our Japanese unit. She found every experience fascinating and worked hard to glean as much from the study as she could. She was very observant during the Seattle trip, making connections whenever possible. Her determination and passion for knowledge brought her many insights into the culture of the Japanese.

Joan has a solid understanding of the whole-number operations, has mastered multidigit multiplication and long division with remainders. She has secured most of her multiplication tables and she has become quick and proficient at solving mental math problems. As she has grown in her ability to sustain academic effort, Joan has brought perseverance to story problems. She is more likely to struggle with a problem, try a variety of strategies and adjust until she finds the tactic that works. She has added many problem solving techniques to her repertoire. Joan has a good conceptual understanding of fractions and decimals. She has built for herself a fine foundation from which to learn and grow mathematically.

Joan has many successes to celebrate this year. Not all have come easily but her willingness to grow has brought her great satisfaction as a learner. She is a serious student who cares about the quality of her work. She is conscientious about dead-lines. Not only has her academic understanding broadened but her social world has expanded. No longer is she on the fringes trying to find an entry into the group. She is a fully vested member of a wide social network with many friends from which to choose. She has come a long way in her fourth-grade year.

Joan, we will miss your determination and voice next year. We hope you have an adventure-filled summer that includes special times with family and friends. Please come next door and check in often so we can keep track of your continued progress.

continued

October 17

Dear Sarah,

   The beginning of the year is a time to get to know each other, find out what you know and find the best way that I can aid your learning. For that reason, I've done lots of watching. The thing that struck me most about you is that you are a reader. You read every single minute you aren't doing something else. Today I watched you read during lunch. You were so intent in the story, you hardly noticed what you were eating. You also smoothly read out loud with much expression. You read many kinds of materials, from fairy tales, picture books to long novels like *Maniac McGee*. Your writing reflects your reading ability. Your text flows smoothly from one idea to the next. Tied into all of this are your art ideas. The pictures from *Peppermint in the Parlor* and *Princess Bride* show that you can listen and create pictures from what you hear.

   I love it when you share your ideas in class. You always add much to the discussion. You are a strong performer. During our musical performance last week, you knew all your lines and followed stage directions well. I could tell that you have been in front of an audience before. You had the same quality of work when you were one of the presidential candidates. You knew your platform and your issues.

   Your work shows that you are a disciplined student. You always know your poem and it's evident that you studied for the several tests we've had. You think through problems. An example of this is gathering and organizing data and creating a highly readable graph. I know that along with breaking some school records, you go to gymnastics three times a week.

   You are a good strong student. I'm really proud of all that you have learned this quarter.

Love,

Mrs A

Figure 13.7
Sample narrative report in the form of a letter to a sixth grader
Source: Reprinted by permission of Terri Austin: *Changing the View: Student-Led Parent Conferences* (Heinemann, a division of Reed Elsevier Inc., Portsmouth, NH, 1994).

intended for delivery to parents, how about if students and teachers work as partners to compose the letter? Shared work results in positive achievement for the student; shared planning and preparation of the narrative assists the teacher; open and effective student-involved communication goes to families; and everyone shares credit for doing a good job! Sounds like a win-win-win situation.

   In addition, as always, we must center the narrative message on the relevant achievement targets. We must take care to transform those targets into rigorous assessments and write about specific achievement results. In other words, we must maintain a clear focus on achievement. To use this option productively, users must regard these reports as far more than "free writing time," when they can say whatever comes to mind about the student. The issue in narrative reports is, What does it mean to be academically successful, and how did this student do in relation to those expectations?

The only way this kind of communication can become practical for a teacher is with careful planning and record keeping. At the time of the writing, all relevant information to be factored into the report must be readily available. The framework for the report must be completely spelled out. And to the extent possible, modern information processing technology should be brought to bear. For example, you might develop a template for narrative reporting on your personal computer. Within this general outline, then, you might merely need to enter essential details.

Remember, however, that narrative reporting places a premium on being able to write well. Teachers or students who have difficulty communicating in writing will find a narrative system frustrating to use and will not use it well.

Continuous Progress Reporting

Teachers in Victoria, Australia, have devised yet another kind of reporting scheme that develops a continuous record of student progress through a series of specifically defined and progressively linked targets (Ministry of Education and Training, 1991). They call these records *profiles* and describe them as follows:

> Profiles are a means of reporting on a student's progress and achievement in key areas of learning. Profiles consist of a series of short descriptive statements, called indicators, arranged in nine levels of achievement called bands. These describe, in order of difficulty, significant skills and knowledge that students must learn to become proficient. A student's progress can be charted over these bands. English Profiles show student progress and achievement in the key areas of reading, writing and spoken language. (p. 7)

The spoken language bands are identified in Figure 13.8, from A at the beginning to I on the high-performance end. Figure 13.9 illustrates one kind of parental reporting form used, the English Profile, focusing on spoken language bands B, C, and D. Note that it highlights the band the student is working on at the time of reporting, and includes prior and following proficiencies for context. Teachers enter brief comments for the record regarding student progress and achievement.

Time for Reflection

What seems to you to be the strengths of this system compared to the two preceding ones? What apparent limitations do you identify? Can you suggest specific remedies for potential problems?

Dealing with the Practicalities.   This kind of reporting overcomes some, but not all, of the shortcomings of the systems described previously. First, it minimizes the amount of narrative teachers must enter. This saves time. Second, it reduces the range of achievement targets and levels over which teachers must comment, focusing on the particular forms of achievement students are working on. This, too, saves time. Third, a concrete record of progress is generated, with cumula-

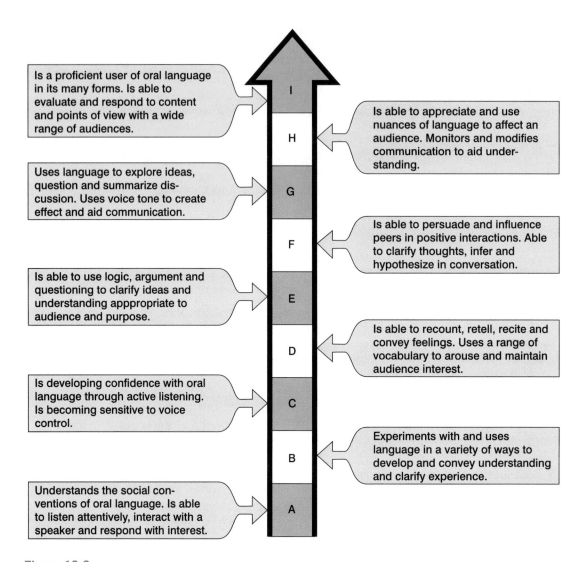

Figure 13.8

The spoken language bands

Source: From *English Profiles Handbook* (n.p.) by the Schools Program Division, Ministry of Education and Training, Victoria, Australia, 1991. Reprinted by permission of the publisher.

tive reports of bands of achievement. This helps with interpretation. Fourth, this is quite a comprehensive and carefully articulated communication system, with the span of achievement covered ranging from elementary levels through high school. This makes the system valuable in contexts where students are expected to make continuous progress in acquiring an interlaced series of outcomes across grade levels.

But there remains the challenge of defining, sharing, and being able to dependably assess the various levels of achievement reflected in the bands. These will take

ENGLISH PROFILE—SPOKEN LANGUAGE

School _____   Class_____

Name _____

Language Spoken At Home _____

Teacher's Assessment
Contexts And Comments   Date

SPOKEN LANGUAGE BAND B

Use of Oral Language

Makes short announcements clearly. Tells personal anecdotes in discussion. Retells a story heard in class, preserving the sequence of events. Accurately conveys a verbal message to another person. Responds with facial expressions. Responds with talk when others initiate conversation. Initiates conversation with peers. Holds conversation with familiar adults. Asks what unfamiliar words mean. Uses talk to clarify ideas or experience.

Features of Oral Language

Reacts (smiles, laughs, etc.) to absurd word substitutions. Demonstrates an appreciation of wit. Reacts (smiles, laughs) to unusual features of language (such as rhythm, alliteration or onomatopoeia).

SPOKEN LANGUAGE BAND C

Use of Oral Language

Makes verbal commentary during play or other activities with concrete objects.

Speaks confidently in formal situations (e.g., assembly, report to the class).

Explains ideas clearly in discussion.

Discusses information heard (e.g., dialogue, news item, report).

Based on consideration of what has already been said, offers personal opinions.

Asks for repetition, restatement, or general explanation to clarify meaning.

Features of Oral Language

Sequences a presentation in a logical order.

Gives instructions in a concise and understandable manner.

Reads aloud with expression, showing awareness of rhythm and tone.

Modulates voice for effect.

Nods, looks at speaker when others initiate talk.

Figure 13.9

English Profile—Spoken language

Source: From *English Profiles Handbook* (n.p.) by the Schools Program Division, Ministry of Education and Training, Victoria, Australia, 1991. Reprinted by permission of the publisher.

considerable investment. Their development and implementation across the curriculum requires that teachers meet across grade levels from primary grades through high school to articulate a continuous progress curriculum, to divide up responsibility for helping students make smooth transitions through the various levels of proficiency.

But imagine the nature and quality of the open, inclusive, student-involved communication environment we could achieve with such bands in place and with everyone able to accurately assess student progress through them. Imagine the power of a portfolio system (including extensive use of student self-reflection on their improvement as achievers) when used in conjunction with such a continuous progress curriculum. And finally, imagine the learning power brought to bear if the *student* is the primary record keeper.

Time for Reflection

At the very beginning of this chapter, I asked you to brainstorm lists of things you thought are good and bad about report card grades. Now that you have completed the chapter, go back to your list of bad things. Based on the material we have covered, can you see ways to overcome them (using better grading practices or other means of communicating) to maximize the effectiveness of your communication?

Summary: Communicating with Report Cards

As in all aspects of assessment addressed in this book, the key to effective report cards is for you, the teacher, to be master of the material your students are to learn. This permits you to translate your clear and appropriate targets into rigorous, high-quality assessments, which, in turn, you can convert to information that you may report in detail or combine into fair and equitable grades.

The reference point for interpreting a report card grade should always be the specific material to be learned, *and nothing else.* Students deserve to know in advance how you will accomplish this in their class, and they need to know the standards you expect them to meet. If you are assessing characteristics other than achievement, you must follow appropriate rules of sound assessment, and should report results separately from achievement grades.

Teachers must carefully plan for gathering information for report card grades. In times when grades served only to rank students, it didn't seem to matter what those grades actually meant. Today, however, we need to produce meaningful communication about student attainment of ascending levels of ever-more-advanced competencies.

This requires a clearly stated set of grading priorities. These achievement expectations are most productively set when a faculty meets across grade levels and across classrooms within grade levels to determine the building blocks of ultimate competence and to integrate them into their classrooms, systematically dividing up responsibility for learning.

You must, however, take responsibility for assembling a strategic assessment plan for generating the information to determine which of your students attain the desired targets. You must then translate that plan into quality assessments throughout the grading period. Students serve as valuable allies in developing and using these assessments, turning assessment for grading into assessment for learning as well.

As you conduct assessments and accumulate results, you must take care to record as much detail about student achievement as is available. To be sure, nearly all of this useful detail ultimately will be sacrificed in our obsession to describe the rich complexity of student achievement in the form of a single letter grade. But don't give up the detail until you absolutely must. And when report card grading time arrives, share as much of the detail as you can with your students, so they understand what is behind the single little symbol that appears on the report card. Then boil the richness of your detail away only grudgingly.

Remember two final guidelines: (1) You need not assign a grade to absolutely everything students produce. It's acceptable to sometimes simply use words and pictures to describe your response. Allow room to explore and grow in between grades. (2) Your challenge is not to rank students in terms of their achievement. Although not all students will learn the same amounts or at the same rates and a ranking may naturally result from your work, the student's next teacher needs more information than a place in the rank order to know what to do next to assist. Remember, our goal is to communicate in ways that help students learn and feel in control of their own success.

When you need to communicate greater detail when using a report card–based communication system, consider the alternatives of sharing your information about student achievement via a checklist of competencies attained, a written narrative report, or a continuous progress reporting system.

Exercises for Self-Assessment

1. Consulting the text, identify several changes currently unfolding in schools that call for changes in grading practices.

2. Create a five-row by three-column chart listing achievement, aptitude, effort, compliance and attitude in the rows. Review the material presented in this chapter and briefly summarize in the first two columns the arguments for and against factoring each into report card grades. Leave column three blank for now.

3. List the five steps in report card grading described in this chapter and identify the specific activities in each step.

4. Compile a two-part list of practical strategies as spelled out in this chapter for avoiding common grading problems. First,

identify a potential problem, then specify a remedy.

5. Rank the three forms of achievement communication listed here according to which are most and least likely to reflect the principles of effective communication. Why do you rank them as you do?

   - A letter grade on a report card
   - An anecdotal narrative description of student achievement
   - A portfolio containing samples of student work

6. In column three of the chart you created for exercise 2, for each factor, explain whether you believe that the arguments for or against should win out, and briefly state why.

7. Analyze the options of grading based on rank order (i.e., on a curve) and grading in terms of student competence (i.e., preset standards) in terms of underlying assumptions about the mission of schools and the nature of student learning, as well as the specific procedures involved in each. Identify similarities and differences between these two procedures for transforming achievement information into letter grades.

 You may go to the Companion Website at www.prenhall.com/stiggins and answer these questions in the Self-Assessment module.

Final Chapter Reflection

1. *What are the three most important new insights to come to you as a result of your study of this chapter?*
2. *Which of your previous questions about assessment can you now answer based on your study of this chapter?*
3. *What new questions have come to mind as a result of your study of this chapter that you hope to have answered as your study continues?*
4. *For practicing teachers only: What do you plan to do differently in assessment in your classroom as a result of your study of this book so far?*

   For those in preservice study only: As you think about the classroom assessment environment that you hope to create for your students, how has your thinking changed as a result of your study of this book so far?

 ## Workbook Activities

Those who are using the workbook, *Practice with Student-Involved Classroom Assessment*, will find the following activities and others included for Chapter 13:

- *Grading Sound Bite.* This activity prepares you for another look at grading with a pre-quiz that can also be used as a post quiz.

- *What's in a "B?"*   This activity provides an opportunity for a discussion of what factors should be taken into account when grading. The discussion centers on a case in which miscommunication was occurring between parents and teachers because groups differed on what the grade meant.

- *When Grades Don't Match the State Assessment Results.*   This case study depicts a phenomenon that is occurring with increasing frequency across the country. What happens when students consistently get high grades but fail to meet competency on the State test? Why might this occur and what can be done to avoid it?

- *Chris Brown's Science Class.*   This case study involves looking at an anonymous grade book to see if you agree with the grades the teacher gave. Various considerations about the vagaries of the grading process are made obvious.

- *Converting Rubric Scores to Grades.*   What are the options? What makes most sense? This activity provokes consideration of the options.

Video Support

The ATI interactive video training package, *Report Card Grading: Strategies and Solutions*, carefully analyzes the key report card grading issues, suggesting ways around common dilemmas and supporting the texts advocacy of grading as a relative pure index of student achievement. Brief video segments alternate with hands-on activities to bring the power of student-involved assessment to the fore.

Portfolios: Capturing the Details

CHAPTER FOCUS

This chapter answers the following guiding question:

How can my students and I communicate effectively about their achievement using portfolios—that is, through collecting samples of their work and their own self-reflections about the quality of that work?

The following overarching principles guide this part of our journey through the realm of classroom assessment:

1. The power of a portfolio communication system resides in its potential for student involvement in record keeping and communication.

2. Portfolios come in many forms, all of which can serve us well if we keep our purpose in mind as we select from among the options.

3. The challenge of portfolios resides in the need to weave them into day-to-day classroom practice in practical ways. But careful planning can remove any roadblocks.

Portfolio Defined

A *portfolio* is a collection of student work assembled to provide a representation of student achievement. The representation conveyed, as you might anticipate, is a function of the context: the purpose for assessing and communicating and the achievement target(s) about which we wish to communicate. Thus, the range of possible applications of portfolios in the classroom is wide indeed, as you shall see in this chapter.

The best depiction of the portfolio concept that I have seen was developed by a professional association of educators (adapted from Arter & Spandel, 1992, p. 36):

> A *student portfolio* is "a purposeful collection of student work that tells a story about the student's efforts, progress, or achievement" in one or more academic disciplines. The portfolio's communication potential and instructional usefulness are enhanced when students participate in selecting content; when the selection of material to include follows predetermined guidelines; when criteria are available for judging the merit of the work collected, and when students regularly reflect on the evolving quality of their work.

Just as artists assemble portfolios of their work to convey their talents and journalists assemble samples of their work to represent their writing capabilities, so too can our students collect examples of their work to tell their school achievement story.

The essential difference between report card grades and portfolios as ways of communicating is that, *with grades, we aspire to the most efficient way to share information and care little about details, whereas, with portfolios, we abandon concern for efficiency and seek to maintain the detail*. Each form meets the information needs of different users.

What Role for Portfolios?

Based on our discussion of grades in the previous chapter, it should be clear to you that we condense a great deal of information into one single little symbol when we assign them. Over an entire semester or year, as teachers, we gather a great deal of detail about student achievement. Visualize a large ball full of information on student mastery of content, reasoning proficiencies, skills, and product development capabilities. To assign a grade, we must force that big ball through a narrow-diameter pipe. When it comes out the other end as an A, B, or C, all of the detail is gone.

Now, here's the problem: some decision makers need that detail that was available before the condensation to do their jobs—to make their decisions. For instance, let's say I am a teacher receiving new students on their journey to excellence as math-problem solvers and all I receive from their previous teacher is a letter grade next to the word "Math" on a report card. That level of specificity tells me nothing about each student's strengths or weaknesses. Based on the report card grade alone, I have no idea what comes next. I need greater detail in this communication.

Or say I'm a parent. My ability to understand, appreciate, and support my child's growth is enhanced if I have access to details regarding that growth, or its lack. A single report card grade only tells me a small part of the story.

This is where portfolios can come in. Typically, they contain details in the form of examples of student work with student reflections on the quality of that work. As a teacher or parent, if I can study those work samples, read the student's reflections, and have that student talk me through the portfolio, describing growth during the past year, I get a clear view of that individual's growth and current needs.

In this chapter, we will explore this communication option, with the goal of having you know and understand the following:

1. Why this record-keeping and communication option has become so popular.
2. The challenges that accompany the use of portfolios.
3. The active ingredients that go into a sound portfolio system.
4. The range of possible uses of portfolios to both improve communication and enhance student achievement.
5. How to manage many of the practicalities of using portfolios in the classroom.

The Popular Culture of Portfolios

The portfolio idea as it is being played out in schools these days brings with it a mixed bag of strengths, limitations, and possible applications. Without question, it is a very powerful and popular example of inclusive, student-involved communication at work in the classroom. By the same token, portfolios can lead to counterproductive and frustrating work for both students and teachers if we don't use them wisely. Let's consider these pluses and minuses.

What's in It for Teachers and Students?

Portfolios, if done well, permit teachers to do the following:

- Track student achievement over time to reveal improvement or the lack thereof. In this sense, they can be diagnostic.
- Preserve the detailed and complex picture of student achievement often lost when we condense everything into a report card grade.
- Afford students an excellent context within which to take responsibility for maintaining and tracking their own files and records of achievement. This is a critical life skill.
- Help students learn to reflect on and see their own improvement as achievers. This involvement has real motivational power.
- Provide important insights into students' academic self-concepts, academic interests, and sense of their own needs.
- Provide excellent opportunities for students to practice their reasoning proficiencies, analyze their own work, compare work over time, draw inferences about their growth or needs, and learn evaluative or critical thinking skills.
- Help students understand the work production requirements of real-life situations. That is, we can establish simulations of life beyond school or connect school experiences with real life, such as developing portfolios for job applications.
- Document student attainment of required district or state standards.

For all of these reasons, teachers experienced in using portfolios find them to be engaging for both themselves and their students.

The Challenges

With all of this encouragement, it's tempting simply to dive in and start developing and using student portfolios. But wait, there's more. Portfolio specialists Spandel and Culham (1995) remind us of three myths about portfolios that you would do well to keep in mind as you study this idea for your classroom.

Myth 1. Creating Portfolios Automatically Makes You a Better Teacher. They advise us that it's not that simple. Without a student-involved assessment environment in place, that is, without a strong foundation underpinning the portfolio structure, this way of communicating will not automatically lead to better teaching. That means we must start with clear targets, organized in a continuous progress manner and feeding into quality assessments (i.e., sound sampling of skills and control for bias and distortion), with students as full partners in assessing and assuming responsibility for their own learning.

Myth 2. Portfolios Are Easy to Manage if You're an Organized Person. Being organized helps, they advise. Over time, teachers report that they become more organized about their portfolios and therefore more comfortable using them. But the lessons they learn along the way are critical to their success. Even if you're organized, it's hard work. It takes time and patience to work into this idea. If you have difficulties early on, it is not because you are disorganized. As one teacher put it, when she first started implementing this idea in her classroom, her students "had portfolios." Now two years later, her students "do portfolios" in her classroom (Austin, 1994). By the time you finish this chapter, you will know what she meant, and will understand what it takes to use them successfully.

Myth 3. Portfolios Make Learning Easy for Students. "On the contrary," Spandel and Culham (1995) tell us, "portfolios offer students a whole new set of challenges: planning, time management, comparing, analyzing, and learning to understand how to learn. What is equally true is that students can potentially gain great insight from the experience, insight equivalent to the effort they put into it" (p. 14). Our challenge as teachers is the same in this case as it has been throughout: Help students see the personal value of assuming responsibility for their learning.

Maintaining Perspective

The immense popularity of portfolios and their rapid evolution have led in some instances to an unfortunate narrowing of perspectives. As you think about and plan for possible applications of portfolios in your classroom, be cautious of the following perspectives.

Portfolio Assessment?

It is not uncommon to see reference in our professional literature to this topic as "portfolio assessment." I don't, however, think of this as an assessment concept per se. In fact, the context (purpose and target) within which we use portfolios may require that we assemble information from several assessments using several different assessment modes to tell a complete story. It is the combination of these multiple assessments that underpin and give meaning to the message. For this reason, I think of portfolios as a communication system rather than an assessment system.

Portfolios and Performance Assessment

In addition, it is common to find the concepts of "portfolios" and "performance assessment" closely linked in current literature. When artists assemble portfolios of their work, they collect the artistic products they have created. When journalists collect samples of their articles, they too gather their work into a coherent whole. These are products. That's one kind of performance assessment. Thus, it is tempting to speak of a portfolio as relying only on performance assessment as the source of its information of student achievement. Resist that temptation. You have four forms of assessment in your repertoire: selected response, essay, performance assessment, and personal communication. We have said consistently that they are all potentially valuable contributors to the story we tell about student achievement. So they all can appear in portfolios. Additionally, portfolios can hold many other types of artifacts, such as photos, letters, rough drafts, schedules, lists (such as of books read), and other evidence relevant to telling a complete story of achievement status or growth.

Time for Reflection

What would you include if you were to develop a portfolio that told the story of who you are as an educator right now—say, as a job application portfolio?

Portfolios and Life Skills

Third, the popular culture associated with portfolios often requires that they focus on real-life proficiencies, for example, that stretch beyond school to the world of work. Some hold that portfolios should be married to the concept of "authentic" assessment, or assessment of skills required in the "real world."

While this represents one excellent application of the portfolio idea, and we should take maximum advantage of it, it is far from the only or even the most valuable application of portfolios. Opportunities abound in classrooms for portfolios to tell powerful stories about emerging academic proficiencies, such as math problem solving, beginning writing skills (including spelling and grammar), social interaction skills, knowledge and understanding of science, and others. These are the academic foundations that ultimately will underpin students' life skills and for this reason they are important. Portfolios can contribute to student success in developing these too, inside the academic world.

The Need for Quality Assessments

The trend that concerns me most about portfolios is the tendency of many users to think that, just because they're using portfolios, they're assured a rich and accurate portrait of student achievement. I have met teachers, administrators, and policy makers who seem to feel that the mere presence of portfolios somehow ensures quality schools, regardless of how well they implement the idea. This is potentially very dangerous. Because any portfolio is really a collection of relevant artifacts, each provides part of the mosaic of student achievement. For this reason, *it is essential that each contributing assessment provide dependable information* about the part of the story it is intended to represent.

Just as high-quality assessments give meaning to report card grades, so too do they permit portfolios to tell rich and compelling stories about student academic growth and development. They can help us to communicate effectively and thus improve schools only if they tell an accurate story. We can ensure the accuracy of the stories they tell only if we maintain a consistent commitment to our five standards of assessment quality: clear targets, clear purpose, proper methods, sound sampling, and control of bias and distortion. Poor-quality assessments will misrepresent student achievement and will place students directly in harm's way, regardless of how we communicate those results. In that sense, everything covered in Parts I, II, and III of this book is a prologue to our discussion of portfolios in this chapter. With these cautions foremost in our minds, then, let's explore the realm of portfolios.

The Keys to Successful Use

The definition of *portfolio* offered at the beginning of the chapter suggested that an effective portfolio system includes several specific ingredients. We'll consider these now. To start with, concentrate on building your portfolios in ways that account for the necessary conditions for effective communication that we framed in the introduction to Part IV:

1. *Maintain a sharp focus.* Place limits on the achievement target(s) of interest. Develop clear guidelines for selecting material to be collected in the portfolio to ensure reflection of those targets.

2. *Rely on quality assessments.* Align targets and purposes to assessment methods that can deliver into portfolios the information needed.

3. *Establish a solid interpersonal environment for communication.*

   a. *Be clear about the purpose for the portfolio.* Know what story the portfolio will tell and why that story is relevant.

   b. *Develop a shared language.* Rely on explicit criteria for assessing student work. These are the standards against which you and your students will gauge success.
   c. *Provide opportunities to attend to the evidence of achievement.* Involve students in selecting some of the work. Do this for the same reason that you would want to be involved in developing your job application. Your students have a stake in the story the portfolio is telling.
   d. *Check for understanding.* Require periodic student self-reflection on their own achievements. This represents the heart of the learning experience provided by portfolios. It will tell you and them if they are "getting it."

Let's discuss these keys to understand the practical lessons they teach.

Sharp Focus on Targets

The effective use of portfolios requires that we apply them in a disciplined way. I have come in contact with several local and even state education agencies that like the portfolio idea so much that they simply order teachers to start one for each student. Envision what I call the universal, all-encompassing, "mega-portfolio." Starting in primary grades, teachers accumulate evidence of achievement. Then each teacher along the way adds more, as the child's school story unfolds. Visualize a file folder that then becomes a file drawer, then a file cabinet, and then a closet full of material. Soon we've evolved to a room-sized collection, leading ultimately to the student driving a tractor-trailer across the stage at high school graduation!

Sound foolish? Of course it does. And I take little solace from technology buffs who tell us not to worry about volume of "stuff" because we can digitize it all and place it on a computer chip the size of your thumbnail. Imagine an "electro-mega-portfolio," still completely devoid of purpose. This lack of focus arises from a lack of understanding or discipline on the part of those who would conceive of such plans. If we start with no focus, no story to tell, no purpose, no clear achievement targets, we end up with a useless and unmanageable portfolio.

To understand how to avoid this, we must visualize a different scenario. We must begin each portfolio application with a clear sense of the target(s) in question. During the schooling experience, students develop and use many portfolios, each associated with a different target. Some will reflect math competence, some reading and writing, and others science skills. Some will be more structured, some less. Some will be more student involving, some less. Some will deal with knowledge targets, others with reasoning, still others with skills or products. Their content will vary. But we hope what will remain in students' minds is a sense that they are in control of their increasing academic competence—a strong and growing academic self-concept. My vision has teachers using portfolios flexibly and opportunistically to communicate information about student achievement and develop a sense of academic well-being. Over the years, most of these portfolio collections will end up in students' hands after serving their purpose. But everyone of them will focus on its own unique and crystal clear set of achievement expectations.

Quality Assessments

By this point in our journey, we don't need to add detail about how quality assessments form the foundation of an effective communication system. We have long since defined our five quality control criteria and discussed how to meet those standards. As we accumulate evidence of student achievement in a portfolio, we must continue to meet those standards. We can use selected response assessments, if they fit the context, to collect some of that information. Essay and performance assessments obviously represent viable options, too, in the hands of qualified users. Written or audio summaries may of course come into play.

I know of a school in which teachers record students struggling to speak a new language and then continue to collect recorded segments on that same audiocassette over the years as each student's proficiency increases. They wrap the cassettes as gifts and present them to their students at graduation along with their diploma. If they have developed high-quality, student-involved assessments, students not only hear themselves improving over time, but also can articulate precisely what it is that makes each new addition to the recording better than those that preceded it. Quality assessments placed in student hands encourage achievement.

Constructive Interpersonal Communication Environment

Sense of Purpose.   To merge effectively into instruction, portfolios must be specifically designed to serve a purpose. There needs to be a reason for telling the story. Thus, we must plan to collect materials that can tell that story. Those plans provide students and teachers with specific guidelines for selecting work for the portfolio. Guidelines will vary according to the purpose and target. Spandel and Culham (1995) provide us with a productive way to think of this by suggesting several structures for portfolios. These are not mutually exclusive categories, and you may blend them to fit the occasion. These structures are the celebration portfolio, the time sequence portfolio, the project portfolio, and the status report portfolio.

The Celebration Portfolio.   A portfolio can be used as a keepsake, which you invite students to create as a personal collection of favorite works and special academic mementos. They might use this to communicate to families the things they are most proud of or to show positive examples of their learning experiences or classroom activities.

In this case, students' guidelines for portfolio selection are driven by this purpose, What do I think is really special about my work and why? This is a wonderful place for young students to begin their portfolio development experience by just collecting favorite pieces of work. They may then begin to categorize and cull for the really special works. The only evaluations are made by the students, according to their own vision of what's "special." No one else's standards have a place here. This is critically important.

Students can use this experience to begin to identify the attributes of special classroom work and to generate personal insights about their own meaning of quality. Over time and through interaction with their teachers and classmates, they can begin to connect these elements of quality into a growing framework that ultimately helps them understand their own sense of what represents "good work." In this sense, the celebration portfolio, devoid of externally imposed standards, can put students in touch with their own strengths and interests, and can help them learn to make choices.

Time for Reflection

If you did a celebration portfolio of your years as an educator, what might you put in? List some things you would enter. Next to each, specify why you would include it. Then, try to capture in a few sentences the story you are trying to tell.

The Growth Portfolio.   Another reason to build a portfolio is to reveal changes or accomplishments in a student's academic performance over time. Two classroom applications of this idea warrant discussion, the growth portfolio and the project portfolio.

In the growth portfolio, the creator (storyteller) collects samples of work over time to show how proficiency has changed. When this is the purpose, guidelines for selection dictate assembling multiple indicators of the same proficiency, such as samples of writing or selections of artwork. If you recall the opening scenario in Chapter 1, Emily shared a sample of her writing from the beginning of the year for the school board to review and critique. Then she wowed them with another sample from the end of the year that revealed how much more proficient she had become. These writing samples came from her writing portfolio—a growth portfolio.

In this case, the evaluation criteria need to be held constant over time. Emily was able to discuss specific improvements in her work included in her portfolio over the year because the writing criteria—word choice, organization, sentence structure, voice, and so on—remained the same for each writing activity. This gave her a yardstick by which to see her writing progress to higher levels of competence. The motivational power of a growth portfolio can be immense.

The Project Portfolio.   Alternatively, the storyteller might depict the completion of steps in a project conducted over time. When this is the purpose, guidelines for selection dictate that the storyteller provide evidence of having completed all necessary steps in a quality manner. For example, students completing a major science project might show how they arrived at a hypothesis, how they assembled the apparatus for gathering the needed data, how they conducted the tests, the test results, and the analysis and interpretation of those results. A project portfolio is an ideal format to use to describe such work carried out over an extended period.

The evaluative judgments made in this case are based on two sets of performance criteria. The first reflect the steps students must have completed within a specified time frame. These typically provide highly structured guidelines for what to collect as proof of work completion. They teach students lessons about the necessity of planning a task and sticking to a timeline. You might also hold students accountable for periodically reviewing progress with you. The second set focuses on the quality of work completed at each step along the way. These, of course, demand that students not merely provide evidence of having done the activity, but also provide evidence that they did it well.

One final comment regarding growth and project portfolios: The span of time covered can range from a brief several-day project to one lasting a full year or longer, depending on the context. These are very flexible options.

The Status Report Portfolio.   Yet another kind of story to tell by means of a portfolio can be that of having met certain preestablished standards of performance. In this instance, the student must make a case within the portfolio for having attained certain levels of proficiency. Therefore, the intended achievement targets determine the guidelines for content selection.

Several applications of this kind of portfolio are relevant in school. As students progress through a continuous progress curriculum in math, for example, we might maintain a portfolio depicting each student's current achievement status. So at any point in time, decision makers could check this record and know what comes next. In this case, when a sample of student work is collected that reveals a new high level of achievement, then the old evidence previously held in the portfolio—now outdated—would be discarded. If there is any portfolio format that might accompany a student across grade levels over the years, this is it.

In another kind of application, in some districts students present a portfolio of evidence of having attained certain essential proficiencies in order to qualify for graduation. Indeed, some states require such evidence to earn a certificate of mastery.

In a much simpler context, we might ask students to assemble evidence of having mastered all requirements for completing a particular course. Or, we might review a status report portfolio to make a course placement decision, such as, What is the next natural course in this student's progression of math instruction?

In all of these cases, the guidelines for selecting material will probably be highly structured and driven by specific academic requirements that provide evidence that students have mastered prerequisites and are ready to move on.

Summary of Purposes and Portfolio Designs.   Clearly, the concept of a "megaportfolio" (a monster file of academic stuff devoid of purpose and structure) makes no sense in assessing student achievement or helping students succeed. However, if we formulate careful guidelines for selection around focused stories to tell, we can use portfolios advantageously to integrate our students deeply into teaching and learning.

We can start them with celebration portfolios in early grades to start students evaluating their own work. We can also help students track their own academic development over time. Sometimes this might center on the growth of a particular set of proficiencies. Other times, it might track the completion of a set of required projects. Either way, the student's skills are the focus of the story.

And finally, we can tap the portfolio idea to describe students' achievement status standards met, courses completed, and requirements satisfied, descriptions that inform our decisions about appropriate next steps.

The possible combinations and permutations of these portfolio options in the classroom are seemingly infinite. Also remember, both the time span covered and amount of material collected for any particular portfolio may vary from a little to a great deal, depending on the learning context and the teaching strategy, thus making this a flexible communication approach.

A Shared Language: Criteria for Judging Merit.   As you well know by now, we need to establish criteria by which to evaluate students' progress, whether judging the merit of writing, charting the expansion of scientific knowledge, or recording increased proficiency in speaking a foreign language. Portfolios can handle a range of target possibilities, relying on a variety of assessment formats.

To illustrate, if a student/teacher team decides that the best evidence of student attainment of a particular target is a score on a multiple-choice test, then the criteria used to judge merit is a high score on the test. If an essay test most accurately reflects the target, then once again, a traditional test score provides the needed information. However, with performance assessments, the applied criteria must reflect proficiency on the skills of interest or reflect the extent to which the student has met quality product standards.

Consequently, we must decide in advance and share with our students how we and they will judge merit. I continue to press the point that *students can hit any target that they can see and that holds still for them.* Obviously, this is equally important with portfolios, and is the essential way to link assessment and instruction.

By the way, some teachers have found it productive to develop and share with their students criteria for judging the merit of the portfolio as a whole. These often center on such attributes as whether the evidence collected reflects the right target(s), whether the evidence shows growth, the organization of the evidence and self-reflections, and the quality of the self-reflections. In fact, one teacher I know begins the year with students analyzing portfolios of varying quality, so they can play a role in establishing the criteria for evaluating the portfolios they will build during the coming year.

Opportunities to Interact: Involving Students in Selecting Portfolio Items.   Let's say you were assembling a job application portfolio. Clearly it would be important for you to take responsibility for selecting the material to be included, for two reasons. First, you know yourself best and can best ensure the telling of a complete and accurate story. Second, selecting the content allows you to present yourself in the most positive light called for in this competitive situation.

Our students are driven, Covington (1992) tells us, by a desire to maintain and to present to the world a sense that they are academically capable. We support and encourage that positive self-image by involving students in recording their own story through their portfolios. But to make this work, they must also actively participate in selecting the work for the portfolio.

In the celebration portfolio described previously, the story is essentially the student's to tell. But there also is much room for student involvement in the growth, project, and status report options. Notice that I am not saying that the student selects everything. Nor does the teacher. We're talking partnership here. Here's how one teacher friend of mine handles this: Her sixth graders maintain files of all work completed, one for each discipline. When it comes time to assemble the representative work for their growth portfolios in preparation for the periodic student-led parent conferences (discussed in detail in the next chapter), students and teacher work as a team to select work.

Davies, Cameron, Politano, and Gregory (1992) advise us that we can maximize the benefits of student involvement in selection by having them describe what they selected and why they selected it. They recommend using a cover sheet for each portfolio entry to capture this information. Figure 14.1 presents an example.

Checking for Understanding: Periodic Student Self-Reflection.   Of all the dimensions of portfolios, the process of self-reflection is the most important. If we are to keep students in touch with their emerging academic selves, we must share our vision of what it means to succeed in understandable terms. We must provide them with a vocabulary to use in communicating about it and keep them in touch with the accumulating evidence of their own proficiency. One way to hold them accountable for achieving a clear sense of themselves as learners is to have them write or talk about that accumulating evidence. With portfolios, this has come to be known as *student self-reflection*.

Clearly *students who learn to evaluate their own achievement become better achievers through the process*. They maintain contact with their own evolving strengths and weaknesses. Figure 14.2 provides an example in two parts, another of Emily's essays, "Visions of Hope," and her reflection on the quality of her work. In this essay, she assumes the persona of a prisoner who uses her art to maintain perspective. Please read the essay carefully first, then the self-reflection. Note that Emily continues to apply the six analytical writing assessment score scales presented in Chapter 7. Here is more evidence that Emily is in touch with her own writing proficiency.

Helping Students Reflect.   Sometimes it's helpful to initiate students into self-reflection by posing some simple questions for them to reflect about, such as the following (adapted from Arter & Spandel, 1992):

- Describe the steps you went through to complete this assignment. Did this process work and lead to successful completion or were there problems? What would you change next time?

- Did you receive feedback along the way that permitted you to refine your work? Describe your response to the feedback offered—did you agree or disagree with it? Why? What did you do as a result of this feedback?

- What makes your most effective piece of work different from your least effective? What does your best work tell you about where you have improved and where you need further work?

When I chose to include this example of my writing in my portfolio I remembered that...

FICTION	NON-FICTION
• has a good story	• gives information
• uses interesting language	• groups information under main headings
• has a beginning, a middle, and an end	• has a table of contents
• uses a variety of sentences, both simple and complex	• has diagrams or pictures to give additional information

I also know that it is important that my work is neat and that it has been edited for spelling and sentence structure.

The piece of work I have chosen is...

It shows...

I want you to notice...

Please give me one compliment and ask me one question after you read my selection...

I put this in my portfolio on _____ _____
                                    [date]   [signature]

Figure 14.1

Summary sheet for student use in describing portfolio selections

Source: From *Together Is Better: Collaborative Assessment, Evaluation and Reporting* (p. 79) by A. Davies, C. Cameron, C. Politano, and K. Gregory, 1992, Winnipeg, MB: Peguis Publishers Ltd. Reprinted by permission.

VISIONS OF HOPE

I call my picture "Visions of Hope." If I'm caught with this picture, I'll be killed. But it's worth it if people outside see it. I want them to know what life was like in the camp and how we kept our hopes up.

You may be wondering how I got the materials I used in this picture. It wasn't easy. I got the materials for the prisoner figures from old pieces of uniforms that had been torn off. This was one of the easier things to get. Uniforms get torn all the time from hard work. All the people look alike because to the Nazis it doesn't matter what you look like—only what you can do. To the Nazis we are all just numbers, without faces and without names.

The buildings in the picture are black to represent evil and death. Most of the buildings, aside from the barracks, you would enter but never come out again alive. I got this cloth from an old blanket that had worn thin from overuse. The Germans didn't care if we were cold or uncomfortable, so they didn't make any real effort to mend things. Everything in our world badly needs mending, too, including our spirits.

Inside the smoke of death coming out of the smokestacks you will see the Star of David. This star represents hope. Hope for life and for living. We will never totally die as long as our hope lives on.

My picture has two borders. One is barbed wire. It symbolizes tyranny, oppression, and total loss of freedom. The barbs are shaped like swastikas to represent the Nazis, Hitler and hate. This is a symbol of true evil.

The other border, outside the barbed wire, represents all the hope and dreams that are outside the camp. The flowers, sun, moon and bright colors were all things we took for granted in our old world. Even though we can see the sun through the clouds and smoke, we can't enjoy it anymore. The feathers represent the birds we barely see or hear inside the camp. We miss the cheeriness of their voices. The tiny brown twigs are as close as we come to the trees we remember. I got the bright cloth from a dress. When new prisoners come to the camp they must take off their own clothes and put on the hated prison outfits. All the nice clothes are sent to Germans outside the camps. My job is to sort through the clothes and pick out the nice things that will be sent away. When I saw this beautiful cloth, I tore off a piece and saved it for my picture.

I hope someone finds this and remembers that we always kept our hopes alive even when they took away everything else. They could never take our hope.

Figure 14.2
Sample of student writing and author's self-reflection

Source: "Visions of Hope," a sample of writing and self-reflection by N. Spandel. Reprinted by permission.

REFLECTION

This piece has always been one of my favorites. It shows not only what I can do as a writer, but as an artist as well. I knew very little of the Holocaust before working on this project. It was almost impossible for me to believe how brutal people could be. It both frightened and horrified me. In my written piece and my picture, I tried to capture that horror but also the courage which kept many people going. I also tried hard to imagine how it would really feel to be imprisoned, locked away from the things and the work and the people I loved. I don't know if anyone can really imagine this without living it, but this project made me think.

In **Ideas and Content,** I gave myself a 5. I thought my ideas were clear, and I thought I created a vivid picture of an artist trying to keep his work alive.

I would also give myself a 5 in **Organization.** My opening does a good job of leading the reader into my paper, especially with the dramatic and honest statement: "If I'm caught with this picture I'll be killed." I want the reader to know right away what is at stake.

My **Voice** is not as strong as I would have liked it to be. It is hard to take on the voice of another person. I am pretending to be someone else, not myself. I guess I just haven't had enough practice at this. Also, my natural voice tends to be humorous, and clearly, this is the most serious of topics. Anyway, I just did not find quite the voice I wanted, and I gave myself a 4.

I gave myself a 5 in **Word Choice.** The language is simple and natural. I did not try to impress the reader with words they might not understand. Also, I tried to capture the mood of what it would be like to live in a concentration camp and think how the people who lived there might talk. What words would they use?

My **Sentence Fluency** was pretty strong. You will notice that I vary my sentence beginnings a lot. That's one of my strengths. It's smooth, whether you read it silently or aloud. I think a few sentences are a little short and choppy, though. Some sentence combining would help. So I rated myself a 4 on this trait.

In **Conventions** I would rate myself a 5. I have always been strong in this trait. Conventions are fairly easy for me, if I think about them, especially with the aid of a computer. I can catch most grammatical errors, and I use a spell checker. I also read through my paper when it's finished to make sure it sounds just right. Rating myself on these traits is very helpful. It allows me to see how I'm doing as a writer, and to see my work as it really is. I think the traits give you a way of teaching yourself.

continued

- What are the strengths of your work in this project (or this series of works)?
- What aspects still need more work? What kind of help will you need?
- What impact has this project had on your interests, attitudes, and views of this area?

These and other related questions can be very helpful in beginning self-reflection. It's human nature to experience some difficulty being constructively analytical and self-critical, at least at first. As we established earlier, this is risky business for most, and especially for those with a history of academic failure. Covington (1992) reminds us that students will go to great lengths to maintain a positive internal sense of academic ability, even to the point of denying or being unable to see, let alone face, the flaws in their work. For this reason, guided practice is a necessity.

It may be helpful for your students to see you model the process by reviewing, analyzing, and self-evaluating some of your own work. Or, consider having the whole class collaborate as a team to compose a hypothetical self-reflection on a particular project. This is the best way I know to show students that your classroom is a safe place within which to risk trying. Either success or problems point the direction not to a judgmental grade, but to a specific path to each student's improvement.

What Makes a Good Self-Reflection?   In effect, self-reflection is a kind of student performance. Therefore, it too can be the focus of an evaluation. When asked to reflect on their work, students unschooled in the process will respond emotionally by saying, "I hate it," or, "I think it's really good." Typically, they will be at a loss as to what else to say. They will be unable to muster evidence to substantiate their judgment. But when schooled in appropriately applying the right performance standards and when they feel safe enough to be honest in making and defending their judgments, they will assert control over the evaluation and speak openly about issues of quality.

Remember the strategy discussed in the performance assessment chapters (Chapters 7 and 10) of having students contrast samples of outstanding and poor-quality performance to uncover key differences? Consider involving older students (mature middle schoolers and high schoolers) in a similar process to discover the key elements of an effective self-reflection. To minimize the risk to students, show them anonymous high- and low-quality self-reflections of some of your work and have students do the contrasting, devising criteria for evaluating their own reflections. Plan to engage students over time in the process of refining their visions of a good self-reflection as needed.

For those who need more specific guidance, consider these key dimensions. But remember, their relevance will vary with the activity (adapted from Arter & Spandel, 1992):

> *Coverage*—Does the reflection address all relevant criteria? Make a checklist of them, and work with the students to review their self-reflection and check them off.
>
> *Accuracy*—Are students developing an accurate sense of their achievement or growth? Compare your evaluations with theirs. Discuss similarities and differences of perspective.

Specificity—Does the reflection include examples to support points made in the self-reflection? Work with students to identify or develop them.

Integration—Have students appropriately synthesized important insights into broader conclusions about their achievement? Work with them to be sure they understand how to draw this kind of inference (excellent practice using an important form of reasoning).

Revelation—Does self-reflection bring students to new insights about their learning? Discuss these new insights with your students.

Time for Reflection

Let's say you wanted to develop a set of five analytical rating scales, one for each of the attributes of a student self-reflection listed above. Further, you want each to include three rating points: (1) Outstanding Reflection, (2) Mid-Range Reflection, and (3) Poor Quality Reflection. What would those rating scales look like? Please take a few moments to draft them. Also think for a moment about how you might involve your students in their development as a means of helping them enhance their understanding of self-reflection.

Dealing with Some Practicalities

As I work with teachers exploring classroom applications of portfolios, several questions seem to come up over and over. I recently sat down with Ms. Weatherby, Emily's teacher and a skilled and experienced user of portfolios, to discuss them.

Time for Reflection

In the following section, after you read each question and before you read Ms. W's response, take just a minute to think through how you would answer it. Then compare your responses to hers.

RICK	Ms. Weatherby, how does your district use portfolios?
MS. WEATHERBY	We start small. Our primary-grade teachers start with a simple celebration portfolio to ease their students into the process. We ask them to answer questions like, What do you like about this piece? What do you think you might be able to improve? In the elementary grades, we have them explore simple growth portfolios, keeping the targets simple and the criteria constant. Then in middle and high school we introduce the status report portfolio. I use the growth one, but our students must assemble a status report, too, during high school.
RICK	Does the long-term experience help?

MRS. W	Definitely. I have really noticed a difference in my students' comfort level when they come to my class with prior portfolio experience. Those who began with them very early plunge with confidence into my project assignment.
RICK	I've seen Emily's growth portfolio. How did you get started?
MS. W	We thought Em did a fine job at the board meeting. She's a perfect example of what happens when the growth portfolio works well, and it works well a lot.

The way several colleagues and I got started was that we wanted to do student-led parent conferences (see Chapter 15). We needed the portfolio to help students prepare evidence of their achievement to share with parents. My particular application of the idea is a writing growth portfolio. Over the grading period, each student has to complete all the assignments and keep a portfolio of evidence of the nature and quality of their work.

RICK	How much time does it take?
MS. W	It varies. It depends. As the scope of the target and time span of the portfolio increase, so does the time commitment. But as students mature and gain experience, they learn to handle most of the work and to enjoy it. You can see that in Emily.

The greater role the students play, the more feasible the idea becomes. But all teachers have to tailor their use of portfolios to fit their available time.

Here again we see deep student involvement helping teachers gain time for instruction—not record keeping.

RICK	You teach high school and face 150 students a day in different classes. Is this idea really feasible for you?
MS. W	You bet! But you have to be crafty about it. As I said, my assessment for my English classes requires my students to complete a series of writing assignments. Their work must meet certain standards of quality. I expect each student to keep a growth portfolio containing evidence of having completed all of the steps in the assignment. I count on heavy student involvement in all phases of the work.

We plan writing exercises together, they assist in devising the performance criteria used to evaluate their work, work in teams to apply those criteria (both for interim revisions and the final product), and maintain complete and accurate records along the way.

At first I was astounded, and I continue to be impressed with their willingness and ability to assume responsibility.

RICK	Can students really manage their own portfolios? What if they cheat?

Ms. W	They can manage it, as long as I provide leadership and insist on those timelines.

Cheating always becomes an interesting topic in my classes. In other classrooms, students can copy someone else's test paper, sneak in a crib sheet, have someone else do their homework for them, and even change grades on assignments before returning them to the teacher. In my years of teaching, I've seen it all.

But my students know that it's impossible to sneak by in the student-involved assessment activities we use in my classes. Those who prepare and deliver stand tall; those who don't, stand out.

And you know what really minimizes cheating? The weekly written self-reflection I require. Students first share them with their study teammates, then put them in their portfolios, where I get to read them. *If you don't know where you are in your own development and don't know what you're talking about, it's very hard to bluff. It stands out like a sore thumb.*

Rick	You've made cheating irrelevant, in effect.
Mrs. W	My students know that I expect to see increasing quality over time on their part. It's as if each self-reflection is more demanding than the one preceding it. Everyone seems to acknowledge that there are no excuses in this classroom. It may sound crazy, but I think you're right, they believe that cheating makes no sense in here. There's no percentage in it. In fact, pretty quickly, they see that it hurts them more than it helps.

Besides, my students quickly learn through the grapevine that they simply can't bluff in the conference with their parents and me at the end of the project, where any attempt to misrepresent their own achievement will be transparent. I ask tough questions in front of their families. They know they're responsible for providing good answers. And you know, I can see the pride in their eyes when they deliver quality.

Rick	How do you convert portfolio work to a grade?
Ms. W	We work as a class to devise a set of grading criteria. Before anyone starts, I share examples of good and bad work from past classes, and we work as a team to identify the differences between them. We establish and define our keys to success, and formulate performance rating scales. Those are all things that Emily told you about.

Frankly, there is a great deal of similarity among the scales developed by my different classes, but that's because I lead their development. My expectations are not open to negotiation. But, I find that student involvement buys ownership on their part. And, I am flexible regarding the vocabulary we use to describe our standards. My students truly have important input.

I base their grade on the quality of the final products at the end of the grading period. We agree on the target in advance, and we define levels of proficiency that equate to different grades—you know, what their profile of ratings must look like to earn an A, a B, and so on. No one gets credit for just doing the work. It's achievement that counts. They know they must set their own aspirations and work accordingly. There's no mystery.

RICK   Who owns the portfolios?

Ms. W   My students keep the growth portfolio. When our purposes have been served, they take them home.

However, the district is experimenting with a graduation portfolio. That requires a record of evidence of student achievement of a specified set of expectations for high school graduation. This might take on the stature of an official transcript. If it does, then this portfolio would become part of the student's permanent record.

RICK   Who has access to your portfolios?

Ms. W   These are official academic records, just like report cards. All normal privacy rights are in force. Only me, my students, their families, and school officials have access, unless families give permission for others to see them.

RICK   Where do you store all of these portfolios?

Ms. W   With their owners—my students. They can be responsible for this. If they wish, they can use a file cabinet in my room. But, the agreement is that each portfolio is private property.

I have heard that there are some electronic portfolio software packages coming on the market. We've begun to investigate this option for the district for the future.

RICK   Thanks, Ms. Weatherby.

About Those Electronic Portfolios

As Ms. W. points out, there are some promising new developments on the horizon for storing student portfolios. A number of computer software developers have created and are refining packages that permit classroom teachers to help students develop electronic portfolios. These purport to allow easy entry of traditional academic records (student background, grades, etc.), as well as actual examples of student work, including everything from written products to color videos with sound. Easy retrieval also is possible using networked personal computers. Profiles of currently available systems can be found on the Internet at www.wested.org/acwt. Those who have access to these kinds of information management systems report immense time savings.

Summary: Communicating with Portfolios

Portfolios offer ways to communicate about student achievement in greater detail than is permitted by report card grades. In this case, the communication arises out of collecting and displaying actual examples of student work. Unlike grades, portfolios can tell a detailed story of a student's achievement. This does not mean that they should replace grades, but rather that we should see them as serving different purposes—different users and uses.

Portfolios have gained immense popularity in recent years because of their potential as a teaching tool that offers many opportunities for student involvement. Portfolios can help teachers diagnose student needs and reveal improvement over time. They can encourage students to take responsibility for their own learning, track that learning, and gain an enhanced sense of academic progress and self-worth. Portfolios help students learn to reflect on their own work, identify strengths and weaknesses, and plan a course of action—critically important life skills. And finally, they give students opportunities for practicing important and useful reasoning and problem-solving skills.

But with all these pluses, they take very careful planning and dedication to use well. The hard work can pay off with immense achievement and motivational dividends if we implement them in calculated small steps. See the big picture, but move toward it in baby steps, one step at a time. Unfortunately, many have drowned in the sea of student papers collected to serve a policy maker's mandated "mega-portfolio" system. We can avoid such problems by preparing carefully.

Specifically, this means the following:

- Collect evidence of student attainment of clearly articulated achievement targets.
- Gather dependable evidence so as to create an accurate picture.
- Use portfolios in a communication environment that lends itself to open sharing by doing the following:
  a. Be sure everyone understands the portfolio's purpose.
  b. Develop a shared vocabulary for discussing levels of proficiency.
  c. Provide plenty of opportunities to interact with students about achievement.
  d. Regularly check to be sure students are in touch with and feeling in control of their own progress.

The possibilities of student involvement in this kind of communication are bounded only by the imagination of the users, meaning you and your students. They can play key roles in identifying the story to be told, devising guidelines for the selection of work to go into the portfolio, devising criteria for judging merit, applying those criteria, reflecting on their own achievement status or growth over time, and communicating to others about their success in learning. That communication process is the focus of our final chapter.

Exercises for Self-Assessment

1. After reviewing this chapter, identify in your own words why portfolios have become so popular in schools beginning in the 1990s.

2. List what you believe to be the major challenges teachers face in their use of portfolios and identify why each is a challenge.

3. Commit to memory the six active ingredients that go into a sound portfolio system and why each is so essential to our success in using them.

4. Create a chart, labeling each line with one of the four types of portfolios discussed in this chapter: celebration, growth, project, and status report. Add four columns headed by these questions: What story will the portfolio tell? What kinds of evidence must it contain? How will we evaluate the information? How does this portfolio type connect to our instruction? Referring to the text, within each cell of this four-by-four chart, briefly answer each question for each portfolio type.

5. In the last section of the chapter, Ms. Weatherby and I discussed a few practicalities of portfolio use in the classroom. Referring to the text, list each question raised in that section, and next to each, answer it in the briefest possible manner, a single word or phrase, if possible.

6. Compare and contrast report card grades and portfolios as means of communication about student achievement. How are they alike? How are they different? What do those similarities and differences tell you about the information users each is likely to serve well?

7. If you were to replace your parent-teacher conferences with student-led parent conferences, what type of portfolio would you have students develop? Why? If you were helping students to prepare portfolios to certify completion of high school graduation requirements, what kind would you help them develop? Why?

 You may go to the Companion Website at www.prenhall.com/stiggins and answer these questions in the Self-Assessment module.

Final Chapter Reflection

1. *What are the three most important new insights to come to you as a result of your study of this chapter?*
2. *Which of your previous questions about assessment can you now answer based on your study of this chapter?*
3. *What new questions have come to mind as a result of your study of this chapter that you hope to have answered as your study continues?*
4. *For practicing teachers only: What do you plan to do differently in assessment in your classroom as a result of your study of this book so far?*

   For those in preservice study only: *As you think about the classroom assessment environment that you hope to create for your students, how has your thinking changed as a result of your study of this book so far?*

Workbook Activities

Those of you using the workbook, *Practice with Student-Involved Classroom Assessment*, as part of your study of this material will find the following activities and others included for Chapter 14:

- *Job Interview Simulation.* When it comes to portfolios, purpose is everything. As in the chapter, this activity makes it clear that the purpose for a portfolio determines what goes in it, who puts it there, who develops performance criteria, who judges the content, and the role of student involvement.

- *How Good Is My Work? Self-Reflection.* This activity provides practice in developing questions for students that provoke self-assessment. It also has you discuss ways to involve students, and perhaps try out some of those ideas.

- *Dealing with Practicalities.* The last section of the chapter discusses practicalities of portfolio use in the classroom. Practicalities relate to time, ownership, storage, grading, and so on. This activity asks you to consider solutions to these barriers for portfolio use.

15

Communicating with Conferences

CHAPTER FOCUS

This final chapter of our journey through the realm of classroom assessment answers the following guiding question:

> How can my students and I communicate effectively with each other and their families about their achievement through the use of various conference formats?

From your study of this chapter you will come to understand the following general principles:

1. As with report cards and portfolios, certain conditions must be satisfied if we are to confer effectively about student achievement.

2. We have choices—we can team students, parents, and teachers in a variety of combinations to meet our communication needs. Each conference format brings with it strengths and challenges.

Let the Conference Begin

"The tablecloths are out, cookies arranged, lemonade cooling, and I'm eating supper—frozen yogurt." Terri Austin, a sixth-grade teacher from Fairbanks, Alaska, begins to tell us what it's like in her classroom the evening of student-parent conferences. Let's listen to the rest of her story.

> It's 5:45. Will they come? No matter how many times I do this, I always wonder if families will show up.

At 5:50, Frank and his mom arrive early. He's all polished, clean shirt and hair combed. As she sits at a table by the window, he quickly finds his portfolio, joins her and begins.

At 6:00, the room fills quickly, Ruth and her mother drink lemonade while looking at the class photographs on the bulletin board.

Chuck says, "Pick a table, Mom." She picks one with a purple tablecloth. Chuck smiles and says, "Oh yeah, you like purple. Would you like some refreshments?" After his mother and brother are seated, Chuck goes to pick up cookies and drinks.

Dennis and his father come in. Dennis's father is still in his military uniform. They find a table by the window. As Dennis shares his work, his father smiles. The father leans closer to Dennis, so they see the paper at the same time.

With his mother sitting across from him, Chuck goes over each paper very carefully. Occasionally, she looks over Chuck's head and smiles at me.

Greg and his mom speak Spanish as they look at the papers together.

Darrin's father rushes in with his family trailing behind. His father asks, "Mrs. Austin, what time are we?" "I scheduled the time wrong," Darrin apologizes. I say, "It's OK. There are no set times. Just find a table and begin." They stop at the refreshment table as Darrin finds his portfolio.

I hear Greg explaining his summary sheet in Spanish.

Steve, his mom, and an unknown lady and child arrive. At the end of the conference, I find out the woman is a neighbor who heard about "Steve's portfolio" and wanted to see it. So Steve invited her to his conference.

Darrin's mom catches my eye and smiles. She listens to Darrin read [one of his papers].

On their way out the door, I talk with Hope's family. They are very pleased with Hope's work. Her mom has tears in her eyes as she tells me how proud she is of Hope. (Austin, 1994, pp. 66–67)

How many workers are sharing the load of communicating here?

Thus, Terri introduces us to the idea of student-led parent conferences.

In this case, we combine the strengths of student-teacher conferences and parent-teacher conferences into a rich and engaging learning experience for students. Terri and her students spend a great deal of time both preparing information about student achievement and preparing to share it with parents. These personal conferences with families add a depth of communication about student growth and development over time that is unattainable with any of other communication option.

After the conferences, Terri checked with her students to see if they thought the hard work and preparation were worth it for them. She was startled at the strength of student feelings:

ANNE   I think it really does make a difference. It's definitely easier because you know the outcome of the conference and you don't get the jitters and all worried wondering about the out-

	come. It teaches you responsibility. You also learn while you're getting ready. I admit it is hard but you are also satisfied knowing you can prepare a conference like a teacher can.
DAVE	Yes, it does make a difference. It is fun and a new experience. I learned patience and responsibility. I learned to tell the truth and to talk about my grades.
SAMANTHA	I have learned that I could explain myself and my grades. It also teaches me to take my time. I learned that I could do more things if I tried because I thought I never could have done them. I also learned that it is a better way to get in touch with your parents.
PHILIP	I learned I can find trust within my grades and show responsibility as in how to make the most of my grades.
MARY	It's scary sometimes.
AARON	It's a very good method.
RICK	I know a lot more about what's going on. Otherwise I don't know what the teacher has said about me. I feel a lot more comfortable doing this. I know my grades and my papers, I seem to know what's going to happen and how I'm doing in school. I'm fair to myself.
DAVID	I learned that I do things that I've never done before and that I can make mistakes sometimes.
MRS. A	Would you recommend this type of conference to other students and teachers? [Everyone agrees they would.]
MRS. A	What do you think? Should we continue this procedure for the rest of the year? [All agree they should.]
MELISSA	Yes. I think parents understand things better when their child answers their questions. Also, we know the answers to all the questions. Maybe a teacher-parent conference wouldn't answer all the questions. (Austin, 1994, pp. 27–28)

Any doubt about the power of Terri's way of setting clear goals, compiling evidence of goal attainment in portfolios, and preparing students to share information about their own achievement is erased when we read this kind of comment from a parent:

The transformation of Jason as a student has been remarkable, from an F and C student to an A and B student. We cannot help but believe that a great deal of the credit must go to the manner in which class materials are presented and the curriculum is organized. Jason certainly has become more focused on his capabilities rather than his limitations. The general emphasis on responsibility for one's own actions and performance has also been most beneficial. Jason was a very frustrated young man in [his former school] and has had a tendency to place blame on others rather than accepting responsibility for his own choices. The last portion of this year has brought welcome changes in this respect. Though not always the most conscientious student, he puts forth serious effort on his studies and assumes responsibility for the results of his efforts. We believe that the "writing classroom" environment has been crucial to Jason's educational development, self-examination and personal growth. (Austin, 1994, p. 48)

I hope this vignette encourages you to explore open, inclusive, student-involved ways of communicating. In this chapter, the final stage of our journey together, I will share an array of ideas for communicating about student achievement that stretch far beyond our traditional teacher-centered report card grades and parent-teacher conferences. But remember, my point is not to negate those ways of sharing information; rather, is it to offer additional possibilities.

Be advised from the outset that these alternative means of sharing information do not represent panaceas that promise to deliver us from our communication challenges. Each option presents its own unique strengths and challenges. And, to be sure, each requires every bit as much work. However, I believe that we can markedly increase our positive impact on students' achievement by using conference formats intelligently.

In addition, never lose sight of the fact that conferences, just like report cards and portfolios, require the use of high-quality assessments as the basis for gathering accurate information about student achievement. *No one has succeeded as yet in inventing a communication alternative capable of converting misinformation into accurate information.*

Necessary Conditions

As in the previous three chapters, before we delve into the topic of conferences, let's do one final review of the keys to effective communication. If conferences are to be conducted in a productive manner, the following conditions must be satisfied:

1. We must be crystal clear and up front with our students about the achievement expectations we hold for them. Those expectations should fit into a continuous progress vision of student growth, both within and across grade levels. And we ourselves must be confident, competent masters of the targets that they are supposed to hit. Without this, we can neither assess nor communicate.

2. Our assessments of student achievement must be accurate. Dependable information lays a solid foundation for effective communication. Inaccurate information lays a foundation of shifting sand. To communicate effectively, the interpersonal environment must be right. That is, all who are involved must

   - Understand what we are trying to achieve by means of our communication about student achievement.
   - Use a common language to convey meaning.

- Take time to be in the moment when information is being shared—take the opportunity to share thoughts about and reactions to the information being shared.
- Check back with each other to be sure everyone understood and felt able to use the achievement information shared.

Our students must be deeply involved in assessing their own achievement over time, so they can understand the meaning of success, watch themselves grow, and develop the vocabulary needed to communicate effectively about their own success.

It is only with these pieces in place that we can meet with each other to share insights into individual students' learning.

Conference Formats That Enhance Communication

We're going to explore three practical conferencing formats:

- Student-teacher conferences
- Traditional parent-teacher conferences
- Student-led parent conferences

In the first format, teacher and student share a common vision and definition of academic success that allows them to share focused discussions of the student's progress. Some teachers are using these strategies to transform their classrooms into workshop settings. I'll share an example.

The second format brings parents or guardians and teacher together to share information on student achievement. While this kind of conference has long been a standard part of schooling, we'll put some new spins on the idea to bring students into the process.

The third case, student-led parent conferences, takes advantage of the benefits of the other two formats, adding some special pluses of its own. Further, it overcomes many of their weaknesses, although it brings its own challenges. With this approach, as we learned from Terri Austin at the beginning of the chapter, the primary responsibility for communicating about expectations and progress shifts from teacher to student. We'll explore some practical guidelines for using this option, review benefits to students and parents, and share some reactions from users.

Student-Teacher Conferences

A classroom learning environment turns into a workshop when the teacher shares the vision of achievement with students and then sets them to work individually or in small groups in pursuit of the designated target. In this setting, the teacher becomes a consultant or coach, working one on one or with groups to improve students' performance. This permits a kind of individualization that works very well when students are at different levels of achievement, such as in the development of their math or writing proficiencies. Much of the communication between teacher and student occurs in one-on-one conferences between them.

These conferences give students personal attention. Besides, students who are reticent to speak out in class often will come forth in conference. As a result, that two-way communication so essential to effective instruction can take place. And finally, the conference provides an excellent context in which to provide specific feedback. Teachers can provide commentary on student performance and students can describe what is and is not working for them.

To understand the kind of dialogue that can emerge from this idea, read the example of student writing shown in Figure 15.1. A conference is about to take place between the teacher, Ms. Weatherby, and the student focusing on this work. Ms. W has been holding conferences with her students since the beginning of the school year. It is now January. She tries to confer with each student every 2 to 3 weeks, and, though it takes a fair amount of time, she feels that the payoff is worth it. The dynamics of the conferences are changing a bit. In the beginning, she had to ask lots of questions. Now, students usually come to a conference with things to say.

Jill, the student, has never been an exceptional writer. Until recently, she didn't like to write and wrote only when forced. She didn't like talking about her writing, and her most frequent comment was, "I can't write."

At first, she didn't want to speak about her writing. The last two conferences, however, have been somewhat different. Jill is beginning to open up. She is writing more on her own. She keeps a journal. She is still, however, reluctant to voice opinions about her own writing; she looks to her teacher for a lead. (Be sure to read Figure 15.1 before continuing.)

"Pretty terrible, huh?" Jill asks Ms. Weatherby.

Figure 15.1
Sample of Jill's writing
Source: Adapted from *Creating Writers: Linking Assessment and Writing Instruction* (p. 105) by V. Spandel and R. J. Stiggins, 1990, White Plains, NY: Addison-Wesley Longman. Copyright 1990 by Longman Publishing Group. Adapted by permission of the publisher.

My Dog

Everyone has something important in their lives and the most important thing to me, up to now, has been my dog. His name was Rafe. My brother found him in an old barn where we were camping in a field near my grandpa's house. Somebody had left him there and he was very weak and close to being dead. But we nursed him back to health and my mom said we could keep him, at least for a while. That turned out to be for ten years.

Rafe was black and brown and had a long tail, floppy ears, and a short, fat face. He wasn't any special breed of dog. Most people probably wouldn't of thought he was that good looking but to us he was very special.

Rafe kept us amused a lot with funny tricks. He would hide in the shadows and try to spook the chickens but they figured out he was just bluffing so he had to give up on that one. When Rafe got hit by a truck I thought I would never stop crying. My brother misses him too, and my mom, but no one could miss him as much as I do.

"What do you think of it?" Ms. W asks, tossing the question back to her. She doesn't answer right away, but her teacher doesn't break the silence. The seconds tick by. Ms. W waits.

"I don't like the ending," Jill volunteers at last.

"Tell me why."

"Well, it just stops. The whole thing just doesn't tell how I really feel."

"How do you feel?"

She thinks for a minute. "Oh, it isn't like I miss him all the time. Some days I don't think about him at all. But then—well, it's like I'll see him at the door, or I'll see this shadow dashing around the side of the barn. Sometimes when we cook out, I think about him because he used to steal hotdogs off the grill, and one time my dad yelled at him when he did that and he slipped and burned one of his feet real bad."

"Now there's the real Jill and Rafe story beginning to come out! You're telling me about Rafe in your real personal voice and I sense some of your feelings. When you wrote about Rafe, did you speak like that? Let's read part of your writing again."

After doing so, Jill comments, "Pretty blah, not much me!"

"If you did write like you were speaking, how do you think it might read?"

"Like a story, I guess."

"Try it and let's see what happens. Talk to me about Rafe in your own personal voice. Besides, stealing hotdogs off the grill conjures up a funny picture, doesn't it? Those are the kinds of mental pictures great stories tell. When I can picture what you're saying, that's 'ideas'. You're giving the story some imagery and focus that I like very much. What kind of imagery do you see in this writing?"

They scan the piece again. Jill says in a low voice, "No images here—just facts."

"How about if you think up and write about some of those personal things you remember about Rafe?"

"Do you think I should?"

"Well, when you were talking, I had a much better sense of you in the story—of how much you missed your dog and how you thought about him."

"I think I could write about some of those things."

"How about if you give it a try, and we'll talk again in about a week?"

"How about the spelling, punctuation, and sentences? Were those okay?" Jill asks.

"Let's leave that 'til later. Think about the ideas, the organization, the voice. We'll come back to the other."

"I don't want any mistakes, though," Jill confesses.

"But is this the right time to worry about that?"

"I don't know; I just don't want to get a bad grade."

"Okay," Ms. W nods. "Suppose we agree that for now, we'll just assess the three traits I mentioned: ideas, organization, and voice."

"That's all?"

Ms. W nods again. "And if you decide you want to publish this paper in the school magazine, then we'll work on the rest."

"We can fix the other stuff then, right?"

"You will have time to fix it, yes."

Time for Reflection

In your opinion, what are the keys to making conferences like this work? What are some of the barriers to effective conferences? How might you remove these barriers?

Dealing with the Practicalities.   Those who have turned classrooms into workshops tell us that conferences need not be long. We can communicate a great deal of information in just a few minutes. However, thoughtful preparation is essential. It is best if both students and teacher examine student work beforehand with performance criteria in mind and prepare focused commentary.

Good listening is essential. If you prepare a few thoughtful questions in advance, you can draw insight out of students, triggering their own self-reflection. Effective conferences don't rely on traditional, one-way communication. Rather, they work best when teachers share both the control of the meeting and the responsibility for directing the communication.

Over time, and with experience in conferences, it will become easier to open the dialogue because both you and your students will become more at ease with each other. Over time, students also will become more familiar with your expectations. They will develop both the conceptual frameworks and vocabulary needed to communicate efficiently with you about their progress. So begin with modest expectations and let the process grow.

Parent-Teacher Conferences

I would be remiss if I failed to insert the traditional parent-teacher conference into our discussion of effective ways to communicate. During our school years, most of us became the "odd person out" of these meetings. We were left wondering, What did they say about me. Further, many experienced teachers who have been on the other side of the desk and who obviously know what was said, wonder if they said the right things and if they were understood.

Analyzing the Benefits.   Parent-teacher conferences offer three specific advantages over report card grades as means of communication. They permit us to do the following:

1. Retain and share a sufficiently high level of detail to provide a rich picture of student achievement. In effect, they provide a personal way to share the checklists, rating scales, and narratives discussed previously.

2. Ask follow-up questions to determine if we have succeeded in communicating. We can provide additional detail and explanation as needed to be sure the message gets through. Parents can ask questions to eliminate uncertainty.

3. Plan jointly with families to blend school and home learning environments for maximum productivity. In some cases, that means we can find out what may be going wrong with a student's home environment and urge adjustments in that environment.

But these advantages should not lead us to infer that conferences should replace report cards or any other record-keeping or communication option. Rather, we can use our various communication options in combination, where part of our conference time is used to explain grades, checklists, ratings, or other symbols, for example.

Anticipating the Challenges.   Of course, challenge number one is time. Parent-teacher conferences take a great deal of time to prepare for and to conduct. Every family must get its share of one-on-one time with you. For junior high and high school teachers working with large numbers of students, again, this option may not be feasible, especially given the number of courses students take at one time.

Challenge number two is that of devising a jargon-free, family-friendly vocabulary and interpersonal manner to use in describing student achievement to parents. If we pile on a great deal of technical language delivered in an aggressive style, we will have difficulty connecting.

Challenge number three is encouraging parental participation in the conferences. Some families care more about their children than do others. Some have busy lives, and competing priorities always seem to win. Some parents feel vulnerable in parent-teacher conferences, especially if things aren't going well in school for their child. There is always the chance in their minds that you might accuse them of failing to support your teaching efforts. Even though you know you would never do that, they don't know it for sure.

Challenge number four is helping students to come through conference time with academic self-concepts intact. This can be risky stuff for our students. If they're left wondering what was really said about them—as they usually are—the effect can be uncertainty, frustration, and even anger. At the very least they may be left with the impression that they aren't important enough in this communication equation to warrant a role.

For any one or all of these reasons, if we use parent-teacher conferences as our means of message delivery, we can be in danger of failing to communicate effectively with students and with some families.

Dealing with the Practicalities.   We can meet these challenges and take maximum advantage of this conference format if we follow some simple, straightforward procedures:

STEP 1:   Establish a clear and complete set of achievement expectations.

STEP 2:   Transform those expectations into quality assessments and gather accurate information.

STEP 3:   Carefully summarize that information for sharing via grades, checklists, rating scales, narrative, portfolios, or test scores.

By pooling your evidence in preparation for the conference, you increase the validity and reliability of the story to be told.

STEP 4:   Conduct a *student-teacher* conference to review all of this material before conducting the parent-teacher conference. This permits students to understand the message to be delivered. In fact, imagine a classroom in which this step was unnecessary because steps 1 to 3 were carried out in a student-involved manner. With targets clarified and shared, students involved deeply in the accumulation of achievement evidence, and students as partners in developing the portfolio that will be the topic of discussion at the parent-teacher conference, everyone shares. The motivational and achievement benefits of such a partnership will be considerable.

STEP 5:   Schedule and conduct the parent-teacher conference. By the way, imagine the kind of ongoing communication link that we might forge with parents if we had our continuous progression of achievement targets organized into bands like the previous Australian illustration (see Figures 13.8 and 13.9). We'd have concrete ways to show parents both how their children are doing with respect to our expectations and, if necessary, in relation to other students of like age or grade.

STEP 6:   Ask for a written follow-up reflection from parents presenting their impressions of the achievement and progress of their children.

Student-Led Parent Conferences

Of all the communication possibilities available to us, this one excites me the most, because it places students at the heart of the process. Notice immediately that I did not label this "student-involved parent-teacher conferences." I used the label "student-led" to emphasize the need to both give students the opportunity to tell, and to hold students accountable for telling, at least some of the story of their own achievement.

This is a more complex communication option than either of the other two conference formats. However, the payoff for the added work can be impressive, to say the least. In fact, I regard this conference format to be the biggest breakthrough to happen in communicating about student achievement in the past century.

Exploring the Benefits.   Among the positive effects reported by teachers who use this idea are the following:

1. *A much stronger sense of responsibility for their own learning among students*. When students understand that, down the road, they (not you) will be

telling their own success (or lack of success) story, they realize that there is no escaping accountability. They realize very quickly that, if they have nothing to share at that meeting by way of success, they are going to be very uncomfortable. This can be a strong motivator. And once they have some positive experience with this process and develop confidence in themselves, they become even more motivated to do well at it.

2. *A much stronger sense of pride when they do have a success story to share at conference time*. It feels good to be in charge of a meeting in which you're the star of a winning team.

3. *A different and more productive relationship between students and their teachers*. When that conference takes place, if the student has nothing by way of success to share, the student won't be the only one who will be somewhat embarrassed. In this sense, students and teachers become partners in the face of a common challenge. Both must succeed together. This kind of alliance can boost student achievement.

4. *Improved student-parent relationships*. Many families report that their conversations about student achievement extend far beyond the conference itself—sometimes weeks beyond. Often what emerges from the meeting is a sense of mutual interest in student projects, along with a shared language that permits ongoing interaction. School–family partnerships can flourish under these circumstances.

5. *An active, involved classroom environment built on a strong sense of community*. Students take pride not only in their own accomplishments and their ability to share them, but also in the opportunity to help each other prepare for and succeed at their conferences. A team spirit, a sense of community, can emerge and this can benefit the motivation and achievement of all.

6. *A reduction in relevance or value of cheating*. Not only is it difficult to misrepresent one's achievement when concrete evidence will be presented at the conference, but also, students seem less interested in cheating. What can emerge is a greater sense of honor and honesty related to their heightened sense of responsibility for and pride in actually achieving.

> One potential source of bias is eliminated.

7. *The development of important leadership skills*. Coordinating and conducting a student-led parent conference requires that the student schedule the meeting, invite participants, handle the introductions, organize and present information to the group, and follow up to discern meeting results. These are important life skills.

8. *Greater parental participation in conferences*. Virtually all schools report that a far higher percentage of parents show up to be part of conferences when students are the leaders. You can probably anticipate why this might be the case. If you are a parent, which invitation is more likely to bring you to a meeting: a mimeographed note from your child's teacher with a date and time filled

in stuck to the refrigerator, or your child standing in front of you looking up with those eyes reminding you that the conference is tomorrow and she will be in charge and "You're going to be there, right?"

Also, remember that some parents' school experiences were less than positive and, for some, things may not be going well in their adult lives. In their minds, there is a danger that, if they come to a parent-teacher conference, you might accuse them of being a bad parent. For this reason alone, they might avoid the meeting. When they know that their child is to lead the meeting, this risk seems to be reduced in their minds. For this reason among others, virtually all users of this conference format report a major jump in the proportion of parents who participate.

Facing the Challenges.   At the same time, this idea of student-led conferences is not without its downside risks. For example, it's not easy for some teachers to share control with students. This requires a kind of trust teachers typically don't grant to their students. When we give up control in this way, we cannot always be absolutely sure what will happen. If difficulties arise, they arise in a fishbowl and some pretty important people will see them. That's scary.

Further, it should be clear that the presentation of student-led conferences is just the tip of a pretty big iceberg. *You buy the whole environment or none of it.* Effective communication is possible only if the conference arises from a student-involved classroom assessment environment. We cannot simply plug in student-led parent conferences in a traditional teacher-centered assessment environment, where students have little idea what the expectations are or how they are doing with respect to those targets. I recently spoke with a parent who's third-grade daughter "got caught" between two adults talking about her. The child was scared before and during the event, according to her mom. She had no idea what was happening, was given no responsibility in planning for the meeting, was asked to answer questions she was totally unprepared to address, and had a completely negative experience. This was a good idea badly implemented and one mother was left very cold about the whole idea. *We must set students up to succeed at the conferences over the long haul or such conferences are not worth conducting.* So from the teacher's perspective, it can be very scary to contemplate such far-reaching changes.

Another challenge is finding the time to prepare for and manage such conferences. Most teachers plan for at least 30-minute conferences. This is especially difficult for junior high or high school teachers, who might face 150 students a day. First, be careful about how you think about time used in this context. There is a strong tendency to think of it as time lost to instruction. Nothing could be further from the truth. The time spent preparing to confer turns into highly focused teaching and learning time.

Beyond this, we need to creatively manage the logistics of holding conferences. Many teachers report that they can have students conducting several at one time, once those students have experience running conferences. In addition, high school teachers I know limit conferences to one or two courses per grading period, thus spreading them across four quarters of the year. In fact, one teacher I know asks that conferences last at least one hour, with only the first 30 minutes taking place in the classroom. The remainder is to take place at home, and students are responsible for reporting back in writing about how the rest of the conference went. To a person, her students report that conferences stretched far beyond the required hour.

But perhaps the most difficult challenges faced by those who would place students in charge of these conferences arise when the student comes from a dysfunctional family. The easiest version of this problem occurs when parents simply fail to show up. More difficult versions have parents showing up and becoming abusive in any of a number of ways.

Time for Reflection

How might we plan conferences in collaboration with our students in ways that maximize the chances that parents will show up? Further, if parents or other invited guests fail to arrive for the conference, how might we handle this in a manner that keeps the student's ego intact? Think about this for a moment before reading on.

Some teachers I know cover the very rare occurrence of parents failing to show up by having a backup "listener" available on conference day. It might be a former teacher, the principal, a janitor, or someone from the cafeteria staff. The only requirement is that the listener be someone whose opinion the student cares about. When this condition is satisfied, students can present enthusiastically and take pride in their achievements. It's okay to reschedule too, if the listener scheduled cannot make it.

Keys to Success.   We overcome these challenges only by attending to some simple fundamental conditions. To make this idea work, we need the following:

- Students who feel confident, safe, and trusting enough to take the risk of describing their own growth to their parents
- Teachers who are willing to take the risk of stepping aside and letting their students take charge, just as a coach helps the players learn the game and then places them on the field or court to play the game themselves
- Achievement targets that have been clearly and completely defined, woven into instruction, and used as the basis for an open and honest ongoing communication system
- Accurate, student-involved assessments fill the portfolios that tell the story
- Both teacher and students who share a common language for talking about attainment of each important achievement target
- Students who have had time to learn about, to prepare for, and to practice their leadership roles

When these conditions are satisfied and students take the lead in evaluating their learning, many good things occur. For example, because students and teacher must work closely together to prepare for the conference, it builds a greater amount of individual attention into instruction. This gives students a greater sense of their own importance in the classroom.

Time spent planning and preparing for student-led parent conferences becomes high-quality teaching and learning time. Students work to understand the vision of success, master the language needed to communicate about it, learn to describe their achievements, and evaluate their own strengths and weaknesses. Is this not the essence of a productive learning environment? Besides, as they prepare for the meeting, students might organize demonstrations, set up exhibitions, and/or develop other documentary evidence of success. It is difficult to envision more engaging student learning experiences.

A great deal of positive motivation can result for all conference participants. As students and teachers prepare, the meaning of success becomes increasingly clear. Clearly defined goals are easier to attain. As evidence of success is compiled, a sense of being in control can emerge for students, spurring them to greater heights—especially in the hope that they might be able to achieve those last-minute gains that will impress their parents even more. Parents acquire new understanding of their children, and of the teacher. In short, the stakes change for students, and so does their opportunity to succeed.

Dealing with the Practicalities.   Here are the steps in conducting a student-led parent conference:

STEP 1:   Establish the relevant achievement targets, be sure all students and parents are aware of them, and plan instruction around their achievement.

STEP 2:   Convert those expectations into quality assessments and use those assessments to help students build portfolios of quality evidence of their own achievement. Note that these can be either growth or status report portfolios, depending on your wishes. You don't have to be there when all of the evidence is gathered. Your students can take the lead—if they're prepared.

STEP 3:   While the evidence is building, keep the channels of communication open with the student's family. This might involve the use of a "take-home" portfolio or a take-home journal that students use to keep their parents informed of progress during instruction. Ask parents to respond to you in writing about their impressions of the progress or about any concerns they may have.

STEP 4:   As conference time approaches, convene a student-teacher conference to assemble the conference portfolio. Work as a team to select the samples of student work that you will use to tell the desired story.

STEP 5:   Model a student-led conference for your students. Role play a good one and a bad one, so they can see what make them work well. Be absolutely sure students know their role (as leader), your role (as coach), and their parents' role (as interested listeners and questioners). Be sure your students understand that we strive for a natural conversation among conferees—an interaction about accomplishments that includes examples, questions, answers, and sharing.

You might consider engaging your students in collaborating to develop performance criteria for a good conference. Remember from the performance assessment design process?

- Brainstorm important elements of a good conference.
- Cluster them into major categories.
- Label and define the categories.
- Analyze and compare conferences of vastly different quality (have your students role play good and bad conferences).
- Devise rating scales or checklists to capture the essential differences between the two.

Your students can be partners with you in building criteria for good student-led conferences. Then you can team up to plan conferences that meet your agreed-on standards of excellence.

STEP 6:   Provide opportunities for students to practice their conference presentations in teams using the established performance criteria to provide feedback and offer suggestions for improvement.

STEP 7:   Establish the time period during which the conferences are to take place. Permit students to select their own specific presentation time. Make them responsible for inviting participants, and for following up the invitation to be sure all are informed.

STEP 8:   When the event happens, be sure students welcome all participants, handle introductions, review the objectives of the meeting, coordinate meeting events, handle follow-up communications, and summarize results. If we have prepared carefully, conferences should unfold productively with few surprises.

STEP 9:   Offer parents an opportunity for an additional one-on-one meeting with you, the teacher, if they wish—just in case there are any personal, family, or risky issues that need attention. In my experience, virtually all parents will decline, but it is good to offer. Incidentally, one teacher I know frames the conference this way: It will last 30 minutes, with the student leading the first 20 minutes. The final 10 minutes is intended for teacher and parents alone, unless the parents invite the student to remain. Almost all do.

STEP 10: Solicit a follow-up written review from parents. You might develop a simple reaction questionnaire that allows parents to participate in planning their children's future goals. Students can take responsibility for collecting this feedback and can be partners in its interpretation and use.

Step 11: Debrief your students on the entire experience. Discuss it as a group or have students evaluate the experience by writing about it. What facets worked? What needs improvement? Be sure you and they learn the important lessons this process teaches both about academics and students' personal reactions.

At the time of this writing, virtually every teacher I have spoken with across the country who has carefully prepared for and conducted student-led parent conferences has found it to be a compellingly positive experience. In fact, a surprising number have told me that it was a career-altering and powerfully rejuvenating experience. Figure 15.2 shares the thoughts of two sixth-grade teachers (Arnold & Stricklin, 1993, personal communication) on their experiences with student-led conferences. Figure 15.3 presents a concise summary of the key points made in this section about student-led parent conferences.

With a combined 35 years of teaching experience, we have rarely found a more valuable educational process than student-led conferences. During preparation the students experienced goal setting, reflected upon their own learning, and created a showcase portfolio.

Once underway, the conferences seem to have a life of their own. We, the teachers, gave up control and became observers, an experience that was gratifying and revealing. It validated our growing belief that students have the ability to direct their own learning and are able to take responsibility for self-evaluation. For many of our students, we gained insights into individual qualities previously hidden from us in the day to day classroom routine.

Students blossomed under the direct and focused attention of their parents. In this intimate spotlight, where there was no competition except that which they placed on themselves, they stepped for a moment into the adult world where they took command of their own convergence as well as their own development. Parents were surprised and delighted at the level of sophistication and competence their children revealed while sharing personal accomplishments.

In order to refine and improve this process, we surveyed both students and parents. Parents were emphatic in their positive response to student-led conferences, with most requesting that we provide this type of conference more often. Students, even those at risk and with behavior problems, overwhelmingly responded with, "We needed more time; a half an hour was not enough."

Figure 15.2
Teacher commentary on experiences with student-led conferences
Source: By Harriet Arnold and Patricia Stricklin, 1993, Central Kitsap School District, Washington. Reprinted by permission of the authors.

Figure 15.3
Student-led parent conference in
a nutshell

Benefits

1.   Stronger sense of accountability among students
2.   Stronger sense of pride in achievement among students
3.   More productive student-teacher relationship
4.   Improved student-parent relationship
5.   Stronger sense of classroom community
6.   Reduced value of cheating
7.   Development of leadership skills among students
8.   Greater parental participation in conferences

Challenges

1.   The uncertainty of sharing control with students
2.   The need to adopt a completely student-involved philosophy
3.   The amount of time required to prepare and present conferences
4.   The logistical challenges of organizing for conferences
5.   The difficulties that can arise with dysfunctional families

Keys to Success

1.   Students willing and able to risk
2.   Teachers willing and able to step aside
3.   Clear targets known to all
4.   Accurate student-involved assessments
5.   A shared language for talking about targets and their achievement
6.   A commitment of time to learn, prepare, and practice

A Final Thought about Your Communication Challenge

If you want your students to use feedback about their achievement as the basis for academic improvement, they need to be able to hear and accept the truth about their current achievement. When that truth is positive, this will not be a problem. But when it is negative—particularly when it seems to always have been negative—acceptance of the message can be difficult. Students can and often do find ways to brush these messages aside, to rationalize them, to discredit the source, or to find some other way to escape. Call this human nature. The problem is, however, that in a learning community, such avoidance is immensely counterproductive.

You must be mindful of conditions you must satisfy for students to really listen to and accept negative information about themselves. For instance, students need to develop certain attitudes and perspectives to be able to receive and act on such messages. They need to see themselves as key players in the search for information about their own achievement. In addition, students need assistance in developing a sufficiently strong academic self-concept so they can acknowledge their shortcomings and not feel defeated. Further, students must see the provider of the feedback as credible, honest, and helpful. And finally, they must come to see the benefits of the message very quickly, so they can muster the resources needed to act purposefully.

From the other point of view, the giver of the feedback (you) must be able to present it constructively, delivering a clear and focused message using understandable language. You must be able to communicate acceptance of students while critiquing their achievement. They must know that you are evaluating their achievements, not them as people. Even more importantly, you must help students understand that you share a common mission: their academic success.

Clearly, it is no simple task to communicate to students that they have missed the target but still have the hope of success and reason to stay motivated. But as a teacher-communicator, that is exactly what you must do. The suggestions offered in previous chapters for clearly defining the meaning of academic success, assessing it well, and involving students throughout, then transforming the results into quality information, are intended to help you fulfill this most important of your teaching responsibilities. As long as students continue to see the target as being within reach and as long as they see their own progress, they will keep trying.

Summary: Finding Effective Ways to Communicate

We explored three communication systems that rely on direct contact among students, teachers, and parents. One turns the classroom into a workshop by using regular ongoing conferences to exchange information between teachers and students. Another is the traditional parent-teacher conference, preceded by a student-teacher conference covering the same material. The third places students in charge of their parent conferences. All require that students understand expectations well enough to be able to converse about them. They also permit students the opportunity of gathering and communicating relatively detailed information about their own achievement. Proficient assessors and communicators rapidly become better performers.

We must continue to explore, develop, and implement these kinds of communication systems as our achievement targets become more numerous, complex, and individualized. Implementation will be made easier as modern information-processing technology evolves and we learn new ways to apply it to the art of assessment. In the meantime, for the immediate future, we will most often use these alternatives in conjunction with or parallel to report card grading systems.

The methods of conveying information reviewed in this chapter hold the promise of allowing students to tell their story about their own academic success. That, in and of itself, represents one of the most powerful learning experiences we can offer them.

Conclusion to This Text

As educators, our job is to teach our-selves out of a job. By this, I mean that we must take our students to a place where they don't need us anymore. Any students who leave school still needing to rely on their teachers to tell them they have done well have not yet learned to hit the target, because they cannot see the quality of their own performance. We must turn our achievement expectations and performance standards over to our students, to make them independent of us. Only then can we assure ourselves that we have helped our students become the lifelong learners they will need to be in the new millennium.

Covington (1992) advises us that, "Indeed, at its best, education should provide students with a sense of empowerment that makes the future 'real' by moving beyond merely offering children plausible alternatives to indicating how their preferred dreams can actually be attained" (p. 3). I submit that we can fulfill this mission only if we rely on student-involved classroom assessment combined with student-involved record keeping and communication.

This ends our journey together through the realm of classroom assessment. By now, each of the four guiding principles that I shared with you in Chapter 1 will make complete sense to you.

Guiding Principle 1: Students Are the Key Assessment Users

Consider the role of students as consumers of assessment results: Right from the time students arrive at school, they look to their teachers for evidence of their success. If that early evidence suggests that they are succeeding, what begins to grow in them is a sense of hopefulness and an expectation of more success in the future. This in turn fuels their motivation to try, which fuels even more success. The foundation of this upward spiral is the evidence of their own achievement, which students receive from their teachers based on ongoing classroom assessments. Thus, classroom assessment information is the essential fuel that powers the learning system for students.

However, when the evidence suggests to students that they are not succeeding in this place called school, what can also begin to grow in them is a sense of hopelessness and an expectation of more failure in the future. This can rob them of the motivation to try, which in turn can lead to more failure and a downward spiral. Here again we see consequences of classroom assessment evidence, but this time as the fuel that drives the motivation not to try.

Strive always for the former. Use your assessments to build confidence.

Guiding Principle 2: Clear and Appropriate Targets Are Essential

The quality of any assessment depends first and foremost on the clarity and appropriateness of our definition of the achievement target we are assessing. We cannot assess academic achievement effectively if we do not know and understand what that valued target is. There are many different kinds of valued achievement expectations within our educational system, from mastering content knowledge to complex problem solving, from performing a flute recital to speaking Spanish to writing a strong term paper. All are important. But to assess them well, we must ask ourselves: Do we know what it means to do it well? Precisely what does it mean to succeed academically? We are ready to assess only when we can answer these questions with clarity and confidence.

Guiding Principle 3: High-Quality Assessment Is a Must

High-quality assessment is essential in all assessment contexts. Sound assessments satisfy five specific quality standards. All assessments must meet all standards. No exceptions can be tolerated, because to violate any of them is to place student academic well-being in jeopardy. These five standards, described here, are illustrated once again in Figure 15.4. This is the last summary of these in this book. I hope that these standards of excellence in assessment will come to guide all of your classroom assessment work.

Clear Targets.   First, sound assessments arise from and reflect clear achievement targets (as in Guiding Principle 2). You can ask this question about any assessment: Can the developer and user provide a clear and appropriate description of the specific achievement expectation(s) it is designed to reflect? If the answer is yes, proceed to the next standard. If the answer is no, realize that there is a very real danger of inaccurate assessment. As educators, we must all be confident, competent masters of the achievement targets we expect our students to master.

Focused Purpose.   This standard admonishes us also to begin the design process with a clear sense of why we are conducting the assessment. It is impossible to develop a quality assessment unless and until we know how we will use the results it produces. So again, about any assessment, you can ask: Does the developer understand the intended uses and has the developer taken user(s') needs into account in developing and implementing the assessment? If the answer is yes, proceed to the next standard.

Proper Method.   A sound assessment examines student achievement through the use of a method that is, in fact, capable of reflecting the valued target. To test mastery of scientific knowledge, we might use a multiple-choice test. But when our challenge is to assess the ability to speak Spanish, we must turn to another method altogether. We have several different kinds of achievement to assess and we have several different kinds of assessment methods to use to reflect them. Our classroom assessment challenge is to know how to match the method with the intended target. About any assessment, you can ask: Is the method used here capable of accurately reflecting the kinds of outcomes the user wishes to assess? If the answer is yes, proceed to the next standard. If it is no, be aware that student achievement is about to be a victim of inaccurate assessment.

Sound Sampling.   Almost all assessments rely on a representative sample of all the exercises we could have included if time were unlimited and the test could be infinitely long. A sound assessment offers a representative sample that is large enough to yield confident inferences about how respondents would have done given all possible exercises. The realities of classroom life require that we generalize from our sample to the total performance arena being assessed. Each different classroom assessment context places its own special constraints on our sampling procedures. Our challenge is to know how to adjust our sampling strategies as context varies to produce results of maximum quality at minimum cost in time and effort. About any assessment, you can ask: Have we

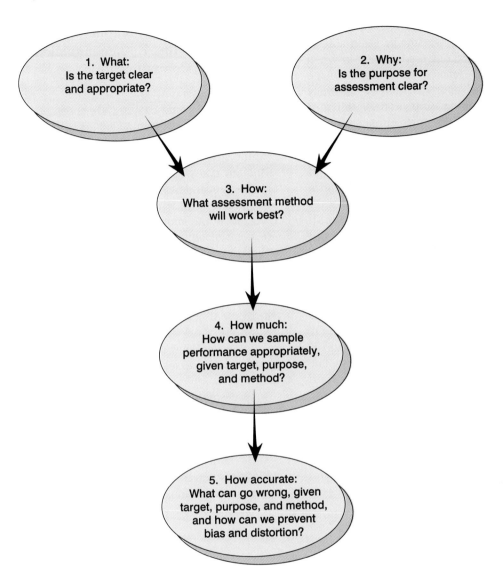

Figure 15.4
Standards of sound assessment

gathered enough information of the right kind, so we can draw confident conclusions about student achievement? If the answer is yes, proceed. If it is no, critical consumers of assessment information should be concerned about student well-being.

Freedom from Bias.   Finally, this standard demands that we design, develop, and use assessments in ways that permit us to control for all sources of bias and distortion that can cause our results to misrepresent real student achievement. Again, each assessment context presents its own unique sources of interference with accurate assessment. Each assessment method permits errors to creep in when we let our guard down. With multiple-choice tests, for example, poorly written or culturally biased test items can harm the quality of resulting scores. With performance assessments, evaluator prejudice can bias judgments. And so it is with all methods. Our challenge is to know all sources of bias and distortion that can rob assessment results of clear and appropriate meaning and to know how to head off those problems before they get a foothold. About any assessment, you can ask: Have the important sources of bias been accounted for during development and use? If the answer is no, you must take or urge action to address unaccounted-for sources of error.

Violate any of these five criteria and you place students at risk. Problems arise when assessments are developed and used by those who fail to understand the valued outcome, fail to identify user needs, select an improper assessment method, sample achievement inadequately, or introduce bias. Unsound assessments can lead to misdiagnosed needs, failure to provide needed instructional support, use of inappropriate instructional approaches, counterproductive grouping of students, and misinformation provided to student and parent decision makers.

Guiding Principle 4: Sound Assessments Must Be Accompanied by Effective Communication

Mention assessment and, for many, the first thoughts that come to mind are those of test scores and grades often attached to forms of achievement labeled very briefly, such as reading, writing, science, math, and the like. Although many assessments do translate levels of achievement into scores and grades, we are coming to understand two important realities more and more clearly. First, numbers are not the only way to communicate about achievement. We can use words, pictures, illustrations, examples, and many other means to convey meaning about student achievement. Second, the symbols used as the basis of this communication are only as meaningful and useful as the definitions of achievement that underpin them and the quality of the assessments used to produce them.

Assessment-literate educators are critical consumers of assessment information. They are constantly asking, Precisely what is being assessed here and how do I know what the results mean? They do not rest until they achieve a sharp focus: clear thinking and effective communication, both in their own assessments and those of others.

How to Continue Your Exploration

I hope our journey has helped you to understand your classroom assessment challenges and solutions more clearly. Please do not permit your personal professional journey to end here, however. I implore you to continue your professional development in assessment by exploring the following readings, and others listed in the references section. As you put into practice all we have discussed during our journey, turn to these readings to enrich your learning.

Thank you for traveling with me, and best wishes in becoming the best classroom assessor that you can become.

To learn more about assessment and student motivation:

Covington, M. (1992). *Making the grade: A self-worth perspective on motivation and school reform.* New York, NY: Cambridge University Press. A comprehensive analysis of the relationship between our evaluations of students and their willingness to strive for excellence.

To further your understanding about student-involved communication:

Austin, T. (1994). *Changing the view: Student-led conferences.* Portsmouth, NH: Heinemann. A teacher's handbook on setting up and conducting student-involved communications.

Davies, A., Cameron, C., Politano, C., and Gregory, K. (1992). *Together is better: Collaborative assessment, evaluation & reporting.* Courtenay, BC: Classroom Connections International. A practical guide to designing and completing student-involved communications.

O'Connor, Ken. (1999). *How to grade for learning.* Arlington Heights, IL: Skylight. Explores grading issues in depth, with a real sense of practicality.

To learn practical lessons about student-involved assessment:

Spandel, V. (in press). *Creating writers: Linking assessment and writing instruction,* 3rd ed. New York: Addison-Wesley Longman. A teacher's guide to integrating student-involved writing assessment with teaching and learning.

Exercises for Self-Assessment

1. Make a three-column by three-row chart on a large sheet of paper. Reviewing the text, use this chart to identify the strengths, limitations, and keys to successful use of the three conference forms discussed.

2. Focus on the system of communication used in your school or in the college or university in which you study. Evaluate that system in terms of the keys to effective communication described in the introduction to Part IV and in each subsequent chapter. In your opinion, is your system sound? Why? Why not?

3. If you are able to identify problems within the communication system that you just evaluated, how might they be overcome?

4. Some who have experimented with alternative communication systems have met with parental resistance. Parents wanted report cards and grades, as they had received when they were in school. If you developed a sound communication system in your school and were confronted with this kind of resistance, how would you respond? Why?

 You may go to the Companion Website at www.prenhall.com/stiggins and answer these questions in the Self-Assessment module.

Final Chapter Reflection

1. *What are the three most important new insights to come to you as a result of your study of this chapter?*
2. *Which of your previous questions about assessment can you now answer based on your study of this chapter?*
3. *For practicing teachers only: What do you plan to do differently in assessment in your classroom as a result of your study of this book?*

   For those in preservice study only: As you think about the classroom assessment environment that you hope to create for your students, how has your thinking changed as a result of your study of this book?

Workbook Activities

Those of you using the workbook, *Practice with Student-Involved Classroom Assessment*, as part of your study of this material will find the following activities and others included for Chapter 15:

- *What's Going Right in This Teacher-Student Conference?* The first type of conference discussed in the chapter is teacher-student. This activity asks you to analyze the dialogue presented in the chapter for adherence to principles of sound communication and keys to success for teacher-student conferences.

- *Let the Conference Begin!* The third type of conference discussed in the chapter is student-involved parent conferences. This activity asks you to analyze the dialogue in this case for adherence to principles of sound communication and keys to successful conferences.

Note also that the workbook offers concluding activities that tie the entire text together.

Video Support

The ATI interactive video training package, *Student-Involved Conferences*, carefully analyzes the alternative conference formats and details the keys to the effective set up and use of each. Brief video segments alternate with hands-on activities to bring the power of student-involved assessment to the fore.

References

American Psychological Association. (1995). *Standards for educational and psychological testing.* Washington, DC: Author

Anderson, L. W., & Bourke, S. F. (in press). *Assessing Affective Characteristics in Schools, 2nd ed.*, Mahwah, NJ: Erlbaum.

Arter, J., & Spandel, V. (1992). Using portfolio of student work in instruction and assessment. *Educational Measurement: Issues and Practices, 11*(1), 36–44.

Austin, T. (1994). *Changing the view: Student-led parent conferences.* Portsmouth, NH: Heinemann.

Bartlett, L. (1987). Academic Evaluation and Student Discipline Don't Mix: A Critical Review. *Journal of Law and Education, 16*(2), 155–165.

Berk, R. A. (Ed.). (1986). *Performance assessment: Methods and applications.* Baltimore, MD: Johns Hopkins University Press.

Bruner, J. (1960). *The Process of Education.* Cambridge, MA: Harvard University Press.

Catlin Gabel School. (1990). Sample student report. Portland, OR: Author.

Central Kitsap School District.

Condry, J. (1977). Enemies of exploration: Self-initiated versus other-initiated learning. *Journal of Personality and Social Psychology, 35*(00), 459–477.

Covington, M. (1992). *Making the grade: A self-worth perspective on motivation and school reform.* New York: Cambridge University Press.

CTB/McGraw-Hill (1996) *Terra Nova: The Only One.* Monterey, CA: Author.

Davies, A., Cameron, C., Politano, C., & Gregory, K. (1992). *Together is better: Collaborative assessment, evaluation and reporting.* Winnipeg, MB: Peguis.

Dunbar S. B., Koretz, D. M., & Hoover, H. D. (1991). Quality control in the development and use of performance assessments. *Applied Measurement in Education, 4*(4), 289–304.

Erickson, H. L. (1998). *Concept-Based Curriculum and Instruction: Teaching Beyond the Facts.* Thousand Oaks, CA: Corwin.

Fishbein M., & Ajzen, I. (1975). *Belief, attitude, intention and behavior: An introduction to theory and research.* Reading MA: Addison-Wesley.

Gardner, H. (1993). *Frames of mind: the theory of multiple intelligences.* New York: Basic Books.

Getzels, J.W. (1966). The problem of interests: A reconsideration. *Supplementary Education Monographs, 66*, 97–106.

Guskey, T. R. (Ed.). (1996). ASCD Yearbook: Communicating Student Learning. Alexandria, VA: Association for Supervision, Curriculum and Development.

Hall, C. S., & Lindsay, G. (1970). *Theories of personality, 2nd ed.* New York: John Wiley & Sons.

Hunkins, F. P. (1995). *Teaching thinking through effective questioning.* Norwood, MA: Christopher-Gordon.

Kohn, A. (1993). *Punished by rewards.* New York: Houghton Mifflin.

Lindquist, E. F. (1951). Preliminary considerations in objective test construction. In E. F. Lindquist (Ed.), *Educational measurement* (pp. 4–22). Washington, DC: American Council on Education.

Marzano, R. J., Pickering, D. J., & McTighe, J. (1993). *Assessing Student Outcomes.* Alexandria VA: Association for Curriculum, Supervision and Development.

Ministry of Education and Training, Victoria. (1991). *English profiles handbook: Assessing and reporting students' progress in English.* Melbourne, Australia: Ministry of Education and Training, Victoria, School Programs Division.

Norris, S. P., & Ennis, R. H. (1989). *Evaluating critical thinking.* Pacific Grove, CA: Critical Thinking Books & Software.

O'Connor, K. (1999). *How to grade for learning.* Arlington Heights, IL: Skylight.

Paul, R. (1995). *Critical thinking: How to prepare students for a rapidly changing world.* Santa Rosa, CA: Foundation for Critical Thinking.

Rowe, M. B. (1978). Specific ways to develop better communications. In R. Sund & A. Carin (Eds.), *Creative questioning and sensitivity: Listening techniques* (2nd ed.) (n.p.). Upper Saddle River, NJ: Merrill/Prentice Hall.

Scates, D. E. (1943). Differences between measurement criteria of pure scientists and of classroom teachers. *Journal of Educational Research, 37*(00), 1–13.

Shavelson, R. J., & Stern, P. (1981). Research on teachers' pedagogical thoughts, judgments, decisions, and behavior. *Review of Educational Research, 41*(41), 455-498.

Skinner, B. F. (1974). *About behaviorism.* New York: Alfred A. Knopf.

Skinner, E. A., Wellborn, J. G., & Connell, J. P. (1990). What it takes to do well in school and whether I've got it. A process model of perceived control and children's engagement and achievement in school. *Journal of Educational Psychology, 82*(00), 22–32.

Spandel, V., & Culham, R. (1995). *Putting portfolio stories to work.* Portland, OR: Northwest Regional Educational Laboratory.

Spandel, V., & Stiggins, R. J. (1994). *Creating writers: Linking assessment and writing instruction, 2nd ed.* White Plains, NY: Addison-Wesley Longman.

Sternberg, R. J. (1996). Myths, countermyths, and truths about intelligences. *Educational Researcher, 25*(2), 11–16.

Stiggins, R. J., & Conklin, N. F. (1992). *In teachers' hands: Investigating the practices of classroom assessment.* Albany, NY: State University of New York Press.

Thurlow, M. L., Elliott, J. L., & Ysseldyke, J. E. (1998). *Testing Students with Disabilities.* Thousand Oaks, CA: Corwin.

Weiner, B. (1974). *Achievement motivation and attribution theory.* Morristown, NJ: General Learning Press.

Wiggins, G. (1993). *Assessing student performance.* San Francisco, CA: Jossey-Bass.

Wiggins, G., & McTighe, J. (1999). *Design for Understanding.* Alexandria, VA: Association for Supervision, Curriculum and Development.

Index

About the Author

Richard J. Stiggins, B.S., M.A., Ph. D., is founder and president of the Assessment Training Institute, Inc., Portland, Oregon, a service agency devoted to supporting teachers as they face the day-to-day challenges of classroom assessment. He received his bachelor's degree in psychology from the State University of New York at Plattsburgh, master's degree in industrial psychology from Springfield (MA) College, and doctoral degree in education measurement from Michigan State University. Dr. Stiggins began his assessment work on the faculty of Michigan State before becoming director of research and evaluation for the Edina, Minnesota, Public Schools and a member of the faculty of educational foundations at the University of Minnesota. In addition, he has served as director of test development for the American College Testing Program, Iowa City, Iowa; as a visiting scholar at Stanford University; and as director of the Centers for Classroom Assessment and Performance Assessment at the Northwest Regional Educational Laboratory, Portland, Oregon. He has also served on the graduate faculties of the University of Minnesota, Minneapolis, Minnesota, and Lewis and Clark College, Portland, teaching educational measurement and program evaluation courses for teachers and administrators.

Rick has turned two decades of classroom assessment research into a national movement to combat decades of assessment training neglect for teachers and administrators. He is helping colleges of education, states and districts across the nation to launch the professional development needed to meet emerging classroom, school, district, and state assessment responsibilities. Rick coined the phrase *assessment literacy* to represent the standards of professional excellence to be attained and has pioneered the use of local learning teams as an effective means of low-cost, in-service assessment training.

Further, to achieve his vision of excellence in assessment, he has pioneered the design and development of print and video assessment training materials to promote practical understanding of sound assessment practice. His unique approach to turning Student-Involved Classroom Assessment into an immensely powerful motivator for students a and time saver for teachers has turned this text into one of the most practical and widely used teacher guides in the country. Rick's very popular interactive videos show teachers how to turn classroom assessment strategies into very engaging learning experiences for their students.